Settlement Sociology in the Progressive Years

Studies in Critical Social Sciences Book Series

Haymarket Books is proud to be working with Brill Academic Publishers (www.brill.nl) to republish the *Studies in Critical Social Sciences* book series in paperback editions. This peer-reviewed book series offers insights into our current reality by exploring the content and consequences of power relationships under capitalism, and by considering the spaces of opposition and resistance to these changes that have been defining our new age. Our full catalog of *SCSS* volumes can be viewed at www.haymarketbooks.org/category/scss-series.

Settlement Sociology in the Progressive Years

Faith, Science, and Reform

Joyce E. Williams
Vicky M. MacLean

Haymarket Books
Chicago, IL

First published in 2015 by Brill Academic Publishers, The Netherlands.

Published in paperback in 2016 by
Haymarket Books
P.O. Box 180165
Chicago, IL 60618
773-583-7884
www.haymarketbooks.org

ISBN: 978-1-60846-642-9

Distributed to the trade in the US through Consortium Book Sales and Distribution (www.cbsd.com) and internationally through Ingram Publisher Services International (www.ingramcontent.com).

This book was published with the generous support of Lannan Foundation and Wallace Action Fund.

Special discounts are available for bulk purchases by organizations and institutions. Please call 773-583-7884 or email info@haymarketbooks.org for more information.

Cover design by Jamie Kerry and Ragina Johnson.

Printed in the United States.

Entered into digital printing January 2023.

Library of Congress Cataloging-in-Publication data is available.

This work is dedicated to my first professor of sociology and life-long mentor
Dr. Sarah Frances Anders
JEW

To my grandson, Cameron
VMM

To our students, past, present, and future
VMM
JEW

∵

Contents

Acknowledgements

We wish to thank the archivists who competently and patiently provided us with efficient services at the University of Chicago Regenstein Library, Newberry Library, Chicago History Museum Research Center, University of Illinois at Chicago Richard Daley Library, Harvard University Schlesinger Library, Harvard University Houghton Library, Smith College Archives, Northeastern University Special Collections, New York Public Library, Columbia University Butler Library, New York University Tamiment Library. We gratefully acknowledge the support of the Middle Tennessee State University's Faculty Research and Creative Activity Committees, and Dean of the College of Graduate Studies Michael Allen and his staff for their generous support of this research. Three substantial grants for travel, archival work and writing made this research possible.

Introduction: In Search of Sociology

Sociology elicits no uniform response from its various audiences. Relatively few students have been introduced to sociology during their public school educations. Journalists prefer the more easily identifiable psychologist or economist when they seek a quick analysis of the daily news. The average citizen often draws a blank as to whom or what a sociologist is or, worse yet, confuses us with socialists or social directors. To the sociologist or to students of sociology, however, the term evokes passion and idealism. This book is written in the spirit of sharing some of that passion and idealism through the history and contributions of a few women and men in the United States who followed their sociological visions—visions such as those captured in the past by Peter Berger's *Invitation to Sociology* (1963) and by C. Wright Mills' *The Sociological Imagination* (1959), or by Dorothy Smith's *The Everyday World as Problematic* (1987), and Patricia Hill Collins', *Black Feminist Thought* (1990). The narrative that follows is about some of the lesser known people and groups who were doing sociology as they understood it in the Progressive Era, defined here as roughly the 1890s to 1920. Their sociology was defined preeminently by the desire to develop a pragmatic science for social reform and social justice. Their vision of social science was unequivocally aimed at combining research and practice to bring about much needed social changes and to help ease the misery and pain caused by emerging social problems. By studying the past we have opportunity to learn important lessons to help us navigate a future path for a sociology grounded in its historical promise as an agent of social change.

Those who write the history of a discipline, or of any phenomenon, in fact exercise both the power of definition and of reification. And such is the case with sociology whose history has been written largely in terms of its white male "founding fathers" and their canonical works. It is no accident, for example, that we know more about the "Chicago School of Sociology" of the University of Chicago than any other sociology in the United States. The University and department controlled and expended significant resources for discipline-building (Williams and MacLean 2005). Less well known however is the Chicago School of Settlement Sociology (Deegan 1990, Lengermann and Niebrugge-Brantley 2002, MacLean and Williams 2012) even though it existed prior to sociology at the University and influenced its development. In the present analysis we seek to contribute to a restoration of a history lost as American sociology was professionalized and institutionalized in academic settings (Lengermann and Niebrugge-Brantley 1998, 2002). Settlement sociology encompassed a sociology of praxis based on a paradigm that informed the work of sociologists active in the social gospel and feminist pragmatist movements of the Progressive Era. The "neighborly relations" paradigm which guided the settlement method of praxis developed among a group of social reformers, some religious, some feminist, and all champions of social democracy and of social justice. These self-identified sociologists believed that social science could be used to bridge the growing gap between the rich and poor in the United States and to address the emerging problems associated with industrialization, urbanization, and immigration.

The chapters that follow explore the various facets of the neighborly relations paradigm in case-by-case analyses of the contributions of key social settlements engaged in early sociological practice. As part of a progressive movement, settlement houses offered a place for service-minded college and seminary educated women and men to move into urban neighborhoods and take up residence in areas housing the poor, particularly immigrants and their families who typically lived in tenements and worked in factories. In many respects settlements were the first graduate programs of sociology, providing laboratories for the collection of data put to use in documenting and remediating the needs of community members who were neighbors. Only by becoming active members of these communities could middle-class residents come to understand first-hand the standpoint and interests of those they sought to help. Most important, by taking up residence and developing neighborly relations, the interests of settlement workers and community members melded and the interests of one became the interests of the other. Thus in conducting research, and in sharing knowledge and education in communities, members were empowered to advocate and to take action in behalf of their own needs.

Sociology as Told

The early history of American sociology exists in various "pieces" but has no comprehensive or comprehendible whole. The lengthiest history of sociology in the US is that written by Luther and Jessie Bernard, *Origins of American Sociology: The Social Science Movement in the United States* (1943). Their narrative history describes the development of sociology as part of the larger Social Science Movement with ideological and associational roots in Europe and in the United States. They examined the origins and development of what they defined as the beginning of "scientific sociology" in the late 19th century. The history they tell is that sociology developed as part of a larger process of "hivings off" of specialized disciplines from the larger multidisciplinary American Social Science Association. Not only is their work focused primarily on the pursuit of scientism as the motivating force for disciplinary development, it is told solely as a history of intellectual men. Moreover, theirs is a narrative constructed to trace the "natural" development of sociology as a social science unfolding through evolving philosophical and theoretical ideas within an academic context. While the history they (chose to) write incorporates many of the antecedents of the discipline, their work is not framed as a reflective critical analysis. It fails to sufficiently address the political contests for legitimacy and the processes of marginalization and exclusion that ultimately defined the traditional sociological canon. Bernard and Bernard's sole pursuit of scientism gives inadequate attention to the fact that both a public as well as academic sociology grew with amazing speed around the turn of the century because it was perceived as the scientific means of "fixing" the problems rampant in urban-industrial society. Their analysis makes no mention of social settlements, social gospel, or early first-wave feminist contributions to sociology. When they do address social reform and social betterment theories they focus primarily on male economic and political philosophers. Yet many of the early social surveys and empirical analyses intended as the basis for reform were conducted by churches, community organizations, labor unions, and social settlements. Some of the best known examples were led by community activists like Jane Addams, Julia Lathrop, and Florence Kelley as documented in *Hull-House Maps and Papers* (1895), by social gospelers such as Robert Woods, as published in *City Wilderness* (1898) and by African-American civil rights activists like W.E.B. Du Bois and his pioneering work *The Philadelphia Negro* (1899).

Schwendinger and Schwendinger covered approximately the same time frame as the Bernards in their analysis of the formative years of academic sociology in the US (1974:161,444). However, they make only brief mention of the Social Science Movement as a form of "moral politics," citing instead C. Wright Mills' brief historical reference to the involvement of sociologists in social reform (1959:84). While Vidich and Lyman (1985) focus on the religious origins of American sociology, acknowledging its theological and moral roots, they focus primarily on its evolution within colleges and universities and fail to adequately acknowledge the contributions of social settlements and the social gospel to the earliest form of public sociological practice. Howard Odum (1951) wrote a chronology of American Sociology on the occasion of its reaching the half-century mark. His is a history told largely through the professional lives and works of the men who were active in building sociology as an academic discipline, presenting its scientific development but essentially separating sociology from its reformist past. Some forty years later, Turner and Turner published a pessimistic institutional history of sociology as *The Impossible Science* (1990) relating its organizational differentiation (into subfields and specialties) to funding and available resources. Although they recognize the early reform roots of American sociology, particularly as funding shifted from private philanthropies and foundations to government-sponsored research, they focus on professional sociology in academia excluding settlement sociology and its public practitioners. Levine's "visions" of the sociological tradition is perhaps more comprehensive and multidimensional, providing a series of narratives including positivistic, pluralistic, synthetic, humanistic, contextual, and dialogical versions of sociology (1995:251). Nevertheless he states unequivocally that sociology in the American tradition is distinguished by "its resolutely empirical character" by which he apparently meant "scientific," value-neutral research. In fact, Levine seems to separate from sociology the "moral roots" that he attributed to the social gospel and to the more secularized transcendentalist movement of the late 19th century. There are other histories, more limited in scope, but also focusing primarily on the scientific origins of sociology or, more generally, of social science (Bannister 1987, Ross 1992, McDonald 1993, Haskell 2000). All of these works tend to view sociology as located within the academy to the neglect of its early public practice and reform impulse.

Most histories of sociology trace its progress as a linear scientific development, constructing a history of systematic sociological theory and methodological formalism; yet these idealized elements are in reality largely absent in the development of early American sociology. An emphasis on systematic theory draws on European influences, but empirical sociology is more an American tradition with roots firmly planted in the social reform movements of the Progressive Era. As Faris pointed out, there was always "a practicality in the empiricism of American methods of sociological research which contrasts with the lofty and dignified sociology of, for example, nineteenth century Germany as the American politician contrasts with European Emperors" (1945:538). Sociology developed very rapidly from its beginnings in the 1880s in a context that was peculiarly American: a unique set of ideas that Ross called "American exceptionalism" (1992:26–30) or what Greek (1992:43) and some historians label "chosen nation status" or "manifest destiny." The view that America was unique in its origin and destiny along with the perception that its destiny was threatened by the problems associated with rapid industrialization, gave rise to a sociology much different from that developing in Europe. American sociology was influenced by European social theory and philosophy; yet it was from the outset practical because it was widely perceived as needed.

"American sociology was created by Americans seeking to understand their own society and respond to its needs in the light of general laws" (McDonald 1993:296). Oberschall notes too that "[t]he reform impulse needed...intellectual legitimacy and respectability because it was in contradiction to the dominant ideology of the time [laissez-faire capitalism] and in fact constituted the most powerful challenge to it" (1972:191). Early sociology was part of a blind faith in American exceptionalism including the belief that the United States could avoid problems such as class conflict and mass poverty that plagued Europe at the turn of the century.

Sociology in the US has at various times been described as experiencing crisis (Gouldner 1970, Furner 1975, Crane and Small 1992), as splintering into generic nothingness (Boyns and Fletcher 2005: 6), as an "impossible science" lacking holistic integration (Turner and Turner 1990), and as heading for a premature death (Lopreato and Crippen 1996). However, for those who live, teach, and study sociology, it is alive and well and we continually work to share its core substance and its spirit of reform. We are passionate about what sociology is and about the works of some who have defined and lived it—some widely known and some relatively unknown. Today students in the United States are typically taught the European roots but not the American roots of sociology. Few are aware that much American sociology actually preceded its European counterparts or developed at roughly the same time. Auguste Comte's six-volume work *Cours de Philosophie Positive* (1830–1842) was popularized in the United States before most of Europe after being translated into English in 1853 by Harriet Martineau (Lengermann and Niebrugge-Brantley 1998:28). *Hull-House Maps and Papers* (1895) came out before Rowntree's (1901) study of poverty in York, England. The University of Chicago's Department of Sociology was founded in 1892, the London School of Economics in 1895, and the first Chair of Sociology in France in 1896. Professional associations were established within a few years of each other: Britain in 1903, The American Sociological Society in 1905, and the German equivalent in 1908 (McDonald 1993:296). What came to be identified as professional sociology in the United States grew in colleges and universities; whereas in Europe professional sociology first grew outside of colleges and universities (Bramson 1961:81) as did applied sociology in the US. By the mid-1880s over a dozen schools in the US were teaching classes identified as social science or sociology; whereas, in Europe, only the University of Bordeaux where Durkheim began his career was teaching sociology (Morgan 1982:35). It was American settlement workers who first brought some of the works of European sociologists to the attention of the American public. In 1884 Florence Kelley translated Engel's *Condition of the Working Class in England* and Ellen Gates Starr brought the influence of John Ruskin and William Morris to her writing on art and labor (Starr [1895]2004:165–179, Lengermann and Niebrugge-Brantley 1998:231). Holden, an early proponent of settlements, used a Marxian analysis to examine social classes in the United States even as most denied the existence of such classes ([1922]1970:80–83). Vida Scudder, founder of the College Settlements Association brought the influences of Fabian[1] Christian socialism and a synthesis of revolutionary Marxism and Christianity to her teachings and sociological practice.

Reclaiming Our History

The case studies woven together in this volume are part of the diverse histories of sociology in the United States and of the visions and works of the women and men who shaped the discipline and on whose shoulders we stand as we look to the future. Sociology in the United States is treated variously as an extension of European sociology, as "Chicago sociology," as the Meadian tradition of social psychology/symbolic interactionism, as the conflict and neo-conflict tradition, or as structural functionalism. Sociology is all of these, but it is much more, some of which have yet to be integrated and melded into its history. From the beginning, sociology has been for some of its proponents a prophetic critique of society; an empirical description of the social world; a theoretical explanation of the social world; or a directive for intervention, amelioration and social betterment. Ironically, the contemporary call for a "public sociology" with greater relevance as set forth by Burawoy in his 2004 Presidential Address before the American Sociological Association (ASA) and in the 2011 thematic of "service sociology" of the Society for the Study of Social Problems (SSSP) represents sociology's coming full circle in a now more

1 The Fabian Society was established in London in 1884 and became perhaps the most influential academic organization of the early 20th century. The Society was comprised of social reformers who advocated gradual over revolutionary change. It was named for a little known Roman general, Fabius Maximus who was nicknamed, "Fabius the Delayer." The first pamphlet published by the Society explained "For the right moment you must wait, as Fabius did most patiently, when warring against Hannibal...but when the time comes you must strike hard" (Shaw 1894:i). The Fabian Society became known in Great Britain for its promotion of universal health care and the minimum wage. Much of the research underlying the Society's proposed reforms was provided by Sidney and Beatrice Webb, early members and co-founders of the London School of Economics and Political Science. Beatrice Webb was a cousin of Charles Booth and worked with him in collecting data for *Life and Labor of the People in London* (1902). Sidney Webb wrote the first Fabian tract (1887) and contributed to Fabian "essays" which settlement workers frequently cited (Shaw 1894).

complex version of its earlier praxis. Originally sociology was seen as a vehicle for understanding the underlying laws of social process and of discovering data that could be applied to the progressive evolution of a more perfectible social order. Burawoy suggests that now, in the 21st century, we are ready to take "knowledge back to those from whom it came, making public issues out of private troubles, and thus regenerating sociology's moral fiber" (2005a:5). Similarly Javier Trevino, as president of the Society for the Study of Social Problems, argued,

> [s]ervice sociology is a sociology of social problems intended to ameliorate conditions of life for those in need of assistance, and to ensure and promote the welfare of the community. ... [It] is aimed at helping people meet their pressing social needs. ... [It] involves the application of sociological knowledge combined with the expression of humanitarian sentiment in neighborly service (2011:1).

Both presidents "hark back to the late 19th century foreparents, for whom scholarly and moral enterprises were indistinguishable" (Burawoy 2005a:9). Burawoy goes a step further, however, in registering the fact that sociology today is more than intertwined scholarly and moral enterprises. In fact, he complexifies sociology by suggesting a matrix of professional, policy, public, and critical sociologies. For some critics, this typology tends to feed the accusation that sociology attempts to be all things to all people. There were rapid reactions to Burawoy's clarion call for a public sociology ranging from the claim that we are and have always been public to a refutation of the need for such (cf. Nichols 2005:3–4, Clawson et al. 2007, Nichols 2007). Among those who contend that sociology is or has always been public are those who emphasize that this history has been erased from our collective memory and/or those contending that they are doing and have always done public sociology.

Early sociology in the United States was a popular movement led by ministers; social reformers with various causes, many of whom were women; independent intellectuals; journalists; a few businessmen; and a few academics (Oberschall 1972). Albion Small's editorial in the first issue of the *American Journal of Sociology* in 1895 makes clear that he perceived sociology as a "movement," not yet a science. He apparently thought at that time that sociology was little more than social philosophy but powerful in its popular appeal as he described the US population as "literate" and maintaining "in perpetual session a lyceum in sociology" (1895:3). This popular movement, according to Small, was because men had broken away from evolutional or theological determinism and had come to realize that "society is what men choose to make it"

(1895:3). Coming from one whose name became synonymous with academic sociology, it is significant that Small made clear in this editorial that he saw the academy as following, not leading the sociological movement. The first textbook in sociology by Small and Vincent asserted that "sociology was born of the modern ardor to improve society" (1894:17). Small's admissions have now been wiped from the hegemonic history of American sociology. Yet, as this work will show, the audiences of early sociology were reform audiences comprised of those critical of the status quo and in search of remedies for the problems of the day. The early practitioners of sociology were as diverse as their audiences—social gospelers, socialists, unionists, and settlement workers—held together by their dissatisfaction with the status quo and by efforts to remedy the problems of the day.

It was the drive to make sociology a recognized science that took it into institutions of higher education where it came to be taught and perceived largely in terms of its European roots. Many sociology students today, even at the graduate level, will not recognize the names, and certainly not the works, of the likes of Lester Ward, Albion Small, Franklin Giddings, or Edward Ross because they have learned a Eurocentric version of sociology taught from the works of Durkheim, Marx, and Weber. As Shils noted,

> The men of learning...of whom Lester F. Ward was perhaps the greatest, have passed without a trace; his works are practically never referred to in any piece of research. The same is true of Franklin H. Giddings, the versatile and erudite incumbent of the chair at Columbia University (1948:6).

It goes without saying that women such as Jane Addams, Emily Green Balch, Mary Simkhovitch, Mary McDowell, Anna Cooper, and Ida Wells Barnett are either unknown or associated with social work or civil rights. Similarly men such as Graham Taylor and Robert Woods who identified as Christian sociologists have been lost in the history of American sociology. Only in recent years, and as a direct result of the civil rights and women's movements, have some texts resorted to an "add and stir" pattern of political correctness by including in their pages the works of African Americans such as W.E.B. Du Bois and women such as Jane Addams and Charlotte P. Gilman. Even though such acknowledgments may be seen as token efforts to correct the omissions of the past, they have, nevertheless, begun to turn us away from a purely Eurocentric, male sociology. While settlement work has largely been incorporated into the history of social work (Trolander 1987), its history as early sociology is still being told (Deegan 1990; Lengermann and Niebrugge 2002, 2007; MacLean and Williams 2012; Williams and MacLean 2012). The narrative we seek to tell is contextualized by the historical separation of a pragmatic community-based "public sociology" practiced for social reform and an institutionalized university-based "community of inquiry" we know today as professional sociology (Oberschall 1972, Haskell 2000). During the Progressive Era as part of a larger Social Science Movement, a sociology of science and reason led the reform efforts of its practitioners. Under the label of sociology, these practitioners were teaching, investigating, interpreting, writing, and advocating for social changes even as they built important programs for community services and advanced social policy, political and business reforms. They self-identified as sociologists even though they were largely working outside the academy in a collective effort to change the class dynamics that fostered social inequalities in a newly industrializing America.

Our critical narrative is told from the perspective of key actors and leaders in the settlement movement. We take as our starting point the assertion that a sociological re-telling of the story is needed because sociology gives theoretical primacy to society as the cause of social problems and as such seeks solutions in the reform of society not in the reform of individuals. Although different versions of this story have been told, most emphasize the role of a group of professional men working in academic settings (Oberschall 1972, Diner 1975, Vidich and Lyman 1985). Few acknowledge the important role that reform-minded women and some less well-known men played in the institutionalization of the discipline-based study of social problems. Discovering and reclaiming for sociology this diverse history is important because it teaches us significant lessons about who we are as sociologists and about why we continue to struggle with defining our professional identities. We particularly struggle with identity issues vis-à-vis lay audiences and students, even as we reproduce many of the same issues and tensions regarding relevance, insularity, and a politics of exclusion in the academy today.

A Politics of Erasure: Knowledge and Knowers in the Sociology Canon

Lengermann and Niebrugge-Brantley began the process of writing women back into the history of sociology and provide an important conceptual framework that restores settlement sociology by linking the first decades of a humanistic social science to the profession today (1998, 2002, 2007). The lost history of sociology's reform roots they argue can be understood as a casualty of a "politics of erasure," a social and political process that has erased collective memories and the actual contributions, or artifacts, of early women founders and many reform-minded men such as the social gospelers. In their day, these "predecessors" were widely influential and enjoyed a large following, successfully influencing and mobilizing public sentiment. These scholar-activists were aware that they were participating in a larger movement to define sociology as a science. They "had their own sense of what that science should be: a project of social critique in which research and theory had as a morally necessary focus the description, analysis, and correction of social inequality" (Lengermann and Niebrugge-Brantley 1998:10). As part of a contest for legitimacy and authority around the turn of the century, a political process began that eventually defined "legitimate" forms of knowledge as "value-neutral" professional scientism, and legitimate "knowers" as academic men (Harding 1991). This process essentially marginalized or erased the contributions and careers of the women and men practicing settlement sociology. During its founding years American sociology was perhaps ninety percent reform and ten percent science (Oberschall 1972). Elite social scientists associated with universities led the march toward scientism and away from social reform although not without struggle. Calhoun notes, for instance that,

> Nineteenth-century social science engaged intellectuals, advocates, and administrators on the basis of a broadly shared concern with social problems and social change. Theirs was not first and foremost an interest in research or knowledge for its own sake but instead for dealing with social (and sometimes personal) problems. Once the disciplinary project launched, however, advancing sociology became more often an end in itself. *This did not go uncontested.* The tension between achieving intellectual authority and being publicly engaged has been present throughout the discipline's history. *Many academic sociologists articulated a commitment to science intended both to claim authority over and to secure independence from extra-academic reformers.* ... Economics and sociology both emerged as disciplines within this broad context. ...sociology... would remain enduringly divided over the primacy of scientific pursuit of generalizable, lawlike knowledge versus engagement with social problems and social change (2007:10–11, emphasis added).

In pursuit of professional scientism and in wrestling authority from a lay population, reform-minded women and social gospel men were easily dismissed as "do-gooders," philanthropists, charity and social workers lacking in professional social scientific training and authority. As will be seen in the chapters to follow, however, these are highly distorted "typifications" that served to diminish and erase the significant contributions of early scholar-activists—contributions scientific in nature and intended to put scientific-based knowledge to work. The early settlement reformers examined in the cases that follow were not only involved in conducting some of the first scientific studies and in pioneering new methods such as mapping techniques but were also educators involved in teaching statistics, survey skills, and observational field methods. They were active in professional associations and in academic sociology; they were prolific writers of books and articles, publishing in such venues as the *American Journal of Sociology*. They earned advanced degrees and many studied in Europe. These "erased" sociologists were not lacking in technical training and sophistication, rather as Lengermann and Niebrugge-Brantley note,

> [t]he erasure of women founders is most basically explained in terms of women's tenuous hold on authority in a man-made culture; that tenuousness can be understood through an analysis of how one person is "present" to, or known in consciousness by, another person (1998:11).

In a feminist reformulation of Alfred Schutz's phenomenological theory of knowledge construction (Schutz 1967, Schutz and Luckmann 1973) they describe the process in which written works and identities are included or lost to the traditional canon.

> For Schutz, the capacity to know another person is learned in the situation of face-to-face relating, the essential relation of human life, in which one consciousness recognizes the other as a human 'like himself.' Schutz calls this the 'thou-orientation,' or 'consociate,' relation. ... [In the] 'contemporary relation'.... individuals are known to each other in consciousness—know each other—through mental constructs, or 'typifications.' A typification may be based on previous firsthand experience, information from mutual acquaintances, documents produced by or telling about the other, or actions the other is known to have undertaken. When a person dies, he becomes a 'predecessor' in Schutz's schema and even more subject to a rigid and lasting typification. Over time, as those who knew an individual also die, the predecessor is increasingly remembered through artifacts—things the person made or wrote, or things others made or wrote about the person. In an academically based profession like sociology, the key artifacts for typifying predecessors are their writings, which may become part of the canon (1998:11).

Adding gender to this model provides an important corrective because male consciousness of women in face-to-face relations is not defined as the "I-thou" relation, but rather as the "I-other" in which male associates view women and their works as "less than," as the mere antics of one who lacks authority (1998:11). Women were well aware that their works were not always taken seriously and many wrote of their dismissive treatment in journals, letters, and autobiographies. For example, Beatrice Webb wrote of a conversation with Professor Alfred Marshall of Cambridge, who said of her proposed project "A book by you on the Co-operative Movement I may get my wife to read to me in the evening to while away the time, but I shan't pay any attention to it" (Webb 1926:352 as cited in Lengermann and Niebrugge-Brantley 1998:13). Although the early women founders were often denied authority because of gender, they nevertheless left an impressive array of sociological artifacts in the form of writings, public policy, and reform work. After these women died and became predecessors, however, they were "truly subsumed within the assumptions of patriarchy" as the symbolic significance of their works came under the evaluative control of men as the legitimate authorities and gatekeepers of the canon (Lengermann and Niebrugge-Brantley 1998:13). The canon represents the "authoritative works" that find their way onto required reading lists, and are "must know" for doctoral exams. A politics of gender has given preference to males over females and a politics of knowledge in sociology has given preference to European roots over American roots and to "scientific" roots over applied or reform roots. In the re-telling of history, some of the works of the women founders have recently been resurrected, but most are still denied a place in the history of sociology. The formative period of American sociology is characterized by a politic about the form that knowledge should take (objectivity versus advocacy) and about who can be a legitimate knower. Its impact fell on both men and women associated with social reform movements in the United States.

> In the period between 1890 and 1947, sociology's academic elites arrived at the consensus that the appropriate role for the sociologist was that of the intellectual committed to scientific rigor, value-neutrality, and formal abstraction. This consensus de-legitimated the work of the women founders, and many men, who practiced the alternative position of a critical, activist sociology of advocacy.
>
> LENGERMANN and NIEBRUGGE-BRANTLEY 1998:14

It is important to reiterate that in the contests over legitimacy and the struggle to develop a science of sociology—one accorded the same respect as other disciplines—that much of the work dismissed and written out of its history was indeed scientific at its base. The primary difference was that the settlement sociologists aimed to create social change and reforms based on sociological knowledge, a venture that became too risky for professional academic sociologists. Particularly as the academic environment became increasingly pro-business and reactionary in its fear of communism, many universities purged their activist and reform-minded faculty (cf. Furner 1975, Diner 1980, Bannister 1987). "[T]he growing emphasis on scientistic expertise was sociology's move into the university as its 'legitimate' work site, a move that was part of its quest for professional authority, social status, and job and salary security" (Lengermann and Niebrugge-Brantley 1998:15). Outside of the halls of academe, settlement houses were home to a variety of social reform, educational, and research activities for both early sociology and social work. Much of the work that was sociological in nature was later rewritten into history by male gate-keepers as social work. For example, on the fiftieth anniversary of the *American Journal of Sociology*, then-editor Louis Wirth, dismissed these sociological predecessors as "social workers, social reformers, social prophets, and social critics who, for want of any other academic refuge, had identified themselves with the adolescent science of sociology" (Wirth 1947:273 as quoted in Lengermann and Niebrugge 1998:15).

The Social Science Movement: Sociology and Social Work

Understanding the politics of erasure builds upon a critical historical narrative of the relationship between sociology and social work.

> [S]ociology and social work began not as distinct fields but as part of a general impulse for social science that emerged out of the reform activism of the mid-nineteenth century. What we today take for granted as the 'natural' division of social science...was a decades-long development out of that original impulse. ... Both fields, at the same time, felt the counter pressure to 'professionalize'...that grew with industrialization and urbanization and with the modern university...individuals who frequently had allegiances to both fields [held] conflicting views about how the fields should relate.
>
> LENGERMANN and NIEBRUGGE 2007:63

The Social Science Movement with its emphasis on research for social reform provided the backdrop for contests over professional definition and the institutionalization of a place or domain for practice. In many respects, a victim of its own success, the social settlement and its varied progressive projects became a contested terrain from which the disciplines of sociology and social work emerged (MacLean and Williams 2012). Between the 1890s and 1920,

> settlement sociology was as complete a school as any in the history of the discipline: it had a coherence of theory, method, practice, and purpose; it had a major theorist in [Jane] Addams; it had an ongoing process of communication through the settlement networks and publications; and it had a research agenda that, consistent with the original purposes of the Social Science Movement, focused on producing major social reforms.
>
> LENGERMANN and NIEBRUGGE 2007: 98

Over time, however, the success of settlement sociology would become its downfall as its organizations and activities were co-opted, fragmented, and institutionalized by more conservative forces, particularly those working to move the science of society and professional training to the academy and away from the settlement and its programs. These forces also erased from history the collective memory of a more radical sociological praxis: the critical practice of science for large-scale societal reform.

The history of settlement work now told has increasingly been presented as precursor to social work; yet this history can as easily be told as a forerunner to a disciplinary sociology that successfully combined theory and practice. Under the umbrella of the larger Social Science Movement, sociology in 1890 was practiced in many locations including "universities and colleges, government agencies, Charity Organization Societies, theological centers, social settlements, labor unions, and by both public intellectuals and ordinary citizens…" (Lengermann and Niebrugge 2007:85). As universities grew and became defined as research centers and producers of knowledge as opposed to mere teachers of classical curriculum, opportunities emerged for building new curricula and professionalizing academic disciplines. The term sociology increasingly replaced social science in the titles of courses and departments (Bernard and Bernard 1943, Williams and MacLean 2005). Sociology, one of the youngest of the social science disciplines, entered into competition with the more established social sciences such as political science and economics. In order to gain a legitimate domain in the university system, it had to demonstrate that it was a science with its own unique body of knowledge. Moreover, its subject matter could not threaten the interests of other disciplines or university stakeholders such as donors, legislators, and trustees (Lengermann and Niebrugge 2007: 86). Forming a consensus on what exactly would become sociology's unique subject matter was not an easy process. In the 1890s, national debates ensued as the American Social Science Association (founded in 1865) began to differentiate into separate disciplinary associations ultimately dissolving itself in 1909. In 1905 the American Sociological Society was formed and defined its objective as, "the encouragement of sociological research and discussion, and the promotion of intercourse between persons engaged in the scientific study of society" (Rhoades 1981:4). While the emerging discipline still lacked a distinctive subject matter, it clearly viewed itself as having a distinctive method and mission—the scientific study of society. Debates about whether this narrow definition would exclude practical sociological work and non-academics dominated the first meetings (Rhoades 1981). Although it was argued that its broad-based description did not preclude practical sociological work, over time academic representation increased in the association while nonacademic representation decreased. Moreover, as sociology and social work emerged as separate professions, they were increasingly sex-segregated ending what Deegan referred to as the "golden age" of women in sociology (1990:195). As Lengermann and Niebrugge summarized the state of affairs,

> By 1921 sociology and social work had assumed separate but distinctly different professional identities. Sociology saw itself as an academic profession, claiming a specialized knowledge based in the value-neutral pursuit of abstract generalizations about human relations. That academic base was overwhelmingly the domain of white privileged-class men. Social work had established itself as a service profession, seeking to counsel the needy and troubled in practical and immediate ways, working primarily in private and public service bureaucracies, and training in clearly demarcated university-based programs. In both the relief agencies and the university training programs, social work professionals were overwhelmingly women, typically white privileged-class women, because the membership rules of the AASW [American Association of Social Workers] excluded many nondegreed workers who performed the routine labors of aid administration (2007:90).

The authors conclude that by 1921 members of the two disciplines were no longer interested in the other's fields, and each became less effective than had they maintained a "mutual basis of thought and practice." Deegan is more pessimistic in her review of the institutional differentiation and sex-segregation of the two disciplines, noting that "the cultural feminism of the early women sociologists was abandoned... [and the tension] ...between social problems and their resolution versus the struggle for [scientific] respectability resulted in not one 'lost dialectic' but two. Sociology buried its concern for humans, social work abandoned its quest to change society" (1990:317). Certainly the institutionalization of the different fields meant that the settlement lost its unique base that had successfully united theory, research, teaching, and reform activism. As a direct result, settlement sociologists lost much of their autonomy of action and independent thought as a basis for social reform (Deegan 1990, Lengermann and Niebrugge-Brantley 2002, 2007; MacLean and Williams 2012).

Methodology

Berg describes historiography as "the study of the relationships among issues that have influenced the past, continue to influence the present, and will certainly affect the future" (2009:296–297). In this work we adopt a collective case studies approach to examine the sociological contributions of some of the most prominent Progressive Era settlements. Our aim is to explore the various components of the neighborly relations paradigm developed by settlement sociologists in response to emerging social problems related to industrialization, urbanization, and immigration. We draw from and build on the theoretical orientations developed in early feminist and critical revisionist histories that identify the class and masculinist biases commonly reflected in the traditional social science canon. Feminist research has been instrumental in creating an important historical corrective, restoring important contributions and agency to women and female organizations (cf. Reinharz 1992 for a review). However, these works have yet to fully incorporate the contributions of settlement sociologists as predecessors whose artifacts are integral to early American sociology. We seek to develop this history further by building on the pioneering works of Deegan (1990) and Lengermann and Niebrugge-Brantley (2002,2007) and revisionist works on the sociological contributions of social settlements (MacLean and Williams 2012; Williams and MacLean 2012). We are particularly interested in learning lessons from the past that can inform the discipline's ongoing debates related to present day tensions and issues regarding sociology's visibility, insularity, relevance and application—all of critical importance to the future of the discipline (Burawoy 2005a,b; Nichols 2005, 2007; McAdam 2007). A burgeoning literature on feminist research methods suggests the importance of standpoint epistemologies and reflexive practices as an alternative to post-positivist science (Smith 1974; Collins 1986, 2000; Harding 1987; Haraway 1988; Reinharz 1992; Naples 2003; Sprague 2005; Jaggar 2008). Standpoint epistemologies, in particular, place emphasis on the "subjugated knowledges" reflected in the paradigms, themes, interests, and values of groups with differential power in the validation of knowledge. Specialized knowledge is always socially located in the standpoint or social positions of groups of people in the larger system of stratification (e.g., by race, ethnicity, class, gender, national origin, sexual orientation, or religion). Situated knowledge is by definition partial, contingent, and politically informed if not subject to bias (Haraway 1988). However, by privileging the perspective of the "outsider within" (Collins 1986) a recovery of the voices of historically marginalized or "erased" groups can potentially provide a more complete knowledge of sociology's history.

In the present analysis we use a collective case studies method, searching for continuities and differences among social settlements in an effort to gain a more holistic perspective on early American sociology and shedding light on the specialized knowledges of settlement sociologists. Initially we selected what we found to be the most visible settlement houses based on a review of existing research on the early contributions of women (Deegan 1991) and settlements (Barbuto 1999; Wood and Kennedy 1911) to American Sociology and Progressive Era reform. In the historical period examined, perhaps as much as 90 percent of settlement work was located in Chicago, Boston, and New York. We thus reviewed archives located in these geographic areas holding collections on social settlements and their associated residents. After searching the archival resources and finding guides of a longer list of settlements, we narrowed our list to three settlements in Chicago (Hull House, University of Chicago Settlement, Chicago Commons), two settlements in New York (Greenwich House and Henry Street), South End House of Boston, and those of the College Settlements Association (Denison House of Boston and the College Settlements of Philadelphia and New York). Settlements were selected primarily based on their representation of the works of prominent settlement leaders in the feminist pragmatist and social gospel movements of the period. The College Settlements Association was included because of its importance in providing a geographic network of opportunity and training for college educated women. As we searched for data we initially cast our net as wide as our resources allowed, not having determined the final list of settlements to be included. Ultimately while not representative of all of the settlements and neighborhood centers in this period we believe that the selected settlements provide an excellent sampling of cases of early sociological practice in scholarly research and reform activism.

A case study method is defined as "research that focuses on a single case, or single issue, in contrast with studies that seek generalizations through comparative analysis or compilation of a large number of instances" (Reinharz 1992:164). Case studies are based on a bounded unit, such as a person or group of people, an organization, an episode, a process, or community. In our analysis the settlement organization was the primary unit for sample selection, and the works of individuals associated with the settlements were included in data collection and analysis. According to Berg collective case studies, as in the present work, allow for "understanding and insight" and for representing contrasting situations (2009:326). Case studies are particularly distinguished by their use of multiple forms of data which are combined into a unitary whole in formulating generalizations or lessons learned from the case (Berg 2009, Creswell 2013). In this work we draw from a variety of primary and secondary data sources including letters, diaries, news clippings, oral histories, autobiographical and scholarly writings, as well as the writings of contemporaries of the period under study. Over a period of several years, we made visits to archival collections related to the selected settlements. We collected primary data from records and papers of the settlement houses and leaders and residents associated with those settlements. We utilized various archival collections in three libraries and a museum in Chicago, three libraries in New York, three in Boston, and one in South Hampton Massachusetts. These archival records produced most of our primary data including historical records of each of the settlements as well as the writings, speeches, and sometimes autobiographies or other artifacts of settlement leaders and residents. Primary data were also found in sociological publications now preserved in on-line archives such as that of the *American Journal of Sociology, Annals of the American Academy of Political and Social Science*, and *The Survey*. Additionally, we were able to access many of the books authored by settlement workers. No doubt, indicative of renewed interest in social settlements, some of these works are now available electronically (some free on books.google.com) and others have been repackaged for publication in recent years, sometimes with original pages copied and released with new bindings and others in new editions with fresh introductions and commentary. Major sources of secondary data were biographies and historical works about the settlement movement and some aspects of that history including the ideas, theories, methods, teachings, and activism of key participants. All of the selected settlements had at least one person, often more, about whom biographies have been written. For the most part, these were considered secondary data although they differ in importance in terms of whether the biography was written with cooperation of the subject or the relationship of author to subject. For example, the only biography of Robert Woods was written by his wife. Jane Addams' nephew wrote one of her many biographies.

According to Reinharz (1992:164), "[f]eminist case studies usually consist of a fully developed description of a single event, person, group, organization, or community" She goes on to note that beyond the goal of generating and testing theory, three major purposes of case studies are "to analyze the change in a phenomenon over time, to analyze the significance of a phenomenon for future events, and to analyze the relation among parts of a phenomenon." With these parameters guiding our analysis, we selected specific cases because of the critical players involved and specific events and issues related to the development of the neighborly relations paradigm as a method of addressing social problems. In our final analysis we seek to show how settlement sociology was practiced, how it shaped the early discipline, and how it can inform a contemporary sociological practice today.

Social and Ideological Context: Feminist Pragmatism, the Social Gospel, and Settlement Sociology

Before launching into the case studies of specific settlements, it is important to take note of the social and ideological context of the Progressive Era that made it possible for scholar-activists of diverse backgrounds to collaborate successfully. The first two chapters contextualize the settlement case studies by locating them within the dynamics of industrialization, urbanization and immigration. These social forces provide some of the framework for understanding the settlement and social gospel movements that shaped and were part and parcel of the Progressive Era. Although the settlement movement was dominated by college educated women (Totenberg 1974, Carson 1990:176–177), it was also driven and sustained by leaders of the social gospel movement. Feminist pragmatists who were typically secular humanists in orientation launched settlements and activities in collaboration with social gospel men who were often led by a philosophy of joining religion and social action. Some women settlement leaders were also social gospelers, successfully combining Christian socialism and feminism in their quest for pragmatic social change.

In a case history of the College Settlements Association Rousmaniere poses the question, "Why did a particular group of women found a strikingly unique philanthropic organization in 1889?" (1970: 45). In other words, what were the social conditions that opened a space for a group of privileged women to practice settlement sociology and social reform at this juncture in history? In part, he answers this question by assessing changes in women's higher education (see for example, Miller-Bernal 2000, MacLean and Williams 2005). But as will be documented in the following chapters, women's education was only one of a myriad of historical, social and political changes that gave rise to the Progressive Era. Rousmaniere addressed the link between social marginality and organizational structure, arguing that women had a collective sense of mission as pioneers, driving them to form "colonies" or settlements that combined both philanthropic work and home. In this way the problematic, deeply entrenched "separate spheres" doctrine (Rosenberg 1982) could be addressed and accommodated. Similarly, Deegan (1990) and Lengermann and Niebrugge-Brantley (1998) argue that Hull House became a base from which a network of women and auxiliary organizations were able to pool their expertise and resources to generate and carry out early sociological research and a social reform agenda. In fact, Muncy (1991) shows how a group of women successfully carved out a "female dominion" in American reform, activism, and public service. The early women of Hull House were able to organize a movement of women's clubs, organizations, and associations to place key women like Julia Lathrop and Grace Abbott in strategic government positions such as the federal Children's Bureau. In turn, the Chicago School of Civics and Philanthropy, under the tutelage of Sophonisba Breckenridge and Edith Abbott, helped train workers to staff the Children's Bureau and conducted research under its auspices. The settlement movement thus became a vehicle for college-educated women to simultaneously launch careers, to shape the civic development of industrial cities, and to craft important social service programs and public policies in a sweeping quest for social justice (Diner 1980).

Deegan describes Addams' feminism as *cultural feminism*, emphasizing that she believed in and "wrote extensively on the superiority of women's values, world-view, and behavior" (1990: 225). Addams "valued the female world and wanted it to be extended throughout society." To the extent that women embodied or viewed the world through a maternal lens this "strength of women...was denied its full expression in patriarchal society" (1990:227). Deegan documented the radical influences on the settlement movement's visionary agenda as reflected in the socialist works and writings of the likes of Florence Kelley and Charlotte P. Gilman.

> [T]he residents of Hull-House, including Addams, were not demurely reading 'proper' or 'saintly' literature, but were interested in radical changes in the structure of society, including feminist alterations in women's power and status. ... Repeatedly, Addams advanced the argument that women were more humanitarian, caring, and 'down to earth' than men. By restricting women's freedom to the home, the larger society was corrupt and unjust. Everyday life functioned poorly because it was based on male values and ethics. This cultural feminism permeated the settlement movement, and provided a system of values for organizing life in these communal homes.
>
> DEEGAN 1990: 229–230

Cultural feminism with its emphasis on the virtues of women-centered values and interests was consistent with socialist materialist leanings, particularly of the British Fabian variety that would more fairly, but peacefully, redistribute wealth in society and close the gap between rich and poor. Vida Scudder, a founder of the College Settlements Association, was influenced by Fabian socialism as she proclaimed her goal of freeing people from the "prison of class," a passion which led her, over the course of her lifetime, to a synthesis of Marxism and Christianity. Addams was influenced by and influenced the early University of Chicago pragmatism, a uniquely American philosophy reflected in the collective works of John Dewey, George H. Mead, William James, and W.I. Thomas (Deegan 1990, Seigfried 1996). Both Deegan and Seigfried, note, however, that Addams' critical pragmatism was of a much more radical variety than the others, particularly in her willingness to forcefully advocate for the minority, less powerful voice, and in her critique and rejection of hierarchical social science. At the heart of the pragmatist tradition is the union of social democracy and education combined with political action and social reform. Deegan states that, simply put, "its central concern is the human capacity for intelligent, purposive behavior" (1990: 247). In the writings of pragmatists, education and improved communications play a key role as a social democratizing force in society. Because humans are viewed as "pliable and shaped through social interaction," social science was thought to play a key role in the evolution of civil society. For pragmatists, social facts and their meanings are seen as created by society through social interaction and are thus qualitatively different from physical facts. In other words, the social world is socially constructed and thus subject to change.

For the most part, cultural feminism was consistent with the critical pragmatist philosophies and with the social gospel that permeated the settlement movement with its emphasis on the union between theory and practice, or social action. Primarily a Protestant phenomenon beginning in the 1880s and 1890s, the social gospel was an attempt to apply the teachings of Jesus, especially those espoused in his "Sermon on the Mount," to social problems. Social gospelers were also proponents of the use of sociology (as they understood it) as a means of helping to alleviate the problems of urban-industrial society and thus hastening the coming of the "Kingdom" of God on earth (Greek 1992:66, Williams and MacLean 2012). Social gospelers in the United States ranged from Christian socialists to moderates who simply wanted to practice the second commandment of "loving thy neighbor as thyself" (King James Bible: Matthew 22:39). This pragmatic social gospel vision, while religious in motivation, nonetheless was consistent in practice with the social constructionist and pragmatic feminism of women settlement workers.

The Sociological Imagination from Margins to Center

While all of the various histories of sociology have contributed to the whole of who we are, or who our publics think we are, none has captured the entire complex history of a discipline that has been many things to many publics and individuals. Nor will this work be the final, definitive history of sociology. It will, however, fill some of the gaps left by the limitations in our current histories. The fact that sociology lacks a core definition or dominant theoretical paradigm has been viewed by many as its weakness and its downfall. We prefer to think that this is not a weakness but rather is the strength of our discipline. Pluralism and diversity are not only the spice of life, but more importantly allow for an open posture in constructing knowledge that is inclusive and holistic. In creating dialogue that moves from disciplinary margin to center, knowledge construction is more complete and truth claims can be assessed from a reflective posture that allows for correction. What we attempt to write in the pages that follow is a part of the history of sociology that can be added to what we already know, providing context as well as density and greater authenticity. We have searched out new pieces of the early history of sociology and we offer new conceptual linkages between these recovered data and the data of our past. In the process we attempt to bring to the center of our early history certain marginal sociologists who are little known, particularly to our students, but who represent for sociology a collective legacy of champions for social justice and equality. Many of our predecessors in sociology have, whether consciously or accidently, been erased from our history and their artifacts lost to time. By examining some of the unknown works excluded from the heterodoxy of American sociology, we aim to create a greater awareness of history and to stoke the flames of idealism and passion in recreating a science *for* society. Our purpose is to illuminate the works of the women and men who were doing sociology in the Progressive years. Toward this end we have attempted to discover, analyze, and bring to interested audiences, and particularly to our students, some of the unknown or little known works that contribute to the sociological imagination even today.

CHAPTER 1

Problems in Search of Solutions: Science, Religion, and Education in the Progressive Era

The Forces of Industrialization, Urbanization and Immigration

The period, from roughly the 1890s until World War I, is labeled by historians as the Progressive Era. It was an era characterized by rapid social change defined and driven by social and economic forces, particularly industrialization, urbanization, and immigration. In fact, the *fin de siècle* in the United States can be summed up in these heretofore unequalled and intermeshed social forces but must be understood also as a reaction to an earlier "Gilded Age" (McGerr 2003, Trachtenberg 2007). Between the Civil War and the Progressive Era, industry grew, businesses expanded into corporations, and wealth became concentrated in the hands of a few families, leaving behind a working class defined by poverty. By 1890, fewer than ten percent of the families in America—a group referred to as the "upper ten"—owned 71 percent of the wealth (Hayes 1957:136, McGerr 2003:5–7). Such wealth was often built on the backs of laborers threatening the ideal of American democracy. Statisticians estimated that a family of four needed about $750–880 a year for mere subsistence. Few, however, earned this much. For example, in New York State, the average factory worker earned $416 per year, assuming no layoffs; dock workers averaged $520–624 per year (Ehrenreich 1985:23–24). The United States was in transition from a rural agrarian society to a complex urban-industrial society where cities rapidly outgrew their immature infrastructures or lacked infrastructures altogether. Waves of European immigrants, in search of jobs and the "American dream"—a promise of mobility and prosperity for those willing to work for it—were part of the urban-industrial growth. However, social problems no more defined the turn of the century than the reform movements that arose to counter the problems. Settlement houses, a new social Christianity, and a new social science worked, sometimes in disparate paths, sometimes together, to alleviate problems of this new urban-industrial United States. The clergy, long deferred to for their authority and leadership, were challenged by the would-be social scientists of the day and by the newly emerging academic men of authority. Settlement workers challenged charity workers and politicians by living among the poor as neighbors. The turn of the century brought new problems and a search for answers mandating changes in social thought, in leadership, and in authority.

From 1860 to 1920, "unskilled immigrant laborers were the dominant factory manufacturing labor force" in the US (Kim 2007:4–5, 22). The captains of industry bent on profit-making and growth turned a blind eye to the needs of workers. Ten to twelve hour days were the norm as were low pay, abysmal working conditions, and no benefits, setting the stage for labor unrest, strikes, and riots to follow (see for example Nicholson 2004). Poor working conditions were exacerbated by equally poor living conditions and sometimes—as in the case of tenement manufacturing (known as the sweating system)—the two were combined (Kelley [1895] 2004). Cities were inadequate in streets, public water supplies, sewage systems, garbage disposal, police and fire protection, parks, playgrounds and recreational facilities as well as public education and housing. "In the 1890s in America not a single one of the major municipalities had adequate traffic facilities. The majority of streets were ill paved, turning into seas of mud during rains, or paved with cobblestones or granite blocks" (Martindale 1958:13). Yet, the masses came in search of work and in pursuit of the dream of prosperity. Lacking transportation, if they found work, they had to live nearby, but not only did industry attract workers, workers attracted industry. "The problem of housing mass populations was met by a building of shanties, rooming houses, hotels of many kinds and inventions such as the tenement house which rapidly formed the slum sections of the cities" (Martindale 1958:15). Urban growth patterns and density in the United States made it necessary, as some proclaimed, to "make a great city in a few years out of nothing" (Hofstadter 1955:176). Business expansion in the nation's cities brought jobs, but often at less than livable wages. Affordable housing was at a premium and was frequently hazardous to the health of its occupants. Immigrants tended to cluster in select city neighborhoods because of ethnic networks that facilitated housing, the transmission of information about the labor market and a support system to help negotiate a new and unknown environment. These networks contributed to the growth of overcrowded neighborhoods and to a division of labor in some markets. By 1890, almost 15 percent of the US population was foreign born, up from 10 percent in 1850 (Gibson and Jung 2006:26). In cities such as Boston, Chicago, and New York natives were outnumbered by foreign-born and their first-generation children (Hofstadter 1955:177–178).

The role of immigration in the building of urban, industrial America cannot be overstated. From 1820 to 1880, over 10 million immigrants came, most from Northern and Western Europe (Bailey 1961:324). They were English, Irish, Scandinavians, and Germans. With the exception of the Irish, these groups were welcomed and accepted into US life because they were of the Anglo-Saxon or Teutonic heritage and culture and not very different in appearance from the nation's founders. Over time, the new arrivals became part of the

English-modeled institutions, culture, and racial dominance of the young nation. The Irish encountered more difficulties in gaining acceptance than other groups. They were Catholic; they came in large numbers (1.6 million), and with a history of British conflict. Compared to other groups, such as Germans, they were "the least mobile both geographically and occupationally" (Kim 2007:4). The unique Irish experience in the US no doubt accounts for their working their way into, and ultimately gaining a measure of political control in cities where their numbers were substantial such as Chicago and Boston. The 1880s saw a change in the flow of immigrants entering the US with most coming from Southern, Central, and Eastern Europe. They found acceptance and assimilation more difficult than earlier groups because they tended to be illiterate, poverty stricken, non-Teutonic, and predominantly Catholic, Eastern Orthodox, or Jewish. Some came not because of their attraction to the United States but because they were fleeing poverty and/or oppression in their homelands. The "Little Italys" and "Little Polands" of New York and Chicago soon were larger in numbers than the villages from which these newcomers migrated, arousing alarm, not only among native-born Americans but also among earlier immigrant groups. "Old-line Americans protested that the original Anglo-Saxon Puritan stock would soon be outbred and outvoted" (Bailey 1961:545). Reacting to such fears, beginning in the early 1920s, the US Congress limited immigration with a series of laws that became known as the National Origins (or Quota) System (Schafer 2006:99–100). However, already, between 1881 and 1920, 20.7 million immigrants had come to the United States (Feagin and Feagin 2008:58). The largest groups were Italian, Polish, Hungarian, Slovakian, Czechoslovakian, and European Jews.

Social Science and Premonitions of Sociology

As the country moved toward the end of the century, the lines between the classes, particularly those who lived in comfort versus all others, were sharply drawn. The Progressive Era brought "an extraordinary explosion of middle-class activism" from the group living between those of extreme wealth and extreme poverty (McGerr 2003:7). For many activists the answer to urban problems was social science, albeit poorly defined and often consisting of little more than repackaged religion combined with unsophisticated efforts at social investigation. In the US, social science acquired something of the character of a moral crusade against the doctrine of individualism and against laissez-faire public policies (Sklar 1998:132). Coupled with this new social consciousness was a move away from an evolutionary deterministic view of life to a belief in voluntarism, offering options for intervention and even changing the course of history and quality of life. The voluntaristic philosophy was a means of coping with urban-industrial problems and daily manifestations of poverty, unfit housing, labor problems, crowding, and lack of sanitation. Evidence of such problems was ubiquitous in the last few decades of the nineteenth century. In addition to squalid tenements, there was labor violence as in the great railroad strikes of 1877 and the Haymarket Incident of 1886. In classless America, "the social question" came to be understood by some as capitalistic exploitation, class conflict, and the deplorable conditions of the working class (Furner 1975, Ross 1992, Stebner 1997: 30). For others, the social question was simply the growing class division or the unequal distribution of wealth (McGerr 2003).

Bernard and Bernard defined the interest in social science in the United States between 1840 and 1890 as a "semi-academic movement for the collection and diffusion of knowledge regarding the conditions and needs of society" (1943:31). For the Bernards, the social science movement was something of an academic construct, an extension of a similar movement in Europe representing the transition from a theologically-oriented to a scientifically-oriented society. They treated it as a precursor of the more specialized academic social sciences rather than the lay movement it actually was. The social science "movement," which was at best pre-science, is epitomized in the American Social Science Association (ASSA) organized in 1865 in Boston. The founders were men and women for whom social science "was an interest and a pastime, not a career" (Haskell 2000:216). Founding of the organization revealed a naive faith in science but with little agreement as to what science was and only a vague consensus that certain problems needed to be investigated and action taken based on "scientific" findings. While the ASSA adopted a name intended to make it a national organization, it was formed in Boston and was always more active in New England than in other parts of the country. In fact, it was an offshoot of the Massachusetts Board of Charities, which later spawned the Conference of Charities and Correction, seen today as the parent organization of professional social work. It was in the context of remedial intervention in pursuit of progress and a better quality of life that the ASSA was born, organized into five "departments": Education, Health, Jurisprudence, Social Economy, and Finance. Haskell concluded that the leaders were not scientists but "men of affairs" such as Franklin Sanborn, the Massachusetts Inspector of Charities and for a time editor of the Springfield *Republican*; David Wells, Commissioner of Revenue; Andrew White, Ambassador to Germany; William T. Harris, Commissioner of Education; John Graham Brooks, Unitarian minister, free-lance writer and social critic, as well as a number of college presidents and elected politicians (2000:164, 228). Such men were the public face of the

ASSA, but women were involved from its creation to its demise. Two of the original 12 members of the executive board were women, and between 1865 and 1880, association membership was always at least 10 percent female (Leach 1989:315). Rosenberg notes that "Women played an active role in the work of the ASSA departments of health, education, and social economy, where they comprised between 20 and 30 percent of the membership" (1982:25). ASSA members were men and women from the upper or upper-middle classes who possessed what was no doubt typical thinking for their day, that is, that they were positioned to know what was in the best interest of the country and of the masses. Social Science to most of the ASSA members was not an autonomous branch of knowledge but the factual underpinnings of the esoteric advice that professional men had always dispensed to the lay public (Haskell 2000:165). The ASSA was rooted in a Christian pragmatist paradigm as is evident in their many publications, speeches, and meetings. Typical was an annual address delivered in 1878 by President Benjamin Peirce who, speaking on the importance of social science, declared, "The only solid basis for an enduring republic is the Rock of Ages. Any other foundation is unstable and insecure...the children of men will reunite in permanent harmony; science and religion will coincide; and the one universal speech will be God's word..." (Haskell 2000:147). Among competing professionals, ASSA members were on the battlefront of the culture wars of their day and in the name of science, often inseparable from religion. Haskell concluded that "The progressive generation owed much to Sanborn and his colleagues for their early groping efforts to articulate and conceptualize the tendencies of an urban-industrial society" (2000:203).

The ASSA existed until 1909 but was gradually stripped of both substance and influence by the formation of more specialized organizations: first the American Historical Association (1884), then the American Economic Association (1885), the Political Science Association (1903), and finally out of these last two groups the American Sociological Society was formed (1905). The Bernards treat the latter as a part of a larger social science movement and as the direct precursor of sociology. They conclude, "we have before us in the history of the Social Science Movement an exhibit of the rapid and panoramic development of a new science of human affairs comparable to the earlier development of the physical sciences" (1943:836–837). It is clear, however, that ASSA members were not scientists, as we know the term today, and the link between the ASSA and science was not as direct as scholars such as the Bernards suggest. Nevertheless, men and women of the ASSA should be credited with helping to instill in the public consciousness a belief that human beings were not helpless victims of a deterministic environment or evolutionary process.

They promoted the belief that people were capable of shaping society and of providing ameliorative relief for the problems of urban-industrial life through science.

The Survey Movement and the Educating of America

Research of the social science variety was largely understood to be synonymous with social surveys, the popularity and frequency of which led to what became known as the Survey Movement that began in the United States in the 1880s and peaked with World War I (Converse 1987:22–32). Surveys dated back to the work of Charles Booth in London and in the US were associated with the work of philanthropy, settlement houses, churches, and progressive politics (Deegan 1991:391–399, Converse 1987). Settlement workers made free use of surveys to present problems associated with urban living and to argue for social reform. Surveys were also widely used by cities and churches, and to learn about rural life. One of the unique aspects of early surveys was that they were designed to involve members of the community although "experts" were typically responsible for their planning and implementation. The involvement of citizens was thought to insure interest in follow-up and use of survey results. It was assumed, naively, that whatever facts were collected via a survey would be put to good use. Such well-known religious and educational leaders as Francis Peabody, Edward Cummings, and Graham Taylor promoted the church's use of surveys to achieve reform and social progress (Vidich and Lyman 1985:127). The most ambitious survey undertaken was begun in 1920 by the Interchurch World Movement and involved 35 Protestant denominations with a budget of over one million dollars.[1] The survey movement was interrupted by World War I and the great depression and never regained its former luster or prominence in scientific, religious, or reform work.

1 The price-tag included anticipated follow-up work. Each county in each state had a paid executive most of whom were clergy although some college professors and students were employed. The writers of the survey insured its failure when they developed an instrument comprised of more than 500 questions that were not standardized and proved difficult to code and tabulate in this pre-computer age. Converse concludes, "The project was an enormous effort to apply sociological concepts to the study of community and church, an extension of the survey's focus on the community to a national and international scale" (1987:29). In 1921 a committee was funded by John D. Rockefeller, to salvage and summarize data that could be extracted. This committee ultimately became the Institute of Social and Religious Research that funded subsequent and better designed works such as the now classics by Robert and Helen Lynd (1929, 1937).

Another Progressive Era phenomenon that contributed to bringing together settlement houses, religion, and the new science of sociology was a search for education—both formal and informal. A public pursuit of knowledge was evident in such adult education programs as Chautauqua, in the programs of the American Social Science Association, the Southern Sociological Congress,[2] and in the survey movement with its community involvement. Numerous summer schools and institutes, such as offered by the American Society for the Extension of University Teaching and Chautauqua, brought together clergy, reformers, social scientists, and ordinary citizens seeking the latest social science findings, survey data, and an exchange of ideas. Oberschall credits the Chautauqua movement with being a powerful lobby for reform and for sociology because its topics contributed to a desire for more education among the public and paved the way for the introduction of sociology courses in seminaries, colleges, and universities (1972:201). Greek concluded that in the 1880s Chautauqua "became committed to the 'sociological movement', hoping to contribute to the Christian regeneration of American society through applying 'scientific' knowledge to the solution of social problems" (1992:138).

America's pursuit of education was evident in the growth of degree-granting institutions. Goldin and Katz report that there were only 49 institutions of higher education established in the US between 1638 and 1819. From 1820 to 1859, 240 more were added, and from 1860 to 1899, 348 were established. By the turn of the century, there were an estimated 721 degree-granting colleges and universities (1999:42). Enrollment in higher education in the United States grew from 30,000 in 1860 to 250,000 in 1900 as institutions reached out to educate more than just the elite (Carson 1990:19). Women's schools came into their own after the Civil War, at first at the high school level. Those with a college curriculum were often labeled "seminaries," such as Mount Holyoke in Massachusetts and Rockford in Illinois. The several decades following the Civil War also gave rise to a number of historically black schools and to a long-running controversy as to whether African Americans should be offered the same curriculum as in colleges for white men or if they should be offered only a vocational-technical education. Some of both kinds of institutions developed and schools founded as vocational-technical gradually began offering a classical academic curriculum as did female seminaries, no doubt contributing to the curricula transformation in higher education (MacLean and Williams 2005). To justify their existence and to allay public fears that women would relinquish

2 An organization based in Nashville, TN devoted at first largely to race relations and later to quality of life issues. Meetings were racially integrated and featured well-known and popular speakers (Bernard 1913, Chatfield 1960).

their traditional roles in society, and not incidentally to secure funding, women's colleges offered a careful rationale for their programs. Sophia Smith who funded Smith College stated in her will, "It is not my desire to render my sex any the less feminine...but to develop as fully as may be the powers of womanhood" (Carrell 1981:66). The first justification that educated women would make better wives and mothers was articulated as a kind of ideal service ethic, an expansion of the traditional domestic and philanthropic roles of women. As Smith put it, "As teachers, as writers, as mothers, as members of society, their power for good will be incalculably enlarged" (Carrell 1981:66). Women's colleges included a strong indoctrination as to the responsibilities of the first generation of female college graduates to work for a better world. For example, Vida Scudder of Wellesley College promoted both social service and social science for women. "Charity becomes scientific, and founds its methods on ascertained law; political economy becomes moral; and recognizes for the first time the truth of universal brotherhood.... Women must be aroused to a sense of their responsibility on the one hand; they must be trained to practical efficiency on the other" (VDSP 1887b:B2, F6)

Oberschall concluded that the rapid expansion of higher education put the United States ahead of Europe in the growth of sociology (1972:187). The last half of the nineteenth century saw a wide-spread introduction of sociology into the American university, an acknowledgment that classical studies such as languages, history, philosophy, and ethics left many areas of social life unexamined. Even as sociology was introduced into the college curriculum, it was associated with social reform and amelioration of social problems (Williams and MacLean 2005). For example, the rationale for introducing sociology at Cornell was that college men were in training to be leaders and should be well informed on the social problems of the day, experiencing "practical instruction calculated to fit young men to discuss intelligently such important social questions as the best methods of dealing practically with pauperism, intemperance, crime...insanity, idiocy, and the like" (Tolman 1902:800). Similarly, Columbia University opened a School of Political Science, where sociology was first included, "designed to prepare young men for the duties of public life" (Tolman 1902:805). In the Progressive Era when growth in education was surpassed only by a growing need to solve social problems, sociology was in the right place at the right time and became established as an academic discipline and as an applied science practiced in social surveys and other forms of social investigation.

Clearly, both the practitioners and academicians gave birth to the discipline of sociology, the women and some men in settlements, in various reform organizations or government agencies, and some, mostly males, in academic settings. As education grew, and perhaps because it grew in an era defined by urban problems, sociology grew along with it as did professional publications geared to the social sciences. Johns Hopkins established *Studies in Historical and Political Science*; Columbia University established its School of Political Science in 1880 along with the *Political Science Quarterly*. The University of Pennsylvania in 1881 established the highly successful *Annals of the American Academy of Political and Social Science*. The fact that sociology was defined largely in terms of social problems and social ethics is clear in the argument made at Columbia to hire a special chair for the division of sociology: "because many special questions of penology, charity, and poor relief could not be treated from the standpoint of pure political economy and many problems of social ethics could not be studied from the point of view of individual ethics" (Oberschall 1972:197). Much of the funding for early educational institutions came from church groups or from private philanthropy that between 1878 and 1898 provided over $150,000,000 for education, funding such schools as Stanford in 1891 and the University of Chicago in 1892 (Bailey 1961:552). The latter included, from its opening, a department of sociology offering graduate degrees and in 1895 launched the *American Journal of Sociology* (AJS) that became the major publication venue for the various sociologies of the day. Under Albion Small's editorship, the AJS published a mix of theoretical, philosophical, reform-oriented, discipline-building, applied, and religious articles. Sociology found early roots in colleges and universities funded by the titans of capitalism. Little wonder then, that the discipline gave rise to some of the early fights to define and secure academic freedom involving issues of activism, free speech, and violations of religious orthodoxy. Silverberg views the split between academic and applied social scientists as overlapping if not identical to the split between men and women in the social sciences and as an indirect product of women's lack of appointments in high profile academic institutions where political activities were monitored by college presidents or boards. She also views the objective and neutral posture assumed by many academic scientists as a retreat from conflict and possible sanctions in academe (Silverberg 1998:7–8).

The Social Gospel in the Progressive Era

A mostly neglected thread in the history of sociology in the United States is that of religion, specifically what became known as the social gospel. The social gospel or what went by other names such as social Christianity, social evangelism or applied Christianity was the religious expression of progressivism in the

United States although it was the product of worldwide forces (Latta 1936:256).[3] Churches and organized religion were unprepared to deal with the complex problems arising at the turn of the century. This lack of preparedness was due not so much to indifference as to a narrow concept of the role of the church in a society where church and state are separate. Furthermore, the church's work was defined largely in terms of saving individual souls from a life of eternal damnation and separation from God, not by saving them from the problems of this life. Recognition that social problems, so blatant in the cities, were compounded if not caused by industrialization and *laissez faire* economics came slowly, due in part to the fact that many churches were not serving the working classes of people, particularly immigrants. In fact, some thought that churches had lost the confidence of the working classes (Latta 1936:259). The capitalist economic system that was working for some while oppressing others seemed on the surface both democratic and Christian and if blame was to be assessed it was individuals who were faulted. Capitalism had a special appeal to those whose beliefs were rooted in Calvinism as was the case with many in the United States during the late 19th century.[4] Calvinists treated wealth as a sign of God's favor and a mark of God's "election" to eternal salvation. The appeal of *laissez faire* economics was further enhanced by the influence of social Darwinism (attributed to Herbert Spencer) and its sanctioning of a survival of the fittest in the marketplace as well as in the biological chain of life. On the other hand, the harsh realities of urban-industrial life at the turn of the century cried out for change and for solutions to problems. Religion could no longer afford to remain associated more with the next life than with this one. The social gospel, or social Christianity, peaked in the US from roughly 1865 to World War I and was motivated by the need for religion to recover relevance lost with the rise of capitalism (Latta 1936:260).

In the United States, the social gospel or social Christianity was never the same as the more radical Christian socialism. In fact, most social gospelers were careful to dissociate themselves from socialism in the narrow sense of its

3 Herein, all of these will be referred to as the social gospel or the terms used interchangeably unless otherwise noted or in quotations.

4 Calvinism in the US dates to the 16th century French reformer John Calvin whose theology became associated with the protestant reformation. Many settlers in the American colonies, including the English Puritans, French Huguenots, the Dutch of New York, and Scotch-Irish Presbyterians were Calvinists and virtually all protestant denominations were influenced to some degree by Calvinistic beliefs. The religion is best known for its doctrines of predestination, as determined by God, and for the inherent depravity of mankind. For a theoretical treatment of the relationship between capitalism and Calvinism, see that of Max Weber (1958).

being state ownership of all or most business enterprises; rather, their mission was to Christianize capitalism through progress, reforms, and social evangelism (Dorrien 2011: 68). The social gospel was not one unified movement, and the phenomenon discussed here as a precursor to secular sociology was one of several variations which can be consolidated as conservative, radical and progressive (Handy 1966:5–6). The conservatives were not far removed from their Calvanistic roots in supporting *laissez faire* economics and even what some saw as a kind of nationalistic theology portending a secular functionalism. The radical version of social Christianity was akin to Christian socialism, favored sweeping reconstruction, and saw social conflict as inevitable for social change to occur. Somewhere in between these two positions was "progressive social Christianity" that became widely known as the social gospel although it had other names and was directly associated with Progressive Era reforms and often publically identified as sociology.[5] The one commonality of the various social gospelers, particularly radicals and progressives, was their mission to apply the teachings of Jesus as recorded in the New Testament, especially in his "Sermon on the Mount." It was fundamentally to love your fellow human beings as yourself, proclaimed by Jesus as the second commandment after loving God (*King James Bible*, Matthew 22:39). The major tenets of the social gospel suggest both a Christian and a nationalist paradigm: (1) belief in the innate goodness of humankind; (2) acceptance of evolution as compatible with God's plan for the universe; (3) rejection of the determinism of evolution in favor of voluntarism; (4) belief in the inevitable progress of society; (5) redefinition of the Kingdom of God as an earthly utopia; and (6) a belief that America was the place where the Kingdom would be established (Morgan 1969, Greek 1992).

More than perhaps anything else, social gospelers were distinguished by their adaptation of the concept of the "Kingdom of God" that in its history had several meanings (Greek 1992:38–42). In the late 19th century, the social gospelers interpreted the Kingdom of God to mean an earthly utopia where God's will would be sovereign. Preachers toned down their descriptions of heavenly bliss in the next life in favor of advocating progress, and final realization of God's Kingdom in this life. Not only did social gospelers predict and seek an earthly kingdom, but they expected its realization to be in the United States. Here it is obvious that the theology of the social gospel intersected with US nationalism such as represented in the doctrine of Manifest Destiny or with similar grandiose ideas such as American Exceptionalism (Ross 1992:22–23) or "chosen nation" status (Greek 1992:43–50, Dorrien 2011:73). These ideal types

5 For more detailed discussion of the various forms and manifestations of social Christianity, see May (1949), Bodo (1954), Handy (1966), and Henking (1988).

relied on divine sanctioning of the great democratic experiment that was the United States, believed to be chosen by God for the building of His Kingdom. The nation was destined to grow and spread democracy, inseparable from Christianity, and finally to become a Christian utopia, God's "new Israel" (Greek 1992:43). Obviously, there was a strain of both racism and ethnocentrism in this nationalistic thinking. For example, social gospeler Josiah Strong provided the logic that was typical in equating the United States and God's Kingdom: Anglo-Saxon people, and especially those in the United States, are the most spiritual and Christian of people; they have developed superior political institutions; the US leads the world in inventions; and English is rapidly becoming the world's predominant language (Strong 1893:54–67). The social gospel was not founded solely on religious sentiment but also on "scientific" knowledge (Greek 1992:64). Strong's last book, *The New World Religion*, mandated "social betterment" as a means of building the Kingdom of God on earth, and he concluded that it was incumbent upon the church to utilize the new tools of social science to accomplish that goal (1915:40).

Because of the influence of Darwinism and of Herbert Spencer in the US and Europe during the late 19th and early 20th centuries, religions were forced to deal with evolution which by some interpretations implied a hands-off approach to social problems as a part of the natural struggle of life leading inevitably to a survival of the fittest. Most social gospelers accepted the basic idea of evolution but not the premise that selection and survival were accidental and unpremeditated. They needed a theory of evolution more compatible with Christianity and thus turned to an earlier Lamarckian concept that recognized God as its driving force, giving divine purpose to change as the source of progress.[6] For example, Henry Ward Beecher, popular preacher and Chautauqua lecturer, was among the first US ministers in the 1880s to voice the belief that evolution was the means that God had chosen to bring about the world's perfection. Beecher was influenced in his thinking by Horace Bushnell, a transitional figure between early and late nineteenth century theologians. His *Christian Nurture* (1847) paved the way for an emphasis on a life-time of work as opposed to a once-in-a-lifetime conversion or "born again" experience. Such early social gospelers as Walter Rauschenbusch, Josiah Strong, and Washington

6 Jean-Baptiste Lamarck (1809) was a French transformational thinker (1744–1829) who offered a theory of evolution preceding that of Darwin (1859). Evolutionary theory could be interpreted as Lamarkian if it allowed for some cosmic force to be directing the process (Greek 1992:23). Since the cosmic force could be divine, this interpretation of evolution was more amenable to Christian thought than was Darwinian evolution which did not necessarily allow for divine guidance.

Gladden made their peace with evolution by simply redefining it. They accepted evolution as rational, as continuous progressive change, and as directed by God. The gospelers accepted the basic idea of organic society, that humankind is bound together and held together in a web of mutual dependence, in a universal brotherhood under a fatherhood of God. They did not, however, accept as inevitable the loss of human beings in a constant evolutionary struggle for survival. Evolution was redefined as culminating in the Kingdom of God: "a reign of God forward [toward] which all creation is moving" (Hopkins 1940:127).[7] This belief led logically to a Christian praxis and to a theology of "inevitable progress" supported by the belief that God's goal was "the ultimate perfection of the common life of humanity on earth" (Greek 1992:33). This perfection, of course, required help from Christian followers, a challenge accepted by the social gospelers who placed their faith in overcoming the problems of a rapidly changing social world in religion, in science, in modernization, and in democracy. Human nature was defined as innately good and constantly improving, moving toward perfection with Jesus Christ as the ideal. However, even good individuals required good environments, mandating a Christian responsibility for social institutions and for intervention in order to alleviate social problems. As social gospelers rejected the Calvinistic doctrine of God's elect, they also subjugated the evangelical concept of individual salvation in favor of a kind of social salvation. Rauschenbusch in his *Theology for the Social Gospel* (1917) seemed to reconceptualize sin as a social condition engaged in by an entire class of people, such as capitalists.

Sociology, Social Reform, and the Social Gospel

Henking proclaimed that in the late nineteenth century, "social gospel, social reform, and social science...all went by the name sociology" (1993:49). The social gospelers, with a goal of facilitating the coming of God's Kingdom on earth, helped to cultivate a sociology that purported to be rooted in science and capable of producing knowledge and facts applicable to solving social problems. According to Mann, "The big question in the new social science was

7 Some have posited faculty at Andover Seminary, near Boston, as the theological link between Calvinism and the Social Gospel as faculty there were among the first to propagate an explanation of evolution as the perfectibility of mankind in the image of Jesus. It was Andover faculty such as William Tucker who began to offer a critique of capitalism in both his classes and in his writings. (For more on Andover's contribution to the social gospel and to sociology see Williams 1970, Williams and MacLean 2012.)

not what is, but what ought-to-be" (1954:111). It was this "ought-to-be" characteristic of the new science that paved the way for social reformers such as those who became associated with the settlement houses of large cities. Greek concludes that sociology's early agenda was driven by social gospel theology and the term "social problems" was selected deliberately to link the positive (social or society) with the negative (problems) (1992:54). Early textbooks by Charles Henderson (1893) and by Small and Vincent (1894) of the University of Chicago as well as by John Bascom (1895) of the Hartford School of Theology, and Arthur Fairbanks (1896) at Yale Divinity School were conscious attempts to relate sociology to the tenets of social Christianity (Greek 1992:73). While denying that most early American sociologists were social gospelers, Swatos acknowledged that for some interest in the church was "merely an extension of their academic commitments [but that] scientific knowledge was the source of the world's redemption, not a crucified and risen Lord" (1984:51). This conclusion suggests that Swatos did not understand the social gospel which also gave more centrality to scientific knowledge than to "a crucified and risen Lord." It was, nevertheless, the strain of reform sociology based largely in social gospel theology that was institutionalized in some colleges, universities, and seminaries as well as being disseminated in Chautauqua lectures, in sermons, in popular and academic writings, and in the work of some settlement houses and institutional churches.

It appears from the writings, sermons, and lectures of the period that persons were identified with the social gospel not so much by their use of the label as by the beliefs they espoused and the praxis they advocated. Hopkins proclaims the "earliest statement of a social gospel in the modern sense" as that of Stephen Colwell, in his book, *New Themes for the Protestant Clergy* (1851). However, Hopkins is crediting Colwell with defining the concept more than coining the term (Hopkins 1940:6). Colwell, for example, admonished leaders of the reformation for leaving charity out of their sermons and works, for overlooking "in their readings of the New Testament, its imperative injunction of brotherly kindness" (1851:111–112). In 1885, Newman Smyth of Andover Seminary[8] attempted to motivate churches to do more to connect with working

8 Andover Seminary began when professor, Eliphalet Pearson broke away from Harvard College in 1807 over a split in Congregationalism between those of orthodox Calvinistic beliefs and more liberal Congregationalists in the Harvard Divinity School. Pearson took his efforts to begin a new seminary to Andover, MA where he helped to establish the first graduate school for the training of ministers. The seminary remained at Andover until 1908 when, because of low enrollments, the trustees voted to move it back to Cambridge to affiliate with the Harvard Divinity School. However, enrollment did not increase as anticipated and

people when he published *Sermons to Workingmen* (1895). Smyth's colleague William Tucker took up the cause of working people by emphasizing that man's attitude toward God is based on his environment and that "souls are social products." He criticized ministers for placing too little emphasis on social responsibility and for continuing to present an individual approach to salvation when the souls of men "are bound up in institutions, in corporations, in unions, in the complicated machinery, industrial, political, and religious of modern society" (Tucker 1891:385). Luker (1991) credits Harlan Paul Douglas as the first in the US to use the term social gospel in his *Christian Reconstruction in the South* (1909). However, White and Hopkins say that the term was first used in 1886 by Rev. Charles O. Brown, pastor of a Congregational church in Dubuque, Iowa in a lecture on labor problems when he referred to the book, *Progress and Poverty* (1879) by Henry George as social gospel (1976: 167). George's book was received by many as "a powerful emotional plea for Christian thinking and action" (Piott 2006:36). George's primary message was an argument for a single-tax on all monopolized, unused, unimproved land held solely for the purpose of speculation. He argued that this tax would have direct and indirect economic benefits as it would increase revenue and lead to land being sold and developed, thus expanding the economy and creating jobs (Piott 2006:35). George was a liberal supporter of labor and explicit in placing the blame for poverty on the "conditions under which people lived, not heredity or individual character" (Piott 2006:40).[9]

Andover never achieved a harmonious working relationship with Harvard or with alumni dissatisfied over the move. In 1931 the school moved back to Andover where it became loosely affiliated with Newton Theological Seminary with both retaining separate campuses and separate administrative structures until 1965 when they merged (*Today's Ministry* 2007: http://www.ants.edu/pdf/todaysministry200anniv.pdf:2–6, retrieved July 11, 2013).

9 George provided what amounted to the social gospel response to an Encyclical of Pope Leo XIII on capital and labor. The Encyclical is sometimes referenced as the church's defense of labor and it does state unequivocally that a worker had a right to receive "what is necessary for the satisfaction of his needs" (1891, Section 5). The same document reminded workers that they had a duty to "fully and faithfully…perform the work which has been freely and equitably agreed on." The Encyclical took a patronizing tone in reminding employers that they were "bound to see that the worker has time for his religious duties; that he be not exposed to corrupting influences and dangerous occasions; and that he be not led away to neglect his home and family, or to squander his earnings." While some, liberal-leaning Catholics (Dorrien 2011:187–195) took the Encyclical as establishing the right of workers to a "living wage," most of the document is unquestionably a defense of capitalism and a renunciation of socialism, leading George to write respectfully to the Pope, "your Encyclical shows you to be involved in such difficulties as a physician called to examine one suffering from disease of the stomach

The influence of science, largely understood as the new science of sociology, was integral to the social gospel. For example, social gospelers such as Josiah Strong declared, "Science, by discovering the laws of nature, reveals the divine methods and enables us, by adopting them, to become efficient laborers together with God unto the kingdom" (1902:104). It was Washington Gladden, considered by many as the father of the social gospel in the US, who identified the mutual need between the social gospel and sociology. Sociology, he thought, could serve Christianity by: (1) providing valuable information on social problems such as vice, crime, and pauperism; (2) suggesting how to rid society of social ills; and (3) elucidating the truths of theology by giving the Christian gospel a scientific foundation. Christianity, on the other hand, could assist sociology by: (1) providing moral invigoration and Christian methods; (2) suffusing theory with Christian ideas in providing a scientific basis for the production and distribution of wealth; and (3) separating sociology from the physical sciences (Gladden 1886: 222–243). Greek concludes that "what ultimately made the social gospel theology intellectually tenable and acceptable to the newly emerging middle-class church was its link to rational scientific thought and methodology" (1992:64). The social gospelers needed a science to rid society of social problems and "the social science which they argued they needed was continually referred to as sociology" (Greek 1992:66). The availability of such a sociology increased toward the end of the century with the proliferation of sociology courses in higher education, the increased output of social surveys and statistics, the settlement movement, and attempts to Christianize industry and politics (Greek 1992). Morgan (1982) as well as Williams and MacLean (2005) have described in some detail the turn-of-the-century growth of sociology in colleges, universities, and seminaries. Along with teaching sociology, many groups claimed to be practicing it in their use of surveys and other data documenting problems in urban living. In the name of science, groups such as the American Social Science Association, churches, the residents of Hull House, students at the Chicago Commons, and individuals such as W.E.B. Du Bois were collecting data by first-hand observation and by door-to-door surveys.

In 1894, the Oberlin Institute of Christian Sociology was formed at Oberlin College, largely the product of Z. Swift Holbrook, a Chicago businessman and writer also on the faculty at Oberlin for a short time (Swatos 1984:15–16), suggesting efforts to link business, the social gospel, and sociology in academia. Holbrook served as co-editor of the *Bibliotheca Sacra: A Religious and Sociological*

---

would meet should he begin with a refusal to consider the stomach" (George 1891:76: http://www.wealthandwant.com/HG/the_condition_of_labor.htm, accessed June 7, 2014).

Quarterly. Washington Gladden, a Board member at Oberlin, served as the first president of the Institute and as the moving force behind Holbrook's "survey" on Christian Sociology, mailed out under the *Bibliotheca* letterhead in 1894. When reporting the survey findings, Holbrook's only methodological note was that he sent out an inquiry to "a large number of the leading thinkers in the United States" asking for their opinions "upon the propriety of using the word 'Christian' as applied to 'sociology' in the phrase 'Christian Sociology'" (Holbrook 1895:458). Holbrook did not report how many surveys were mailed, the selection criteria, or the number of responses. He did, however, publish 126 responses, presumably in their entirety as some are quite long, along with names and, for most, titles or institutional affiliations. A brief analysis of the responses, now more than 100 years old, are revealing of how decisively the Christian thought of the day was wedded to sociology in the minds of many prominent academic and religious leaders. Of the 126 responses published, 96 (76%) were from academics, the vast majority college or seminary presidents with such prestigious institutions as Vassar, Cornell, Stanford, MIT, and Brown represented. Of the remaining 30 respondents, 22 were clergymen, and 8 others were mostly heads of organizations but with a few disparate individuals such as a judge and the Secretary of Labor. From the names or titles, it seems a safe assumption that all respondents were white males. About 40 percent of the academics and an equal proportion of the clergy replied in the affirmative that they thought it appropriate to use the phrase "Christian Sociology." A typical response was from a professor at the University of Chicago, "A Sociology which leaves out this prime element of Christian motive is itself unscientific" (Holbrook 1895:460–461). Only about 25 percent of the "other" category agreed with the propriety of Christian Sociology. More than one-third (37.5%) of both the academic and other respondents gave an outright "no" in answer to the question, compared with 14 percent of the clergymen. Those who said no were about equally split in their reasons between thinking that science was neither Christian nor nonchristian and saying that it depends on how you define sociology, recognizing that sociology at the time lacked a common definition. What was even more interesting about the responses is that 25 percent of the "other" category, 18 percent of the clergy, and 10 percent of the academics gave neither a "yes" or "no" answer because they saw Christian and Sociology as tautological. Typical of such responses was that of the President of Oberlin College, "if Jesus alone can save his people from their sins, then the principles of Christianity are the fundamentals of Sociology." An emeritus college president (unnamed institution) similarly replied, "Christian principles correctly applied to society and a correct Sociology are identical." Only three prominent sociologists were identified among the respondents: Small, Giddings, and

Ward. All argued that science is neutral and should not be paired with the Christian prefix. Small gave the most opinionated response, charging that the phrase gave credence to "unscholarly Christians." This survey is the source of Ward's well known quote: "Christian Sociology sounds to me about as would Christian Mathematics, Mohammedan Biology, or Buddistic Chemistry" (Holbrook 1895:459–460).

Scholars differ as to how deliberate or accidental was the reciprocal relationship between sociology and the social gospel. All agree, however, that the gospelers needed concrete data describing social problems, and sociologists could supply it. Greek suggests that without this push sociology might have developed into a more qualitative discipline along the lines of Max Weber and other phenomenological German philosophers (1992:76). It was the quantification of social problems that separated sociology from muckraking journalism, and it was religious leaders more than the sociologists in institutions of higher education that pushed for an empirical sociology that they could use. Of those who heard the call and responded to the challenge to get the facts about social problems were some of the early settlement house workers who defined themselves as sociologists: Jane Addams, Robert Woods, Florence Kelley, and Graham Taylor. Nor did sociologists in academic settings ignore the emerging demand for an applied sociology and often a "Christian sociology." Charles Ellwood, at the University of Missouri, for example, proposed teaching sociology dealing not only with the introduction of the scientific study of social problems but with the treatment of those problems (1907:590–591). At the University of Chicago, Albion Small felt it necessary to address the subject of Christian Sociology in the first issue of the *American Journal of Sociology* (1895), perhaps not unrelated to the fact that there was a strong tie between his department and the School of Divinity. "[A]ll work given in the department of sociology carried credit toward a degree in divinity" (Diner 1975:541–542). In the Progressive Era, many schools of theology, added sociologists to their faculties. Graham Taylor, professor of Christian Sociology at Chicago Theological Seminary, held a joint appointment in the Department of Sociology for a number of years. It was Shailer Mathews at the University of Chicago Divinity School who, at Small's invitation, undertook the task of providing a definitive treatise on Christian sociology published in the AJS (Mathews 1895, 1896). Social gospeler, Richard Ely at Johns Hopkins and later at the University of Wisconsin, was the editor of a series of books that included *Hull-House Maps and Papers* and is credited with having encouraged the residents to publish their research documenting and describing some of Chicago's urban problems. Vidich and Lyman say of Ely and other Wisconsin economists and sociologists, they "were committed to a Christianization of the social sciences as part of a larger effort that would make professional social scientists responsible for creating a new social covenant" (1985:154). Ely was sympathetic toward unions, gave advice to strikers, and encouraged state intervention in the economy. "He admonished businessmen to replace the profit motive with altruism and laborers to seek Christ in their hearts.... He prophesied that the Kingdom of God would find expression in a benevolent state society" (Vidich and Lyman 1985:154). In 1919, John Barker, professor of Sociology in Boston University's School of Theology, published a manual for Christian laymen and ministers on how to implement the social gospel so as to move toward realization of the Kingdom "where God's great thought for society will be fulfilled" (1919:17). Barker relied on use of sociology as then understood to ensure that "the Christian theory of social progress proceeds on a scientific and rational basis" (1919:220–221). He instructed the church to "fulfill its social function...[by awakening] the interests of its members and constituency in the work of social research in the school of life about them." Barker concluded, "Jesus could weep over [the city of] Jerusalem [*King James* Bible, Luke 19:41–42] because he had an intimate knowledge of its conditions and needs" (1919:48–49). He further pointed to the "survey of Springfield, Illinois" (1917) as a model for other communities to follow in gaining intimate knowledge of their cities in order to implement reforms. Advocates of this search for facts or scientific knowledge saw it as scriptural, citing Jesus' admonition, "Ye shall know the truth and the truth shall make you free" (*King James* Bible, John 8:32).

While the social gospel departed from traditional protestant faith and variations of it can be found among Catholics, it was still largely articulated and disseminated by white, educated, protestant males who were as reliant on science as on salvation, and with whom the working class immigrants—Catholic, Greek Orthodox, Jew, or non-believer, had difficulty identifying.[10] The social gospel was evoked by urban problems and "developed in part as a means of reclaiming the proletariat" (Latta 1936:268), reason enough that the same genre of social gospel did not develop in the South or in rural areas. Stebner wrote that the social gospel and the settlement movement were similar in their desire

10 For balanced discussions of manifestations of the social gospel among Catholics, see Kerby (1900), Cross (1958), Blasi, (2005b), and Dorrien 2011:185–215). Some historians have sought to place Catholics, particularly women of the religious order, in the social gospel movement, some simply by virtue of their praxis and others because they were actively involved in settlements such as the Madonna Houses in New York and Chicago (Delio 1995). Others have sought to separate Catholics from a social gospel seen as humanitarianism that "bends one of the religious virtues into a quantitative expertise whose principal purpose is a planned advancement of the human economic condition" (Harnish 2011:97).

to bring Christianity closer to the people. However, she also points to their differences.

> The social gospel was male dominated and emphasized theological proclamation; its key leaders were either clergymen or male academics. The social settlement movement was female-dominated and emphasized praxis and community; its key leaders were women who could not be official leaders within either institutional churches or educational institutions (1997:103).

The author goes on to point out that some settlement house men, such as Robert Woods and Graham Taylor, were also social gospel leaders but that the founders of Hull House, Jane Addams and Ellen Gates Starr "were never defined as within the social gospel movement. This was perhaps not due as much to the incompatibility between their work and beliefs but as to their gender" (Stebner 1997:103). Greek, however, did identify Addams as a social gospeler, in fact labeled her as "the major female spokesperson for the social gospel" (1992:77). His justification comes primarily from Addams' speech on "the subjective necessity of the settlement" in which she articulated "the desire to interpret democracy in social terms...to aid in the race progress; and...the Christian movement toward Humanitarianism" ([1892a] 2002:25). Sklar characterized the Hull House women as "in but not of, the Social Gospel Movement" (1985:663). Over time, Adams translated Christian idealism into a secularized praxis. For her, the gospel message "must be put in terms of action" ([1892a] 2002:23). Dorrien referred to Addams as following a "secularized version of the social gospel" and asserts that she "did not believe in the sacred/secular distinction" (2011:184). In belief and in praxis, Adams measured up to the male social gospelers although she never identified herself as such or spoke of working toward realization of the Kingdom. Some women within the settlement movement, such as Vida Scudder and Ellen Gates Starr, called on religion as justification for their work but identified themselves as Christian socialists rather than social gospelers. Vidich and Lyman characterize both the settlement and the social gospel movements as a "university mission to the urban proletariat" (1985:63). Greek credits the settlement house movement with incorporating a "domesticized version of the social gospel into sociology in America" (1992:84).

Despite all of the evidence that the social gospel was a compelling force in the development of contemporary sociology, the religious influence has been erased or denied in efforts to strengthen and retain what Lengermann and Niebrugge (2007) refer to as a "natural history narrative." For example, Swatos saw religion as an impediment to the recognition of sociology as a science, suggesting that early American sociologists have been written out of discipline histories because they were "unsophisticated Protestant churchmen intent on reforming society by means of Christian theology and morality" (1984:iii). Swatos, like many others, dismissed the influence of these predecessors and concluded that the "dominant forms of sociological thought in America have from the beginning to the present been essentially Comtean in character [and further American sociology] has always been dominated by functionalism" (1984:54–55). A re-telling of history, however, finds that the pathways of sociologists, social gospelers, and reformers intersected, borrowed from and enriched each other during the Progressive Era as they moved toward the common goal of a more just society.

CHAPTER 2

Neighborhood Settlements: Residence, Research and Reform

Settlement Houses have been largely relegated to history with those surviving their prime having taken other names and assumed other functions. Yet neighborhood settlements were a vital link between the harsh realities of urban living and the families of recently arrived immigrants or rural populations. "Social democracy was their secular goal, human brotherhood their religious aim" (Stackpole 1961:18). Not only did the settlements provide assistance in the process of acculturation, but their workers learned about and came to understand and advocate for these "new Americans." As Spain put it, the settlements "saved strangers from being defeated by the city. They also saved cities from being overwhelmed by strangers" (2001:14). The unique aspect of social settlements is that they brought middle or upper-class volunteers, of varying motives, to live (settle) among the poor and usually foreign-born populations. Many of these settlement workers were the predecessors of American sociology. Between the 1880s and 1920s when the discipline was first coming into being in the United States, sociology was not confined to the academy but in fact enjoyed a presence in public practice and discourse. As Lengermann and Niebrugge-Brantley aptly remark,

> A nineteenth century contemporary looking at "sociology" would have as easily turned to the settlement as to the university—indeed, we could argue perhaps more easily, because the university did not necessarily contain a sociology department (the first being founded in Chicago in 1892); but the settlement always acknowledged itself in some way as concerned with "sociology". ...settlements as a collective enterprise and many settlement workers as individuals saw themselves as doing sociology (2002:7–8).

Woods and Kennedy reported that there were 74 American settlements in 1897, 103 in 1900, 204 in 1905 and 413 in 1910 ([1911]1970:vi). The settlements were largely a phenomenon of the Progressive Era and thrived in the Midwest and Northeast, with 40 percent located in the cities of Chicago, Boston, and New York (Davis 1984:268, n59). It was Woods who described settlements as "the most distinctive new social institution in an age of unparalleled discovery and invention" (Pacey 1950:154). The early settlement houses became the first laboratories for the gathering of social statistics in the form of surveys done in the neighborhoods where they were located. According to Vidich and Lyman, these settlements "became the first major extra-university loci for the merger of two strands of *fin-de-siècle* sociology—Social Gospel theology and rational, planned, scientifically grounded municipal action" (1985:128). Theory, research, and action were truly inseparable to settlement workers who resided in neighborhoods, observed daily life, collected data, and advocated for social reform. All of these endeavors were situated in a *neighborly relations* paradigm—i.e., knowing one's neighbors through direct contact and relations and sharing in their daily lives so that interests and needs melded. Although it can be said that settlements functioned as the first social science laboratories, clearly settlement epistemology rejected restrictive definitions of science as detached, indifferent or disembodied. Settlement workers were often idealists who, as characterized by Davis, "came perilously close to believing that, if they gathered enough statistics and found out enough information about the social evils in America, the solution would follow naturally" (1964:513). Sociological praxis was not to be confused with academic sociology per se, nor was it to be mistaken for charity work or what later became professional social work. Ultimately, in a pragmatist philosophical vein, the goal was to find solutions to urban problems through a union of theory and practice. Practical results were not conceived as part of a specific research agenda, political platform, or social service program. Rather, results were seen as the natural outgrowth of knowing and experiencing first-hand the plight of immigrants, the poor, and the disabled through direct relational contact and social advocacy.

The English Background

The settlement house movement in the United States was inspired by the work of the Rev. Samuel Barnett and his wife, Henrietta, of St. Jude's Parish, in East London's Whitechapel district. The first settlement house was named for Arnold Toynbee, an economist of socialist leanings on the faculty at Billiol College. Before he died at age 32, Toynbee had educated the public about poverty and linked college students with work among the poor (Davis 1984:6, Mallon 1950:263). Charles Booth is also important in the history of the settlement movement for his pioneering social survey work best exemplified in his *Life and Times of the People of London* (1889–1903). His investigation of poverty began with documenting the needs of the Whitechapel area and in making an effort to define poverty because he believed that a scientific approach was better than a benevolent one in bringing about social reform. Even before Toynbee

Hall, as early as the 1840s, two Christian socialists, Frederick Denison Maurice and Charles Kingsley, clergymen and professors, were at work on the problems of London slums. Maurice opened the Working Men's College in 1854. He was helped by John Ruskin, a professor of fine arts at Oxford who taught drawing and art history at Working Men's College because he believed that art could make a difference in the lives of ordinary people and that they had a right to enjoy the aesthetic beauty of life even in the dismal atmosphere of a slum. He encouraged college students as well as young artists such as William Morris and Edward Denison to live in the slums and to interact with working people. Before Toynbee Hall, Octavia Hill, a friend of Barnett's wife, purchased a tenement house in London and moved in, at the same time acquiring vacant lots to create small parks in the midst of the slums (Tucker 1917:642). Thus the first settlement house, Toynbee Hall, was a culmination of several decades of work that brought together the interests of religion, education, art, labor, and scientific research. It was as much an effort to bridge the chasm between the social classes as to alleviate poverty.

The United States Settlements

William Tucker, the moving force behind the establishment of Boston's Andover House, once commented that "settlement work is too personal to be standardized" (1917:643). His observation is supported by the different practices and agendas that came to be included in US settlements although many of the founders had visited Toynbee Hall and subsequently adapted that model to the needs of their neighbors. Where early English settlements were under the auspices of the church, most early settlements in the US, even if inspired by religion, were not formally affiliated with a church or denomination. In many cases this was deliberate because most of the settlement workers were Protestants and the people they served were Catholic, Greek Orthodox, or Jewish if affiliated with a religion at all. Those who did become involved in settlement work for religious reasons were often inspired by the social gospel, Christian but more humanitarian than sectarian. Also, in comparison with England, US settlements were more gendered institutions in that women played a decisive role in their origin and history. Finally, settlements in the US were peculiarly American because of the role they played in the acculturation of large numbers of immigrants whose first contact with America was often through the settlement houses. As in England, many of the US settlements had either a formal or informal association with colleges and universities. Low-budget settlement houses utilized the labor of college students or recent graduates in an environment that expanded their education about the real-world problems of urban-industrial society. Students, most of upper-middle or upper class backgrounds, were critical to the settlement's goal of bridging the gap between classes and between immigrants and the dominant American culture.

The term "settlement house" refers less to the physical structure of a place than to the practice of persons—often labeled as outsiders, because of their education, social class, or national origin—settling into or moving into a house in a poor neighborhood where they would live and work with local residents. Clark Tibbetts found that the only people listed in *Who's Who* in such areas were those living in social settlements. "It is evident that the people who are doing the work of the settlement are those who have relinquished their claims upon the communities of their origin, and have elected to live among the underprivileged" (EWBP: B139, F10). In some cases the founders purchased, rented, or persuaded owners to donate as the "settlement house" a once-luxurious residence, vacated due to the encroachments of urbanization and industrialization. In other cases, settlements were begun in dilapidated tenements, much like those of the populations they would serve. Occasionally the settlement began out of the residence of its founder. Although most settlements began in just one building, they often grew to include a complex of buildings, added to meet needs and as donor support allowed. For the first settlement workers, bringing the classes together involved bringing a middle or upper-class life style with their residence. Some arrived at the settlement house with nice furnishings, linens, books, musical instruments, and art work. The contrast with their neighbors' standard of living was obvious and not without its problems and contradictions as the following quote from Carson illustrates.

> Addams suggested that the 'style of living' should be one 'the residents would naturally have if they lived anywhere else....' Though residents were expected to keep their own rooms neat, the houses usually hired servants, as most of them might have done in their own homes or at college. Still, some felt nagging doubts about whether hired service was self-indulgent or inappropriate in the settlements (1990:58).

All of the settlements recruited upper or middle-class volunteers and/or college students as residents, and all relied on the economic support of wealthy donors. In addition to bringing together the different social classes, all settlements articulated or pursued some of the same goals of aiding in the process of Americanization, of education, and of meeting the diverse needs of their "neighbors." They "tried to replace the typical nineteenth-century charity worker's air of superiority with one of neighborliness" (Trolander 1987:9). In order to assess and represent to policy makers the needs of the neighborhoods, settlements workers engaged in varying amounts of scientific investigation. Regardless of differences in programs, philosophical origins, or sponsorship, the daily routine of settlements and some of the services offered were very similar.

> An average day at the settlement around 1900 began at 9:00 A.M. with the kindergarten. A Legal Aid Society and a loan office were open all day. After school let out at 3:00 P.M., the club rooms, study room, library, and rooftop playground came alive. In the evening, teenagers gathered for clubs or games, and a trade union might meet. People also used the settlement's public baths, the first in New York.
>
> TROLANDER 1987:9

While Hull House is remembered by many as the first social settlement in the US, it was actually the Ethical Culture Society in New York that established the first settlement although it was called a Neighborhood Guild. However, even as the first Guild was organized by Stanton Coit, other settlements were in the planning stages. It appears that various settlements began almost simultaneously in the United States with no coordinated planning. Although the early settlement leaders later came to know each other and to work cooperatively, they did not know each other as they undertook the founding of their respective settlements (Davis 1984:8–14).

The Ethical Culture Society and Neighborhood Guilds

The first of three neighborhood guilds was established in New York under the auspices of the Ethical Culture Society, a non-sectarian, ethical-spiritual and educational movement established by Felix Adler in 1876. This New York organization was the first of many ethical culture societies founded in the United States and Europe by Adler who hoped to transcend the limitations of both Christianity and Judaism. His emphasis was on moral principles and on participation in practical endeavors to solve human problems.[1] Adler demonstrated

1 Adler was born in Germany in 1851 to Jewish parents who immigrated to the United States when he was six years of age. His father became rabbi of the Temple Emanu-El in New York City, and Adler studied in Germany to prepare for the rabbinate which he subsequently rejected in favor of a transcendental spiritual but non-sectarian philosophy based on moral principles and ethical treatment of fellow human beings. He taught Hebrew and Oriental Literatures at Cornell University but gave up the academic life to pursue a more active one. He founded the New York Ethical Culture Society in 1876 with a speech at Carnegie Hall calling for a new religion seeking "common ground where we may all grasp hands as brothers united in mankind's common cause" (Carson 1990:18).

his commitment to pragmatism by proclaiming the importance of "deed, not creed" (Barbuto 1999:6). Inspired by Adler and Ethical Culture, Stanton Coit opened the Neighborhood Guild on the lower east side of New York in 1886.[2] He began his work among the largely Jewish immigrant population by inviting a group from the Workingmen's Club to meet in his apartment. Shortly after this initial meeting, he rented a "dilapidated tenement no better looking than its neighbors" (Davis 1984:32). Apparently his early work was patterned in part on Maurice's Working Men's College in London (Davis 1984:40). Coit's neighborhood guild emphasized community organizing, the empowerment of the people in the targeted neighborhood, and the natural emergence of leadership and programs. After two years, Coit turned the Neighborhood Guild over to two associates, Charles Stover and Edward King, and left for England to carry on the work of Ethical Culture in that country.[3] After Coit's departure, Stover and King struggled to keep the New York Guild alive and in 1891 reorganized and renamed it the University Settlement although not affiliated with a university. After 1894, with the appointment of James Reynolds as head resident, the settlement became more involved in "careful and scientific investigations of the social, moral and civic conditions of the lower east side," sometimes cooperating with other settlements on studies such as housing and unemployment (Recchiuti 2007:92).[4] The second settlement sponsored by the Ethical Culture Society was the Hudson Guild, established by John Elliott in 1895, and in many ways more exemplary of Coit's model than was the Neighborhood Guild (Barbuto 1999:147). Madison House was established in 1898 as the Down Town Ethical Society to serve the largely Jewish populations of New York's lower East Side and, more than the Neighborhood or Hudson Guilds, represented Felix Adler's effort to "advance the social/philosophical ideals of the Ethical Culture Movement." With the help of a group of friends, Henry Moskowitz opened the

2 Coit graduated Amherst College as did Robert Woods and several other males involved in the settlement movement and, as was the case for many educated males in the US in the late nineteenth century, he traveled to Germany to earn a Ph.D. at the University of Berlin. He subsequently spent three months working as a volunteer at Toynbee Hall where he was inspired to introduce the settlement concept in the United States.

3 Once settled in England, apparently in an effort to insure the continuation of guilds, Coit (1892) wrote and published a manual as a guide for others to follow the model attempted in New York.

4 During the first decade of the century, the University Settlement published the *University Settlement Studies Quarterly* co-edited by head worker James H. Hamilton and resident, Walter E. Weyl. While the *Quarterly* served largely as an outlet for reports on work at the University Settlement, it also included regular contributions from other New York settlements and occasionally from those outside the city.

settlement, renamed Madison House several years later, and served as its first head resident (Barbuto 1999).[5] The major contribution of settlements sponsored by the Ethical Culture Society was in community-building and not in research or activism. They bear mention here because they were first and because some of their work has survived and reappeared and been recycled in other times and places. The concept and practice of community organizing declined after World War I but was revived again in the 1960s when community action programs, integral to President Johnson's Great Society, took a page from Ethical Culture's emphasis on empowerment and community organizing. Although the history of the Ethical Culture Society's direct involvement in settlement work is limited and largely confined to the three houses described here, there were linkages with other settlement house pioneers and through them many indirect influences.

Feminist-Pragmatism and Settlement Houses

Feminist pragmatism is best represented among the women social reformers and settlement leaders prior to World War I. It is characterized by theoretical primacy attributed to the social structural nature of industrial-urban problems and its emphasis on the importance of legislation, social policy, and jurisprudence as a means of reform, particularly in areas relating to families, women, and children. Many of the largest and best known US settlements were founded, led and/or staffed by women, perhaps the most notable being Hull House of Chicago (Jane Addams and Helen Gates Starr), the University of Chicago Settlement (Mary McDowell), Greenwich House of New York (Mary Simkhovitch), Henry Street of New York (Lillian Wald), and settlements in New York, Boston and Philadelphia founded by the College Settlements Association

5 All three of the neighborhood guilds survive today as neighborhood centers, still serving in their same locations. Although none of the three acknowledges a current association with Ethical Culture, the Hudson Guild mission statement continues to reflect the original goal of empowerment (http://hudsonguild.org/about_mission.html, accesseded April 12, 2013). University Settlement still operates under the same name and its webpage claims its history: "As the first settlement house in the United States, founded in 1886, University Settlement embodies the settlement ideal — working from within the community to buoy the lives of individuals, families and the collective whole" (http://www.universitysettlement.org/who/index.html, accessed May 12, 2013). In 1954 Madison House merged with Hamilton House founded in 1902 by Lillian Wald of the Henry Street Settlement as a small "outpost" in an area suffering from epidemics of tuberculosis, pneumonia, and other contagious diseases (Woods and Kennedy [1911]1970:203). Today, Hamilton-Madison House still serves the residents of New York's Lower East Side with a variety of social services and neighborhood organizations (http://www.hmhonline.org/, accessed May 12, 2013).

(including Vida Scudder, Emily Balch, Kathryn Coman among others). Settlement houses established by women were to give meaning and purpose to the lives of college-educated women, first by utilizing their abilities and experiences and, second, by providing a place and a practice to aid in closing the gap between the classes. These dual functions became what Addams conceptualized as the subjective and objective necessity of the settlement (1892a, b). The latter goal was to be achieved by sharing, in neighborly fashion, some aspects of the privileged life style with the less privileged. Additional roles were added in the settlements as the women became aware that to share their life-styles must, in reality, become secondary to a more practical approach to enabling people to achieve a descent quality of life.

Jane Addams and her friend Ellen Gates Starr began the neighborly relations model in 1889 with the establishment of Hull House in Chicago which quickly became an institutional anchor for a network of women in sociology[6] (Deegan 1990, 2002a; Lengermann and Niebrugge-Brantley 1998). It also served as a meeting place and as an important liaison for academic sociologists, particularly from the University of Chicago. Although initially influenced by Toynbee Hall, Hull House quickly came to represent a new organizational model informed by an egalitarian and pragmatic approach that guided the work of most early women sociologists in the United States. It was a place where knowledge could be tested and if found valid, applied to solve social problems. Addams and Starr were friends from their days at Rockford Female Seminary. As with many other settlement founders, they had visited Toynbee Hall, were familiar with its work, and were, no doubt, influenced by its history. In fact, both Addams and Starr maintained a relationship with the Barnetts and visited them several times on their respective trips to Europe. However, their plan, or "scheme" as they called it, seemed more driven by their own idiosyncratic motives and their work began without institutional affiliations. In her first autobiography, Addams wrote of her years following Rockford as filled with health problems, despondency, and without direction or goal. She began to focus on finding purpose for her life while traveling in Europe in 1888. The turning point may have been when she became conscious and alarmed that she had viewed a bull fight in Italy with indifference even though it resulted in the wasteful death of "five bulls and many more horses." This new consciousness and her exposure to Toynbee Hall prompted a plan for opening a settlement house, a "scheme" first shared with

6 While Jane Addams led much of this innovation in thinking it was also influenced by the ideas of other women associated with Addams including Edith and Grace Abbott, Sophonisba Breckinridge, Charlotte Perkins Gilman, Florence Kelley, Julia Lathrop, Mary McDowell, and Ellen Gates Starr (Deegan 1991).

friend and traveling companion, Ellen Gates Starr. Clearly, Addams' idea was the result of what she perceived as a need for educated women to use their abilities and to work on the social problems that were becoming increasingly obvious as a part of urban life in the United States and Europe. Presumably Addams saw women as having a particular vantage point given their traditional responsibilities to family and community.

Another organization brought to life by women, the College Settlements Association (CSA), was as much to meet the needs of educated women as to meet the social needs of the day, again seen as most effectively accomplished by women. The CSA began to take shape in 1887 in the thinking of a group of Smith College alumnae. The driving force was Vida Scudder, recently returned from study at Oxford University where she had attended lectures by John Ruskin. The strategic role of women in the settlement movement was inextricably linked with the higher education of women and Vida Scudder was critical in that linkage. As Carrell points out, in the late nineteenth century, "it was necessary to form a specific rationale for the education of girls" (1981:65). Colleges for women carved out a place in higher education by developing and promoting a service ethic as the purpose driving women's education. It was a timely message in the context of the growing social problems of urban-industrial society. A service role for women was non-threatening and still within the gendered doctrine of separate spheres. Women could help to ameliorate the social problems of the day by teaching, Christianizing, and ministering to the poor and needy—by doing the things that women typically did in the home or as community volunteers. Scudder recognized "the ennui…that besets the rich lady" and expanded the restrictive female role to include a service ethic that was publically palatable as an extension of the traditional feminine place in society. For the first generation of college graduates, "[t]he settlement house was the symbol of the moral fervor of their generation" (Carrell 1981:13). The settlement also became the domain where women would engage in their subversive version of separate spheres— "municipal housekeeping" (Spain 2001:63–65).

Like Addams, Scudder floundered for several years after graduating college and experienced a time when she was alarmed by her lack of emotion, acknowledging with horror her failure to grieve over the death of her grandmother (1937:50,38). Her life began to take on meaning when she received a faculty appointment at Wellesley College where she would profoundly influence college women for almost four decades. The year of Scudder's Wellesley appointment was also the year she returned to Smith to reunion with a group of friends and alumnae. Scudder, no doubt influenced by her days at Oxford where she became acquainted with Toynbee Hall, promoted the idea of an organization for settlement work in the city slums with classmates Helen Rand

and Jean Find. She argued that settlement work was naturally the purview of women and that women should be ashamed for not having inaugurated Toynbee Hall, "For obviously such work is woman's work; it has for its very essence the power of home-making, which has always been supposed to be a feminine prerogative" (VDSP, 1890, B2, F3). The idea appealed to the Smith alumnae, not only as a needed humanitarian project, but also as a project for the fulfillment of educated women. The women set in motion what became the College Settlements Association (CSA), an organization formalized even after they opened the Rivington Street Settlement in New York in 1889, according to Scudder, two weeks before the opening of Hull House (1937:135). The CSA was supported by a network of women's college alumnae with control vested in the CSA rather than the local settlement. The women founders deliberately formulated an organization intended to live on beyond them.

Some of the women founders may have been motivated by religious zeal but not as overtly as the men who came into settlement work through the social gospel movement. If anything, the religious motivation of the women was more representative of European Christian socialism and pragmatism than of the American social gospel. Scudder, in fact, seemed to see social settlements as a new type of social order in keeping with socialistic principles (Williams 1970:153). Both Starr and Scudder were influenced by the teaching of Christian socialist John Ruskin and came to believe that no civilization could call itself Christian if it permitted the poor to go hungry or without shelter. Religion was a less definitive motive for Addams who resisted the idea that she must go through a "conversion experience" and once wrote to Starr, who was constantly in search of a religious epiphany, "I do not think we are put into the world to be religious, we have a certain work to do, and to do that is the main thing" (EGSP 1879: B3). Outside of Starr and Scudder, other settlement women, while considering themselves religious, took a secular approach to their work and were sometimes called upon to give witness to their religious convictions. For example, Mary Simkhovitch, founder and head resident of Greenwich House, writing in *The Churchman* summed up what she saw as the relationship between settlement workers and religion, "the settlement as a group is through its associated life gathering convictions rather than expressing them" (GHR: B22, F42). The stated object of Hull House when it was founded in 1889 was the same as that of the Chicago Commons, founded in 1894 by social gospel minister Graham Taylor, except for the addition of "religious" to the beginning of the list of enterprises of the Chicago Commons: "to provide a center for the higher civic and social life; to institute and maintain *religious* [emphasis added], educational and philanthropic enterprises, and to investigate and improve the conditions in the industrial districts of Chicago" (Woods and Kennedy

[1911]1970:40,53). Denison House, founded by the all-female CSA stated simply that it was "for social and educational work and neighborhood co-operations for better conditions" (Woods and Kennedy [1911]1970:109).

In a speech at Lincoln Center in 1907, Mary McDowell articulated the spirit of service and the philosophy of feminist pragmatism when she addressed the topic of religion and the settlements.

> As long as people live in overcrowded tenements, in rooms so dark that you cannot read without an artificial light, where the sun never shines, where children grow up knowing nothing of privacy or space that gives freedom; as long as the aged poor are not tenderly cared for; as long as mothers and children must work to make a family budget equal to the demand of a growing standard of living, just so long shall we have to meet the social needs with scientific accuracy and human sympathy, for 'vain will be higher education, music, art or even the Gospel unless they come clothed in the life of brother man.'
>
> MMSR: B1, F3

Although McDowell did not invoke the words of Jesus she no doubt expected that any Christian-leaning person would be reminded of his admonition: "Insomuch as ye have done it unto one of the least of these my brethren, ye have done it unto me" (*King James Bible*, Matthew 25:40). Most of the settlement women practiced, if not publicly professed, an ecumenical, humanistic faith in universal brotherhood and sisterhood as opposed to any denominational or sectarian-driven faith. Even stronger than religious motivations, women leaders in the settlement movement promoted the moral responsibility of educated women and men to bridge the gap between the privileged and the disenfranchised through their cultural resources and works.

Women's leadership in the settlement movement, while motivated by a "social responsibility," was also motivated by opportunities for meaningful work at a time when women's careers were still highly circumscribed. Increasingly settlement residents were both female and male "graduate students in sociology and economics and a wide variety of reformers and writers interested in studying the city and its problems" (Davis 1984: 29–30). Publication of pioneering studies such as *Hull-House Maps and Papers* (1895) and *City Wilderness* (1898) gave settlements increasing visibility as sociological laboratories for the study of urban life. Young people graduating college often viewed settlement residencies as a continuation of their college training and as a place for gaining experience prior to taking on other jobs. As social service agencies began to develop, they found settlements to be their most viable source of experienced workers. Women, in particular, were drawn to the settlements, and applications for residency soon outnumbered available positions. By the early 1900s women comprised about 77 percent of residents and 84 percent of settlement volunteers. Approximately 70 percent of the head residents were women (Woods and Kennedy [1911]1970). It is not surprising then that settlement sociology reflects a distinctively feminist and pragmatist orientation.

The Social Gospel Structural Transformation Model

Although most early settlements in the United States were not formally affiliated with churches, religion, especially of the social gospel variety, permeated the settlement movement, more among the men founders than the women. "Graham Taylor, Robert Woods, and Stanton Coit found in settlement work a practical field for their essentially religious callings.... The urge to reform a flawed society shaped their professional decisions" (Carson 1990:49–50). Many men inspired by the social gospel chose settlement work as an alternative to the ministry, a choice due in large measure to the fact that the social gospel ascribed to a foundation of scientific knowledge as much as religious sentiment (Greek 1992:64). Settlements were seen as a new and unique tool in God's plan for the progress of the United States. By the late 19th century, the hope for a Kingdom of God on earth was threatened by the myriad of social problems evident in cities. Both the social gospel and the new science of sociology offered a critique of society and a promise of bringing scientific evidence to bear on urban problems. Both emphasized the fact that social injustice associated with wealth and capitalism contributed to poverty and other problems of urban-industrial society and that individual salvation was insufficient to solve these problems. The turn to settlement houses, seen by many as the locale of a composite social gospel and sociology, was in a real sense a pursuit of the Kingdom by means of practical action.

Settlements inspired by the social gospel reflect linkages with social research or the public sociology of the day—undifferentiated from Christian sociology—in a more overt way than the houses established and staffed by women. Although both engaged in research, the women were always clear that research evolved from and enhanced the "neighborly relation," whereas, some of the male founders conceptualized it as more integral to the mission of the settlements. For example, Graham Taylor wrote that he made his acceptance of a faculty position at Chicago Theological Seminary in 1892 conditional "upon permission to conduct social-educational work on the field, such as the medical schools do in the clinic and the schools of science do in their laboratories." Taylor went on to explain that he felt he needed "direct contact with the home and work-life of the people" in order to be an effective teacher and to facilitate students' learning about the real world of urban problems (Taylor 1936:5). Taylor and Robert Woods both epitomized the social gospel creed that justice for your fellowman was more important than individual experiences of salvation in achieving the Kingdom of God on earth. Robert Woods wrote and lectured on settlements as "laboratories in social science" a concept he introduced and that apparently included both the collection of data and the application of that data to solve problems ([1893]1970:30–46). In his version of the neighborly relation, Woods expressed the conviction that "science and sympathy" must unite to provide realistic knowledge of the poor while "The close scientific study of the social conditions in the neighborhood about a settlement is indispensable to its success" (Woods 1893:68–69). Woods advocated the anthropological method of living among the people and allowing social reform to emerge from what "the people are accomplishing for themselves" (Vidich and Lyman 1985:63). Jane Addams' pragmatic approach was simply "investigate to see what needs to be done, then do it" (Philpott 1978:71). However, she expressed some reservation about the concept of the settlement as a laboratory.

> I have always objected to the phrase 'sociological laboratory' applied to us, because Settlements should be something much more human and spontaneous than such a phrase connotes, and yet it is inevitable that the residents should know their own neighborhoods more thoroughly than any other, and that their experiences there should affect their convictions ([1910]2008:197).

Andover Theological Seminary, affiliated with the Congregational Church and located near Boston, Massachusetts, seems to have been an early nexus where the social gospel, settlement houses, and social science came together. Their publication, *The Andover Review*, begun in 1883, served as a vehicle to spread the new social gospel philosophy as the editors and contributors explored the connections among theology, social science, social problems, and human welfare (Tucker 1889, Carson 1990:13). Vida Scudder published several articles in the *Review*, one on college settlements (1892). In addition to the usual theological articles, the journal carried a section on "Sociological Notes." Faculty involved in the publication of the *Review* included Professor William J. Tucker who formed the Andover House Association for the purpose of founding a settlement house in Boston. Most of the Association's members were affiliated with Andover Seminary and Tucker served as board president for many years. According to a prearranged plan, he selected his student, Robert Woods, to become the first Head Resident and sent him to England to observe work at Toynbee Hall. Through Woods, Tucker's influence is evident in the key male leadership of settlement houses. On the occasion of the 25th anniversary of South End House (1917), Tucker wrote an article in the *Atlantic Monthly* praising the settlement as a "new social unit of very great possibilities" and citing its approach to the alleviation of social problems and social inequality as "marked by a comprehensiveness which is seldom found elsewhere" (1917:642–645). Linking settlements with the new sociology, he referred to surveys completed by settlement residents as tools of legislative and policy reform. On the matter of residents, Tucker recommended those with "advanced training in economic and sociological studies." Tucker went beyond the settlement neighborhood to recognize a number of prominent professionals and policy-makers of the day who were "better public servants" because of their experiences as settlement residents. And finally, Tucker credited settlements with giving women "their first opportunity to enter upon public service" and proclaimed that women had achieved influence "proportionate to their numbers" (1917:648).

Commonalities and Differences

While always denying that the primary purpose of settlements was evangelism, nevertheless, some form of religious observance was characteristic of the male-identified social gospel settlements. For example, Woods reported to his mentor, Professor Tucker, an early and failed attempt to institute daily prayers among residents and staff although he saw such practice as "essential to the idea of moral and spiritual unity" (Woods 1929:51). There was no word on how this matter was resolved although at the end of the first year Woods reported no prayer service but a Sunday "music hour" that included the singing of "hymns of the faith" (SEHR: B1, F53). Religion apparently played a more overt role at the Chicago Commons where, according to Taylor, religious observation was part of the routine through the years.

> We have also found it profitable to devote a half-hour after dinner to our household vespers before going to our evening classes, clubs, and other appointments. No one is required to attend, but we naturally linger for it in the residents' living-room. Someone plays a few moments on the piano or violin; selections from the Scriptures are read; a hymn is sung and we unite in the Lord's Prayer—all tending to weld us together in spirit (1936:25).

In contrast, Hull House, more secular than many of the settlements, had no regular religious observances although there are no shortage of examples of the spirituality of Addams and the Catholic orthodoxy of her co-founder Ellen Gates Starr. Even though various religious groups met at Hull House, these were just some of a myriad of community groups to find space there. For many years, Sunday evenings at Hull House offered lectures on topics of common interest, often presented by faculty at the University of Chicago. These lectures, however, were begun after an attempt at a Sunday evening religious observance which Addams described in a rather humorous vein as follows.

> ...[W]e made an effort to come together on Sunday evenings in a household service, hoping thus to express our moral unity in spite of the fact that we represented many creeds. But although all of us reverently knelt when the High Church resident read the evening service and bowed our heads when the evangelical resident led in prayer after his chapter, and although we sat respectfully through the twilight when a resident read her favorite passage from Plato and another from Abt Vogler, we concluded at the end of the winter that this was not religious fellowship and that we did not care for another reading club ([1910]2008:285).

Despite religious and other differences, the settlements had many things in common, one of the most obvious their democratic ideals. The Americanization of immigrant groups was an explicit goal in all of the settlements. Democracy, social science, and the social gospel were often indistinguishable, more perhaps among male settlement workers than their female counterparts. There are democratic themes intermeshed with those of the social gospel in the writings of Robert Woods with titles such as *Americans in Process* (1903) and *The Neighborhood as Nation-Building* (1923). Woods often treated democracy as a part of the evolution of human progress (see, for example, "Democracy a New Unfolding of Human Power," 1906). Yet Tucker, Woods' mentor, wrote a scathing criticism of Andrew Carnegie's *The Gospel of Wealth*, charging "If the few can administer wealth for the community far better than it could or would do for itself, then democracy has reached the limit of its willingness and responsibility" (1915:291). On the other hand, some settlement leaders such as Mary Simkhovitch voiced a less critical acceptance of the ideal of a working democracy: "There is certainly one belief that all 'settlers' have in common, and that is faith in democracy.... And further there is the belief that it is worthwhile to work for democracy and that it will prevail" (GHR: B22, F42). Over a period of several years, Jane Addams delivered a series of lectures emphasizing the importance of socializing democracy (2002b). Her writings on social relations in the workplace and between charity workers and clients illustrate the difference between individual and social ethics. Moreover she made an important distinction between democracy as a form of government and democracy as a fundamental principle that guides social relations and social interaction, an element of her feminist pragmatism (Addams 2002b).

It seems clear that in the early stages of settlement work the labels social work and sociology were used interchangeably by all. Although in later writings Woods seemed to use sociology to mean information gathering and social work to mean the application of the information collected, he clearly treated these as inseparable as is evident in his overview of the settlement movement (Woods and Kennedy [1922]1990). Pioneer settlement leaders such as Addams, Woods, and Taylor had all the credentials of sociologists of their day in that they were members of the American Sociological Society and published in the organizations' journal. All the settlement workers had in common an identity differentiating them from "charity visitors," often seen as the first social workers. Most notably, "charity workers emphasized the individual causes of poverty; settlement workers saw social and economic conditions as causing poverty" (Greek 1992:81). As one Hull House resident put it, "Instead of pulling Mr. and Mrs. Jones out of the ditch, fix the ditch." The settlement workers' view of the cause of the problems they confronted daily was in sharp contrast to the visitors who were likely to blame the people for their own problems, whether poverty, unemployment, or illness. The settlement workers saw the problems of their neighborhoods as rooted in the avarice of capitalism and in the failure of political-economic systems as well as in a lack of urban planning with the people's interest and welfare in mind. Nor were the settlement workers inclined to blame urban problems on "foreign cultures," or on lack of motivation or immorality on the part of individual families and workers. Even though settlement workers were not without some of the prejudices and ethnocentrism of their generation, they were more inclined toward a structural critique of their social world than many of their contemporaries. Davis, historian of the settlement movement, concluded that while churches and community organizations may have had greater impact on local neighborhoods than did settlements, "the settlements and their residents had a greater impact on the nation" because of their research and reform activities (1984:xxii). The basis of all settlement activities whether research, reform, or service was the neighborly relation. The settlement was the method by which workers lived among their neighbors, learned from them and shared in their needs.

Networking and Federation

Settlements were always about neighborhood but they were also up front in recognizing the need for macro-level social reforms. Settlement workers were among the first to differentiate what C. Wright Mills (1959:8–11) later conceptualized as personal troubles versus public issues. They recognized that in order to make life substantively better and sustainable, they had to attack the constellation of structural problems associated with industrialization, urbanization, and immigration, and in order to do this they needed to move beyond the neighborhood and they needed the political clout of numbers. They needed to educate policy-makers, civic leaders, and the public about the commonality of problems associated with industrialization, poverty, and urban living. This awareness led ultimately to settlements joining together organizationally in order to send a concerted message and reinforce their agenda of social reforms.

Perhaps the first time that some pioneer settlement workers met and interacted was at an 1892 summer institute sponsored by the Ethical Culture Society. Thereafter, the personal papers of many of the settlement leaders document regular correspondence and travel-related visits among settlements. The need for some kind of cooperative organization for settlement workers to exchange ideas and information emerged at the 1908 annual meeting of the National Conference of Charities and Correction (NCCC) to which many early settlement workers belonged.[7] For the next several years settlement workers sponsored a number of sessions focused on their special interests while remaining a part of the NCCC. In

7 Over the years settlement workers intersected on many fronts with representatives of the National Conference of Charities and Correction (NCCC) and with Charities Organization Societies (COS). While they cooperated on many endeavors, they were sometimes in disagreement over both methods and goals. The NCCC evolved from the American Social Science Association (ASSA) when a group of interested persons began meeting as a subgroup at ASSA annual meetings and in 1875 founded the Conference of Charities and a few years later began meeting separately from the ASSA. In 1884 they merged with the American Prison association and changed their name to the NCCC. In the 1890s, settlement workers were in regular attendance at NCCC meetings but sponsored sessions geared to their own interests, for example in 1896 they held a special meeting on settlements and labor. In 1897, Mary Richmond delivered her speech calling for the training of charity workers, seen by many as the beginning of the profession of social work. The NCCC was very influential in writing the Progressive Party platform in the 1912 election and in 1919 morphed into the National Conference of Social Workers. The Charities Organization Society (COS) began in 1880 with an organization in Buffalo, New York but was heavily influenced by a similar movement in Europe. Charity Organization Societies spread to other cities and by the turn of the century numbered more than 90. The served as a clearinghouse for charitable organizations already at work and dealt largely with individuals or families. They were transparent in their belief that most poverty was due to moral deficiency (Barbuto 1999:41). Their goal was to eliminate poverty by making people self-sufficient and toward this end they purported to investigate, evaluate, and coordinate work among the poor and needy. During the Progressive Era, COSs, settlement workers, social workers, and those representing the leadership of the NCCC coexisted but not without tensions and sometimes fundamental disagreements. However, there were overlapping individuals, active in more than one of these organizations, who no doubt managed to utilize the best in all for the greater good. For example, some of the leading

the meantime cities with multiple settlements such as New York, Boston, and Chicago began to establish citywide federations, and the College Settlements Association with houses in three cities comprised its own small federated organization. In 1908, representatives of all known settlements were invited to attend the annual meeting of the NCCC and, as a subgroup, to consider the special needs of settlement workers. From this meeting, ten representatives, mostly from the largest and best-known settlements, were selected to determine a future course of action. As a result of that meeting and perhaps as an effort to identify who they were and what they were doing, Robert Woods and Albert Kennedy of South End House in Boston were commissioned to collect information on settlements across the United States, subsequently securing funding from the Russell Sage Foundation. The result was the *Handbook of Settlements* (1911) that identified 413 settlements across the country by state and city, providing descriptions of each in terms of residents, volunteers, programs, research, and publications. In the Preface, the authors pay tribute to their predecessor, the *Bibliography of Settlements* published since 1897 by the College Settlements Association.

At the 1911 meeting of the NCCC, almost 200 representatives of settlements formally organized the National Federation of Settlements (NFS). Jane Addams was elected the first president and Robert Woods the first secretary (Barbuto 1999:140). Goals of the new organization were stated as developing policies regarding settlement issues, cooperating with other reform organizations to achieve common goals, sponsoring research studies and publishing the results. Indicative of commitment to the latter goal, shortly after formation, the NFS launched a study of young working girls, the results of which were published two years later (Woods and Kennedy 1913). In addition, the NFS was committed to attracting and sponsoring college men and women to participate in settlement work (Barbuto 1999:140). These and other goals were formalized and expanded by the NFS in their 1920 Articles of Incorporation where they vowed to: (1) federate settlements, neighborhood houses and similar institutions to promote the welfare of settlements and their neighborhoods; (2) encourage development and maintenance of settlements in cooperation with neighborhoods; (3) organize conferences, groups, and studies; (4) cooperate with private and government agencies; (5) consider and act on matters of interest to settlements and their neighbors; and (6) act in an advisory capacity to settlements.[8]

settlement workers of the day served as presidents of the NCCC: Jane Addams, Graham Taylor, Robert Woods, Julia Lathrop, and Grace Abbott.

8 In 1949, the NFS became the National Federation of Settlements and Neighborhood Centers, and in 1979 the United Neighborhood Centers of America which continues to advocate nationally for social legislation and to work with local agencies to address social problems (Social Welfare History Project, National Federation of Settlements and Neighborhood Centers:

Perhaps as important as the formal organization of settlements was the informal network of settlement leaders, particularly among the first and second generation; and the network among the women was apparently more intense than among the men. This fact becomes apparent when reading the records of settlement workers preserved in various archives. They wrote frequent letters; when traveling they stayed overnight at other settlements, sometimes giving guest lectures while visiting; they cooperated in research projects; they reviewed each other's books and writings; they acknowledged friendships and debts of gratitude in autobiographical writings;[9] they sometimes wrote about others in the movement as in the case of Addams' *My Friend Julia Lathrop* ([1935]2004); and they gave eulogies at each other's funerals or memorial services as in the case of Graham Taylor for Jane Addams and for Mary McDowell, and as Emily Balch did for Helena Dudley. It was not unusual for some active in the movement to live in more than one settlement. For example, Florence Kelley moved from Hull House to the Henry Street Settlement. Mary McDowell began at Hull House before becoming head resident at the University of Chicago Settlement. Mary Simkhovitch lived at the New York College Settlement before establishing Greenwich House.

Contributions to Sociology

The Settlement Idea and Social Class

Vida Scudder once proclaimed that she "wanted people set free from the prison of class" (VDSP 1930: B1, F3). Early settlement workers like Scudder grasped the meaning of social structure as it related to the "social question." If they were not aware when they entered settlement work, they quickly became aware of the interconnectedness of wealth and poverty, and as they treated the symptoms of poverty they were in search of underlying causes.

> Out of the striving for greater justice and humanity came an understanding of the interdependence of society, of the cost to all when some suffer, of the contagion and danger to the social structure and public well-being when a part of it is left neglected, cramped, and without opportunity....
>
> PACEY 1950:1

---

http://www.socialwelfarehistory.com/organizations/national-federation-of-settlements-and-neighborhood-centers/, accessed June 14, 2014).

9 Vida Scudder, for example wrote in her autobiography of the "splendid women" (settlement pioneers) with whom she was fortunate enough to have a friendship: "Jane Addams, greatest of all; Ellen Gates Starr, Lillian Wald, Mary Simkhovitch... Helena Stuart Dudley" (1937:101).

Perhaps nothing captures the contrast between the settlement and charity workers' approach to social class better than a 1896 incident at a meeting of the National Conference on Charities and Corrections,

> ...a charity organization speaker made the usual allusions to the failings of the urban poor and the need for 'moral force' to lift them up. The next speaker, Mary McDowell of the University of Chicago Settlement...commented that she could not bring herself to criticize a filthy tenement apartment when she knew that smoke and soot were pouring into it from unregulated factories nearby. 'When I try to apply some of that 'moral force' ...somehow I don't know how'.
>
> BOYER 1992: 155–156

Settlement workers in the US were recognized as the experts on social class inequality before their peers in academia began to theorize and research the topic. In 1908 John Commons, a University of Wisconsin professor, presented a paper at the American Sociological Society on class conflict in the US. The first two persons selected as discussants of Commons' paper were Graham Taylor of the Chicago Commons and Jane Addams of Hull House. Lorene Pacey edited a collection of papers and speeches by settlement workers, a perusal of which reveals thematic references to social class and to the interrelatedness of poverty and wealth. According to Julia Lathrop (Hull House), residents were trained to "look for causes" and she went on to offer her conclusion that the "social question" hinges on industrial and economic questions (Pacey 1950:44). William Noyes (NY Federation of Settlements) was alone in acknowledging the contradiction of settlements acting as advocates for the poor and laboring classes while depending on financial support from the wealthy. He offered no solution to this contradiction but was unrelenting in his criticism of industrial society as he proclaimed, "What the poor need is not so much upper-class culture or upper class morality as freedom from industrial bondage" (1950:65). Jane Addams (Hull House), in discussing the role of settlements vis-à-vis unions referred to the "power-holding classes—capitalists as we call them" (1950:39). Vida Scudder (College Settlements Association) described the "conditions of life forced...upon vast numbers of the working classes, especially upon the poor" as "undemocratic, un-Christian, and unrighteous" (1950:72). Alice Hamilton (Hull House) thought that social investigations should be about "searching for the cause of wrong conditions instead of merely relieving the effects" (1950:77). Violet Carruthers (English social reformer) spoke in behalf of the working classes whom she described as "in no mood today to tolerate the ministrations of superior persons" (1950:150). Percy

Alden (Mansfield House, England) called for representation of the working class in all public bodies (1950:48). Noyes concluded: "class distinctions were never so clearly and unequivocally based upon the fundamental basis of life, viz, the economic basis.... Possession or non-possession of the resources of wealth, is coming to be the test of class superiority and inferiority" (1950:63). Robert Woods (South End House) lauded the settlement for having been "engaged for a generation with an enterprise in social structure" as applied to the "reorganization of industry" (1950:150). William Tucker (Andover House) challenged workers to aim "not simply at the relief of the poor, but at a reduction of poverty itself corresponding at least with the increase of wealth" (1950:290).

Of all the writings about the settlement movement, one work by Arthur Holden is of particular value as a definitive statement on the purpose and meaning of settlements vis-à-vis the social question.[10] To Holden, for urban-industrial society the "social question" was the issue of class: "The plight of the low grade unskilled workman...forced into a condition of abject poverty and 'wage slavery'" ([1922]1970:21). Holden's history of wage labor is Marxian in substance although he was careful to discredit socialist revolution, instead embracing the settlement idea of bringing the classes together in a neighborly relation as revolutionary in concept.

> Ours is the opportunity of applying on a greater scale a conception and a method wherein lies a great hope. It is possible for any man to extend his circle of living to meet laboring men and by offering himself as a friend learn to understand the laboring man's point of view, his despairs and his aspirations.
>
> HOLDEN [1922]1970:32

Holden is one of the few writers on the settlement movement to attempt to delineate and define the social class structure in the US and to relate the settlements to that structure. He was well ahead of his time in describing the "line of advantages or privileges" that we have today come to understand as the unconscious privilege enjoyed by whites and by the affluent. Using a pie-chart, but avoiding quantification, he diagramed a four-fold class structure and asserted that settlements should have a major role in educating individuals and groups about their relation to the whole structure of society. His four classes were: (1) a

10 Holden, a New York City architect, and expert on housing, was for many years involved in various civic and social organizations with reform agendas. He taught for a time at Princeton University and served as secretary of their Committee on Social Service. While not directly associated with any one settlement house, he was familiar with the work of settlements and over the years served with residents on a variety of boards and committees.

privileged class enjoying "all of the advantages which money and position can procure" but insensitive to any social responsibilities to other classes; (2) a larger group comprised of under-privileged who look up to the class above them but rather than assessing blame for their less fortunate position, are grateful for what they have; (3) an under-privileged but class-conscious group, ranging from revolutionaries to educators, who understand the "social forces and social relations" among groups; and (4) a small and privileged class (such as settlement residents) who enjoy the advantages of wealth, education, and travel but who understand that they have a relation and a responsibility to society as a whole. Holden drew a "line of advantages or privileges" depicting social responsibilities, concluding that "It is difficult...to keep fresh in one's memory the fact that oneself and one's possessions are alike part of the world and exist only as part of the whole" ([1922]1970:80–83). For Holden settlements provided a ready means of social practice and problem-solving for those with a pre-developed social consciousness. A Marxian influence is evident in his final chapter.

> I believe the writings of Karl Marx to be of the very greatest historical value...his criticism of economic conditions...was certainly just.... His conclusions gave society a terrible scare. His method taught men in greater numbers than ever before to seek an economic system more endurable to live under.... The influence of socialism has been a healthy one... [bringing] about a revolution in methods of thought. With its program of a reconstructed human society, it has given the inspiration for the quest of a society molded according to human design. It has given to humanity the inspiration that man can by conscious effort control his own destiny ([1922]1970:175–176).

Holden ended by asserting that the social settlement was not just an idea but a method, the application of which would lead to a more just society. Settlements for him were not only for the fulfillment of privileged people who wanted to do good but were about bringing the classes together and maximizing the influence of those with a developed social conscience who could use their influence to restructure society. Holden connected the settlement idea to what he termed "social evangelism" and declared that whatever may be life in the hereafter, we must, in our own time, seek "the social good." He cited as the first and last commandment of Jesus to "love one's neighbor as oneself." For Holden, the settlement mission was for workers and neighbors to interpret one to another so that they could, in fact, come to love one another. Finally, Holden saw settlements as,

> the best agency yet devised for the improvement of the social structure because it is the most human. It does not have to wait for any automatic

> breakdown of capitalism nor for any general strike.... It is the only method yet devised which takes into consideration both ends of society ([1922]1970:87–88).

Clearly, most of the early settlement residents were from upper or upper-middle class backgrounds. Consequently they brought with them certain aspects of the life to which they had been socialized, not only books, music, and art, but also domestic workers—a source of some discomfort and philosophical disparity. All of the larger settlements had some domestic help and they made every effort to incorporate them into the settlement community. Jane Addams and Helen Gates Starr are widely known and recorded as the original residents of Hull House even though three women moved into this new residence. The third was cook and housekeeper and a friend of the Addams family, Mary Keyser, who died prematurely at age 36 after five years of residence (Stebner 1997:95–98). Addams acknowledged Keyser's contributions to the beginnings of Hull House when she wrote that she "began by performing the housework, but...quickly developed into a very important factor in the life of the vicinity as well as in that of the neighborhood" (Addams [1910]2008:61–62). South End House began with only four male residents and three female housekeepers which Robert Woods obviously felt somewhat apologetic about as he wrote to his board chair, "Of course it looks from the outside rather absurd to think of having three women to take care of four men. But the fact is that the work of taking care of the house already represents a good deal more than that." He referred to the frequent need for these women to answer the door when neighbors decided to drop-in and residents were engaged in other tasks leaving the housekeeping staff as greeters and representatives of the settlement. Woods went on to make his point, "It seems as if when we get six or seven men in the house, we should have to have the housekeeper and two capable girls." Even though Woods clearly saw a household staff as essential, and wrote that there was no point in "experimenting" with the need, he still demonstrated discomfort with managing the personnel. In his early days as head resident, he wrote that "domestic matters are still uppermost...two girls leaving...partly on their own choice and partly by request" (Woods 1929:50). The Chicago Commons also employed domestic help and a committee of residents, apparently grappling with the question of the relationship between the staff and residents, in 1899 recommended the signing of a voluntary agreement by all probationary and permanent residents. The agreement was an overt effort to bridge the class disparity between the domestic help and residents and read in part as follows.

> I. I AGREE that in the spirit of brotherly love and consideration, I will treat each and every helper in the work of this household, as a member

> equally with myself, of the family circle, especially endeavoring to share with them the life and privileges of the Settlement.
>
> II. I AGREE that I will do all in my power to avoid causing them unnecessary labor or inconvenience, and that I will assist as I have opportunity in the manual labor for the comfort and convenience of the household...to the end of limiting the working day of our hired helpers to eight hours, and of releasing them to the fullest possible extent, from Sunday work.
>
> III. I AGREE to afford with regularity, promptness and thoroughness, the morning care of my own room, and to prepare my room for its periodic sweeping and cleaning.

The document also asks residents to agree to gender-specific household chores. For example the men were to assist in the care of the stoves by providing coal, kindling wood, and disposition of ashes. The females were to assist with dishes and cleaning up after meals. Out of respect for the household staff, all residents were asked to pledge to be prompt at breakfast and other meals. The Committee ended by stipulating the purpose of this agreement as,

> not merely to ameliorate the excessive toil of those who faithfully serve our comfort and convenience; but rather, to revolutionize the spirit and method of our domestic life, more especially our relations with our hired servants, to the end that we shall:
>
> abolish so far as in us lies, lovingly, helpfully and considerately, the social classification palpably existing between ourselves and our servants.
>
> share, so far as we may be able and as the general convenience of the household will permit, in the spirit of helpful love, the menial drudgery caused entirely by our own life and in the service of our own comfort.
>
> recognize, candidly and unmistakably, the dignity of manual labor in the service of daily life and comfort, and the duty of each person to bear his own share of that labor occasioned upon others by his own leisure and convenience, but most of all,
>
> begin to create, within our own household, a living example of Christian co-operation and brotherhood.
>
> GTP: B50, F2312

The Chicago Commons agreement is an unobtrusive measure of efforts to bridge the gap between the classes in the daily life of settlement workers. It is unknown whether other houses made comparable efforts, but here is evidence that at least one settlement demonstrated social consciousness and attempted to reduce the social distance between residents and domestic help.

Cultural Pluralism

The settlements were intersections of social classes and ethnicities (in those days referred to as races) and settlement workers often found themselves interpreting to the "natives" the cultural differences and national loyalties of working-class immigrants. Many members of the dominant Anglo/Teutonic population had little tolerance for the cultural diversity presented by immigrants and wanted assimilation as rapidly as possible. Settlement workers, in daily contact with immigrant populations, were able to appreciate the unique differences of each group and were likely to encourage remembrances of their histories, traditions, dietary differences, and religious observances. Many settlement leaders were early advocates of what later became known as ethnogenesis or cultural pluralism, a sociological concept traced to Horace Kallen (1915).[11] It is difficult to say if Kallen influenced the settlement idea of "immigrant gifts" or if it was settlements that contributed to Kallen's concept of cultural pluralism. As a student at Harvard, Kallen lived for a time in a Boston settlement where he instructed immigrant children in various subjects (Konvitz 1987:100). As Carnevale observed, "The cultural pluralism articulated by Horace Kallen in 1915 found its nearest approximation in the settlement house movement" (2009:70). Kallen, who later taught at Harvard, Wisconsin, and the New School in New York, rejected the melting pot theory of assimilation in favor of cultural pluralism although he did not use that term until 1924 when it appeared in his book, *Culture and Democracy*. Before Kallen, however, settlement workers were supporting if not advocating for cultural pluralism and understood the implications of the concept in action. In fact, the archival records of settlement leaders document their many speeches and formal lectures delivered in a variety of settings—college classrooms, churches, synagogues, Chautauqua circuits, and civic organizations—devoted to the topic of immigrants. As Geraldine Gordon of Denison House explained, the settlements

11 Kallen's concept embraced the preservation of a group's unique cultural heritage as evidenced in language, religion, art, literature, holidays, and rituals within the context of a common use of the English language and acceptance of the prevailing political and economic systems. Kallen studied under William James at Harvard, and James philosophical works on pragmatism influenced both Addams and Kallen.

needed audiences in order to utilize their role as social scientists, to "understand and interpret" the lives of their neighbors to others (DHR 1913, Headworkers Annual Reports:M141,R4). Their targeted audiences were ordinary people who were or would be neighbors and always, directly or indirectly, policy makers, capitalists, and other influential decision-makers. A typical example is a speech delivered by Lillian Wald at a synagogue in 1907 where she decried our "national vanity that says 'if we can't make them like ourselves, let us make them as nearly like ourselves as we can'" (LDWP, NYPL: Reel 24, B35). In 1908 Jane Addams addressed the National Education Association on the topic of immigrant children, taking a strong stance in support of respect and maintenance of cultural diversity.

> ...[T]he schools ought to do more to connect these children with the best things of the past, to make them realize something of the beauty and charm of the language, the history, and the traditions which their parents represent. It is easy to cut them loose from their parents, it requires cultivation to tie them up in sympathy and understanding...it is the business of the school to give to each child, the beginning of a culture so wide and deep and universal that he can interpret his own parents and countrymen by a standard which is world-wide and not provincial ([1908]2002:236).

Henry Moscowitz, of New York's Madison House Settlement wrote that social settlement residents were "among the first to appreciate the cultural heritage which foreigners bring to the new country, the first to combat that cheap notion of assimilation which exacts of the foreigner that he abandon what constitutes his distinct contribution to American life—his best traditions" (1911:462). Settlements, for the most part, placed no obstacles in the way of people of the same nationality who preferred to meet by themselves on special occasions. Some even facilitated such meetings as is evident from the following by Addams.

> Saturday evening, our Italian neighbors were our guests... [Hull] house became known as a place where Italians were welcome and where national holidays were observed. ...
>
> Friday evening is devoted to Germans... They sing a great deal in the tender minor of the German folksong or in the rousing spirit of the Rhine, and they are slowly but persistently pursuing a course in German history and literature ([1892b]2002:34).

In fact, some public criticism of settlement houses was because they were perceived as discouraging assimilation by showing too much respect for cultural differences and national loyalties. Through the years, however, scholars have recognized and documented the work of the settlements in offering common ground and opportunities to find human similarities and to deconstruct prejudices through association and education (Carson 1990:57–58). White (1959), for example, provides a comprehensive examination of the relationships between settlements and their immigrant neighbors, drawing heavily on the writings of Jane Addams, Robert Woods, and Gaylord White from New York's Union Settlement. The papers of Graham Taylor show his unwavering appreciation of immigrant cultures as evident in an untitled and undated manuscript, for what purpose we do not know.

> We are all children of immigrants.... Our country wants what you bring from the land of your birth. Do not lose it on the way. Bring with you to us your language. Tell us the stories and songs of your childhood. Show us the games and dances of your youth. Let us share with you what you learned in the old country, at school and church, in the fields and shops. It will enrich our lives and make better Americans of us all.... Never be ashamed of the land or the people which gave you birth. Add their best things to the good things you find here.
>
> GTP: B32, F1857.

Addams is the settlement worker most frequently recognized for her support of cultural pluralism. Stackpole, for example, surmised that "Jane Addams reveled in diversity... Hull House's idea of Americanization was to encourage a respect for the immigrant heritage, and at the same time expose the foreigner to American ideas naturally, not artificially" (1964:69). In New York, Mary Simkhovitch of Greenwich House believed that "worthwhile Americanization could not be imposed from without, but must grow from within through the experiences of the immigrant in the community" (Stackpole 1961:73).

Boston settlement workers were perhaps the least likely to embrace cultural pluralism and Vida Scudder was even described as an "Anglophile" or "cultural snob" although she recognized that inevitably the Anglo-Saxon would not be "the American" (Stackpole 1961:38, Scudder 1902:822). As noted by Carson and others, the language in some settlement research occasionally slipped from generalization to stereotype (1990:102). One such example can be found in the recorded characteristics of certain groups in a South End House report on "The Invading Host" (Woods [1903]1970:40–70). While Robert Woods worked with all groups in his settlement neighborhood, his annual headworker reports suggest that he saw some as a threat to the "best values" of American life and hoped to "control" them by "encouraging association (and discouraging ethnic sectionalism) among the different groups" (Streiff 2005:179). Woods was accused by some of being a restrictionist, particularly with regard to the "new" immigrants from Southern and Eastern Europe, and he did eventually support "reasonable limitation of immigration in the interests of all" ([1903]1970:364). Woods' lifetime of work at South End House shows his pragmatism in conceptualizing Americanization as "an evolution" and conceding,

> It is beyond measure better for this country that newcomers should settle with their own people and reproduce their native life, with its churches, benefit societies, and cultural institutions, that they should either live isolated in the midst of an American community or become part of a commercialized cosmopolitan slum ([1922]1990:327–328).

A final work by South End House Residents, unpublished at Woods' death, is characterized by ambivalence, with writings that sometimes lament the loss of ethnic cultures and at other times disdains them (Woods and Kennedy 1969). Although some historians such as Hofstadter accused settlement workers of condescension (1955:181), as a whole, they were out front in support of immigrants and of their cultural contributions to American life. Milton Gordon's comprehensive treatment of assimilation in the United States singles out settlement workers as exceptions in otherwise "monolithic attempts" to Americanize immigrants irrespective of cultures and heritage.

> As far back as the 1890s the settlement houses had begun a gentler process of dealing with the adjustment of the hordes of impoverished newcomers from Southern and Eastern Europe, and some of them had shown an appreciation of the immigrant's own cultural heritage and its potential contribution to American life (1964:99).

Settlement workers originated and propagated a doctrine of "immigrant gifts" to tout the positive contributions that these newcomers could make to the developing democracy of the United States (Eaton [1932]1970). Promotion of this doctrine was as much about pragmatism as cultural diversity because settlement workers learned early on that the assimilation process could be destructive to the immigrant family as parents clung to their old and familiar ways while their children, craving acceptance, readily became Americanized. Settlement workers were among the first to discover that they could,

> ...check family disorganization by extending an appreciative welcome to Old World heritages... In encouraging the newcomers to preserve the

> "best" in their own traditions, settlement leaders argued that each immigrant group had a tangible contribution to make to the building of American Culture.
>
> HIGHAM 1981:121

A "trends" history of sociology published in 1929 recognizes settlements for their contributions to the concept and to the reality of cultural diversity and also documents that some settlement workers were household names with audiences constituting pockets of influence.

> The settlement was one of the first agencies to recognize the importance of the immigrant's own culture in effecting a constructive accommodation to our society. Sympathy, understanding, and proper appreciation of the interdependence of culture patterns have been marked characteristics of the 'settlement house idea.' Who has not heard of Jane Addams, the saint of social work and most beloved woman in America; Lillian Wald and the House on Henry Street from which emanated the visiting nurse movement and ungraded school classes; Robert Woods and South End House; Graham Taylor and Chicago [Commons] and University [of Chicago Settlement].
>
> BAIN AND COHEN 1929:350

Race Relations

Some have represented settlement leaders rather matter-of-factly as products of their time and social location in matters of race. Carson, for example, asserts that "the settlement movement did not ameliorate, or even directly address white society's systematic discrimination against black Americans" (1990:195). Trolander made a similar claim while offering "reasons" for this: fundraising, lack of a wide spread civil rights movement following the Civil War, resistance to integration from white neighbors, and a certain blindness with regard to "white privilege" (1987:94–95). The National Federation of Settlements failed to develop a policy with regard to Black settlements and/or race relations, and not until the early 1940s did they make an effort to address the problem by engaging in a long-overdue analysis of interracial policies (Lasch-Quinn 1993:24). Davis gives settlement workers credit for having "a greater sympathy for the lot of the Negro...than most of their generation" (1984:84). Although settlements were established and maintained primarily to assist immigrant populations, race relations were not ignored nor were the needs of southern rural-to-urban Black migrants who were met with diverse responses.

> [A] settlement confronted by the appearance of blacks in its environs responded either by closing down, by following its white immigrant neighbors and moving out of the neighborhood, by excluding blacks, by conducting segregated activities, by establishing or urging the establishment of a separate branch for blacks, or by attempting integration.
>
> LASCH-QUINN 1993:24

Some settlements or settlement leaders took public positions in opposition to segregation and racial inequality in their day. They also helped in the formation of institutional supports for racial justice (Moore 1994). Of the 60 signers of the 1909 Call for the Lincoln Emancipation Conference that resulted in the formation of the National Association for the Advancement of Colored People (NAACP), one-third were settlement workers including such familiar names as Jane Addams of Hull House, John Dewey of Hull House and the University of Chicago Settlements, William Walling of Hull House and later University Settlement, Florence Kelley of Henry Street, Henry Moskowitz of Madison House, Mary White Ovington of Greenpoint and Greenwich House, Lillian Wald of Henry Street, and Charles Zueblin of Hull House and the Northwestern University Settlement (Davis 1984:99–102, Moore 1994). Initial plans for the organization of the NAACP were drawn up by three settlement workers: Walling, Moskowitz, and Ovington (Davis 1984:101).

Settlements sponsored some of the first research on urban Blacks. The Philadelphia College Settlement was a cosponsor, along with the University of Pennsylvania, of W.E.B. Du Bois' research on the *Philadelphia Negro* (1899); his associate, Isabel Eaton was a CSA fellow. Mary White Ovington with the support of a Greenwich House fellowship undertook the same kind of exhaustive study of blacks in New York resulting in *Half A Man* (1911). The research of Louise de Koven Bowen of Hull House resulted in *The Colored People of Chicago* (1913). South End House resident and fellow John Daniels produced *In Freedom's Birthplace* (1914), a study of Boston's black population. In 1905 a special issue of *Charities* was devoted entirely to problems facing urban blacks with articles reporting on local research conducted largely by settlements (Davis 1984:98). With the exception of Du Bois, these studies were carried out by whites; they did, nevertheless, refute some of the widely held beliefs that the problem with blacks was their lack of a work ethic, their intelligence, or/and their morality. As Davis put it, "The overwhelming effect of settlement investigations was to show that the position of the Negro could be improved through organization and social reform" (1984:98). When behavioral or culture problems were described stereotypically, the authors were generally consistent in positing their roots in slavery and in the failure of Reconstruction.

In what is the most comprehensive overview of the settlement movement vis-à-vis blacks, Lasch-Quinn faults settlement leaders for "failure to reorient their own movement toward their black neighbors" and with their erroneous perception of the "nature of African American individuals and culture" (1993:11). She did not, however, paint all settlement leaders with one broad brush. Rather, she selected four to portray some of their similarities and differences in approaching the problems of blacks in US cities: Jane Addams, Louise De Koven Bowen, Frances Kellor, and John Daniels. She also singled out Lillian Wald as having "earned a reputation as an advocate for blacks and for interracial advancement" (1993:29). Deegan (2002b) has thoroughly examined the complex and multi-dimensional work of Addams and other Chicago women as well as early men of the University of Chicago in what she termed Chicago's neo-abolitionist movement (2002b:16–47). Addams referred to the plight of blacks as "the gravest situation in our American life" (1930:401). Although her analysis placed some of the problem on black families, it was ultimately a racist social structure shutting blacks out of jobs, a living wage, and descent housing that she faulted. Bowen, however, was critical that Hull House was more willing to confront the problems of blacks in other areas of the city than in their own neighborhood (Lasch-Quinn 1993:15–16). Most of the settlements did not turn blacks away, particularly children, but attempted to meet their needs without falling victim to the status quo segregation and racism that could threaten their overall programs and donor supports. Thus concessions were made with separate programs and assistance in organizing separate black settlements (Streiff 2005:179). In fact, many of the best known settlements became sponsors of or assisted in the founding of black settlements. By 1910 there were ten settlements in the US serving largely black populations and a few institutional churches functioned for the black community much as settlements did in immigrant communities.[12] Most of the black settlements were non-segregated but few whites took advantage of their services. Some of the settlements offered meeting spaces for black groups and risked public criticism. Lillian Wald, for example, hosted some of the developmental meetings of the NAACP at Henry Street Settlement in New York (Moore 1994). She wrote

12 There is little research on black settlement houses or institutional churches and we cannot do justice to them in this work. We do, however, call attention to the fact that here is a subject in need of research. Lasch-Quinn (1993) provides the most thorough examination of settlements and race relations although her treatment of black settlements deals largely with those in the South. Both Lasch-Quinn (1993) and Luker (1984) note that the black settlement movement has been overlooked and little researched, in part because scholars have been more likely to define such settlements as missions.

that she invited members of the NAACP to the settlement for a party because she thought them "too serious unless some social provisions were made." However, the group protested that if blacks and whites were to sit down together for supper the occasion would draw negative publicity for Henry Street. Mrs. Wald countered with the fact that the house was too small for a sit-down supper for 200 and that they would have to "stand up for supper." She reported that all agreed "then it would be all right...and the party was successful" (1934:49). Henry Street was also among early settlements to invite for residence, "A young Negro woman, a graduate of Oberlin doing postgraduate work at Bryn Mawr, who...wanted to study the new group of colored people in our neighborhood" (1934:28). In fact, many of the settlements, including Hull House, counted Blacks among their early residents. Most settlement leaders were astute enough not to take sides in the infamous Washington-Du Bois debate. Both men were visitors at settlements such as Hull House and Henry Street, and settlement personalities such as Addams, Kelley, Wald, Taylor, and Woods sometimes shared speaking platforms with both men. When racial conflict emerged in cities such as Chicago, settlement leaders were called on to mediate or to study such conflicts. For example, Graham Taylor of Chicago Commons was among a group of prominent leaders called together to discuss the crisis following the city's race riot of 1919. He was instrumental in the formation of a commission to research and write the final report on that incident. Taylor's son, Graham Romeyn, and sociologist Charles Johnson served as co-directors of the project (Chicago Commission on Race Relations 1922). Clearly, settlement workers, along with most of their peers, could have done more for their Black neighbors. However, it is unfair to indict them as absent leaders in the fight for racial justice or to suggest that they spoke or acted as one.

Theory and Method

An interesting and under-cited article by Cravens (1971) is very relevant to our appreciation of the contributions of the settlements to sociology although unfortunately he does not make this connection. Cravens approached the early history of the discipline via seventeen "founding fathers"[13] whose works

13 Cravens specifically lists only sixteen of the seventeen although he was presumably also including Lester F. Ward. The sixteen listed were: Frank W. Blackmar (Kansas), Charles H. Cooley (Michigan), James Q. Dealey (Brown), Charles A. Ellwood (Missouri), Franklin H. Giddings (Columbia), John M. Gillette (North Dakota), Edward C. Hayes (Illinois), George E. Howard (Nebraska), Albert G. Keller (Yale), James P. Litchenberger (Pennsylvania), Edward A. Ross (Wisconsin), Albion W. Small (Chicago), William G. Sumner (Yale), W.I. Thomas (Chicago), George E. Vincent (Chicago), Ulyses G. Weatherly (Indiana).

between 1890 and 1920 he examined for efforts to define sociology while at the same time moving it away from evolutionary theories modeled on the physical sciences. He credits these men as ultimately, but not linearly, coming to search for causation in social rather than natural forces, thus portending the influence of social structure on human behavior, "perhaps the distinctive contribution of the discipline of sociology in the twentieth century" (Cravens 1971:6). The men at first looked for "natural laws" but until Charles Cooley's *Social Organization* (1909) focused on a study of individuals over groups. Cravens concludes, "They agreed that social forces were psychological and mental in character, that the proper focus of sociological theory was the individual, and that society might be defined as the mental interactions of individuals" (1971:10). Franklin Giddings, for example, argued that sociology should be a psychological rather than a biological discipline (1899). Albion Small pursued his theory of "interests" as the basis of sociology for years before having it refuted and rejected by graduate student, Luther Bernard. Ellwood finally came around to acknowledging the importance of social over natural causation but never shifted his unit of analysis from individual to group. Schwendinger and Schwendinger assert that between 1906 and 1929, male presidents of the American Sociological Society were "busily involved in grounding the entire sociological discipline in psychology" (1974:360). Only after exploring natural and psychological causation as the purview of sociology, and only after positing the individual in his or her sociocultural environment, did the male founders go where settlement sociologists had already been, to social structure. However, we do not find among the works of these founding fathers as clear a definition of social class structure in the United States as that described by Holden ([1922]1970). Nor is there recognition of structural causation of social problems as demonstrated in the many writings and speeches of settlement workers (Pacey 1950). Phenomena that are today accepted as basic to the conceptual and analytical framework of the discipline of sociology were recognized and articulated first by settlement sociologists (Deegan 1990; Lengerman and Niebrugge 2002, 2007; MacLean and Williams 2012; Williams and MacLean 2012).

The critical pragmatism that informed both the social gospel and the settlement mission and method formed the basis for a social science of reform based on a theory of social relations that posited social structure as the cause of people's problems while calling for social action (Lengermann and Niebrugge 2007:99, 108). Settlement sociology treated social relations or the social connections of individuals within their own groups, with others, and with society as the essential focus of sociology (Addams 1892b, Brandt 1903, Lengermann and Niebrugge-Brantley 2002:13–18). By definition then, social problems were the result of "disconnections" (as between the classes). Woods, long-time Head

Resident of South End House, gave theoretical attention to social relations between settlement house residents and their neighbors, arguing that social reform must spring from the cooperation of all classes, the underlying assumption of the neighborly relations paradigm. Woods relied on an organic explanation of interdependence by using a parable that narrated the spread of a "dread disease" from the servant or workers quarters to the manor house, taking a terrible toll on both. Woods conclusion: "Thus was it burned into the souls of those in the great house and those in the cottage that there is one human family" ([1903]1970:356). The foundation of settlement theory was the proposition that middle class residents could "grow into a sense of relationship and mutual interest" with the poor and working classes, thus the neighborly relation was offered as an alternative to Marxian revolution. There should be no theory without accompanying methodology, and the settlement itself was the method as settlement sociologists in their day-to-day relations collected data and used these data to alleviate the problems they saw as impacting the quality of life in their neighborhoods.

Urban Sociology and Beyond

Chicago sociologist, Nels Anderson (1929:261–296) attributed the development of urban sociology to three distinct post-Civil War forces: the social gospel, applied sociology, and settlement houses. Although Anderson offered specific examples of all three of these forces, our work makes clear that they were not only overlapping but often indistinguishable. Because university faculty were slow to turn from what Anderson termed arm-chair philosophy to research, social science found other locations, namely in the social settlements which, "as social laboratories or, better still, observation posts...were surpassed by no other institution at the time" (1929:269). Robert Park, while often denouncing reformers, acknowledged that "Social settlements...became outposts for observation and for intimate studies of social conditions in regions of the city that up to that time had remained *terra incognita*" ([1925]1967:5). He also cited *Hull-House Maps and Papers* and *The City Wilderness* as "in the nature of an exploration and recognizance, laying the ground for the more systematic and detailed studies which followed" ([1929b]1967:6). Park was referring of course to subsequent studies of the city of Chicago carried out by sociology faculty and students in his department in the 1920s and 1930s that became generally known as Chicago Sociology. However, settlement sociologists provided earlier and more detailed ethnographies of city neighborhoods in which they made their homes. Comparing the work of Chicago sociologists such as Robert Park and Ernest Burgess with settlement sociology, particularly that of South End House, reveals that settlements provided more than ground work for urban sociology.

Settlement workers were the first urban sociologists, and the neighborly relation was the ultimate form of participant observation. Their data provided the foundation for a sociology of structural inequality and use of these data to effect reform social policies impacted the quality of life for all workers. There is evidence that the urban sociology later developed at the University of Chicago by Ernest Burgess and Robert Park was influenced by settlement sociology although neither man does more than recognize such work as exploratory or pre-sociological. An examination of some of Burgess' papers, however, reveals that several of his courses taught between the mid-1920s and the mid-1930s used bibliographies including works by Addams, Woods, and Taylor (EWBP: B27, F1). Further, Burgess was chair of the University's Local Community Research Committee in 1927 when they conducted a study of neighborhoods and social settlements (EWBP: B139, F10). In personal correspondence with Graham Taylor about a manuscript, Burgess suggested that he should be more specific in calling attention to sociological "studies which settlement residents instituted" (GTP 24 December, 1927: B12, F580).

The settlement house movement was in many respects a nucleus of interlinkages formed out of the changing roles of women in 19th century society, higher education, the social gospel, and the new discipline of sociology. Regardless of motivation, however, all of those involved in the settlement movement had in common the goal of alleviating the social problems of urban-industrial society, especially class inequality. Based on their social investigations as well as their neighborly relations, settlement workers were inclined to define the problems of their neighbors and neighborhoods as structural rather than personal, an inclination that increased over time and led to clear distinctions between personal troubles and social problems.

CHAPTER 3

Hull House: Feminist Pragmatism and the Chicago Women's School of Sociology

Chicago's winning bid for the Columbian Exposition of 1893, in celebration of the 400th anniversary of the discovery of America, won international recognition for the city as attendance averaged over 150,000 people per day during the 179 day run. Indeed, the Exposition announced that despite the great fire of 1871, Chicago had risen from the ashes to become the model of a progressive city. Determined that the Exposition would not gloss over Chicago's problems, settlement workers such as Jane Addams took advantage of the event to educate the public about urban problems. They used speeches, lectures, and exhibits to contrast the ideal "white city"[1] with the "real Chicago of slums, disease, and corrupt politics" (Davis 1984:187). And Ida B. Wells staged a protest when the city announced a "Colored People's Day" promising 2000 free watermelons (*Chicago Tribune* May 1, 1893). In many ways Jane Addams, Hull House, and Chicago became synonymous with reform and during the Progressive Era the settlement served as a community-based school for the study of social problems and the practice of sociology. Hull House, founded in 1889, developed a distinctive school of women social scientists who practiced sociology with the leadership of Jane Addams. Fundamental to Addams' sociological work was the belief that the privileged classes had a responsibility to the less fortunate.

The Hull House legacy is one of programmatic developments, sociological investigations, and reform activities, particularly during the peak period of sociological practice in the settlement movement from 1890 to World War I. By 1920, with the establishment of the graduate School of Social Service Administration at the University of Chicago, sociology was formalized as an academic discipline, essentially sex-segregating sociology and social work and rendering "public sociology" as practiced by the social settlements obsolete (Deegan 1990, Lengermann and Niebrugge 2007, MacLean and Williams 2012). Prior to WW I, a strong pacifist stance emanating from the feminist pragmatism of many in the settlement community, most notably Jane Addams, added

1 The term "white city" originated as a derisive description of Exposition buildings, most erected in haste, a composite of plaster, cement, and jute fiber called staff. The buildings, most intended to be temporary, were painted white giving them an apparent gleam especially when lighted.

to other emerging forces to mark the decline of settlement sociology and the institutionalization of early settlement activities as a form of social work. Deegan (1990, 2002a) describes the years prior to the 1920s, as the "golden era of women in sociology." Subsequently, a dark era of patriarchal ascendancy would marginalize, obscure, or entirely erase women's early contributions to sociology until the 1960s social movements began to revive them.[2] Similarly Lengermann and Niebrugge (2007) provide an insightful critical social history of the shared interests of sociology and social work in Progressive Era social reform activities and of their eventual separation as academic disciplines and fields of practice. They note that this process was part and parcel of a larger "politics of knowledge" encompassing political contests centered on both gender and social reform (Lengermann and Niebrugge-Brantley 1998:10–17).

Jane Addams and Her Journey to Hull House

Jane Addams, born prior to the Civil War in 1860, died on May 21, 1935 at the age of 74 from complications following intestinal surgery which revealed a growing cancer. The outpouring of love and affection demonstrated at her death is just a small indication of her legacy and life's work of 46 years as the head resident of Hull House.[3] News articles preserve the details of Addams' memorial service

2 By the 1920s most of these women were no longer practicing in domains or with titles bearing the name sociology but were practicing in the gender-segregated fields of social work, household administration, education, and applied psychology. The archival records suggest that there were both "push and pull" factors involved in this process of disciplinary differentiation and segregation. While there is good evidence that what became the formal discipline of sociology was increasingly an unfriendly, if not hostile, environment for women at the University of Chicago, women also actively carved out their own domains for practice. At times they no doubt sought job security, at other times the freedom to seek solutions to social problems unencumbered by the professional agendas of their male colleagues and of university politics.

3 Jane Addams always hyphenated Hull House although the reason and significance of her doing so are seemingly lost to history. Most speculations are that it had to do with the hybridization of the classes and of the different ethnicities and nationalities in the Hull House neighborhood (Jackson 2001:59–60). Addams may have believed, as expressed later by John Dewey, that "the hyphen connects instead of separates" (Dewey 1916:185–186). Rachel Glass, education coordinator of the Hull House Museum, says the answer, or puzzle of the hyphen, is lost in "the mists of time." In recent years most writers opt not to hyphenate Hull House, a practice traced back, whether intentionally or unintentionally, to Victor Weybright, editor-in-chief of New American Library when they began releasing some of Addams works in new editions (Tower 1961:39).

and provide impressive photo coverage of the thousands of people who gathered outside of Hull House to pay their respects upon the news of her death. The service was speaker-amplified into the surrounding streets as the small courtyard could accommodate only 1,000 people. Addams' benediction was given by her close friend and associate of many years, Dr. Graham Taylor, then 81 years of age, and retired head resident of the Chicago Commons settlement. On the day of her death, the *Chicago Herald and Examiner* reported that, "When Miss Addams' temperature rose to 107¼ at 5:30 P.M. it was obvious the death would be only a matter of minutes. In the terse cold language of medicine the doctors reported the end of the large-hearted, tireless, broad-visioned woman whose long career had been one of constant labor for those who need help" (HHC: B1, F2). Apparently, before slipping into a comma, Addams was asked whether she might like a drink of water. To this she purportedly replied, "Oh, I am always ready for a drink of water." The symbolism of this last act of kindness and her final words reveal a role-reversal apropos of her life's work at Hull House that was always about providing respite and succor to those in need.

Much more is known of Jane Addams' life than is the case for many other settlement workers because she has come to symbolize the movement as a whole.[4] She was born to middle-class parents, John and Sarah Addams, near the fledgling village of Cedarville, Illinois where her father purchased a small saw and gristmill and planted Norway pines brought from Pennsylvania. Ten years later he had prospered enough to build a large mill and the largest home in the area. John Addams invested in railroads, banks, mines, and a life insurance company. He served in the Illinois State Senate from 1854 to 1870. He was present at the founding of the Republican Party and thereafter remained a loyal Republican. All of Addams' biographers emphasize the fact that her father was the dominant influence in her life; she herself described her affection for him as "doglike" ([1910]2008:6). According to one biographer, Jane was aware "that her father was the wealthiest and most prominent person in the

4 There are more than a dozen biographies written about Jane Addams as well as several compilations of her writings and speeches, some with analyses and biographical notes. The biography by her nephew (Linn [1935] 2000) is the only one that Addams participated in and is considered by some as the definitive biography while others see it as lacking in objectivity. Some of the best known biographies are those by Diliberto (1999), Davis (2000), Elshtain (2002a), Berson (2004), and Knight (2005, 2010). Thematic biographies include Knight (2010) which traces Addams' political career from dreamer to ambassador, Joslin (2004) which documents Addams' life as a writer, and Deegan (1990) which restores her contributions as a sociologist. In addition to the biographies, Addams wrote her autobiography in several formats, perhaps more completely in *Twenty Years at Hull House* (1910). The definitive biography of Addams' life as a feminist has yet to be written.

village and her house was bigger than all the other houses...she had advantages that many other children did not have, such as drawing and music lessons" (Davis 2000:8). Despite this awareness, however, Addams' playmates were the sons and daughters of mill hands and village life in Cedarville had an egalitarian feel to it. Her father described himself as a Hicksite Quaker; however, Davis concluded that "her father's Quakerism was so vague that he was not even a pacifist, and helped recruit a regiment during the Civil War" (2000:135). Jane's mother, Sarah, died at the age of 49 shortly after giving birth to an infant who also died. The couple had nine children but only four survived to adulthood, Jane being the youngest and only two years of age when her mother died. Accounts differ as to Addams' age when her father remarried; she reported that she was eight although others have reported her as younger (Addams [1910] 2008:7, Davis 2000:6). The new stepmother had two sons, one about Jane's age and the other, 18 at the time, later married Jane's sister, Alice. Addams became quite close to both of her step brothers, particularly the younger one. While Adams' relationship with her step mother was generally a warm one, there were tensions after her father's death with regard to financial matters and expectations that Jane would assume the family caretaker role typical in that day for the unmarried "maiden aunt." Addams grew up suffering from a number of physical ailments, the most significant of which was diagnosed as "tuberculosis of the spine" that left her with a slight curvature of the back later requiring surgery to relieve the pain (Davis 2000: 6).

Jane Addams is usually considered a member of the first generation of college women although in reality her education was secured in a female seminary, not quite equal with the women's colleges that had recently opened their doors. Rockford Seminary had been chartered by the Presbyterian and Congregational churches and as with other seminaries for women it taught piety and domesticity, but was more academically rigorous than many, having been patterned after Mount Holyoke's classical curriculum of languages, literature, and science. It was Addams' fervent desire to attend Smith College but her father insisted that she enroll at Rockford where two older sisters had attended. Reluctantly she entered Rockford in 1877 and left with a seminary degree in 1881, the year that Rockford began offering a BA degree for an additional year's work. Addams opted not to remain for this additional year, planning instead to enter Smith the following fall to earn her BA as had been her dream before Rockford. Davis speculates that the importance of Smith was that, in comparison with other women's colleges, it was patterned after the more challenging curricula of male institutions, an observation supported by MacLean and Williams as well (2005). According to Davis (2000:14) and other biographers, Addams never considered marriage for herself but rather set her sights on a career although the path ahead would be a circuitous one. While she may not have contemplated marriage, Addams had learned feminine domesticity and tried to make it compatible with later career goals. For example, in one of her college essays, she wrote, "She [women in general] wishes not to be a man, nor like a man, but she claims the same right to independent thought and action" (Davis 2000:20). Even though Addams went through a period of floundering in search of a meaningful life pathway, the feminist pragmatism that was to characterize her career is clearly evident in embryonic form during her Rockford days. For example, her senior essay that also became her valedictory address, centered on the tragic heroine of Greek mythology, Cassandra, daughter of the King of Troy who was endowed with great powers which were denied because she was a woman.[5] As Addams wrote,

> ...to Cassandra...suddenly came the power of prophecy. Cassandra fearlessly received the power, with clear judgment and unerring instinct she predicted the victory of the Greeks and the destruction of her father's city. But the brave warriors laughed to scorn the beautiful prophetess and called her mad. The frail girl stood conscious of Truth but she had no logic to convince the impatient defeated warriors, and no facts to gain their confidence, she could only assert and proclaim until at last in sooth she becomes mad ([1881]2003:428).

This particular writing captures the special feminist qualities that Addams perceived as being essential to the best interest of society (truth, clear judgment, and unerring instinct) but also captures Addams' frustration because Cassandra lacked the credibility or respect that must come from others. Addams only hints that this lack of credibility was due to the fact that Cassandra was a beautiful woman; instead she suggests that men would see the woman as credible if she had logic and facts behind her prophecy, the logic that science and factual observations could give her to support her prophecy or insight. Women lacked what Addams termed *auethoritas* (or *auctoritas*), what we would translate as authority or agency today. The speech emphasized the importance that Addams attached to facts and to logic, more likely a part of the education of males than females in that day. Addams had not yet reached the point of addressing systemic sexism; instead she put the onus for change

5 Addams' valedictory took place at a time when Rockford Trustees were embroiled in a controversy on whether women should be allowed to sit on the Board and when the Seminary was about to exercise the right included in its charter to assume the status of college as well as seminary.

on women, "Let her not sit and dreamily watch her child; let her work her way to a sentient idea that shall sway and ennoble those around her" ([1881]2003:429). Toward the end of her speech, Addams turned to the ultimate goal of justice which she asserted "must be established in the world by trained intelligence; by broadened sympathies toward the individual man and woman who... embrace the opposing facts and forces." She concluded by giving women parity with men in the pursuit of justice, saying "The opening of the ages has long been waiting for this type of womanhood" ([1881]2003:429). In fact, Addams' vision emboldened a generation of college-educated women to embark on a life of social investigation linked to social reform (Schultz 2007:12). Later, of course, Addams' reputation at Hull House and in Chicago came to be associated with her pragmatic use of science based on facts collected by settlement residents and on her own systematic observations. She always held true, however, to an idea expressed in her Rockford valedictory, "to express herself not by dogmatism, but by quiet, progressive development" ([1881] 2003:420). Addams' development came through her years of experience at Hull House.

Addams never realized her dream of earning a degree from Smith. After graduation from Rockford, she returned to Cedarville where she became ill and suffered a bout of depression. In an effort to improve her health, her father took his wife and daughter on a trip to Michigan where he owned mining property and where he became ill and died, at the relatively young age of 59, of a ruptured appendix. Shortly after her father's death the Addams family moved to Philadelphia where her step brother Harry was enrolled in medical school and where Jane entered the Women's Medical School, a decision that still puzzles many of her biographers. Addams herself did not explain her decision to enter medical school although she did explain that she left because of the "spinal difficulty" that had "shadowed" her from childhood and finally required surgery and six months of immobility. She also apparently felt caught between the demands of being a student and of her family responsibilities. As she recalled in her autobiography, "I was very glad to have a physician's sanction for giving up clinics and dissecting rooms and to follow his prescription of spending the next two years in Europe. ...my brief foray into the profession [of medicine] never resumed" ([1910]2008:43). At her father's death Addams received a small inheritance that provided her with economic independence. However, for Addams her father's death was followed by illness, inertia, depression, a sense of failure, and years of unfocused activity that included several trips to Europe. Perhaps in seeking to find meaning in her life, she received the rite of baptism into the Presbyterian Church; she assumed management of family affairs, and even at one point ventured into farming. Thus began a circuitous route that would eventually take her to Chicago and to Hull House. It was during her European travels, undertaken as diversion, that she was introduced to urban poverty and to labor unrest, especially in the streets of East London where she saw "hideous human need and suffering" such as she had never witnessed before. She later recalled her distress over the first up-close view of poverty that was "suddenly driven into my consciousness" ([1910]2008:47). Shortly thereafter, in 1888, Addams' plan to open a settlement house began to take shape.

> I gradually became convinced that it would be a good thing to rent a house in a part of the city where many primitive and actual needs are found, in which young women who had been given over too exclusively to study, might restore a balance of activity along traditional lines and learn of life from life itself; where they might try out some of the things they had been taught and put truth to 'the ultimate test of the conduct it dictates or inspires' ([1910]2008:55).

Later that same year while traveling in Europe, Addams shared her "scheme," with friend, Ellen Gates Starr, who gave her support and would become with Addams the cofounder of Hull House. It would be overly simplistic to say that Addams and Starr needed something worthwhile to do in an era when women of "proper" upbringing were, even if college-educated, role-restricted although this more than other motives may have driven their pioneering work. The fact that Hull House was in many ways unique among settlements is no doubt due to the fact that it came to revolve around the person and the feminist pragmatism of Jane Addams.

When Addams next returned to London to visit Toynbee Hall, it was with more than a tourist's curiosity and interest. Instead, she was in search of "as many suggestions as possible" for the work that she envisioned ahead of her. It seems clear that Addams was seeking to satisfy her own inner needs, and perhaps those of other women such as herself, as well as to heal the blight of poverty for those around her. Like Vida Scudder and other college-educated women, she lamented the divergence of expectations coming from the "elaborate preparation" of education versus the reality of "no work provided [for women]" and a corresponding feeling of "waste" ([1910]2008:78). Following her trip to England, in 1889, Addams and Starr[6] established Hull House on South

6 Although Ellen Gates Starr founded Hull House with Addams and remained a resident and associate until 1929, she did not play a prominent role in the governance or financing of the Hull House Association. Addams began paying a small pension from Hull House funds to Starr when she retired to a nunnery after back surgery left her paralyzed from the waist

Halstead Street in Chicago's 19th ward, a poor neighborhood populated by immigrants in tenements and sweat shops. An article, "To Meet on Common Ground" appeared in the *Chicago Tribune*, March 8, 1889, apparently introducing Chicagoans to the novel settlement idea.

> ...[W]ithin a few months an interesting departure in humanitarian work will be undertaken in this city. ... The plan is proposed by a young lady of independent means and generous culture, who has recently come to Chicago to interest educated women in her project. ...a mutual exchange of the advantages of wealth and poverty. It assumes that these are by no means so one-sided as generally supposed, but that the poor have joys and opportunities for growth that would enrich the lives of the well-to-do could they be brought within their influence. The barriers of class needlessly circumscribe life.
>
> HHC: B1, F648

The article provides as background a description of England's Toynbee Hall stating that it was "founded by men" and presents Addams' project as its female counterpart although she is never named. The explanation sounds somewhat patronizing and certainly foreshadows none of the radicalism that later came to be associated with Hull House.

> A similar plan will be adopted by the young lady in Chicago. She will take a house in some poor district, furnish it attractively, and make it a centre of helpful social life. A young lady friend will be her companion, and it is hoped that a few daughters of the rich will at all times be found in her home. Living with her for varying periods they will enter into her plans. Several have already promised assistance and a number of our leading clergymen are enthusiastic supporters of the idea.
>
> HHC: B1, F648

Hull House began in a decaying nine room mansion (originally built by Charles Hull) belonging at the time to philanthropist Helen Culver. Residents first occupied a top floor of the home but gradually expanded to include the entire house as well as a city block of buildings. The Hull House complex provided

---

down. This small pension became a matter of dispute by Louise Bowen in the management of funds after Addams' death. Bowen apparently was unaware of the arrangement documented in correspondence between Addams and Starr, and perhaps Bowen did not fully appreciate Starr's role in Addams' life due to coming on board in 1903, some 14 years after Hull House was originally founded (EGSP: B1, F10).

meeting spaces for social clubs, educational programs, and trade unions. Over time, a library, art gallery, labor museum, coffee shop, theatre, health infirmary, public park, and cooperative apartments became a part of Hull House in a neighborhood with high concentrations of Italian, Greek, Russian and Polish immigrants. Residents established comprehensive programs to improve living conditions and to ease the strains and problems associated with immigration, rapid urban growth, and industrialization. The Hull House archival collection suggests that Chicago's several newspapers gave considerable and positive coverage to the early years of Hull House where sometimes it was recognized as a new form of sociology but was referenced by such headlines as "Chicago's Toynbee Hall," a "new social movement," "a noble work," and as "two women's work." Sometimes, the papers reviewed research in which Hull House residents had assisted, for example in 1891, a study of the "Working Girls of Chicago." More often, however, local news coverage emphasized the noble philosophy and sacrifices of the women who chose to live among the poor while overlooking the class reciprocity and mutuality of interests stressed by Addams' neighborly relation. Local news stories of this early period also provide understanding of why many came to refer to Jane Addams as "Saint Jane" (HHC: B1, F506). Indicative of the overlap of settlement work and sociology at that time, an article in the religious publication, *The Pilgrim* (1901) proclaimed Addams and Starr's European visit to Toynbee Hall as of "marked sociological importance" because it "gave birth to a great and important movement." Although neither of the women formally studied sociology, the article credited their settlement initiative to "their education in the study dearest to them—sociology" (HHC: B1, F647).

Addams the Sociologist

Although humanitarianism is certainly an important aspect of her legacy, Jane Addams' contributions to the practice of sociology are no doubt greater than any other woman living in this time period (Deegan 1990, 2002a; Schultz 2007:1–4). During her lifetime she authored some ten books and several hundred articles and essays (see Appendix A). The exact number of Addams' writings is difficult to establish because after her death a number of composite works that combine her speeches and essays have been published and republished as have some of her college essays. Her writings substantially impacted social theory, research methods, and practice related to the looming social problems of the day. The relatively recent and wide dissemination of Addams' writings has been propelled not only by gender studies but by demands that women and minorities be included in sociology texts, leading to the "discovery" of Addams the sociologist, thanks in large part to the early work of Deegan

(1990). Addams and the women[7] who worked with her, often in collaboration with leading male academics at the University of Chicago, occupied a gendered space that promoted the distinctive growth and production of a social science practice in social reform influenced by feminist values (Deegan 1990, Muncy 1991, Silverberg 1998, Sklar 1998, Ross 1998). Unfortunately Addams' sociological work has been overshadowed by other aspects of her career in the many biographies and writings about her life and work. However, one indication of the multifaceted and compounded impact of Adams' life is reflected in the range of newspaper headlines appearing upon her death. Some emphasized her personal relationships and humanitarianism such as "Good Friend Gone" and "Hull House Folk Recall Long Life of Kindness." Others emphasized her career as a sociologist or social worker, reading "Jane Addams, Famous Social Worker, Is Dead," "Mrs. Roosevelt Joins Tributes to Sociologist," and "Campus Joins Slum in Honor of Sociologist." As these headlines suggest, not only was Addams well-known in her day as a great humanitarian and social worker, but among those who commemorated her death, some saw her work as encompassing applied sociological investigation, intellectual scholarship, and social reform activism (HHC: B1). She was a charter member of the American Sociological Society, was identified publically as a sociologist, and published regularly in the early years of the *American Journal of Sociology*.

Hull House and the Practice of Sociology

While the majority of Hull House residents were women, men were also in residence from its earliest days. Some residents worked fulltime for the settlement while others paid room and board and held outside jobs but were

7 Most of these women had formal or informal linkages with the University of Chicago (UC) as graduate students, instructors, researchers, and occasionally as heads of female-segregated departments or units. For instance, Marion Talbot served as the Dean of Women from 1892–1925 and Sophonisba Breckinridge served as her Assistant Dean and worked in the Chicago School of Civics and Philanthropy (CSCP). Annie Marion MacLean, Francess Kellor, Sophonisba Breckenridge, Grace Abbott and Edith Abbott were graduate students taking masters or doctoral degrees. Many of the women, including Addams, taught courses at the UC, some in research methods and statistics. The women were members of the same professional associations such as the American Sociological Society, the National Conference of Charities and Correction, the American Association of Social Workers, and the Association of Collegiate Alumnae (later AAUW). Other professional associations that tied them together included the National Association for the Advancement of Colored People and the National American Woman Suffrage Association.

expected to volunteer evening and/or weekends in the variety of educational programs, social investigations, clubs, recreational activities, or classes offered at Hull House. Residents were not assigned activities but "discovered their own special fields of service" (Kemp 1985:34). Among the early residents and workers as of January 1895, including Jane Addams and Ellen Gate Starr, were 14 women living in the original Hull House mansion at 334 South Halsted St. Five single men and two couples resided at the neighboring Polk Street and Ewing Street addresses; fifty Jane Club apartments housed working women on Ewing Street and the Phalanx Club housed ten male members on Polk Street (HHC: B1, F474). At the time she wrote *Twenty Years at Hull-House*, Addams reported that most of the present roster had been in residence for more than 12 years and among them were two practicing physicians, several attorneys, newspaper men, business men, teachers, scientists, artists, musicians, professors, officers in the Juvenile Protective Association and in the Immigrants' Protective League, a visiting nurse, and a sanitary inspector ([1910]2008:286–287). Hull House archives include a list of all residents between 1889 and 1929 categorized by occupations: business, education, authors or journalists, artists and musicians, law, medicine, government service, social and civic work, and homemakers. The residents listed numbered 338 and another 22 were listed as deceased. Of these, the largest number, 22%, were categorized as in "social and civic work," followed by 17% in business and 15% in education. Interestingly, 12% of residents were listed under the occupation of "homemakers," all female, and with only two exceptions all with Mrs. preceding their names. Judging from names of males appearing in other categories, some of these women must have been wives of male residents and some may have been housekeeping staff as Mary Keyser's name appears among the homemakers (HHC: B1, F294).

Hull House provided an alternative space for shared sociological practice critical to freedom from constraints imposed by university or special interest politics. Addams consistently refused overtures that would have made Hull House an ancillary of the University of Chicago or its "sociological laboratory," seemingly aware that the mission, spirit, and vision of Hull House could be compromised if governance were shifted to the Rockefeller-dominated board of trustees, or to university professors advancing their own professional agendas. Correspondence between President Harper and Addams in December of 1895, when Helen Culver donated a million dollars to the University, suggests that Harper was eager for a merger and that Addams feared the settlement would be overpowered if it were to occur. In response to a *Chicago Tribune* article announcing the Culver gift and alluding to the possibility that Hull House would be included, Addams fended off interest and refused absorption into the department of sociology or another University program. She warned

Harper in a strongly worded letter that such an arrangement "would work most disastrously to our institution, and require constant explanation which would be embarrassing for the sociological department of the University as well as for ourselves" (Addams to Harper 19 December 1895, as cited in Deegan 1990:38). Presumably, Addams' reference to "embarrassing" contained a thinly veiled reminder that Hull House activism would continue in behalf of underrepresented populations, taking stances that would not always be compatible with vested interests of the University. Addams further voiced her conviction that the usefulness and value of Hull House was to be measured by "its own interior power of interpretation and adjustment" noting that its residents were pioneers "living in the 19th Ward, not as students, but as citizens, and their methods of work must differ from that of an institution established elsewhere, and following well defined lines." She wrote Harper unequivocally that "any absorption of the identity of Hull-House by a larger and stronger body could not be other than an irreparable misfortune, even though it gave it a certain very valuable assurance of permanency." Addams' fears that the University might attempt to absorb Hull House in a kind of "hostile takeover" were apparently well founded because Harper was seen by some as too closely associated with the corporate model of his benefactor, John D. Rockefeller. Harper's corporate tendencies included the absorption of smaller educational units (five small colleges for example), consolidations such as with the Chicago Theological Seminary, and affiliations with public high schools (Bachin 2004:62–66). Addams' determination to maintain Hull House's autonomy and integrity no doubt insured the many valuable contributions that its residents would make to public sociology and to social reform. Hull House records leave little question that for over four decades Addams maintained primary control as president of the board and head resident. Over this time span she had a very stable board and they clearly gave her wide berth in decision making. A total of only 19 individuals served on the Hull House board from its founding until Jane Addams' death in 1935, and eight of these served for over 12 years (HHC: B1, F1).

There is a rich and varied legacy left by Addams and other academically trained women practicing sociology through settlement work (Rousmaniere 1970; Deegan 1978, 1987, 2002a; Lengermann and Niebrugge 2007). Their philosophy of critical feminist pragmatism was the driving force behind many of the sociological projects and reform activities of the social settlements in their heyday. A good example was the multiplicity of problems surrounding young people, especially those who were poor and lacked supervision from working parents or those who dropped out of school only to lose their childhood in an exploitative labor market. Hull House women, especially Julia Lathrop and later Louise De Koven Bowen, helped to organize the Juvenile Protective

Association (JPA) that worked to improve social conditions for children, lobbied for a mother's pension law, and established the first child guidance center and the first juvenile court in the nation. The JPA was responsible for collection of the earliest and most thorough statistics on the needs and problems of miners, giving them authority as one of the most aggressive child welfare agencies in the country (Barbuto 1999:106–107).

While many saw settlements as seedbeds of socialism or even of revolution, the vast majority of settlement workers saw themselves as striving to make real the promises of democracy. As Julia Lathrop once put it, "The settlement may be regarded as a humble but sincere effort toward a realization of that ideal of social democracy in whose image this country was founded, but adapted and translated into the life of today" ([1896]1950:45). Quite naturally then, immigrants and their related class inequality were another area of Hull House practice. For the most part, settlement pioneers did not question immigration but assumed that the health of the United States democracy depended on the country's ability to include newcomers in the American dream. They did, however, question the differences between classes and saw such inequality as endangering democracy. And, most controversial, they asserted that capitalism was responsible for a growing class inequality and must be regulated by government intervention. Thus, Addams proclaimed: "The crucial question of the time is, 'In what attitude stand ye toward the present industrial system'?" ([1895b]2004:193). Social progress, according to settlement workers, was dependent on all classes accepting mutual responsibility—each for the other's well-being—because "no part of society can afford to get along without the others" ([1895b]2004:203).

The Chicago Women's School of Sociology

The *Chicago Women's School of Sociology* (CWSS) is a term developed to characterize the informal collective activities of "a network of women who worked collaboratively to produce a body of sociology linking social theory, sociological research, and social reform" (Lengermann and Niebrugge 2007:229). These women worked primarily out of Hull House, the University of Chicago, and the community-based Chicago School of Civics and Philanthropy. Hull House was without doubt the hub and seedbed of sociological work and other settlements, organizations, and agencies were pulled toward this center, including a number of University men. Network ties and collaborative relations extended well beyond Chicago to other cities and other centers that supported women's sociological work between the 1890s and 1920 (cf. Deegan 1978, 1987; Morgan 1980). Their scholarly work was often sponsored by civic organizations, clubs, and agencies that formed community action committees, as well as by philanthropic benefactors like Helen Culver and occasionally by governmental agencies seeking to collect statistics. Hull House was founded prior to the development of a formal sociology department at the University of Chicago and quickly became a home base for women scholars and activists, providing them the freedom and moral support to investigate, write critically, and to follow their convictions in advocating for social reforms.

Appendix A provides a summary of selected scholarly works, books, reports, and essays authored by Jane Addams and by others in the Chicago Women's School of Sociology. While this listing is far from inclusive of the scholarship produced, it provides a representative sampling of the volume and substance of their body of work. Inclusion of many more pamphlets, reports, news articles, bulletins, speeches and unpublished papers would enlarge this compendium even more. There is convincing evidence to support Lengermann and Niebrugge's claim that "settlement sociology was as complete a school as any in the history of the discipline" and that it included theory, method, practice, purpose, and a major theorist in the person of Jane Addams (2007:98). Addams provided strong leadership in scholarly productivity, particularly in the area of social theory. Other prominent members of the early CWSS include but are not limited to Julia Lathrop, Florence Kelley, Alice Hamilton, Edith Abbott, Grace Abbott, and Sophonisba Breckinridge. Those in a more extended network of scholars include Frances Kellor, Annie Marion MacLean, Marion Talbot, and Mary McDowell (Lengermann and Niebrugge-Brantley 1998:229–256). Their overt critique of capitalism and the use of a macro-level structural analysis are largely attributable to the influence of Florence Kelley who was steeped in European socialism of the Marx and Engels variety. The fact that her socialism was toned down into what she called "bourgeoisie philanthropy"(Kelley 1986:91–104) is no doubt due to the pragmatist leanings of Jane Addams and her strong ethic of social democracy (Addams 2002b).

The Hull House women published in academic as well as service-oriented journals including among others, the *American Journal of Sociology*, *Journal of Political Economy, Annals of the American Academy of Political and Social Science, Charities, The Survey, Social Service Review* and the *New England Quarterly*. Their collective body of work is distinguished by its theoretical primacy focusing on the *social structural* nature of industrial problems, attributing the origins of such problems to the organization of society rather than to the personal deficiencies of individuals and families. The work of the CWSS is also distinguished by its emphasis on the importance of *jurisprudence*[8] or the

8 The concept of sociological jurisprudence in the United States is traced to the work of Roscoe Pound (1943) and its subsequent popularization in the work of Supreme Court Justice Louis

science of law as a medium for social reform (Lengermann and Niebrugge-Brantley 1998:243). As noted by Lengermann and Niebrugge-Brantley, "[t]o study a problem out of only abstract scientific interest with no attempt at remedy is, for the Chicago Women, practically illogical and morally indefensible" (1998:244). Rather, the researcher's goal, as they saw it, should be "both to discover such [inequitable social] arrangements and to advocate measures for their reform." A final characteristic of the work of the Chicago women was an emphasis on *social democratic principles* for guiding human relations. This guiding philosophy directed societal reform beyond merely guaranteeing civil liberties to individuals. It sought reforms that would advance the interdependence and mutual respect of different groups in society. Epistemologically the body of work associated with the CWSS is perhaps best understood as sharing critical feminist pragmatist and the standpoint orientations of Addams both in its emphasis on situated knowledge grounded in experiences, especially the experiences of women and the working poor, and on the importance of producing practical knowledge for creating effective social change (Seigfried 1991, 1996; Deegan 2002a). Seigfried notes for instance that, "consistently in tune with pragmatist principles, Jane Addams pays particular attention to women, ethnic minorities, and the often destitute working-class while covering a dizzying array of social issues in *Twenty Years at Hull-House*" (1996:235). Emphasizing Addams' standpoint epistemology grounded in the "neighborly relations" and interpretive tradition, Charlotte P. Gilman wrote, "Her mind had more "floor space" in it than any other I have known. She could set a subject down, unprejudiced, and walk all around it, allowing fairly for everyone's point of view" (1935:184). This ability to "pivot the center" giving voice to the experiences of minorities is the unifying thread if not the hallmark of the Chicago Women's School of Sociology.

Among residents who were the most active in public sociology, in addition to Addams, the names of Florence Kelley, Alice Hamilton, Julia Lathrop, Edith and Grace Abbott, and Sophonisba Breckinridge come immediately to mind (Lengermann and Niebrugge-Brantley 1998:229–275). The women had much in common. All were college graduates in an era when women's opportunities were gender-restricted; all came from upper middle-class backgrounds; all had a strong fatherly influence and, with the exception of Hamilton, had fathers who were not only businessmen or lawyers but involved in government service

Brandeis and other reform-minded lawyers practicing during the Progressive Era. Brandeis was critical of the tendency of the law (as actualized by judges) to "lag behind the facts of life." He advocated for an infusion of a "social spirit" into interpretation of the Constitution and to bringing the law into harmony with the needs of society (Piott 2006:127–130).

at various levels. All were exposed to the forces of abolition and their fathers were supporters of Lincoln. So productive were these women that it is impossible to examine the entirety of their works; some selections, however, will serve to establish their importance as a part of settlement sociology in Chicago. As Jane Addams stated matter-of-factly the settlements antedated by ten years the establishment of the first research foundations and also predated sociology at the University of Chicago (1930:405). The women of Hull House represent the liberal wing of the Progressive Era and as such many became public figures. Addams, in later life, was more associated with the Women's International League for Peace and Freedom than with Hull House. Helen Gates Starr ran unsuccessfully for Chicago city council on a socialist ticket and later became involved nationally in the labor movement before retreating to a nunnery in her final years. Hamilton became a successful physician and the first woman hired by Harvard Medical School. Lathrop became the first head of the federal Children's Bureau where she used her office to focus attention on the plight of child workers (and often their mothers) and to lobby for governmental action in behalf of the nation's children, finally leading to passage of the Sheppard-Towner Maternity and Infancy Act in 1921. Addams wrote of the contributions of Hamilton and Lathrop, two of her closest friends (Addams [1910]2008). In fact, her final book published after her death was *My Friend, Julia Lathrop* ([1935]2004). Of Kelley, Addams stated, she "galvanized us into more intelligent interest in the industrial conditions all around us" (Addams [1935] 2004:82). Some Hull House residents became associated with the Chicago School of Civics and Philanthropy which was started by Graham Taylor at Chicago Commons but became well known for its research, scholarship, and activism due largely to the work of Hull House residents Julia Lathrop, Sophonisba Breckinridge, and Edith and Grace Abbott. The latter "ennoble threesome" became well known for research on Chicago housing, women and children in industry, immigration, and finally for taking the Chicago School of Civics and Philanthropy into the University of Chicago to become the School of Social Service Administration (MacLean and Williams 2012).

The published works of Hull House residents are substantial compared with other women of the Progressive Era, and their archival records have been more carefully studied. The selection of women whose works are discussed briefly in this and other chapters are based on agreement among feminist scholars that these are the best known of the Chicago Women's School of Sociology (Fish, 1986; Deegan 1990, 1991; Lengermann and Niebrugge-Brantley 1998; Silverberg 1998; Schultz 2007) or they have been grouped according to their relations to each other and to their overlapping works, overwhelmingly focused on women, children, and the poor. For example Fish (1986) characterized Hull House sociologists as consisting of two circles with Addams at the center of both. The first circle was comprised of three women who came to live and work at Hull House between 1890 and 1897: Julia Lathrop, Florence Kelley, and Alice Hamilton. The second and generationally overlapping circle of younger women were active in research and reform during the first decade of the century: Grace and Edith Abbott and Sophonisba Breckinridge (Fish 1986: 185–227, Stebner 1997:16). Their works and contributions to public sociology are examined here briefly.

Hull House Maps and Papers: Change-Oriented Knowledge

For some Hull House residents their first publication was a contribution to the collaborative volume, *Hull-House Maps and Papers* (1895). Since being brought out of moth balls and examined by feminist scholars beginning with Deegan (1990) and others such as Sklar (1998), Ross (1998), and Lengermann and Niebrugge-Brantley (1998), *Hull-House Maps and Papers* has now gone through several reproductions and many analyses. Although some scholars have identified more than twenty investigations conducted by Hull House residents between 1892 and 1933 (Schultz 2007:14), *Maps and Papers* is without doubt the quintessential work of Hull House sociology. It is a primary description of the various dimensions of poverty that some rank in importance with Henry George's *Progress and Poverty* (1879) and Jacob Riis' *How the Other Half Lives* (1890), or even Booth's *Life and Labor of the People of London* (1902–1903). These works emphasized the interdependence of rich and poor and the blight on democracy presented by poverty. Congress apparently got the message that the existence of poverty could threaten the success and progress of democracy in the United States and authorized a study of the poor in large cities with Carroll Wright, head of the Bureau of Labor, designated to oversee the work. It was the collection of data for *The Slums of Baltimore, Chicago, New York, and Philadelphia* (Wright et al. 1894) that gave Florence Kelley her first job doing research in Chicago and that led to the publication of *Maps and Papers*. The work is important because it provides a factual repudiation of the working of *laissez faire* economics. Addams' assertion that "the settlement is pledged to insist upon the unity of life...to work toward the betterment not of one kind of people or class of people, but for the common good" ([1895b]2004:203) stands in sharp contrast to Charles Sumner's proclamation that the social classes owe each other nothing (1893). For Addams, the pressing issue of the day was labor and the responsibility of industrialists toward workers.

All of the contributors to *Maps and Papers* had been in residence for at least five years and wrote about aspects of settlement work familiar to them, for example: Florence Kelley on the "sweating system" of labor; Kelley and Alzina Stevens on wage-earning children; Charles Zeublin on the Jewish ghetto; Ellen Gates Starr on art and labor; and Addams on the labor movement. In introducing the work, Addams acknowledged the use of the same color scheme used by Charles Booth in his "wage maps." She also acknowledged some limitations of *Maps and Papers* by pointing out that the work did not represent the totality of the settlement's methods or results but, rather, "record certain phases of neighborhood life with which the writers have become most familiar" (1895:viii). The significance of the Hull House research often goes unrecognized in that it preceded by several years Rowntree's work in England. McDonald lauds the work as pioneering "the quantitative methods that would later make the University of Chicago's Department of Sociology famous" when they were taken up by Robert Park and Ernest Burgess in the 1920s and 1930s (1993:298). Deegan describes *Maps and Papers* as "a scholarly classic...erased from the annals of sociology" because credit for the survey methodology has been reassigned to male academic sociologists (1990:55). Deegan documents the fact that male sociologists such as Albion Small were anxious to access and use the Hull House data produced by the women. Richard Ely, at the University of Wisconsin and editor for Crowell's Series on Economics and Politics, served as Addams' "sociological godfather," and sometimes nemesis in getting the work in print (Deegan 1990:55–69, Joslin 2004:73–76). Methodologically, the Hull House residents were quite sophisticated for their day. They recognized that their work was both educational and empowering. They showed respect for their neighbors who participated in the research by posting results in the settlement house, easily accessible to all (Elson 1954:6, Deegan 1990:46–47). Because of a dispute with the publisher about the expense involved in including the color-coded maps, Addams waived all royalties in exchange for their inclusion (Deegan 1990:58). She thought it important that local residents and political decision-makers see their neighborhood represented graphically.

The authors of individual chapters of *Maps and Papers* are identified but the volume as a whole was published under the authorship of the Residents of Hull House. Two of the ten contributors were male residents (Zeblin and Mastro-Valerio). In introducing the volume, Jane Addams noted that the energies of those collecting the data had been "chiefly directed, not toward sociological investigation, but to constructive work" ([1895a] 2004:viii). *Maps and Papers* attracted some limited attention when first published including positive reviews in several newspapers. One such review published in a Brooklyn, New York paper drew a response from Richard Ely. First he complimented the paper on its "Reports from an Experimental Station in Sociology" as showing appreciation for the significance of the book but goes on to take exception to the last paragraph of the article which apparently recommended that a chair of sociology be found for Addams. Ely's response leaves no doubt that he considered Addams as a fellow sociologist, practicing in a venue more public, and perhaps more important, than the university.

> If she were a professor of sociology she would be simply one professor among many others. At the head of Hull-House she is a teacher of teachers and her work is followed with interest in a hundred different educational institutions. ... Miss Addams' work at Hull-House in all its phases is work for the nation. ... Hull-House itself should become the true 'people's University'.
>
> HHC: B1, F507

It is clear that sociological investigation was never the end goal of the Hull House sociologists. Rather, they were about "constructive work," social reform that emanated from a factual base as Addams had envisioned even in her valedictory address when she asserted that justice could be attained by those "who...embrace the opposing facts and forces." Regardless of the area of investigation, Hull House sociologists did not miss an opportunity to call for government intervention where they saw it as necessary to alleviate the systemic problems they documented. In one of her essays on democracy, Addams called attention to the fact that European governments had stepped up to regulate industry as the need arose while the United States was "slower than these old Powers to protect it humblest citizen" (1907:121). Addams was not only critical of the government's inaction in the regulation of industry but also in refusing to "administer to the primitive needs of the mass of people" as in health care, housing, and descent wages (1907:84–85). Needless to say, such admonitions did not endear the female sociologists to the proponents of *laissez fair* capitalism and adherents to the creed that less government is better government.

Some Members of the Chicago Women's School of Sociology

Florence Kelley (*1859–1932*) is included among the residents of both Hull House and the Henry Street Settlement in New York and she was one of the most prolific writers associated with either. Her contributions in both Chicago and New York were substantial and the success of her work with the National Consumers' League in New York was enabled by her Chicago network of support. Kelley was trained in sociology, political economy, and the law; and while she conducted an impressive amount of research, she is perhaps best remembered for the application of her sociological work to the betterment of the lives of women and children and downtrodden workers in general. Her life's work can be summed up as investigate, educate, legislate, and enforce (Kelley 1899:289–304, Sklar 1995:252, Recchiuti 2007:133). Between investigations and the passage of legislation, Kelley often found that agitation was necessary because as one of her biographers put it, "to evoke that sense of social responsibility was Florence Kelley's special gift. ... She was unequaled in her ability to arouse moral fervor" (Goldmark 1953:3). In his biography of Jane Addams, her nephew described Kelley as "the toughest customer in the reform riot, the finest rough-and-tumble fighter for the good life for others, that Hull House ever knew" (Linn [1935]2000:138).

Kelley's involvement in social investigation at Hull House came about as a result of her being employed by Carroll Wright with the Bureau of Labor Statistics to assist in data collection for a study of poverty in large cities. Her job was to investigate the sweating system[9] in Chicago. Armed with this research, Kelley took the lead in introducing state legislators to the tenements and factories of Chicago. With guided tours for legislators and the press and using irrefutable statistics, including health reports and employment of underage workers, Kelley declared that the "sweating system was that winter a sensation" (Goldmark 1953:34). Kelley also took the lead in proposing legislation that became the first factory law for Illinois, revolutionary in that it limited women's work to eight-hour days, prohibited the employment of children under 14, established control of tenement sweatshops and created a state factory inspection system. Providing opportunity to put her investigative work into action, in 1893 the governor appointed Kelley as Chief Inspector of Factories for Illinois. Although she achieved several legislative victories for the workers of Illinois, especially women and children with the passage of the Sweatshop Law of 1893, Kelley soon learned that legislative success did not mean her work was

9 The sweating system was a typical part of the manufacturing industry in large cities. One form of this system was the renting of a room in a tenement building and setting up an off-site mini-manufacturing plant without regard for any regulations or protection for workers. Another variation of the sweating system involved sending or delivering materials to homes, usually located in tenement houses, where products were assembled largely by women and children working long hours for low wages based on piece-rate prices. Entire families often lived and worked in one room leading to unsanitary conditions for manufacturing and unhealthy life-styles for families. Garment manufacturing was the most frequent offender, but sweating was also found in the manufacture of cigars, artificial flowers, dolls, brushes, and purses. Women would do this kind of work even to the detriment of their health because it allowed them to stay at home with their children and to increase their income by putting their children to work.

accomplished but often was only the beginning of the reform process. Frequently legislation was not accompanied by enforcement or by judicial affirmation. Kelley experienced a failure of the system to enforce the new law, and then the eight-hour day for women and girls as prescribed in the Sweatshop Law was declared unconstitutional in the courts. Determined to have a greater influence, Kelley registered as a law student at Northwestern University where in 1894 she was awarded a law degree. Knowing that legislative statues were of little value if overturned in the judicial process, Kelley came to place great emphasis on the success or failure of court challenges to reform legislation that she worked to pass in Chicago, New York, and at the federal level. Although Kelley was a long-time socialist, she worked within the system of American legislation and jurisprudence and made "interpreting the effects of court decisions upon American life" her lifelong mission (Goldmark 1953:46). Nor was Kelley averse to attempting to influence the court, to bring the judges around to her way of thinking. She stated after one negative court decision, she felt a need to "rescue the fourteenth Amendment" (Goldmark 1953:144). It was her work on what became known as the Brandeis Brief (named for Louis Brandeis) that changed how cases were argued before the high courts. The Brandeis Brief set the precedent for the introduction of social science research into the information presented to judges as they weighed their decisions. As an indication of her influence, Supreme Court Justice Felix Frankfurter wrote that Kelley played "a powerful if not decisive role in securing legislation for the removal of the most glaring abuses of our hectic industrialization following the Civil War" (Goldmark 1953:v). Much of Kelley's investigation of the sweating system in Chicago was preliminary to her leadership in the production of the *Hull-House Maps and Papers* and subsequent to her appointment as Chief Factory Inspector for the State of Illinois. As inspector, Kelley located her office near Hull House and drew heavily on the settlement's network of support. She took her causes to the public and to state legislators and politicians armed with both first-hand observations and carefully tabulated statistics. With data made readily understandable for public consumption she lobbied for and often succeeded in securing reforms in work place safety and sanitation, sweating shops, the length of the working day, and child labor. Kelley, of course, was not without controversy and her appointment as Chief Factory Inspector was not renewed when the Illinois governorship changed.

Julia Lathrop (1858–1932) like Jane Addams was a native of Illinois and attended Rockford Seminary, one year prior to Addams and Starr, but subsequently transferred to Vassar College from which she graduated in 1880. After graduation, she worked for almost a decade as secretary to her father and other lawyers in Rockford but decided in 1890 to move to Chicago after hearing a speech by Addams and Starr about their plans for a social settlement. Lathrop's interests began in philosophy and theory and her first service assignment at Hull House was leading the Plato Club. As Lathrop interacted with the Hull House neighbors her "interests moved very quickly from the theoretical to the practical. She began to investigate relief applicants in the Hull House neighborhood" and became the inspiration behind the *Hull-House Maps and Papers* (Stebner 1997:113). Her contribution to that volume was a chapter on Cook County charities that would portend her life-long interest in public institutions for the poor, the sick, juveniles, and other dependent groups. Lathrop believed that it was the institutional structure of society and not individuals that were responsible for poverty and human need. One of her first publications as head of the Children's Bureau was to document the relationship between income and infant mortality (Lathrop 1919). She was the first Hull House resident to receive a state appointment when Democratic Governor John Altgeld appointed her in 1893 to the State Board of Charities, an unpaid position she held until 1901 when he left office and she resigned because of partisan politics (HHC July 18, 1901, Letter from Lathrop to Governor Richard Yates:B32, F306). She accepted reappointment to the Board under the term of Republican Governor Charles Deneen, from 1905 to 1909. One of her early publications grew from her work with charity organizations and was influenced by her frustration with volunteer workers who unnecessarily institutionalized persons better assisted in their communities. She was a critic of the view that the poor are unworthy and responsible for their own problems and in an effort to change this philosophy, she wrote *Suggestions for Visitors to County Poorhouses and Other Public Charitable Institutions* (1905). As is first evident in Lathrop's report on Cook County charities in *Hull House Maps and Papers*, she often used vivid descriptions of these institutions from an insider perspective, foreshadowing Erving Goffman's much later insider presentation in *Asylums* (1961). In 1908 Lathrop accepted the position of research director for the Chicago School of Civics and Philanthropy (CSCP). Although the CSCP was established by Chicago Commons' founder, Graham Taylor, its research arm functioned much of the time out of a room that Addams provided at Hull House where Lathrop's two research assistants and protégés Sophonisba Breckinridge and Edith Abbott lived.

The CSCP was a community-based school that served as a training center for research and activism before sociology and social work became distinctive and sex-segregated disciplines (MacLean and Williams 2012:251–256). With funding established by a five year grant from the Russell Sage Foundation, Lathrop served as head of the research department and co-director of the school until 1912, when she was appointed to the Children's Bureau in Washington

(GTP: B61, F2420, F2524). Lathrop played an important role in the establishment of the first juvenile court in the nation (Chicago) as well as in the creation of the Juvenile Protective Association, the Immigrants' Protective League, the National Committee for Mental Hygiene, and the Children's Bureau. Lathrop's first significant work at the Children's Bureau was to document the problem of infant mortality and to establish a uniform system of recording births and deaths of infants and young children. Indeed, she saw such statistics as representative of the health of the nation as she explained, "The infant death-rate measures the intelligence, health, and right living of fathers and mothers, the standards of morals and sanitation of communities and governments, the efficiency of physicians, nurses, health officers and educators" (1912:322). Although Lathrop always possessed a penchant for statistics, they were not valued simply as a method for the quantification of problems but as a means of solving them. As Scott aptly notes, "As firmly as [she] believed in the possibilities of social science as the basis for dealing with social problems, she never thought research was an end in itself. The essence of her definition of the 'scientific spirit' was science applied to human purposes" (2004:xvii).

Alice Hamilton (1869–1970) is described in her archival papers as the "mother of industrial medicine" and as a "Crusader, Pioneer, Physician, Scientist, Teacher, Author, Humanitarian, and Gentlewoman" (AHP 1935, prepared for *Who's Who in Industrial* Medicine: B1, F1). She moved into Hull House in 1897, eight years after its founding when she began teaching pathology at the Woman's Medical School of Chicago's Northwestern University. She remained at Hull House for more than 20 years and during that time formed close relationships with Addams' inner circle, particularly Kelley and Lathrop, and also with Lillian Wald of New York's Henry Street settlement with whom she joined in various research and reform projects. Hamilton was a native of New York, one of five siblings, the second of four girls close in age and a brother born when Alice was 17. Most of her formative years were spent in Fort Wayne, Indiana where her father, a graduate of Princeton, was a whole-sale grocer. Summers were spent on Mackinac Island in northern Michigan. Her family was of the Presbyterian faith. The Hamilton girls were largely home-schooled by private tutors and by their mother, described by Alice as "an extraordinary woman." From 1886 to 1888, Alice attended Miss Porter's finishing school in Farmington, Connecticut as did all of her sisters. Subsequently, she decided that she must follow a career path not only of service but one that would provide a livelihood. She wrote that she chose medicine because as a doctor she "could go anywhere...to far-off lands or to city slums—and be quite sure that I could be of use" (1943:38). Hamilton received her doctor of medicine degree in 1893 from the University of Michigan, Ann Arbor. She did not plan to go into private practice but to specialize in bacteriology and pathology. After an internship and a year of postgraduate study in Germany, Hamilton was offered the faculty position in Chicago where she would also fulfill her wish to live at Hull House (Sicherman 1984). Even though Hamilton held a full-time job, her service to Hull House was significant; her greatest accomplishment in her first years was the establishment of a well-baby clinic. Living in the slums was totally new to Hamilton as was the male-dominated academic world in which she was thrust by her teaching job. With her Hull House associates, she developed a political awareness of economic and political inequality, but she soon became exhausted and frustrated with attempts to balance her Hull House duties with teaching. Her life became somewhat less demanding when in 1902 the Women's Medical School closed and she went to work at a research laboratory. As testament to her development of the pragmatism characteristic of Adams and the women of the Chicago network of scholars, one of Hamilton's biographers wrote,

> Her first research was on typhoid, her problem being to get actual confirmation of the then unproved hypothesis that flies carry typhoid bacilli. This work, done in connection with the practical study of a thousand homes in the Hull House district, where an epidemic was raging at the time, had highly successful results, both pragmatic and scientific; the problem was proved and the district and the city administration were 'cleaned up.'
>
> But Alice Hamilton was coming to realize that 'pure research' was not a field in which she could hope to make a contribution important enough to compensate for the absolute and narrow abnegation of human relationships which such a career demands. She well [knew] by this time that she was more a member of Miss Addams' family than she was a teacher or a research worker. The emotional center of her life was not in a laboratory or a class room. The human need at Hull House in the days of its strenuous youth was inescapable. …
>
> AHP 1935, prepared for *Who's Who in Industrial Medicine:* B1, F1

Hamilton became interested in industrial diseases after reading *Dangerous Trades* by Sir Thomas Oliver and this interest would determine her life's work from that point forward and would shape her early contributions to industrial sociology. After receiving an appointment to the Illinois Commission on Occupational Diseases, she supervised an investigation on lead poisoning in the workplace and began her career of exposing the dangerous excesses of industrialization. Her residency at Hull House also exposed her first-hand to laborers who suffered from diseases, disabilities, and early deaths because of their work. Her documentation and exposure of dangerous factory working conditions in the state marked the beginning of Hamilton's work as a scientific reformer. Of the importance of this transition in her career, Hamilton wrote,

> It was in April, 1919, while I was living in Hull House...that I left the laboratory of bacteriological research...and took a year's leave of absence in order to assume charge of a survey of the poisonous trades of Illinois for a commission just appointed by Gov. Deneen. Taking charge proved to mean doing much of the survey myself, and so interesting did I find it that I never went back to the laboratory, and ever since then I have been following the trail of lead, mercury, nitric acid, carbon disulphide, carbon monoxide, explosives, aniline dyes, benzol, and a long list of chemicals with complicated names which are interestingly varied in their uses and in their effects on that more or less unconscious victim, the worker.
>
> AHP 1935, *Who's Who in Industrial Medicine:* B1, F1

In 1910, Hamilton was named a special investigator for the Labor Bureau and in this position investigated work conditions in mines, mills, and smelters where she found alarmingly high mortality and morbidity rates among workers due to poisons. Later, Hamilton did similar studies in other industries and did research for the government during World War I. She became well known for her scientific approach to problems and applications of research to improve the lives of workers who were often without an advocate.

In 1919 Hamilton was the first woman appointed to the faculty of the Harvard Medical School after she negotiated a contract which allowed her to teach half a year while maintaining a residence at Hull House and continuing her industrial research the remainder of the year. At Harvard, she became recognized as a world-wide authority in industrial toxicology and wrote one of the classic textbooks in the field, *Industrial Poisons in the United States* (1929). Her international reputation was further enhanced by her appointment to two terms on the Health Committee of the League of Nations. Hamilton retired from Harvard in 1935 but remained professionally active well into her eighties. She conducted her last field research in 1937 and 1938, demonstrating high levels of toxicity in the processing of rayon and prompting passage of the first compensation law for occupational diseases in the state of Pennsylvania. Although Hamilton was an industrial scientist and toxicologist she deserves a place in the history of settlement sociology and her work is testament to the importance of interdisciplinary research in matters of worker safety and public health. Her work was one of the earliest to link industrial labor and social environments to specific pathologies that could be remedied with workplace and safety reforms. She committed her career to scientifically documenting these relationships and to advocating for industrial workplace reforms and government regulations.

Sophonisba Breckinridge (1866–1948) came from a background very similar to that of other Hull House women. She was one of four children born to upper middle-class parents whose father was involved in Kentucky business, law, and politics. She entered Wellesley College in 1884 and graduated in 1888. She subsequently moved to Washington DC where her father was a US Congressman and where she taught high school mathematics for two years. In 1893 after studying law in her father's office, she passed the bar exam and was the first woman admitted to the bar in Kentucky. In the years to follow, however, she floundered as she encountered setbacks because she could not attract sufficient clientele to support herself as a lawyer; she suffered several illnesses, and her mother died. She moved to Oak Park, a Chicago suburb, to visit with friends, regroup, and explore other career options. There she renewed ties with Marion Talbot, formerly of Wellesley, now Dean of Women and teacher of Sanitary Science at the University of Chicago. Talbot arranged for Breckinridge to enroll as a student in political science and to earn her room and board by working as a dormitory assistant. In 1899, she was hired as a lecturer to teach courses in sanitary science located in the Department of Sociology until 1904 when it was organized as a separate department of Household Administration. With the assistance of a fellowship, in 1901 Breckinridge completed a doctorate in political science and in 1904, a doctorate in law (Coghlan 2005:10–11).

It was 1907 when Breckinridge was 41 years of age that she and Edith Abbott moved into Hull House after accepting jobs as researchers and teachers with the Chicago School of Civics and Philanthropy. Research and teaching at the CSCP were products of Chicago Commons, Hull House, and the sociology department at the University of Chicago (for a detailed case study of the CSCP, see MacLean and Williams 2012). In the early 1900s most social work training was reform-oriented rather than case oriented and occurred outside of the University in settings such as the CSCP. Breckinridge had already begun to focus her research on working women and had published in the *American Journal of Sociology* and in the *Journal of Political Economy*. However, according to Deegan, it was not until her move to Hull House in 1907 that her work and "power as a social critic blossomed" (1991:82). Once with the CSCP, her work became more diverse and publications more frequent in areas such as housing, the family, immigrants, child labor, and juvenile courts. Some of Breckenridge's best work was done in collaboration with Edith Abbott or Marion Talbot. One work that stands out as representative of the Hull House genre is a qualitative study of immigrants' adjustments to their new homes in the United States, *New Homes for Old* (1921). Perhaps because of her legal training, Breckinridge tended to present the facts and often neglected analysis or theory. However, Silverberg cites a 1923 article on "The Home Responsibilities of Women Workers and the 'Equal Wage'" as one of her best works because it utilized both her legal and her analytical skills (1998:53). After becoming a full-time faculty member in the School of Social Service Administration at the University of Chicago, her writings turned more to public welfare, family welfare, social work and the courts although in 1933, she published *Women in the Twentieth Century*, a comprehensive history of women's social, economic, and political successes and failures and in some cases men's efforts to block their successes. Breckinridge is better known and better chronicled than many of the other Hull House women, but largely because of her role in establishing the first graduate school of social work at the University of Chicago. Before this accomplishment, her work was primarily that of a sociologist, most of it done between 1910 and 1924 under the auspices of the CSCP and she held interlocking positions between and among the three institutions. Although Coghlan (2005) has argued that Breckenridge was not a sociologist, the disciplinary identity she chose late in her career is less important than her work and associations which established her as a vital member of the CWSS.

Edith Abbott (1876–1957) was the second of four children born to upper middle-class parents in Nebraska. Her mother, a graduate of Rockford Seminary, was a feminist, abolitionist, Republican, and Quaker. Her father was a Civil War soldier, a lawyer, banker, and the first lieutenant governor of the state of Nebraska. He suffered financial failure during the country's economic depression in 1893, an event that altered the life style of his family and the education of his children, including college for Edith and her sister Grace. Before entering the University of Chicago in 1902, Edith had taught high school for several years and had studied part time at the University of Nebraska, a progressive school that gave her the opportunity to study sociological jurisprudence with Roscoe Pound and sociology with E.A. Ross. She earned a degree in 1901 and entered the University of Chicago in 1902 where she studied political economy and political science with J.L. Laughlin and Thorstein Veblin. She graduated with a Ph.D. in political economy in 1905 (Fitzpatrick 1990:49). After graduation, Abbott worked for a time with the Women's Trade Union in Boston and lived in Denison House where she assisted with a research project on women's work, thus beginning her long-term landmark project, *Women in Industry: A Study of American Economic History* (1910). In 1906, she was awarded a Carnegie fellowship for the London School of Economics and Political Science where she studied with Beatrice and Sydney Webb (Deegan 1991:30). She returned to take a teaching position at Wellesley College, disappointed because teaching positions in other than women's colleges were closed to her. She was some ten years younger than most of the other women of the Chicago-Hull House cohort when, in 1908, she was recruited by Lathrop to become director of research at the CSCP and to move into Hull House. Shortly thereafter she also began teaching part time in the sociology department at the University of Chicago where, until 1920, she taught classes in statistics and research modeled after those taught in England by Beatrice Webb. She was never, however, admitted to full-time faculty status in the department.

Edith Abbott did not begin as a reformer or activist but apparently had hoped for an academic career in a co-educational institution. Between 1904 and 1913, she published seven articles in the *Journal of Political Economy,* most on women's employment and wages, and one in the *American Journal of Sociology* (Silverberg 1998:46). Interestingly, the cumulative research that made her the recognized expert on women's work, *Women in Industry*, was published under two institutional affiliations, neither of them academic, Hull House and the little known Chicago School of Civics and Philanthropy. In this work she used the "historical rather than the statistical method" to show that women had from the beginning of colonial America, always been in the workforce and that there was no evidence they were displacing men. "Any theory… that women are a new element in our industrial life, or that they are doing 'men's work,' or that they have 'driven out the men,' is a theory unsupported by facts," she concluded (1910:317). In seeking to answer the question of whether differences in male–female wages were attributable to differences in skill-levels or restriction of opportunity, Abbott examined work skill requirements, positions, wages, and opportunities across various industries and across time. Her findings led her to conclude that gender wage differences were due to differential opportunities and would be diminished by unionization, a growing class-consciousness among women, and the effects of the woman's movement. Abbott's closing sentence drives home the fact that restricted opportunities for women were responsible for gender inequality: "The woman of the working classes finds it, so far as her measure of opportunity goes, very much as her great grandmother left it" (1910:323). In 1934, when President Roosevelt formed a comprehensive advisory committee on economic security, Edith Abbott was appointed to the Committee on Public Employment and Public Assistance.[10]

---

10 The Committee on Economic Security was established by Executive Order of President Franklin D. Roosevelt on June 29, 1934 and is the body largely responsible for writing the Social Security Act of 1935. A five-member oversight Committee was comprised of Frances Perkins, Secretary of Labor; Henry Morgenthau, Jr., Secretary of the Treasury; Homer Cummings, Attorney General; Henry Wallace, Secretary of Agriculture; and Harry

Grace Abbott (*1878–1939*) was similar in background to her older sister. She graduated from Grand Island College in 1898 and taught high school for several years prior to doing graduate work at the University of Nebraska. She moved to Chicago in 1907, took up residence at Hull House, and in 1909 earned a master's degree in political science at the University of Chicago (Barbuto 1999:2–3). She published five articles in the *American Journal of Sociology* as well as other articles in the *Annals of the American Academy of Political and Social Science*, criminology journals, and law reviews. In Chicago, most of her publications were focused on immigrants and immigrant workers. Like one of her mentors, Julia Lathrop, Grace was described as diplomatic and as possessing administrative ability. These were characteristics which brought her to head Chicago's Immigrants' Protective League founded by Breckenridge and other Chicago reformers in 1908. In fact, Abbott became known as an authority on immigrants and immigration policy, a topic on which she published articles in popular magazines and newspapers as well as in publications such as *The Survey* and the *American Journal of Sociology*. Her book, *The Immigrant and the Community* (1917) was widely read and positively reviewed. It is a comprehensive look at various immigrant groups, for some beginning with their journey to the US. Using her years of experience at Hull House and her involvement in the League, Abbott wrote with first-hand knowledge of the immigrants' problems related to finding work and housing while sometimes becoming victims of exploitation. She gave particular attention to the vulnerabilities of young female immigrants and examined what some of the most essential institutions—courts, schools, government, and the work place—were doing to serve their needs as they moved toward citizenship. The book is both a retrospective look at the treatment of immigrants and a look ahead at the need for developing programs and policies to absorb these new Americans. Abbott was a supporter of multi-culturalism as she took on Anglophiles and the assumed superiority of white, Anglo-Saxon Protestants. Her interest in improving the lives of immigrants and her resistance to assimilation of the Anglo-conformity variety are well-reflected in a passage from one of her books:

> ...we have expected by a sort of faith-cure process to hasten the coming of that happy time when all those who come to the United States shall have

---

Hopkins, Federal Emergency Relief Administrator. Other groups served with the Committee in various advisory capacities: a 23 member Advisory Council, a two-member Technical Board, and several specialized advisory committees on employment, health, hospitals, nursing, public assistance, and child welfare.

> become exactly like the native American. This policy is as wrong in principle as it will always be unsuccessful in practice. ... Many of the habits and customs which the immigrants bring would form a valuable contribution to our community life. None of them should be foredoomed to extinction simply because they are different from those that have existed here (1917:293).

At the behest of Lathrop, Grace Abbott went to Washington in 1917 to head the Child Labor Division of the Children's Bureau, created to administer the first child labor law (*Keating-Owen Bill* of 1916). This job did not last, however, as the legislation was ruled unconstitutional by the Supreme Court in 1918 and Abbott returned to Chicago. Later, in 1921, she followed Lathrop as the second head of the Children's Bureau in Washington, DC and subsequently her research and writing focused largely on issues associated with children and with child labor. Had Grace Abbott followed her own preference, she would no doubt have spent the remainder of her professional life in Chicago. However, the Chicago-Hull House women's circle decided for her that she was to replace Lathrop as head of the Children's Bureau, and they lobbied the president in full force to make this happen. They had one of their own as the first woman to head a national agency and were not inclined to relinquish such power. Muncy described this as "the settlement spirit" that required women to subordinate individual ambitions and interests to the more general social reform agenda (1991:90). Abbott served as head of the Children's Bureau from 1921 to 1934 and as a member of the Advisory Council of the President's Committee on Economic Security she had direct input into President Roosevelt's New Deal programs. Trolander quotes sources close to the President as crediting her "above everyone else...for the child welfare provisions which occur in the Social Security Act" (1975:87). Upon retirement, she returned to Chicago where she taught part time at the School of Social Service Administration and served as editor for their journal, *The Social Service Review*. Two books marked the end of her remarkable career, *The Child and the State* (1938), a summation of her work with the Children's Bureau, and her last book, *From Relief to Social Security* (1941). The latter was a defense of the newly enacted social security law, attempting to deflect some of the misgivings about the new program from both the right and left, including in the social work community. Abbott died in 1939 from multiple myeloma. Her last book in defense of the social security system was published posthumously, compiled by her sister, Edith, from a wealth of notes, lectures, and research Grace had collected during her years in Washington.

Contributions to Sociology

For Addams, the concept of the neighborly relation evolved from her observation of relationships among the poor which she described as "primitive and genuine," characterized by,

> ...a willingness to lend or borrow anything, and all the residents of the given tenement know the most intimate family affairs of all the others. ... There are numberless instances of self-sacrifice quite unknown in the circles where greater economic advantages make that kind of intimate knowledge of one's neighbors impossible (2002b:13–14).

She contrasted the relief of one poor neighbor toward another with the guarded care dispensed by a charity visitor to a charity recipient and chose the neighbor-to-neighbor model as her own. Addams insisted that settlement residents "must be content to live quietly side by side with their neighbors until they grow into a sense of relationship and mutual interests" ([1892a]2002:26). Sounding both a pragmatic and a social gospel theme, Addams asserted that "residents should live with opposition to no man, with recognition of the good in every man, even the meanest" and should express "in social service, in terms of action, the spirit of Christ" ([1892a]2002:24). Perhaps because of this overarching paradigm of the neighborly relation, the contributions of Hull House and the Chicago Women's School of Sociology were unique in perspective and outcome, providing lasting though largely unacknowledged contributions to the discipline of sociology in the foundational areas of theory, methodology and social inequality.

Social Theory: Critical Feminist Pragmatism

John Dewey credited Addams with shifting the traditional paradigm of democracy to that of a lived democracy (Seigfried 2002:xi). The body of work that was developed through Hull House and the Chicago Women's School of Sociology grew out of Jane Addams' philosophy of feminist pragmatism and from her theory of civil society. This theory is deeply embedded in sociological praxis, a conjoining of theory and action that calls for an adjustment between the organization of production in industrial society and a new social ethics that fundamentally transforms social relationships and human interaction not merely as a political system but as a way of life. As Addams saw it, knowledge entailed social obligation ([1895b]2004:185). Hull House was "opened on the theory that the dependence of classes on each other is reciprocal" (Addams [1910]2008:59).

Egalitarian principles were central to what was perceived as a needed shift in social relationships, but equality by definition required a collective commitment and transformation in consciousness. According to pragmatist philosophy, such an emergent consciousness would embrace the realization of a socialized democratic society that minimized gender, class, and ethnic differences. Addams believed that problems could not be solved merely through individual ethical transformations, a belief that set her apart from many community leaders and academicians of the day. A collective transformation, to Addams, required an expanded socialized ethic that would holistically transform the social arrangements of organized society and its group relationships. Governments at the municipal, state, and federal levels had an important role to play in this transformative adjustment. However, the kind of social change advocated could not be paternalistic in nature. Policies and programs would not be effective in solving social problems unless they were defined, directed, and implemented in direct relationship with, and in the common interest of, the poor, immigrants, women, children, and the laboring classes they were intended to serve (Addams 2002b). Added to Addams' mix of pragmatism and transformational democracy was, of course, her special brand of feminism, one espoused in her Rockford Seminary days when she perceived women as possessing truth, clear judgment, and unerring instinct but lacking authority. It was the Hull House experience and social investigation resulting in an accumulation of facts that gave the Hull House women authority and thus their feminist pragmatism.

Democracy and Social Ethics (2002b) compiles a series of Addams' essays illustrating the typical nature of social relations and the transformative social ethics needed for a *socialized democracy* to be realized. The thematic reflected in these essays includes the adjustment of relations of charitable efforts among families, households, work, education and the polity. A common interpretive thread running through each of her essays is the use of a critical pragmatist lens to describe authority relations between the powerful and less powerful. Each addresses relational problems inherent in patrimonial interactions and ties that fail to give autonomy and choice to those in dependent relations such as charity workers and the poor, parents and children, husbands and wives, employers and workers, teachers and students, and government officials and their constituents. Through her anecdotal writings Addams revealed a pragmatic social ethics deeply embedded in the American Revolutionary tradition that "condones neither the tyranny of the majority nor the right of moral authorities to coerce those who do not share their moral standards" (Seigfried 2002:x). Seigfried notes that the ideal type democracy embraced by pragmatists embodies a set of values that constitutes much more than a political system; it essentially represents a way of life. Such values include faith in the possibilities of human nature "irrespective of race, color, sex, birth and family, of material or cultural wealth" (Dewey as quoted in Boydston 1988:226). Pragmatists were aware, however, that a democratic ideal was not sufficient to remove personal prejudices such as those based on race, class, and gender nor was belief in the ideal of the dignity and worth of every human being. Rather, democratic principles embraced as a life style require taking action that will help to create the conditions for the fulfillment of human potential. Moreover, democracy as a way of life includes a reflexive social process that allows for its ongoing renewal and re-visioning in light of what is evaluated as problematic and what is found to be a social good that should be more equitably refined and extended. This shift in the definitional meaning of democracy from a static political system to a dynamic system of social ethics represents a radical paradigm shift that guided the works of early feminist pragmatists.

Multi-Cultural Feminism

Scholarship is divided on whether Addams and her Hull House associates pioneered the philosophy of multiculturalism or tried but failed to rise above the ethnocentrism, racism, and nationalistic thinking of the day. Representative of these two perspectives are Deegan (2002b) on the side of multiculturalism and tolerance and Lissak (1989) who viewed settlement workers through a less positive lens. Weighing both sides of the argument leads to the conclusion that in some respects the early sociologists were products of their own upper-middle class Anglocentric upbringing but largely rose above this to become advocates for immigrant groups and for their cultural gifts to the United States. One of Addams first essays, "The Subjective Necessity for Social Settlements" ([1892a]2002) portends her life-long concern with social justice for marginal groups—immigrants, children, former slaves—who as she expressed it, "desire to share in the race life." The Immigrants' Protective League (IPL) was housed at Hull House because most of its founders either lived there or were associated with it. The first director was Grace Abbott who later wrote a book (1917) detailing the work of that organization. Many cite the IPL that served as a clearinghouse for information, advice, and social services for immigrants as evidence of Hull House's support for immigrant communities and, more generally, the cultural diversity they represented (Barbuto 1999:103–104). Others, however, saw the League as an agency of Americanization and social control, citing causes in which the IPL was involved that were of questionable value for immigrants. For example, the League opposed the recruitment of immigrant children into private schools where they were taught primarily in their native languages and thus were slow to learn English. On the other hand, the League employed on its staff social workers who spoke the language of the newly arriving immigrants. Lissak (1989) charged that the League had a "one-sided" relationship with the immigrant community and that the board never included an immigrant woman. In fact, the board did include immigrants although none was elected to top leadership positions until the 1920s (Costin 1983:68–99). Lissak also questioned the benefit of the League's efforts to remove immigrant services from ward politics and for undermining the immigrant networks established by some leaders while cultivating the favor of others (1989:62–76). Offering a contrary view, White concluded that

> ...settlement workers were the pioneers in recognizing and appreciating the positive significance of the pluralistic nature of our culture, and they were literally the first representatives of the English-speaking group purposefully to seek out the alien and to communicate with him on an intimate basis (1959:55).

White credited Addams with addressing head-on the fear that American "civilization was being imperiled" by large streams of immigrants from Southern and Eastern Europe. In fact, Addams used a variety of speaking platforms and writing venues to address the need to respect immigrant differences. For example, in a speech on the importance of recreation, she wrote, "There is no doubt that the future patriotism of America must depend not so much upon conformity as upon respect for variety, and nowhere can this be inculcated as it can in the public recreation centers" (1912:617). In a convocation address at the University of Chicago, Addams admonished scholars for neglecting the study of immigration and asserted that the "immigrant situation" should be "frankly regarded as an industrial one" (1905:282). Concern with a growing social divide between immigrant parents and their Americanized children led Addams and other Hull House residents to create the Labor Museum in 1900 with the aim of keeping alive the handcraft skills of immigrant groups that seemed to be disappearing and to show young people the relationship between raw materials and finished products. In the Museum workshop immigrant Americans demonstrated skilled craftsmanship indigenous to their countries such as metallurgy, woodworking, and textile manufacturing. The Museum was, according to Addams, to "reveal the humbler immigrant parents to their own children," to "build a bridge between European and American experiences" ([1910]2008:151). Lissak, however, concluded that in the end, Hull House was about assimilation.

> Hull House was not an immigrant institution in the sense that it represented a pluralist cultural view of society. It was, rather, an American

> institute that sought to integrate individual newcomers of different backgrounds into a cosmopolitan, American-oriented society by breaking down ethnic barriers and ending segregation....immigrant children and youngsters who were ethnically oriented did not usually attend Hull House. Those who came were attracted by its American programs rather than by its ethnic-cultural ones. They came to Hull House to become Americanized... (1989:47).

Jackson also saw Hull House as assimilationist and as comprised of upper middle-class women who were well-intentioned but often working "against the politics of cross-cultural engagement" (2001:128). Jackson represents some of the Hull House residents as a modern version of "going native" or "slumming." For example, she quoted from a letter by Ellen Gates Starr in which Starr divided her friends into "friends from civilization" and "friends from the neighborhood" (2001:48). Of such attitudes, Jackson offered a harsh assessment: "such cross-cultural sociality between settler and neighbor occurred from within the former perception of the latter's deficiencies" (2001:51).

Despite these criticisms, we cannot help but note the similarity in Addams support of diversity with that of Horace Kallen (1915, 1924) who is credited with developing the concept of cultural pluralism. In one of her early speeches, Addams compared the Hull House neighborhood to a rendition of the Hallelujah Chorus in which one would surely appreciate all the solo voices but in the end it would be the joining of all voices that "produced the volume and strength of the chorus." Ever the proponent of democracy, Addams went on to analogize the chorus as working as democracy does—when all voices "have authenticity and are heard" ([1892a]2000:25). Some years later, Horace Kallen, also used a musical metaphor in likening ethnic group differences to a division of labor in an orchestra, "the free and well-ordered cooperation of unique individualities toward the making of the common tune" (1924:180). In comparing Addams' theories of multiculturalism with those of other scholars or philosophers or her day, Brown found that "Addams was way ahead of them" (2012:8). With regard to the criticism that she was at heart simply an assimilationist, Brown concludes,

> Addams approach to assimilation was too complex to make her easy to categorize. ... She added a new idea to the concept of assimilation, pointing out that it was a two-way street in which Americans learned from the newcomers. She developed practical programs for both immigrant-to-American and American-to-immigrant assimilation (2012:10).

Addams herself summarized the position of Hull House vis-à-vis immigrants when she said, "We believed that America could be best understood by the immigrants if we ourselves...made some sort of a connection with their past history and experiences. ...early settlements practically staked their future upon an identification with the alien and considered his interpretation their main business" (2002a:244). Addams understanding of ethnic differences also carried over to Chicago's black citizens. According to Diner "She was among the few Chicagoans in the Progressive Era for whom the plight of blacks was a major interest," perhaps predictable given the fact that Addams' father was an abolitionist (1970:398). More than many of her contemporaries, Addams demonstrated insight into the cost of slavery as she noted that African cultures had been broken during slavery while blacks were denied entry into the core culture. She lamented our "national indifference to the spirit of the Emancipation Proclamation" (1930:396–398). Diner also argued that Addams close Hull House associates shared her interest in blacks, citing specific writings and/or activism on the part of Julia Lathrop, Sophonisba Breckinridge, and the Abbott sisters as well as Hull House board member, Louise De Koven Bowen who wrote *The Colored People of Chicago* (1913). According to Diner, these women approached the problems of Chicago's black population from what he described as an "environmental" perspective rather than one of racial inferiority or personal failures (1970:399–400).

Standpoint Epistemologies

Standpoint epistemology was embodied in feminist pragmatism as an understanding of the experience of others, in this case the people that settlement workers were living among. As Mary McDowell put it, "settlement residents do not go to people with a plan, a policy or a proposition; they go as friends, as neighbors with a keen sense of the commonness of all that is best in all. Theirs cannot be a handing down of culture or a going down to live with the poor" (MMP: B4, F20). Lengermann and Niebrugge-Brantley (1998), Deegan (1990), and Seigfried (1991, 1996) have all described the Chicago women's methodological orientation as a critical feminist pragmatism grounded in standpoint epistemology informed by their own experiences as neighborhood residents and as women building community and transforming social structures. Their reform agenda required a methodology that embraced a subjective understanding of the groups oppressed by social structural arrangements. It further required collaboration with those groups as opposed to merely offering a charitable helping "hand-up" to the less fortunate. In this way sociological inquiry was directed toward changing situations perceived by the actors as problematic. "Social situations cannot be solved pragmatically if such resolutions satisfy only those with the power to force a resolution or if it excludes those for whom the situation is problematic in the first place" (Seigfried 1996:263). As with other settlement workers, Addams saw the settlement as a method, an approach to the "social question,"

> ...an experimental effort to aid in the solution of the social and industrial problems which are engendered by the modern conditions of the great city. ... It is an attempt to relieve...the over accumulation [of wealth] of one end of society and the destitution at the other ([1910]2008:83).

The settlement method of inquiry initiated by Addams and her colleagues was not based on *a priori* classifications of knowledge or on objective scientific methodology. Rather it was grounded in a search for knowledge specific to the social situation or to the problem needing resolution. Knowledge could not be generated in the absence of those in need of a solution. Similarly the usefulness of knowledge could be judged only by those who benefited from it. Addams never addressed a Chicago audience on the subject of the settlement or its community without inviting a neighbor to accompany her, "that I might curb any hasty generalization by the consciousness that I had an auditor who knew the conditions more intimately than I could hope to do" ([1910]2008:63). For example, Hull House residents worked with women laborers to develop trade-union associations and by lobbying for the passage of legislation to limit the hours of working women and to curtail child labor. These efforts to improve work conditions were born of observation of the human misery lived daily by their working neighbors: a little girl, age four, pulling basting threads hour after hour in a home sweatshop; women who worked nights and were unable to sleep during the day because of household responsibilities; young girls who walked the streets alone in the early morning hours, exhausted and debilitated after working ten hour night shifts (Addams [1910]2008:129–137).

Similarly, the importance of understanding social problems from the vantage point of women was central to the scholarship of the feminist pragmatists and of Jane Addams working from Hull House and in the expanded Chicago network. In an age when the world was presumptively patriarchal, Davis describes Addams work in *The Spirit of Youth and the City Streets* (1909), as "practical, realistic, and useful, with special feminine insight into the problems of urban America" (1972:viii). Addams' contemporary William James wrote in a review of the same book,

> All the details of the little book flow from this central insight or persuasion. Of how they flow I can give no account, for the wholeness of Miss

> Addams' embrace of life is her own secret. She simply inhabits reality, and everything she says necessarily expresses its nature. She can't help writing truth (1910:553).

His words reflect an awareness of Addams as a "knower" in relation to her personal social location or standpoint as both woman *and* social scientist, a distinctive standpoint that bridged the worlds of public and private within the emergent political culture of women (Muncy 1991; Sklar 1995, 1998; Ross 1998; Silverberg 1998). Addams demonstrated the ability to use the reflexive anecdotal narrative approach to weave a story depicting the full complexity of human conditions and social relations while making them personal in their presentation of common humanity. As Davis notes, "The memories of her childhood became a reference point for evaluating and understanding the massive changes taking place in America during her own lifetime, and they enabled her to become an interpreter of those changes" (1972:xv). Similarly in *City Streets* Addams is sensitive to gender as a central analytic variable. About the city's exploitation of girls and their experience of liberation she wrote:

> Apparently the modern city sees in these girls only two possibilities, both of them commercial: first, a chance to utilize by day their new and tender labor power in its factories and shops, and then another chance in the evening to extract from them their petty wages by pandering to their love of pleasure. As these overworked girls stream along the street, the rest of us see only the self-conscious walk, the giggling speech, the preposterous clothing. And yet through the huge hat with its wilderness of bedraggled feathers, the girl announces to the world that she is here. She demands attention to the fact of her existence, she states that she is ready to live, to take her place in the world ([1909]1972: 8).

Addams deliberately adopted a style that rejected the cool detached statistical approach to facts and figures that disembodied people from their social circumstances. Her work in this way represents a long and deep tradition in feminist epistemology (see e.g. Smith 1974, Hartsock 1983, hooks 1984, Collins 1986, Harding 1987). The Chicago women combined an adroit use of qualitative and quantitative data. For such problems as inadequate housing, they provided objective measures such as the number of persons per square foot along with vivid descriptions of families huddled into one room where they cooked, cleaned, slept, and sometimes worked.

The methodologies of the settlement sociologists differed from the scientific model that was emerging simultaneously in the universities. Schultz notes that men "founded the first university departments and embraced objectivity and theory for a social science modeled on the natural sciences" (2007:14). On the other hand settlement workers, led by Addams, "envisioned social science knowledge as coming from civic participation across class, race, and ethnic divisions; systematic collection of data was to be rigorous and based on information that came from direct engagement with the subject" (2007:13). In the academic environment, activism was often seen as a threat to the development of science as universities were dependent on benefactors or boards who disliked activists and the liberal causes with which they were associated, especially those critical of the negative consequences of unbridled capitalism. Settlement sociologists and reformers worked outside of these academic restrictions utilizing the core principles of collaboration, community building, and social action (Fabricant and Fisher 2002:25). The settlement method involved reciprocity between residents and "neighbors" who were never defined or objectified as "subjects," and both were inseparable to the process just as study or "investigation" was inseparable from action. The scientific process demanded of residents "patience in the accumulation of facts and the steady holding of their sympathies as one of the best instruments for that accumulation" (Addams [1910]2008:83). Indeed, Addams and her Hull House colleagues shaped a form of humanistic sociology, a *verstehen* sociology that was dropped from the discipline's mainstream as male academics pursued a value-neutral, detached scientific sociology modeled after the physical sciences.

The Social Survey Method and Other Primary Data

Certainly one of the important contributions of the settlements to sociological research is reflected in the development of the survey method. *Hull-House Maps and Papers* (1895) became the flagship example of scientific analysis of the working-class poor in the United States. The research is known for its use of detailed colorful maps illustrating the concentration of ethnic groups by city block and the relationship between ethnicity and income. The work paved the way for similar studies in other settlement districts (e.g., South End House of Boston) as well as in some states and municipalities (Stivers 2000) and later at the University of Chicago (Sklar 1998). According to Holbrook who wrote the methodology of the volume, *Maps*, in comparison with Booth's work, emphasized "the greater minuteness" of the Hull House neighborhood, and she predicted that this precision "will entitle it to a rank of its own, both as a photographic reproduction of Chicago's poorest quarters...and as an illustration of a method of research" ([1895]2004:11). Florence Kelley who led the Hull House *Maps and Papers* project had the support and resources of the U.S. Department of Labor and of Carroll D. Wright, U.S. Commissioner of Labor from 1885–1905.[11] Consistent with a pragmatist philosophical orientation, the survey project sought to systematically collect data reflecting the experiences and lives of community members that could be consumed by them and used to promote social reforms benefiting the neighborhood. As Schultz explained this process for *Maps and Papers*, once door-to-door survey schedules were completed, but

> ...before a form was sent to the commissioner of labor in Washington, D.C., it would be copied by a Hull-House resident—the nationality of each individual, his or her wages when employed, and the number of weeks she or he was idle during the year beginning April 1, 1892. The information was then color-coded and transferred to maps (2007:18).

The maps were prominently posted in Hull House so that community members could learn more about their environs and have input in community projects and programming (Deegan 1990:46–47). The Hull House mapping was especially significant and extended beyond that used by Charles Booth in London. While Booth's maps provided information for the entire city of London, and also included the work and writings of collaborative researchers from Toynbee Hall, much of the poverty data provided were extrapolated statistical estimates. By contrast the Hull House maps drew from household-level data for every street in the ward. Kelley's contributions were particularly important in bringing "the statistical techniques of social investigation to Hull House, as well as Marxist Theory; and [she] developed them into a powerful tool of social reform" for workers in industry (Ross 1998: 236). Under Kelley's direction and the work of four Department of Labor "schedule men," the Hull-House surveys provided in-depth and detailed household information for the 19th Ward. Most significant in illustrating the congested and hierarchical living conditions, and unlike Booth's maps, the Hull House maps recorded and illustrated both ethnic nationality and wages, creating "vivid spatial depictions." Sklar notes:

---

11 Wright held a number of other important government positions and apparently his confidence in the work of settlement investigators caused him to contract with them periodically for special projects. In 1893 he was placed in charge of the Eleventh Census; in 1894, he chaired the commission that investigated the Pullman Strike of Chicago and in 1902, was a member of the Anthracite Coal Strike Commission. He taught statistics and social economics at Catholic University of America, at Columbian University, and at Harvard. In 1902 he was appointed president of Clark College, while still retaining his position as Commissioner of Labor, and in 1903 served as president of the American Association for the Advancement of Science.

> ...through their omniscient perspective on social problems, maps empowered the observer in ways that prose or statistics could not match. ...the maps...also depicted, along with the concentration of certain ethnic groups in certain blocks, a striking range of moral relationships: between poverty and race; between the isolated brothel district and the rest of the ward; between the very poor who lived in crowded, airless rooms in the rear of tenements and those with more resources in the front: between the observer and the observed. If in many respects social science replaced religion as the interpreter of moral priorities, maps best exemplified this substitution. They conveyed more than information. They also communicated moral imperatives (1998:137).

Maps and Papers was not only the result of a penchant for securing accurate data, but also of a driving moral consciousness and a desire to link social data with social action. This philosophical orientation informed the Hull House methodology and is illustrated in the short prefatory note of Jane Addams.

> The residents of Hull-House offer these maps and papers to the public, not as exhaustive treatises, but as recorded observations which may possibly be of value, because they are immediate, and the result of long acquaintance. All the writers have been in actual residence in Hull-House, some of them for five years; their energies, however, have been chiefly directed, not towards sociological investigation, but to constructive work ([1895a]2004:vii–viii).

Embedded in the larger settlement paradigm of the "neighborly relation," Addams emphasized the validity of research conducted by residents who subjectively shared the social realities of those studied and had an investment in their well-being as opposed to maintaining an "objective" detachment from the subjects of research. Similarly the first section of the book, "Map Notes and Comments" written by Agnes Holbrook ([1895]2004: 3–14), reflects the desire to create grounded knowledge situated in a context that can illicit an impulse for social change.

> [T]here is surely great reason to suppose that Chicago will take warning from the experience of old cities whose crowded quarters have become a menace to the public health and security. The possibility of helping toward an improvement in the sanitation of the neighborhood, and toward an introduction of some degree of comfort, has given purpose and confidence to this undertaking ([1895]2004:10–11).

Her notes further illustrate the "up close and personal" qualitative involvement of the researchers with their work and suggest a critical and reflexive awareness that *Maps and Papers* was pioneering and would become a model for future investigations.

> It is also hoped that the maps and papers may be of value, not only to the people of Chicago who desire correct and accurate information concerning the foreign and populous parts of the town, but to the constantly increasing body of sociological students more widely scattered. ... The manner of investigation has been painstaking, and the facts set forth are as trustworthy as personal inquiry and intelligent effort could make them. Not only was each house, tenement, and room visited and inspected, but in many cases the reports obtained from one person were corroborated by many others... ([1895]2004:11).

Finally, Holbrook's words convey the strong moral imperative reflected in the body of feminist pragmatist research that would follow, pioneered by the collective work of the early Hull House residents.

> [T]he aim of both maps and notes is to present conditions rather than to advance theories—to bring within reach of the public exact information concerning this quarter of Chicago.... While vitally interested in every question connected with this part of the city, and especially concerned to enlarge the life and vigor of the immediate neighborhood, Hull-House offers these facts more with the hope of stimulating inquiry and action, and evolving new thoughts and methods, than with the idea of recommending its own manner of effort.... Merely to state symptoms and go no farther would be idle; but to state symptoms in order to ascertain the nature of the disease, and apply, it may be, its cure, is not only scientific, but in the highest sense humanitarian ([1895]2004:13–14).

The history of the discipline of sociology as typically recorded gives men at the University of Chicago rather than the women of Hull House credit for the survey and mapping technique and for field studies in general. The University men were largely without the reform activism that drove the Chicago women and have subsequently been labeled as empirical scientists and the women as "do gooders." Recent scholarship, however, has exposed the fact that the Chicago school, under Park and Burgess, relied more on data collected by others than by themselves. In fact, much of the data used by the Chicago men were collected by the CWSS or social service agencies such as the Immigrants'

Protective League and the Juvenile Protective Association, both associated with Hull House (Platt 1994). Perhaps one reason so much methodological sophistication and innovation have been attributed to Chicago sociologists is that their works provide little information about their methods of data collection. Such works were typically labeled as "case studies" and appropriately used multiple sources of data but often from unnamed sources identified simply as "documents" that included interviews, observations, reports, life histories, and agency data. As Platt concluded,

> It is not clear that the university added anything to the repertoire of methods of data collection and presentation already in use elsewhere. ...a close reading of the classic monographs suggests that the extent to which they rely on firsthand data collected by their authors has been exaggerated. Most of them contain large quantities of secondary data, and many of the data which look firsthand turn out to be so at one removed—collected firsthand by others. ... The 'firsthand' data provided by others most often come from the records of social work agencies (1994:61).

Platt makes her case by examination of four classical works of the Chicago male sociologists: *The Taxi-Dance Hall* (Cressey 1932), *The Gang* (Thrasher 1927), *The Unadjusted Girl* (Thomas 1923), and *The Gold Coast and the Slum* (Zorbaugh 1929). She concluded,

> ...a number of studies of slums, immigrants and other aspects of urban life in Chicago had been carried out at Hull-House and by the women associated with it before the well-known university work. Juvenile delinquency had...already been studied by Breckinridge and Abbott (1912). A report on the dance halls of the city had already been published by Bowen (1917) of the JPA long before Cressey started work on the subject. Prostitution and promiscuity was a hackneyed topic by the time Thomas came to it; Addams (1912) [*A New Conscience and an Ancient Evil*] may be taken as the book-length example most closely associated with Chicago. ...there is even a near-predecessor to *The Polish Peasant* (1919) ...in Balch's *Our Slavic Fellow Citizens* (1910).
>
> PLATT 1994:71

Platt pointed out similarities between the works of the Chicago university men and the CWSS. Both, for example, made recommendations for action and neither was objective, value-free science. The women, however, felt compelled to follow up their recommendations with action while the men left that to other individuals or social service agencies. Platt concluded, "It is not at all easy to distinguish between [the research of] the two groups, and indeed to treat them as two separate groups could be seen as misleading" (1994:72).

Social Reform and Feminist Jurisprudence

While a belief in the theoretical primacy of structural causes of social problems informed the research practices of the Chicago Women's School of Sociology, their strong adherence to humanistic principles of jurisprudence informed their social reform activism. Edith Abbott studied with Roscoe Pound who is generally credited with propounding the concept of sociological jurisprudence in the United States. Pound's explanation aptly describes the Chicago Women's School of Sociology.

> [Sociological jurisprudents] regard law as a social institution involving both finding by experience and conscious making—an institution which may be improved by conscious effort; they lay stress upon the social ends which law subserves rather than upon sanctions; they look on legal precepts and doctrines and institutions functionally and regard the form of legal precepts as a means only. Philosophically they are chiefly positivists or neorealists. They employ a pragmatist method which is consistent with different metaphysical starting points.
>
> as quoted in BARNES 1925:458

Because of problems created by the organization of industry, the Hull House sociologists recognized and documented the need for societal change that would require a concomitant transformation of the system of production as well as community and of urban infrastructures. Successful change or even adjustments would hinge on the emergence of a transformed collective consciousness or *democratized social ethic* based on the principles of equality. This emergent social ethic was expected to drive collective demands for legal remedies and state-sponsored programs designed to create a more equitable distribution of resources and to ameliorate problems of unemployment, poverty, and substandard living conditions caused by capitalist industrial organization. Some of those associated with the Chicago Women's School of Sociology studied law in addition to the social sciences. They became familiar with legal briefings and engaged in political dialogue and debate in order to advance the progressive agenda for social reform. They organized women's groups and clubs even before women had gained the vote, arguing that it was women's civic duty to draw attention to social problems and to lobby politicians to pass legislation, create watch-dog organizations, and to systematically study the problems of the poor, of women and children, of immigrants, and of the sick, infirm and institutionalized inmates, patients and residents of our large cities. Lengermann and Niebrugge-Brantley reflect on the importance of jurisprudence to their reform efforts.

> [J]urisprudence, which for them was the philosophy that law is a medium for social reform—[was] a generally accepted Progressive faith. Lathrop, Kelley, Breckinridge, and the Abbotts had fathers who were lawyers and legislators.... Kelley, Breckinridge, and Kellor all got law degrees themselves, and Lathrop and Grace Abbott both read law for a time. The Chicago Women had a keen interest both in the drafting of reform legislation and in its implementation and administration. They viewed legislation as the means to implement a caring and democratic social state (1998:243).

The Chicago Women enacted their philosophy of feminist jurisprudence in at least three ways: through providing a critique of the separation of public and private spheres (Kemp 1985, Lengerman and Niebrugge-Brantley 1998), by organizing associations to press for change (Addams 1932a,b; Lengerman and Niebrugge-Brantley 1998; Sklar 1998), and by securing government appointments and by drafting and lobbying for specific legislation (Lengermann and Niebrugge-Brantley 1998:250–252). Importantly, the robust women's network and associations helped pave the way for many of the appointments that women secured and in the rise of a strong women's political culture (Sklar 1995, 1998). In research, writings, and lectures, these women collectively critiqued traditional understanding of the private sphere and the public good. In examples of the public-private linkages, the women sociologists documented the public impact of private troubles such as inadequate childcare, recreation, and education (Addams 1908, 1909, 1912; Kelley 1903, 1905). They pointed out how the failure of fathers to make child support payments was an economic as well as a family problem (Breckinridge 1910); how domestic violence, particularly among immigrant women, reduced worker productivity and contributed to family poverty (MacLean 1925); and how inadequate housing impacted employment practices as well as public health (Breckinridge and Abbott 1911, Abbott 1936). Kelley put some of the burden of worker exploitation on private consumer practices (Kelley 1899). Talbot made access to education a public responsibility (Talbot 1910). Kellor drew associations between criminal behavior and inadequate sanitation, sewerage systems, and bathing facilities (1900abc, 1901) while Addams made individual prejudice, immigrant suffering and illness public and moral issues (Addams [1910]2008). Women were uniquely situated to shed light on how private experiences and practices have direct impact on the public good. As traditional care-givers and stewards of community affairs women more than male decision-makers were aware of how private matters were both product and cause of public problems. Ultimately the goal of the Chicago women activists was to generate awareness and to motivate the public will to demand government intervention in the creation, enforcement, and support of programs and legislation to alleviate private suffering and, thereby, social problems.

The Politics of Erasure

Both a "politics of gender" and a "politics of knowledge" have shaped the course of sociology and applied the historical eraser to settlement work even as the university-based academic canon was legitimized (Lengermann and Niebrugge-Brantley 1998, 2002). The massive amount of sociological work produced by the Chicago Women's School of Sociology includes empirical research, critical theory, and a sophisticated methodology. Without changes in the content and context of what we teach and of what we publish, unfortunately, this is a history lost to future generations of sociologists. In their critical historical narrative of the separation of sociology and social work, Lengermann and Niebrugge (2007) made a strong argument that during the Progressive Era social work and sociology were one and that their confluence is found in settlement sociology. Settlement sociology as epitomized in the Hull House practice was a theory of social relations that propelled investigations, the assemblage and dissemination of facts relevant to problems of urbanization, industrialization, and immigration and, based on these facts, plans of action to solve or alleviate social problems. During this period, however, some practitioners formed competing allegiances to one another, to social science reform, and to the emerging fields of sociology and social work. In 1909 Jane Addams became the first female president of the National Conference on Charities and Correction (NCCC), the forerunner of the National Association of Social Workers. This election may signify the beginning of settlement sociology's submersion into social work as settlement workers in the past had a somewhat conflictual relationship with charity workers, and some years were not even welcome at annual meetings of the NCCC. In fact, in 1897 Jane Addams seemed to feel it necessary to apologize for her presence, explaining that "settlement workers are accused of doing their charity work very badly" (as quoted in Davis 1984:21). This was the same year that Mary Richmond, known today as the founder of modern social casework, delivered her speech calling for the training and professionalization of social workers, in essence calling for the training of caseworkers to focus on individuals and families. Addams and Richmond often disagreed, sometimes publicly (Franklin 1986). One of Addams' essays in *Democracy and Social Ethics* is an indictment of the practices of the charity visitor (forerunner of the social caseworker) described as blaming "the individual for his poverty, and the very fact of his own superior prosperity gave him a certain consciousness of superior morality." Despite the masculine language of the day, charity visitors were almost always women who Addams described as "daintily clad" and insisting that those in need of help "must work and be self-supporting" because the "most dangerous of all situations was idleness" (2002b:12). Addams was critical of the individualistic and paternalistic orientation of charity work, and of the psychologically oriented casework version of social work that was evolving. In the tradition of the old Charities Organization Society (CSO), poverty was blamed on the inadequacy of people, a viewpoint disputed by settlement workers who called attention to the underlying causes of poverty. In the minds of some, however, the settlement position came to be associated with socialism, radicalism, or Communism and the COS position a more acceptable alternative to the treatment of poverty. Also, no doubt because of the prominence of Hull House and Addams in the Settlement Movement, this position was closely connected with what was sometimes labeled as "social feminism" (Reisch and Andrews 2002:22–23).

Even if women achieved sociological authority in their contemporary lives, it was sometimes stripped from them in death. For example, Jane Addams has been made into a secular saint, her contributions to sociology forgotten and erased until recently. At her death, University of Chicago sociologist and once Hull House resident, Ernest Burgess, wrote a long tribute poem in which he praised her as "mother of the poor and helpless," and as "supporter of every good cause." Presumably to show her extensive influence, the poem goes on to credit her with inspiring the work of other settlement people: "Graham Taylor went forth from your side to found Chicago Commons;" "Mary McDowell left to live Back of the Yards," "Florence Kelley to defend the toiler;" "Edith Abbott to train youth for social work" "Sophonisba Breckinridge, to right old wrongs" (the poem is quoted in its entirety in Deegan 1990:150–151). Although a touching tribute, there is nothing in the poem that acknowledges Jane Addams the scholar, the theorist, the author, or the sociologist.

Demise and Dissolution of Hull-House

Perhaps the ultimate victim of erasure is Hull House itself. Unlike many of the early settlements that have survived as community centers or as neighborhood social service programs, Hull House, the most famous of the settlements, has not survived. In the 1950s and 1960s Hull House was part of Chicago's inner-city property targeted by Mayor Richard Daley for urban renewal and for development of the University of Illinois campus. In 1963, responding to the pleas and protests of former Hull House neighbors and residents, the University purchased the property on which the original settlement building was located, the old Culver home, and agreed to preserve the building that was subsequently declared both a Chicago and a National Historic landmark. This building which today is maintained by the University as the Hull House Museum (a self-supporting organization) is all that remains of the original Hull House complex of thirteen buildings. Before demolition, social service programs were dispersed, under the auspices of the Hull House Association, from the Halsted site to various locations across the city. By 1985 Hull House Association sites numbered 29 and by 1990 had a budget of $40 million but that plummeted to $23 million by 2011. In early 2012, the Association announced that it would cease operations in the spring. However, the agency abruptly closed a few weeks later and filed for bankruptcy, leaving some 300 employees without jobs, severance pay, or pension benefits. As one critic suggested, had Jane Addams lived, "with the staff fired with little notice and without benefits...she would be organizing them for protests" (Cohen 2012:4). By some analyses the Association tried to do too much, was too diversified, and too dependent on government funding. Others thought it belatedly fell victim to "founder's syndrome." One journalist wrote the Hull House obituary as an ignoble ending to a noble history, elegantly capturing the essence of Addams and the Progressive Era Hull House cohort.

> ...[B]elieving the importance of fact and data, Addams led Hull House into investigations of sanitation, truancy, tuberculosis, infant mortality, and cocaine use in Chicago, prompting changes in laws and public programs. In the first few decades, the Hull House of Jane Addams was a beacon for social change and the delivery of services was secondary, or even tertiary, in the original settlement house concept....
>
> Addams' successors in no way measured up to her or perhaps didn't even grasp some of what she might have meant by the socialization of democracy or Hull House as a "cathedral of humanity." Some shoes are almost impossible to fill.
>
> COHEN 2012:2

A Legacy Worth Preserving

Hull House and its network of women, and a few men, is without doubt the most complete and the first school of sociology to evolve in the United States, a product of the Progressive Era's penchant for the alleviation of human misery. The theoretical core of Hull House sociology was critical feminist pragmatism infused with an ethic of social democracy. Their methodology was that of the neighborly relation exercised through the vehicle of the settlement and the unique standpoint epistemology of the residents. The pioneering sociologists of Hull House gave us a first community survey and subsequently researched almost every aspect of urban life where suffering and need were apparent. They provided quantitative and qualitative descriptions of the poor who were the backbone of our labor force but inadequately remunerated for their work and consequently inadequately housed, fed, educated, or cared for when sick, old, or disabled. Their descriptive research was always a means to an end, the end goal to reform work conditions, to raise the quality of housing, to improve the standards and inclusivity of the schools, to abolish sweatshops and child labor, and to move democracy in the United States toward its ideal form. They saw the future of America in the welfare of immigrants and in its women and children and gave them voice through their work. The fact that so few people today will recognize names such as Florence Kelley, Alice Hamilton, Julia Lathrop, or Grace and Edith Abbott is sad testament to the effectiveness of the politics of erasure but simultaneously a call for a recovery of this history.

CHAPTER 4

Back of The Yards: The University of Chicago Settlement

The University of Chicago Settlement (UCS) was begun in 1894 by the University of Chicago Christian Union, an organization comprised of male faculty vested with responsibility for the University's religious life. Barrett's history of the Stockyards asserts that one of the university's "prime motivations" in establishing a settlement was "to provide its budding social scientists with a window into the world of the immigrant worker" (1987:66). The faculty committee appointed to determine a plan for a settlement included J. Laurence Laughlin, Economics; Frederick Starr, Anthropology; Richard Moulton and Robert Lovett, English; and George Vincent, Sociology (Hill 1938:127). In the spring of 1893, four students were recruited to conduct a survey of the stockyards district which had been determined in advance as "the most needy and the nearest" industrial area of Chicago suitable for a settlement. George Waldron wrote the final report for the group as he recalled at the 20 year anniversary celebration (MMSR B2, F3). While the faculty committee represented different disciplines, the settlement was most directly linked with sociology. "The new agency, taking its philosophy from Hull-House, was to serve as a 'window' for the Department of Sociology of the University, the first such department in the country, and at the same time to minister to the needs of a Chicago neighborhood" (Wilson 1928:22–23). Acting on the recommendation of Jane Addams, Mary McDowell was hired as head resident. In 1898, the University of Chicago incorporated the settlement in the state of Illinois, as "a center for educational, religious, and philanthropic work" with management vested in a board of twelve directors (later expanded to twenty four) with three *ex-officio* members: the president and chaplain of the University, and the head resident (Wilson 1928:40). The University itself offered no regular financial support except to designate Sunday chapel collection once monthly to the settlement, and a "Settlement Sunday" each quarter was given to news about settlement activities and solicitation of funds for special projects. Although President William Harper took a personal interest in the settlement, he never secured an endowment for it (Bachin 2004:122). Most UCS income came from "members" and "associate members" who paid an annual fee and assisted with solicitations from larger donors. The University of Chicago Service League, a support group comprised largely of faculty women and wives, assisted with fund-raising and with programs such as art and music (UCSLR 1897–1994).

Many settlement residents created pleasant municipal homes in some of the worst areas of early cities. Some settlements became gathering places for artists, activists, and intellectuals, somewhat akin to the salons of Europe, designed both to please and to educate, albeit in the midst of poverty. Visitors to Hull House, Henry Street, and Greenwich House, for example sometimes described them as "the hottest spot in town" (Briggs 2008:92) or as the "best club in town" (Davis 1984:31). Along with diverse "neighbors" and adventurous residents, the settlements often hosted public figures, even celebrities; and always there were informative lectures or club meetings, and stimulating conversation prevailed at the dinner table. One did not, however, hear such comments about the University of Chicago Settlement located in the district known as Packingtown or "back of the yards" in the slaughter house and stockyards area identified with filth and unpleasant odors. It was the 29th Ward in the city's political structure and as Breckinridge and Abbott described it,

> No other neighborhood in this, or perhaps in any other city, is dominated by a single industry of so offensive a character. Large numbers of live animals assembled from all sections of the country, processes of slaughtering and packing, the disposition of offensive animal waste, constitute an almost unparalleled nuisance.... In the Stockyards ...are the mingled cries of the animals awaiting slaughter, the presence of uncared-for-waste, the sight of blood, the carcasses naked of flesh and skin, the suggestion of death and disintegration—all of which must react in a demoralizing way, not only upon the character of the people, but the conditions under which they live (1911:434).

Visitors could hardly tolerate the sights and the odors of Packingtown, and those who came either had business there or were committed to the cause of reform. The area, as described by McDowell, was

> bounded on the east by one square mile of stockyards and packing houses which, with the forty-two unelevated railway tracks, separated this "New City" from the other side of town. On the west were the prairie brickyards and many clay holes which the city used for garbage dumps.... The south boundary consisted of more unelevated railroad tracks. On the north was Bubbly Creek...a cesspool for the sewage of the packing houses and adjoining district...a noxious, nearly dead end of the south fork of the south branch of the Chicago river...[V]acant land on Gross Avenue and Ashland Avenue had been used as hair fields, where the hair from the hogs had been put to dry.
>
> MMSR 1914:2

Wilson added to this description,

> On the south the community gave way to open but bedraggled prairie.... Except for Ashland Avenue and Forty-seventh Street there were no paved streets, only roads deep with dust which was stirred up in heavy clouds by the feet of horses in the summer times and was converted into a succession of mud holes bordered with dirty pools of stagnant water littered with trash in the spring and autumn. Neither were there any concrete sidewalks, only board planks on stilts a few inches above the ground, and with almost as many planks broken as in good repair....
>
> WILSON 1928:25–26

In the fall of 1894, in the midst of an economic recession, the University of Chicago Settlement opened its doors and Mary McDowell (1854–1936) established her home in four small rooms on the second floor in the rear of a tenement building at 4655 Gross Avenue in the southwest corner of Packingtown. The street extended from near the intersection of 47th Street and Ashland Avenue into the yards. In fact, near the end of Gross Avenue where it intersected with Ashland, a vacant lot served as a receptacle for drying animal hair. When the stockyards first came to Chicago, they were located well away from the main business district and residential areas; the growth spawned was obviously not anticipated. Packing plants followed the stockyards, and workers, mostly recent immigrants, were drawn to any area offering jobs and housing was quickly assembled to accommodate them. At the time of McDowell's move, back of the yards included five packing plants and stockyards that received hogs, sheep, and cattle from as far away as Texas. By 1919, reportedly over one billion dollars' worth of meat and by-products such as soap, glue and combs were sent from Packingtown to every country (McDowell 1914:5). The invention of refrigerated rail cars gave impetus to the industry, but many meats were still canned on site, some exported to other countries or purchased by the US government for soldiers' rations. The meat industry in the United States was one of the early and most successful forms of monopoly capitalism. "The grip which the 'Big Five' packers—Swift, Armour, Morris, Cudahy, and Schwarzschild and Sulzberger (later Wilson)—held on the developing national and international markets shaped the character of labor relations in the industry from the late nineteenth century on" (Barrett 1987:13). Packing houses, the employers known as "packers," determined the way of life for some 30,000 workers, ages ranging from 11 to forty and over, who were dependent on the meat industry for their livelihood. The workers lived in a one square mile area surrounded by garbage dumps, stockyards, packing plants, and railroad tracts with a population density of 75 per acre

(Barrett 1987:74). Workers were at first Irish, but they moved out and were replaced by more recent Slavic immigrants, the largest groups being Polish and Lithuanian still limited in their use of English. A few Irish remained on "Whiskey Row," but there were very few native-born Americans in Packingtown.

As head resident of the UCS, McDowell's first speaking engagement was before students in the sociology club at the University of Chicago. When she told them she had moved in and begun a settlement but had no cooking utensils, one of the students proposed that they give her a "shower" which they did, helping to furnish the settlement's first home. Several months into its existence, the settlement received its second resident, Caroline Blinn who came because of a newspaper article about the opening of the UCS; she remained, working mostly with juveniles, until her death almost 30 years later (McDowell 1914:10). Although people in the neighborhood did not understand the mission of the settlement and were at first distrustful of its residents, the programs were welcomed and described by one reporter as an "oasis in a desert of vice and ignorance." Women were the first to benefit from the settlement, not only because of its programs but because it became for them what the saloon was as a gathering place for men (Barrett 1987:85). The intention of the University in sponsoring the settlement was to use it as practical, hands-on experience for students, and both faculty and students assisted in teaching classes and in initiating programs and activities. Services were added as needs were determined and support available: a trained nurse, nutrition classes, child care, music, painting, and English classes. As McDowell saw it, "The settlement was like a window opening in the wall which separated socially different classes of people" (Wilson 1928:37). A year after the settlement opened, it expanded to occupy another floor of the same tenement building, and in 1896 moved to a frame building on Ashland Avenue where four small flats and a nearby storeroom were rented (Wilson 1928:35). In 1897, the board of trustees purchased two lots located on Gross Avenue, just across from the original location of the settlement. In 1899, a gymnasium with a stage in one end was the first building to be erected on this new site. In 1905, a second and larger building was erected on the property containing living quarters for residents, a kitchen and dining room, as well as club meeting rooms and a first-aid station. In 1924, the last building was added to the settlement plant, a new and modern gymnasium and boys' building. During the second decade, the settlement added a camp and a bus to transport kids out of the city during the summer months. McDowell described the settlement as "almost the most permanent factor of neighborhood life" in an area that had doubled its population in a decade and was changing its nationality every fifteen years (Wilson 1928:43). On November 30, 1956, the name of the University of Chicago Settlement was officially changed to the Mary McDowell Settlement. Later, the organization merged with the Chicago Commons Association. The original buildings of the settlement are gone today, but Gross Avenue has been renamed McDowell Avenue and a Chicago Tribute Marker is in place to commemorate where the settlement stood.

Mary McDowell: Standing in the Breach

Graham Taylor wrote of his friend Mary McDowell that through forty years she "bravely stood in the breach between employing capital and underpaid labor, between the native and foreign born, between the white and colored races" (1938:xi). Unlike some of the other settlement women about whom multiple biographies have been written, there is only one about Mary McDowell, titled, simply *Neighbor* with a Foreword written by Jane Addams. Howard Wilson's work is drawn from primary sources: interviews with colleagues, former residents of the settlement, McDowell's personal papers and records as well as "long conversations with the Settlement Lady" herself (Wilson 1928:vii). McDowell reported that she was the first of six children (MMSR 1971, Biographical Dictionary: B1, F1). Wilson focused on the close and influential relationship between Mary and her father with less mention of her mother. In an unfinished autobiography McDowell credited her mother for her "desire to share in whatever work was going on" and her father for encouraging her to be independent. McDowell wrote, "My own childish heroes had all been doers—the blacksmith, the fireman, and my father who was helping Abraham Lincoln to free the slaves" (1914: Foreword). Mary was born in Cincinnati, Ohio to Jane Gordon and Malcolm McDowell. Her mother came from the Gordon family of steamship builders and her father was from a family that produced iron and steel. Malcolm McDowell, also an inventor, became very successful and moved his family to Columbus, Ohio and then to Providence, Rhode Island. When called to serve during the Civil War, he moved his family back to his wife's childhood home on the banks of the Ohio River and went to Washington where President Lincoln appointed him paymaster, responsible for the distribution of pay to soldiers in the field. Mary spent her formative years in the Ohio River community where her playmates were children of boat and lumber yard workers. She was close to her father and recalled vividly his sadness at the assassination of his hero, President Lincoln. Mary began life in the Episcopal Church but after her father returned from the war, the two began attending services at a "little Methodist chapel whose members were mostly workmen in the industrial section of the Cincinnati water front" (Wilson 1928:12–13). After the War, the McDowells moved to Chicago where Malcolm established a successful steel rolling mill. It was in Chicago that Mary began her career in social service when at just 17 years of age she worked as a volunteer, assisting victims of the 1871 Chicago fire. In the 1880s, her family moved to Evanston, Illinois where Mary attended the same church as Frances Willard, founder of the Woman's Christian Temperance Union, and taught a Sunday school class that gained a reputation in the community for its emphasis on the applied principles of Christianity (Wilson 1928:17). Although little else is known of Mary McDowell's birth family, a UCS publication in 1901 listed as residents both her parents and another McDowell (Hanson) who could have been a brother. Since settlements often listed temporary as well as permanent residents, the length of their stay is not known (UCSLR: B15, F6).

McDowell differed from most leaders in the settlement movement in that she was not a college graduate, "nor did she come to the Chicago district by way of Toynbee Hall and its influence" (Boynton, MMSR: B1, F1). She attended public and private schools in Ohio and Illinois and in the 1880s completed training at the Chicago Kindergarten College after which she taught briefly in New York and returned to Chicago in 1890 where she became interested in settlement work and moved to Hull House as one of their early kindergarten teachers. A few years later she was called back to Evanston because of her mother's illness but used her time there to engage her father's associates in discussions about labor and industry. As labor unrest grew and culminated in the Pullman strike of 1894, McDowell made it her business to understand both sides of the dispute. She recalled,

> I was living in the nineties in a university town near the great seething, restless Chicago, where the workers, the mass of the population, were struggling for something as to which our community...was restfully ignorant.... Evanston saw no reason why wage-earners who had work should be disturbing the peace.... Reverend Carwardine, pastor of the Methodist church at Pullman...helped me to see that the Pullman strike was only typical of the great world unrest which *must* be understood.
>
> WILSON 1928:21

From this awakening, the next phase of Mary's life was as head resident of a new settlement in the midst of what Upton Sinclair was later to make famous as *The Jungle* (1906), the heart of Chicago's most profitable industry—meat. McDowell brought to her new work the Hull House philosophy of becoming a neighbor, "the new kind of neighbor who gossips in statistics" (Wilson 1928:44). She became known throughout the city and state for her activism on behalf of immigrants, blacks, and all workers but especially children and women. She helped to found the Women's City Club, was the first president of the Illinois Women's Trade Union League, a post she used to get black women admitted to the union. She established the first interracial committee for women in the city after the Chicago race riots of 1919. In 1907, she lobbied in Washington, along with other female activists, for funding of a comprehensive study of women in industry. She was an active member of the Illinois Equal Suffrage Association, the National Child Labor Commission, the American Sociological Society, the National League of Women Voters, and Chicago's Immigrants' Protective League. In 1914, she ran on the Progressive Party ticket for Cooke County Commissioner but was defeated. For more than four decades, McDowell was about improving the quality of life of her neighbors in the stock yards. In 1923 her influence was expanded when Chicago Mayor William Dever appointed her Commissioner of Public Welfare, a post she used to establish a Bureau of Employment and a Bureau of Social Survey. She resigned as UCS head resident in 1929 after which George H. Mead led an effort to make her an honorary member of the University of Chicago faculty and to pay her a small sum for lecturing and for writing the history of the settlement. The University, while welcoming her work in these roles, rejected any form of remuneration leading a group of McDowell's friends to raise funds to insure that she had some income during her retirement years (MMSR May 18, 1927, Correspondence: B1, F1). McDowell began but did not complete work on her autobiography in 1914 and, at the urging of friends, resumed work on it again in the summer of 1927; there are parts of ten chapters in her papers (MMSR: B1, F1). Beyond the first several chapters, others are largely stand-alone essays on social issues, some of which are preserved in a tribute volume compiled by Caroline Hill, *Mary McDowell and Municipal Housekeeping* (Hill 1938). This volume also contains tributes from friends and colleagues who worked with McDowell on various issues and projects over the years. For as long as health permitted following her retirement, McDowell remained active in the UCS and other social causes in the city. She was always a promoter of the enfranchisement of women, of adequate housing, of vocational and increased compulsory education for school children, of racial equality, and of restrictions on the labor of women and children in industry. Sometime adversary, head of the Swiss Packing Company, and later president of the UCS board, Harold Swift said of McDowell after her death,

> She strove to provide for material and mental wants, to build our people into better, loyal citizens and into healthier, happier, wiser men and women. She chose the sincere, sure course of friendship, living with

> and for her neighbors. She struggled to bring a ray of reality to those fantastic stories of a land that flowed with milk and honey, stories that drew peasants first from the northern and central, and later from the southern countries of Europe. That their hopes would not be entirely lost; that they might get a measure of security and happiness out of chaos; that they and their children might have a decent American living—to this end Mary McDowell devoted her life (1938:117).

In her years at the UCS McDowell was known as "Fighting Mary," "the Garbage Lady," "the Duchess of Bubbly Creek" and as the "Angel of back-of-the-yards." She suffered a paralytic stroke in 1935, and died in Chicago on October 14, 1936, at the age of 81. The high esteem accorded McDowell by her associates, is exemplified by George H. Mead when he closed a University introduction with: "she has provided [the University] with a soul" (Hill 1938:129). Many would agree that she was the soul of Packingtown as well.

University Research

For a number of years little research was conducted from the UCS other than surveys that could be used for immediate programming or lobbying of city officials, for example to document the disproportionate occurrence of certain diseases in Packingtown and the need for public baths and playgrounds. However, some University students pursuing masters' theses or doctoral dissertations did take advantage of the stockyards area for research. One of the most comprehensive works was that of Charles Bushnell who earned a doctoral degree in sociology in 1901. His dissertation, "Some Social Aspects of the Chicago Stock Yards" was subsequently published in four installments in the *American Journal of Sociology* (1901–1902) and provides a thorough description and analysis of the stockyards in the context of the city. Bushnell used mostly available data and mapping techniques to describe what the area looked like, how it worked, who its chief stakeholders were, and what its relation was to the city as a whole and, for the meat packing industry, to the nation as a whole. Bushnell began with an informative and objective description of the livestock and meat-packing industry and all stages of their operations. The chief packing plants were named and information provided on their organization and their role as employers of some 30,000 workers. Perhaps because of the location of Packingtown next door to the affluent Hyde Park, Bushnell drew frequent comparisons between the two, for example, contrasting statistics on diseases and infant mortality. Hyde Park was home to the University and many faculty and administrators as well as to some of the titans of the meat industry. While Bushnell acknowledged that Hyde Parkers were generous in supporting the settlement and other service organizations in Packingtown, he nevertheless made the stark observation that one exists because of the other,

> ...that the very community...helping to support the agency [settlement] which is trying to rescue the people of the Stock Yard district from the effects of their bad sanitary and economic conditions, is at the same time...sending its garbage over into the Stock Yard district to make its sanitary and economic conditions worse (1901:310).

Without specifying meat packing, but having used data from that industry, Bushnell indicted industry in general and the profit-making class in particular because,

> ...the tendency of the blind principle of hostile competition in business would so lengthen working hours, reduce wages, limit air and light, and employ women and children, as to cause a retrograde movement toward a barbarous stage of society among the wage-workers.... Undue emphasis upon production for its own sake—that is solely for the sake of profits to be productively reinvested—becomes a menace to all the other social functions by limiting their influence chiefly to a small favored class... (1902:436).

Bushnell ended his work with suggestions for reducing class contrasts between Packingtown and Hyde Park and for achieving "a greater measure of democratic benefit." With reference to labor unrest and its ominous warnings, Bushnell concluded, "only when men become intelligently, morally, and masterfully conscious of the great forces that environ them can we have a truly organic society, maintaining itself through the free and normal participation of all of its members in all of its social functions" (1902:702). In addition to what Bushnell's work tells us about the Chicago stockyards district, it also speaks to the state of the discipline of sociology at the turn of the century. Sociology had not yet reached the stage of a "neutral science" void of any moral or value-laden tone. Further, the end of Bushnell's work demonstrates what appears to be a taken-for-granted pragmatism, its application to problem solving. He offered specifics suggestions for reforms ranging from federal government supervision and regulation of interstate corporations to public school education. McDowell herself recognized that being a university settlement carried with it a special responsibility. She wrote in her autobiography, "Being a university settlement we must further the study of facts as data for certain dependable conclusions; we must know about the conditions of industry and the lives of the people in the crucible of American civilization." However, she, like Jane Addams, rejected the idea of the settlement as a laboratory without purpose, "It is more than an observer; it is a student of the situation...discovering proper lines of conduct, not primarily facts" (MMSR 1914:44–45).

Sociological Research and the Settlement

In the early years of the University of Chicago Settlement, little research was conducted compared with other settlements. The explanation according to Board member and University of Chicago professor, Percy Boynton, was that McDowell "was so concerned with making herself a good neighbor that she steadfastly held off the university investigators...until personal relationships had been unassailably established" (MMSR: B1,F1). The absence of research in the early years of the settlement was also noted by McDowell's biographer as deliberate.

> For many years after the opening of the Settlement it had been the policy of Mary McDowell to avoid the making of formal surveys, because she believed those surveys would be valuable only to the degree in which the people of the neighborhood co-operated in them. Hasty attempts at 'prying into neighborhood affairs' might defeat the entire investigational purpose of the Settlement. Miss McDowell's first consideration was the making of friends; it was not until friendship had become a tried and constant factor that adequate investigations could be undertaken.
>
> WILSON 1928:67–68

While this explanation is no doubt true, there were other reasons for the lack of research. First, in the early days of the settlement, Packingtown was considered unsuitable for individuals doing the house-to-house canvassing typical of survey research at that time. It was, for example, passed over in a survey of housing conducted about the turn of the century. It was not until almost a decade later that Sophonisba Breckinridge and Edith Abbott of the Chicago School of Civics and Philanthropy conducted a study of housing back of the yards (1911). Secondly, the packers and the University were forces to be reckoned with in any research project. To some extent all of the settlements were located in that contradictory space between the lower class workers they purposed to neighbor with and the upper classes on which they were dependent for support. As settlement workers reached out in a spirit of neighborliness to the masses around them, they were obliged to reach out with the other hand for donations from the affluent. For the University of Chicago Settlement, however, there was another layer to contend with. The incorporator of the settlement bearing its name was a private university also reliant on the upper classes for economic support, especially in its early history. Meat was the largest industry in Chicago and the three largest meat packers were Armour, Swift, and Morris, all stakeholders in the University. For example, in his history of the University of Chicago, Goodspeed (1916:493–497) listed P.D. Armour, one of the founders of the Armour Meat Packing Company, along with five members of the Swift family as among the University's "larger contributors." Edward Morris, head of the third company, was also listed as a large contributor and was married to Helen Swift, daughter of his competitor. When Morris died in 1913, his widow was a significant contributor to the University of Chicago Library. The packers served interlocking positions as supporters of the Settlement and the University. Harold Swift served on the settlement board, including one term as president, and later served as president of the University's board of trustees. William Bond was for many years vice president of the UCS board as well as later serving on the University's board of trustees. It appears then that the UCS was independent neither of the University nor the packers. No doubt, the packers looked upon the settlement as an extension of the University and as a charitable agency that must continually earn their support. The settlement's list of donors consistently included names of the Swift and Armour families (Slayton 1986:175). Understandably, ties with the university and with the packers made many residents of Packingtown suspicious of the settlement and explain McDowell's concern with earning their trust:

> ...the Settlement House's funds were of alien origin. They came from Hyde Park, the home of the University of Chicago, which was snobbish, condescending, middle-class, and Protestant, or from the very rich, the bankers and business leaders in faraway North Shore suburbs like Evanston and Winnetka—worlds apart from the residents of Back of the Yards. Worst of all, some of the money came from the Swift and Armour clans themselves, the hated overlords of the packing plants.
>
> SLAYTON 1986:175

It was some sixteen years after the settlement was established that John C. Kennedy was employed to conduct investigations intended to produce six reports: (1) the effect of conditions in the stockyards and the packing plants on the standards of living in the community, (2) family budgets in workers' homes,

(3) housing and sanitary conditions, (4) general sanitation and health, (5) children behind in educational achievement, and (6) vocational training and guidance (Wilson 1928:66–67). The UCS minutes state that funds for the research were donated by "generous friends," making possible "systematic and comprehensive investigations" that the settlement was ready to begin. The same minutes laid out "general principles" to "control the investigation," more about what investigators would *not* do than what they would do and clearly designed to diffuse any objections to the research. They *would not*: study one industry only, make a case for a particular point of view, violate the privacy of either home or business, provide any inducements or make any threats against anybody. They *would* include all classes of workers and all classes of employers and all varieties of conditions within the district. They would get "facts and not rumors or suspicions" (MMSR February 9, 1910, Minutes: B4, F21–22). Kennedy and other researchers were hired by the UCS Committee on Studies and Publications comprised at the time of board members Charles Henderson and George H. Mead, both University of Chicago faculty, businessmen William Bond (also board vice president) and Sherwood Larned, and McDowell (US Commission on Industrial Relations 1916:3462, Deegan 1990:112–114, Cook 2006:68).[1] Given obvious concerns reflected in the "principles," Kennedy was a curious choice for the work as he was at the time secretary of the Illinois Socialist Party and very pro-labor.[2] Much of the decision-making in initiating

1 William Scott Bond, Jr. served as vice president of the UCS board from 1909–1917. He was a graduate of the University of Chicago, a prominent real estate lawyer and was elected to the University board of trustees in 1922, the year that Harold H. Swift, of Swift meat packing, became president of the University board. Sherwood J. Larned was a member of the Settlement board from at least 1909–1917 when he was superintendent of the Chicago Telephone Company where he patented a devise to improve telephone circuitry. He was a trustee of the Art Institute of Chicago for many years and was listed in the Chicago Social Register. Charles Henderson was a member of the original sociology faculty at the University and served as University chaplain. He was a founding member of the UCS and served on the board until his death in 1915. Mead served as UCS treasurer for a time and as a member of the Finance Committee. He chaired the Committee on Studies and Publications for at least ten years beginning in 1911 and served as President of the settlement's board of directors from 1919 to 1922 (Cook 2006:68).

2 In testimony before the Congressional Committee on Industrial Relations John Kennedy identified himself as secretary of the Socialist Party of Illinois; alderman of the twenty-seventh ward in Chicago; economics professor at the University of Chicago, 1908 and 1909; a "sociological investigator" in the Stockyards in 1910 and 1911 at which time he was also a resident of the UCS; and a "housing investigator in 1912 (USCIR 1916:3460). In 1918 and 1919 he engaged in a series of debates with William Darrow at the Garrick Theatre in Chicago, introduced by socialist Arthur M. Lewis. After leaving Chicago, Kennedy traveled while working as

the research was apparently left to Mead and Henderson as the social scientists on the committee. Wilson reported all six research projects as if they had been completed although this was not the case. An altered agenda is not surprising given the fact that there would have been considerable overlap had the work proceeded as planed and in all likelihood Kennedy soon realized this. It is apparent also that as the research got under way investigators learned of existent or ongoing research and revamped their design so as not to be duplicative. Records of the UCS survey project indicate that Kennedy presented the board with a progress report at the end of six months listing the areas of investigation somewhat differently from the six initially laid out. A study of organizations and churches, a study of saloons, and a study of employer-employee relations had been added, the latter apparently to collect statistics on industrial accidents and insurance benefits (MMSR June 31, 1910: B4). Kennedy emphasized that it would not be necessary for the research team to collect all of these data because some were available from other sources, particularly the new census. Kennedy indicated that data were being collected on wages and family expenditures and that housing data collected in 1909 by Breckinridge and Abbott would be used, supplemented by "information which we have gained by visiting houses in all sections of the district." He referred to the health study as if it were concluded although apparently what the settlement ended up using was their own study of diarrheal diseases and other available data on tuberculosis, respectively the major diseases of children and adults in the area. The work ongoing dealt with wages and family budgets and school children, the latter begun by Louise Montgomery and completed by a Miss Bugby working with Dr. Caroline Hedger. Kennedy ended his report on an optimistic note, "we will get most of the information that we originally planned to get, and the investigation will be completed on schedule." In fact, all did not progress as smoothly as Kennedy's report suggests. The research ultimately fell victim to "back of the yards politics" that interfered with its execution as well as outcome and publication. Although many details have been lost to history, Deegan concluded that "this massive community study was continually hamstrung by the politics of the meat packers, university interests, and the question of the appropriate relationship between sociology and its application" (1990:112). Apparently the settlement board acquiesced to special interests when they agreed in advance to submit the report to some of the packers before going to press. It was clear from the beginning that the settlement committee was very intent on not alienating the packers and some of the research

a writer and labor activist and for a time he was a lecturer at Brookwood Labor College in New York.

required data from the packing companies. Such data were released reluctantly and only after members of the settlement board assured the packers that the data were sought for accuracy and that the report would be submitted to them for comments in advance of publication (MMSR July 25, 1910, letter from Scott Bond, representing the settlement board, to Mr. Stratton, legal counsel for Armour and Company: B4, F21).

Piecing together the history of the UCS surveys shows that data were collected in 1910 and 1911 and, although not following precisely the original format, three UCS studies were completed and published by the University of Chicago Press: *Opportunities in School and Industry for Children of the Stockyards District* by Ernest Talbert (1912), *The American Girl in the Stockyards District* by Louise Montgomery (1913), and *Wages and Family Budgets in the Chicago Stockyards Districts* by John Kennedy (1914). Both Montgomery and Kennedy were UCS residents at the time of their research. Talbert was a doctoral student at the University of Chicago. The first two of the three reports apparently combined research topics outlined in the initial agenda, adding a focus on young working girls and their wages. The UCS eventually combined several sources of existing data for a health survey, and the housing survey planned by UCS was already underway by Sophonisba Breckinridge and Edith Abbott of the Chicago School of Civics and Philanthropy. The Preface to the first volume of the UCS surveys summarized the entire project, naming all those who assisted in collection and analysis of data; six investigators were identified as social scientists and graduates of the University; the other four (apparently UCS and community residents) were selected because of their familiarity with local conditions and their language skills. With one exception, all were paid workers and all except two were full-time workers for varying periods of time. The research yielded copious data and observations and conclusions delimited by the data. Survey techniques were used, and standardized schedules completed by door-to-door canvassing provided qualitative and quantitative data. The Preface of the first volume is written as if all facets of the initial research design were completed. Talbert acknowledged Kennedy as having "general charge of the survey" and as having conducted "the study of wages and working conditions in the packing-houses, the study of health and sanitary conditions, and parts of the studies covering family budgets and housing conditions" (Talbert 1912:3). Suggestive of the sensitive political nature of some of the reports, the first volume includes a disclaimer that "the Settlement does not necessarily indorse all the conclusions and suggestions of the investigating staff" (1912:3–4).

The first report was based on records and interviews drawn from almost 500 students and former students and was actually intended to be the last report but was completed first and thus published ahead of the others, perhaps not incidentally because the education and training of school children was less controversial than some of the other topics. Talbert concluded that the public schools were not meeting the needs of adolescents and that parents were ignorant of the benefits of children remaining in school as opposed to going into the labor force early. Compounding the problem was the fact that no significant increase in earnings was found for children continuing school beyond the mandated years as opposed to dropping out to begin working. Recommendations made by Talbert were to: (1) reorganize the school and increase its scope; (2) increase the incomes of families to lessen the need for children to go to work; and (3) institute a vocational guidance program with economic benefits as opposed to just "staying in school" as long as legally required.

The second report, authored by Louise Montgomery, was based on data from some 500 young women (ages 14 to 24) working in the stockyards. It was timely as the age of compulsory school attendance was under discussion as was the role of women in the labor force, particularly the type of work they would be hired to do and the number of work hours allowed. Perhaps the most revealing finding of Montgomery's work was that almost all of the young female wage earners were supplementing their families' incomes and had no control of their earnings, a pattern true for young women more than young men. Families were clear, however, that young women were considered unreliable wage earners because they were expected to marry and leave the home. The most obvious recommendations to emerge from this study were to raise the compulsory education age from 14 to 16 and to institute systematic industrial and commercial training for females in the seventh and eighth grades prior to their entering the work force. Other recommendations were less explicit and likely controversial only to the careful reader. For example, the author concluded that "children must be relieved of the need to become premature breadwinners, an unnatural burden forced upon them by the ignorance, disability, or low wage of the parents" (Montgomery 1913:65). While the author was critical of families that garnished the wages of young women, she was more critical of industries that paid workers less than a living wage (Montgomery 1913:66). The first two studies were published in their entirety and with recommendations. The final survey, authored by Kennedy, was much more controversial as it dealt with the most basic fact of life for stockyard families—income and family budgets. Its publication was delayed because of negotiations between the UCS Committee on Studies and Publications and the packers, explaining one reviewer's criticism that "its publication comes four years after the larger part of the data was gathered" along with praise that the "investigation deserves a place with the best...studies of family budgets" (Stbeightoff 1914:952). The research was based on data from some

350 personally canvassed employees as well as payroll reports furnished by two packing companies and timekeeper reports furnished by four of the largest packing companies. To provide an up-close look at how families spent their incomes, 184 families were trained to keep detailed records of every expenditure for periods of time ranging from two to twelve months. Kennedy first submitted his work to the UCS Committee on Studies and Publications, at the time chaired by George H. Mead (Cook 1993:102) and, as with the two earlier reports, he included conclusions and recommendations. The final report however was published without conclusions or recommendations and with a new chapter written by Alice Durand[3] providing comparable wage data for workers in other locations and in other industries. Her work was no doubt intended to deflect criticism of the meat packers' labor practices by documenting that their wages were comparable with at least some other industries in other cities. In the end, as Kennedy later testified before a hearing of the Commission on Industrial Relations (USCIR 1916),[4] only the findings

3 Alice Durand was a Fellow in the Department of Sociology at the University of Chicago. She had previously studied at the New York School of Philanthropy, done research for the US immigration Commission, and been an instructor in English composition at Oberlin College (University of Chicago 1910).

4 The History of the Industrial Relations Commission (1912–1916) is an example of the Chicago-New York reform network in action (Davis 1963:211–228). After a 1910 labor-management dispute at the *Los Angeles Times* resulted in the deaths of 21 employees and imprisonment of two labor activists (John and James McNamara), settlement leaders and other supporters of labor mobilized to demand a federal commission to investigate industrial relations. They first met in New York at the offices of *The Survey* in late 1911. Among those present were Jane Addams, Paul Kellogg, Lillian Wald, Florence Kelley, and Samuel Lindsay. At a later meeting, they were joined by others such as Mary Simkhovitch, Edward Devine, John Glenn of the Russell Sage Foundation, and Henry Moskowitz of Madison House. These individuals came to identify themselves as the Industrial Relations Committee and drew in most of the major reform organizations of the day. Their work led to a symposium and a resolution for presidential appointment of an Industrial Relations Commission, a request that President Taft sent to Congress. The Committee actually drafted a proposed bill and hired two men to lobby it through the Congress. The Hughes-Borah Bill was passed in August, 1912. However, because the committee did not like the names Taft floated as appointees, they stalled actual appointments until President Wilson took office. Apparently the Committee responsible for bringing the Commission into being was also unhappy with most of Wilson's appointments and over the course of the next few years lost interest in it. The Commission continued until 1916, producing an 11 volume report (http://archive.org/search.php?query=creator%3A%22 United%20States.%20Commission%20on%20Industrial%20Relations%22, retrieved June 17, 2013). As Davis summarized, "The war and the internal dissensions and difficulties of the Industrial Relations Commission made the final report in 1916 of little concern to the social

portion of the research was published by the Committee on Studies and Publications which Kennedy referred to as the Settlement's three member "editing committee" comprised of Sherwood Larned, William Bond, and Professor Charles Henderson. "They went over the report and decided that it would be best simply to publish the statement of fact and leave out the recommendations and the interpretation of those facts.... So, that part of the report which I considered most important, personally, was left out" (USCIR 1916:3462). Controversial parts of the report were apparently modified by the Committee and further changes were made later when Mead met with packers (Deegan 1990:114).

Kennedy's major finding was that stockyard workers earned less than needed for meeting the essentials of food, clothing and shelter, what McDowell, and later the unions popularized as an "American standard of living" (Barrett 1987:143). The average male worker in the stockyards earned $10 per week or less and females earned $6. Kennedy testified,

> ...no ordinary workingman can support a family decently on $10 a week in Chicago ...[meaning] a low standard of living for thousands of families in the stockyards. ...boarders will be taken in to help pay the rent, and this generally means overcrowding and lack of family privacy. ...there is strong economic pressure to send the wife out to work. ...the children are sent to work as soon as they become 14. Even with the income. ...derived from boarders and the labor of the wife and children it is sometimes impossible to feed, clothe, and educate the family decently.
>
> Instead of strong, vigorous, well-educated children being reared for our future citizenship, we are certain to get a group who are weak physically and woefully undereducated.
>
> USCIR 1916:3519

Kennedy did eventually have opportunity to publish his conclusions and recommendations, not to the intended audience, but as material entered into evidence at the request of the US Commission on Industrial Relations in hearings held in 1915 and 1916 and for which he was a key witness in several days of testimony devoted to Chicago and to "life and labor conditions of Chicago stockyards employees." Others who gave testimony about conditions in Chicago included Mary McDowell, J. Ogden Armour and John O'Hern, president and

workers who had been responsible for its creation. The social workers' campaign, however, remains an important illustration of the realistic tactics of a group of idealistic progressives" (1963:228).

general superintendent respectively of the Armour Meat Packing plants, and Dennis Lane of the Amalgamated Meat Cutters union. The testimonies before this Commission reveal some of the behind-the-scenes activities that led to the censorship of the Kennedy report (USCIR 1916:3462). Curiously, Kennedy did not mention Professor Mead who was, according to his biographer and UCS minutes, chair of the Committee on Studies and Publications and the initiator of the UCS surveys for which he personally raised funds and hired Kennedy to conduct (Cook 1993:102–103). This omission may be due to the fact that Mead was not present at the board meeting where the final decision was made to publish the report without the controversial material (MMSR 15 November, 2012, Settlement Minutes 1910–1928:Vol 2). Deegan reported that it was Professors Mead and Henderson who were responsible for the studies but that it was Mead who finally acquiesced to the packers (1990: 112–114). Henderson died unexpectedly in March, 1915 but was actively involved with the UCS board until shortly before his death. Kennedy speculated that his recommendation for a labor union as the best protection of workers against low wages and poverty was no doubt objectionable to the packing companies. "I emphasized that point very strongly.... It seems that the editing committee thought that that was a personal idea that had no place in a scientific report. So it was left out, *and the material which bore out that part of my conclusion* was left out entirely" (USCIR 1916:3462 emphases added). The packers' objections to the Kennedy report were cloaked in the guise of scientific objectivity. Kennedy, on the other hand, thought his recommendation justified because he had documented that wages actually declined for stockyards' workers after the 1904 strike. That strike resulted in the defeat of unions in the stockyards after which some workers were required to present written proof of resignation from union membership or be fired; still others had their wages reduced to pre-strike levels. Among other things, the Kennedy report recommended that the state set a minimum wage for all packinghouse workers and require improvements in the work environment such as lighting, ventilation, and bathing facilities. Citing data from some European cities, Kennedy's recommendations went beyond the work place to a call for a minimally acceptable quality of life that included public housing and shorter workdays. In addition to suggesting the need for unionization, Kennedy documented the fact that wages were inadequate to support a descent standard of family living. Quoting from an earlier report by Neill and Reynolds, he testified that "The lack of consideration for the health and comfort of the laborers in the Chicago stockyards seems to be a direct consequence of the system of administration that prevails" (USCIR 1916:3477). Kennedy commented further on health issues, pointing to the fact that one of every three children in the stockyards died before reaching age two. He associated unsanitary working conditions with the high rates of tuberculosis (cause of over 30 percent of deaths) among stockyard workers, explaining, for example, that victims of this disease "expectorate on the spongy wooden floors of the workroom, from which fallen scraps of meat are later shoveled up to be converted into food products" (USCIR 1916:3477). The following is a quote omitted from Kennedy's published report but revealing his justification for a descent standard of living in exchange for undesirable work, no doubt why the packers argued that he went beyond "objective science."

> When society demands of any worker that he shall spend his life 'shackling cattle', 'trucking feet' or 'pumping kidneys' then society must see to it not only that the work is done under the best possible conditions, but that the workers should receive sufficient compensation and have sufficient leisure to secure for themselves the development and culture which are absolutely denied to them in daily work.
>
> USCIR 1916:3524

In response to questions from Commission members about the circulation of his report prior to publication, Kennedy reported that it had been submitted to several packers and that while he did not know the reactions of all, he knew that Mr. Armour objected to his conclusion about unionization because it was partisan and did not belong in a scientific report. A letter entered into exhibit from the representative of Armour and Company objected that the report developed an "argument in favor of a particular cause [unionization]...and the moment the field of disputation is entered *the value of it as a scientific study is gone*" (USCIR 1916: Appendix emphases added). The letter (author not identified by name) raised numerous objections to specific portions of the report such as lack of any mention of a relatively new workmen's compensation law. Disputed also were statistics on child labor violations as well as differences in earnings during slack and busy seasons. Kennedy entered into testimony a letter from Sulzberger and Sons (one of the smaller packers) saying they had no objection to the report and would be glad to cooperate as needed in the future. A letter from Swift and Company was not read or entered into exhibit but was referenced in Kennedy's testimony as commenting on the report in general. Perhaps picking up on the contradictory location of the settlement as an explanation for the censored report, one Commissioner asked Kennedy if the packers contributed to the financial support of the settlement. Kennedy answered that he did not have access to donor information and could cite only one example known to him personally involving packers' support—payment of a nurse headquartered at the settlement. Kennedy's testimony included the fact that he had lived at the UCS and was somewhat familiar with the work of all Chicago settlements, leading Chairman Walsh to departed from his script and ask questions about settlements in general. Apparently assuming that all settlements were associated with colleges or universities, he questioned "the methods used by college professors and instructors in studying and ascertaining sociological and economic truths and in disseminating those truths." Walsh further questioned whether the "great economists and sociologists in our colleges and universities can be relied upon to lead the way in the advancement of social and industrial justice?" (USCIR 1916:3478). Walsh was obviously ignorant of the fact that the vast amount of research was put to use not by academicians but by nonacademic sociologists such as in the settlements. Kennedy applied a partial corrective by replying that the knowledge of most professors came from books and not "conditions as they actually are."

Despite the original research agenda, no health and sanitation study was published as part of the UCS work. As ample health and sanitation research in Packingtown had already been conducted or was underway, some existing as internal reports, this work was updated but not duplicated. Almost every publication on health in the city of Chicago singled out the stockyards area for it high rates of infant mortality and deaths from diseases such as tuberculosis. A report in McDowell's papers dated 1908 summarized a door-to-door survey on childhood diarrhea that included every family in the southwest corner of the stockyards. The survey team included an interpreter for the various language groups and where cases of diarrhea were found a nurse gave instructions on treatment and prevention. No information was reported on the total number surveyed, but 127 cases of children under five years of age were found suffering from diarrhea, most of long-term duration. The report attributed wide-spread childhood diarrhea to improper diet and to environmental causes such as dirt and dust from the unpaved streets, alleys with unsanitary water closets, crowded living conditions, and lack of bathing facilities. The report concluded that baby deaths follow the poverty line and "to make the death rate what it should be [consistent with the city at large] would be difficult 'til poverty was abolished" (MMSR 1908: B2, F13). Another report referenced in speeches and papers was a study of tuberculosis conducted by local physician, Dr. Caroline Hedger (1906). In a report on industrial research for *Charities and the Commons* (1906b:208–209), Graham Taylor reported on Hedger's house-to-house survey of the incidence of tuberculosis in the stockyards area, and identified the work as being for the University of Chicago Settlement. Hedger herself wrote about this research, reporting a rate of tuberculosis 10 times higher in the stockyards than in the city and death rates 55 percent higher. Hedger's conclusion was that living conditions in the stockyards were conducive to tubercular infections and other diseases because of low wages associated with unsanitary living conditions, overcrowding, lack of ventilation, fresh air, and fresh food (1906:7507–7510). Working conditions for meat packers were equally hazardous to their health: deficient sunlight and ventilation exacerbated by air pollution, water closets insufficiently separated from food preparation, and stress due to the speed of the work line. In the same publication as Hedger's article was another by W.K. Jaques, supplemented with vivid pictures of the Chicago meat packing industry. The author's message: "The packing houses are the kitchens of the nation, and they ought to be clean. They are very far from it" (1906:7491).

It seems likely that the UCS research team did not conduct a comprehensive health survey as originally announced because by the time they could commence such work it would have been redundant. Sanitation and health in the stock yards had already reached the office of the President of the United States. As Davis (1984: 120–122) reconstructed the events, an article by McDowell and an editorial by William Hard, journalist and former resident of Northwestern University Settlement, caught President Roosevelt's attention in 1904 and he forwarded these to Carroll Wright, Department of Commerce and Labor, asking him to investigate conditions in the stockyards. Wright complied by dispatching Ethelbert Stewart to the UCS where he stayed for several weeks and in 1905 wrote a report, largely irrelevant to working conditions but positive about the unions' contribution to the Americanization of immigrant workers. Shortly thereafter, a serialized version of Upton Sinclair's book, *The Jungle*, began to appear in a socialist newspaper and Roosevelt, dissatisfied with Stewart's investigation, and after conferring with both McDowell and Jane Addams, dispatched Charles Neill and James Reynolds for a report specific to health and sanitation. Reynolds was former head resident of University Settlement in New York and had just completed an investigation of housing in Washington, DC. Neill was a professor of political economy at Catholic University and a resident at the UCS before becoming Commissioner of Labor in early 1906. The two men stayed for several weeks at the UCS and made surprise and random visits to the packing plants. Although word of their work had leaked to the packers and frantic efforts were immediately begun to "clean house," Reynolds and Neill's on-site observations confirmed that Sinclairs' book was not a total work of fiction and that, in fact, eating meat was probably not safe. Roosevelt did not immediately release the Neill-Reynolds report but instead used it to pressure Congress to act on a pending bill for federal inspection of meatpacking plants and to persuade packers not to oppose the bill. Pending a congressional hearing, the packers continued cleaning their plants, invited inspections, and lobbied against the bill. The packers, at least for a time cleaned as they worked, removing dead animal carcasses and washing manure from floors and walks. They even installed new bathrooms for workers although they could not change statistics documenting disproportionate death and disease rates. Roosevelt was angered by the packers' opposition to the pending legislation and their argument for self-monitoring. In June of 1906, he released the Neill-Reynolds report resulting in the Meat Inspection Act of 1906. So, in fact, a study of health and sanitation was conducted; the UCS was a part of it; and it was legitimized at the highest level of power.

The other research included in the initial UCS agenda was a survey of back of the yards housing. Presumably, after the six-part research project was adopted by the board, it was discovered that a housing survey was already underway by the Chicago School of Civics and Philanthropy.[5] As Kennedy reported,

> ...a careful study of housing conditions in thirteen blocks in this district was made in the Autumn of 1909 by the Chicago School of Civics and Philanthropy. The information gathered...supplemented by information which we have gained by visiting houses in all sections of this district, should enable us to give an accurate description of housing conditions in this vicinity. This information should be used in a practical way in securing provisions in the new building code to be adopted next Fall....
>
> MMSR JUNE 31, 1910:B4

Sophonisba Breckinridge and Edith Abbott of the Chicago School of Civics and Philanthropy (CSCP) with ties to Hull House and the Chicago Commons more than to the UCS were experienced researchers and had students at the CSCP who helped with the collection of data which, like the other surveys, involved a large number of cases. Personal interview schedules were collected in 1909 from 1,562 families, most living in 15 blocks of what the authors described as "typical houses" and a smaller group of homes along "Whiskey Row," selected because they frequently included lodgers. With the exception of the latter group, the vast majority of families canvassed were recent immigrants of Slavic

5 The back-of-the-yards study was part of a larger survey of housing conducted by the Chicago School of Civics and Philanthropy with the cooperation of the Chicago Department of Health. Breckinridge and Abbott directed the entire project and personally conducted the Packingtown work. The other surveys included housing among various special populations: single males, families living in furnished rooms, African Americans, Italians, Slovaks, Lithuanians; and neighborhoods such as the West Side, Hull House, and the steel mills. All were published in a ten-part series in the *American Journal of Sociology* from 1910 through 1915.

origin, mostly Polish and Lithuanians, typical of packing house hourly-wage workers. The authors noted that newly arrived immigrants were the most likely to be exploited with high rents for the poorest housing. Using Chicago housing ordinances and regulations as their standard, the authors allowed the facts to speak for themselves as they reported statistics and personal observations on light, cubit air space per person, toilet facilities, and number of rooms per family not used for sleeping. Overall, they found "in many instances people...living and sleeping in shockingly overcrowded rooms, that...are dark and ill-ventilated, that there is a demoralizing lack of privacy, and that toilet accommodations are often disgracefully inadequate" (1911:467). This survey and several others documented a surprising proportion of houses that were owner-occupied in the stockyards area—approximately 20 percent. Strangely, home ownership was part of the problem because it was directly associated with an excessive number of boarders and consequent overcrowding. To own a home was the dream of most immigrants and to realize it they were willing to take in borders, sacrificing space, privacy, and comfort to make the home affordable (1911:462). Unencumbered by University-packing house politics, Breckinridge and Abbott presented their findings using Chicago housing statutes as their point of reference, noting violations as well as the need for new or updated regulations as appropriate. By framing their findings with these delimitations, their recommendations could be faulted only by city officials who were derelict in enforcing or updating housing standards. In fact, the authors noted that Chicago had the mechanism for enforcing a standard of adequate housing but this mechanism was not enabled because of lack of staff and budget. They faulted the city for substituting "the shadow for the substance in dealing with the problem of city housing" (1911:468).

Mary McDowell was also called to give testimony before the Commission on Industrial Relations where she identified herself by saying that she was neither a sociologist nor economist but a "neighbor" (1916:3328). In advance of Kennedy, she testified in general about the situation for industrial workers in Chicago and of her personal involvement with workers during the 1904 Packingtown strike. When asked a direct question by a member of the Commission as to whether she believed that labor organization has had "an upward tendency" for workers, she replied, "Oh decidedly. I didn't know anybody thought any other way" (1916:3332), a rather strange comment given the controversial position of unions in the US economy at that time. Her testimony did not reveal the fact that McDowell had a long history of pro-labor activism although in the stockyards this was an interest that she, of necessity, had attempted to balance with the interests of the packers. In 1902, McDowell had called in Michael Donnelly, of the Amalgamated Meat Cutters and Butchers Union, to help women workers organize. Local 183 was born with only 14 workers, but by the 1904 strike they numbered over one thousand (Slayton 1986:83). Nor did McDowell reveal in her testimony that she had personally been involved in ending the strike, first by enlisting the help of a stockyards physician, Dr. Cornelia DeBey to appeal in person to J. Ogden Armour for a meeting with union leaders. Armour refused to meet with union representatives but did agree to meet with McDowell, and McDowell, in turn, invited her friend Jane Addams to accompany her to the meeting. Ultimately, the only concession won by the union was an agreement for workers to return to work at prestrike wages and with no punitive actions taken—a promise soon broken. McDowell rationalized that a lost strike was not a dead cause. However, for Michael Donnelly, the lost strike meant not only the end of his career as a union leader but the end of his ability to find employment in his trade as a butcher (Wilson 1928:113–114). McDowell testified that a few workers were organized after the strike but that they lacked the leadership of Michael Donnelly of whom she spoke very highly (USCIR 1916: 3329). In her testimony, McDowell several times referenced the Kennedy research but was not questioned about the controversy surrounding his work nor did she volunteer any comment about it. She, like Kennedy, saw low wages as the basic cause of problems in Packingtown, summing up what she called a consistent theme heard in "every language in the neighborhood.... We cannot live a decent American life on 15½ cents an hour with 40 hours a week." In questioning McDowell, a member of the Commission attempted to lead her to say that workers were better off at the present, even without unions, than in the past. She stood her ground, however, and quoted from the Breckenridge and Abbott study showing that many children would not have sufficient food if their families did not take in lodgers. McDowell was adamant that such lodgers create an unhealthy space problem and that some families are forced to choose between space and food. The Commissioner asked if there were no such cases 20 years ago; she replied that there was no such crowding 20 years ago (USCIR 1916:3332).

McDowell wrote about her experience with the 1904 strike in an unpublished paper perhaps written for a speech or her autobiography (MMSR: B3, F15). She noted, as Kennedy had done, that this strike broke the union and that many workers were subsequently punished or fired from their jobs. With typical optimism, however, McDowell enumerated some positive outcomes of the strike. For example, she thought that Mr. Armour better understood the workers' point of view as a result of the strike. He did not know, for example, that when some employees came to work in the morning they did not know how many hours they would work because their work day was determined by the number of animals to be slaughtered. Nor was Armour aware that each day long lines of workers formed outside the plant office waiting to be hired as day laborers. Many waited and few were hired, and those hired were not compensated for the hours they spent standing in line. After the strike Armour began employing nurses and increased the number of showers available for workers in the butchering facilities. McDowell even acknowledged the packers' economic reality by stating the obvious, that wages would not be increased "as long as there are thousands waiting for a job every morning."

Several undated pages in McDowell's papers entitled, "Notes on Packing Town Situation and Recommendation to Packers" (MMSR: B2, F7a) provide a fitting final note on the UCS ambitious research projects. The document in draft form is comprised of recommendations to be submitted by the UCS board to the packers after the stockyard surveys were completed. Recommendations include some hard-hitting facts such as packers' profits: "Statistics show that total amount paid for the support of the 25,000...[workers] to be but 5% of the value of the business done." The document makes several references to large sums that packers spend on advertising but concludes that, "the public really judge you by what they see of the people [workers] and their homes...and also by what they smell. We confidently say that the occasional packing town smell counteracts a very large sum spent yearly in advertising." In the end, the recommendations challenge the packers to step forward and clean up their own houses, to make Packingtown a model community. Packers are admonished to pave the streets and alleys, to make loans to needy property owners, to cultivate health and sanitary living conditions in the area, and to eliminate the economic necessity of the "vicious" boarding system among families. The document several times alludes to the poor reputation of the meat packing industry, admonishing them to form an organization that will "clean up and civilize back of the yards." Pragmatically referring to the economic benefits of such actions, the report concluded that all of this should be "conducted not as a human or charitable effort, but as a business scheme, like any other department." The historical record is not clear on whether this document or some version of it was actually sent to the industrial packers. However, in the minutes of later board meetings there are references to "recommendations" made to the packers, suggesting that some recommendations drawn from the stockyards surveys found their way to the intended audience.

Contributions to Sociology

The career of Mary McDowell and her work at the UCS were dedicated to the reduction of poverty, inequality, and the improvement of the quality of life for workers, particularly those whose daily activities were carried out amidst the garbage and waste of industry and next door to the economically advantaged.

Toward the goal of reducing inequality, the UCS made contributions to the art and technique of survey research and to the use of community studies to influence political decision-making. McDowell's definition of the university settlement's role sounds the theme of early public sociology.

> This new kind of neighbor gossips in statistics gathered by trained sociologists and used as a basis for helping the neighbors—for humanizing facts about the wages and housing conditions of those in the struggle for existence; making a public opinion that leads to change for the better, and for legislation in the interest of those who cannot bring it to pass themselves.
>
> MMSR 1914:46

University of Chicago settlement sociologists were among the first to learn to navigate the mine fields of the politics of knowledge, as they were located at the juncture of interlocking interests of University, workers, and industrial powers. McDowell knew how to compromise, how to assume the role of the other—even of the barons of industry. She stands as an early advocate of environmental justice because she lived much of her adult life back of the yards, in the wastes of Chicago and of the meat-packing industry. In 1900, McDowell led a group of stockyard residents to city hall to protest the health hazards and nuisances of the district. Most of the workers had given up a day's pay to take a stand for their health and welfare and that of their families. The more politically astute among them were also aware of the politics of garbage. The large open pits in their neighborhood were repositories for the garbage of the entire city and were owned by a city alderman who was leaving the holes where his brick-making business excavated clay. He wanted the garbage to fill in the holes, but profited doubly by charging the city 25 cents for every load of garbage deposited there by open wagons that left a trail of raw waste as they moved along the streets. A young lawyer for the city countered the description of health-hazards presented by McDowell with the statement that "in all great cities there must be a place segregated for unpleasant things, and of course the people living there are not very sensitive." According to McDowell's account of what happened, "the people living there" stifled their rage and instead burst into laughter at every other comment the young lawyer made until "it became apparent that he was gaining a new consciousness of the common people" (1938a:1). A "place segregated for unpleasant things" is the very essence of the concept of environmental justice and sociologists along with other social scientists have produced an interdisciplinary environmental literature inclusive of theory and research that extends into social policy and planning. Their focus on the distribution of environmental benefits and burdens has led to recognition of the unequal costs for people, their communities, their health and quality of life when they inhabit those "places segregated for unpleasant things." But McDowell stated unequivocally, "I firmly believe that ugliness is brutalizing" (1914:51), and her life's work was about making Packingtown less brutalizing. This quest led McDowell to travel to Europe to study the scientific disposal of waste, a trip financed by the Woman's City Club of Chicago. In Glasgow and in Frankfort, McDowell learned about two scientific methods for the incineration of garbage, both of which would result in the production of electrical power or useful by-products. McDowell brought information about these methods back to Chicago where subsequently two incineration plants were begun but construction halted when a new mayor and his administration took office; they preferred to simply hide the garbage holes under a dirt cover. It was not until the late 1920s that the city moved toward scientific improvements in waste disposal and passed statutes requiring industries to dispose of and clean up their own waste. It was not until industries needed additional land that Bubbly Creek was filled in and covered with railroad track.

Along with other activists in Chicago, McDowell lobbied for an inclusive study of women and children in industry, one that she felt must have government sponsorship and funding in order to accomplish the scope needed. Because of the networking of Chicago-New York women, Congress passed a bill in 1907 "to authorize the Secretary of Commerce and Labor to report upon the industrial, social, moral, educational, and physical condition of woman and child workers in the United States" and to be printed as a public document. The final report included 19 volumes published between 1910 and 1913, most of the data collected in 1908.[6] The report dealt with different industries that employed large numbers of women and/or children such as cotton textiles and garment factories. Some of the final report dealt with such topics as the relationship between infant mortality and mothers' employment, labor laws in different states, and the history of women in industry in the United States. McDowell was among the first to write and speak on the concept of equal pay for equal worth. In her essay on women laborers, "Proxies in Industry," she called attention to women doing jobs traditionally thought of as men's work yet receiving less pay. Specifically, she wrote about women munitions workers in Europe in World War I. These women were so vital to the war effort that French Marshall Foch proclaimed "if for 20 minutes, those munitions women

6 For a summary of all 19 volumes as well as title and publication information on each, see U.S. Department of Labor (1916) or googlebooks.com for *Summary of the Report on Condition of Woman and Child Wage Earners in the United States*, accessed January 28, 2013.

would stop work, the allies would lose the war." McDowell also called attention to the fact that these women sometimes continued their work in factories filled with explosives during bombing raids (MMSR: B3, F15). She declared that "One of the very few good results of the war was the revelation to men of the adaptability and versatility of women in lines never before open to them" (1938b:44).

McDowell was an early advocate of racial equality beginning at Hull House where she organized clubs for Negro women. In writings and in speeches, she made comparisons between immigrant groups and Chicago's southern Negroes, pointing out a critical difference: "To the foreign born, color of the skin does not present a fixed line" (1938c:29). Knowing first-hand the importance that union membership could be for workers, she advocated for blacks to be admitted to unions and she deplored their exploitation as strike breakers. She pointed out that blacks who had migrated to cities such as Chicago were driven by the same "legitimate impulse common to all mankind...to better their conditions of living" and deserved the opportunity to realize their aspirations (1938c:30). She expected blacks to move up the socio-economic ladder and worked to see this happen in her lifetime although she was discouraged when race riots erupted in 1919. Witnessing the violence around her in Chicago, McDowell reflected that she was stirred emotionally to the point that she "was ready to apologize for being white" (1938c:34). Harriet Vittum head of Northwestern University Settlement wrote of her friend and colleague,

> During the last ten or fifteen years of her active service the race-relations campaign was probably Miss McDowell's most compelling interest.... She did more to promote racial understanding between the white people and the negroes than any other Chicagoan. Probably her greatest satisfaction during these years came from seeing the negroes farther forward on the way, largely through her interest and work (1938:25–26).

As McDowell reflected on the problem of race prejudice, her message to fellow Chicagoans was a pragmatic one: they are "a people who are here to stay and who must be understood" (1938c:38).

The Settlement and an Early Politics of Knowledge

In some respects, Hull House and the University of Chicago Settlement are case studies in contrast, but there are also similarities. Hull House under the leadership of Addams attracted a group of scholar-activists and grew an independent school of settlement sociology that made lasting contributions to the discipline, especially in early methodology and feminist-pragmatist theory. The University of Chicago Settlement under the leadership of Mary McDowell was free to engage in service and charity and made important contributions to local and national social reforms to improve the quality of life for workers. Apparently this freedom did not extent to research. Investigations generated by Hull House residents under Addams' leadership, and the research produced by the CSCP under the leadership of Julia Lathrop and Graham Taylor were unfettered by university politics and more likely to reach targeted audiences free of censorship. In contrast the scholarship produced at the University of Chicago Settlement was suppressed by the interlocking stakeholders of the University, the meat-packing industry, and the settlement. Even though some of its scholarly works were produced by settlement residents, they were more products of the University than of the settlement and, if anything, paved the way for today's institutional versions of "objective, value-free" sociology as opposed to knowledge applied to change. In a politics of knowledge, ownership of knowledge was contested and ultimately settlement research was thwarted and controlled by the academic interests of the university in deference to powerful stakeholders. On several occasions this contest resulted in McDowell making public disclaimers that she was not a (trained) sociologist or economist, yet she frequently referenced social scientific data. Her refusal to identify herself as a sociologist was perhaps due to her daily interactions with social scientists from the University of Chicago and perhaps to the fact that she herself was not a college graduate. It may also have been a practical strategy to distance herself from the politics of the university sociologists and to maintain her relationship vis-à-vis the community as *neighbor*. There were no such reservations among the women of Hull House, and it is no doubt significant that they did not work *for* academic men but worked *with* those of their choosing (Deegan 1990). Despite these differences Addams and McDowell had similar goals; both aimed to be "good neighbors" and to close the gap between classes or, as McDowell said, to "throw a level bridge over a social chasm" (1914:41).

CHAPTER 5

Chicago Commons: Settlement and Social Gospel in Action

> The good will to understand one another, to interpret misunderstood attitudes and situations, to reconcile and be reconciled to differences of taste and temperament, race and religion, heritage and aspiration, and through service and sacrifice to promote the unity of spirit in the bond of peace, this is the way toward the peace of God that passeth all understanding. Such is the meaning of our forty years experience here. Is it not now the hope for the best that it is yet to be everywhere?
>
> GRAHAM TAYLOR, 1851–1938

The above is a quote from Graham Taylor on the occasion of the fortieth anniversary of the Chicago Commons settlement. It was later included on the cover of a memorial edition of the publication *Social Action* at the time of Taylor's death in 1938, obviously intended as a fitting summary of his life and work. He established the Chicago Commons settlement in 1894, modeled after Hull House. Prior to moving to Chicago, Taylor read and was inspired by Coit's *Neighborhood Guilds* and had visited with Jane Addams, seeking advice as he considered his own life's work. Both of these influences apparently motivated him to accept a faculty seminary position in Chicago and begin to formulate plans to open a social settlement. Addams' pragmatism and Taylor's social gospel are both reflected in the fact that the mission statements of Hull-House and the Chicago Commons, chartered five years later, were identical except that the latter added the word "religious" at the beginning of a list of enterprises to be "instituted and maintained" (Woods and Kennedy [1911] 1970: 40, 53). Addams' support of Taylor's work is evident in the fact that she served until her death on the Commons' board of trustees.

If Taylor is known and remembered today, it is in the annals of social work and the history of social settlements. Yet, in his day Taylor had many identities—social gospel minister, professor of sociology, educator in diverse venues, a public voice for sociology, a newspaper columnist, and the founder and head of the Chicago Commons—but in all of these he is most aptly described by Henking's label as a sociological Christian. This identity represents a pattern "in which religion is maintained as the primary identification with sociology subsumed under the religious perspective" (Henking 1988:263–266). Being a sociological Christian defined and determined all of Taylor's other identities. After being hired as the first professor of Christian Sociology at the Chicago Theological Seminary, and with the understanding that he would begin a social settlement, Taylor found a needy neighborhood in the lower northwest side of the city populated by recent Irish and Scandinavian immigrants. He sent four students to spend a summer in the neighborhood and to study its family life, churches, industry, and politics. This advance team was authorized to locate housing suitable for a settlement as well as for the Taylor family and the students. Housing was very limited, and they settled on a former boarding house that had stood vacant for some time and was thought by most to be unfit for family living. Taylor, lacking any financial backing, rented the house at 140 North Union Street with his own funds and described occupancy as "disputed...by great gray rats and other smaller inhabitants" (Taylor 1936:11). The building had been relinquished as a single-family residence after factories and tenement houses occupied by first and second generations of German, Irish, and Scandinavian immigrants began to encroach on the neighborhood. The settlement name, the Commons, was chosen for its English meaning of free use by the entire community. "So we hoped that Chicago Commons might be a community center where all people, without distinction of class, color, race or sect, could meet and mingle as fellowmen to exchange their social values in something like a clearing-house for the Commonwealth" (Taylor 1936:15). The Chicago Commons perhaps accomplished this goal best in its well-known weekly "Free-Floors" chaired by either Taylor or his associate John Gavit and advertised as "all sides to free speech with no favors." While many free-floor discussions were political, dealing with such controversial issues as labor or war, they also included topics such as family, marriage, health, housing, budgeting, manhood and womanhood. These Free Floors were almost always educational and sometimes "safety valves" for free expression on volatile topics (Taylor [1930]1976:323).

Taylor moved his wife, Leah, and four children, along with four students, into the old, once fine, dwelling that daughter, Lea Taylor, later recalled as follows.

> The outlook from those second story windows was on a mass of tenements at the rear, crowded in two and three on a lot with a saloon next door which was quite a lively place and had a famous horse trough in front of it which had a sign, 'Water your horses, but don't forget yourself'. ... There was a furniture factory on the other side which ran a buzz saw all day and caught on fire once or twice a month. ... There was mainly dust and no particular pavement. The sidewalks were wooden and were at a different level from the street because Chicago was trying at that time to get to a level above the swamp. This area was almost downtown, just on the border of the north branch of the river....
>
> LDTP 1968: B1, F2

Once in the neighborhood, Taylor described himself as

> ...between two frontiers. The one on the front faced me with its advancing lines of academic research and its picket lines of social pioneers, who were followed by the supporting ranks of the more progressive citizens. And there was that frontier in the rear, across which lived and labored the vastly outnumbering multitude of wage-earning people and commercial middle men and their families who constituted the mass life to which religion was also to be interpreted and applied ([1930]1976:5).

After living in the Union Street building for several years, in 1899 an arrangement was worked out with Tabernacle Church on the corner of Grand Avenue and Morgan Streets for a 99 year lease on the property for one dollar per year. The Commons agreed to erect a new building, the auditorium of which was to be used by the Church's declining urban congregation for Sunday services and other programs. Taylor moved the Commons family to the new location in 1901. Over the next ten years, additional buildings on Grand Avenue were purchased for residence and neighborhood activities, and land on rear lots was cleared for children's playgrounds. In 1919 the church property was sold to the Commons with an understanding that they would continue to accommodate the needs of the dwindling church membership (CCAR: B19, F5). In 1923, a farm camp in Michigan, to be used for summer activities and recreation outside the city, was added to the Commons by an estate gift. While none of the original buildings remains today, thanks to the financial endowment secured by Taylor, the Chicago Commons survives as an active part of Chicago's social services network. With name still intact, the Commons continues to offer programs in a number of Chicago neighborhoods and is especially known for services to senior citizens and children (http://www.chicagocommons.org/pages/home.html, accessed July 12, 2014).

Graham Taylor: Sociological Christian

Pathway to the Settlement

Unlike most of the settlement pioneers, Taylor had not visited Toynbee Hall, in fact never traveled abroad until 1903, and he came to embrace the social gospel through his own associations, observations, and study. His first direct contact with social gospelers was in 1885 at an Inter-Denominational Congress in Cincinnati focused on urban problems, social Christianity, and working-class alienation from the church. There he listened to and interacted with Josiah Strong, Richard Ely, Washington Gladden, and Lyman Abbott (Wade 1964:33).

His move toward the social gospel was simultaneous with his embrace of what he saw as the science of Christian sociology, and for him the two became inseparable. In his autobiography ([1930] 1976), Taylor first used the term sociology in describing his evolution from a sense of individual responsibility to one of social responsibility. To the Biblical command, "Ye must be born again," Taylor was fond of adding that the church had an equally important obligation to improve the hereditary and environmental conditions of birth and life in this world (Taylor [1930]1976:387). The influence of sociology is evident in his teaching, preaching, and writing—all frequently connected by what he saw as the primary units of human association, "life spheres:" family, neighborhood, economics, politics, and religion "which are woven through all sociological theory and social action" ([1930]1976:354).

Early Life and Ministerial Development

Taylor was born in Schenectady, New York but spent most of his childhood years in Philadelphia and New Brunswick, New Jersey where his father was a minister in the Dutch Reform Church. Taylor graduated from Rutgers College in 1870 and subsequently entered the Rutgers Theological Seminary to pursue a ministerial career, the fifth generation of Taylor males to follow this path (LDTP: B1, F2). His first pastorate was in 1873, a Dutch Reform Church in the small rural community of Hopewell, New York where he spent seven years. It was in Hopewell, in 1873, that Taylor married Leah Demarest, the daughter of one of his seminary professors. Two of the four Taylor children were born in Hopewell, daughter, Helen and son, Graham Romeyn. Apparently Taylor was a typical Calvinist in this first phase of his ministry as he later reflected with embarrassment that he had subjected his congregants to sermons about hell-fire and damnation if they were "without Christ." Despite his beginning as a traditional Dutch Reform minister, in Hopewell he began "placing less emphasis on divine election and more on Christian action" (Wade 1964:15). Taylor's explanation of this change was that he "was led by a new consciousness of the needs of my fellow men, begotten by close touch with their lives" (as quoted by Russ 1960:18). This change came not through any formal training; in fact, he observed that his college and theological training did not help him to interpret his fellow men or Mother Nature (Wade 1964:19). It was Taylor's observations of class differences between the wealthy land-owners and the poor tenant farmers in the Hopewell area that caused him to change his thinking and his approach to the ministry. He reflected on these years as marking "the beginning of my transition from a sense of individual responsibility to a community or civic consciousness" ([1930]1976:360). This transition led him to change his affiliation from the Dutch Reform to the Congregational Church, an early leader in the social gospel movement and in social reform. In a letter of reflection shortly before his death, Taylor credited Congregationalism with allowing him to "develop my teaching and practice of the social gospel" (GTP: B9, F324).

In 1880, Taylor moved to Hartford, Connecticut to pastor the Fourth Congregational Church, a debt-ridden urban church but offering a more liberal theological environment than Taylor had known in his former pastorate.[1] It was in this urban setting amid the budding influence of Congregationalism that Taylor developed an institutional church, and immersed himself in social gospel thinking. In Hartford, he was influenced by the legacy of Horace Bushnell, social gospeler and Congregational minister, who had died in 1876 although his widow and daughter still lived there and became friends and supporters. Conscious efforts to develop an institutional church "to cover the entire life of man" also reflect the influence of William Tucker who Taylor several times named as one of his role models although he had not studied with him (Taylor [1930]1976:393). In Hartford, Taylor was viewed with some suspicion by fellow pastors who were ministering primarily to the upper classes and blaming poverty on the poor. There were, however, fragments of liberal support in the community. In addition to the Bushnells, there was the Nook Farm nearby with residents such as Harriet Beecher Stowe and Mark Twain (Wade 1964: 25–26). Taylor formed an alliance with Henry Gillette, another social gospel minister known through his work with the Connecticut Bible Society. Taylor, however, felt inadequately prepared for the new challenges of an urban ministry and entered into a program of self-improvement by enrolling in elocution and voice lessons and by hiring a German tutor. He also became an avid student of the developing science of sociology (Wade 1964:40–47).

Taylor's Hartford congregation was experiencing what was to become a pattern for inner-city churches. The most affluent and influential members moved out of the city compromising the church's financial base and leaving behind tenement residents, newly arrived immigrants, and the working poor. Churches that remained oblivious to these changes had little to offer their new neighbors, and some closed their doors or moved to the suburbs. Taylor was determined to meet these challenges and began with direct and consistent contacts and personal visits within the vicinity of Fourth Church. In 1889, he assisted Henry Gillette with a comprehensive religious census of Hartford for the Cincinnati Bible Society. This early foray into social science caused Taylor to report in his autobiography that the *Religious Census of the City of Hartford*

1 An in-depth history and analysis of Taylor's Hartford years and the significance of this period for his development as a sociologist and social gospeler can be found in a dissertation by Hartford student, Charles T. Russ (1960).

(1890) "may claim to be one of the earliest taken in this country...since no reference to any prior city-wide canvass is found in the Russell Sage Foundation's department of surveys and exhibits" ([1930]1976:418), a claim supported by his biographer (Wade, 1964:45). Taylor's experience with the Hartford survey introduced him to what he saw as the power of sociological data, and was influential in moving him toward an increasingly social emphasis in his ministry. The Hartford survey showed that three-fourths of the city's poor immigrants were crowded in an area near Fourth Church. Taylor used the facts gathered to criticize his church and others in the city for their lack of relevance and responsiveness to these populations. In fact, he came to believe that the urban church had a mission to solve the problems of urban-industrial society. Taylor's outreach programs for the urban poor added new, if atypical, church-goers to his congregation; the church debt was paid, and Taylor's reputation as a pioneer in urban ministries was established. His sermons were often messages about social democracy and the new social gospel. Indicative of his efforts to develop an institutional church, he established an inter-denominational Pastors' Mission Project, hired Gillette as its director, involved students from Hartford Theological Seminary, and secured some support from other churches. Outreach programs were developed for alcoholics, gamblers, criminals, and their families. Taylor served as chaplain for the state prison and his interest in former inmates led him to begin a prison follow-up program, causing some to refer to Fourth Church as the "church for ex-convicts" (Henking 1988:298).

In 1888, Taylor was appointed as Professor of Practical Theology at Hartford Theological Seminary where he had been teaching part-time and had involved students in much of the church's outreach work (LDTP: B1, F2). Once appointed full-time to the Seminary faculty, the Fourth Church allowed him to retain his position as pastor by hiring an associate to take on many of his responsibilities. He was also encouraged to use the church as an urban laboratory for his students which he did with compulsory field work. Many other churches in Hartford disapproved of Taylor's dual role and withdrew support of his Mission Project although the Seminary picked up some of the loss. Taylor's professorship brought him more exposure to scholarly writings even though he expressed disappointment at finding no adequate text for training students in Christian field work. He was, however, profoundly influenced by William Fremantle's *The World as the Subject of Redemption* (1882) and a subsequent journal entry reveals his focus on social over individual salvation.

> No less, but not only, is the one soul to be sought and saved, but the world itself. And the world as the divinely constituted order of human life and relationships is to be won back to what it was made and meant to

> be—the Kingdom of the Father. Never again was it to be misinterpreted as wholly evil, fitted for destruction. ... Emancipated from that final fear, which had beclouded the horizon of hope, the shadow was lifted from my teaching. ... Not to 'leave the poor, old stranded wreck and pull for the shore' with one soul at a time, but to be world-savers, Kingdom-builders, I was to teach my students.
>
> as quoted in WADE 1964:44

In his inaugural address at Hartford in 1888, Taylor declared his commitment to the developing science of sociology: "The channel through which life is now sweeping is less individualistic than sociological in its formation." He saw the world as moving toward science and if the church wanted the science to be Christian, "she must formulate a Christian sociology and train her leaders and her people in it" (GTP: B30, F1711). Russ credits Taylor with being the first to introduce the term sociology to the Hartford community when he declared in his inaugural address that "Sociology is the substance of progressive social change according to God's great plan. ... There is to be, if there is not now, a science of Sociology" (1960:84–85).

In 1892, after much agonizing and rejecting an attractive counter offer from the Hartford Seminary, Taylor moved to Chicago to accept an appointment to the faculty of Chicago Theological Seminary where he would head the newly established and first ever, department of Christian Sociology. Ultimately, his decision hinged on Chicago's promise of "unrestricted liberty" and the "call of the West to pioneer on its social frontier" (Taylor [1930]1976:381–382). About his decision, Taylor wrote, "Christian sociology is the door...that can make the remainder of my life more effectual." It was in Chicago that Taylor was to bring to fruition his idea of linking the church and the city through the vehicle of a social settlement. He made acceptance of his faculty position contingent on being able to establish a settlement house, a place to "live and work among the masses of the people, which would serve me and my students with a point of view and actual contact with fellow-men, thus furnishing a clinic for my classroom and a laboratory for me" ([1930]1976:383). It took some two years for Taylor, with the help of several students, to find a building that would accommodate their mission and their residence which they named the Chicago Commons. Taylor remained at the Commons until his death in 1938 although he turned over responsibilities as head to his daughter, Lea, in 1921. Through his writings both in professional and popular venues; through teaching generations of students; as a public speaker; and by service on boards, committees, and other community, state and national organizations Taylor's influence reached into almost every area of social, spiritual, intellectual, and economic life in the city of Chicago and beyond.

Family Life

Taylor was one of the few settlement leaders to move his family into residence and to raise his four children there. Lea Taylor's memoirs suggest awareness of how unusual her family life was as part of the larger family of the Commons. She reflected on how difficult this must have been for her mother but observed that her mother never complained. In fact, daughter, Lea, provides us with some of the little information available about Taylor's wife Leah.

> As I have grown older, I think I have appreciated more and more what my mother must have gone through in this rather exciting life she lived and in which she was the mainstay of all the members of the family. She, like my father, had a background of ministers in the Dutch Reformed Church, was the oldest of a family of seven, and had a good education in a small school in New Brunswick, New Jersey. She was very intelligent, broadminded, keenly interested in people, quiet, responsible, and through all of her life was a firm and calm person. She had an understanding of other people and their problems, but rarely asserted her own ideas unless she was asked. ... She was a great resource to the rather miscellaneous group of residents who had moved into the family circle. ... As I have grown older, I have appreciated more and more mother's contribution to father's work, for she was always available and always interested in everything he was doing. I realize now how much he relied on her judgment in the decisions he was always having to make.
>
> LDTP: B1, F2

Leah Taylor died in 1918; her husband outlived her by some 20 years, in fact remarried in 1921 to a childhood friend and distant cousin who preceded him in death in 1926 (Wade 1964:214).

In many ways, Taylor's life was lived on the economic edge. His daughter states that he never took a salary from the Commons, that his income came from his Seminary teaching and occasionally from writings, lectures and some family bequests (LDTP: B1, F2). The Chicago Commons records indicate, however, that the Commons Board, for the first time in 1918, voted to pay Dr. Taylor $1500 for the upcoming year (CCAR 1916–1924, Trustee Minutes: B19, F5). It is not indicated if this was to be an ongoing salary or a one-time stipend possibly related to loss of a small income he had been receiving from administering the Chicago School of Civics and Philanthropy which was at that time in financial straits and soon to be merged with the University of Chicago. Taylor was constantly raising money for the School and for the Commons and while he took none of this for his own salary or living expenses, he was sometimes assisted personally by benefactors, particularly in paying for travel or vacations. Lea Taylor recalled in her memoirs that her father once apologized for signing a scholarship application for her because he was having difficulty meeting college expenses for two children at the same time (LDTP: B1, F2). Daughter, Lea, a graduate of Vassar, followed her father in working for the Commons after first becoming interested in women's trade unions and attending meetings at Hull House. In 1911, Lea traveled in Europe with her older sister, visiting settlements in France and England, including Toynbee Hall. Upon returning to Chicago, she began assisting her father with administrative work at the Commons while her sister, Helen, lived a more traditional life as the wife of a prominent architect but was also involved in various organizations and social causes in her home near Chicago. The youngest Taylor child was daughter Katherine who graduated and taught at Vassar before becoming director of Harvard's Shady Hill School. The one Taylor son, Graham Romeyn, was Harvard educated in the social sciences and worked both as a researcher and a journalist focusing on urban problems. While employed by the *Survey* he wrote a well-known sociological work, *Satellite Cities* (1915). He worked for the State Department from 1916 to 1918, stationed in Russia. Upon returning to Chicago, he was appointed Executive Secretary for the Chicago Commission on Race Relations and with University of Chicago sociology student Charles Johnson directed an inquiry into the Chicago race riot of 1919 and issued an extensive report, *The Negro in Chicago* (1922).

Taylor the Public Sociologist

Taylor's practice of working outside the traditional boundaries of the church began during his years in Hartford which he credited with training him "both for the religious work...and for the sociological study and teaching" ([1930]1976:366) It was in Hartford that Taylor first proclaimed his belief that "Christian Sociology is the door—wide and effectual—open to me" ([1930]1976:381). It was in Chicago, however, where Taylor walked boldly through this new door of opportunity. He became the city's best known public sociologist and, next to Hull House, the Commons was the best known settlement in Chicago. Taylor was known for his teaching at the Seminary as well as for his teaching of classes for community workers at the Chicago School of Civics and Philanthropy (CSCP) which he founded in 1903 as the Social Science Center for Practical Training in Philanthropic and Social Work (MacLean and Williams 2012). The CSCP was identified with Taylor's name and became well known for its training programs for settlement and charity workers as well as for research directed toward problems and reforms associated with urbanization and industrialization. Taylor was also deeply involved in writing and publishing. He began *The Commons*, a publication that came to represent the settlement movement.[2] He served on a number of committees and boards and chaired the local draft board during World War I. He wrote a weekly column for the *Chicago Daily News* for many years. He helped to organize the National Federation of Settlements and served for a time as its president. He was active in the National Conference of Charities and Correction and served one term as their president. His research, which he saw as necessary to rational planning for the amelioration of urban problems, identified him as a practical or applied sociologist. He was a founding member of the American Sociological Society and published in the *American Journal of Sociology*. In his day he was the target of critics who labeled him as dangerous because of his consistent linking of sociology, Christianity, and social reform. One newspaper editorial identified Taylor as "a prominent socialist, best known for his connection with Chicago Commons," then denounced Taylor's identity as a Christian sociologist by proclaiming, "Christianity is not a system of sociology. It is a method of getting sin pardoned. ... The trouble with a large section of the Christian ministry is that they are trying to substitute sociology for theology" (Taylor 1936:146).

Taylor began as a Christian reformer, but in both Hartford and Chicago he came to recognize the necessity of government intervention in the remediation of social problems. In Chicago he was heavily involved in governmental reform, particularly at the ward level. He served as a member of the Executive Committee of the Legislative Voters League and as a member of the Civic Federation of Independent Voters. He was a member of the Executive Committee of the Municipal Voters League for 33 years. Davis concluded that Chicago Commons was "more successful than Hull House, South End House, or Greenwich House in influencing the politics in their ward," a fact attributed to Taylor. After preliminary and unsuccessful attempts to cooperate with the ward "boss," the settlement men's club managed to defeat him, and then for nearly two decades effectively controlled elections for alderman in the ward. Instead of running an independent candidate the settlement concentrated on getting good candidates nominated from the major parties and supporting them in the electoral process.

> Settlement workers controlled enough votes so that their endorsement was tantamount to election. ... But Taylor alone could not have made his settlement into a successful political machine. He was aided by a group

2 The *Commons* was absorbed by the *Charities*, publication of the Charities Organization Society, in 1905 to become *Charities and the Commons*. In 1909 the name was changed to the *Survey*.

> of young, politically oriented social workers who, unlike the settlement pioneers, consciously sought to make the settlement a base for political reform in the ward and in the city. ... They made surveys, filed reports, checked for voting frauds, organized political rallies and torch parades, distributed posters and handbills. Most important they became acquainted with the people and the politicians....
>
> DAVIS 1964: 507–508

Taylor was the early face of Christian sociology in Chicago and, along with Addams, Lillian Wald of New York, and Robert Woods of Boston, among the best known of the first generation of settlement workers in the United States. Taylor's influence beyond the city of Chicago and state of Illinois is evident in the fact that approximately one-half of the contributions to the Commons came from outside of the Chicago area. Wade reported that by 1914 his financial contributions came from 23 different states (1964:154). He had, of course, established a reputation during his years in New York and in Hartford, but much of his national reputation came from his popularity in the Chautauqua lecture circuit and from the early Chicago Commons School of Economics. The "School" was a series of summer conferences, beginning in 1895, for settlement workers, ministers, teachers, and the public featuring speakers such as social gospelers Washington Gladden and John Graham Brooks, Christian sociologists George Herron and Charles Henderson, and from the settlement movement, Jane Addams and Robert Woods. Taylor also worked diligently to establish university fellowships and internships with schools such as the University of Michigan where Charles H. Cooley sent his students to serve a residency. Fellowships at the Commons were also funded by Auburn Theological Seminary, Rockford College, and the University of Chicago.

Taylor was appointed to the Chicago Vice Commission, "vice" apparently being code for prostitution. Both through his work on this Commission and in his newspaper column, he was influential in closing Chicago's South Side "red light" district, in the public identification of "vice lords," and in passage of the Mann Act (Taylor [1930]1976: 90–91). As a member of the Immigrants' Protective League of Chicago, Taylor participated in research with immigrants, engaged in lobbying to secure protective safeguards for immigrants, and was a frequent speaker and writer on the subject. He was equally well known as a writer and speaker on the topic of labor. He wrote a series of articles for the *Commons* about the rise, development, and significance of the labor movement. He served on the Industrial Commission at both the city and state levels, charged with studying the working conditions of employees and recommending reforms with regard to their health, safety, and comfort. His research and experience provided him with ample data and insight for a course at the seminary on the "Ethics of Industry." Taylor was sometimes called on as a labor arbitrator but would engage in such activity only when invited by both parties. He served on the Illinois Mining Investigation Commission and in 1909 was called on to investigate the Cherry Mine disaster that resulted in almost 300 deaths (Taylor [1930]1976:162–173). He opened up the Commons for weekly "Free Floor" discussions, a safe venue where all sides of disputes, frequently involving labor, could be heard. Taylor was not among those who feared that laborers would develop into a class of anarchists. Indeed on that topic he observed that fear of labor came from those removed from "the field of action" while "those in the thick of the struggle are most optimistic in regard to the mass movements of American labor, most optimistic of its peaceful and evolutionary and triumphant struggle for justice and equity" (1908:770). At the outbreak of World War I, Taylor was appointed to head the local draft board and provided space at Chicago Commons for this work. His daughter, Lea, served voluntarily as secretary. They combined these tasks with sociological research to determine the qualifications of young men, 18–21, in the Chicago Commons ward to serve in the armed forces ([1930]1976:210–211). Taylor supported the war, but only after much agonizing, no doubt intensified because his good friend Jane Addams stood staunchly against the war.

Despite the fact that Taylor sometimes tended toward "oratorical self-dramatization" in his writings and public statements, he is described as radiating "avuncular warmth and infectious optimism" (Carson 1990:94) which seemed little diminished with age and more than three decades of service at Chicago Commons. Taylor's personality, however, did not protect him from public attacks as both he and the settlement movement, by association, became identified with Christian socialism, often undifferentiated from sociology. Two Chicago newspapers, *The Chronicle* and the *Inter-Ocean* were avid opponents of Taylor and other settlement workers. In a series of editorials the papers charged settlement houses with "abetting anarchy" and settlement workers, sociologists, and socialists each "in their respective ways" with "undermining the moral fiber of society." The Commons settlement was singled out as "dedicated to the proposition of Christian socialism." Luckily, the larger and more influential *Chicago Daily News* was a supporter of Taylor and the editor and publisher, a generous supporter of the Chicago Theological Seminary, insured that Taylor's job was not impacted by the negative publicity (Wade 1964:100–101). Taylor himself never wavered in proclaiming the need for sociology and his belief in a social gospel as a necessary path to bringing people together to work on the problems of society which in its ideal form was God's Kingdom.

Taylor, the Social Gospel, and Sociology

In his farewell sermon upon leaving Hartford, Taylor asserted his claim that "the church must supply men with decent homes to be born in before it can hope to have them born again" (Russ 1960:69). For Taylor, religion must change to meet the needs of changing times: "To manifest and transmit the life of God through the lives of men is the problem of religion in this and every age" (1913:94). Taylor's writings and speeches demonstrate his work toward realization of the Kingdom of God on earth, and for him this entailed bringing the church and Christianity as practiced into a sociological context. An example of Taylor's sociological orientation can be found in his address on the occasion of his inauguration as Professor of Christian Sociology in the Chicago Theological Seminary (1893) which he lauded as the "first institution of its kind to have established a department exclusively devoted to Christian sociology." The speech reflects his inseparable social gospel and sociological orientation as he declared that a "Christian science of society should be undertaken as a fundamental service to the Kingdom." He was explicit in his claim that students trained in sociology "for the world work of the Kingdom" would have the advantages of the sociological point of view: of the methods of sociological study, of practical forms of social work, use of the English Bible, and new inspiration for service to society (GTP: B25, F1472). Clearly, Taylor did not separate theoretical or analytical sociology from its methodology or from its application nor any of these ingredients from Christian training and service. He consistently proclaimed "the gospel of the Kingdom is sociology" (GTP: B26, F1515). He elaborated on this theme in an article in the *American Journal of Sociology*: "The gospel of the Kingdom is sociology with God left in it, with Christ as the center of human unity, with the new birth of the individual for the regeneration of society and the indwelling Spirit as the only power adequate to fulfill its social ideals" (1899:309). Taylor summed up his sociology/social gospel: "The acme of sociology is to develop the life of the individual out of a mere self-conscious existence into a personality that shares the life of the whole brotherhood of man and the fatherhood of God" (GTP: B25, F1472). The rapid growth of Christian sociology intermingled with the social gospel is evident in Taylor's compilation of a fourteen-page bibliography, *Books for Beginners in the Study of Christian Sociology and Social Economics* (GTP 1895: B25, F1487) meant to compensate for a dearth of appropriate publications for teaching Christian sociology.

Taylor's greatest contribution to sociology may well be in his early teaching of the subject in seminary settings and at the University of Chicago. In 1928, at the dedication of Chicago Theological Seminary's Graham Taylor Hall, a former student wrote, "Sociology was a new word 20 odd years ago, and you helped to blaze the path that has led your students into confident interpretation of the times now through far seeing conclusions" (GTP: B64, F2560). Interestingly, in perusing the life histories of over 200 sociologists collected by L.L. Bernard, it was faculty identified with the social gospel movement such as Taylor, Shailer Matthews, and Francis Peabody who were most frequently identified as influential teachers (Henking 1988:222). Ewing credits Taylor with turning theological training at the Seminary toward "sociological interpretation." Symbolically he saw Taylor's textbook as "the settlement" and the "final exam" as the transformation of society (1955:4). A 1895 pamphlet from the Seminary laid out the importance of sociology according to Taylor: "The province of the department is defined by that of the sociological sciences. .... Under the term Sociology, society is viewed as a whole, and the scientific observation, classification, relationship and methodical study of social phenomena are taught" (GTP: B64, F2561). Taylor's first syllabus for General Sociology (undated) includes in its bibliography books and journal articles by the likes of Comte, Ward, Small and Vincent, Giddings, and Spencer. Notes from another course simply labeled Sociology appear to focus on Giddings' *Principles of Sociology* (1896) with chapter by chapter notations (GTP: B64, F2555). Taylor's syllabus for Biblical Sociology demonstrates his adherence to social gospel themes: "the Biblical conception of the social ideal [to be sought here on earth] is disclosed in the idea of the Kingdom of God" in the Old Testament and in the life and teachings of Jesus in the New Testament (GTP: B32, F1813). Biblical Sociology was among the first courses taught by Taylor at the Chicago Theological Seminary and one that was a prerequisite for other courses. The syllabus demonstrates Taylor's conceptualization of both the Kingdom of God, as deduced logically from the Bible, and of sociology and the sociological method and its usefulness to achieving the "Kingdom." Taylor understood sociology to be the science of society as it deals with *society considered as a whole*. This definition of sociology seems to predate and to surpass the work of better-known academic sociologists of the day who defined sociology as the study of individuals and were unable to separate it from psychology (Cravens 1971, Schwendinger and Schwendinger 1974:360–362). Further, Taylor saw sociology as a tool to be used to collate and classify social phenomena and relationships and "to apply inductions from these to the development of life, individual and social, in accordance with the Divine Ideal." Taylor's course in Biblical Sociology, taught from his beginning days at Chicago Theological Seminary and before that at Hartford, examined the concept of the Kingdom in the Old and New Testaments and according to the variations of individual writers. In the New Testament, he searched for terms comparable to society, winnowing down to Kingdom and generic references to the Church but then reasoned that Kingdom subsumes or transcends the Church. Ultimately Taylor equated the sociological concept of society with the Biblical concept of Kingdom. His course summation is a conclusion that places him firmly in the social gospel camp: "The kingdoms of this world become the Kingdom of our Lord.... The social ideal is realized in the city of God wherein no temple was seen, for society itself had become the sanctuary, the habitation of God through the Spirit" (GTP: B32, F1813).

For Taylor, the social gospel combined the relationships between man and God and man and man with that of social action, the latter directed by sociology as "the gospel of the kingdom" (GTP: B26, F1515). He further asserted that "sooner or later no one will be recognized as a Christian who does not possess faith in the ethics of Jesus as the rule of practice" (1899:315). Taylor decried *laissez-faire* economics, described as "the lisping of the infancy of economic science." Without qualification, he found any system of industrial or social order "untenable which attempts to incorporate such diametrically opposite ethical standards as that upon which the 'competitive system' is based and the principle of neighbor-love inculcated by Christ" (1899:319). While advising that churches should not be turned into lectureships on economics and politics, he, nevertheless, asserted that the reformers' conscience should claim the "right to audit the books of society" (1899:315). In this context, Taylor positioned social settlements as "incarnating the spirit of Christ in their ministry to the physical and social, educational and civic, moral and spiritual necessities of our city centers, not only saving souls out of the wreck, but also helping to save the wreck itself" (1899:311).

In the 1920s and 1930s, L.L. Bernard solicited autobiographical statements from members of the American Sociological Society, data that have yet to be fully examined (Henking 1992). Taylor sent Bernard a ten-page statement (typed with handwritten notations) the first line of which reads, "My sociological teaching began in 1888 with my unexpected call to the professorship of Practical Theology in the Hartford Theological Seminary." He goes on to explain his personal evolution of "social consciousness" from "very individualistic prepossessions." With regard to his teaching of sociology, he outlined the content of some of his early classes such as Population, Group Life, the Function of the Church, and The Function of the Church in Industry and his search for an appropriate literature when none existed although he went on to include an extensive bibliography of works in which he was able to find relevant materials. He asserted that he based his teaching "upon the psychological bonds of association, rather than upon biological analogies which were more fanciful than factual." He told Bernard that he found the writings of Lester Ward and Franklin Giddings "constructive help" and recommended as collateral reading but not suitable as texts for his classes. Taylor also reported on some of his experiences with "public misapprehensions" about that label sociologist, again recalling that he and his settlement were regularly attacked by two Chicago newspapers. He cited as an example one editorial entitled, "Socialism, Sociology and Crime" apparently alleging a cause and effect relationship between the first two and the latter (GTP: B6, F82). Taylor's biographer surmised that "The classroom experience kept Taylor constantly reevaluating and explaining his own religious convictions. In the process he became an articulate spokesman for social Christianity, an effective propagandist for the social gospel" (Wade 1964: 106). Taylor's social gospel—propounded in the classroom and in his neighborly relations—made it incumbent on every Christian "to care for the life and limb, the livelihood and standard of living, the health, and wellbeing, the growth and the happiness of our fellows" (Taylor 1913:94).

Works by Taylor and Chicago Commons Residents

That Taylor always felt somewhat torn between the academic world of teaching sociology and doing research versus the real world where he saw himself as applying sociology is evident in the following statement from his autobiography.

> Voices called me both ways. Those in front were more familiar to me, as they were to my fellow-teachers and most of my students, since they too were in the privileged minority to which we belonged. From the rear, where were the vast majority of fellow-men, came voices from the great inarticulate multitude—heirs of industrial, political, social, and racial disparities. Cries reverberated from nearby deserts of poverty, wastes of want, and the underworld habitations of cruelty ([1930]1976:5).

This strain of the academic versus the "real" world is evident in Taylor's volume of writings. He was a prolific writer, but mostly for public consumption as opposed to academic or scholarly audiences. He authored three books: the first, *Religion in Social Action* (1913) was a collection of writings or speeches used in his teaching of Christian Sociology; his autobiography, *Pioneering on Social Frontiers* (1930); and a history of *Chicago Commons through Forty Years* (1936). His work appeared only twice in the *American Journal of Sociology*, once as author of "The Social Function of the Church," (1899) and once as a discussant for a paper on class conflict in the US (1908). More typical of Taylor's writings were short articles or speeches published in abundance over the course of his career. His biographer identified 366 publications in outlets as divergent as

The Kingdom, and the *Jewish Tribute and Hebrew Standard*. More typically, his publications were in the *Commons* and later in *The Neighborhood* published from 1928 to 1932 by the National Federation of Settlements. Taylor wrote on topics such as labor, immigration, politics, churches, vice and crime, education, and industry. A thematic analysis of his publications by title reveals that if industry, industrial relations, labor, working conditions, strikes and labor legislation are combined these were the subject of fully twenty percent of his writings. About an equal number of his writings dealt thematically with social Christianity, the social functions of the church, ethics and morality. By comparison, writings on settlements per se comprised only about ten percent of his topics. In publications, Taylor's by-line typically included the Chicago Commons as his affiliation and less frequently the seminary. Indicative of Taylor's longevity and statue in the city, he appeared to deliver, in written and oral form, an inordinate number of eulogies, including that of Jane Addams, and often in more than one venue. In his role as educator, Taylor published, in pamphlet form, lectures and course materials such as syllabi and bibliographies. In his role as citizen and public Christian sociologist, Taylor published a weekly column in the *Chicago Daily News* from 1902 to 1938, as he described it, "from the settlement point of view" ([1930]1976:33). Given his writings and the diverse audiences who must have read them, it is little wonder that for several generations, in Chicago and beyond, Taylor was the face of reform and of Christian sociology. For some, this was inseparable from socialism and he was sometimes attacked for "radical" views and even, along with other settlement workers, with "abetting anarchy" (Wade 1964:100–101). Some of these accusations must have been personally painful because years later, in his autobiography, Taylor included an excerpt from one very public attack, in the *Chicago Chronicle*, calling for his dismissal from the Chicago Theological Seminary (Taylor [1930]1976:402–403).

It appears that Taylor's own sociological investigation was limited but that he was a major figure in initiation, interpretation, and dissemination of work carried out by others, particularly Chicago Commons residents and later staff and students at the Chicago School of Civics and Philanthropy. Taylor referred to the settlement's first ventures into sociological research as "social interpretation" and in this he included the Social Economic Conferences held twice annually between 1895 and 1897, sponsored jointly with Hull House. He explained their work as subsequently progressing into more empirical ventures such as "investigations and surveys...devoted to studies of the changing conditions and movements of population, especially in our own and adjacent wards of the city" (1936:173). In fact, residents carried out annual surveys of demographic and economic changes in the Commons' neighborhood

(CCAR: B23-24, F2). As a member of various local, state, and national organizations that undertook data collection, Taylor was frequently the one to summarize findings, present them publicly, and suggest directives for social policy. In "The Social Evil in Chicago," the official report on prostitution, Taylor wrote, in rather oblique terms, about "a broad survey of the sources and resources of the social evil, its secret and open operations, its relation to drink and narcotics, crime and the police..." ([1930]1976:87). In another venue, Taylor reported that he had made "personal inspection...of vice resorts and interviews with their keepers" (CCP, B24). Taylor, along with a team of researchers, interviewed some 2,400 girls and women, most incarcerated and presumably prostitutes. From these data, the Commission concluded that a majority of the women had entered the trade because of bad home conditions, economic hardships, lack of healthy recreational outlets, or enslavement. The problem, they emphasized, was exacerbated by lack of sex education. The researchers made comparative investigations of cities where prostitution was legal or geographically confined and pronounced these patterns of containment a failure.

Taylor participated in several studies of immigrants, one conducted by the Immigrants' Protective League, one by the National Conference of Charities and Correction (NCCC), and a later one by the National Conference of Social Workers. In a presentation of the NCCC findings, he warned that "invidious comparisons" are being drawn between the earlier and later immigrants. He offered policy suggestions for the "distribution and assimilation of immigrants" and to protect "their persons and property" as well as to "inform and train them for citizenship" (GTP: B27, F1571). This report, as well as a later chapter in his autobiography, provides an astute sociological analysis of immigration laws enacted in the 1920s that became known as the "quota system." He pointed out the difference in public acceptance of "old immigrants" who came to the US from Northern and Western Europe prior to 1900 and "new immigrants" who came from Southern and Eastern Europe after 1900 and before quotas were imposed in 1921. Taylor correctly pointed out that the old immigrants were of the so-called "Nordic" racial stock such as those coming from the British Isles and not unlike "native Americans." After 1900, immigrants of what Taylor termed "Latin and Slavic races" came to dominate in numbers. They were typically perceived as "different" from and less desirable than the Nordic racial stock preferred in the US, a fact that became evident when the new legislation (National Origins Act) assigned large quotas to countries from Northern and Western Europe and small quotas to those from Southern and Eastern Europe ([1930]1976: 203–219).

Another topic in which Taylor combined civic volunteer work with sociological investigation was the sale, distribution, and consumption of alcohol, both before and after passage of the Eighteenth Amendment and the Volstead

Act that ushered in a period of prohibition in the US from 1919 to 1933. One of the early sociological investigations based at the Commons was a study of saloons in Chicago carried out by University of Michigan student and Commons resident, Royal Melendy. The work was published in two parts in the *American Journal of Sociology* (1900, 1901) and was later included in reports issued by the prestigious Committee of Fifty as part of a nation-wide investigation of liquor in the United States.[3] The work clearly depicted the neighborhood saloon as a resource which, if abolished, would leave many unmet needs. Methodology for the research included extensive observations, correspondence, and personal interviews and is still cited as exemplary of early urban ethnography (Mattson 2007:75–94). The functional analysis made clear that the saloon was much more than a place for men to drink. Many saloons were meeting places for neighborhood groups of similar nationality, occupation, or political interest. Their function in the community was little different than that of trade unions, culture clubs, recreational associations, charity and philanthropic agencies, public libraries, social settlements, missions and churches. The report argued that if saloons were closed, the community would have an ethical obligation to provide substitutive community organizations because,

> ...their back rooms and halls provided the only meeting places...for weddings and private parties, club dances, and political meetings...their toilets met a necessity. ... They cashed the pay checks of the wage workers and were places where employment was sought and through which certain employers engaged all their help. In one period of long unemployment, 68 percent of the saloons throughout the city furnished free lunches to anyone whether he patronized the bar or not...homeless, destitute men...were allowed to sleep on the floors.
>
> TAYLOR 1936:176

---

3 The Committee of Fifty had its beginnings in an upper-class, reform oriented organization called the Sociology Group. It was founded in 1889 to study questions relating to major social issues, especially what it termed "labor reform and the government of cities." Over the course of four years it published position papers and analyses of family life, labor, politics, and cities. In 1893, the Sociology Group enlarged its membership and reorganized itself in order to concentrate "on the drink problem in the United States," renaming itself "The Committee of Fifty for the Investigation of the Liquor Problem." It attempted to use contemporary social scientific methods to study the subject and to avoid moralism. The Committee authorized and funded a thorough investigation of "the liquor problem" that was carried out between 1893 and 1903, and subsequently published in five volumes by Houghton Mifflin. For more about this organization and activities related to prohibition see Levine (1983:95–116).

Many settlement workers were more concerned with control of alcohol and/or finding a workable substitute for the neighborhood saloon than they were with prohibition per se. Alcohol was a continuing topic of research for the Commons and for settlements in general. Shortly after prohibition became law, the National Federation of Settlements (NFS) began a longitudinal survey on the impact of prohibition with an emphasis on family life. The NFS questionnaire was divided into three periods: (1) before wartime prohibition and the 18th Amendment, (2) from 1918–1921 when national prohibition was in effect, (3) from 1921 to the time of the survey (1926–1927). Each settlement was to gather data in its own and surrounding neighborhoods. Minutes from some of the meetings of the Chicago survey committee indicate differences of opinion as to how the work should be executed. For example, Jane Addams was interested in collecting human interest stories that would indicate before and after effects, and she suggested Mary McDowell was being "too sociological" because she wanted to collect categorical data, such as by sex and ethnicity. The data collected suggest that both prevailed. The final report to the NFS did include some personal case histories and, as evident in the Chicago Commons records, categorical reports such as by age, ethnic group, and family status (CCAR: B24). This survey became a reality due to the influence of Graham Taylor and other settlement leaders anxious to demonstrate the benefits of the Federation. As part of the NFS study, under the direction of Martha Bruere, survey questions were mailed to almost 100 cities and towns in 41 states. Almost 200 returns were received from settlements and other social service agencies as well as from some private citizens. The survey responses were analyzed and results summarized in *Does Prohibition Work?* (1927). Although findings were mixed, there was some agreement that the impact of prohibition on community and family life was generally positive for at least the first few years. The preponderance of data suggest that with the growth and institutionalization of the illegal production, sale, and distribution of alcohol, community and family problems increased proportionately.[4] Kennedy, writing for the NFS shortly before the end of prohibition, examined several different surveys dealing with the impact of prohibition and concluded that "between 1920 and 1923 prohibition really prohibited." Subsequently the effectiveness of prohibition depended on enforcement and the capital or efficiency of "bootleggers." Kennedy also cited

4 The design of the survey was complex as was the history of prohibition and the pre-prohibition era which really began two years before mandated by the 18th Amendment due to the temporary Wartime Prohibition Act of 1918 designed to save grain for the war effort. Also, some states had enacted state-wide prohibition even before participating in ratification of the 18th Amendment, and thus had been dry for several years.

a decline in public support for prohibition, pointing to the fact that "The wealthy and educated no longer believe that they and their offspring are injured by ingesting small amounts of liquor…" (1933:206–207). Indeed, looking at the recommendations that emerged from the NFS and Committee of Fifty surveys, we see much of what became "liquor policy" in the US today—particularly control and taxation of the manufacture, distribution, and sale of liquor as well as for what has become known as "local option," a policy allowing residents of municipalities, counties, or states to determine by ballot if they want to be "wet" or "dry." On another front, Taylor was responsible for mobilizing the Chicago Federation of Settlements to conduct a survey of Chicago's unemployment problem several years prior to the great depression of the 1930s. Once results of the Chicago work were made public in 1928, the NFS stepped up to conduct a national study as all settlements were finding their resources inadequate to deal with a growing unemployment problem and its ramifications for communities and families. The findings of the national survey were written by Helen Hall of University House in Philadelphia and were solicited for presentation before a subcommittee of the Senate Committee on Commerce considering legislation ultimately embedded in the National Recovery Act and other New Deal legislation (Taylor 1936:179–183).

Chicago Commons' records show that residents were continually canvasing the neighborhood to collect data that could be used to improve quality of life. For example, trend data on registered voters in the ward, complete with bar grams and pie charts, showed a gradual decline between 1902 and 1912 due to an increase in the number of foreign-born. Another study by a resident and student at the Chicago School of Civics and Philanthropy examined employment opportunities for young people ages 14 to 18 when most were leaving school to enter the work force. Many in this group were found to be negatively impacted by new legislation requiring employers to abide by an eight-hour work day for those under age 16. With practical application, this research also included an inventory of businesses and opportunities for employment in the Ward. Another work indicated the settlement's interest in shifting patterns of immigration as researchers examined the characteristics (ethnicity, age, religion) and year of arrival of over 2000 immigrants living in the Commons neighborhood. Before prohibition residents constructed an inventory of neighborhood resources which they labeled "Constructive Agencies" (schools, churches, settlements, playgrounds) and "Destructive Agencies" (saloons, pool rooms, and "greek coffee houses"). Commons residents apparently assisted with and made use of census data. Settlement records, for example, preserved street and block census reports in an area populated by almost 58,000, complete with color-coded and hand-drawn pie charts and graphs constructed from the 1920 census. Most of these records were used to track nationality, citizenship, age, occupation, family size, and type of housing (CCAR: B23, Fs 2–4). Sometime in the late 1920s, a student or students of Ernest Burgess at the University of Chicago did a survey of residents in the Commons area that provided rich qualitative data about the meaning of the settlement for the "neighbors" (CCAR: B23, F9). A Norwegian immigrant recalled putting up "twenty-five dollars for that pool table…[and as being] one of the fellows that made the big clock in the lobby." Another resident credited Taylor with getting the people a park and a school, "We didn't used to have nothin' but a dirty old vacant lot where the Washington School is now." A female Polish resident stated simply, "The settlement does a pretty good business. The people like it." Yet another resident gave Taylor credit for honest elections:

> He [Taylor] sure did a lot of good for the people of Chicago. … There was a time when if we voted for anybody but [name omitted] crowd we would get slugged. Taylor went over to the station before election one time, and said, 'Now I want protection at the polls tomorrow. You can give it to me if you want to. If you don't I'll go to the chief and if he doesn't give it I'll go higher up yet.' He got it and we voted.
>
> CCAR circa 1928, Lower Northwest Side Study: B23, F9

Another Burgess student, Clark Tibbitts, working under the auspices of the Local Community Research Committee at the University, conducted a study of the "social forces and trends" in areas that became the "habitat of the settlements" (Tibbitts 1928).

These are but some of numerous examples of applied sociology that Taylor participated in; however, two works perhaps more than others demonstrate his ability at sociological analysis: an article on the social function of the church (1899) and the other an analysis of the social impact of the industrial revolution (1906a). The latter was a paper delivered at the 1904 Universal Exposition in Saint Louis which drew attendees from throughout the US and much of Europe. Taylor assessed the impact of industrialization as "the most radical transformation through which civilization has ever passed" (1906a:694). His analysis treated industrialization as representing movement from an era of independence to one of interdependence with potentially positive outcomes for individuals, classes, workers, communities, and nations. He discussed such changes as the move from individual contracts to collective bargaining, the changing status of women who as workers outside the home should be able to take their "rightful place of equality" with their husbands, and the move from "racial populations" to "a cosmopolitan composite citizenship" (1906a:682,

686). Taylor's examination of the social function of the church is an equally sophisticated sociological analysis in which he conceptualized an "ideal type" church with formative social functions in a progressive, democratic society. This writing also demonstrates Taylor's proclivity toward pragmatic Christianity as when he declared, "Worship is, therefore, social service of the highest type and the most practical utility" (1899:306).

Taylor and the Chicago School of Civics and Philanthropy

In 1903 Taylor began offering classes for those interested in doing community work such as in the settlements. To differentiate these classes from the Chicago Commons and from his teaching at the Chicago Theological Seminary, Taylor offered them under the auspices of the Social Science Center for Practical Training in Philanthropic and Social Work (MacLean and Williams 2012). The program was launched with a single course on "Dependency and Preventive Agencies" taught by Professor Charles Henderson of the University of Chicago sociology department. University of Chicago President, William Harper became interested in this project and allowed Taylor to list the classes taught as a part of the University's downtown extension program. Harper also suggested the name be changed to the Institute of Social Science and Arts. For the academic year, 1904–05 the Institute opened with 44 registrants and four classes: Industrial Relations taught by Taylor; Dependency and Charities taught by Henderson; Public Charities taught by Julia Lathrop of Hull House; and a series of guest lecturers in an Open Lecture Course. Although Taylor received no money from the University, Harper did provide a nominal stipend from his private funds until his death in 1906 at which time the Chicago Commons assumed responsibility for the Institute, renamed the Chicago Institute of Social Science. By 1907, the number of students had increased to almost 200 and the Russell Sage Foundation financed a Research Department and allocated a training grant of $10,000 for five years. With these funds, Taylor hired Julia Lathrop as supervisor and co-director of the Institute and she in turn hired Sophonisba Breckinridge and Edith Abbott as part-time instructors and researchers (Taylor 1936:154–159). From that time on, most of the research published in conjunction with Chicago Commons came out of this organization.

In 1908 the Institute became incorporated under the new name of the Chicago School of Civics and Philanthropy (CSCP) with Taylor as President and a Board of Directors that included such notables as Jane Addams, Julia Lathrop, and Julius Rosenwald (of the Sears Roebuck business and later the Rosenwald

Fund) as well as several professors. The Charter was approved by the state of Illinois on May 11, 1908, with the stated objective: "to promote, through instruction, training, investigation, the efficiency of civic, philanthropic and social work, and the improvement of living and working conditions." Not only did the Institute and later the CSCP provide classes to train community workers but a Department of Social Investigation conducted research with applied potential. They also did some contract research and produced useful pamphlets such as a *Handbook for Women Voters* (1913), very timely since women in Illinois and several other states had been granted the right to vote and a campaign was underway that would ultimately lead to national enfranchisement. The CSCP also issued *The Charity Visitor: A Handbook for Beginners* (1913). A memorandum summarizing the school's history, accomplishments, and activities makes it clear that the School was engaged in "social investigation" and in teaching both sociology and social work (GTP 1991–1920: B61, F2524). There is substantial evidence of research produced and published under the auspices of the CSCP. One study, that of Chicago housing, demonstrates the quality of the research as well as the involvement of students and other community agencies. The *American Journal of Sociology* published the housing research in a series of ten articles, the first appearing in late 1910 and the last in late 1915. As noted earlier with reference to the University of Chicago Settlement, Breckinridge and Abbott directed this mammoth work and wrote four of the articles. Data were collected by CSCP students who wrote the other reports. A research note explains that data were collected by house-to-house canvasing and from other observations and reports. The data are qualitative and quantitative, making use of maps, tables, charts, and pictures representative of housing in each area. Some of the quantitative data involve violations of housing codes, for example requirements of space per occupant, number of water closets, adequate light and ventilation. Antidotal materials are used to humanize the living conditions, particularly with regard to family life.

After the Russell Sage grants ran out, the CSCP struggled from year to year, dependent on donations that Taylor personally solicited and on students' tuition. Finally, in 1920 it was subsumed by the University of Chicago and became its Graduate School of Social Service Administration. In his autobiography, Taylor reported,

> After eighteen years of steady progress, the Chicago School of Civics and Philanthropy faced the crisis of its success. Its trustees and faculty realized that the weight of its work in meeting country-wide demands for its service could no longer be borne either by the generosity of the few contributors to its financial support or by the loyalty of its students and alumni, whose tuition fees covered a remarkably large proportion of the budget.

> ... Then the feasibility of affiliating the school with a university was considered. The University of Chicago was found to be favorable to the overture. By action of the Boards of Trustees of both institutions in August, 1920, the school was taken over by the University and became its Graduate School of Social Service Administration ([1930]1976: 310).

Despite the mater-of-fact tone of Taylor's record, this transition represented one of the most painful of his career and was resisted until he became convinced there was no other way to save the School. This time period was made even more stressful for Taylor because his wife Leah was ill for a number of months prior to her death in July, 1918. He resigned as President of the CSCP in April, 1918 with a letter to the Trustees and in a separate letter informed Breckinridge of his decision (GTP: B6, F102). Apparently, negotiations with the University of Chicago were initiated and handled by Breckinridge and Abbott, both of whom had ties with the school as graduates and as part-time faculty, before being presented to the Board. Correspondence with the Board, with Abbott and Breckinridge, and with others is civil and reflective of Taylor's benevolent personality. It is understandable, however, that Taylor attempted for possibly too long to hold on to the school and to continue it even without reliable financing. Taylor had begun the School, nurtured it, always with insufficient resources, given generously of his time and energy, and for most of its existence taken no salary for his work. It is understandable also, that he felt some sense of betrayal as Abbott and Breckinridge, in many respects his protégées, had wrestled the school from his control and handed it over to the University of Chicago (MacLean and Williams 2012). Negotiations over the location and future mission of the CSCP represent a clash between generations and in some respects a clash between settlement sociology as represented by Taylor and the training and professionalization of social workers on the part of Breckinridge and Abbott. Taylor's biographer did an excellent job of piecing together all sides of this very complex and protracted situation which reverberated into the future of both sociology and social work (see Wade 1964:161–185, MacLean and Williams 2012). Taylor's correspondence in later years, long after the CSCP was institutionalized as part of graduate education at the University of Chicago, reflects a collegial and sometimes cordial relationship with both Abbott and Breckinridge.

Contributions to Sociology

Although few today associate Taylor's name with sociology's founding or its early history, he was recognized as a sociologist in his day and accepted the good and the bad that went with that label. There is considerable evidence that men in the University of Chicago sociology department knew and accepted Taylor as a fellow sociologist. Not only did he have a close working relationship with Charles Henderson, in fact, delivered one of the eulogies at his funeral, but he was also associated with Albion Small and later with Ernest Burgess. Small was Chair of the department of sociology when Taylor held a joint appointment there between 1902 and 1906. During that time, Small invited him to give one of the presentations for the International Congress of Arts and Science, part of the Saint Louis Exposition of 1904, for which Small was a vice president (AWSP: B1, Fs 2–13). Another interesting documentation of Taylor's identification as a sociologist is found in letters from Ernest Burgess, at the time a young professor at the University of Chicago. In early 1927, Burgess wrote to thank Taylor for sending him a copy of a speech he made on the occasion of ground-breaking for the Graham Taylor Assembly Hall. Burgess wrote of the speech, "I shall wish to keep it both because of its historical value in relation to the origins of sociology in this country and because of the insight that it gives into the social and civic movements of Chicago to which you have contributed so distinctly" (GTP, letter dated 4 March, 1927: B12, F580). In this speech, Taylor attempted to establish his place in the history of sociology vis-à-vis the University of Chicago as well as to indicate that seminary teaching of "sociology" had been reduced in scope as academic sociology had grown since his inauguration as Professor of Christian sociology at the Seminary in 1892.

> Professor Albion W. Small opened the first university department of sociology here at Chicago the very same month in which my courses at the Seminary were offered. And through all the years of his pioneering teaching and authorship, I shared his fraternal fellowship until his recent death as I did the ever helpful friendship of the late Professor Charles R. Henderson. The Seminary is greatly advantaged now by close co-operation with the Sociology Department of the University of Chicago, which frees my successor from covering in outline the more diversified scope of my teaching, and allows him to concentrate his instruction within the bounds now properly designated as "Social Ethics."
>
> GTP 1927:B64, F2559

In another letter, later in the same year, Burgess commented on his review of Taylor's manuscript on the history of the Chicago Commons.

> ...you might quite properly stress the contribution of the settlement and settlement workers, not only in calling attention to social problems, but

> in providing concrete materials on family and neighborhood life from their own intimate experience. The recent trends in sociology seem to me to be following up the types of observations and studies which settlement residents instituted.
>
> GTP: B12, F580

In addition to the teaching and dissemination of sociology, Taylor made contributions to urban sociology, especially in his use of social surveys to identify and ameliorate problems and to the dissemination of Christian sociology in churches and in institutions of higher education. Taylor wrote few lengthy pieces of sociological research as we know it today, but he was among the most prolific writers of a public sociology. His sociological observations, perspectives, and research findings (his own and those of Chicago Commons or CSCP researchers) frequently appeared in settlement publications. The *Commons*, for example, regularly disseminated facts about urban life gleaned from settlement surveys and observations, thus creating in the minds of its readers a reciprocal link between the settlement movement and the new science of sociology. With Taylor's initiative, The *Commons* began monthly publication in 1896 under the editorship of John Gavit, a social gospeler, who later went on to become a well-known journalist. While published by the Chicago Commons for nine years, The *Commons* came to represent the voice of all Chicago settlements and, unofficially, the settlement movement in general with circulation growing to some 4000 (Taylor 1936:163). Contributors to this publication were not only settlement workers and social gospelers but also academics such as Charles H. Cooley, Richard Ely, and Charles Henderson. For years Taylor wrote a column for the *Commons*, "From Sociological Classrooms," used to describe new research, books, or classes related to sociology. Taylor's voice also found public and diverse audiences in his weekly column in the *Chicago Daily News* for over 30 years.

Taylor's work was as theoretical as that of some of his peers in early sociology. His teaching espoused an early version of grounded theory with action serving as the data antecedent to theory. In a course syllabus for Introduction to the Study of Social and Philanthropic Work which Taylor taught with Charles Henderson, he stated that theory did not begin until the work of Auguste Comte. This "late development" was, according to Taylor and Henderson, "accounted for by the fact that theory awaited accumulation of fact." Taylor's explanation of the development of theory included what is typically identified as the "ideal type," for example, in the work of Max Weber (not yet translated into English). According to Taylor, people "acted socially before they thought it." Thus the development of theory was gradual and based on tested action in a process that began with use of an "ideal," then a test of methods of action, followed by making whatever modifications were needed and finally with the "coordination of principles with each other and with life" (GTP: B62, F2532). Much of Taylor's work was devoted to the development of a theoretical framework that united theology and sociology with an explanation of the institutional roles uniting the two (Taylor 1913, Ewing 1955: 68). Taylor organized his theory by initially analyzing personality and social structure. As for personality, Taylor saw every human life as "a social product, produced by the co-operation of many other lives" (1913:2). Sounding much like George H. Mead, a contemporary of Taylor at the University of Chicago, Taylor thought that consciousness of self was formed and developed as the individual becomes conscious of other selves in the social world ([1930] 1976:339). For Taylor both individuality and community were key to the development of full humanity. Taylor's examination of social structure was largely in terms of the roles and relationships within the "life-spheres" of family, neighborhood, economics, politics, and religion. Beyond personality and social structure, Taylor turned his attention to explaining the forces and aims of Christianity. Life and religion were one and the same for Taylor: "the relationship which each one of us actually has to God as Father, and to fellow men as brothers" (1913:87). Taylor's theory indicates a transition from his early Dutch Reform roots and the focus on saving souls to a redefinition of saving souls by loving and caring for them in a social sense as in taking action in order to create a healthy, safe, and enabling environment. For Taylor, the proverbial Christian "calling" came to be a call of people to action—to usefulness (1913:65). Such action, however, must be predicated on facts and understanding and this, of course, required sociology. Taylor once proclaimed that "only in our own times have religious and social ideals been held close enough to earth to be applicable to the local community" (1913:238). Sociology was, in fact, the tool that put these "ideals" to work in alleviating the problems of the local community, "to manifest and transmit the life of God through the lives of men" (1913:94). As Taylor saw it, the adjustment of the church and the forces of religion to the scientific forces of sociology were "necessary both to the winning of the soul and the coming of the kingdom" ([1930]1976:388).

The records of Taylor's life leave little doubt that he was publicly identified and self-identified as a sociologist, more specifically as a Christian sociologist which no doubt accounts for his absence from the history of the discipline today even though he maintained a perspective more sociological than that of some of his academic peers. Despite the substantial evidence that Taylor both thought of himself and was thought of by others as a sociologist, he was not granted a place in the history of the discipline, and there are some suggestions that he felt slighted by this omission. For example, an address by president John Gillin of the American Sociological Society in 1926 on the development of sociology in the United States carried a note when it went to press that read, "Since this was put in type Professor Graham Taylor tells me that about the same time [as Small began at Chicago], he became the first teacher of sociology in a Theological Seminary" (Gillin 1927:2). Taylor obviously felt that he had helped to pioneer the discipline and was not given his just recognition. He wrote in his autobiography, as if to set the record straight, "I began to teach the very same month in 1893 that Professor Albion W. Small entered upon his pioneering undertaking at the University of Chicago" ([1930]1976:4). Taylor's biographer declared that his ultimate goal as a professor was "to teach the new science of Christian Sociology" for which his early role models were Francis Peabody at Harvard and William Tucker at Andover Seminary (Wade 1964:42). Unfortunately, Taylor's omission from sociology has been repeated to the present even though he described his life as tied together at both ends by sociology—beginning his academic career by teaching the first sociology courses at Hartford and ending his career teaching sociology at Chicago Theology Seminary ([1930]1976:385). Taylor's erasure from sociology was not only because of his identity with the social gospel and with social reform, but also because he offered the first classes for "social workers" through a quasi-extension program with the University of Chicago that ultimately paved the way for the Graduate School of Social Service Administration (Williams and MacLean 2012). Graham Taylor had many publics: neighbors, students, fellow citizens, academic colleagues, settlement colleagues, and fellow social gospelers. He lived and worked as a sociological Christian, a role and identity rejected as the discipline struggled to gain identity as a science.

CHAPTER 6

Boston's South End House: A Sociological Laboratory

Andover House, named for the seminary, opened in Boston's South End in 1892, the sixth settlement in the United States and the first in that city. Its stated objectives: to be a center of learning for students; to be a good neighbor to the people, to churches and other organizations in the neighborhood; to serve as "a medium between different social elements of the city" and "to advance in general the cause of Social Christianity" (SEHR, Articles of Association, Circular No. 3, Reports: F53). The name was changed to South End House (SEH) in 1895 to divest the settlement of any perceived religious affiliation. It was once described as a "University for the Overlooked" (Brooks 1925:732), and the South End, as an area where "good citizens literally or figuratively hurried by it and strove to forget it" (Woods 1929:354). Robert Woods spent more than three decades as head resident and over the years the settlement became synonymous with his name and was very much the product of his training, preparation, and formative influences, many directly related to the social gospel. The settlement was first named for the seminary from which Woods was graduated and the Andover Association provided initial support and direction in the person of Dr. William Tucker, Woods' mentor. For Tucker and other social gospelers, the settlement was a form of Christian pragmatism and the best manifestation and use of the Christian personality (Carson 1990:56). According to Tucker, an integral part of Christian pragmatism was "social investigation" and while the settlement's motive was religious, its method was to be educational. Eleanor Woods wrote of this "education,"

> It was clear enough that this new type of education was needed by no one class of people, but was a requirement for the direction of the social consciousness of every condition of society. ...The plan which Dr. Tucker and Mr. Woods undertook...was to let themselves be taught, however it might come, what society needed to learn for bringing the poorest of its members up to the level of a reasonable existence, and for giving strength and energy to life among all the less favored. Upon such knowledge they were to lay foundations for social education both as to aim and technique (1929:46).

Boston's South End is a peninsula, at the time cut off from the main section of the city by a long arm of the Boston Harbor over which stretched three bridges.

Robert Woods described the South End as a community of some "40,000 souls." His wife, Eleanor, described it as,

> A vicious circle of tuberculosis and drunkenness centered in miserable houses built of wood, and undermined the health and integrity of the young. There was scarcely any recreational resource. The multiple assortment of drinking-places, the sordidness of the lower section of the district extending out to desolate unbuilt flats along the harbor, gave to the task of 'scientific charity' a hopeless setting, with no hand held out to do more than the day's work in relieving acute need (1929:146).

Woods and three other young men took up residence at 6 Rollins Street in 1892. Unlike other settlements located in the very heart of slums, Andover House was located on a "quiet byway" but not far from one of Boston's most "troublous centers." The settlement house, "a swell-front red brick" of "mid-nineteenth century respectability" was near but not in the slum. The settlement was, however, at a crossroad location because of nearby Dover and Washington Streets, "Mecca of drifting fragmentary humanity." The area was a strategic hub of transportation for people from commercial and industrial quarters of the city; a residential area for industrial workers; home of bars, cheap eating places, and entertainment of questionable reputation on the periphery of the theater district. "It was into a world of complicated activity that Robert Woods turned as he swung the corner of Rollins Street with its misleading appearance of quietude" (Woods 1929:48). The settlement occupied just one building until 1895 when a Club and Class Center was added. There were no female residents until 1900 when the first Women's Residence was opened, then a second in 1906. For several years South End House also maintained buildings that housed work among the black population. In 1908 these activities were spun off to become the independent Robert Gould Shaw House (Woods and Kennedy [1911] 1970:128). Eleanor Woods wrote that at the 30th anniversary of South End House the settlement occupied ten city lots in six different Boston locations and four summer vacation residents for children. Such expansion and decentralization was part of her husband's pragmatic belief that "flexible manifold adaptation" was required of settlements (Woods 1929:299). In time, there were as many as 30 persons in residence at South End House. Woods was careful and methodical in the selection of residents, aiming for diverse interests while resisting specific assignments. According to his wife, Woods allowed residents to pursue their own ideas, to follow their own causes as long as they did not go "too far afield" and as long as their activities contributed to the "fabric of public spirit" (1929:230). Woods' early correspondence with Dr. Tucker reported that residents were allowed "all the scope they could wish" and that each man was to "manage his own work from the beginning" (SEHR nd, letter from RA Woods to William Tucker:F18). While encouraging residents to follow their own interests, whether in doing social investigation or initiating youth activities, Woods held them accountable as "trustees of the house" with reminders that they were engaged in "a social experiment of vast importance" and it was "essential not to jeopardize it by taking...extreme positions. Thereby one weakens the emphasis on the main undertaking" (Woods 1929:224). His philosophy: "The settlement is a group of experts...living intimately together constantly stirring each other to fresh interest by the result of new information and discovery" ([1923]1970:43). Research conducted by residents is evidence that they did follow their own interests, studying diverse problems in the city and beyond. Woods was the first among settlement pioneers to formalize the concept of the settlement as a laboratory for sociological study of neighborhoods and communities for purposes of social reform and the alleviation of social problems ([1893]1970). From the founding of SEH, until Woods' death in 1925, significant studies were carried out by the residents. Today, as with other settlements, South End House has become a community services center, still in its old neighborhood but part of a consortium of United South End Settlements (uses.org).

Robert A. Woods, His Wife, and Associates

Woods: The Man and His Calling

The only complete biography of Woods (1865–1925) was written by his wife, Eleanor Bush Woods, after his death. In describing his philosophical, theological, and ideological roots, she drew heavily on Woods letters, speeches, and writings all of which suggest influences from the social gospel. By her account, Woods, the fourth of five children, was born in 1865 near Pittsburgh of Scotch-Irish immigrant parents. His father was a successful small businessman in Pittsburgh and an active leader in the Presbyterian Church although having Episcopalian roots. In high school, Woods was remembered as a serious but happy young man, optimistic, and an arbiter among his peers. His father died when he was 15 and a year later Robert, along with four classmates, entered Amherst College near Boston. His initial impression of the College was that it provided a culture "unafraid of either science or religion" (Woods 1929:8). In some of his letters, Woods lamented the limited interaction with Amherst faculty; yet, he obviously found an intellectual home there. He apparently drew early inspiration from Amherst President Seelye who declared frequently that "no career could be of higher service to the nation than that of the educated man who should go among the people and in largeness of mind and heart join with them in working out the labor problem" (Woods 1929:13). Woods noted also that philosophy Professor Charles Garman helped students to reconcile the new scientific thought with the religious thought of the past. As Woods saw it, "the old philosophy of individualism was eliminated and the new teaching of the organic unity of mankind developed" (Woods 1929:14). At Amherst, Woods heard lectures by social gospelers such as Lyman Abbott and Washington Gladden and by progressive theologians such as Francis Peabody of Harvard and William Tucker of Andover Seminary; all talked of preparing a way for better men in a better society. While not planning to enter the ministry, nevertheless, Woods and several of his Amherst classmates decided on further study at Andover Seminary where Tucker was known to be "blazing new trails" with his knowledge and teaching about city problems (Woods 1929:17). The teachings of Tucker, for example, included the works of such controversial scholars as Henry George and Karl Marx. Tucker himself taught that "distribution and not redistribution of wealth was the central economic issue, and that charity was no substitute for economic justice" (Carson 1990:29). Upon arriving at Andover, Woods wrote that he and his fellow "Amherst men" had already made a transition in their thinking not reversed by the "heresy trial" of several Andover faculty which began shortly after their arrival. Woods recalled that his admiration of these men—whose only offense was that they were too "progressive" in their thinking—was intensified after attending the first day of the trial. He wrote that he was "more than ever impressed with the depth of soul of Professor Smyth [one of the defendants]", described as "the seer of the new Theology" (Woods 1929:20). How Woods perceived the role of Dr. Tucker in the education of future generations is captured in his biography as well:

> Dr. Tucker had gone to the Seminary to aid the next generation of men entering the ministry in meeting the moral questions of modern life, in adjusting the teachings of Christianity to a world confused by the issues of industrial problems. A previous generation 'saw the religious peril of materialism, but not the religious opportunity for the humanizing of material forces.' 'The fundamental idea [of the Church] was still that of charity, and the whole trend of events was showing the insufficiency of the idea for social reform and advance. The greatest social grievance came from those who, if in need of charity, did not want it—the vast army of unskilled labor. Their grievance...changed the whole problem from that of charity to that of economic justice'.
>
> WOODS 1929:25–26

It was Tucker who introduced Woods to the problems of laborers and to the labor movement, an interest that was to serve him well in settlement work. In fact, it was a course taken with Tucker that sent Woods to New York to learn from interviews with labor leaders something of their attitudes toward socialism, a topic he then reported on in the Seminary *Bulletin* (Woods 1929:26). Perhaps it was this early field work and later observations in London that shaped Woods life-long preference for facts over dogma. As Woods saw it, Tucker encouraged a "benign and heterodox socialism," an influence that shaped Woods' philosophy that all of social life was interconnected, a perspective he carried throughout his career.

Woods was clearly drawn intellectually to the "new theology" and even to thoughts of Christian utopian communities (Woods 1929:18). At Andover, from 1886 to 1890, he was surrounded by other males who were planning to enter the ministry, and he apparently tried but failed to receive a "calling." Consequently, he spent his last two years at Andover in something of a state of depression, a period of self-doubt, and a search for purpose as his life lacked future direction.[1] Woods delivered some sermons as a lay minister but leaned toward a career in Christian journalism, having been a correspondent for the *Christian Union* and published several articles in the *Andover Review*. He wrote to his mother of his interest in securing a newspaper position and that Dr. Tucker recommended he seek a position with a secular paper that would allow him to report on religious happenings. "If I had such a position I could be of help to every sort of good work going on…and perhaps introduce some new schemes" (Woods 1929:24). His writing did not lead to a job after graduation as he had hoped, and his time of seeking direction apparently ended with the conclusion: "The object of the individual life…is to work out its possibilities. But each race unit has currents of its life out into its immediate environment, into all the race, and into all the universe. All a man's powers then are simply potentialities of relationship" (Woods 1929:32). It was Professor Tucker who helped Woods to work out his "potentialities" by selecting him to head up Andover's planned settlement house in Boston after an internship at Toynbee Hall.

Apart from the social problems and issues of the day, Woods was always drawn to the classics in literature (he wrote poetry) and to understanding the "character" of individuals with whom he came in contact. His wife wrote that understanding facts about people's lives and his own reaction to others were among his primary interests and an integral part of what he perceived

1 A period of personal floundering, a search for direction was reported by some of the best-known settlement founders, such as Jane Addams and Vida Scudder, prior to their becoming invested in the settlement movement.

as his Christian "calling." Integral to the calling was "enthusiasm of humanity" and a reflection of "the spirit of God in the material universe" (Woods 1929: 21–22). Wood's interest in the character study of people seems in contrast with some descriptions of him as aloof and reserved, lacking in personal warmth and charisma. One writer, observing Woods in the company of Jane Addams remarked, "The impersonal Woods was the loser in her comparison." Alice Hamilton wrote to a friend, "Mr. Woods...has the highest ideals and very clear rational convictions, but he has no warmth, no human impulsiveness and personal interest in his attitudes toward people" (Hamilton family papers as quoted in Carson 1990:94). Despite such perceptions, Woods was an effective settlement worker and was highly respected in all of Boston, and, toward the end of his career, on the national scene. Woods' neighbors came to love and accept him, as one wrote: "when Mr. Woods kept staying on and we got used to having him going through the streets and seeing him so often, we got to think that he belonged to us" (Woods 1929:55). Offering a eulogy at Woods' funeral, John Graham Brooks, labor activist and writer, told the story of a "half bantering dispute over the meaning of the word gentleman" among a group of social workers who ended the discussion with the suggestion, "why not take Robert Woods for the definition, and let it go at that?" (SEHR:B1, F82).

In preparation for his beginning the work of a settlement, in 1890 Woods spent six months in England under the sponsorship of Professor Tucker. He learned first-hand of the work of the Barnetts at Toynbee Hall and of Booth's poverty research. His time in England brought him into contact with other students as well as Christian socialists and Fabians. In fact, he expressed his appreciation for the work and thinking of Fabians such as Vaughn Nash, William Clarke, and Graham Wallas whose ideas were not new to him. As a student at Andover he had declared himself an "unswerving disciple of John Ruskin" (Woods 1929:39). Even with these influences, however, Woods never completely gave up theological orthodoxy, but instead mixed it with the philosophy of Christian Socialism. For example, he wrote to an English correspondent shortly before he assumed his post at Andover House,

> I hardly think I could say the Apostles' Creed if I denied the virgin birth, though I know some wise and conscientious men are perfectly honest in doing so. I am rather glad they can do so. ...I am doing everything I can to get fellows who deny miracles to stay in the Congregational ministry. ... The Congregational churches must be made broad enough to admit all Christians.
>
> WOODS 1929:42

In his person Woods was a mild-mannered man who was uncomfortable with authority. When he assumed duties as head of Andover House, he was only 26 years of age. Thus it is understandable that he often wrote to Professor Tucker (his board chairman) about problems with the housekeeping staff, with whom there was considerable turnover at first, and with some of the residents. For example, in his early months he attempted to institute daily mandatory prayers for residents and staff which, as he wrote Tucker, he thought "essential to a moral and spiritual unity...not a thing that I could submit to a ballot" (SEHR February 12, 1892, letter from Woods to Tucker:F18). Several residents rebelled, resulting in prayers being made voluntary, often with only the maids attending. At common meals at the House, Woods insisted on "Grace before Meat" but was not, according to his wife, a regular church goer although he was always ready to assist his church. Woods on various occasions expressed disappointment in local churches for failing the populations they should be serving, and he often admonished them to get out into the real world with the people and not wait for the people to come to them. Local churches, he thought, rarely rose to the challenges of their immigrant neighbors. Pragmatically, Woods recognized that the future of Christianity depended on its ability to change the dominate forces of business and politics (Woods 1929:274–275).

Robert Woods was an unlikely reformer. Although he was the consummate advocate for immigrants and the poor working people served by South End House, he was never one of them. Described by his associates as always immaculately dressed and giving off the "impression of ministerial aloofness" he, nevertheless, wanted neighboring immigrants and laborers to accept him as one of their own, knowing full well that they did not. In fact, in a letter to Anna Dawes of the International Congress of Charities and Corrections, he expressed ambivalence about the success of the neighborly relations model while mindful of its importance.

> The relation between the settlements and their neighbors is an artificial one. I don't know that it can ever be otherwise. Dr. Coit, Miss Addams, and Miss Scudder all think that this difficulty can and will be remedied by having settlements of families in working class quarters. This I do not believe. I think it is far harder to make the family democratic in its outward attitude than it is to make the individual so. There are also certain dangers in the experiment with the family which seem to me too great to be risked. Yet I am quite ready to believe that people in general will become tired of being shut in with a single class in society; so tired that they may seek some unmistakable way to escape. What a blessing it would be to Fifth Avenue to have a settlement of mechanics.
>
> SEHR DECEMBER 20, 1893: B1, F18

While not of the working class, and never altogether comfortable with them, Woods admired laborers and early in his career came to perceive them as a force capable of bringing about a universal brotherhood. He wanted to give reality to the American promise of equal opportunity. He saw human waste in the uncultivated abilities of workers and young people and saw settlements as part of a network of churches, schools and other social organizations that would assimilate workers and their families into the fabric of America. He worried that the most capable workers of ethnic identity were moving up and out of their original neighborhoods and that those remaining fell somewhere between an aristocracy of labor and a dependent class. For these he thought the settlements must foster human associations such as neighborhood improvement groups, schools, and labor unions (Woods [1903]1970:356–383).

Eleanor Bush Woods

Woods' letters reveal some of the sexism of his generation when he admitted to his future wife, "Men are savages. They don't really respect women's minds. I don't think I even...respected a woman's mind until my mind touched yours" (Woods 1929:153). In another letter prior to marriage, Woods wrote that he always expected to be married but "I didn't expect to find such comradeship in a woman" (Woods 1929:158). Eleanor Bush, as the future Mrs. Woods, had much to bring to settlement work. She was a Smith College graduate who had completed a year of graduate work at Radcliffe. She had some training in social work and had been employed for four years prior to her marriage with the Associated Charities of Boston. She met Woods as a result of her work; she explained, "I had been transferred to South Boston to bring the work of the Associated Charities there up to the new standards" (Woods 1929:146). The letters Woods wrote to Eleanor before their marriage make it clear that he did not intend her to become directly involved in the work of the South End House. In fact, one of his letters is explicit that she would not have to live at the settlement because he had found a small house nearby. These letters suggest that Woods expected Eleanor to be a traditional wife and to keep a home that would provide him with a respite from the outside world, even mentioning in one letter that she might keep his appointments, allowing him maximum flexibility, and on another occasion asking her to promise never to be on a committee (Woods 1929:164, 157). There are indications, however, that Mrs. Woods continued her interest in social work. Davis reports, for example, that Eleanor Woods was on the committee that organized the first State Conference of Charities in Massachusetts in 1903, shortly after her marriage (1984:21–22). By Mrs. Woods' own account, her husband increasingly came to include her in the work of the South End House.

> In spite of his hope that I would keep myself free from many engagements, it was Mr. Woods himself who began first to make special claims for 'the work' upon my time. There was always more than enough to be done. ...We soon came to see that I, too, should have some very definite identification of my own with the people of the district. Mr. Woods gave me an assignment to the new venture in the lodging-house district, then far more a city wilderness than any tenement-house section.
>
> WOODS 1929:180–181

Upon their marriage in 1902, the newlyweds moved into a small house near the settlement which, over time, became part of the South End House complex. At one point when Woods was away on one of his many trips, Eleanor must have written (letter not available) asking his opinion of her involvement in the suffrage movement locally. His response suggests awareness that his wife needed her own cause although he ended with a cautionary note.

> As to municipal suffrage for women I want you to do just what you think is right. Of course at times we have to consider the general interests of the Kingdom before taking marked steps in some new direction. But I don't see anything to interfere with your supporting this movement on practical grounds. I would not be pushed into a position of leadership where you would have to bear the responsibility for what others say and do.
>
> WOODS 1929:234

There is no indication in Mrs. Woods' writing as to whether she did become involved in the suffrage movement in Boston although much of her work was focused on women's issues. It is evident that over time Woods made his wife a partner in South End House activities and that she established her own reputation in Boston where she served on the Board of Associated Charities, founded the South End Women's Club, and was an active member of Boston's Federation of Women's Clubs. She was also involved with local schools and with a study of the conditions of female office workers in Boston, an involvement that led her to establish the first Business Women's Club in the US (Woods 1929:278; USESR February 15, 1957, Eleanor Woods news obituary: B2, F29). One of her most important projects culminated in the licensing and registration of rooming and lodging houses in the city. There were over 2,000 lodging houses in Boston, many in the South End, and little if any regulation. Following a study by resident, A.B. Wolfe that identified the needs and problems of the lodging house population, another resident was assigned the task of doing the preparatory work for lodging house regulation and registration. Dissatisfied with the resident's work, Mrs. Woods took over the project and recommended that the resident be "set free" of her responsibilities and of her salary (SEHR nd, The Room Registry: F58). In the South End House Annual report in 1905, Ms. Woods wrote about the opening of a lodging house especially for women and also about beginning efforts for a lodging house registry (SEHR, 13th Annual Report: F80). She subsequently worked to secure standards and regulations for the city as a whole (SEHR 1912–1918, Lodging House Registry Project: F58). Indeed, Eleanor Woods became associated closely with the reform and regulation of lodging houses and wrote several articles on this topic, one in the *Survey* (1907). She also coordinated and wrote a *Report on Unemployment among Boston Women in 1915* (1916) for the National Civic Federation Woman's Department. The Woods had no children which may account for the fact that over the years she became an integral part of settlement work and is listed in a 1917 report as General Co-operating Director, a position she held until her husband's death. Woods died in 1925 at the relatively young age of 59 of heart failure, a problem that apparently became known only shortly before his death. Eleanor remained at South End House for several years, working with her husband's papers to write his biography. She then moved to Los Angles and headed a settlement there where she is reported to have done "an outstanding piece of work in a predominantly Mexican community" (USESR February 15, 1957, Obituary: B1, F85). She returned to South End House in 1945 where she remained until shortly before her death in 1957 when poor health took her to live with family in her home town of Concord.

South End House Associates

Woods maintained a busy schedule as he always served on several civic committees simultaneously, was frequently called upon for speeches or presentations about the work of the settlement, was active in federated settlement activities, at first in the city and then nationally, and was a regular lecturer at Andover Seminary, Antioch College, and Harvard. For the day-to-day working of the settlement, he must have relied heavily on trusted associates. For example, William Cole, like Woods a graduate of Andover, remained in residence from 1894 to 1913, leaving to chair the newly created department of Sociology at Wheaton College. John Whitman spent many years at South End working with boys clubs and other organizations; Ester Barrows served as head of the Women's Residence for more than 20 years; and Mary Strong served for more than a decade as the settlement nurse (Woods 1929:222). A number of residents came to South End House as recipients of fellowships from over a dozen institutions, the largest number coming from Harvard and Amherst with women's colleges such as Smith, Simmons, and Radcliffe contributing to the fellows once a women's residence was added. No doubt, Woods' closest associate over the years was Albert Kennedy (1879–1968), a social gospel minister who became Director of Investigations, Associate Head Resident and, after Woods death, Head Resident. Woods coauthored four books with Kennedy who was born in Rosenhayan, New Jersey and graduated from Marion Collegiate Institute in New York, then attended the University of Rochester where he earned a bachelor's degree in 1904. It was his Rochester study that exposed Kennedy to the social gospel through the teachings of Walter Rauschenbush. After seminary, Kennedy served one year as a pastor in Minnesota then began study at Harvard from which he received a theology degree in 1907. He was in residence at South End House for several years before being appointed Director of Investigation in 1908 and six years later as Woods' associate. Kennedy lived at SEH for 17 years and was among the few settlement workers to raise a family while in residence. He and Woods were instrumental in the founding of the National Federation of Settlements with Woods being the first executive secretary, a post he held until 1923 when he became president and was succeeded by Kennedy as secretary. After Woods' death, Kennedy served three years as Head Resident of SEH then left to accept the position of head resident at University Settlement in New York. Kennedy remained in New York until he retired in 1944 but in later years became something of a controversial figure in settlement work because of a divorce and because he came to emphasize the cultural aspects of settlements over their reform work. He promoted the visual and performing arts and became a strong proponent of cultural pluralism (Barbuto 1999:113–114, Warner 1969:4).

Since several of Woods' books based on settlement data were coauthored with Albert Kennedy, it is difficult to know their division of labor. There are some clues, however, that Kennedy's contribution was more in collection of data than in the written product. This is borne out by the fact that their last work, *The Zone of Emergence*, remained unpublished after Wood's death because it lacked his final editing although the data had been collected and drafts of most chapters completed. Kennedy's first paid appointment at SEH as Director of Investigations suggests that his primary responsibility was the collection and perhaps analysis of data and that it was Woods who did the editing and writing for publication. This can be surmised from Eleanor Woods' statement that her husband spent some ten years on the final preparation of *The Settlement Horizon* although it is coauthored with Kennedy. While Trolander acknowledges that little is known about the working relationship of Woods and Kennedy, she concludes, "The publication patterns of the two authors illustrate that Woods was, by far, the more capable writer" (1990:xii). Woods, however, did not use his position to affix his name as author or coauthor of every publication associated with the South End House. His belief was that the personality of one person "should not overshadow the rest" ([1923]1970:24).

Woods and Academic Relations

Woods closest academic ties were with his two Alma Maters, Amherst College and Andover Seminary, the latter because of his long relationship with Professor Tucker who chaired the Andover Foundation Board and remained a Board member of South End House even after Woods' death. In 1908, Andover Seminary returned to its original Harvard affiliation and to the Cambridge campus and was located there at the time of Woods' death. The Andover-Harvard history no doubt accounts for the fact that Woods developed strong ties with the University that in 1910 awarded him an honorary degree. He served as Director of Student Volunteer Work at Harvard for several years beginning in 1900 (SEHR: F 80). He was a frequent guest lecturer in classes in religion and philosophy and in the summer of 1912 presented a class on "Practical Christianity." Once Mrs. Woods completed work on her husband's biography, she donated the official records of the South End House and many of her husband's personal papers to Harvard. Harvard and Boston also appear to link Woods and University of Chicago sociologist Robert Park. The Boston suburb of Wollaston was home for the Park family from 1903 until 1916 although for much of that time Park lived elsewhere (Rauschenbush 1979:78). Park attended Harvard for the academic year 1897–1898 and worked as an assistant in the Philosophy department from 1903 to 1905. During his time at Harvard, he also worked as the Editorial Secretary for the Congo Reform Association and was responsible for his friend John Daniels' appointment as Corresponding Secretary. In 1904, Daniels was also the recipient of Harvard's South End House Fellowship which brought him to residency at the settlement where in 1905 he began his study of Boston's Negro population. Apparently Park was a mentor to Daniels who may have been a common link between the two men and a source of information with regard to their respective works. The American Sociological Association meeting in 1913 established a further link between Park and Woods as both presented papers, Park's on racial assimilation and Woods' on "The Neighborhood in Social Reconstruction," both subsequently published in the AJS in 1914. Daniel's research, *In Freedom's Birthplace* was initially published in 1914 with an introduction by Woods. Daniels' Preface acknowledges the "constant guidance" of Robert Woods and the assistance of Albert Kennedy and William Cole of South End House in reading and providing criticism of his manuscript. He credits Park with first suggesting the work and for guiding him in a "historical and descriptive" as opposed to "argumentative" direction. In a review of Daniels' book for the *Survey*, Park praised it as "unquestionably the best study that has been made thus far of the Negro in a northern community" (1914:100). In 1905, Park moved to Tuskegee, Alabama to become secretary to Booker T. Washington, a position he held until 1912 when he returned to Boston for a year prior to accepting a teaching position in 1914 at the University of Chicago. During his time in Tuskegee, Park's wife and four children remained at their home in Wollaston with Park absent except for summers and vacations. Several sources have documented the fact that Park's wife, an artist and published writer, was well known for her work with reform and women's groups in Boston and later in Chicago (Traverso 2003, Deegan 2005). It is quite likely that Clare Park and the Woods moved in the same circles.

Woods and the Social Gospel

Woods can easily be placed in Henking's typology of the sociological Christian (1992:334–336). He came to religion before sociology and while never deviating from certain orthodox beliefs, he nevertheless saw his religion as preparatory to his social mission to humankind which was his work in the settlement movement. Woods is often described as a social gospeler (Williams 1970:150–154, Trolander 1987:11, Barbuto 1999:237) and while he did not use this label to describe himself, his work and beliefs identify him as such. His formal church affiliation seems somewhat incidental to the more secular social gospel influence. He was born into a Presbyterian family, and as a student became a Congregationalist, presumably because that denomination was more identified with the new social gospel. In later years, commensurate with his wedding, he became an Episcopalian which he explained as follows.

> The change is a natural and, in fact, a long contemplated one. I was brought up a Presbyterian. My ancestral traditions were of the Church of England. I have never seemed to myself other than a generously treated guest in Congregationalism. I have always felt very grateful for what it was for me at Amherst and Andover, and have endeavored loyally to return the great obligations which it had placed upon me. ...My intimacy with Episcopalians in matters of present-day Christianity is more and more a vital thing (1929:164–165).

Woods was known for his lofty rhetoric and poetic prose expressing an optimistic belief in the goodness of humankind and in the progress of society toward a kind of nationalistic, religious utopia. Despite evidence of utopian thinking, Woods is often cast as a Christian pragmatist (Woods 1929, Snedeker 1950, SEHR: B1, 24) and South End House was Christian pragmatism at work based on Woods' proclamation that the "expression of the settlement in the neighborhood should be by deed" (1929:352), and deeds were always to be based on knowledge and understanding. When the occasion allowed, Woods was capable of reverting to a religious rather than secular frame of reference as when he was asked by the Russell Sage Foundation to observe and report on the work of foreign missions during his sabbatical year abroad. The resulting report is more religious in tone than most of his writings, but it is also replete with references to Christian deeds over evangelism. For example he wrote, "As one reads the life of Christ, one finds that on at least half the occasions when he came in direct touch with people's lives, he did the helpful deed and passed on" (SEHR: B1, F83, Woods 1921:4). His message to the Foreign Mission Board was that the *deed* is "an essential way of instilling the meaning of the gospel into the mind and heart of the world" (Woods 1929:5). The most obvious religious and social gospel thematic in Woods work is his life-long vision of the Kingdom of God on Earth. He was steadfast in his evolutionary vision of the Kingdom as achievable on earth and warned against more messianic visions.

> ...[W]hile we may tolerate the form of Utopia which implies the sudden passing of the present order and the catastrophic introduction of some new order let down from the clouds, we shall teach with our utmost conviction that there is to be a peaceful, growing cooperative, comprehensively human growth and progress directly out of our present way of social life into that which is to come.
>
> WOODS 1929:275

William Cole, long-time resident of South End House, in delivering a Woods' eulogy, summed up his religion as "little more than love to God and love to man," and he wrote Woods' epitaph as "Friend of humanity. Servant of God" (USESR: B2, 1925).

Woods, the Civic Leader

Robert Woods' active life in Boston both promoted the cause, and justified the existence, of settlement houses. He was aware that he could not separate the man from the House and apparently chose his involvement in social and political issues outside the settlement carefully and encouraged his associates to do the same. The inseparability of the man from the settlement is evident in his weekly column, “The Social Settler” that appeared in the *Boston Evening Transcript* for some 20 years. Regardless of his cause, his motivation was always that of “moral uplift” by which he meant improving the quality of life for the working poor of Boston. His involvement in many aspects of Boston’s civic affairs is testament to the influence of South End House and to Woods personally. His work in behalf of communities, the city, the state, and ultimately the nation chronicles the career of Woods the reformer; yet his reform activities were always firmly positioned on empirical research and facts. During his Boston years he was appointed to numerous city and state committees and commissions to work for the alleviation of social problems. Some of his early ventures into city politics were obviously in behalf of the settlement neighborhood as he lobbied for public baths and recreational facilities in the South End. In recognition of his efforts to bring these needs before city decision-makers, he was appointed to and chaired the Boston Committee on Public Baths and Gymnasiums, resulting in the location of a pubic bath on Dover Street and later a South End gymnasium and playground (Woods 1929:120). In 1893 during a period of high unemployment, the Governor appointed Woods to his Special Commission on Unemployment (Woods 1929:309). Woods’ public activism for industrial education led to his appointment as chair of the Committee to Promote a State System of Industrial Education and later as secretary of the State Commission to Establish Industrial Schools (Woods [1923]1970:331). His promotion of industrial education came from daily observations as young people, especially young men, dropped out of the public schools to become immediate wage-earners but in jobs with no future such as newsboys, bootblacks, and messengers (Woods 1929:190–191). In writing for local papers and publications such as *The Commons*, and in sermons and speeches, Woods took up the cause of industrial education, in the process indicting the public schools for concentrating on the ten percent of students who were headed for higher education. He was concerned that industrialization and the growth of a working class had brought about a division between culture (as in appreciation of the arts) and work and that the public schools were contributing to this division. By Woods’ definition industrial education did not have to limit young people to manual labor but could include leadership training and cultivation of “executive capacity” as well (1929:261).

Woods was in favor of the benefits that organized labor brought to workers, but often disapproved of their tactics. On one occasion he wrote, “Think how vast the gain...if the next two or three great industrial revolts in this community could be anticipated; the concessions which they will compel, granted in advance; and a new order established by which all such difficulties could be peacefully negotiated" (Woods 1929:263). He was often called upon to arbitrate strikes or threatened strikes. He served for several years as a member and chair of the Relief Committee of the Central Labor Union and was able to secure funding for the Committee to offer assistance in times of high unemployment. Related to Woods' interest in labor, he apparently shared some of the public sentiments of his generation that led to restrictive immigration legislation in the 1920s (Davis 1984:91, 93). He was a member of the Immigration Restriction League's[2] executive committee (Trolander 1990: xv). In fact, one of the few criticisms found in retrospectives on Woods have to do with his inclination toward nationalism or ethnocentrism. Stackpole offers perhaps the most pointed criticism, concluding that he "feared immigration would harm both the economic and racial standards of the nation" (SC 1961:78–81). She noted that Woods joined with sociologists such as E.A. Ross[3] in petitioning President Wilson to pass a literacy standard for immigrants and that Woods was "relieved by the passage of the quota laws of the 1920s" (SC 1961:79). Some have even gone so far as to characterize Woods as a racist or at the very least an Anglophile (Solomon 1972:140–143). Woods' wife defended her husband, asserting that his views on immigration restriction were misrepresented and that his real concern was the practice of bringing immigrant workers to the US when needed and then dumping them on the community when their labor was no longer in demand (1929:350). On another controversial issue, Woods favored the 18th Amendment and predicted that it would "reduce poverty, nearly wipe out prostitution and crime, improve labor organization, and 'substantially increase our national resources by setting free vast suppressed human potentialities'" (Davis 1984:226). In fact, many settlement workers favored prohibition because their research had placed the neighborhood saloon at the center of neglected families, urban crime, prostitution, and political corruption (Carson 1990:167). Woods was not so much an opponent of drinking as he was the social problems associated with drink, and because of his belief in this causal association he became actively involved in the temperance movement and chaired the Massachusetts committee to secure state ratification of the 18th Amendment. Before throwing his support behind the national campaign for prohibition, however, he

2 The Immigration Restriction League was founded in Boston in 1894 by several Harvard graduates and gained nation-wide support with chapters in many major cities. Its purpose was to stem the tide of "undesirable immigrants" coming into the US from Eastern and Southern Europe. The League used speeches, sermons, and lectures as well as articles and pamphlets to sway public attention and also lobbied Congress for legislation.

3 Ross' views on immigration were much more restrictive, particularly against Asians, and contributed to his dismissal from his faculty position at Stanford University (Weinberg 1972).

supported more local and state control of the sale of liquor, beer, and wine (Woods 1929:296). He worked for and secured passage in Boston of a Bar and Bottle Law calling for separate licensing for the sale of individual drinks and the sale of liquor by the bottle. This change prohibited bar owners from selling a bottle of liquor to a patron to take home after he had been drinking at the bar all evening (Woods 1929:286). Woods also worked to alleviate the association between liquor and prostitution by restricting the sale of liquor in cafes and hotels worked by prostitutes. Woods was not without sympathy for those who fell victim to drink and was chair of the board of the State Hospital for Inebriates. He was, no doubt, ahead of many of his peers when he began a speech with the declaration that "Inebriety, considered in its simplest sense, is a disease" (SEHR 1912–1923:F30).

Despite his civic engagements and lobbying efforts in behalf of poor neighborhoods, Woods, with few exceptions, avoided direct political involvement for most of his career. He and other residents of SEH worked to reform the representation of Boston's city alderman by backing a proposal for at-large elections and to have the mayor run without party affiliation. Boston became one of the first cities to adopt these kinds of reforms and subsequently Woods, for the first time, endorsed a candidate. In fact, in 1908 he worked to overthrow John Fitzgerald, the maternal grandfather of President John F. Kennedy, as mayor of Boston. Woods only other overt involvement in politics was the endorsement of Theodore Roosevelt's Progressive Party in 1912.[4] The US entry into World War I came as the first serious division among settlement workers in the National Federation of Settlements (Davis 1984:220–221). For social gospelers such as Woods, the war was particularly problematic because it represented an obstruction in realization of the Kingdom and the ideal democracy in the United States. The war was therefore rationalized as necessary for removal of these obstructions toward social progress. Thus World War I became the "Great War" or what some referred to as the "War to end all wars." Woods came to support the war and saw the necessity of keeping the settlement work going during the war as a means of "maintaining national vitality and spirit." He chaired the Boston War Camp Community Service Committee, formed to provide service men with wholesome leisure time activities and opportunities (Woods 1929:319). He used his weekly newspaper column to support the War and put SEH resources behind the war effort, describing the settlement as "always on duty."

Woods gave settlements a broadly defined visibility and a mission inclusive of the neighborhood, the city, and society-at-large. Indicative of Woods

4 Other settlement workers, including Jane Addams, also endorsed Roosevelt and it was said that the social workers turned the Progressive Party Convention of 1912 into a revival meeting (Davis 1984:201).

influence beyond South End House, yet directly related to its mission, was his work toward an organization of settlements, first the Boston Social Union (comprised of 26 settlements) and then in the National Federation of Settlements. He saw settlements as "unifiers, interpreters of moral issues" and not meant to become agents for the views of any particular class or group but able to explain and bring understanding to all sides of an issue. Woods wife said of him that he had the ability to "sympathize with those with whom he did not agree" (1929:266). In conferring an honorary degree on Woods in 1910, Harvard president Lowell said, "Robert Archey Woods—A man who labors to raise his fellow-men—trusted alike by those who toil and those who think—a knight of Christ's chivalry, without fear and without reproach" (USESR: B1, F30).

The Work of Woods and South End House Residents

Woods wife concluded that his first two publications from the South End House (*City Wilderness* and *The Neighborhood as Nation Building*) "brought him out of the classification of either theoretical socialist or reformer. He remained steadfast...to a policy of social construction" (1929:183). To Woods, the settlement was a tool in the construction of the ideal society, a constellation of interrelated, interdependent communities. Woods always knew that the settlement was something more than charity work. On one occasion he wrote to Jane Addams that they should "keep the settlements from being merely part of the drudging machinery of charity" (Carson 1990:122). In fact, Woods redefined charity by prefacing the noun with the descriptor "scientific." He believed in the "potent notion that social science would explicate and resolve the problems of urban industrial society" (Carson 1990:49). It was Woods who first laid out the concept of the settlement as a sociological laboratory and annual reports of the South End House provide a record of his fidelity to this mission and attest to the fact that the sociological enterprise included the gathering *and* application of data for the alleviation of class differences. In his third year at South End House, Woods wrote that the settlement,

> prepares a certain number of persons identified with the more favored classes who can...put themselves in the place of the less favored and so act as means of communication and sympathy and even as arbitrators of justice between opposing classes...all study should be carried out in such a spirit and from such a point of view.
>
> USESR 1894:B2

In the ninth annual report Woods emphasized the importance of the application of their investigations. "The residents...look forward to the day when statistics will be gathered not only about conditions to be remedied, but about concrete net results of effort toward remedying such conditions." He used as an example of research, application, and traceable results, work on juvenile law-violators, systemic reforms, and recent statistics revealing a decrease in numbers of delinquents. "We are confident...that future statisticians will...prove... that such work not only benefits those on the verge of being law-breakers but... enhances the welfare of the vastly larger class of struggling but self-respecting working people" (USESR 1901:B2). The thing that no doubt insured Robert Woods and his South End House associates of continuing involvement in the public affairs of Boston was the credibility they brought to their roles as reformers and as participants on local and state committees and commissions. They came armed with facts because South End House residents had conducted "investigations" in most of the areas of public life where their voices came to be heard. Carson says of Woods that he was "the most thorough of the early American observers of the English settlement movement," observation and knowledge that he made use of in Boston (1990:36). Woods was the author, co-author, or editor of nine books and numerous articles that appeared in journals or other periodicals. The preponderance of his work is focused on the problems of cities and with efforts to identify, confront, and resolve the problems associated with the lives of the working poor in cities. The theoretical underpinning of Woods' work was that of social relations within the context of a social democracy and the disconnects between classes and between workers and industry; his methodology at the most general level was the settlement itself. Woods pragmatism was built on the concept of social construction or problem-solving reconstruction as in neighborhood-building (1914) and nation-building ([1923]1970). His writings follow three tracts: (1) explorations of poverty and class inequality in Europe and the US; (2) local studies carried out by settlement residents or associates in a systematic study of the South End neighborhood and other working class neighborhoods in Boston; and (3) the nation-wide scope and impact of settlement work.

European Background Brought to the United States

In the first category of writings, *English Social Movements* (1891) was based on Woods' experience in London, including his time at Toynbee Hall and is comprised of lectures given at Andover Seminary following his return in 1891. Part theory, part method, and part empirical observation, Woods provided the rationale and philosophy for the settlement movement. The book went to three editions in his lifetime. Woods endorsed a multifaceted approach to poverty such as was underway in England with the combined efforts of the labor movement, the new Christian socialism, settlement work, university extension programs, church, charitable and educational programs. *English Social Movements* did not allow readers in the United States any feeling of smugness as they read of poverty in England. Woods reminded readers in his Introduction: "We do not…need to go over the sea to learn about evil conditions." He also sought to prevent any sense of superiority emanating from the new democracy of the United States when he pointed out that "Our class system is not less cruel for having its boundaries less clearly marked" (1891:vi). His time in England served as the basis of Woods' life work because it was there he first moved beyond text book and classroom hypotheticals to learn of poverty and its precipitators first hand. Woods edited his second book, *The Poor in Great Cities* (1895) which brought poverty closer to home while giving it international impact. *The Poor* is less theoretical than the first work and more descriptive of various manifestations of poverty and of reform efforts underway in cities across the US. The book includes chapters on New York tenements, the children of the poor, and the poor of Chicago but contains more on reform efforts such as undertaken by model organizations. While the book is primarily focused on the United States, it includes chapters on Riverside Parish in London, street children in Paris, and the poor of Naples. Woods offers a subtle acknowledgment of ethnocentrism and racism in the US by his observation that American citizens would be more disturbed by a drive through East London than by a tour of an American slum because in London, they would be more likely to see themselves in the faces of the poor (Woods 1895:1–3). As with Woods' first book, this one attends to remedial efforts, their successes and failures.

Local Studies in Boston

It is the second and local category of Woods' work, in collaboration with South End House residents and associates that clearly establishes him as a sociologist. He laid out a plan for study of Boston to be published in three volumes as explained in the fourth annual South End House report. The first phase of the work was to be

> …a comprehensive social analysis of the lower half of the South End. …The study will include such topics as history, population, and economic condition of the district; the housing of the people; their relation as consumers, with the small shop, the installment store, the cheap restaurant, the saloon, the pawnshop; popular amusements; crime and criminals; local organizations, political, economic, recreative; charitable, educational, philanthropy, and religious activities. It is the determination of the editors to give

> thorough unity and consistence to the completed picture. A final essay will point out the total drift of things in the district, showing what its special needs are, and what practical steps can be taken to meet them.
>
> USESR 1896: B2

The culmination of the first phase of the local work was publication of *The City Wilderness* (1898) that followed by three years *Hull House Maps and Papers*, no doubt inspired by it, although both were obviously modeled after Booth's work in London. *Wilderness*, edited by Woods, is comprised of a Preface and twelve chapters along with maps and charts and other illustrative materials. The authors are all males as there were yet no female residents and, with one exception, all were SEH residents. Woods is identified as the author of the Preface and of the two final chapters. He also wrote, but did not claim authorship of chapters on politics and education which appeared without a byline but with an explanation that the "writer withholds his name out of consideration for certain interests that involve outside persons" ([1898]1970:iv). In fact, the interests were likely those of the settlement as Woods was increasingly involved in civic affairs and did not want to be rendered ineffective in the city. Woods' authorship of these chapters is confirmed later by Eleanor Woods (1929:169).

The City Wilderness provided demographic and historical descriptions of the area of Boston most immediately served by South End House. Data for some of the maps were collected by residents while others were compiled using data from Tenement House and Census reports. The color-coded maps depicting types of buildings show a preponderance of tenement houses followed by a smaller number of lodging houses and fewer apartments. In the lower portion of the neighborhood there were rows of factories but very few stores were located in the South End and even fewer public buildings.[5] The chief industries were those associated with coal, lumber, wood working, and other businesses dependent on the waterfront for supplies. Labor statistics in the area showed both unskilled and skilled workers, but laborers connected with municipal departments—most the result of political patronage—were said to "constitute the aristocracy of the unskilled" ([1898]1970:88). Many of the people living in the South End did not work there but made their way to jobs outside the area and returned to their tenements or rooming houses in the evenings. The living conditions were described as tending "to lower not only physical but mental

5 There is no indication in Woods' writings as to whether Houghton-Mifflin's publication of the color-coded fold-out maps created the same obstacles that Jane Addams dealt with a few years earlier in her efforts to insure that Thomas Crowell included the maps in *Hull House Maps and Papers* (see Deegan 1990:56–58).

and moral standards of health" ([1898]1970:81), this no doubt leading to the conclusion in the final chapter that "the individual... [is not] the main cause of difficulty...the trend of his physical and moral existence is practically determined for him by his outward conditions" ([1898]1970:289–290).

Woods' unsigned chapter on politics described local caucuses as the control center of the city's political machine and documented the relationship between boys' gangs and machine politics. Political bosses cultivated these gangs and exploited the young men for their own purposes such as using their supply of "votes" gathered from deceased persons or non-voters. The young male gang members enjoyed a degree of power within their neighborhoods as they were rewarded with some of the spoils of the system but were pulled into the city's political corruption in the process. The biggest prize was always a municipal job or a political appointment. Woods used the facts gathered for this chapter later in leading efforts to reform Boston's election procedures. The other chapter authored anonymously by Woods was on education, no doubt controversial because he attributed to the school much of the responsibility for the assimilation of immigrant children of the first and second generations, a task at which he saw them failing ([1898]1970:233). On vocational training in the public schools, Woods was also emphatic. "For poor children whose material welfare and moral salvation very largely turn upon getting started in some skilled trade, our system of education is obviously deficient" ([1898]1970:238, 240). The "anonymous" author also advocated for evening schools and adult education and finally, on the broadest level, put the onus of justice, even the realization of the democratic ideal, directly on the schools.

> There is a special question of justice involved, in so far as the working people have distinct intellectual ability, the value of which is largely lost to themselves and to society on account of their lack of early opportunity. It is necessary to prevent this waste, not only because of the welfare of the uneducated, but also for the patriotic reason that ignorance means weakness and corruption in our democratic system ([1898]1970:243).

City Wilderness drew on the neighborhood as a social laboratory and was meant to form the basis of programmatic work at South End House and to provide compelling evidence for broader policy reforms at the city and state levels some of which are laid out in the final chapter. In spite of its many positive features, the book suggests that the settlement workers, while living in close proximity to African Americans, held the same prejudices as most of their contemporaries. Resident Bushee, for example, described the Negro population (the terminology used at the time), mostly migrants from the South, as exhibiting "the usual characteristics of the Negro race: loud and coarse, revealing much more of the animal qualities than of the spiritual" ([1898]1970:44).

Apparently Boston's north, west, and south ends comprised the largest populations of recent immigrants and most of the tenement and lodging-houses in Boston. Study of the North and West Ends demonstrate Woods' view of the organismic interdependence of the different sections of the city and the fact that he did not wish his influence to be confined to the South End. The various chapters of *Americans in Process* (1903) were written by SEH residents who had "long familiarity with persons and affairs in the North and West Ends. ... [although, Woods acknowledged] the writers do not have so intimate a knowledge of the life of these districts as of the section of the city in which most... lived and worked" ([1903]1970:vi). Of the ten authors, five were women (by now South End House had female residents) who contributed chapters on the history of Boston; public celebrations, feasts and holidays of the various ethnic and racial groups; and immigrant children in the public and parochial schools. The major theme of this volume is the Americanization of immigrants or in some cases their exclusion from the process. The book covers most of the same topics as the first, including chapters on how residents of the two areas make their livings and how the livelihood of citizens is tied to industrial development in the city. In this volume Woods claimed authorship of the chapter on politics, which continued his criticism of the local political machine and in which he took on two unnamed politicians, apparently easily identifiable by those familiar with Boston politics. Woods did not, however, exonerate ordinary citizens from culpability, charging that they were less interested in reform than in electing men who will be "fair" in sharing the spoils of their power ([1903]1970:148–149). Woods detailed how the political machine worked in the North and West Ends, linking ward corruption with that at the city and state levels. Both parties were taken to task for their corruption and for their use of the "spoils of the system" to seduce young men into politics. On the other hand, Woods recognized pragmatically that for no small number of constituents in these two wards, politics are economics and economics are politics and for as long as this was the case, the system would endure ([1903]1970:189).

There is no overt theoretical perspective in these two works as it was always Woods' contention that theory was to emanate from the building of neighborly relations. There is however, an assumption that settlement work must contribute to the promises and to the potentials of a social democracy and that a foundation for reform was established in the documentation of Boston's social problems. Both books are qualitative and quantitative descriptions of Boston's poorest residential areas. Both are responses to the macro-level forces of urbanization, industrialization, and immigration as reflected in their similar thematic—structural inequality tied to urban-industrial growth, and labor exploitation, all exacerbated by inadequate education and corrupt political machinery. Both books rest on the assumption that assimilation of the masses of European immigrants is in process and offer a warning that the urban relocation of blacks from the South and other rural areas will present a problem for the future. Although a much more understanding tone is evident in the second book, it is apparent that the authors do not expect African Americans to assimilate as well as European immigrants. For example, one writer commented, "notwithstanding the Negroes' desire for assimilation, color remains an almost insuperable obstacle to them" ([1903]1970:60).

While these two books constitute the local investigative portion of South End House research, a third volume was anticipated by Woods as explained in the 9th annual report.

> Having finished the investigation of the North End, the West End, and the lower part of the South End, the residents now look forward to some studies of the outlying working-class districts, Charlestown, East Boston, South Boston, and lower Roxbury. This belt of districts, while it includes real poverty, yet on the whole represents the more enterprising working people who have established their homes beyond the area of the greatest congestion. Several years will probably be taken for these new investigations. As the result of them will come the third volume in the series of which *The City Wilderness* and *Americans in Process* are volumes one and two.
>
> USESR 1901: B2

The third volume of the South End House series as initially laid out by Woods was incomplete at the time of his death and was apparently abandoned by Kennedy who, as Woods' associate and successor, would have been expected to complete the project. The work was published much later, after a chance discovery of the incomplete manuscript, as *The Zone of Emergence* (1969). At the same time the systematic research program was underway locally other social investigations were conducted (some published) by individual residents and by Woods and Kennedy. The *Handbook of Settlements* ([1911]1970:128–130) lists more than two single-spaced pages of investigations along with other pages of "Efforts for District Improvement." Residents conducted studies on the lodging house population, the "tramp problem," public baths, women wage-earners, tenement housing, saloons, factory workers, Negroes in Boston, churches, recreational facilities for adolescents, family budgets, tuberculosis and other health problems. Resident Alvan Sanborn, who later became a journalist, did exhaustive participant observation study (some of the earliest of this kind) of "cheap" lodging and the life that went with it in Boston's South End. From this work, he published in the *Andover House Bulletin* (1895) "Beggars and their Lodgings" and "Anatomy of a Tenement Street." He later published a book inclusive of these essays, *Moody's Lodging House and Other Tenement Sketches* (1895). Another early empirical work on lodging houses was conducted by resident Albert Wolfe and published in 1906. Some of the South End House studies were disseminated as internal reports or as pamphlets for the City and for social service agencies (Woods and Kennedy [1911]1970:128–130). Some books written by residents were published by major presses of the day and other works in periodicals such as *Current Affairs, Charities and the Commons, Scribners, The Independent,* and the *South End House Bulletin.* The extensive research on lodging or boarding houses, which became the special project of Eleanor Woods, resulted in several publications including a Boarding House Registry listing all houses in the area that met standards and their current vacancies. A South End House resident, sometimes Eleanor Woods, made regular visits to each house to insure that they met "moral standards" as well as those of sanitation, privacy, and space (Woods 1929:184). Boarding houses participated in this registry because it gave them a stamp of approval and also brought them referrals for preferred lodgers.

The National Scene

The final category of Woods work is national in scope and resulted from his leadership in the settlement movement. Two works were coauthored with Albert Kennedy and undertaken for the National Federation of Settlements with much of the cost underwritten by the Russell Sage Foundation. Their exhaustive research produced an annotated catalog of all settlements in the United States, organized by states and cities within states, as of approximately 1910. The sheer volume of data collection required to produce *The Handbook of Settlements* (1911) no doubt explains the gap between Woods previous book in 1903 and this one. According to the preface, *The Handbook* "presents an outline of the material facts about every settlement in the United States, including non-residential neighborhood centers." Woods and Kennedy reported having visited "the large majority of the houses" and read all of their publications ([1911]1970:v). The quantity and quality of information for settlements is uneven, depending on what was available from a variety of sources; however, some information is presented on 413 settlements. As might be expected, the most complete data came from the largest and oldest settlements: a brief history; mission statement; founding date; sponsorship; address (or addresses); name changes; a brief description of the neighborhoods served; head residents, and number of male and female residents and volunteers; activities, including social investigations (with some reports and publications named) as well as social services, clubs, and organizations. Apparently Kennedy did much of the data collection for the *Handbook* and Woods, the disciplined and methodical writer, the organization and final editing. The *Handbook* was an invaluable resource for social workers and settlement workers of the day and, because it was reprinted and reissued in 1970, remains a resource for researchers. The *Handbook* was conceived not only as a reference tool but also as a symbol of unity for the National Federation of Settlements of which Woods and Kennedy served as "joint secretaries" from 1911 to 1923 (Trolander 1990:xii). In quick succession, and shortly before his death, Woods produced two final books. *The Settlement Horizon* (1922) was co-authored with Kennedy and Woods' final book, *The Neighborhood in Nation-Building* (1923), marked his 30-years at South End House. *The Settlement Horizon* is the companion volume to the *Handbook* and most of the content was no doubt a part of the data collected for the first volume, the latter, according to Eleanor Woods, intended as an amplification of it (1929:356). She reported that publication was delayed because of the war and because of a trip she and Woods took around the world in 1919 and 1920. Whereas, *The Handbook* was a compendium of vital statistics on settlements in the United States, *Horizon* describes the origin, philosophical underpinnings, and substance of the settlement movement. The book is organized into five rather autonomous parts and the organization of each sometimes defies logic for today's reader. For example, hidden away in a chapter on families is an excellent methodological protocol for community study ([1922]1990:305–315).

The targeted audience for *Horizon* was apparently settlement workers and secondarily a concerned citizenry. The authors seemed most intent on introducing a new generation of settlement workers to a proud history and on resetting a national reform agenda. The book is in many ways the single best description of settlement work in the United States although filtered through the social gospel perspective of Woods and Kennedy. One reviewer described the work as "a history of the [settlement] movement, an interpretation of its philosophy, a critique of its purposes and its methods, a declaration of its goals, a recognition of its failures, an appraisal of its achievements" (North 1923:621). The value of *Horizon* is not in its presentation of new data or ideas but in its thorough history and accounting of settlement work over more than 30 years. It was also an attempt to position settlements for the post-war era but as Trolander points out in a new edition published in 1990, the authors ignored trends destined to change the nature of settlements and settlement work, namely the professionalization of social work, and an evolving funding plan designed to consolidate solicitation of charitable contributions (1990:ix). The basic framework of *Horizon* was no doubt planned in advance of these movements gaining the ascendancy they eventually did. The authors continued to voice the necessity of the educated classes carrying the university into the heart of the city ([1922]1990:59) and applying "the gospel to the imperious demands of the new [more just] order of life" in urban-industrial and post-war America ([1922]1990:40). In fact, there are frequent reminders of the social gospel mission of the settlements, for example: "Original American settlement groups, in nearly all cases, came to their tasks under the dominating religious motive of the Kingdom of God as a new earthly order to be built out of broader and deeper human relationships" ([1922]1990:56). *Horizon* includes general descriptions of the activities, educational, and cultural programs common to all the settlements, such as boys and girls clubs, along with selected exemplary programs (some of these included in Appendices). After describing the deplorable working and living conditions of many laborers, the authors take a stand for organized labor, asserting that "The trade union suggested itself as the best weapon with which to meet such conditions" ([1922]1990:170). The authors, however, play down the role of settlements in labor organization and emphasize their role as arbitrators of labor disputes, bringing together "the better inclined in both groups" ([1922]1990:171). Some chapters are particularly revealing of the settlement position on social class in the context of a capitalistic economy. While the authors are critical of the tendency of some to blame the poor for their own economic hardships, unlike some other settlement workers, they do not place the blame directly on capitalism. Rather, they conclude that poverty is "clearly traceable, *not* to defects of character but to accident, sickness, death, unemployment, unforeseen responsibility, fluctuation of industry" ([1922]1990:190). Following their assertion that "poverty is unnecessary and should be abolished" Woods and Kennedy endorsed the controversial citizenship right to a decent standard of living, citing Greenwich House in New York as having established an empirical urban working-class standard of living ([1922]1990:204). A chapter on "Race and Place" addresses the various groups that settlements have worked with, including African Americans, and sheds some light on the controversy with regard to Anglo-assimilation versus pluralism ([1922]1990:327). Perhaps in defense of criticisms that settlements were too aggressive in their work toward assimilation, the authors state, "The whole career of the settlement shows that its emphasis upon American standards has not failed to conserve the best traditions which immigrants bring with them" ([1922]1990:329–330). With regard to blacks, and indicative of an attempt to cover the gamut of settlements and to be pragmatic, the authors suggest that "large groups of colored people in a neighborhood predominantly white may force a settlement, against its inclination, to choose between the two. In this case, the soundest practice is to establish a separate branch" to work with this population which is, of course, what many did ([1922]1990:337).

A major theme of *Horizon* is its emphasis on how settlements have made a difference in people's lives through investigations, activism, and consciousness-raising. Because of settlement work, the authors claim that "an increasing circle of people [are] unwilling that their comfort should be based on the hardship of their fellows" ([1922]1990:72). Using specific examples, various settlements are credited with bringing transparency to the evils of ward politics; improving the quality of life through campaigns for public baths, garbage disposal, and recreational facilities; and garnering support for the war effort. The final section of *Horizon* includes a roll-call of well-known settlement pioneers and the authors are not timid in their recitation of accomplishments, systematically citing the impact of settlements on institutions such as government, churches, schools, higher education, medicine, and charity work and even in moving social science away from its Darwinian roots.

> Thirty-five years ago economic thinking both within and without the universities was still based on the theory that unrestricted competition would somehow secure the common good...during the transitional period settlements have had a significant influence in bringing human facts and motives within the range of the social sciences ([1922]1990:391).

In between the *Handbook* and *Settlement Horizon*, Woods and Kennedy edited a research monograph for the National Federation of Settlements, a study of *Young Working Girls* (1913), summarizing data from two questionnaires completed by settlement and social workers across the nation. Facts assembled in this volume were used by settlement workers to lobby for, and in some cases secure, better work place regulations for young women.

Woods' final book, *The Neighborhood as Nation-Building*, was published less than two years before his death. Although there is no indication in any of the biographical data that he was in poor health or knew that his death was imminent, his last two works suggest an awareness of the passage of time. Whereas the *Settlement Horizon* was Woods' attempt to record for posterity the settlement movement, his last book is a life-time retrospective—a collection of papers, speeches and other writings, almost all published earlier. The chapters are arranged in chronological order and reflect "the development of a consciousness," of a man driven by the social gospel and by his passion for the settlement movement ([1923]1970:Preface). The first three chapters are reprints of Woods' early efforts to articulate in public speeches and writings his concept and vision for social settlements: "The University Settlement Idea" (1893), "University

Settlements as Laboratories in Social Science" ([1893]1970), and "Settlements: Their Point and Drift" (1899). In these early presentations Woods justified the linkage between universities and settlements and placed responsibility on the educated class to give "what they have in such abundance" ([1923]1970:7). He conceptualized the settlement as a "home" established in the turbulent context of the "industrial revolution, of a new immigration, and the unmanageable growth of cities" ([1923]1970:14, 53). Both theory and method were treated as integral to the "study and practice of scientific charity" ([1923]1970:17) with Woods arguing that settlement theory was to emanate from the building of "relations of friendliness and intimacy," in a "living experience" between the classes. He argued that the democratic ideas of settlement work would override the sentiments of pity and mercy characteristic of charity work ([1923]1970:14, 12). His methodology was grounded in the development of knowledge learned from the people themselves and from intimate study and analysis of the settlement community. The local community, however, was treated in terms of "those larger phases of social conditions of a city as a whole...the government...business enterprises...and the public school system" ([1923]1970:32). Reform must be based on study and analysis and must be developed *with*, not for, the people. In the end, Woods expressed confidence that the settlement experience through its practice of scientific charity would function as a change agent moving from the individual, to the neighborhood, the city, and ultimately to society at large.

The book-end chapters of Woods collection, perhaps not coincidentally, move not only chronologically but also spatially from neighborhood to the international scene. The final chapter is obviously a post-war analysis and prospective on the future of settlements. "The Settlement Foothold" was written as a speech to be delivered at the first International Conference of Settlements in London, although for reasons not stated, Woods did not deliver the speech, instead sent it to be read as a "communication." It reveals Woods' cognizance of the fact that the war had made the world both smaller and more complex and that there were questions about the viability of settlements in a post-war society. Woods message took into account the necessity for change while reiterating that "the settlement, in its essence, must continue through the generations." "The day of the settlement has only begun" he declared ([1923]1970:321). Woods referred to settlement workers as "social workers," but declared that "the true meaning of social worker is found where it undertakes to deal with totals" ([1923]1970:322). The totality of the social worker was to Woods one engaging in communal, educational, and mediatory roles using knowledge gained from science, from the arts, and from the generations. Woods ended his message by acknowledging the dynamics of post-war society but with steadfast adherence to his social gospel vision.

> In a period of disintegration, which our neighborhoods are sharing in common with the world, it is all the more possible for the settlement to touch the underlying universal forces that can bring the moral unity of mankind. It is perhaps, above all a settlement privilege that in it the social worker may nourish, 'the firm conviction that beneath all the forms of economic and social change he is striving to bring about, there is proceeding a great spiritual movement toward the millennium of the City of God' (([1923]1970:327) 327).

Contributions to Sociology

Next to Hull House, South End House produced the greatest volume of sociological work. Because of the need for some delimitation we focus here on contributions to the development of theoretical and applied urban sociology, to the concept of cultural pluralism, to recognition of the social structure of class inequality, and to the methodology of urban ethnography.

Urban Sociology

Robert Park and his young colleague Ernest Burgess wrote the first widely adopted introductory textbook in sociology in which they described the works of Woods and Jane Addams as presenting "sympathetic and arresting pictures of city life" (1921:331). They cited Woods no less than eight times in the text; Addams was cited three times, only once for anything other than *Hull-House Maps and Papers*. In Park and Burgess' chapter on Conflict, the entire section on "The Gang and Political Organization" is attributed to Woods' chapter in *The City Wilderness* (Park and Burgess 1921:610–613). Lannoy's (2004) explanation of the authors' preference for Woods over Addams, their Chicago neighbor, is that Park saw Addams as a threat to his yet unestablished reputation as a sociologist in Chicago and that he looked derisively upon Addams and all the settlement women as "do gooders" or reformers.[6] Perhaps rivalry in Chicago did play a part in Park's lack of recognition of Addams or perhaps Woods was seen as more academic because of his ties with Harvard and the fact that Park

---

6 Lannoy (2004) draws this conclusion because of the obvious fact that Addams worked in Chicago where Hull House was an established institution and was well known nationally as well as in Europe. Further, Lannoy points to the fact that Park had only one scholarly publication prior to his Chicago appointment and that he was 54 years old and unknown as a sociologist. The author also suggests that Park's initial appointment (as a professorial lecturer) may have been the faculty position first offered to Jane Addams but as a full professor (2004: 41).

knew him and had first-hand knowledge of his work through his friend John Daniels and through his Boston residency. However, there appears to be a link and an influence, if not actual borrowing, between the sociology of Woods and his South End House associates and the now classical Chicago School of Sociology most prominently identified with Robert Park, his colleagues and students in the 1920s and 1930s. Deegan traced the idea of the settlement as a laboratory directly to Woods and a speech he made at the Summer School of Ethics in 1892 (1990:35). Woods later published the speech after delivering it at the International Congress of Charities, Correction and Philanthropy ([1893]1970). It was more than twenty years later when Park wrote "The City: Suggestions for the Investigation of Human Behavior in the City Environment" positing the idea that the city could be thought of as a "laboratory or clinic in which human nature and social processes may be most conveniently and profitably studied" (1915:612). It was more than three decades later when Park revised his initial essay on the city with the title, "The City as a Social Laboratory" (1929). In the original essay Park defined the city as an institution and seems to suggest that because it is there it presented an opportunity for research. For Woods, the laboratory concept presented an opportunity for collection of data to be applied toward the solution of urban problems. Park's original essay includes a number of research questions and suggestions for collection of data but without specific methodologies and techniques. Most of Park's suggestions were consistent with use of descriptive data such as would be collected in field work or with secondary data found in agency reports, census, crime statistics, and surveys although the word survey appears in the article only once. Lannoy (2004) speculates that Park's initial essay on the city was his effort to move away from studying the city as a means of social reform, that is, divorcing himself from the "do gooders" he was known to ridicule (Bulmer 1984:148, Deegan 2005:18). Park twice revised and refined his first essay (Park 1925, 1929), and while the first two publications had the same title, they were not the same; the 1925 piece was more than an update of the 1915 one and was clearly meant to replace it. Some scholars have interpreted Park's original work as laying out his plan for teaching a class on the city. However, Lannoy argues that this was not the case because Park was not hired to teach such a course and, in fact, urban sociology did not yet exist at Chicago and when introduced, someone else taught it. Rather, Park was hired to teach a course on social surveys with which he was unfamiliar and of which he was disdainful because he associated surveys with social control and reform. Thus, apparently what was scheduled as a social survey course was taught, according to former students, as a course on the city as conceptualized by Park in his 1915 article (Lannoy 2004:38). Whatever his original intent, Park's essay on the city has been canonized as the beginning of urban sociology and has made his name synonymous with that specialized area of sociology and with treatment of the city as a laboratory.

Perhaps because of rampant problems associated with urban-industrial society at the turn of the century, urban sociology (although it had yet to be named) became one of the earliest areas of specialization: focused on that segment of population dwelling in the city and on other segments of society as they relate to the city. However, before sociology was identified as an area of study in the university, it thrived in America's settlements through the likes of Jane Addams and Robert Woods and their pioneering works in urban ethnography. Yet it is the oft-quoted and oft-labeled "seminal essay" of Robert Park (1915) that is credited with making urban sociology a viable specialization within the discipline. This attribution has endured even though Park himself labeled settlement residents as "pioneer students of urban sociology" ([1929b]1967:5). Some who wrote early histories of the discipline did recognize Woods and settlement sociologists for their contributions to urban sociology (Anderson 1929, Bain and Cohen 1929). Park's first essay on the city used a lengthy quote from a paper by Woods (1914) defining the neighborhood as "the simplest and most elementary form of association...in the organization of city life" (Park 1915:580). In fact, Park's research agenda for using the city of Chicago as a sociological laboratory begins with acknowledgment of the neighborhood, "a locality with sentiments, traditions, and a history of its own"(1915:579), a definition elaborated on with a quote from Robert Woods:

> It is surely one of the most remarkable of all social facts that, coming down from untold ages, there should be this instinctive understanding that the man who establishes his home beside yours begins to have a claim upon your sense of comradeship (1914:580).

Park began his prospectus for city investigation with suggestions for studying the local neighborhood that sound remarkably like those offered by Woods in a 1913 presentation, for which Park was present at the American Sociological Association. Park offered research questions covering essentially the same areas of community life: housing, demographics, history, division of labor, social classes, leadership, and population mobility. Both Park and Woods suggested utilization of some of the same resources: surveys, vital statistics, and newspapers. Park, however, did not like surveys used as a means of educating the public for the purpose of social control (1915:605), and he was concerned that data collected should have generalizability for the "predictable character" of communities (1915:581–582). Woods simply assumed that to study the local community was to study a microcosm of the city and nation (1914:578).

Woods' influence on Chicago sociology is easily observable in Park's social-anthropological field tradition of research and there are many similarities in Woods' treatment of the neighborhood and Park's concept of "natural areas." These respective units of analysis served much the same function in their visions of sociological work, but beyond the actual conceptualization as research target, the similarity ends. For Woods, research was of value for its applicability in solving social problems; for Park, research was of value in building a scientific base for studying the city. For Woods the neighborhood was the smallest unit of social analysis, "comprehensible and manageable," but a microcosm that included the "essence of all the problems of the city, the state, and the nation...it includes all the fundamental international issues" (1914:578). Similarly, Park saw the city as a constellation of natural areas serving an important methodological function for what they can tell us of society as a whole.

> They constitute...a frame of reference, a conceptual order within which statistical facts gain a new and more general significance. They not only tell us what the facts are in regard to conditions in any given region, but insofar as they characterize an area that is natural and typical, they establish a working hypothesis in regard to other areas of the same kind.
>
> PARK [1929a]1952:198

Woods charged that "Sociology as an art, no less than a science, must find its primary essential data in the fully understood neighborhood in building organically from the neighborhood up to the nation" (1914:589–590). Natural areas were key to Park's view of the city in that they allowed people to "satisfy fundamental needs and to solve fundamental problems" (Stein 1960:22). They are "products of forces that are constantly at work to effect an orderly distribution of populations and functions within the urban complex" (Park [1929a]1952:196). Both Woods and Park were organismic in their approach to the city, its study and its meaning. Park saw the city as a complex of interdependent units making it possible for "unassimilated peoples to live together, participating in a simple economy, but preserving at the same time, each its own racial and cultural integrity" ([1925]1967:9). Woods saw the city as "one of the great nerve tracts of the social organism" and the people as "intertwined humanity" ([1923]1970:22–27) and where "the supreme task of men and women is to learn to work together for the highest destiny" and with "joint responsibility for human society" (Woods 1929:65). However, Woods and Park differed on what they saw as the origin of social problems. For Woods, social problems were "the worst results of the industrial revolution, of a new migration, and of the unmanageable growth of cities" ([1923]1970:73). In contrast, Park saw social problems as "fundamentally behavior problems" ([1929b]1967:12).

Of the many empirical works of Woods and South End House residents, *The Zone of Emergence* is the most closely linked in theoretical conceptualization and methodology with the Chicago sociology of the 1920s and with the urban sociology most often attributed to Park and his colleague Ernest Burgess. Based on research conducted between 1905 and 1914, the unpublished manuscript was discovered in an unused coal bin at South End House in 1958 (Warner 1969:3). In an interview before his death in 1968, Kennedy reported that Woods supervised the project, coauthored the introduction, and made handwritten comments in the margins of the manuscript as author queries (Warner 1969:1, USESR: B2, F38). Kennedy remembered that the study was interrupted by the War and abandoned afterwards because it was thought to be outdated. It is also likely that Woods and Kennedy had to give priority to completion of the *Settlement Horizon,* under contract to Russell Sage (Warner 1969:7). Kennedy confided to an associate that the *Zone* perhaps should not have been published because it contained ethnic and racial stereotypes with which, toward the end of his life and post-civil rights era, he was uncomfortable (Trolander 1990: xviii–xix). The manuscript, unedited but largely complete except for a chapter that John Daniels was to have written on Negroes, was subsequently edited and placed in publication, first in 1962 and a second edition in 1969, by Sam Warner, Jr., MIT Professor of Urban Studies. As Lannoy noted, "In this Woods developed a vision of the city growth peculiarly similar to Park's" later one (2004:57n32). It is possible that Park read parts of the manuscript or discussed the work with Woods or John Daniels who was apparently occupied with getting his book out and failed to submit his chapter (Warner 1969:6). During the time work was underway on the *Zone of Emergence,* Park's family residence was near Boston and he spent much of his last year (1912) there before moving to Chicago and before writing his first essay on the city (Lannoy 2004:36–37,57, n 32). Although it cannot be stated unequivocally that Park or other Chicago sociologists were familiar with the *Zone,* some of the similarities with their urban sociology are striking, and it remains today the most sociological of the volume of work produced by the South End House residents. *Zone* continued their tradition of community studies, but is also a longitudinal study of working class families and individuals, a majority of them first or second generation immigrants, who were pursuing the American dream by moving to "better" neighborhoods. While they are not necessarily the same residents that lived in the tenement neighborhoods studied earlier, they are of the same demographic.

The *Zone* consists of empirical studies of eight working-class Boston neighborhoods carried out by Kennedy and six other residents, including Eleanor Woods. As can be seen in Appendix B, these communities are placed in relation to the city of Boston in much the same circular pattern conceptualized by Burgess in his Concentric Zone Theory and restated by Park in several writings (Woods and Kennedy 1969:31–33, Park and Burgess [1925]1967). The zone of emergence, comparable to Burgess' zone of workingmen's homes, was comprised of workers in industry who had bettered themselves by moving out of inner city slums (Burgess [1925] 1967:47–62). Woods and Kennedy referred to these "deteriorating areas" as the "inner belt" of congested tenements while Burgess called this the zone of transition (from single-family dwellings to business, industry, and tenement slums). Warner and others suggest that the manuscript was abandoned by the authors because they were disappointed in their findings which they interpreted as a loss of community relative to the settlement neighborhood that served as their frame of reference. *The Zone of Emergence,* in fact, identifies many of the patterns of change with which urban sociologists have become familiar. A growing anonymity was identified in several of the communities such as Charlestown where the population was said to have "become so disintegrated that purchasers seldom have a personal relation with those from whom they buy" (1969:55). The authors also found a disintegration of ethnic culture, leading Warner to characterize the book's theme as "the sterile discipline of American life" (1969:2) or a lack of what we label today as diversity. Kennedy was ahead of his time in pointing out dangers of bedroom communities where "a considerable portion of the population goes cityward [Boston] to work and feels itself far more at home there than in the Port" (1969:85). The communities studied were also experiencing an early version of "white flight" and of ethnic segregation. In East Boston, for example, it was observed that "Since 1895 the American remnant of the population has decreased with great rapidity" being replaced by the Irish Catholics, described as having "developed a life of their own, parallel and more or less apart from that of the rest of the community" (Woods and Kennedy 1969:198).

> [I]ndeed the zone of emergence is the great Irish belt of the city. They entered the zone on the wake of the industries which drove out the American population. The departing Americans sold their property to the newcomers, who, at a single stroke, often thus secured living accommodations that represented a decided advance over any they had dreamed of previously.
>
> WOODS and KENNEDY 1969:36

Some of the authors indicated disapproval of the flight of Dorchester "natives:"

> In the face of the outward march of Hibernian and Jew the Yankees have girt their garments well about them, snatched up their skirts that so much as a hem might not be defiled by contact with 'foreigners,' and have betaken them elsewhere in a spirit little and shallow, if not mean and snobbish.
>
> WOODS and KENNEDY 1969:149

An early form of ethnic succession was observed in some neighborhoods where "the more capable Irish have moved away, and their places have been taken by the laggards in the general progress of the main body of the race" (Woods and Kennedy 1969:143). In Dorchester, the succession was pronounced: "The first movement brought those of German and English nativity of a more assimilated type, but the Chelsea Fire[7] marked the beginning of an immigration of Russian Jews which has yet to cease" (Woods and Kennedy 1969:157). Although lacking in sophisticated analysis, which Woods might have provided had he returned to the manuscript after the war, there is no stretch in labeling this work as sociology. Its themes are readily recognizable in present day urban research and theory.

Despite the fact that Burgess had earlier acknowledged the contributions of settlement sociologists to the discipline, his association with Park apparently led him to critique their work as falling short of scientific rigor.[8] In an essay entitled, "Can Neighborhood Work Have a Scientific Basis?" ([1925]1967), Burgess presented "neighborhood [settlement] work" as laying the foundation for, but not achieving the level of scientific sociology. He argued that to achieve a scientific basis, settlement research should demonstrate three stages. First, *contact with social reality* which the settlements achieved as they moved into

7 The Chelsea fire occurred April 13, 1908, devastating the manufacturing tenement and retail sections of the Chelsea area of Boston in the extreme southwest section of the city and eventually covering more than a mile. The fire took four lives and injured many more. It destroyed churches, hospitals, a public library, city hall, schoolhouses, twenty business blocks, factories, and some 300 tenements and dwellings. The damage was estimated at $10,000,000 and some 10,000 persons were left homeless.

8 Interestingly, Burgess had once lived at Hull House (Rauschenbush 1979:182, Deegan 1990:144) and his early career was very much involved with reform and what later came to be labeled as social work. However, as documented by Deegan and Burgess' own writings, he later renounced this affinity and as Deegan put it "went back in time and made this difference appear to have always existed" (1990:146).

poor neighborhoods and extended "friendly relations." Second, *discovery of facts* was also achieved by the settlements as they produced works such as *Hull-House Maps and Papers*, *City Wilderness*, and *Americans in Process*. The third stage, according to Burgess, a *study of social forces* was not achieved by the settlements because they studied *factors* rather than *forces* as the cause of social problems. His differentiation was that factors are local and may be established as the cause for events or problems at the local level. Social forces, on the other hand are generic, macro-level abstractions that can be studied, described, measured, and analyzed. In fact, Burgess concluded that "no comprehensive study of the human community from this standpoint has yet been made" although he credited McKenzie[9] for laying out a prospectus for such a study ([1925]1967:63–79) and refered to studies currently under way at the University as treating social forces rather than factors.[10] On the one hand, Burgess can be seen as critical of settlement workers for not advancing to the scientific stage or, on the other hand, he can be seen as crediting them with providing a scientific foundation for sociological work as Park did in writing that they laid "the ground for the more systematic and detailed studies which followed" (Park [1929b]1967:5–6). According to Burgess, it should be possible by studying the community as an ecological, cultural, and political entity, to establish the "cause" of events in general because the processes of urban life in one community are typical of all. Burgess seemed to be advancing a criterion of science drawn from the Park and Burgess introductory text and subsequently labeled as "reliability:" "Sociology...will become...science...as soon as it can state existing problems in such a way that the results in one case will demonstrate what can and should be done in another" (1921:45). From Burgess' perspective, settlement sociology did not reach this level of reliability. In short, Burgess accused the settlement workers of being too local and too myopic in their approach to social problems. At first, Burgess seemed to use neighborhood and community interchangeably but then went on to describe communities as comprised of a number of different neighborhoods. Ignored in his discussion is the fact that all of Woods' work did implicitly and explicitly recognize the social forces of industrialization, immigration, and urbanization ([1923]1970:73). In fact his AJS article argued for studying the neighborhood as a microcosm of society (1914:578). It is clear that Woods' concept of neighborhood was not confined to his South End of Boston as he explained that the "new meaning of the

9 Roderick D. McKenzie was a student of Park and Burgess at the University of Chicago.

10 Presumably he refers to such studies as those by Anderson (1923), Thrasher (1927), Wirth (1928), or Zorbaugh (1929), all "natural area" studies directed by Park.

neighborhood" was "developed at four hundred settlement houses which have sprung up in America during this generation" (1914:581). Woods saw the city as organically integrated through its neighborhoods and in an argument comparable to Burgess' call for ecological, cultural, and political study, Woods argued for moral (his term for quality of life) and political study (1914:580). Although Burgess was unwilling to accept settlement sociology as scientific, his essay identified settlement work as the foundation of scientific sociology that was developing at the University of Chicago. The table in Appendix B compares Woods and Kennedy's conceptualization of Boston's growth patterns with those of the now canonical Concentric Zone Theory of Ernest Burgess and compares Park's concept of the natural area with Woods' concept of the neighborhood. Both the concentric zone and natural areas are ideal types, integral to urban sociology as developed at the University of Chicago in the 1920s. In fact, by the time Park began his work on the city many of his suggestions dealt with subjects which settlement sociologists such as Jane Addams and Robert Woods had been researching, writing and speaking on for two decades (Scott 1967, Lannoy 2004). Warner says of South End House sociology, "Taken as a whole the series constitutes an impressive body of pioneer studies of urban poverty. It will endure as one of the most complete American records of the obstacles then confronting native and immigrant poor" (1969:1).

Cultural Pluralism with Reservations

The body of work of Woods, Kennedy, and other South End House residents reflects a respect for cultural pluralism muted by a nationalistic, assimilationist paradigm. Unlike Jane Addams who is said to have "reveled in diversity" (Stackpole 1961:69), Woods' respect for ethnic diversity was tempered by his promotion of assimilation. In *Americans in Process*, he praised the Irish, Jews, and Italians as "three brilliant races...bringing forth a new brood" each "in its different way, making valuable contributions to the city's economic and moral welfare" ([1903]1970:374,380). With this recognition of ethnic cultures, Woods at the same time advocated for reciprocity in the assimilation process.

> The immigrant nationalities are already adding variety and fresh impulse to the city's industrial and social interests. It is essential that the established civilization of Boston should much more fully lay hold upon the body of feelings and traditions which are represented. ...The motive should be to have them affected by the American spirit, but also to have the American spirit affected by what is real in them...honoring and seeking to preserve much in the genius of each nationality ...([1903]1970:382).

Woods' only publication in the *American Journal of Sociology* seems to endorse a modest version of cultural pluralism when he wrote of the settlements as "holding together the fabric of all that is best in the immigrant home, while patiently integrating it into the common local relationships" (1914:587). Woods seldom wrote or spoke his appreciation of immigrant cultures without acknowledging the need for assimilation or Americanization. His goal was to "honor what is genuine in the spirit of nationality among each of the complex elements of our working populations while exalting those American loyalties which can unite them into a common citizenship" ([1922]1990:53).

Interest in the various immigrant communities (sometimes referred to as colonies) making their homes near South End House led to several investigations by residents, for example, a study of Italian immigrants in 1897 by Frederick Bushee, and a study of African Americans conducted by John Daniels beginning in 1904. While both works indicate that these residents were not free of the prejudices and ethnocentrism of their day, they also reveal appreciation for the difficulties peculiar to each group, and group strengths are acknowledged along with weaknesses. For example, in summing up his report on Italians, Bushee concluded:

> ...we have in the Italians a large colony of immigrants held together by a combination of clannishness and ignorance...a people who are physically strong but intellectually untrained; perhaps no worse morally than ourselves, yet who offend and shock us because their vices are of a different nature. ...It is only by a careful study of the people themselves and an observation of their actual life amongst us that we shall be enabled to judge of them correctly and estimate their contributions to American life.
> LDTP 1897, South End House Bulletin NO. 10: B3, F38

Likewise, Daniels did not hesitate to point out the many problems found among Boston's black population, most being recent migrants from the South. Yet their "shortcomings" were treated as rooted in generations of slavery, and he concluded on a positive note:

> A people grown up, from a forlorn and helpless band of slaves brought hither from the African jungle, into ten millions of free citizens, constituting a tenth part of the total inhabitants of the United States to-day; a people which has been in this country from the beginning, and has had an honorable and, indeed, a vital part, both in its establishment and preservation by ways of war, and in its manifold upbuilding by ways of peace—this people will eventually attain the position at once of self-respect and worthy recognition ([1914] 1969:441).

Further insight into the South End House approach to ethnic groups is found in Woods introduction to Daniels' book in which he suggested a tactic that would later prove very powerful in the civil rights of African Americans, economic boycotts used in pursuit of economic and political equity. "If the Negro in Boston could...consolidate their purchasing power, and direct it as they collectively chose, they could quickly double or treble the number of their representatives who should be holding responsible positions in industry and mercantile establishments" ([1914]1969:xii).

Appreciation of the diverse ethnic cultures of immigrant communities seemingly increased over the course of the South End House work and is most obvious in the *Zone of Emergence* where Kennedy and his colleagues revealed a preference for strong ethnic communities. Such communities were perceived as conducive to a healthy assimilation by providing a support system while immigrants were in the process of Americanization, as Kennedy noted with recent immigrants to the East Boston community.

> Common traditions and loyalties keep the individual in touch with the moral traditions of his race or nation while he is becoming socially acclimated and he does not become that most helpless of all beings, a man without friends or country...national loyalties perform a function whose importance cannot be overestimated.
>
> WOODS and KENNEDY 1969:193

This appreciation may have been strengthened as researchers observed the waning influence of immigrant cultures and a simultaneous loss of community and increasing anonymity. For example, in Kennedy's chapter on Cambridgeport there is a note of regret that the Irish are "American to the core of their being" (Woods and Kennedy 1969:72) and a tone of sadness in his description of the newly arrived Lithuanians and Poles who "cling to the old customs. But this soon changes in the American atmosphere" (1969:81). Woods' support of ethnic cultures was sometimes overshadowed by the appeal of democratization of immigrants and his continual search for the utopian Kingdom of God. Perhaps the strongest evidence of these interrelated influences is contained in an essay written in honor of his former Amherst professor, Charles Garman. The essay suggests that his social gospel and his faith in democracy were one and the same; his ideal democracy was indistinguishable from the Kingdom of God.

> The Utopia of democracy, in its true interpretation different in no principle from the Kingdom of God on earth, gathers up into itself all the

> great dreams which have illumined and fired the democratic prophets and martyrs, and constitutes in itself one of the deepest sources of power for making personality adequate to its present and confident of its future, and for bringing on the day when...the moralization of human society shall be complete (1906:99).

Seemingly Wood's faith in the democratic process was his reason for the acceptance of diverse cultures: "Only under a democratic system could any such variety of racial types and groups as there are in this country be held together in a common unity while retaining a very large degree of social distinctness and special loyalty" (1906:91). Woods acknowledged various concerns sweeping the nation that would lead later to passage of immigration restrictions. He discussed options for meeting the challenges of population quality, including suggestions for "artificial selection" which he rejected as "entirely beyond human ken." Instead, he favored minimizing "social sectionalism while giving due emphasis to all phases of the heredity and tradition of our different racial groups" and working toward the "full democratic development of education." Woods saw improved and increased education as the most viable means of "raising the standard of humanity." Ultimately, he looked to democracy to accomplish such uplift because democracy "furnishes an inspiration which comes from a fresh outlet to the moral imagination" on the way to the Kingdom (1906: 93–96). Woods, in his typical lofty, poetic style ended this essay with a utopian prophesy: "as humanity reaches upward and onward...there are vaster energies working in affinities undreamed of, by avenues inconceivable, to sustain and relate all the protean diversities of being in a unity that grows toward omnipotence" (1906:99–100). Woods concluded that "America is a federal union [and] in its racial character and its type of civilization...it must be that also" ([1923]1970:94). Overall, work from the SEH residents and associates gives evidence of appreciation for the contributions of their immigrant neighbors and awareness of their own ethnocentrism but ultimately an integrated social democracy was their goal.

Class and Racial/Ethnic Inequality

Woods often stated the obvious, "the curse of the poor is their poverty" and, less obvious perhaps, that the labor of the disadvantaged makes possible the life of the privileged classes ([1923]1970:11). As he saw it, bringing the classes together in settlement neighborhoods would hasten the realization of privilege on the part of the advantaged classes, both for the settlement residents and for those who would be influenced by them. He did not deal directly with class consciousness or class conflict in a Marxian sense, but implicitly recognized these. Woods' position seems to be what Lengermann and Niebrugge called the "radical middle," that is Marxian class conflict could be avoided by bridging the gap between classes in the settlement way, by the "neighborly relation" (2007:109). For consciousness-raising,Woods relied on class interaction to produce "an increasing circle of people unwilling that their comfort should be based in the hardship of their fellows" ([1922]1990:72). South End House writings offer numerous examples of class-consciousness and reflect perceptions of a three-tiered social class structure comprised of industrialists, a middle class of professionals and small business owners, and the working classes. Without using Marxian terminology, most of the South End House writings reflect concern with the dichotomized industrialist-worker classes. Their writings also deal with differences within the working strata, sometimes based on national origin, sometimes on labor skill, and at other times housing that was of course a function of economics. Over the course of his career Woods found various ways to characterize what he saw as a semi-permanent working class structure in the United States. For example, he described the population of Boston's North and West Ends as "broadly separated into three different strata."

> There is a residuum at the bottom characterized by some chronic form of dependence or degeneracy. There is the aristocracy of labor at the top, those who are likely to rise out of working-class life altogether, including all who are born with special capacity, whatever their surroundings may be. Between the two levels is a great middle class of labor, the working class proper, made up of those who will neither rise nor fall out of their grade, and most of whose children will not pass above it ([1903]1970:371).

In the same writing, Woods referred to the residuum at the bottom in Marxian terms as an "industrial army" ([1903]1970:371). Interestingly, Kennedy's working class distinctions in Cambridgeport were made in terms of housing, typically combined with work skill: "half-skilled workmen and unskilled laborers attracted by cheap rents;" "home-owning mechanics and clerks;" "highly paid clerks, salesmen, commercial travelers and small business men" seen as escaping the responsibilities of homeownership by apartment-living; and finally those young people who still live at home and work in Boston (Woods and Kennedy 1969:68). Kennedy also recognized the association between national origin and social class. His ranking moved from the oldest to the newest immigrants: those from the British Isles and Canada followed by Swedes and Portuguese, and finally Russian, Baltic, and Eastern Mediterranean groups (Woods and Kennedy 1969:70). Not unrelated to the fact that 85 percent of the residents of Cambridgeport were descendants of "English-speaking stock," is Kennedy's conclusion that the Port was "a stronghold of the great and powerful social grouping known as the 'middle class'" (1969:69). His discussion of "social classes," in Cambridgeport reflects both residential and life-style considerations. The "old Cambridge group," was described as a stable group of renters identified with the interests of their neighborhoods. In contrast were "peripatetic families" who moved frequently and had few ties and the boarding-house group or lodgers described as living in the area as "casual onlookers" (Woods and Kennedy 1969:86).

The "social question" in the Progressive Era was most often a veiled reference to social class and to the unequal distribution of wealth, veiled because the founding fathers established and successfully perpetuated the ideal of America as a classless society where success or failure was a product of individual meritocracy. Woods and Kennedy captured the fallacy of this ideal in their history and contextualization of the settlement movement in the United States.

> [U]p to 1885 only a few of all the responsible leaders in different walks of life were conscious that there was, in any real sense of the term, a social question. Every attempt at association among laborers was looked upon as an irrelevant and dangerous intrusion from out of the decaying civilization of Europe. The thought of any form of control over industry and commerce by government, except through a protective tariff, was hardly in the national mind. That the municipality should assume responsibility for conditions under which its citizens lived...was considered subversive of the principles under which alone American citizenship could thrive. It was still a matter of public confidence that the opportunities of American life were sufficient for everyone and would satisfactorily assure national well-being.
>
> WOODS and KENNEDY[1922]1990:35–36

Woods proclaimed his belief in class interconnectivity or mutuality of interests in a statement illustrating the importance of the underlying industrial system.

> There cannot be any more important message to the settlements everywhere than that which will bring them with fresh thought and purpose, into participation with their neighbors in meeting the economic issues that confront them in all their relations to the industrial system and process ([1923]1970:314).

A consistent theme in Woods' writings is his recognition that real reform must go beyond the individual case or family approach. As he put it, "the settlement movement strikes at the root of the tree" ([1923]1970:27). However, his proposals for ameliorating inequality held to the ideal of a social democracy and were little more than declarations of equal opportunity: "Social democracy does not hold that all men must be kept at exactly the same stage of progress. It does hold that each man shall have constantly held out to him his fair and just opportunity" (Woods 1929:106). Woods spoke often of the "waste of ability and genius" in American industrial society. In his early days, he promoted a class-free society, but in his later years he seemed to accept the reality of a stratified laboring class, some of whom would move up while others would not. He also came to accept that settlements should offer different opportunities to different groups within the working class because some had "exceptional gifts" while others were of the "vast unremarkable majority" (Carson 1990:118). One of Woods early writings explains the function of the settlement "as a connecting link between the two great sections of society...the commercial and professional classes, on the one hand, and the working class on the other" (1899:11). Functions such as social investigation, education, and charity were seen as necessary to achieve this class linkage. As Woods put it, the settlement motive must be carried "up into education and down into charity" (1899:15–16).

Methodology

More than perhaps any other settlement worker, Robert Woods has left among his artifacts a sophisticated methodology for community study. In one of his first public speeches as head of Andover House, Woods laid out his vision and plan for settlements as "laboratories in social science." He made clear that the settlement is a vehicle for social reform and that its "particular territory for study and experiment...includes the whole reach and depth of human life in that little world which lies within the narrow limits of the neighborhood of which the residents are part." Woods subsequently moved from the neighborhood to "all the neighborhoods of the city," urging residents to use a comparative methodology in studying neighborhoods other than their own and ultimately, "this leads the settlement out into the broad field of social economics as studied and practiced the world over" ([1893]1970:31–33). Woods conceptualized settlement residents as working in a new kind of sociological laboratory where they would use the "analytic and synthetic methods of science" in their careful and persistent investigation of social facts. So careful was to be their work that they must "differentiate every flower from every other flower and every fruit from every other fruit" ([1893] 1970:36). For Woods settlement workers were engaged in "careers in reconstruction;" their work had to provide guidelines for social action and, "in due time present some substantial results" ([1893] 1970:32). The methodology by which this work was to be accomplished was laid out with Wood's usual attention to detail as he prescribed what researchers today know as participant observation but taken a step beyond to the "neighborly relation." For residents, the settlement itself was their strategic instrument for data collection and they were urged to get to know the neighborhood by learning "a complete schedule of what life means in the particular street or court where...new found friends live, including the outer conditions of the place and the inner nature of the people" ([1893] 1970:36). Woods and Kennedy later outlined specific suggestions for researching a community including the collection of multiple and exhaustive sources of data ([1922]1990:305–308). Residents, students, or other researchers were instructed to first collect all available data (census, vital statistics, on births, deaths, marriages, crime, and disease) before determining what additional data were needed. Researchers must know their community's physical and social geography—the streets, alleys, vacant lots, public buildings, recreational areas, railroads, factories, schools, political parties, churches, and saloons. Equally important was to tap the community's collective memory and history. Although many settlement communities were new and fluid, Woods and Kennedy emphasized that they still had traditions, memories, loyalties, shrines, heroes, leaders, celebrities, and local historians. Researchers were reminded of the valuable resources to be found in the files or "morgues" of newspapers. Woods' first rule of social investigation was to start where the people are. He was among the first of urban ethnographers and he trained residents and students to be "neighbors and observers." He stressed the use of the inductive method over the mechanical and inquisitive method of census takers or charity visitors. In his first annual report from Andover House, Woods described the work done over the past year as "getting acquainted with the streets, learning their character, finding out about the way the law is administered, and in seeing in general how life is lived." According to Woods, "scientific charity" must begin with residents conducting a careful analysis of the social conditions of the neighborhood and the experiences of its people, attempting to see life as they did, to assume the role of the "other" (SEHR: BI, F53).

In a chapter in his final book, Woods offered an exercise for teaching sociology students how to study a neighborhood ([1923]1970:172–178). The fact that he specified sociology is no doubt because such classes were feeding residents into the settlements at that time. The exercise was designed to take students back to the neighborhoods in which they grew up and have them write down everything they could recall: geography, character, people, institutions, and problems. Students were to write papers based on their recollections and then read their papers in class where an analytical and critical discussion would follow. For instructors who wanted to formalize this classroom research, an appendix included a questionnaire for the purpose of guiding students through the exercise as he had done in a class at the Boston School of Social Work.[11] Although Woods did not say who originated this teaching tool, presumably it was constructed in collaboration with Kennedy. Woods suggested that this same exercise could be adapted to high school students who were still living in their neighborhoods and could learn skills in observation and investigation. Another tool of settlement sociology provided by Woods was "Twenty-One Kinds of Visiting" ([1923]1970:170–171). Inherent in these research tools was Woods consciousness of the importance of class reciprocity as "representatives of the more favored classes come to the less favored...observing the effect... upon the life of the poor and by observing from the new point of view the effect of the life of the poor upon the more favored" ([1893]1970:31). Settlement residents were representatives of the "more favored classes" and were to live among their "neighbors" and come to know their needs, their families, organizations, traditions, and customs, not as a "visitor" or census taker but as "neighborly caller." Wood stressed that settlement residents were to respect their neighbors and develop a reciprocal understanding so that they could "put themselves in each other's place."

Clearly, Robert Park built on the work of Woods and other settlement sociologists, describing their work as "a new literature...telling us how the other half lived" ([1929b]1967:4). He offered cautious but qualified praise that the settlement studies "do not yield generalizations of wide or general validity but... have furnished a body of materials that raise issues and suggest hypotheses which can eventually be investigated statistically and stated in quantitative terms" ([1929b]1967:8). Park seemed unaware that his own work or that of his students was subject to the same lack of generalizability. The "natural area" studies supervised by Park such as *The Hobo, The Ghetto*, and *The Gold Coast and the Slum* were also local studies of limited generalizability. Park's use of "natural areas" as the primary unit of analysis is similar to Woods use of the neighborhood. Similarly, both suggested some of the same sources of data; for example, the study of institutions and organizations in a given community. Beyond these similarities, however, directives for using the city as a laboratory differ, particularly in theoretical perspective and in methodology. Woods thought it absolutely essential that researchers (in his case, settlement residents) live among the people they studied (1914:582). Park encouraged his

11 He also indicated that Stuart Chapin had used this exercise at Smith College.

students and colleagues to study the city's natural areas but to do so as a journalist, observing and reporting the facts while not losing the objectivity of an outside observer ([1929b]1967:5). He placed emphasis on population demographics because "the proportion of age and sex groups shows extraordinary variations in different parts of the city and...are indices of other cultural and character differences in the population" ([1929b]1967:11). Settlement researchers linked social problems with a structure of inequality brought about by the forces of industrialization, urbanization, and immigration. Park took an ecological approach choosing to focus on individuals in their environments because social problems "frequently terminate in problems of individual behavior" and are often solved "by transferring the individual from an environment in which he behaves badly to one in which he behaves well" ([1929b]1967:12).

It was Woods' assumption that to know poverty and inequality through the eyes of one's neighbors would impel those of privilege to work toward a reduction of inequality. Woods did not have the personality or experience to become one of the working class for whom he advocated; nevertheless, he pioneered a participant observation and urban ethnography that furthered understanding and knowledge of the working class. For Woods, sociological investigation was all about studying and knowing the neighborhood and the neighborhood was to society what the circulation of blood was to the body ([1923]1970:148). Woods looked to the new science of sociology for discovery and understanding of the myriad complexities of communities and then of the nation ([1923]1970:161). Franklin, credits settlement workers, led by Addams, with use of Dewey's techniques of rational inquiry, a form of experimental design that involved defining a problem by moving from hypothesis through experiment and confirmation to a further hypothesis, a process of critical importance to practitioners (1986:520). For Woods, the beginning of this experimental process evolved from the people and from living among them and learning of life from their perspective.

Sociology, Social Work and the Politics of Gender

Woods papers contain two newspaper obituaries, the headlines of which are telling. One is captioned, "R.A. Woods, Social Worker, Dies Suddenly." The other reads, "Robert A. Woods, Noted Sociologist Dies" (SEHR nd: F 82). Woods followed the trajectory of many of his contemporaries who first identified as sociologists and subsequently as social workers as the discipline of sociology moved toward scientism and social work toward case work. We find fewer references to sociology in Woods' later writings than in his early ones and more to social work. By then he seemed to identify as a social worker, perhaps because of his serving as president of the National Conference of Social Workers and because, by this time, the bifurcation of sociology and social work was near completion (Lengermann and Niebrugge 2007:90). As with many other settlement workers, however, Woods traced his journey through sociology. He was a charter member of the American Sociological Society, published in the *American Journal of Sociology,* and all of his books were reviewed in the AJS between 1896 and 1923. Like many of his peers he was also a member of the National Conference of Charities and Correction, later the National Conference of Social Work (NCSW). Woods was one of several settlement workers who served as president of the NCSW (Barbuto 1999:138–139). Woods and Kennedy's observations on social work in their later writings suggest that they saw it as separate from sociology, but no less influenced by settlement history. Before settlements, they assert that charity workers dealt only with individuals or families; whereas, settlement workers came to realize the need to deal with "family after family" while building on the "case work technique developed by charity organization societies." At the same time they saw settlement work as having "liberalized its [casework] spirit and extended the range of its influence to include many new forms of advice, assistance, and education" ([1922]1990:396). Woods and Kennedy credited sociological studies in the settlements as contributing to disciplinary growth.[12] They also cited an impact on higher education as former residents filled faculty chairs in sociology or economics and as holders of settlement fellowships returned to report their experiences to classes and to student volunteer organizations ([1922]1990:392). The authors expressed regret, however, that "nowhere yet has there been complete cooperation on the science side between settlements and universities." While acknowledging that lack of cooperation was in some cases due to limitations on the part of settlement workers, they nevertheless saw universities as being "unwilling to apply their resources to the hard conditions of life" ([1922]1990:392).

Clearly, there is no shortage of examples of the contributions of Robert Woods and the South End House residents to the discipline of sociology, and those cited here speak for themselves. Chicago sociologist George Vincent in an article for the *Encyclopedia Americana* (1904) acknowledged the contributions of Woods, along with Graham Taylor and Jane Addams in "social technology" or "sociological practice." Barnes, in his history of sociology, classified Woods, along with Jane Addams and Graham Taylor, as "social economists" or "practical sociologists" (1948:741). In a later work, Odum adopted Barnes'

12 In fact, three South End House residents went on to teach in or to chair departments of sociology, one being William Cole who chaired the first department of sociology at Wheaton College (SEHR 1913:F77).

classification and listed Woods as among the "notable leaders in social work and public welfare" who published in the early issues of the *American Journal of Sociology* (1951:404). Other histories of the discipline, if they acknowledge Woods at all, do so in the context of his early neighborhood studies of the area surrounding the South End House (Vidich and Lyman 1985) or he is recognized for his introducing the concept of the settlement as a sociological laboratory. Woods' vision of social settlements as laboratories embraced both social investigation/research and its applications as integral to the improvement of city life. He closed a speech by saying that "settlements stand as laboratories in the greatest of all sciences," presumable sociology based on the earlier text of his speech. He subsequently identified the functions of such laboratories as "to develop skilled social workers, and to send them out, not merely into professional charity and philanthropy, but into every kind of human activity" ([1893]1970:45–46). Toward the end of Woods' life, social work was evolving into a profession largely defined by and associated with women. Gender dominance was established before social work was fully defined. The first two decades of the twentieth century saw various academic turf wars over social work in Boston, New York, and Chicago. These conflicts involved disagreements as to how and where social workers should be trained and efforts to separate social work from the emerging academic discipline of sociology and from the politics of socialism as well as the politics of gender (Shoemaker 1998, Lengermann and Niebrugge 2007, MacLean and Williams 2012). Woods evidenced an early awareness of these emerging issues when he chose the topic of "Social Work: A New Profession" for his address before the Harvard Ethical Society in 1905 (reprinted in [1923]1970:88–104). His platform for the speech is also indicative of the fact that this was both an academic and a nonacademic debate, and the speech is carefully crafted to address major issues surrounding the emerging profession. Woods began with a definition of social work as "seeking first to understand, and secondly to affect the problems of the community by means of direct contact" ([1923]1970:91). His definition includes both sociological study (to understand) and social work practice (to affect), suggesting that the two were inseparable. Woods articulated the social work role as "in the nature of unofficial statesmanship," but that is how he saw the role for *males*. When Woods referred to the settlement's "claim upon the university man," he was not simply using generic language as he went on to specify a patriotic duty as calling "upon young men to enter upon a definite and absorbing career of public service" ([1923]1970:95). Woods' description of male social workers sounds like Haskell's description of leaders in the American Social Science Association some three decades earlier as "men of authority" or "experts" (Haskell 2000:164–167). In fact, at one point, Woods said that social workers should train people to "trust the experts" ([1923]1970:92). This speech was also designed to keep social workers in their role of nation-building in the settlements, where "One social worker is primarily a doctor, another a lawyer, another a teacher, another a clergyman, another an artist, another a musician, another a businessman, another a sanitary expert, another a politician" ([1923]1970:97). A different picture emerged when Woods turned his attention to *women* in social work, asserting that the profession offered "peculiar opportunities to women." In contrast to the statesman role for males, he described women as carrying out a "natural extension of the interests and duties of the woman in her own home and in normal neighborhood society...the enlightened woman is simply making new and large adaptations of the specialized capacities which she has by nature and by training" ([1923]1970:99). In these complementary roles, Woods argued that men and women would be brought together "in a common work in which their cooperation is based on an unmistakable sound and real type of equality between the sexes" ([1923]1970:99–100). Unfortunately, his description of male and female social work sounds like a modified version of the doctrine of separate spheres.

It is not important, nor is it possible to establish Woods along with other settlement workers as sociologists or social workers. In fact they were both because as Lengermann and Niebrugge (2007:94) point out both sociology and social work found a home in the settlements of the United States between 1885 and 1920 and were combined into a science of reform. Settlement social scientists saw themselves as part of both sociology and social work, but as the authors argue settlement sociology turned on a politics of gender and after approximately 1920, settlement workers were marginalized and ultimately erased from the history of sociology because most were women. They do not speculate as to why workers such as Robert Woods were also vanished from the history of sociology. There are two possible reasons, the first and simpler is that if the women settlement workers were not sociologists then neither could the men be; however, this may assume a gender parody that was non-existent. A second reason could be that the men, most social gospelers, were too religious and sociology as a science has chosen to construct a history more secular than sacred. Even some academics may have fallen from the sociological canon for the same reason and, in fact, this may be one reason that European masters have remained in the canon while the likes of Albion Small, Charles Ellwood, and E.A. Ross are remembered, if at all, only as founding fathers.

South End House was, perhaps more than any other settlement a sociological laboratory and "'intellectualized' its religious motives into sociological research" (Stackpole 1961:31). This examination of Woods, his work, and that of other South End House residents, demonstrates that their contributions to sociology were substantial and that, in fact, there are parallels to be drawn between the South End House sociology and the now canonical Chicago School. Employing the neighborly relations paradigm, South End House contributed to a theory of a socialized democracy as begun by Jane Addams, to the substantive area of urban sociology, to a methodology of urban ethnography, and to advancing the critical concepts of structural inequality and cultural pluralism.

CHAPTER 7

The College Settlements Association: Breaching Gender and Class in Cities

At the same time that Hull House was beginning work in Chicago and the Neighborhood Guild in New York, a group of young women near Boston, associated with Smith and Wellesley colleges for women, were founding settlements in the Northeast. From an organization known as the College Settlements Association (CSA) formed in 1890, three social settlements emerged: the College Settlement in New York (also known as the Rivington Street Settlement) in 1889, College Settlement in Philadelphia, and Denison House in Boston, both opening their doors in 1892 although in the case of Philadelphia, the CSA assumed responsibility for on-going work. In 1910, the CSA added a preexisting settlement in Baltimore. The CSA was the product of women's college graduates and the settlements were continuously supported, managed and staffed by CSA and a network of women's colleges. In the beginning, the CSA was little more than the dream of a group of Smith alumnae who met in Northampton, Massachusetts in 1887 for a reunion: Vida Scudder, Jean Fine, and Helen Rand. This trio was shortly joined by other women associated with Smith or Wellesley: Katherine Corman, Katherine Lee Bates, Cornelia Warren, Jane Robbins, and Helena Dudley. An undated and anonymous note in the archives of the Settlements Collection reads as follows,

> Vida Scudder, Clara French, Helen Rand, all of '84, and Jean Fine of '83, when in college being much interested in settlement work planned later to open a settlement under the auspices of the women's colleges. Thinking it might be possible to open a settlement in '87 Miss Scudder and Miss French went to Oxford for a year's study. Miss French died and the other three lost their courage for the time being. However, they did form an organization of women's colleges and opened the first college settlement at Rivington Street in New York with Miss Helen Rand in charge. The following year a settlement was opened in Philadelphia in December 1892. Another house was established at 93 Tyler Street, Boston, known as Denison House after Edward Denison of England.
>
> SC:B1, F3

Scudder, recently returned from study with John Ruskin at Oxford and newly appointed to the faculty of Wellesley, was apparently the moving force in the group whose primary motivation seemed to be to break the restrictive bonds of gender and class. According to Scudder the young women founders knew nothing of Hull House or other efforts in the social settlement movement in the United States although they were familiar with the movement in England. In her autobiography, Scudder wrote of their beginning, "We followed the all-too-frequent American method; we began with an Organization, then we established centers, then we sought for people to carry out our ideas. We had splendid women among our organizers and our early residents but we had no Jane Addams" (1937:136). Scudder credited Katharine Bates as being the one to "outline the form in which our Eastern movement crystallized, a 'College Settlements Association,' with a governing board composed of delegates from the several women's colleges" (1937:110). This proposed organization was to be supported and controlled by college women and was later formalized in a simple thirteen-article constitution. The stated aims of the CSA were to further the education of college women and to reduce the distance between the classes, both to be accomplished in the real world of the college settlement (SC 1890, First Annual Report:B2, F1). Over the course of its history, the CSA established or came to manage four settlements, and their public presentation of settlements as women's work impacted the movement as a whole.

Membership in the CSA was both of an individual and organizational (colleges and universities) type, but governance was female-centered. The Constitution was at first written that "any woman" could become a member by paying an annual fee of five dollars; this was amended, in their first year of operation, to read "any person" (SC 1890, First Annual Report: B2, F1). Every college with at least 20 members would be entitled to two representatives on an Electoral Board, one elected by CSA members who were graduates or former students of member schools and the other elected by undergraduate members. "Two women" were also to be elected to the board to represent non-collegiate members. Interestingly, this latter provision states specifically women whereas this stipulation is not attached to other representatives. Theoretically it was possible for males to end up in governing positions since coeducational institutions could become members as could "any person" who paid the five dollar annual fee. However, the fact that most collegiate support came from, and was recruited from, women's colleges meant that by default this was to be a female-led organization. The Constitution also stipulated that "The majority of the residents in a Settlement at any one time shall always be College women." Decision-making power was vested in the Electoral Board with two-year terms, half the members being elected each year. Vida Scudder rotated on and off the strategic Electoral Board and the first Annual Report makes clear that "while all are welcome," presumably including men,

> ...the Settlement aims to be a distinctive work of college women, to express their conviction of their responsibility toward the social needs of the times and their faith in the method of fellowship and personal communion, as the most direct mode of ministering to that need. The management of the enterprise lies chiefly in the hands of college women. Responsibility for its success is theirs also.
>
> SC 1890:B2, F1

Approximately ten years after their founding, a CSA Bulletin listed fourteen institutions as constituting the organizational membership: Barnard, Bryn Mawr, Bucknell, Cornell, Elmira, Mt. Holyoke, Packer, Radcliffe, Smith, Swarthmore, Vassar, Wellesley, Wells, and Woman's College of Baltimore. With the exception of Cornell, an early pioneer in coeducation, all were women's colleges located in the Northeast. Representatives of these institutions comprised a CSA governing board to: (1) found, support and exercise general control over settlements, (2) train women for social service, and (3) accomplish an educational work of a broad scope. The document goes on to affirm:

> The Settlement stands today as the best embodiment of social democracy, and the College Settlement is the expression of the highest social ideals of college women.... By the simple method of residence among the poorer classes, women in our Settlements are finding a larger interpretation and a deeper significance for the relation of friend and neighbor.
>
> SC, College Settlements Association: B1, F6

Scudder and other CSA leaders saw themselves as involved in a "great modern movement" and always stated their belief that the organization would go as far as their funding and support would take them or be stymied by limits "such as we shall ourselves assign" (SC 1891, Second Annual Report: B2, F1).

The CSA Constitution specified that each settlement would have an Elective Committee comprised of three elected members and *ex-officio*, the head resident, and one other member added by the committee. At some point it was also specified that over one-half of the membership of these decision-making committees must be female. A majority of the Committee was to be chosen from members of the CSA residing in the neighborhood of the Settlement, suggesting that members of the Committee did not have to reside in the settlement itself but in the geographic area. This local, Elective Committee was essentially responsible for day-to-day management: hiring of the head resident, budgeting, programming, annual reports, and fund raising. The CSA Electoral Board shared decision-making with this local Elective Committee and as time went by the settlements became more and more dependent on local fundraising. The CSA parent organization offered each settlement an annual stipend but rarely more than $1200. Beyond that, budgets and facilities were met by local communities. Buildings, for example, were almost always donated or paid for by special benefactors. In some cases, the head resident ended up spending more time fundraising than in programmatic activities. Over time, the settlements added local boards of trustees or advisory boards to their work, often to assist with fundraising. As each settlement was expected to become an integral part of the neighborhood in which it was located, and management was in the hands of a local committee, it is not unexpected that the CSA settlements each developed their own special culture and sometimes moved in different directions as reflected in the Third Annual CSA Report.

> In New York the Settlement is, first of all, social; it aims to bring pleasure into lives from which pleasure is crowded out by the unrelenting round of toil. In Philadelphia the condition is practically reversed; the people in St. Mary Street and vicinity are anything but hard-working; the need is not for pleasure and rest, but for employment and the self-respect begotten of honest labor. In Boston the work is too new to afford a sufficient basis for generalization, but we may say that the outlook there is largely toward sociological investigation.
>
> SC 1892: B2, F1

There were not only differences among the CSA settlements but substantial differences also existed between the CSA and other settlements. The CSA was a group effort and was never identified with any one individual as were houses in Chicago—identified, for example, with Addams, McDowell, or Taylor—and even in Boston where the South End House became synonymous with Robert Woods. The CSA settlements were very much the product of the first generation of college-educated women, and more specifically of women's colleges. If associated with any one individual, it would most likely be Vida Scudder because of her frequent public appearances and speeches on behalf of the CSA work. The CSA founders were all in their twenties and, as Scudder admitted, "We had no influence and, except for Cornelia Warren, no money.[1] Nobody in America within our range of contacts had ever heard of the idea that possessed us.... And not a scrap of sympathy that I remember did we receive from any of our elders in this crazy notion of ours" (1937:111). For a time, plans for the CSA

1 Cornelia Warren was a Smith College graduate and member of the wealthy Warren family of Massachusetts. She supported many philanthropic causes. Her donation of the first several buildings for Denison House and her friendship with many of the CSA women made her an influential person in that organization.

seemed fated to the scrap pile of history, but Scudder was motivated by a certain emptiness in her life and a longing for something more meaningful, spurred on it seems by the death of her dear friend Clara French who died shortly after accepting a teaching appointment at Wellesley. This early and unexpected encounter with death seemingly renewed Scudder's determination to invest in, and motivate others to invest in, settlement work. In a statement reminiscent of Betty Friedan's (1963) the "problem that has no name," Scudder wrote of "the ennui of restless luxury that besets the rich lady" (1890:4). From its inception, the CSA held steadfast to its dual aims of reducing the distance between the classes and of providing a meaningful service role and continuing education for college women. CSA literature and speeches often referred to their work as part of a "great movement for social reconstruction" (1890), and social science was the "engine of effective change" (Carson 1990:100). A ten-year retrospective document from the CSA history states that the breaking down of "the wall of ignorance and prejudice which causes the separation of classes" was to be accomplished by "the method of friendly intercourse" (SC:B1, F6), what Addams and others described as the "neighborly relation."

Mann asserts that this first generation of college women was "more concerned with the profitable use of their time than with the effect of their progressivism on the masses" (1954:228). Similarly, some critics suggest that the CSA settlements were more effective in meeting the needs of educated single women than those of slum dwellers (Vicinus 1985:222). In describing and questioning the work of the College Settlements Association, Recchiuti wrote,

> They bought or rented houses or tenements and moved in after graduation from Smith, Vassar, Amherst, Columbia, City College, and NYU, making homes there, primarily among immigrants, fueling discussions in settlement-sponsored clubs, mobilizing the community for political action...far from the charity alms of past patrons of the poor.... But...in bringing social science to the slums, what was to be the relationship between the educated scholar-activist elite and the mostly ill-educated working poor (2007:65–66)?

Rousmaniere argued that the CSA settlements were women's colonies and extensions of women's colleges such as Vassar, Smith, and Wellesley. In fact, these three schools provided all of the 16 first-year residents, almost half of all residents in the first five years of CSA operations, and a majority of the long-term residents. He also argued that residency in the CSA settlements was very much a function of peer-group alliances as more than three-fifths of all college-educated CSA residents knew at least one other woman who was also to become a resident (1970:47–49). In comparing the CSA settlements with others, Mann drew a sharp contrast, particularly between two Boston settlements, Woods' Andover (later South End) House and CSA's Denison House.

> Unlike Andover House, the woman's settlement did not produce a social survey of the neighborhood…it is here that we touch on a crucial difference between Robert A. Woods and Vida D. Scudder. Woods believed that the well-situated must identify themselves with and uplift the poor, but the *sine qua non* of the settlement was to reclaim a blighted neighborhood. It would collect data on the life of the area, discover the causes of poverty, cooperate with trade unions, serve as a neighborhood center of public pressure, and above all, recommend…how to eliminate want and woe from American cities. Miss Scudder regarded all of this as fine, but the settlement 'should feel that it vindicates its existence, though it give not a statistic to the world, if only…it renders possible life among the people for those whose heart belongs to the people'.
>
> MANN 1954:224

Settlements established by the CSA were less involved in sociological study than were many other settlements, seeing their task as more social in enriching the lives of those around them and thereby reducing class inequality. An entry from the New York settlement in one annual report states, for example,

> We have no statistics to record, no tabulated additions to economic science to deliver, but we have found that simple healthy living is possible in the midst of poor conditions…that genuine Christian neighborliness is no chimerical vision, but a happy prophecy of a reconciled world.
>
> SC 1892, Third Annual Report: B2, F1

It would be a mistake to suggest that social investigation was not important in the CSA houses or that none was produced, but simply that it lacked the primacy given it in other houses. Scudder, the chief spokesperson for the CSA frequently solicited support for the "establishment of fellowships for women who seek to pursue sociological studies in College Settlements," touting such study as so important as to "help our movement more than any other one thing" (SC 1891, Second Annual Report:B2,F1). Indeed, early in their existence, the CSA did begin a program of fellowships to support residents who wanted to conduct sociological research or later to gain more training and preparation for the profession of social work.

Jane Addams once referred to settlements as providing a "socialized education," in other words a pragmatic education in the real world of urban problems. More than other settlements, the CSA formalized a structure guaranteeing that women would not be subordinate to men while living, working, and studying in the settlement environment. It seems clear that Scudder envisioned settlements as places where women could live and work in areas of need and, at the same time, continue the study of sociology or political economy begun in college (Ryan 2006:51,133). For example, a paper from Denison House, "Information to Candidates for Residence" invited residents to participate in the "opportunities for study" offered by the Boston settlement and stated further that residents were expected to "give at least one hour a day to sociological readings." Suggested resources included the house library as well as study with persons such as Emily Green Balch, John Graham Brooks, Vida Scudder, or the Rev. W.D.P. Bliss (Williamson 1895:237, Ryan 2006:137). Formal sociological study at Denison House was apparently situated in the Social Science Club which sometimes met with residents of South End House and sometimes clergymen, students, and labor leaders. The topics could be as diverse as organized labor, capitalism, or "charity visits." Usually someone would present a paper and this would be followed by a general and "animated" discussion presenting viewpoints from all sides (Williamson 1895:237). This kind of in-house education was also apparently prevalent at other settlements such as the one in Philadelphia, and all of the settlements seemed from time to time to offer what amounted to college or university extension classes taught by local professors for a nominal fee. Often times these classes were designed to meet the needs of resident workers, such as learning about city government in Boston or Philadelphia or learning about Jewish history or even Yiddish classes (Ryan 2006:140). The CSA attempted to provide post-graduate or on-the-job training for women, beginning with the simple distribution of a list of suggested readings for women considering settlement work (Rousmaniere 1970: 61). A formal "Syllabi for the Study of Social Questions" was prepared and distributed to the CSA settlements where it was apparently used by some in formal classes and by others for meetings of social science clubs. One syllabus, obviously intended for continuing education, was authored around 1904 by Caroline Williamson, a resident of Denison House, and a graduate of Wellesley. It shows the influence of her mentor, seemingly having been drawn from Scudder's book, *Social Ideals in English Letters*, and her Wellesley class of the same name. The syllabus included 27 readings authored mostly by English males; there were only seven Americans among the authors. In fact, reminiscent of today's often weak effort toward diversity, the syllabus included the writings of only two females, Dorothea Dix and Sister Dora, and one black male, Booker Washington (SC:B1, F6, Ryan 2006: 92–124). For several years, Williamson, by then Caroline Williamson Montgomery, compiled a *Bibliography of College, Social, University, and Church Settlements* for the CSA.

Apparently in an effort at outreach, the CSA offered syllabi for sale to any organization or individuals interested in education about settlement work and/or the training of workers. For example, the 1905 bibliography offered a syllabus by Emily Greene Balch on "A Study of Conditions of City Life" for 15 cents and syllabi on "Biographies of Social Leaders" and "Modern Philanthropy" for five cents each (Montgomery 1905:9). Balch's syllabus included a 12 page bibliography grouped into the headings: citizens, housing, health, education, recreation, art, and municipal functions.

In 1917, the CSA became the Intercollegiate Community Service Association (ICSA), obviously shifting attention from settlements with resident workers to community service and social work. Interestingly, it was Vida Scudder who wrote the final chapter of the old organization just as she had written the first. She reported on the outdoor meeting at Mt. Ivy, New York, where "the old CSA, still full of faith and fire, decided to rebaptize itself and to widen its appeal and its ambition...grey-haired...founders sat in a row; around them clustered college women from all succeeding generations...the CSA was reborn" (SC, Intercollegiate Community Service Quarterly, Vol. 3: B1, F11). The decision was to change the name and to widen the appeal of the organization to community service, but great care was taken to protect, maintain, and continue support of the four CSA settlements. At the time of this transition, Scudder announced the appointment of Susan Kingsbury then director of the School of Social Studies at Bryn Mawr and also Director of Research of the Women's Education and Industrial Union[2] as Executive Secretary of the ICSA and Helen Greene as her assistant. The emphasis going forward was to be on social justice and civic health. Recruitment of workers and support was still to be from colleges. The fellowships were to be continued although descriptions reflected a change in emphasis from research to social work. However, Kingsbury's connection with the WEIU did bring attention to the availability of research fellowships for graduate students. All four former settlements remain active in various specialized programs of community service today.

2 The WEIU was established in 1877 in Boston by Dr. Harriet Clisby, one of the first female physicians, to respond to those social problems that were severely impacting the well-being of women and children such as crowded housing, poor sanitation, and exploitative working conditions. The organization was restricted to women until 1903 when men were admitted as associate members. Other chapters were formed in New York. Over time the WEIU provided services such as legal aid, employment training and placement, a credit union, and funded scholarships and research (http://ocp.hul.harvard.edu/ww/weiu.html, accessed July 14, 2014).

The Women Founders

Scudder: The Voice for Educated Women

Vida Dutton Scudder (1861–1954) was born in Madura, India where her father was a Congregational missionary who drowned when she was hardly a year old. Following her father's death, Vida and her mother returned to their home base in Boston where both parents were members of prominent families. Her mother was a Dutton of the E.P. Dutton publishing house, the publisher of several of Vida Scudder's books. Her paternal uncle, Horace Scudder was a long-time editor of the *Atlantic Monthly* and a well-known writer. She enjoyed an unusually good education and, between her two extended families, a privileged upbringing. She was a member of the first graduating class of the Boston Girl's Latin School in 1880 and graduated from Smith College in 1884. It was at Smith where Professor John Bates Clark introduced her to the writings of Frederick Denison Maurice that Scudder began to think about social problems. After graduating Smith, she traveled and lived in Europe with her mother. In England, she and her friend, Clara French, were the first women admitted to study at Oxford University although because of their gender they were not awarded degrees. It was at Oxford where Scudder's social consciousness was further awakened as she studied with John Ruskin and delved into the works of Christian Socialists such as Charles Kinsley and further into the work of Maurice. After returning to her home in Boston, Scudder earned a master's degree from Smith in 1887 and subsequently accepted a position teaching English literature at Wellesley College. She was also offered a position at Smith but accepted Wellesley because it allowed her to continue to live in Boston in a house that she shared with her mother and an aunt. In fact she lived in that same Boston house until 1912 when she built a home in Wellesley and moved there with her mother who died in 1920. Scudder retired from full-time teaching in 1927 but continued to live in Wellesley where she remained active as a writer and public speaker. Much of her work in later life was focused on Christian Socialism. She traveled and occasionally taught a class at Wellesley or elsewhere until her death in 1954. Scudder was well known because of her teachings and writings and as a pioneer in the use of literary criticism as a vehicle for social reform, the best example being her *Social Ideals in English Letters* (1898) and a Wellesley course by the same name. Among her writings is a semi-autobiographical novel, *A Listener in Babel* (1903) which explains much of how she conceptualized the split between the classes. In this work she explored the geography of the city of Boston, with its economic and ethnic diversity, through the eyes of an advantaged young woman torn between the comfort of her own familiar way of life and that of settlement work in the city's

South End. As she traversed the city and took note of contrasting human conditions she engaged in disappointing discussions with several clerics, causing the young woman to conclude that the church was "on the side of wealth" and "the greatest instrument of moral self-deception ever invented by the race" (1903:141, 252). Scudder did not, however, disavow her own Christian faith but vowed to work toward reform of the church as she prayed "Come and save us from Thy Church, O Carpenter of Nazareth" (1903:157).

Religion was an important part of Scudder's life. Although she grew up a Congregationalist, the church of her father, when she was 14, both she and her mother joined Phillips Brooks' Episcopalian Trinity Church in Boston. Through the years, however, she was a supporter of and frequently attended the Church of the Carpenter a congregation formed by the Rev. W.D. Porter Bliss and comprised largely of Christian Socialists (Scudder 1937:165). As a young woman Scudder also joined an organization that was to have a major influence on her religious and spiritual life, a semi-monastic group of Episcopalian women known as the Companions of the Holy Cross, dedicated to intercessionary prayers and social reconciliation; not incidentally, most were Christian Socialists (Barbuto 1999:186–187). Scudder identified as a Fabian Socialist early in life, although she said in her autobiography that she could not remember when she "took out [her] red card [Socialist Party membership]" (1937:161). Many of her writings and speeches suggest a continuing effort to reconcile her religion and her socialist leanings (VDSP:B2, F4). Her ardent work in organizing the College Settlements Association and in taking the initiative in the establishment of three settlements suggests that this work was perhaps one way that Scudder attempted to alleviate guilt over her own privileged background and to assuage her conscience, awakened as a result of her education and exposure to the problems of urban poverty. The CSA was a secular institution but the social gospel or Christian socialism motivated many of its supporters and participants. "Because they were members of the dominant WASP culture, however, the early headworkers and residents were unaware that what they considered secular was overtly religious," for example Sunday night Vespers or Christmas celebrations (Ryan 2006:57). In fact, some scholars have treated Scudder as a social gospeler and, indeed, some of her writings are of that genre. For example, she wrote in the *Atlantic Monthly*,

> The best, the final work of democracy will be to give us all the freedom of the City of the Common Life. This all Americans know in theory. Let us beware lest we deny it in deed by withholding our faith from the great class-conscious movement of the working people, which alone holds in practical form the ideal of a world where divisions based on economic

> accident and arbitrary causes shall be obliterated, and life be lifted to new levels of freedom.
>
> VDSP 1911: B2, F2

Some, such as Stackpole, have suggested that while good intentioned Scudder was never able to get beyond her own cultural snobbishness (1961:39). It was, nevertheless, Scudder who, more than any other person, made settlement work the "cause" for educated women and brought a somewhat modified version of feminist pragmatism to CSA settlements (1887a). She made the pressing social problems of the day equal in importance to the need for women to get involved in the work of finding solutions, thereby casting off the "ennui of restless luxury" that beset many of the privileged class. Scudder's philosophy is well articulated in an 1890 address to the Association of Collegiate Alumnae (later the American Association of University Women). The speech represents an early effort at public education in order to gain support for the idea of women in social service which she referred to as "sociological work," its broad scope spelled out as involving "the reconstruction of the whole social order" (1890:6). Scudder elaborated clearly one of the primary motives of settlement work by placing this first generation of college women in "an intermediate position between the two great orders of the rich and the poor" (1890:4). She waxed eloquently in her description of the role of an individual worker: "Let her visit the schools, the homes, the work-rooms, the saloons, and learn, not only through eye, but through ear and heart; and then, when she has watched, when she has thought, let her speak. She will have something to tell" (1890:12). Without referring directly to the doctrine of "separate spheres," Scudder made her case by educating the public as to the appropriateness of settlement work for women, presenting the settlement as a public home (1890:10). In a speech before an all-female audience, she proclaimed, "Put half a dozen young men together, and they instinctively evolve a club; put half a dozen young women together, and they instinctively evolve a home" (1892:341). Scudder also served up a heavy potion of responsibility to the first generation of college women and for the several generations to follow, positing them as "a new factor in the social order," as responsible participants in a "moral organism" where "if one member suffers, all the other members suffer with it" (1890:6). Scudder also demonstrated the influence of the "new sociology" in her thinking, and in her socialist tendencies. She dismissed Herbert Spencer as "the characteristic figure of the later years [of the nineteenth century]" and Karl Marx as more likely to be representative of the twentieth century. She spoke approvingly of "the transition from scientific speculation to sociology" and credited Comte with spurring passage from "the metaphysical to the positive [scientific]" (1890:1–2).

As with many of the socially conscious leaders of her generation, Scudder referred to social service and social investigation as "sociological work" for which she saw college women as having "a peculiar effectiveness" (1890:3). Settlement work for women was seen as practical, intellectual, and spiritual, providing opportunity to live, not singly but in colonies, as neighbors among the poor because "the only way to know life is to share life" (1890:10).

Perhaps more than any other settlement leader, Scudder linked settlements with colleges and universities, particularly the women's colleges which she saw as especially equipped to "establish centers in the midst of our industrial population" (1900:141). She saw colleges, indeed higher education in general, as imbued with "a definite responsibility toward the social needs of our times, and a definite contribution to make toward their solution" (1900:140). A settlement connected with a college should be of a distinct type which she elaborated in detail.

> It must...stand for life rather than for work, for attitude rather than achievement, and must have for its firm foundation personal fellowship with the unprivileged; it must not neglect practical work...but it will emphasize and develop the opportunities for sociological study which settlement life affords; it will continue the tradition of the colleges in doing its evangelical work indirectly, and will therefore not narrow its scope as must be the case with the avowedly religious settlement...it will...offer a systematic training of workers to a high standard of social efficiency; and it may well place...stress on presenting to working-people...some of the most life-giving results of academic studies.... [Workers] shut up in the prison of ceaseless daily labor...have been unable to discover for themselves the worlds of art, of thought, of learning. But it is surprising to see how quickly love and intelligence can open these worlds to them (1900:140–141).

Perhaps because Scudder idealized the role of higher education and of educated people, particularly women, she was critical of colleges and universities for accepting what she called "tainted money" from wealthy industrialists because the money came with strings attached. Her writings and speeches denouncing "tainted money" got Scudder in some trouble with the Wellesley Board of Trustees. She considered resigning but did not and they did not fire her. Of course, the fact that her uncle, Horace Scudder was on the board may have helped her (Scudder 1937:180–184). Scudder's name was prominently associated with early labor organization and activity. She wrote about and made speeches in support of labor. She publicly supported the textile workers' strike in Lawrence, Massachusetts, traveling there to get a first-hand perspective

(1937:184–185). Many today will see Scudder as an early feminist, and she doubtlessly was; however, she was very critical of the feminists of her day. For example, she raged against the suffragists as women "devoting their energies to the embroidery of doilies, while they mourn the narrowness of their lives" (1887b:12).

Others Founders of the College Settlements Association

Of the women who helped to found the CSA, most remained directly or indirectly involved in the settlement movement with Scudder and Dudley demonstrating life-time commitments. Some of the other founders, although unknown today, made contributions in various ways and deserve mention here because they stepped out of their comfort zone at a particular juncture of history to advance the cause of gender and class equality.

Jean Fine (1861–1935) was an 1883 Smith graduate from Ogdensburg, New York. She taught math and science at Clinton College in Kentucky after her graduation until 1888 when she left to take a post with the Neighborhood Guild, in charge of women's and girls' clubs. She was in transition between teaching and her pioneering settlement work when she became one of the group of women who founded the CSA. She was deeply involved in the initial work of the organization and served as the first head resident of the College Settlement in New York, a position she held until 1892 when she left to marry Charles Spahr, an economist and later editor of the *Outlook*. After her marriage she remained active in the CSA organization and in fund raising (Recchiuti 2007:68).

Jane Robbins (1860–1946) from Wethersfield Connecticut, attended Smith College for one year from 1879–1880, later other schools in New Jersey and Kentucky, eventually studying to become a physician at Women's Medical College of New York. She lived at the Neighborhood Guild prior to moving into the New York College Settlement which she viewed as both "a gathering place for the neighborhood residents and as a tool of social investigation" (Barbuto 1999:177). After the departure of Fine, Robbins became the head worker at the College Settlement and was known as a strong supporter of labor and of improving the working conditions of women and children. She was also a supporter of public school education and at one time worked as a school inspector in New York and advocated for using school buildings after hours as neighborhood centers. She left the settlement in 1897 to resume private medical practice and over the next 30 years provided medical services in different fields including to those in need after WWI and as a member of the Red Cross.

Helen Rand (1863–1935) was a member of the Rand family of New York that began the Rand School of Social Science, a school for those of socialists leanings started in 1906 by George Herron (son-in-law to Carrie Rand), Christian sociologists who was fired from his position as professor of applied Christianity at Iowa State College. In 1935 this school became the Tamiment Institute and Library. Helen graduated Smith College in 1884 and later married Lucius Thayer and became the mother of two children while remaining active in the CSA, with the Smith Alumnae and with various philanthropic organizations and social causes such as woman's suffrage and child labor.

Katherine Coman (1857–1915) was a Wellesley professor, frequent visitor and long-time supporter of Denison House in Boston. Her life's work was primarily as an academic where she encouraged many female students to enter settlement work and helped to establish a fellowship program for young women to spend a year in residency. She was one of the first women to earn a degree from the University of Michigan (1880) and then accepted a position as instructor of rhetoric at Wellesley. In 1893 she moved into her real area of interest with appointment as professor of economics and sociology, a position she held until she retired in 1913 and subsequently worked in Progressive party politics. While never a settlement resident, she was a long-time supporter of the CSA and persuaded her friend Cornelia Warren of Boston to become the association's first major financial contributor. She chaired the committee that opened Denison House in Boston in 1892. She was a member of Phillips Brooks' Trinity Episcopal Church in Boston as was Scudder. She was very involved in union activities and helped to make Denison House headquarters for union activity. She and Cornelia Warren helped to organize women garment workers and supported them in a number of strikes. In 1910, for example, she traveled to Chicago to assist in a strike of seamstresses seeking union recognition which they won the following year (James 1971:365–367). Coman joined the Consumers' League and used it as a vehicle to bring pressure to bear on manufacturers' for improved treatment of workers.

Katherine Bates (1859–1929) helped to found the CSA and was largely responsible for writing the initial plan of organization after which her direct involvement was limited. She is best known as the author of the words to "America the Beautiful" and as head of the English department at Wellesley from which she graduated in 1880. She taught English at Wellesley until near the time of her death and believed that values could be revealed and developed through literature. She shared a living arrangement with Katharine Coman for almost 25 years. Scudder said of Bates,

> Katharine was never active in the movement; poetry, friendship, scholarship, and the service of her College, were to fill her life; but she contributed the initial plan of organization. And she did more, for she introduced me to a young teacher in the department of history, who was to become

> her dearest friend.... Katharine Coman. She adopted the settlement idea at once, and interested her friend, Cornelia Warren of Boston, the first person with any money to welcome the scheme (1937:110–111).

Helena Dudley (1858–1932) was a member of the first graduating class of Bryn Mawr in 1889. While a student, she heard Scudder, Fine, and Rand discuss the new social settlement movement and subsequently volunteered to represent Bryn Mawr at a meeting of the CSA in 1890. In 1892 she become the first head resident of the College Settlement in Philadelphia. The following year, she moved to Boston to replace Emily Balch as head of Denison House where she remained until 1912. She joined with Robert Woods and residents of the South End House to investigate housing conditions in Boston and to campaign for public baths. With Scudder, she organized a Social Science Club at Denison House to hear lectures and engage in discussions about social issues. She was actively involved in unions and union activities; she joined the Federal Labor Union and the American Federation of Labor. She and Scudder were delegates to the Boston Central Labor Union and she helped to organize the Women's Trade Union League. She was sympathetic to the militant approaches of industrial workers and, in fact, her support for the IWW 1912 textile workers' strike in Lawrence, Massachusetts led to her resignation as head resident of Denison House because she feared her support of labor would alienate benefactors of the CSA. However, she remained actively involved with the settlement as a volunteer and in 1917 was given the title of Headworker Emeritus at Denison House. Her "retirement" years were filled with activism in support of labor and in support of the peace movement during and after World War I. She was a charter member of the Fellowship of Reconciliation, was actively involved in the Women's International League for Peace and Freedom, and in promotion of the League of Nations. Her labor interests eventually led her to join the Socialist Party. She died while attending a meeting of the Women's International League in Switzerland in 1932 (Barbuto 1999: 66).

Clara French was one of the founding members of CSA and Scudder's best friend. After graduating from Smith, she traveled to England with Scudder and her mother where she studied at Oxford and came under the same influences as her friend Vida. French was offered a faculty appointment at Wellesley the year after Scudder. She accepted the appointment but died of typhoid fever near the beginning of her first semester, a loss which Scudder lamented for the remainder of her life.

Mary H. Mather (1861–1925) was another of the founding members of CSA but little is known about her beyond her Smith College affiliation. After college she apparently became active in women's causes, especially education for women. In the early part of the century, as a resident of the state of Delaware, she organized the Women's Committee of Fifty to lobby for women's higher education in a state that "spent not one cent on higher education for women." Efforts of this and other groups culminated in the establishment of the Delaware College for Women. She is also currently listed in the Delaware Women's Hall of Fame.

The CSA and the Movement for Social Reconstruction

The CSA settlements are less well known than some of their contemporaries; however, settlements in New York, Boston, and Philadelphia each made distinct contributions to what the leaders conceptualized as the "movement for social reconstruction." They did not have the dominating presence of a Jane Addams; they lacked the social gospel mission of a Graham Taylor; they did not produce the sociological studies methodically engineered by Robert Woods in his South End House "laboratory." While each CSA settlement produced or inspired some important sociological work, their overall contribution to sociology is that they gave us a better understanding of ethnicity/race, class, and gender and of how a group of educated, middle and upper-class women could breach the boundaries of urban geography, of social class, and of gender roles. These CSA women carved, out of the fabric of the old doctrine of separate spheres, a new role and a new voice for women—the kind of women heretofore plagued by purposelessness and ennui. Clearly Scudder and her fellow CSA founders were aware of the new science of sociology and saw it as an important tool for reform when they began their adventure in settlement work. As early as 1892, the CSA began awarding from one to four student fellowships for the purpose of "sociological investigation" and after 1911 for "practical training in settlement work." Pursuant to the initiation of these fellowships, Vida Scudder wrote for the Electoral Board in 1891, "The establishment of fellowships for women who seek to pursue sociological studies in College Settlements would perhaps help our movement more than any other one thing" (SC 1891, Second Annual Report: B2, F1). Apparently the first fellowships were endowed by individual donors with names such as Upham and Dutton attached to the fellowships; later the Sage foundation underwrote the fellowships for several years, and in 1912 Carola Woerishoeffer provided an endowment for fellowships, as did some colleges. These awards were competitive and residency was required of recipients along with well-defined projects with the promise of "usefulness" for both the research and those who carried it out. In most cases, the fellows followed their own interests, perhaps extensions of classroom study; however, on some occasions, members of CSA or others interested in "the movement" suggested problems in need of research. The CSA Annual reports document that Fellows produced papers on such topics as "The Obstacles to Sanitary Living Among the Poor," based on research in New York and Boston; "Diseases and Accidents Incipient to Occupations" based on research in Boston and Philadelphia; and "Receipts and Expenses of Wage Earners in the Garment Trades." While the annual reports were very uneven in their documenting ongoing research projects, beginning in 1893, most included some mention of fellowships and the research underway. For example, it was reported that fellowships assigned for 1892–93 went to Amelia Shapleigh of Cornell to study "The Dietary of the Poor" and to Maud Mason of Wellesley to study "The Use the Poor Make of their Leisure Time." Most of the fellows were female college students and their work was supervised by faculty members in their respective schools, further solidifying the link between the CSA and its college supporters. Apparently it was not uncommon for fellows to split their year's residency between two houses, not always CSA settlements, as in the case of Chicago. In some years only one fellowship was awarded due to lack of funds and the chair of the Fellowship Committee appealed in the Annual Report to "all interested in this most promising experiment in sociological work to use their influence to secure funds for a second fellowship for next year" (SC 1894:B2, F2). Largely as a result of the fellowships, each of the CSA settlements produced research that made a contribution to a sociology of urban problems, to women's equality, to labor reform, and ultimately to what would become the interdisciplinary academic program in women's studies. Over the years, there were changes in the size of stipends, the number of fellowships, and at one point there was differentiation between fellowships and scholarships, the former being specifically for research, the latter for social work training. Most fellowships were for one year but some were renewable, particularly when research was underway. Both fellowships and scholarships were awarded on the basis of financial need and in the beginning provided just enough financial assistance to pay for a fellow's room and board since all of the CSA houses required that residents pay their own expenses. A 1914 CSA 25-year anniversary report summarized the outcome of some of the fellowships, not only in scholarly products but in the application or practical outcomes of the work of the fellows.

> Such, for instance, are Mary Sayles, who investigated tenement-house conditions and became a tenement-house inspector; Isabel Eaton, who investigated conditions among colored people, and is now at the head of settlement working among that race; Frances Kellor, who made a study of

> employment offices and has since been at the head of the New York State Bureau of Immigration; Mary Gove Smith, who, through her study of the Italian immigrant, was prepared to take up and develop a remarkable work for the Italians at Denison House; Mary Van Kleech, who investigated the overtime work of girls in factories, and is now connected with the Department of Women's Work of the Russell Sage Foundation, a department which was a direct outgrowth of Miss Van Kleeck's work.
>
> SC 1914, 25th Anniversary Report

Indeed, among names of promising and productive sociologists associated with the College Settlements Association during the first half of the century, are those such as Frances Kellor, Mary Van Kleech, Emily Balch Green, and Mary Simkhovitch. These women were beneficiaries of CSA fellowships and continued their work by bringing in other agencies and organizations to fund expanded work and to assist in the application of their findings by advocating and implementing reforms.

The New York Settlement

The establishment of the New York Rivington Street settlement in the city's lower East Side preceded the formalized incorporation of the College Settlements Association. In keeping with the CSA, however, the expressed motive behind the New York settlement was two-fold: the British tradition of the responsibility of the educated to the poor, and the self-conscious need of the first generation of college-education women in the United States to be of service. In retrospect, the CSA settlement in New York may have made the best adaptation to the needs of America's poor. In the fall of 1889 two women, Dr. Jane Robbins and Jean Fine opened the doors of the College Settlement at 95 Rivington Street very near the location of Coit's Neighborhood Guild, becoming the second settlement in the United States and the first under the auspices of the CSA. Robbins took up full-time residence and was joined on week-ends by Fine, who was then teaching uptown. They began by sponsoring social clubs for girls. Fine resigned her teaching job to become the first head resident and held that position until 1892 when she resigned to marry. As head resident, Fine moved from programs for women and girls to a full range of programs for all settlement neighbors. She also established a small library in the settlement and opened two baths for use by women and children (Barbuto 1999:75). The College Settlement was staffed entirely by women until 1907 when men were added to the staff but not as residents. This all-female operation was consistent with the mission of the CSA and also complemented rather than competing with the services of the nearby, male-led Neighborhood Guild. Although the two settlements were located just blocks apart and both were nonsectarian in programs and cooperated on many endeavors, they were very different. The Guild was more structured in its programmatic efforts to involve the community in uplift and self-help while the College Settlement saw itself as a kind of intellectual, social mission and, although unplanned, the settlement became known for its hospitality to organized labor, a center for labor meetings and activities. In its first year, even though required to pay room and board, 80 women applied for residency, far more than could be accommodated. Eleanor Roosevelt worked as a volunteer at the New York settlement and several times taught dance and calisthenics classes there between 1903 and her marriage in 1905.

A *New York Times* report on a speech by Dr. Robbins about the work of the College Settlement suggests that journalists and, perhaps consequently, the public had difficulty understanding just what the settlement workers were doing and little wonder based on the press account of Robbins' speech. Reminiscent of an article several years earlier in the *Chicago Tribune* about Hull House, the *New York Times* report described the College Settlement as "open for general hospitality" and as having attached to it "a teacher, a doctor, two assistants, and three members, whose chief office is to disseminate gracious influences" (March 15, 1894). There was no mention in the report of research underway at the settlement as a result of social science fellowships, even though at the time of Robbins speech, Isabel Eaton was writing up her research on the garment workers of New York and Chicago, later published in the *Journal of the American Statistical Association* (Recchiuti 2007:69). After Robbins left the Rivington Street settlement, she was succeeded by Mary Kingsbury who served as headworker for one year before leaving to accept a position at the Friendly Aid House. In 1898 Elizabeth Williams, another Smith graduate (1891) with a master's degree from Columbia, became head resident and remained through the years of World War I. When the CSA celebrated its first 25 years of service, they reported that the New York Settlement then occupied two houses, a gymnasium and club house, and a summer camp at Mount Ivy.

Several pieces of research with important social reform implications were begun or conducted at the New York College Settlement. One of the earliest was that of Mary Buell Sayles, an 1890 graduate of Smith who began her work at the College Settlement but, upon being granted a CSA fellowship to study housing in Jersey City, moved to become a resident of Whittier House, an early settlement in Jersey City where she worked as a CSA fellow for two years. Her work was a massive undertaking for a one-person project. She interviewed over 500 families and collected statistics on over 2,000 apartments in the city.

Her investigation was subsequently published (1903) and led to a meeting of political leaders that produced housing reforms for the city and the state when the Governor appointed the first statewide Tenement House Commission. Sayles went on to do other research and continued to write, with reform in mind, about foster children and the need for home services for families.

The work of Frances Kellor is perhaps the best known of those associated with the New York College Settlement and is an example of the interfacing of various settlements in that she had ties with Hull House, College Settlement in New York, and later lived at the Henry Street Settlement and studied at the New York School of Philanthropy. When she was awarded a CSA fellowship in 1902 and went to live at College Settlement, she was almost 30 years of age, older than most residents. She was familiar with settlement work because of her years in Chicago as a resident of Hull House. While a student at the University of Chicago she studied sociology, political science, and political economy. Before arriving at the New York CSA, Kellor had already published a text on *Experimental Sociology* with an introductory chapter by Charles Henderson and several articles in the AJS, edited by Albion Small (see Appendix A). Most of her work dealt with female criminal behavior or with the general topic of criminal behavior. Perhaps because she never received any financial support from the University, Kellor left without taking a degree although she was awarded a law degree from Cornell in 1897 prior to going to Chicago. Her research on working women and girls, begun as a CSA fellow, burgeoned into work that Kellor continued for years beyond her fellowship. Her earlier work on women in prison led her to make an association between criminality and unemployment, an interest that led her into extensive research on unemployment and resources available to assist in the search for work. Her research, published as *Out of Work* (1904), linked the problem of unemployment with corrupt practices in many New York employment agencies and was deemed important enough that the CSA renewed her fellowship for 1903–04 and subsequently helped to finance a job for her. Kellor's project was big enough that it involved the help of other fellows and students in field work and in the use of innovative methods, today known as participant observation, in the collection of data. In investigating the practices of employment agencies, Kellor studied two kinds, those serving all kinds of workers, male and female but primarily male and the second kind, known as Intelligence Offices, that specialized in supplying household workers, often female immigrants. With only antidotal evidence of wide-spread corruption in the beginning, Kellor determined that she must get a true picture of the business practices of the agencies and that she could do this only if she went in and asked direct questions. Thus she elected to sometimes assume the role of an employer looking for workers and at other times to pose as a worker looking for a job. She justified this bit of deception as being in the interest of science and saw the end as justifying the means. She studied over 800 agencies in four cities: Chicago, New York, Philadelphia, and Boston. Her analysis emphasized structural problems that kept the corrupt employment offices open and exploiting clients, especially immigrants and southern blacks. She advocated reforms that relied on facts, state intervention, and government centralization. Later, Kellor worked with another reformer, Mary Dreier, to draft actual legislation (the Prentice Bill) in New York State to correct some of the corrupt practices her research had uncovered. Because of their lobbying, their effective use of research findings and of the press, they succeeded in getting both municipal and state reforms passed, including a rather comprehensive state-wide regulatory bill in 1906 (LDWP, NYPL:Reel 2, B35). Kellor's expose' of employment agencies led to her appointment to head the Inter-Municipal Committee of the New York Women's Municipal League[3] overseeing the organization's various committees and an information clearing house to conduct research and disseminate findings (Fitzpatrick 1990:135–137). Following her work with the Women's Municipal League, she was appointed by the governor to head the New York Bureau of Industries and Immigration, part of the state Department of Labor. In 1912, like many of her fellow settlement workers, Kellor became involved with the Progressive Party and persuaded Theodore Roosevelt to establish, within the party, a research bureau devoted to important political, social, and economic issues. The result was the National Progressive Service, an agency intended to fuse scientific research and social reform (Fitzpatrick 1990:149). Indicative of Kellor's networking, was the "parade of social welfare leaders, academics, and public figures she was able to assemble to serve on departmental subcommittees."

> John Dewey headed a group interested in "public education problems," while Booth Tarkington directed the Division of Motion Pictures. Edith Abbott served on a subcommittee investigating women's labor under the guidance of Chicago settlement worker Mary McDowell. Kellor herself agreed to launch a committee on immigration, whose members included

3 The Boston Women's Municipal League (BWML) was formed in 1908 by a group of well to do women "to promote civic betterment." The founders believed that housekeeping of a great city was women's work. It was their challenge to see that the city was kept clean which would, in turn, help to keep their own homes clean. The League grew to include chapters in other cities such as New York and some 2,000 members. Their dues funded studies and programs carried out by paid professionals or sometimes students (internetarchive.org, accessed May 12, 2013).

> Wellesley professor Emily Green Balch, writer Jacob Riis, and Edith Abbott's sister Grace, then head of Chicago's Immigrants' Protective League. Chicago professor Charles Merriman, U.S. Commissioner of Corporations Herbert Knox Smith, settlement leader Lillian Wald, juvenile court innovator Judge Ben Linsey, George Kirchwey, dean of Columbia's Law School, and *Survey* editor Paul Kellogg....
>
> FITZPATRICK 1990:150–151

During her years with the Progressive Service, Kellor oversaw the drafting of a series of legislative bills embodying key elements of the Progressive Party platform and carefully positioned on research findings. Most of the bills, however, were doomed from the start as eventually was the Progressive Party. By 1914, Kellor shifted her efforts to immigration by heading an organization known as the Committee for Immigrants in America which resulted in the creation of an informational clearing house within the federal Bureau of Education on problems of the foreign-born. With the approach of World War I, this agency took on added importance for the government and changed its focus from immigration reform to concerns about the loyalties of foreigners living in the United States. Kellor herself became less an advocate for immigrants and preservation of their native cultures and involved herself more in various Americanization programs. She eventually came to support United States involvement in the war, thus becoming part of a split within the settlement movement with leaders such as Robert Woods, Graham Taylor, and Mary Simkhovitch supporting the war and the likes of Jane Addams, Vida Scudder, Lillian Wald, and Emily Balch taking a pacifist stand. Kellor's career is but one example of the far-reaching impact of work begun by CSA fellows and is also exemplary of the consistent theme running through the life's work of many—that research must be the basis of reform and social policy.

Denison House of Boston

Of the three CSA settlements, Denison House (DH) most nearly reflected English inspiration and aspirations. It was named for Edward Denison an English social reformer and advocate of living among the poor, as he himself did. Although Denison died at the young age of 30, his influence lived on through publication of his letters and speeches. The Boston settlement was the only CSA settlement to be named for an individual and this fact suggests the presence, influence and vested interest of Scudder more than was true of the other houses. In fact, during the years that Scudder lived in Boston she maintained a room at Denison House and was very involved in the day-to-day working of the settlement. She wrote of this involvement in her autobiography and of stimulating "group social study" that included the likes of labor leader, Edmund Billings; writer, John Graham Brooks; and Rector, Charles Brent. But she also wrote of getting out and mingling with the "neighbors" (1937:159). Located in what was known as the Old South Cove area of Boston, interest in sharing culture with the masses was more prominent in the atmosphere and programs of Denison House than the other CSA settlements. Indeed, Denison was located in what was known as the "most cosmopolitan district of Boston" populated by Syrians, Armenians, Italians, Greeks, Chinese, French, and Eastern European Jews (DHR 1910, Report of Headworker Dudley). Despite its being named for a male, Denison House was very much a female domain and, in fact, is one of three such domains in the city of Boston examined by Deutsch in *Women and the City*, the other two being the Fragment Society, founded to assist the poor, and the Women's Educational and Industrial League founded to aid all women in gaining economic and intellectual self-reliance (2000:136–160). Even the three buildings into which Denison House grew in its first decade were donated by a wealthy female benefactor, Cornelia Warren.

> Denison House...headed first by Emily Balch and then by Helena Dudley but with Vida Scudder always in evidence, was situated in a less "Fetid" district.... The aristocratic desires to share culture with the masses were more basic to Denison House than self-identification with the poor. The house...never lost its British aristocratic tone, and failed to join in the great fact-finding drive of the early Progressive years.
>
> STACKPOLE 1961:25–26

Descriptions of Denison House raise questions as to its purpose in comparison with other settlements. One patron of the CSA compared Denison House with the busy, almost frenetic pace of the New York settlement.

> At Denison House there is something of a mission and a school atmosphere: prayers after breakfast etc.... Pictures all madonnas or the Botticelli kind, doubtless one ought to admire them but I think the neighbors would enjoy other subjects better. Children don't seem to come in and hang around.
>
> FCKP, JOURNAL: B1, F8

Interestingly, an early quote from the CAS Third Annual Report indicated expectations that the Boston settlement would lean toward "sociological investigation." However, the Boston settlement produced less sociological research than either the New York or Philadelphia settlements. The expectation for sociological work was not met and as one critic put it, "the only record of anything remotely investigational at Denison House is the description of the women's visits to their neighbors during the first couple of months" (Capitanio 2012:57–58). Dudley, however, reported that Denison House residents in 1897 began a thorough house-by-house investigation of the district's lighting, sanitation, tenement house ventilation, and crowding and that the results were sent to the city's Board of Health (DHR 1897, Report of Headworker Dudley). In fact, Robert Woods and residents of the South End House investigated and described the South Cove Area more thoroughly in *The City Wilderness* (1898) than the residents of Denison House ever did. This omission was apparently deliberate as head resident Dudley and her friend Vida Scudder, unlike other settlement workers, felt it more important to focus on reaching the individual than the entire community. Dudley once proclaimed, "The settlement worker is occupied generally not in securing the larger reforms of conditions which must come gradually through public action, but in caring for the individual" (DHR 1903, Report of Headworker Dudley). This seems contradictory, however, to the language Scudder frequently used in referring to the CSA as the "great social movement of reconstruction." In comparing Denison House with nearby South End House, a virtual sociological laboratory, Streiff concluded,

> Although Denison House residents did not pursue social scientific surveys in quite the same vein as did South End House residents (and Denison House never published reports on the scope of *The City Wilderness*), the settlement still represents one of the first neighborhood-based social reform efforts in Boston, as well as in the country (2005:165).

More than research and club activity, Denison House came to be associated with labor organizations and activities such as those of the Women's Trade Union League. The Fourth Annual Report of the CSA in 1893, only the second year of operation for DH, states that the Executive Committee had set a direction: "our leading interests at Denison House will be twofold.... University extension and the organization of labor" (SC:B2, F2). Denison House did become best known for their support and advocacy of labor unions and labor activists. In fact, head resident Dudley eventually resigned because she feared that her association with labor was an impediment to fundraising. Apparently the thing that caused Denison House to become increasingly associated with labor was the economic depression of 1892 and1893 which rendered so many jobless. Dudley personally worked to raise funds to put people to work at Denison House in order to ensure the survival of families. Before that economic crisis, as Scudder observed, "it had been possible to live in a tenement house district, happily absorbed in pure neighborliness" (1937:154). In fact, the labor activity centered at Denison House was a direct response to the needs of workers, but at first it was a need observed by Denison House residents and outsiders more than a need voiced by workers themselves. Several events converged in the early 1890s to set in motion Denison House's turn toward labor. Mary Kenny arrived, fresh from labor organizing at Hull House; Helena Dudley visited a women's garment basement work room and was shocked by the deplorable conditions; and Jack O'Sullivan, labor reporter for the *Boston Globe*, began visiting Denison House. O'Sullivan kept returning, bringing labor organizers and women workers to tell horror stories of their working conditions. Neighborhood meetings were called and Dudley began going out into work places to invite workers to organizing meetings. Scudder called on a friend who was a female factory inspector to begin inspections of some unknown work places they were hearing about. But female workers were hesitant to get involved, partially because they saw unions as men's work and because they feared losing their jobs, bad as they were. In the beginning, Denison House residents took on the work of organizing more than the workers themselves. Dudley and Scudder were delegates to the convention of the Boston Central Labor Union as early as 1893 and helped to organize the Federal Labor Union and in 1903 the Woman's Trade Union League (Scudder 1937:155). Another organizer of the League was Mary Kenney who married Jack O'Sullivan and the couple frequently held labor meetings at Denison House (Scudder 1937:154–155). The settlement came under criticism because some observers felt that the Denison House women should adhere to the advice of Robert Woods that settlement houses should remain publically neutral in matters involving labor. Although perhaps overshadowed by labor activism, the settlement was also involved in the typical neighborhood clubs and classes, activities which they apparently did quite well. Their most famous resident may well have been Amelia Earhart who lived there from 1926 until her transatlantic flight in 1928. In fact, before leaving, she cleared her plans with head worker Marion Perkins and promised to be back for summer school (Ware 1993:42).

Although Denison House was never a powerhouse of sociological research, it did have a secondary impact on such work through former residents who while living at the settlement became familiar with sociological investigation and hence were motivated to do their own research. Denison had an active social science club and heard frequent lectures and discussions led by those who were involved in research. South End House sometimes met jointly with the Denison Social Science Club. Some residents were involved in various sociological projects. Henry Bruere, for example, lived for a time at Denison House and later, as head of Chicago's Bureau of City Betterment, spent time in Hull House and Chicago Commons.[4] In New York where he headed the Bureau of Municipal Research, he lived at both the College and University settlements. In discussing Bruere's municipal research, Stivers offered the following observation, "his experience as a settlement resident (Boston's Denison House) and his interactions with residents of Hull House, Chicago Commons, and New York's University Settlement might well have given him the term [survey] and almost surely inspired the approach" (2000:78). Another example of sociological work associated with Denison House is that of Emily Greene Balch, whose interest in Slavokian immigrants no doubt evolved from her experience while at Denison House with various immigrant groups in the South Cove area of Boston. Balch was the first head resident at Denison House, long-time board member, and after leaving residency, professor of economics and sociology at Wellesley for almost 20 years. She used her first sabbatical and an additional year at her own expense to undertake this first inquiry into the lives of Slovokian immigrants in their native European environments and later in the United States.[5] She combined available demographic data as well as observations, primary documents, and interviews in weaving together descriptions of conditions that shaped the people and motivated their emigration as well as their culture which they could transport only in part to their new home in America. The second part of her study involved the collection of data (again quantitative and qualitative) from these same groups in the United States as she visited Slavic colonies from New York to Galveston, Texas, and sometimes lived with the people she was studying and at other times at various settlement houses (Randall 1964:116–117, Gwinn 2010:66). Her ethnography, *Our Slavic Fellow Citizens*, has much in common with Thomas and Znaniecki's *The Polish Peasant in Europe and America* (1918–1920) and preceded it by more than 10 years, but while the latter has become a classic in sociology, Balch's work (1910) is little known.[6] The scope of Balch's work was, in fact, broader than that of Thomas and Znaniecki although the objective of both works was similar: to look at a group of immigrants from the perspective of forces at work in their homelands and to examine the lives of

4 During the administration of Franklin Roosevelt, Bruere worked for the treasury department and served for a time as a media advisor to the president.

5 These were Polish; Slovaks; Croatians and Slovenians; Ruthenians; Bohemains and Moravians; Bulgarians, Servians and Montenegrins; Russians; and Dalmatians, Bosnians, and Herzegovinians.

6 Parts of Balch's research on Slavic immigrants were first published in a series of articles for *Charities and the Commons*. She later revised these essays and increased the volume of both qualitative and quantitative data for an inclusive publication (1910).

these groups after they settled in the United States. While the work of Thomas and Znaniecki was more sophisticated methodologically and theoretically, the work of Balch was more inclusive and involved first-hand interviews and observations of large numbers of people representing the various groups known at the time as "Slavs." Thomas and Znaniecki relied primarily on analysis of documents from a limited number of Polish immigrants and their causal analysis seemed to impose, after-the-fact, a discordant social psychological theory of values and attitudes. They also seemed to dwell on the negative aspects (social disorganization) of Polish life in the United States. Reflective of the neighborly relations paradigm, Balch's work had no agenda other than to acquaint readers with Slovakians now part of the U.S. tapestry. Balch readily pointed out the strengths of native cultures transported to their new homes. She clearly leaned toward cultural pluralism and predicted losses for both Slovakians and the United States if these immigrants became Americanized to the extent that they lost vital cultural traditions.

In 1913 Denison House filed papers for incorporation, allowing it to own property and engage in fund-raising on its own while affirming a continuing association with the CSA (CS, 25th Anniversary Report). In 1941, after neighborhood studies by Denison House and the Boston Council of Social Agencies, the decision was made to move Denison House to the Dorchester-Roxbury area of Boston. The move took place in 1942 and for six years the office and programs were located in several different buildings. In 1949 Denison House moved into permanent quarters in the renovated Howard Avenue School and in 1965 merged with three other settlements to form Federated Dorchester Neighborhood Houses (FDNH). Each house retained its own director and program staff, with FDNH responsible for program coordination, fund raising, and fiscal management. In 1975, after a fire destroyed the Howard Avenue building, Denison House moved to Codman Square, Uphams Corner, where since 2008 it has focused on educational programs. In 2009, Denison House became College Bound Dorchester targeting college education as a means of community transformation (http://www.fdnh.org/about/history, accessed April 2, 2013).

The Philadelphia College Settlement

Compared with other settlements, there is a dearth of information on the College Settlement of Philadelphia (CSP). As Ryan noted in beginning her research: "[T]he literature on settlement houses generally treats the Philadelphia settlements as mere footnotes, even though Philadelphia

…participated fully in the settlement movement and afforded numerous educational and social opportunities for college-educated women" (2006: 34). According to Davis, although Philadelphia had eleven settlements at the turn of the century, only the CSP had an important impact on social reforms in the city (1984:23). Compared with cities such as Chicago, Boston, and New York, Philadelphia's immigrant population was small. However, only Baltimore, Washington DC, and New Orleans had larger populations of African Americans. In attempting to trace the history of the CSP, it is sometimes difficult to differentiate the histories of other organizations that were an overlapping part of CSP history, particularly since some were often identified by the same names: Starr Center, Wharton Center, Whittier Center, the Saint Mary Street Library, and the Wharton Settlement. According to several accounts, the College Settlement of Philadelphia evolved from the Saint Mary Street Colored Mission Sabbath School, founded in 1857 by wealthy merchant George Stewart. Other philanthropists were involved in this area of the city, later to become known as the Fifth and Seventh Wards. For example, Theodore Starr added to Stewart's work with a day care, kindergarten, playground, coal club, and Penny Savings Society. Inspired by the example of Octavia Hill in London, several wealthy Philadelphians including Starr, and cousins Susan Wharton, Hanna Fox and Helen Parrish, began buying houses in the African American community, restoring them, and renting them at affordable rates. The Seventh Ward, while of mixed socio-economic and racial composition, was home to about one-fourth of the city's African American population and as with most such communities of that day it contained some of the poorest and "some of the best Negro families" (Du Bois [1899]1996:60). Wharton, Fox, and Parrish, influenced by their Quaker roots and a history of family activism, began assisting in programs at the Starr School; Fox, for example, taught in the kindergarten. In 1884, Theodore Starr died and Wharton purchased a house on Saint Mary's Street, expanded the programs of the school and opened a library.[7] The Saint Mary Street Library (SMSL) functioned in many ways as a settlement without live-in residents; in addition to loaning books, classes and vocational training were

7 Susan Wharton's Father, entrepreneur Joseph Wharton, established the Wharton School of Finance and Economy at the University of Pennsylvania in 1881, "to prepare young men to assume control of the complex economy" that was unfolding. This was the first business school in the US established at a university. Interestingly, while their printed bulletin did not list the appointment of WEB DuBois as a Research Assistant from 1896–1898, he is today listed on their website as having been awarded a fellowship to undertake "an intensive two-year study of the social and economic conditions of urban blacks" (http://www.wharton.upenn.edu/about/wharton-history.cfm, accessed February 21, 2013).

offered in carpentry and cooking. In 1891, a six-member Executive Committee (four men and two women) invited the CSA to join them in Philadelphia in assisting with and expanding programs in the Saint Mary Street neighborhood. This invitation and its positive reception by the CSA no doubt came about because of networking on the part of the women. Wharton and some of her cousins were graduates of Vassar and since Vassar was a supporting member of the CSA, they were familiar with the organization through the women's college network. A house owned by Susan Wharton at 617 St. Mary Street was offered to the CSA rent free for two years. The CSA, eager to expand its settlements and opportunities for young women, readily agreed to the SMSL offer and joined the work in Philadelphia in 1892, naming the St. Mary Street house the College Settlement of Philadelphia. In contrast with other CSA settlements, The Advisory Board included not only males and females but also African Americans and whites (SC 1891–1892, Report of the St. Mary Street Library: B4, F2; Katz and Sugrue 1998: 4–6; Ryan 2006:46, 195–199). About a year after the SMSL Executive Committee joined with the CSA to found the College Settlement of Philadelphia, Susan Wharton founded the Whittier Centre for the "study and practical solution of Negro city problems" which over time came to focus on such quality of life issues as housing, health care, and recreation and came to be referred to locally as the Whittier Center and/or the Wharton Center. To further confuse matters, there was the Starr Foundation with programs and property carried over from the old Sabbath School. The library formally ceased to exist in 1893 when it became a branch of the City Library of Philadelphia.

Helena Dudley became the first head resident of the Philadelphia settlement but remained for only one year and left to assume that same position at Denison House in Boston. She was replaced in Philadelphia by Katharine Davis, a Vassar graduate (1892), who remained as head resident for four years (1893–1898) before leaving to pursue graduate study at the University of Chicago.[8] Ryan suggests that the Philadelphia women were apparently networked with Jane Addams and Hull House because both head residents to follow Dudley at

8 Davis did not return to settlement work after completing her degree in political economy at the University of Chicago. She became involved in prison reform and was appointed Superintendent of the women's reformatory in Bedford Hills, New York. In 1914, she was appointed New York City Commissioner of Corrections, the first woman to hold a cabinet-level position in the history of the city. As commissioner, among other things, Davis became known for doing away with stripped prison uniforms for women saying, "you cannot reform a woman who is wearing bed ticking." She headed New York City's first parole commission and ended her career as head of the Bureau of Social Hygiene funded by the Rockefeller Foundation where she became the center of public controversy surrounding a large-scale survey of women's sex behavior (Fitzpatrick 1990:92–129, Rosenberg 1982: 197–203).

the College Settlement of Philadelphia were referred by Addams as was their best known research fellow, Isabel Eaton, a former resident of Hull House and a contributor to *Hull-House Maps and Papers* (Ryan 2006:262). The College Settlement was Philadelphia's first full-fledged settlement and the first to be established in a predominantly African American neighborhood. Its first home was on St. Mary Street between Sixth and Seventh Streets, just south of Lombard Street. Over half of Philadelphia's black population lived in or near the Fifth and Seventh Wards that included one of the worst areas of the city but also included some of the most prominent whites. "[P]roud stone and brick row homes, many with ten or twelve rooms, which housed some of Philadelphia's elite" remained from an earlier day (Katz and Sugrue 1998:10). These whites knew each other, moved in the same social circles, and some served together on the executive committee of Susan Wharton's SMSL and in other civic and charitable positions. Most of the nearby black population was comprised of those who worked for wealthy white families in private homes, in hotels, stores or other businesses, and a sizeable segment were live-in domestics. But as Katz and Sugrue described this nineteenth century "walking city," rich and poor, black and white could not avoid each other, and from time to time, the stench of the nearby congested housing (whites and blacks) must have drifted into the fine homes on the Ward's periphery. Blacks and some poor whites lived in close proximity but the poor lived in dank alleys with crude outdoor facilities, a family with several children usually occupying one or two sparsely furnished rooms in unventilated row homes with no indoor water or toilets and where toxic smells were so prevalent that some labeled Philadelphia "Filthydelphia" (Katz and Sugrue 1998:8–10, Ryan 2006:29–31). Abysmal conditions in the city were no doubt one reason that in 1892 Charles Harrison, University of Pennsylvania Provost, donated a furnished country home for settlement children to enjoy summers out of the city. According to Alewitz (1989), Philadelphia politicians were committed to low taxes and high tariffs and failed to see the need for street paving, garbage collection, sewer and water systems. Unlike some other settlements, however, the Philadelphia one did not move into a community lacking in organization or indigenous institutions, especially for African Americans. There were numerous churches, clubs, small black businesses, and several newspapers. In fact, Du Bois found the number and richness of black institutions, so little removed from slavery, to be remarkable ([1899]1996:233–234). Another unusual demographic of the black population was that it was disproportionately female, presumably because women found jobs as domestics in the city.

In 1899, after considering several possible locations, the CSP moved to Fourth and Christian Streets because their house and others on St. Mary's (later Carver) Street were taken by eminent domain and the city tore them down to be replaced with Starr Garden Park. The settlement had always served diverse races and ethnicities although some clubs and activities were apparently race-segregated, ostensibly based on interests (Katz and Sugrue 1998:8–9). The new location was more an immigrant neighborhood than a black one, meaning that by default the settlement would no longer serve primarily a black population. However, their old location was also becoming more diverse as additional immigrant groups moved in. The new location was near intersecting streets spanning both the Seventh and Fifth Wards of the city, populated by blacks, German and Russian Jews, Italians, and Poles who formed a "mixed population with no prevailing elements" (SC, Second Annual Philadelphia Settlement Report: B1, F14). What united these diverse groups, with the exception of some white families representing an earlier and more prosperous history, was poverty. Internal dissention among members of the settlement's Executive Committee over the move and new location can only be surmised by the fact that shortly after the Christian Street location was decided, both Hanna Fox and Susan Wharton resigned from the Committee although Fox later agreed to remain as treasurer. Ryan and others suggest that the women were disappointed in the committee's decision to move away from the black community which had always been their "neighborhood." Around the same time, it was announced that the settlement kitchen, coal club, and visiting nurse programs would be separated from the settlement because they were independent enough to survive on their own. In fact, records are unclear as to what happened between the settlement and the remnants of the old SMSL and the programs begun there by Starr and continued by Wharton and Fox. Lasch-Quinn says that Wharton, wishing to continue serving the black community following the move of the CSP, established Whittier Center. That Center, while active in health and housing programs, "faltered" and Wharton subsequently regrouped and established the Wharton Settlement (1993:33–35). The *Settlement Handbook* further confuses the status and relationship of these organizations by listing separately the College Settlement of Philadelphia, the Starr Center, and the Wharton Settlement. Whether connected to the move or to the Fox and Wharton resignations, at about the same time, Katharine Davis announced her resignation as headworker. Davis was followed by Anna Davies who remained as head resident for 43 years. Davies was a graduate of Lake Forest College and was attending the University of Chicago working on her Ph.D. when Jane Addams suggested her for the Philadelphia position. Davies accepted the position and never returned to Chicago to take her doctoral exams (AFDC, http://collections.lakeforest.edu/items/show/2904, accessed June 13, 2014).

The Philadelphia settlement pioneered in a number of areas such as neighborhood libraries, kindergartens, and music programs. In fact, the settlement music program was so successful that it was spun off into a separate program in 1908 and still functions today, serving some 15,000 students and awarding over a million dollars in financial aid programs that reach beyond the city (Ryan 2006:56). The Philadelphia College Settlement has earned a place in the history of both social work and sociology. In social work, it is known as the first institution in the city to offer classes seen as early social work training or at least prerequisite to such. In fact, Ryan's work (2006) is a very thorough treatment of the settlement as a center of early education. In her first years as head resident, Davis, began a series of classes for the purpose of providing training for volunteer workers in order to raise "the standard of social work among the poor and of meeting an increased demand for trained workers." For one dollar, students could enroll for "Practical Sociological Study," a series of seventeen lectures, some delivered by local college professors and some by persons working in the field (Ryan 2006:54). Davis' method of teaching involved a lecture followed by a lively discussion and then application (Ryan 2006:55). Ryan reported that a course on "Recent Social Economic Legislation" was taught in 1896 by E.R.L. Gould, Professor of Statistics at the University of Chicago, as preparation for social work courses to follow. In announcing the class, the headworker explained, "The Settlement, with its social ideals on the one hand and its practical experiences on the other, seems to us to be the place...where this all-round knowledge may be gained" (SC January 12, 1896, Executive Committee Minutes: B4, F11). Gould's course was followed with a lecture by Jane Addams that kicked off the College Settlement Conference for Workers, a series of lectures by experts in the field and open to the public for a ten cent admission fee. The Conference ended a year later with a lecture by head resident, Katharine Davis on "The Settlement Movement." These and similar educational activities led Ryan to conclude that the "College Settlement of Philadelphia offered post-baccalaureate training in social work to its residents, volunteers, and other interested charitable and philanthropic workers before the establishment of the New York Summer School in Philanthropic Work and the New York School of Philanthropy" (2006:147). The College Settlement of Philadelphia continued for the next several years offering a series of classes or lectures as "Practical Sociological Study" designed to be both theoretical and applied. In the fall of 1896, 35 students registered for a class in "Preventative Philanthropy." In fact, Ryan says that some of these courses later appeared in the curriculum of the New York schools and treats this early work as "an overlooked yet integral feature of the history of social work education" (2006:156).

It is unclear how much sociological research was done at the CSP in comparison with other settlements. However, the settlement has a place in the history of sociology if for no other reason than that the now classic ethnography, *The Philadelphia Negro*, by W.E.B. Du Bois and the thorough investigation of domestic servants living in the Seventh Ward conducted by Isabel Eaton were both products of the settlement. Apparently Du Bois' work was jointly sponsored by the settlement and the University of Pennsylvania. However, due to confusion regarding programs and institutions, the *Handbook of Settlements* (Woods and Kennedy [1911]1970:262–265, 271–75) credits Du Bois' work to the Starr Center, founded in 1884 by Susan Wharton, and reorganized in 1900 after the College Settlement of Philadelphia moved its location, apparently because Wharton wanted to maintain a presence in the African American community. There was, however, no formal break between the Starr Center and the College Settlement and the research of both Eaton and Du Bois' was completed before the move took place. Just as Du Bois had expected his work to lead to a faculty appointment at the University of Pennsylvania, Eaton had been led to expect a position at the College Settlement. Neither received the expected appointment, Du Bois' no doubt because of race, and Eaton speculated that her rejection was because of union activities. Finding that many jobs required union membership but that African Americans were locked out of unions, she helped to organize the League of Colored Mechanics at the College Settlement in 1897. Based on correspondence between Eaton and Jane Addams, Sutherland suggests that Eaton did not leave the settlement of her own volition (1973:59). Nevertheless, Eaton remained committed to working for the betterment of the African American community and later headed the Robert Gould Shaw House in Boston, an African American settlement spun off of the South End House.

One of the earliest sociological works to come out of a settlement and to have survived to the present day, or more accurately to have been revived, is that of the *Philadelphia Negro* by W.E.B. Du Bois. This work is a comprehensive ethnography of the Seventh Ward of Philadelphia where the College Settlement was located at the time. In his Introduction to the 1996 edition, Anderson describes the work as "a link in an empirical chain engaged in the central social scientific...work of the settlement" (1996:xviii). Anderson goes further to say that the work of Charles Booth of London and Jane Addams of Hull House served as models for Du Bois, and credits him with anticipating the later work of Robert Park and the Chicago School of Sociology.[9] Du Bois' appointment to

9 In fact, Addams and Du Bois did know each other and later worked together in the formation of the National Association for the Advancement of Colored People. Du Bois was very familiar with the work of Hull House where he was a frequent visitor and lecturer when visiting

conduct this research was directly associated with the CSP and was initiated by Susan Wharton, then on the settlement's Executive Committee. Wharton appealed to her neighbor, Charles Harrison, for the University to join with the settlement in a sociological study of the African American population in the Seventh Ward and suggested that the person to carry out such a study should be an African American. Because Harrison lived in the area and had a vested interest in it, he agreed that the University would act as a cosponsor and appointed university sociologist, Samuel Lindsay to take charge of the project. Lindsay secured the services of Du Bois who he had met when studying at the University of Berlin where both attended lectures by Max Weber. Harrison specified that Du Bois, was to be charged with finding out, "how this class of people live; what occupations they follow; from what occupations they are excluded; how many of their children go to school; and to ascertain every fact which will throw light on this social problem." Du Bois, however, had his own agenda, "He proposed to find out what was the matter with the area and why." The politics behind his appointment were unimportant to him (Lewis 1993:188–189). He was very happy to have the assignment because he had been unable to secure a faculty appointment in white institutions, and was teaching outside his fields of sociology and history at the all-black Wilberforce College in Ohio. Du Bois accepted the University of Pennsylvania offer which, although it paid only $900, he hoped would lead to a faculty appointment. Some reports say that he was appointed as assistant instructor of sociology and others that his appointment was simply that of "assistant in sociology" (Anderson 1996: xv, Katz and Sugrue 1998:17–18, Ryan 2006:213). In the summer of 1896, Du Bois and his wife Nina, moved into the settlement's Kitchen and Coffee House building comprised of residential quarters on the third and fourth floors, a library on the second floor, and a restaurant on the first. The living quarters were newly renovated and pleasant; however, as with most settlement residential facilities, they had no kitchen and Du Bois and his wife took their meals with other residents (Ryan 2006:227). The couple, newly married and experiencing slum life for the first time, were able to look out their windows at one of the worst poverty-stricken areas of the city as Du Bois acknowledged in a footnote, "The investigator resided at the College Settlement, Seventh and Lombard streets, some months, and thus had an opportunity to observe this slum carefully" ([1899]1996:312). It is unknown if Nina Du Bois participated in any of the

---

Chicago. Deegan labeled Du Bois a "critical pragmatist" and argued that while he was not accepted by white male sociologists, he was accepted by the Hull House and CSA women who were practicing community sociology and who became an important part of his socialization as a sociologist (Deegan 1988).

settlement activities. Her husband was likely working most of the time although records reflect that he did teach a history class one evening a week and that he participated in Sunday evening lectures (Ryan 2006:215). Du Bois remained in Philadelphia for over a year, collecting all of the research data himself. His methodology—reflecting the influences of Max Weber, Charles Booth, and the women of Hull House—combined the use of urban ethnography, social history, official statistics, interviews, and community mapping. Du Bois reported using a house-to-house canvas in which he talked with over 5,000 people in interviews reportedly lasting from ten minutes to one hour (Du Bois [1899]1996:63, Katz and Sugrue 1998:23). He used six different instruments for collection of data: a family schedule, an individual schedule, a data sheet on which he recorded the physical properties of occupied houses, a record and mapping of various streets and alleys, an inventory of community organizations and institutions, and finally a schedule for domestics living at their place of employment (Du Bois [1899]1996:2). Incredibly, in this pre-computer era, Du Bois completed his work in fifteen months and the final product is replete with maps of every block with legends depicting socioeconomic differences and frequencies. Also used were bar charts, line graphs, and often comparisons with other populations (black and white). The published work was ignored for years, described by Du Bois as a "fat volume" which "few persons ever read" (Du Bois 1968:198). He was no doubt correct about this until the sixties brought a recognition and resurrection of the work of early and unknown black sociologists such as Du Bois and Oliver Cox. Since the 1960s *The Philadelphia Negro has* been reprinted in at least seven different editions, some exact reprints of the original, others with new introductions by the likes of E. Digby Baltzell and Elijah Anderson. Still unknown by most, however, is the fact that Du Bois' work was a product of early settlement sociology. Although nominally identified with the University of Pennsylvania, it was apparently not considered important enough to have received mention in their first history of sociology at Penn State (Katz and Sugrue 1998:18).

As with many early practicing sociologists, Du Bois believed that problems would be solved by presenting people, especially decision-making leaders, with facts. Thus, it was his idealistic belief that, as a young sociologist, he could contribute to the betterment of the Negro race by the use of sociological data. The Philadelphia project was his first opportunity to put this belief into practice although, unfortunately, it did not produce the end result hoped for. The work is packed with descriptive statistics and is remarkably objective as perhaps best illustrated by the final chapter in which he analyzed "the meaning of all this." It is here that he made his only recommendations for action including a section on "The Duty of Whites" and a section on "The Duty of Blacks." In the case of the former, Du Bois saw quite simply "the Negro problem so far as the white people are concerned is the narrow opportunities afforded Negroes for earning a decent living" ([1899]1996:394). His anger surfaced periodically as, for example, when he lambasted the city for preferring immigrant over Negro employees: "The policy of the city today simply drives out the best class of young people whom its schools have educated and social opportunities trained, and fills their places with idle and vicious immigrants" ([1899]1996:395). Du Bois did not lack facts in filling page after page with examples of real people with either formal education or skilled vocational training who because of "color prejudice" could not find work allowing them to use either ([1899]1996:322–355). As for Negro women, Du Bois asserted that they had but three careers open: domestic service, sewing, or married life" ([1899]1996:323). Du Bois' balanced approach is evident in his suggestion that the African American must "bend his energy to…solving…his own problems, even if as a people, they have been "consciously and intentionally wronged" ([1899]1996:389). He admonished African Americans to "make the best of themselves." In addition to self-improvement, he recommended that blacks engage in institution-building and "rational means of amusement" beyond the black church ([1899]1996:391). It is clear that the seeds of Du Bois' theory of the "talented tenth" began to germinate in his Philadelphia study. That is, the best and the brightest of the race, if not held back by color prejudice, had the ability to lift and lead the race to assume its rightful place of equality in the United States. He did not publicly articulate this theory until 1903, but it was no doubt given impetus by the fact that in Philadelphia he saw many talented and capable African Americans held back simply because of the color of their skin. Indeed, this was also his lived experience. Du Bois was better trained than many of the early academics of his day, having earned a Harvard Ph.D. and having followed the recommended educational path of studying in Germany before seeking a professorial position. The only academic positions open to him, however, were in all-black institutions. Even though he was hopeful that the Philadelphia research, co-sponsored by the University of Pennsylvania, would lead to a faculty appointment, this did not happen. He was never allowed to teach a class except at the College Settlement.

In Philadelphia, Du Bois worked with a CSA fellow Isabel Eaton who already had research experience from her work on *Hull-House Maps and Papers* and her study of garment workers in New York and Chicago. Eaton investigated the lives of African American domestics in Philadelphia's Seventh Ward, providing work complementary to that of Du Bois' in expanding on this segment of the black working population [1899]1996). Eaton later went on to Columbia University where she was able to use the Philadelphia research as her master's thesis. Apparently Du Bois worked closely with her and provided guidance in her analysis of data, and perhaps even her writing although he had no official position at Columbia (Deegan 1988:307–308, Hunter 1996:425–426). To his credit, Du Bois included Eaton's work as a part of his book and gave her full authorship. Professor Lindsay worked with both Du Bois and Eaton in their development of interview schedules and he also wrote the introduction to the first edition of *The Philadelphia Negro* (1899). While a revival of interest in the work of black sociologists has brought Du Bois some of the recognition he so richly deserves, Eaton, whose work is equally impressive if not as expansive, has not received the same recognition. Eaton lived at the College Settlement and conducted her research at the same time that Du Bois did. The only comparable research was that just completed by Eaton's friend and mentor, Lucy Salmon (1897). Salmon, a Vassar history professor had drawn data from employers and a smaller number of domestic workers, almost all white European immigrants on the east coast. For a comparative frame of reference, Eaton used both Salmon's work as well as Booth's research in London, but she was the first to focus exclusively on African American domestics, an appropriate area of investigation given the fact that almost 60 percent of African American working men and over 90 percent of working women in Pennsylvania were in domestic service. She estimated that 30 percent of the African American wage earners in the Seventh Ward were domestics. She followed the same pattern of data collection used by Du Bois, a house-to-house canvas that produced interviews with 677 men and 1,612 women. Interviews with 55 white employers in the Seventh Ward, many of whom had employed both black and white servants, provided an added dimension to Eaton's research and documented employers' favorable attitudes toward their servants' reliability, honesty, and hard-work. Like Du Bois, Eaton's work was comprehensive, using descriptive statistics sometimes cross tabulated by sex and age, sometime differentiating live-in from live-at-home workers, and utilizing secondary data for national and state-wide comparisons where available. She presented data on wages, expenditures, savings, marital status, illiteracy, health, and use of leisure time. Overall, Eaton's data provide both a quantitative and qualitative description of the lives of domestic servants in Philadelphia's Seventh Ward, thus giving depth and breadth to Du Bois' work and giving us an early occupational ethnography.

The College Settlement of Baltimore (Locust Point Settlement)

According to the CSA's twenty-five year anniversary report, in 1910, the Locust Point Settlement of Baltimore, a preexistent institution since 1896, made application "similar to that made from Philadelphia," for affiliation and "such union took place in the following October" (CS 1914, 25th Anniversary Report). Beyond annual reports for the next several years, little is known of this settlement. The reports suggest that they were involved in the usual educational, recreational, and economic programs although on a smaller scale than the other three settlements. There is no indication of any sociological research taking place at this settlement.

Contributions to Race, Class, and Gender Studies

Founders and spokeswomen for the CSA never gave up their dual mission: the education of women in real-world settings that would put them in the forefront of what they saw as the social movement of their day, and secondarily to reduce the distance between the classes by "bringing brightness and help to a limited neighborhood" (SC 1891, Second Annual Report: B2, F1). When Woods and Kennedy published their *Handbook of Settlements*, they offered affirmation that CSA had worked successfully toward both goals. The authors gave special coverage to three collective organizations: the College Settlements Association, the National Conference of Settlements, and the Women's Home Mission of the Methodist Episcopal Church ([1911]1970:2–4). The latter two include an umbrella organization for settlements nation-wide and a church group that established Wesley Houses in the South. However, the *Handbook* gave the most detailed coverage to the CSA which included not only acknowledgement of their role in the establishment and management of settlements but also their substantial contribution to the research and literature of social settlements, most by CSA fellows. Listed are works such as Katherine Woods' "Queens of the Shop, the Workroom and the Tenement" published in 1891 in *Cosmopolitan.* Both Isabel Eaton's "Receipts and Expenses of Wage-Earners in the Garment Trades" and Katharine Woods' work on "Accidents in Factories and Elsewhere" were published in 1895 in the *Quarterly Publication of the American Statistical Association.* Eaton's later work on Negro domestic workers was, of course, published as a part of Du Bois' *Philadelphia Negro.* Sayles investigation of "Housing Conditions in Jersey City" was published in the *Annals of the American Academy of Political and Social Science.* Kellor's exposé of employment agencies was published in its entirety in book form as *Out of Work* (1904). Mary Kingsbury's survey of "Women in New York Settlements" was published in *Municipal Affairs* (1898). A number of research reports were also published in *Charities and the Commons* and later in the *Survey* on such diverse topics as working girls who were elementary school drop-outs, the condition of seamen in port, child labor in New York, and working girls' clubs. Significantly, all of the research cited here was carried out by CSA fellows, consistent with the mission of educating women, and all the research had potential for application in reducing the distance between the classes. The *Handbook* also documented the CSA's work in furtherance of the education of settlement workers, particularly female workers. For example, the CSA published five editions of a *Bibliography of College, Social, and University Settlements* from 1893 to 1905. The organization was also credited for its publication of various syllabi to be used in settlement classes or for discussion groups in social science clubs. These syllabi were written by Emily Balch, Caroline Williamson, and Vida Scudder. Finally, the *Handbook* authors recognized CSA leaders for their role in educating the public about the work of college settlements and the role of women in this "great social movement." Numerous speeches and publications were cited by founders and former residents such as Vida Scudder, Helena Dudley, Katharine Coman, and Emily Balch.

History records settlement houses, along with their other functions, as centers of education—whether kindergarten, adult education classes for immigrants, or post-graduate classes for workers. For young people seeking to find solutions for social problems, the settlements provided opportunities for leadership as well as serving as centers of activity, of intellectual stimulation, and pursuit of knowledge that could be applied to the problems evident around them. McClymer and several who followed him referred to settlements as "ad hoc graduate schools" and Bulmer, et al. used the description of "proto-graduate schools of social policy" (McClymer 1980:14; Bulmer, Bales, and Sklar 1991:28, 37). Before there were formalized curricula in applied sociology, social policy, or social work, there were settlement houses that functioned as centers of practical education. Indeed, "the settlement method of living among the people and 'staying with them a long time'" was Jane Addams legacy of pragmatic education (Addams as quoted in Silverberg 1998:243). The educational function of settlements was of particular importance to women college graduates who, having proven that women could master the same education as males, albeit typically in separate institutions, were graduated, prepared for jobs that were not open to them. Settlements, however, opened new opportunities; they were the female hope of the Progressive Era. They provided useful work in service to the needy; they provided hope for restructuring society by reducing the gap between the classes; they provided opportunities for leadership and for engaging in research expected to translate into social reforms. As Davis put it, "For some, settlement work was merely an extension of graduate school, while for others it was a place to test the new ideas and theories discovered in college" (1984:38).

The CSA settlements were among the first schools of service-learning sociology. Because of their function in offering real-life education for women, these settlements and their operating philosophy stand as a contribution to women's initiative and agency more than to any substantive area of sociology. Always the settlement founders saw themselves as involved in a "great social movement" with women leading the way. Writing in CSA's First Annual Report, Helen Rand acknowledged a frequently raised "serious question" about whether settlement life would prove "unwholesome" and too demanding for women. Her response: "the colony plan makes the life a reasonable and natural one. The family life of educated women with congenial tastes, common interests and independent convictions is a relaxation in itself" (SC 1890: B2, F1). It was Scudder, educator and the chief spokesperson for the women's settlement movement, who called on the first generations of college-educated women to prove their worth by taking up a cause—the cause of the settlement house and the cause of reducing the social distance between the classes—a movement which she earnestly urged "upon all college women as their primary collective duty." Reflecting on the importance of settlements in her autobiography, Scudder admitted that "[b]y the end of the century, the inadequacy of settlements was clearer and clearer ...they were one small element only in the social unrest which was sweeping the country" (1937:164). However, she still thought that women with settlement experience would have a part in changing the world because they would be changed: "women who entered into settlement residence would be transformed and enlightened. They would return to their natural milieus ...with crusading spirit, equipped to contribute to the Great Awakening" (1937:160). Of later workers Scudder was not so optimistic. She was critical of what social work had become—its evolution into casework, which she termed "an awful phrase" because it neglected to "look at social questions in the large" (1937:161).

The archives of the CSA show that on at least two occasions they attempted to assess their work through the opinions of those once closest to it, then somewhat removed—former residents. One survey, which unfortunately has no date, consisted of questions written by then residents to construct a questionnaire sent to more than eighty former residents (SC:B2, F3). Forty-two former residents, all women, responded. Some of the questions stand as a good measure of how well the CSA experience served to meet its dual aims of reducing class inequalities and as an educational experience for college women. In response to a question about the importance attached to the different kinds of work carried on in the settlements, the prevailing opinion identified "unorganized work," that is visiting and interacting with neighborhood residents "of various classes and conditions" as the unique and most important function of settlements thereby affirming the neighborly relation model. The importance of settlement life as informal education came through spontaneously on a question asking whether settlement life was seen as a form of deprivation. Overwhelmingly, the answer was in the negative, that the benefits far surpassed whatever physical disadvantages were involved in settlement living. Typical was one resident who said, "In the six months spent in the Settlement, I consider that I gained more knowledge of life than I could in almost any other experience." In response to a direct question as to whether settlement life can do away with class distinctions, answers were mixed but realistic. For example, one former resident wrote that "Settlement life is a great destroyer of theories, and the belief in the speedy disappearance of caste is usually possessed by the theorist alone." One of the most optimistic responses was, "When I am in the atmosphere of the Settlement, class distinctions seem so artificial that it seems possible to do away with them." Interestingly, most residents who expressed doubt that the settlement could do away with class differences displayed their sociological literacy in noting the need for macro-level, structural changes. For example, one respondent said, "I do not think that the Settlements can work materially toward doing away with class distinctions so long as economic conditions outside work so powerfully to produce them." Another said, "I do not believe such distinctions will be destroyed without a radical change in our industrial scheme." It is also interesting that when asked what reforms or changes were most urgent with regard to class inequality the most frequent responses were changes in the economic and political structure, in housing, organization of labor, eight-hour work days, improved schools and compulsory education laws.

Another survey, with questions written by a committee was conducted in 1914 "to test the reactions of settlement life upon settlement residents" (SC:B1, F6). This survey is presumed to be later than the one just referenced because of the number of subjects involved and because of the fact that there were, by this time, some male residents. The survey was sent to 450 residents and former residents and 145 were returned, 105 from women. Questions were of a general nature as to the importance of settlement work subjectively and objectively and were written and responses compiled by a CAS committee. Again, some of the responses speak to the value of settlement education and to the reduction of class disparities although the questions asked addressed neither of these directly. One respondent stated emphatically, "my years at 95 Rivington Street gave me a training invaluable in self-reliance and resource." Another credited the settlement experience with giving her "a most intimate viewpoint on social questions...I must always feel that they deal with real men and women, boys and girls, such as were my friends so long and are still in many cases." Almost half of the respondents saw settlements as furthering democracy by spreading fellowship across class lines although some specified that this worked more for the residents than for their neighbors. Spreading democracy across class lines reemerged on the question of the "distinctive contribution of the settlements to the general development of social work." Although there was no consensus as to this distinction, the awakening of class consciousness and the settlements' "democratizing influence" were frequently mentioned; but cited also were research, training, and for settlements "being laboratories, the channels of truth, as opposed to mere theory."

CHAPTER 8

Henry Street: Where Health Became a Public Issue

During the Progressive Era New York evolved a scholar-activist network of interlocking academic and social reform organizations and individuals intent on linking theory and practice and making the laboratory concept a reality for the City. Schools involved were the School of Political Science at Columbia University, the New School for Social Research, the Rand School, and the New York School of Social Philanthropy. Some of the most influential organizations included the New York Charities Organization Society, the National Child Labor Committee, and the National Consumers' League as well as various settlement houses, labor unions, and some women's groups. Goldmark described "well-known figures" in the Charities Building at Twenty-second Street and Fourth Avenue where some of the key participants in New York's scholar-activist network were officed or tended to collect:

> Edward T. Devine, the head of the Charity Organization Society, whose vision led to the extension of relief into constructive tenement house reform and tuberculosis work; Lawrence Veiller, then head of these new divisions of the Charity Organization Society; Samuel McCune Lindsay and Owen Lovejoy of the new National Child Labor Committee; George Hall of the recent New York Child Labor Committee; Mrs. [Florence] Kelley and others of the national and state consumers' leagues; Paul and Arthur Kellogg of the *Survey* and *Survey Graphic*...(1953:68).

Settlement house leaders such as Lillian Wald and Florence Kelley of Henry Street were important network actors in this "time of intellectual and educational ferment" (Goldmark 1953:68). What began as a Nurses' Station became New York City's fourth settlement, founded in 1893 by Lillian Wald and Mary Brewster. Unlike many other settlement founders, the two young women were not familiar with Toynbee Hall and the settlement movement in England or the US and did not set out to found a settlement house. However, Wald and Brewster had in common with other early female pioneers their search for a meaningful role in life. Before finding their first location for a nursing station, Wald and Brewster were assisted by workers in two other settlements. Charles Stover and Edward King of University Settlement escorted the two women around the neighborhood and assisted them in finding a suitable tenement, on one occasion steering them away from what might have otherwise been suitable rooms in the red-light district. Stover and King also took the two women to the College Settlement on Rivington Street where Jane Robbins was head resident and where, as Wald recalled, several young women had "taken a house...for something like my purpose." The women at College Settlement suggested that Wald and Brewster live there temporarily until "finding satisfactory quarters" [and] "during July and August, we were 'residents' in stimulating comradeship with serious women, who were also the fortunate possessors of a saving sense of humor" (Wald [1915]1991:10). Wald and Brewster actually began offering their visiting nurses' services when living at the College Settlement while they searched for a place appropriate for treating those who came to them as well as a station for nurse-visitors. By September of 1893, Wald reported that they found two rooms and a hall bathroom, in a tenement on Jefferson Street ([1915]1991:10). No doubt because their work began and functioned for several months as a visiting nurses service within the College Settlement, the groundwork was laid for future networking and friendships among residents and headworkers of these New York settlements. In the beginning, and for many years to come, the primary benefactor for the nurses' work was New York banker and philanthropist Jacob Schiff and his mother-in-law, Betty Loeb. For the first year, these two guaranteed the nurses $120 per month for living expenses and supplies (Siegel 1983:28). In April of 1895, Schiff bought a house on Henry Street and arranged for its repair and furnishing to be used as a permanent nurses' center. The neighborhood was comprised primarily of immigrants, the largest groups Italian and Irish Catholics and Russian and German Jews. Wald, who was only 28 years of age, soon realized that the badly needed visiting nurses service was not enough to meet the needs of the community. In 1903 she reorganized and renamed the Nurses Settlement as the Henry Street Settlement. Its expanded programs began with club activities for the children in the neighborhood and soon included a full range of social services, social research, and reform activities, the latter two sometimes in cooperation with University and College Settlements. As Wald recalled their expansion,

> I do not know who originated the idea of a "club" as a means of guidance and instruction for the young. Our inducement to organize socially came from a group of small boys in the summer of 1895, our first in the Henry Street house. We had already acquired a large circle of juvenile friends.... When these boys of eleven and twelve years of age...called to ask if they could see me sometime when I 'wasn't busy', I made an appointment with them for the next Saturday evening, whereupon the club was organized ([1915]1991:179–180).

Although the primary focus of Henry Street remained nursing, Wald acknowledged, with her early expansion of programs, that the health of her neighbors was not an entity apart from their social location. Healthy neighbors required adequate income, housing, food, recreation, and education. It is not surprising that Henry Street became a center of reform activism in the Progressive Era, but their primary focus was always public health delivered mostly in the form of home nursing where people paid what they could afford or not at all. In times of wide-spread medical emergencies, Wald and her team of nurses were on the job. In 1902, following an epidemic of contagious diseases among newly-arrived Italian immigrants on Hamilton Street, she opened a small nurses' station there. In 1918, she organized her nurses to assist the city through the influenza epidemic. Because of poor living conditions, death rates, including infant mortality, in the wards surrounding the settlement were higher than in the city as a whole, and the Henry Street nurses worked tirelessly to change this statistic. Wald was also there for her neighbors in times of joblessness and economic depression. She wrote in her autobiography that Henry Street had "seen five major depressions in...forty years" (1934:230–231) and she recounted some of the many ways that the settlement was organized to help their neighbors, even sometimes providing jobs and job training ([1915]1991:138–139). Wald always maintained that services and programs at Henry Street were open to those of all races and there were from the early years black nurses in residence at Henry Street. Although their services were not confined to the black population, they did eventually assist in the opening of the Lincoln Center in the black community (Recchiuti 2007:74). Over the years, in addition to medical and social services, education, and reform activities, Henry Street became active in the arts, supporting a neighborhood playhouse and music school. The nursing service became a separate entity in 1937 and in 1944 incorporated as the Visiting Nurse Service of New York. The Henry Street Settlement continues today to serve New York's lower East Side as a community center offering a "wide range of services—from after-school to employment and senior programs [serving] more than 50,000 New Yorkers of all ages" (http://www.henrystreet.org/about/history/, accessed June 30, 2014). Lillian Wald lives on through the Henry Street legacy as well as in a Lillian Wald Research Award supported, since 1982, by the National Association of School Nurses for research impacting the health of school children.

Founders and Residents

Lillian Wald: The Woman and the Nurse

Wald (1867–1940) was born to Jewish parents in Cincinnati, Ohio, the third in a family of five children. Her father was the son of Polish immigrants brought to the United States as a young child as was her mother whose parents were

German immigrants. Both parents were from prominent Jewish families in their native countries, descendants of merchants, rabbis, scholars, and professionals who left their homelands in search of opportunity and to avoid anti-Semitism. Lillian was close to both sets of grandparents but her colorful maternal grandfather was seemingly a strong influence on her life and was much mourned when he died. Lillian's father was a successful salesman of optical supplies who traveled frequently and moved the family from Cincinnati to Dayton, Ohio, and then, when Lillian was age eleven, to Rochester, New York which she came to consider home and where she grew up in middle-class comfort and in the midst of a large extended family. While Lillian was apparently not raised with a strong sense of Jewish identity, the Wald family attended Berith Kodesh, a reformed Jewish synagogue in Rochester, and her parents, one brother, and she are buried in the temple cemetery. Wald was known publicly as Jewish and never denied her heritage although one of her biographers described her as "ambivalent" about her Jewishness (Daniels 1989:9). However, she had no tolerance of anti-Semitism and on one occasion wrote to a "restricted" hotel inquiring whether it was true that Jews were unwelcome there, stating, "I am of that race." At another time she apparently thought it necessary to investigate discrimination against Jews in sororities at Swarthmore College. During the era of Hitler's holocaust, Wald became more public in her Jewish identity but was always quite clear that religion did not motivate her work. In fact, Daniels speculated that Wald "was probably a non-believer" (1989:9–10). During her years at Henry Street she joined the Ethical Culture Society and attended their services.

Wald admitted to a spoiled, privileged childhood where she enjoyed every opportunity in life, including a good education. She attended Miss Cruttenden's boarding and day school for young women, a nonsectarian, prestigious, private school with students of both Jewish and Christian parentage (Siegel 1983:7). The school had a college preparatory division—sending its graduates on to Vassar, Wellesley, Bryn Mawr, and Smith—and Lillian learned not only the standard Latin of the day but also German and French. Wald was a very attractive and intelligent woman and was known as always being conscious, perhaps even vain, of her dress and appearance. One of her biographers reported, for example, that Wald was "particularly upset by pictures of herself that she considered to be unflattering" (Daniels 1989:14). This bit of information humanizes the woman known for her many and selfless accomplishments in nursing, social service, women's rights, race relations, labor organizing, and the peace movement. Wald wrote two books about the Henry Street Settlement, more histories of the house than autobiographies (1915, 1934). However, she has no less than six biographies, apparently only one (by Duffus) written with her cooperation. Wald shared with Addams, Scudder, and other young women of her generation a search for a meaningful life. Even as she watched her older brother, Alfred, preparing to follow an uncle into a career in medicine, Lillian could only picture herself as his aide, working at his side in caring for the sick. Yet she never seemed to move toward the traditional roles of wife and mother expected of young women of that day. As one of her biographers put it, "the outside world attracted her and not marriage" (Siegel 1983:8). A college education eluded Wald when she applied to and was turned down by Vassar because she was too young, only 16 at the time. Lillian floundered, continuing at Miss Cruttenden's for another year, attending dances and teas, helping with her sister's wedding, working part time at several clerical jobs, and attending her mother who took to her sick bed after the untimely death of her son, Alfred. One biographer described this period of Lillian's life.

> In the secret of her days there was often the panic of uncertainty, of emptiness, of being adrift. She had not gone to college as a new generation of middle-class women had; she had no profession, no career, no training. And in rejecting the traditional feminine role defined by the circles in which she moved, she was without direction.
>
> SIEGEL 1983:10

Lillian came of age in Rochester with all the problems of industrialization, immigration, and urbanization in evidence although she was apparently sheltered from these and knew nothing of the experiences of the working poor. She found a career before she found a cause. While spending time with her sister during a difficult pregnancy, Lillian met and talked with nurses who came to the home to care for her sister and learned of nursing as a career opportunity for women. In their work, she saw a possibility for her own life, leading her to apply to the New York Hospital School of Nursing. She wrote in her application of days devoted to society, study, and housekeeping but went on to say, "This does not satisfy me now.... I feel the need of serious definite work.... I choose this profession because I feel a natural aptitude for it and because it has for years appeared to me womanly, congenial work, work that I love and which I think I could do well" (Siegel 1983:16). Lillian began her nursing program in 1889, with practical work in the New York Hospital among patients housed in a large basement ward and many more using an out-patient clinic on a daily basis. Her training covered two years that she called "strenuous," but during this time she felt herself embedded in a "sisterhood" with other nurses, one being Mary Brewster who later helped her to found the Henry Street Settlement. Wald completed the nursing program and worked for a year as a staff nurse at the

New York Juvenile Asylum after which she enrolled in the New York Women's Medical College, feeling the need to broaden her medical knowledge as much as to actually earn an MD degree. The city of New York also brought into sharp focus all of the problems of urban-industrial society. A new social consciousness caused her to volunteer to teach a class in home health care and hygiene that the Medical College offered off-site to immigrant women. It was at the end of one such class that a small girl appeared, asking help for her sick mother, having heard on the street that a nurse was in the neighborhood. As Wald later recalled, this experience determined her life course from that point on. She followed the young child and as she traversed the short distance to the child's home, she described witnessing "all the maladjustments of our social and economic relations...epitomized in this brief journey and what was found at the end of it" ([1915]1991:6).

> The child led me over broken roadways...over dirty mattresses and heaps of refuse...between tall, reeking houses whose laden fire escapes, useless for their appointed purpose, bulged with household goods of every description. The rain added to the dismal appearance of the streets and to the discomfort of the crowds which thronged them, intensifying the odors which assailed me from every side...the streets were a marketplace, unregulated, unsupervised, unclean; past evil-smelling, uncovered garbage-cans; and—perhaps worst of all, where so many little children played.... The child led me on through a tenement hallway, across a court where open and unscreened closets were promiscuously used by men and women, up into a rear tenement, by slimy steps whose accumulated dirt was augmented that day by the mud of the streets, and finally into the sickroom ([1915]1991:4–6).

Wald never returned to medical school, but she did seek the help of a classmate, Mary Brewster, and proposed to her that they find a house, move to the East Side, and "live in the neighborhood as nurses, identify ourselves with it socially, and, in brief contribute to it our citizenship"(Wald [1915]1991:8). Wald always said that in the beginning she had little inclination except to "be of use in some way." As she went from the protection of her parental home to that of a female residential nurses program, she was naive about what was going on in the world outside and, as she put it,

> ...ignorant of the various movements which reflected the awakening of the social conscience at the time, or of the birth of the 'settlement'.... Indeed, it was not until the plan of our work on the East Side was well

> developed that knowledge came to me of other groups of people who, reacting to a humane or an academic appeal, were adopting this mode of expression and calling it a 'settlement'.
>
> WALD [1915]1991:2

Wald's Network of Nurses and Other Associates

There is limited information about Wald's co-founder Mary Brewster who, little more than a year after helping to found the Visiting Nurse Service, was described by Wald as having "broken down" under the work load. She was forced to leave the service and spend time in a hospital and in recuperation. She attempted to return to the work shortly after the Henry Street house opened but her health was too fragile; she was forced to retire and died a few months later in 1895. Other nurses joined Wald, however, and by 1900 the number in residence reached 15, young women who came to constitute an inner circle of support and friendship for Wald.

> Without ties to husbands and children...they gave their creative minds completely to their work. Imaginative programs proliferated out of Henry Street.... Lillian Wald, centered and supported within the house, became the public figure, the face that represented Henry Street. She was the visionary; she had the executive ability and the personality to ally Henry Street with the larger world—to financial supporters, to related movements, to the march of people pressing government to assume responsibility for public welfare.
>
> SIEGEL 1983:47–48

At the time of the publication of the *Handbook of Settlements* in 1911, there were 41 women, most of them nurses, in residence on Henry Street and five males who worked in various recreational and teaching capacities. In the beginning, nurses' salaries were paid by individuals or organizations that could support the program by funding a nurse. Such was the case with benefactors such as Henry Morgenthau who supported a nurse for 22 years or the Ethical Culture Society that funded a nurse for seven years. Lavina Dock, known affectionately as "Doc" was among the first nurses to join Wald in residence at Henry Street after the death of Brewster. She arrived in 1895 and remained for the next 20years. She was a graduate of the Bellevue Hospital School of Nursing and had worked in disaster relief and in the yellow fever epidemic. She was also an academic having been head of the Johns Hopkins School of Nursing for five years and authored one of the first international nursing textbooks. Dock was a well-known crusader for women's suffrage, encouraging Wald and other nurses to join in marches for women to get the vote. Siegel described her as "a militant suffragist...a linguist, musician, scholar, and pacifist" (1983:46). In relation to Wald, "she helped...give shape to the profession of public health nursing, putting her scholarship into many of Miss Wald's speeches and articles" (Siegel 1983:46). During her years at Henry Street, Dock coauthored with Adelaide Nutting, head of the Columbia School of nursing, a widely acclaimed four-volume history of nursing (Siegel 1983:45). Indicative also of the quality of Henry Street nurses is the fact that their superintendent of nursing, Annie Goodrich, was called into military service during World War I as dean of the Army School of Nursing and as chief inspector nurse; she was subsequently awarded an Army Distinguished Service Metal (LDWP Feb. 28, 1918, Henry Street News: Reel 78, B66). Another well-known Henry Street nurse-resident for almost a decade beginning in the nineteen twenties was Marguerite Wales who later authored *The Public Health Nurse in Action* (1941), the Foreword of which was written by Wald shortly before her death. In this last publication, Wald established for posterity ownership of the label and the concept of public health nursing as she titled her Foreword: "We Called Our Enterprise Public Health Nursing" (1941:xi). Wald was by training a nurse but in practice most considered her a nurse-social worker. She is today credited not only with the origin of the term "public health nurse" but also with its definition in practice (Wald [1915]1991:72). It is thus fitting that she served as the first president of the National Organization for Public Health Nursing. Wald was also a pioneer in nursing education and became internationally recognized for post-graduate nurse-training programs at Henry Street and for helping to create and affiliate with the settlement a Department of Nursing and Health at Columbia University, ([1915]1991:64).

Wald: Good Neighbor and Civic Leader

Wald became, along with Jane Addams, one of the most influential women in America. She was not only involved in the obvious—public health and the settlement movement—but also in public education, recreation, immigrant protection, housing, labor disputes, the rights of workers, prohibition, women's suffrage, civil rights for blacks and, later in her life, international peace. Her archived papers document the memberships and activities of a woman whose name was associated with all the major issues of the Progressive Era. Her papers, particularly her correspondence, tell us much about the kind of conscientious person Wald was in that she sometimes refused membership or withdrew from an organization, even though she believed in its cause, because she did not have time for active involvement. Her correspondence provides ample evidence of Wald's public influence in that she was often solicited simply for name-endorsement. She did not, however, lend her name to a cause without careful consideration, mindful that her name was synonymous with the Henry Street settlement. For example, in 1929, when Franklin Roosevelt was governor of New York, she refused a request from Eleanor Roosevelt to lend her name to the Women's Division of the Democratic State Convention while tactfully assuring Mrs. Roosevelt that this was "in no way a lessening of her support of him [Franklin Roosevelt]" (LDWP, B8, FN-R). Unlike many of the other female leaders of the Progressive Era, Wald was not college educated; she had nurse's training and some few months of medical school education. However, because Wald was quick to recognize causal relationships between health and social-economic conditions, she took her place as a Progressive Era leader along with peers such as Addams, McDowell, Scudder, Kelley, and Simkhovitch. In the end, most of the public forgot that Wald was a nurse; they saw her as a settlement leader, and as a spokesperson for various causes related to quality-of-life and social justice. A fellow nurse characterized Wald as the "great interpreter" because of her ability to "interpret one class to another, one nationality to another, one race to another, and the under-privileged to the over-privileged" (Daniels 1989:116). But Wald never forgot she was a nurse, always her primary identity, and she remained loyal to that profession until the end of her life. She was, however, equally true to the neighborly relations paradigm as evidenced by the fact that Henry Street programs were developed in response to the needs of the people and the fact that Wald always required her nurses to live either in the settlement or in the neighborhood where they worked. In an address before the International Congress of Nurses, Wald explained how settlement nursing provided a natural environment for discovering and reporting on the social and political aspects of health and diseases: "not only were the nurses' services needed for the sick, but...their friendly offices were needed as interpreters for bringing to the proper sources the larger and more general matters that affected the life of the people they were in contact with" (1902:570). From her neighbors, Wald learned of abuses in the work place leading her to become a leader in unionization of workers, especially women, and for reforms to keep young people in school. Henry Street nurses' systematic observations on the linkages between diseases such as tuberculosis and infant mortality and unhealthy housing conditions caused Wald to lobby for improvements in tenement conditions and for housing codes and their enforcement. Seeing children in the neighborhood without playgrounds and living in crowded tenements where they rarely saw the sun caused her to work for and to secure playgrounds and summer camps. In all of these activities, Wald was always adamant that settlements were to be "free from the institutional form of philanthropic work" (Wald 1902:568).

Florence Kelley

Next to Lillian Wald, the name most associated with social research and reform at Henry Street is that of Florence Kelley (1859–1932). As did Alice Hamilton (M.D.) at Hull House, Kelley and Wald documented the empirical association between labor and health and through an influential network of organizations and individuals worked to change some of the negative impacts of one on the other. Kelley had training in the social sciences and, from her studies in Europe, was widely read in the socialist literature of her day. Prior to Henry Street, she was established at Hull House where she lived and worked for almost ten years and was an integral part of the Chicago network of women sociologists. She can also be located in her home town of Philadelphia, an area that her father represented in Congress for almost 30 years, or in New York and the Henry Street Settlement where she established her longest residence. Kelley was in reality an international citizen and the impact of her work was felt throughout the United States and in Europe. She was born near Philadelphia into a prominent family where her father was a leading Republican Congressman after having served in various local and state political positions, including that of judge. William Kelley began as a Democrat but, after helping to found the Republican Party, switched his membership, largely because of his anti-slavery commitment. As a Congressional Representative from 1861 until his death in 1890, he was a life-time supporter of working people, of the rights of women and the poor. For much of his time in Congress, he was a member of the powerful Ways and Means Committee, serving as its Chair in the early 1880s. He was a leading advocate of black male suffrage, helping to pass the 15th Amendment. It was in the anti-slavery movement that Kelley became aware of the potential power of dissenting women, an awareness he transferred to his daughter. Sklar says that Florence Kelley "grew up within the most radical network in women's public culture—Garrisonian abolitionism" (1995:15). She was heavily influenced by her father and his world of electoral politics and by a maternal great aunt, a single female who was a teacher and almost a "full-time reformer." Sarah Pugh had a proclivity toward collective action for various social causes, especially in women's organizations. She espoused values that caused Florence to consider her as "conscience incarnate" (Sklar 1995:4, 16). No doubt Kelley's later interest in children's rights, and particularly in children's health, had its origin in her family history. In Philadelphia where Kelley grew up, about one-third of children died before they reached age ten. Even middle-class families such as the Kelley's were vulnerable to infections from contaminated food, milk, or water. Kelley lost five sisters, ages seven months to six years, to various childhood or infant maladies. Only Florence, who herself suffered from unknown illnesses in early life, and two brothers survived. These deaths took their toll on Florence's mother and it was her father who became her confidant and mentor. Perhaps because the family became overly protective of their one surviving daughter, Kelley's early formal education was limited to a few years at a Quaker School, although it was one of the best in Philadelphia. She was largely self-educated as she took up residence in her father's study during his long periods away from home. There she became a vociferous reader of his library that offered an escape from her mother's grief (Sklar 1995:35). It was in her father's study that she found a brochure from Cornell University offering "equal intellectual opportunity to women," whereupon, Kelley began preparing for the admissions examination. She entered Cornell in 1876 and graduated in 1882, having her studies interrupted several times because of health problems. While at Cornell, Kelley developed an interest in social science although at the time there were few courses offered beyond history and ethics. She helped to found the Social Science Club at Cornell and, although the only female member, became a leader in the club's activities (Sklar 1995:61). Kelley's senior thesis was written between 1879 and 1882 when she lived in Washington D.C. with her father and had opportunity to work in the Library of Congress on a daily basis. Her topic was a legal history of children which led her logically into a history of the legal status of women and their role in civic culture (Sklar 1995:63).

Because of the influence of her father, Kelley's thesis tracing the transition of children from chattel to personhood through legislation and legal precedent was published in *The International Review* the year of her graduation (1882a). A few months later she published, also in *The International Review*, what Sklar characterized as her "manifesto about women and social science," an article touting the strengths and benefits of working women (including immigrants), for themselves and for the nation. Kelley examined the changing roles for women as they left what she termed "farmers' work" and began to enter more diverse jobs. She discussed both the necessity and opportunities for females in the labor market laying the basis for her argument that there were two essentials vis-à-vis the public interest: women's health and their education and training to give them the skills and knowledge needed to be good workers. Kelley discussed some of the more traditional areas of female work, which she described as overcrowded, then ventured into new territory encouraging women to become involved in "brain work." Prominent among the "brain work" to be claimed by women was the new field of sociology as she wrote,

> In the field of sociology there is brain work waiting for women which men cannot do. While the science of man was a science of wealth, rest and self-interest there was slight inducement for women to touch it. The new social science has humane interest, and can never be complete without help from women. It is the science of human relations. These must be studied as they exist, with patient care; but exact tabulation of facts is the beginning only; afterward comes the work of interpretation (1882b:521).

Kelley was astute and ahead of her time in calling attention to the need for equal pay for equal work, an issue still with us today. She also pointed to the need for woman's universal suffrage as a means for women to improve their power in the marketplace. She noted the various ways that men had improved their position simply by virtue of their vote: "The workman's prime necessity... he has secured by his ballot" (1882b:524). Kelley's first two publications laid the foundation of what was to become her life's work: protection of children and securing equality and dignity for female workers and for women in general. The means for securing these goals Kelley believed to be in the combined power of social science and the legislative-judicial process: gather the facts, interpret those facts to the public and to decision-makers (especially legislators), lobby for the needed legislation and social policies, and follow these through adjudication as necessitated by legal challenges.

Upon graduation from Cornell, Kelley returned to her home in Philadelphia and applied for graduate work at the University of Pennsylvania to study Greek but was turned down because women were not to be admitted there until some three years later. In autobiographical notes written many years later, she reflected on the irony of this experience.

> This conservative university refuses a young woman a chance to study, of all things respectable, Greek—and what happens? Seeking the chance denied her, she goes to Zurich and is thrust at once with German socialists and Russian revolutionists who waste no time in giving her an insight into things never heard of in the philosophy of Plato and Aristotle.
>
> FKP ND "Notes on Sixty Years": 21

Although, at the time of her death, Kelley had two grandsons, it was to her one granddaughter, and namesake, that she addressed pages of lengthy memoires.[1]

1 Drafts of this memoir to her granddaughter are undated. Her papers contain four rather complete chapters and outlines and notes for ten additional chapters. The four completed are largely personal history but the incomplete chapters deal with labor, business, trade unions,

And lest the granddaughter take for granted her opportunities, Kelley pointed out the importance of education in her day, writing, "out of this first wave of education of women, came this strong impulse to share in the lot and in the release of all women" (FKP "Notes on Sixty Years": B10, F4:32). Interestingly, the gender-restrictive University of Pennsylvania, in refusing Kelley admission, may have determined the course of her life from that point forward. Hearing that women could earn graduate degrees in Europe, she traveled abroad to study government, political economy and law at the University of Zurich and the University of Heidelberg where she was introduced to the writings of Marx and Engles.[2] As a student there, she became a socialist and met Polish-Russian physician Lazare Wischnewetzky who became her husband in 1884 and the father of her three children. While in Germany, Kelley began a correspondence with Fredrich Engels (Marx had recently died) and persuaded him to allow her to translate into English *The Condition of the Working Class in England in 1844*, a task that she accomplished during her first pregnancy. Kelley actually met Engels in person only a few times but carried on a correspondence with him until his death (see some of these letters in Sklar and Palmer 2009).

In 1886, Kelley and her husband returned to the United States to live in New York where he did further study and opened a failed medical clinic. The couple had three children, but the marriage was not a happy one as her husband was controlling and sometimes prone to physical abuse. In 1889 Kelley left him, moved to Chicago and to Hull House where Jane Addams helped her to find suitable accommodations for her children with a family nearby.[3] Kelley did not move from Hull House until she left the city in 1899; in the meantime, she attended Northwestern University and earned a law degree in 1895. During her years in Chicago, Kelley divorced her husband and had the court restore

legislatures, courts, suffrage, and other topics that constitute Kelley's life's work. Some of this same autobiographical material, although less personal, seems to have been published in four installments in the *Survey Graphic* in 1926 and 1927 and much later the Survey articles were collected in a single volume with an introduction written by Sklar (1986). These autobiographical writings are available in their original in the New York Public Library's Manuscripts and Archives Division (FKP 1881–1932: B10, F4–9).

2 Deegan reported that Kelley was awarded a doctorate in political economy from the University of Zurich in 1886 (1990:42). However, in her autobiographical writings, Kelley said of her studies at Zurich, "I listened and studied, but never presented myself for a degree" (1986:68).

3 Kelley's three children were boarded with the Henry Demarest Lloyd family who lived some 20 miles outside the city of Chicago. Demarest (1847–1903) was a lawyer and journalist with the *Chicago Tribune* but after receiving a family inheritance, he devoted himself full-time to social activism and was a friend and supporter of settlements.

her maiden name for herself and her children of whom she gained custody. After her service as factory inspector for the State of Illinois ended, Kelley was without steady work for a time and was forced to survive on part time jobs until she again moved to New York to accept a position as General Secretary with the National Consumers League (NCL) and to take up residence at Henry Street Settlement where she maintained her home for almost 30 years.[4] The *New Republic* editorialized in 1924 (November 12) that "No single individual has done more than Mrs. Kelley, through her long years of keen participation in local, state and federal campaigns, towards securing the body of social legislation which exists in the United States today." Florence Kelley's life's work can be summed up in her own oft stated credo: investigate, educate, legislate, enforce (Sklar 1995: 252).

The Kelley-Wald Alliance and Network

When Kelley moved to New York in 1899, she brought with her a valuable and multilayered professional and social network from Chicago, and in New York Lillian Wald and Henry Street became for her what Jane Addams and Hull House had been for her in Chicago (Goldmark 1953:66–67). At Henry Street, Wald and Kelley were a combined, if unlikely, force for reform. Wald was known for her quiet disposition, her tact and persuasion, and as a nurse-healer. Kelley was known as a socialist who was zealous and often abrasive in her challenges to the status quo; she was outspoken and had little tolerance for injustice in any form. On one occasion she walked out of a meeting with President Theodore Roosevelt because of a joke he made about his wife (Goldmark 1953:99). Former residents of Henry Street were fond of recalling

4 The NCL grew out of the Working Women's Society established by Alice Woodbridge who made a study of the hours and working conditions of women in large retail establishments (1893). The research led to the formation of the New York Consumer's League (NYCL) and the beginning of a movement to pressure consumers to accept responsibility for ensuring that the goods they purchased were made under safe, sanitary working conditions and, on the other hand, to pressure factory and retail stores to improve working conditions or suffer public boycotts. The NYCL published a "white list" of stores and industries that met minimum standards, thus recommending these to the public. Consumer leagues were subsequently established in Philadelphia, Boston, and Chicago and in 1899 delegates came together to form a National Consumers' League with Florence Kelley, formerly of Hull House and chief factory inspector for the state of Illinois, as president. Shortly thereafter, Kelley took up residence at the Henry Street Settlement and became a natural ally of labor activists, often combining forces with the New York Child Labor Committee and the New York Women's Trade Union League (Barbuto 1999:57–58).

Wald and Kelley's interactions over their breakfasts and their reading of the morning paper. As one resident put it, Kelley would "practically demolish her opponents" while Wald showed "forbearance and understanding" (Siegel 1983:51). In New York, from her bases at Henry Street and the National Consumers' League, Kelley developed a national and international nexus of "middle-class reformers, labor leaders, rank-and-file working people, women suffragists, academics, politicians, intellectuals, and businessmen" that shaped reforms during the Progressive Era (Sklar and Palmer 2009: xxi). Her work was in large measure a product of these overlapping networks. Her first office in New York, with the National Consumers' League, was located in the Charities Building which placed her strategically in the scholar-activist network of the city. Intermittently Kelley came under attack and her message was subverted because she was labeled a socialist, an affiliation that she steadfastly maintained even though she learned to compromise on her reform goals. Sklar attributes Kelley's autobiographical pieces in *Survey Graphic* in the 1920s as well as the more personal writings for her granddaughter as her defense against public acrimony. Attacks against Kelley were more vitriol than those aimed at other female reformers because she was labeled a socialist and communist although, in fact, Kelley always distanced herself from communism. Some organizations, such as the Daughters of the American Revolution, publicly denounced both Addams and Kelley for their anti-war activities, referring to Kelley by her married name, no doubt because it was Russian (FKP:B10, F12). Kelley's desire to defend herself is understandable in that her affiliation with the socialist party made her vulnerable at a time when socialists such as Eugene Debs and Kat Richards O'Hare had been imprisoned and non-citizens deported. Sklar speculates that while Kelley was often denounced publically as a socialist, she was spared more direct actions because she was "more closely affiliated with the social settlement movement than with the Socialist Party." However, her FBI file noted in 1923 that Kelley had been "a radical all the sixty-four years of her life," and she was refused a passport in 1915 (Sklar 1986: 1–19, back cover).

Members of the large and well-connected Goldmark family were often associated with Kelley and her work with the NCL. For example, one Goldmark sister was married to Felix Adler of the Ethical Culture Society and another to Louis Brandeis who performed critical work for the NCL and was later to become a Supreme Court Justice. Two other sisters, Josephine and Pauline, were prominently associated with the settlement and labor movements. Josephine lived at Henry Street; Pauline had spent time at settlements in Chicago, Philadelphia, and New York. Both were educated at Bryn Mawr with additional work at Barnard, Vassar, and Columbia. Both were active in the New

York Child Labor Committee, in the New York Consumers' League, and worked with Kelley in the National Consumers' League. Josephine and Pauline, along with Kelley, provided their expertise and reservoir of data to the work of the New York Factory Investigating Commission in the aftermath of the Triangle Shirtwaist fire. Pauline went on to teach at the New York School of Philanthropy where she headed their Bureau of Social Research while Josephine became Kelley's invaluable assistant and ultimately her biographer. Josephine worked for the NCL in several different capacities and was trained by Kelley as a researcher known for her thorough and detailed work, most of which today will be viewed as early industrial sociology. With brother-in-law, Louis Brandeis, Josephine Goldmark, Kelley, and other NCL volunteers supplied the social science data used in the adjudicatory defense of laws involving workers' rights. This work was later published in the form of legal briefs: *The Case for the Shorter Work Day* (Frankfurter and Goldmark 1916) and *The Case Against Nightwork for Women* (Brandeis 1918). Josephine Goldmark's work, *Fatigue and Efficiency* (1912) was based on research done for NCL court cases. Although Goldmark was primarily a social researcher and activist for industrial reforms, she also brought her research skills to the nursing profession. In 1919, as secretary of the Rockefeller Foundation's Committee for the Study of Nursing Education she examined over 70 schools of nursing resulting in the publication of *Nursing and Nursing Education in the United States* (1923). This work, as well as her association with Henry Street no doubt accounts for the fact that Goldmark served for a time as director of the New York Visiting Nurses Service (Barbuto 1999: 81–83, jwa.org/encyclopedia, accessed February 6, 2014).

The Intersection of Health and Industry

Social Investigation

Nowhere is the impact of industrial labor on health and all of its human ramifications more clearly documented than in the work of Wald's Henry Street nurses and Kelley's industrial researchers. Their investigations were far-reaching and collaborative, encompassing some of the earliest work in the US on public health in its social context. As Wald expressed it in one of her first reports, "poverty augments the misfortune of disease" (1901:685). Social investigations at Henry Street were diverse, ranging from a study of dispossessed tenants conducted in 1897 in collaboration with University and College Settlements to a study of settlement magazines conducted by a resident in 1929 (LDWP: B34). Studies in which Wald was directly involved or had a supporting role included a study of midwives, conducted by Henry Street nurses with the cooperation of two other organizations and published in *Charities* (Crowell 1907); an investigation of children's street games (Wald [1915]1991:66–98); investigations of the conditions surrounding working girls in various industries published later by the National Child Labor Committee (1910) and by the New York Factory Investigating Commission (1913,1915). Henry Street nurses investigated the well-being of babies boarded out in foster families (LDWP: B29, F2); children kept out of school because of illness or physical defects; and children who had been issued working papers at or before age fourteen (Wald [1915]1991:138–139). There were also publications by committees or commissions of which Wald was a member and whose reports she helped to shape and disseminate such as the report by the Mayor's Pushcart Commission (1906); a report on *Trade, Industrial and Art Schools of Greater New York* (1909); and the report of the State Immigration Commission (1909). Wald supported, promoted, and did some of the background research for New York's comprehensive study of the need for pensions for mothers and children (LDWP 1913–1914: B23, F2.1).[5]

One piece of research for which Wald did go into the field and collect data was carried out with Frances Kellor for the State Immigration Commission. She and Kellor personally toured work camps housing laborers, most of them immigrants, for two long-term construction projects, New York City's construction of a new aqueduct and the state's expansion of its basins and barge canal. Wald and Kellor wrote detailed descriptions of living, sleeping, and eating facilities as well as provisions, or lack thereof, for health care and leisure-time activities in the work camps. Most of the camps lacked basic sanitation; provided poor food; crowded workers into small, unventilated, often unlighted spaces; and provided for no health care or leisure-time activities other than drinking. Since, in most camps food and lodging could only be purchased from the "company store," often the workers ended each week owing most of their wages. The report included some demographic data but it was the vivid descriptions and pictures of camp conditions that received public attention (LDWP 1910: Reel 24, B36, F2). Another piece of research in which Wald was personally involved was the treatment of sick school children and the relationship between the children's health and their living and working conditions (LDWP: Reel 24, B35, F5). Wald lectured on the relationship between mental "dullness" and physical illness and campaigned successfully for "medical

---

5 Copies of many of these unpublished reports are available in one or both archival collections at the New York Public Library (LDWP Reels 24–27, Writings and Speeches) and at Columbia University's Rare Book and Manuscript Collections (LDWP General Subjects Boxes 17–41 alphabetical).

inspectors" and then nurses in the public schools. In writings and in speeches, she consistently presented the health of school children as a public concern because of the spread of diseases among home, school, and the workplace. Wald helped to inaugurate a system that provided a medical inspector physician to report to schools each morning to examine children sent by teachers because they were suspected of being ill. The medical inspector subsequently determined which children should be returned to class and which ones sent home. Sending sick children home from school made for healthier schools and lessened the spread of contagious diseases but presented other problems such as unsupervised and untreated children at home during the day or sick children being conscripted to work in home manufacturing. On an experimental basis, Wald offered the services of one of her nurses for one month to assist schools and the department of health in working through these problems. This school nurse was vested with the responsibility of seeing that sick children were not only removed from the classroom but that they were treated before and after being sent home. Follow-up statistics were impressive in documenting shorter school absences, a decrease in student drop-outs, and healthier classrooms and homes (Wald 1905:88–96). Wald was heavily involved with public schools in other ways. For example, she convinced the schools to provide vision tests and to treat eye diseases as well as to assist students with vision problems in getting glasses (LDWP 1905: Reel 24, B35). Another service that Wald performed for the public schools was the implementation of "vocational scholarships" to keep children between the ages of 14 and 16 in school rather than sending them into the labor market, an idea already tested by Hull House. Often the wages earned by these young people were needed by the family and they were encouraged to drop out of school and go to work. A Scholarship Committee at Henry Street screened and approved children for a scholarship of $150 per year, paid at three dollars per week. Wald wrote in 1917 that the Scholarship Committee had granted "500 Scholarships and has had ample opportunity to prove the constructive effects of this work on wage earning children." In the same writing, she offered the services of the Henry Street committee in helping other communities to set up similar programs (Wald [1915]1991:137–144, LDWP: Reel 25, B37, F2). On another front, Wald announced that research by her nurses, under the direction of Marguerite Wales, found hospital care to be more costly and less effective than home nursing care in the treatment of four contagious diseases (Wald 1934:81–83). This research was part of a larger study conducted by Anna Phillips on communicable diseases in the Bronx (1932:48–53).

More than collecting data herself, Wald encouraged others to collect data that could be used to solve social problems. This was particularly true of her nurses' records and observations which she used in giving testimony before groups such as the Factory Investigating Commission. She was frequently called on as a conference speaker or as a speaker for religious and civic groups throughout the country. She wrote a substantial number of articles in public health or nursing journals as well as in social science and social service publications such as the *Survey* or *Charities*. Through these various venues of speaking and writing, Wald was very skilled at summarizing and disseminating data relevant to the problems of urban-industrial society. Over the years, Henry Street moved well beyond its origin as a nurses' station, establishing authority nationally as a center of social welfare reforms associated with public health, child labor, labor protectionism, and education. Some of these reforms were a result of the fact that Florence Kelley lived at Henry Street for many years, maintained her office nearby, and was often the motivating force behind research as well as organized activism focused on the well-being of women and children. Wald and Kelley and their network of researchers, nurses, and activists became the first intersection of the public's health and the public's work.

Henry Street and Labor Activism

In a profile of Lillian Wald in 1929, a writer for the *New Yorker* described her as on the "one hand…converting bankers and the other…coaxing strike leaders into clean collars, in her undying ambition to make extremes meet" (Smith and White [1929]1968:34). The Henry Street Settlement did not set out to become involved in labor organizing or advocacy, rather labor activism evolved in the settlement as the need was either voiced or evidenced by the Henry Street neighbors. After the Settlement expanded in 1904, Clinton Hall was opened and used for many union meetings. Wald and Kelley helped to organize the Women's Trade Union League (WTUL) in 1903 which, among other things, was to investigate conditions of working women and encourage women's membership in unions or to help them to organize where no unions existed (Daniels 1989:99). The WTUL was comprised of both working women and upper middle class women such as philanthropists and settlement workers; Mary Dreier and Eleanor Roosevelt were active members along with some of the most experienced labor organizers of the day such as Rose Schneiderman (Wald 1934:31- 32). One of its goals was to recruit female workers into the labor movement and to secure support from the leadership of the American Federation of Labor (AFL), the largest and most successful union at the time. The WTUL supported women strikers by providing meeting spaces, raising money for relief funds and for bail. Wald, along with other Henry Street residents, was always acutely aware of the importance of legislation to provide the proper protection and controls for workers. Henry Street nurses supplied much of the data on home sweatshops used by Wald and Kelley in their frequent appearances as expert witnesses before legislative bodies. Both women were adept in depicting home sweatshops as an endangerment to the health of workers, their families, and to the public at large. As cases in point, they could cite examples of contagious diseases such as small pox and typhoid fever being spread by means of garments stitched at home by infected workers (Sklar 1995:265–268).

During the shirtwaist strike in 1909 and 1910, a representative of Henry Street sat in the courtroom all day, bailing out arrested picketers. In 1912, the Settlement served as one of the headquarters for hearings on "fair consideration" of the Lawrence textile strike. In her history of Henry Street, Wald tells the story of a young girl from the neighborhood who first knocked on the door of the settlement to speak with residents about the "troubles of her shopmates" and to present an argument about how a union would bring relief. Wald speculated that the young woman sought help from the Settlement because of their English-speaking ability and "perhaps with a hope that the union might gain respectability from the alliance" ([1915]1991:202–203). Wald further confessed that her ignorance sent her to the library the following day "for academic information on the subject of trade unions." Her initial study convinced her that collective power might be employed to insure justice for otherwise powerless individual workers and eventually as a source of power for the whole of the working class ([1915]1991:203). Despite solicitations from fellow workers, however, many young women were hesitant to become involved in labor organizing. They had two primary fears, one being that such activity would be considered "unladylike" and would hamper their marriage opportunities; the other was a fear of losing their jobs because they knew first-hand of fellow workers fired when they dared complain about working conditions, pay, or hours. Wald observed that union organizing was further complicated by a lack of what she called "permanency" as young women were constantly on the look-out for better jobs, often leading to short-term employment. Wald, however, cited two particular incidents that caused her to support and work for women's trade unions. Shortly after taking up residence on Henry Street, she found herself in agreement with the grievances of women cloak workers in the neighborhood and took the initiative in organizing a union when they went on strike. Another time that Wald and other Henry Street residents gave unqualified support to unionization was in 1911 after more than 140 employees of the Triangle Shirtwaist Company, most of them women, burned or leaped from windows to their deaths because they were locked into the loft where they worked. Wald concluded,

> Little wonder that women who had never known the bitterness of poverty or oppression found satisfaction in picketing side by side with the working girls who were paying the great cost of the strike. Many, among them settlement residents, readily went bail or paid fines for the girls who were arrested ([1915]1991:210).

Personal experiences with her Henry Street neighbors convinced Wald of the importance of union organization for female workers and she used her name and her influence to actively promote such organization; in fact she saw unions as the only effective means of wiping out sweatshops. In 1906 she addressed the American Academy of Political and Social Sciences on the need for organization among five million female workers. She made the case that women workers should be recognized as a permanent part of the labor force and that they needed the same kind of collective protection from unions that men were beginning to realize. She gave an approving nod to the American Federation of Labor because it had gone on record as "heartily in sympathy and ready to cooperate with any movement to organize women" (Wald 1906:180). In the same speech, Wald dismissed the contentious argument about "favorable discrimination on account of sex" and argued that such "discrimination" would eventually lead to just pay, safe working conditions, and a reasonable work day for all laborers. Over the years both Wald and Kelley came to appreciate the importance of judicial as well as legislative actions as they sometimes spent years in promoting and securing reform legislation only to have it overturned by judicial decision. Such was the case with early legislation that limited work hours and provided special protections for women and children.

Florence Kelley: A Life in Search of Justice

As head of the National Consumers League, Florence Kelley engaged in a national campaign of public education to teach the responsibility of the individual consumer vis-à-vis the public good. Consumers were vested with the responsibility of becoming "enlightened purchasers" who must find "trustworthy assurance" that the goods and products purchased were "free from participation in the employment of children, in starvation wages and in the continuance of the sweating system."

> Before the individual purchaser can vindicate his own personal rights, the whole body of purchasers are constrained to save childhood for the children, and home life for the workers who dwell in tenements.... On no

> easier terms can the conscience of the citizen as purchaser be freed from participation in the meanest forms of cruelty, the sacrifice of the weak and the defenseless to the search for cheapness (1905:230).

Kelley frequently began her many speeches throughout the country with a statement designed to provoke consumer responsibility and guilt: "The people of the United States do not wish to use the products of child labor" (Goldmark 1953:114). Kelley's work with the NCL did not stop with sweating shops; she also went after food products, lobbying for legislation that required articles of food or medicine, when offered for sale, to state clearly and truthfully the ingredients. Ultimately, Kelley never veered far from her socialists beliefs, in recognizing that the problems associated with and emanating from labor practices were integral to industrial capitalism. One of her harshest critiques was delivered in a lecture at Columbia Teachers College where she had this to say about the sweating system.

> For twenty years the state of New York has proclaimed through its highest court that it cannot protect the homes of its industrially weakest citizens from invasion by the materials of their industry. These materials are owned by the rich and powerful employers, strongly organized locally and nationally, and are foisted upon the meager dwelling of the poor solely for the purpose of saving to the employers the cost of heat, light, cleaning and far more important, rent of workrooms. For the convenience of the powerful, the weakest individual factors in the community, the widows burdened with young children, the daughter, kept at home by bedridden parents, have been invaded by industry (1905:245–246).

Kelley was the first person to recognize and to use the power of consumers to attack the problems of US workers. Along with capitalists and workers, Kelley posited consumers as the third leg of the triangle, and she did not hesitate to use a moral argument in enlisting consumers in her fight for workers' rights. At times, she added an element of fear, as with a reminder of the "danger...of buying smallpox, measles, scarlet fever, infectious sore eyes, and a dozen forms of disease of the skin in...new garments" (1899:296). Kelley argued that every person is a consumer and that "the consumer ultimately determines all production" (1899:290). But all persons were not equally important as consumers and Kelley recognized that in empowering consumers she was also empowering women who "since the exodus of manufacture from the home, the one great industrial function of women has been that of the purchaser" (1899:298). Under Kelley's leadership, the NCL began a "white label" guaranteeing articles were manufactured under safe and fair working conditions; they also offered a "white list" of businesses that dealt fairly and appropriately with their employees. According to Sklar, under Kelley's leadership, "the NCL became the single most successful lobbying agency on behalf of legislative protections for working women and children—lobbying based on social data, carefully collected and analyzed" (1998:138). Unlike today when consumer organizations are primarily for the purpose of protecting and informing consumers, the NCL was focused on work conditions and consumers' responsibility to workers. The bulk of the League's membership was comprised of middle and upper-class women, industrial society's chief consumers (Wolfe 1975:378–379). Acting as a critical, analytical social scientist and with a supporting network from the Consumers' League and Henry Street, Kelley took on capitalism and abusive labor practices, especially those impacting women and children. With her analytical and legal skills she used statistics and she used the press, often disputing the claims and data provided by employers or politicians. She criticized the methodology, the research, even the operational definitions (for example who is a child worker) employed by some agencies and businesses. She insisted that "child laborers" must include all those under the age of 16, and she insisted that when reports presented so-called "trend data" that they take into account changes in the population base (Sklar 1995:156–167). Kelley's most exhaustive studies were those on the "sweating system" that involved primarily women and children stitching garments in the cramped quarters of their homes. Lillian Wald and her nurses often provided pertinent data, collected from home visits where they witnessed the conditions in which entire families lived and worked, and too frequently became ill and died. As a nurse Wald was able to authoritatively link child labor, education, and health.

Kelley was a collector of facts subsequently used in efforts to secure policy and legislative changes for workers. She was a prolific writer, authoring over 300 articles in publications as wide-ranging as the *American Journal of Sociology* and *Annals of the American Academy of Political and Social Science* to the *Woman's Home Companion* (Sklar 1995:409–411, Sklar and Palmer 2009:xxviii). Kelley also authored several books and translated Friedrich Engels' *The Condition of the Working Class in England in 1844*, the only English translation until 1958 and, according to some scholars, still the preferred one (Sklar 1995:100). Her work is largely associated with the rights of women and children, but in truth these groups served a more general purpose for Kelley. She knew that policy makers could be relied on to act on measures dealing with women and children out of a patriarchal sense of protective obligation more than would be the case for all workers or for the general social good. In the end her work on behalf of women and children served to secure social and human rights for all. For example, her use of data on accidents causing deaths or lifetime disabilities for workers under age 16 was the beginning of workplace safety and health requirements for all workers (Kelley 1889). Former Supreme Court Justice Felix Frankfurter said of Kelley that she "had probably the largest single share in shaping the social history of the United States during the first thirty years of this century" (Sklar and Palmer 2009:xxvii). Most of her work was directed toward three kinds of human rights: children's right to an education; adult workers' right to adequate wages for meeting the necessities for living and maintaining health; and the workers' right to leisure. Among Kelley's many writings, one volume perhaps more than any other epitomizes her life's work. *Some Ethical Gains through Legislation* is a compilation of writings and speeches delivered in various venues the Preface of which summarizes her career as a scholar-activist and acknowledges the influence of friends and associates from the settlements.

> The substance of this volume has grown out of the writer's experience as special agent for the Bureau of Labor Statistics of Illinois for an investigation of the needle-trades in the tenements of Chicago, in 1892; as Chief Inspector of Factories of that state from 1893 to 1897; as agent in charge of the Chicago division of the investigation of the "Slums of Great Cities" for the Department of Labor at Washington; and as Secretary of the National Consumers' League from 1899 to the date of publication; but chiefly as a resident for thirteen years beginning in 1892, first at Hull-House in Chicago and afterward at the Nurses' Settlement in New York. Lest it seem strange that one of the laity should discuss statutes and the decisions of courts of last resort, it may be well to state that the writer has for many years been a member of the bar of Illinois (1905: vii).

The book devotes two chapters to her interests in children, making a factual case that labor robs children of their right to childhood, protection of which she argued was "the noblest duty of the Republic...cherishing all its children that they, in turn, may become enlightened self-governing citizens" (1905:3). Kelley devoted several chapters to the right to leisure, again relying on her observations and statistics to make a case for unfair labor practices that strip workers of their right to enjoy life outside the work place, thereby diminishing the quality of life not only for workers but for families and for the nation as a whole. Giving voice to her support of women's suffrage, Kelley wrote a chapter on women's right to vote, at the same time documenting the societal loss because women lacked this right nation-wide. She presented facts to illustrate that in states where women were not allowed to vote, they were also missing in public service and in political appointments. In short, public officials preferred men who could vote and the result, was to "deprive the community of...useful service which cannot be available until the constituency attains its full complement of women voters" (1905:177–178). On another front, Kelley connected the women's vote to public education, pointing out that a "broad line divides the communities in which women perform the duties of voting citizens in all matters relating to the schools, from those in which they are prevented from exercising those functions." Kelley pointed to the contradiction in public education where the teaching staff, in daily contact with children and "intimately acquainted with their needs," was largely women but the "business of the schools, the work of the board of education, is conducted either wholly by men or by boards on which men constitute the majority" (1905:178–179). As always, Kelley's bottom line was the cost to society at large when the rights of certain groups are restricted. As a lawyer, she was astute in her awareness that the Constitution guarantees individual rights but not social rights, the latter must emanate from the former and often this was a matter of public education as was the case with consumers.

> The more closely the rights of purchasers are scrutinized, the more clearly it appears that they are social rights. However much they may present themselves to the mind as individual, personal rights, the effort to assert them invariably brings the experience that they are inextricably interwoven with the right of innumerable other people.
>
> KELLEY 1905:229

Kelley's campaign for the prohibition of women and minors' working at night was the beginning of movement toward the uniform ten-hour work day and later the eight-hour work day for all workers. Both in Chicago and in New York, however, Kelley experienced the triumph of protective legislation for adult workers and children only to have these laws challenged and overturned in the courts at the state and national levels. Ultimately, when victories were won in the courts, it was due in large measure to a new tactic, the use of social science data presented in the form of a legal brief. This brief, accepted and considered by the Court, and subsequently labeled the "Brandeis Brief" came to serve as a model for future social science briefs and their acceptance in judicial arguments. Such briefs deviate from the typical citation of case precedent and instead focus on humanitarian and health and welfare issues posed by industrial conditions unfit for workers in a democracy. Goldmark explained the background and significance of the social science brief following a disappointing loss in the courts.

> ...[I]t became more than ever apparent that a new emphasis was needed in the defense of labor legislation, and we awaited the opportunity in which to put this belief into practice.... Such an opportunity offered in the very same year. A laundryman was arrested for violation of the Oregon law fixing a ten-hour day for women employed in factories and laundries. The validity of the law was affirmed by the Oregon courts, and in December, 1907, an appeal was taken to the United States Supreme Court at Washington [*Mullen v. Oregon*]. Here, then, was an opportunity to present the real issue to the highest court in the land, concerned for the first time in its history with a statute limiting the workday of adult women. By good fortune, the active interest of a distinguished lawyer [Louis D. Brandeis] was enlisted and he proposed to put these issues before the court in a new way. His argument and brief marked a radical departure in the defense of labor laws. It confined itself to the tangible human elements involved—health, welfare, and economic efficiency. In a brief of more than 100 pages, he devoted two to the legal aspects of the case, and over 100 to a new kind of testimony—mankind's experience, physical and moral, with respect to women in industry and the duration of their working hours. The document was made up from the accumulated mass of British and Continental factory inspectors' reports, commissions and enquires, as well as the observations of medical men and economists. It was well received by the court, which in its decision upheld the validity of the Oregon law. Quoting from the new empirical evidence contained in the brief, the court stated that it 'took judicial cognizance of all matters of general knowledge', thus in a single phrase warranting the new emphasis upon practical data. The decision in the Oregon case was indeed no narrow victory. It was the most sweeping decision ever rendered by the federal Supreme Court in relation to working hours.
>
> GOLDMARK 1912:251–252

Following the precedent of *Mullen v. Oregon*, cases subsequently argued by the NCL used such briefs and judges came to expect them. Perhaps the best known legacy of the Brandeis brief is the accompanying social science brief presented the Supreme Court in the case of *Brown v. Board of Education* (1954) documenting the harmful effects of segregation and racism on school children (Lengermann and Niebrugge-Brantley 1998:252).

Although Kelley's interests always seemed to be primarily for women and children, more often than not this emphasis was a means toward the end of finally achieving social justice for all workers. Kelley was astute enough to know that in order to secure reforms for the public as a whole the best course of action was to begin with the most vulnerable members of society. Men, in theory, had the power of the ballot box and were better positioned to defend themselves than were women and children. However, issues such as minimum working hours, minimum wages, and safe working environments were clearly linked to the wellbeing of all members of society because they were inseparable from housing, use of leisure, and family life. Kelley differed with leading authorities of the day who saw women's power as resting in their moral transcendence of political life. She theorized that women would be empowered by the political process, and full participation in that process required universal suffrage. Therefore, achieving the ballot was achieving the ability to shape public policy with regard to the rights and needs of children, women, and families. Left to run its typical course, without intervention, Kelley saw that the political process tended to lessen the position of women and children, keeping them as patriarchal dependents (Sklar 1995:65). In her organizational positions, Kelley learned to work within the system, but ideologically, she was a socialist and thought that real reform had to come from revolutionary change. This is made abundantly clear in an 1887 speech in which she laid out two kinds of philanthropic work: bourgeois philanthropy and philanthropy of the workers. The former is what Kelley saw as the art of "applying palliatives," or of "propping up a system of society which is based upon the exploitation of the working class" ([1887]1986:94). In contrast, the working class "fix" to the problem was a "radical cure of the social disease" but would also mean "the end of the system of exploiting the workers." Obviously, Kelley was enough entrenched in bourgeois life to see the problem with the working class "cure" and acknowledged that "to stop exploiting [workers] would be suicide for the class that we are born and educated into, and of which we college-bred women form an integral part" ([1887]1986:95). With some resolute acceptance, Kelley went on in the same speech to promote the possible and the pragmatic. "The foundation of our social order being accepted, [there remains]...much field for critical research, and collegiate activity in the domain of economics and sociology... with subordinate questions of practical politics" ([1887]1986:99).

Henry Street and the Factory Investigating Commission

Tragic as the Shirtwaist fire of 1911 was, some saw it as a turning point in reforming work conditions. The public outcry that followed in New York brought legislative formation of the Factory Investigating Commission (FIC), chaired by Robert F. Wagner and Alford E. Smith, later US Senator and New York Governor respectively. Suggestive of the intricate and wide-spread reaches of industry, the work of the Commission was extended in time and scope until their final report was issued in 1915. Apparently the FIC found it could not stop with a local investigation as their findings led to an unfolding of the complex layers of industrial capitalism. Not only did they investigate factories such as that where the shirtwaist women were employed, but they also investigated tenement manufacturing, sanitary and safety conditions of workers in different industries, workers' health, and the relation between work and poverty. A retrospective on the work of this FIC by the US Department of Labor reads as follows.

> The New York Commission was by far the broadest, most thorough study of workers' safety and health done up to that point. It was comparable to the Pittsburg Survey, only covering the entire state. Through the Commission, in the words of Frances Perkins, the flames of the Triangle fire were magnified into 'a torch that lighted up the industrial scene' (dol.gov/dol/aboutdol/history/mono-regsafepart07.htm, accessed June 24, 2014).

The FIC held nine public hearings, heard from 472 witnesses including employers, workers, unions, public officials, health providers, social scientists, settlement workers, and reformers. Among those who shared the results of their research and worked with the Commission in various capacities, including staff, advisors, and witnesses, were some well-known persons associated with the Henry Street Settlement and with the National Consumers' League such as Wald, Kelley, Josephine and Pauline Goldmark, and Frances Perkins. Wald, for example, provided statistics collected by her visiting nurses on home sweatshops, the workplaces of thousands of women and children. She cited also the association of such work with children's lack of education and reported that there were some families with as many as seven working children under the age of 14, none of whom had ever been to school. Wald testified that she had no exact figures on the numbers of working children, but did know that their incomes were often essential for family survival, and she concluded that, in such cases it would be absurd to say that these children were not "forced to work" (NYFIC 1913. Second Report Vol 4:1562–1572). One FIC member estimated that there were as many as 40,000 children working in their homes. Pauline Goldmark presented the FIC with findings from her research on women workers in retail stores. Florence Kelley and Josephine Goldmark gave testimony on minimum wages and facts to support the association of low wages with "physical, moral, and economic problems" in the country. In testimony packed with statistics both from the United States and Europe, they argued for the formation of a Minimum Wage Commission to establish and oversee a system of fair standard wages in different industries (NYFIC 1915. Fourth Report, Vol

1:701–705). Pauline Goldmark provided extensive testimony and data about the negative effects of night work for women, arguing that women should not be required to work before six in the morning or after ten at night. Night work was documented as being more detrimental for women than men because women's responsibilities in housekeeping and child care prohibited their getting adequate sleep during the day. She presented evidence from some industries, such as book binderies and textile mills, where women typically worked 20 to 21 hours consecutively (NYFIC 1913. Second Report Vol. 4:1649–1658). The Commission issued a series of reports from 1912 to 1915 providing complete records of its work and ultimately took credit for the passage of twenty laws targeting improvements and regulations of safety and health in the work place. Lange described work of the FIC as "the longest, most thorough investigation and evaluation of workplace safety and workers' health ever undertaken" (2008:78) and Frances Perkins, later Secretary of Labor, pronounced it a "turning point in American attitudes toward social responsibility" (Lange 2008:81). Testimony presented in these hearings provides ample evidence of the importance of practicing sociologists to an emerging sociology of health and industrial organization. Indeed they represent the intersection of activism and social science that produced a substantial body of social policy reforms for industrial workers.

Some Contributions to Sociology

Theory and Method

In this case study of settlement sociology at Henry Street, much of the focus has been on Florence Kelley because she was clearly a sociologist in both theory and method. Kelley was at heart a Marxist, adopting what she termed in a letter to Engels a theory of scientific-materialism (FKP, December 29, 1887: B1, F4). She explained in a speech in 1887 that scientific materialism was simply the critical analysis that unskilled workers were being paid only part of the value of what they produced, the rest, what Marx termed surplus value, was as Kelley explained it, profit for investors and owners. While Kelley understood the need to change this system of labor exploitation, she nevertheless worked pragmatically within the system of which she was a part—a system she labeled "bourgeois philanthropy." She was not without hope, however; she saw her work and that of others involved in bourgeois philanthropy as engaged in "theoretical preparation" for the more fundamental changes needed and for which she saw organized labor as the best hope. In the meantime, Kelley pursued her own agenda of seeking social justice by a gradual system of legislation and social reforms that would ultimately expand the rights of all workers thereby improving the quality of life for the nation. Kelley understood the United States and its collective fear of Marxism, socialism, and centralized government. She knew that she could not go into court or lobby using a Marxian theory of class oppression. She knew also that she lived in a patriarchal society where paternalistic male decision-makers perceived themselves as protective of women and children. Thus women and children became her surrogates for the working class, a tactic that sometimes brought critical reactions from feminists who saw her "protective" work for women as countering the cause of gender equality. Kelley cared no less for all workers, but saw women and children as dependent on others to speak for them because their voices went unheard, perhaps because they could not vote. Pragmatically, Kelley understood that male decision-makers were more likely to act in behalf of women and children than in behalf of workers in general. She admitted most directly to her surrogacy tactic in a publication written in German and perhaps not intended for an American audience. There is no date on the article (later translated) except that it is included with a collection of essays written between 1885 and 1908. It is a personal article about her role as the first female factory inspector in Illinois and how she used this position for the improvement of conditions for workers in general. Toward the end of the article is Kelley's most revealing statement as to why her work was focused on women and children.

> It is much easier to find approval by appealing to the sympathy of the masses for the welfare of helpless working women and children than to find it by suggesting absolutely necessary measures to protect the lives, bodies, and health of men, who are the fathers, husbands, and breadwinners of the same women and children...for these male workers...it is assumed that they can protect themselves [they after all had the ballot].
>
> KELLEY [ND]1998:103–104

According to two of Kelley's biographers, rights and righteousness were inextricably linked for her and her quest was always perceived as a moral one (Sklar and Palmer 2009:xxiii). However, regardless of the degree to which Kelley was personally and passionately invested in what she did, she always worked from and argued from a factual base and trained her colleagues to follow this same practice. The use to which data could be put was Kelley's reason for collecting and analyzing it, both of which she did very well. Goldmark, a long-time research associate, admired Kelley's ability as a social scientist and cited one example where a young field worker had collected data on over a thousand cases of child labor and was "struggling with the perennial difficulty of organizing a mass of details."

> Miss Kelley undertook to help Helen Marot write up the findings. In so doing she began that generous aid to younger colleagues in mastering their material which she was to continue all her life. I recall her offering similar assistance in later years in training other investigators-in-the-making who subsequently became well known in their own right .... I well remember how Mrs. Kelley issued an edict setting aside Saturday morning as the time for a weekly meeting of the committee to go over the various sections of Helen Marot's report.
>
> GOLDMARK 1953:81

While Kelley is more obviously a sociologist than Lillian Wald, Wald was, nevertheless, true to the tradition of using the settlement as method for both research and for problem-solving and proclaimed it "the most pliable tool for social service that has been developed" (Wald 1934:6). Wald, however, had little tolerance for studying something simply because it was there and pronounced such work "a hindrance rather than a source of help" (1934:124). The work of the Factory Investigating Commission presents several examples of how Wald, Kelley, and other "Henry Streeters" came before the Commission as witnesses, armed with data to document the atrocities industrial workers were subjected to on a daily basis. It was such public appearances by Wald that caused many to think of her as a sociologist, the typical label for the female reformers of the day. For example, a 1933 entry in *The National Cyclopedia of American Biography* began by identifying Wald as a "sociologist and author" (LDWP:Reel 1, Biography).

Industrial Sociology

The study of work and industry and their impact on other aspects of social life, such as health, childhood, and family has produced a massive body of sociological work, empirical and theoretical. Indeed, much of sociology rests on the assumption that the means and mode of production are the bases of social life. It is, in fact, a loss to the discipline of sociology that the early history of research and reform relating to industrial conditions has not been recognized and that the development of industrial sociology has been dated as much later than its actual beginning with settlement sociology. An early and important phase of industrial sociology in the US began in 1893 with Florence Kelley's appointment as the first factory inspector for the state of Illinois, one outcome of which was her report on the sweating-system of manufacturing in *Hull-House Maps and Papers* (1895). The settlements practiced industrial sociology in documenting a lack of standards, lack of sanitation, lack of safety regulations, inadequate pay, and child labor abuses characteristic of many workplaces. Sociologically, these investigators connected the dots from workplace problems to health problems; from school dropouts to child labor abuses; from inadequate wages to unhealthy living, to health contagions and to family dissolution. These facts were presented to legislative bodies and regulatory agencies that could make a difference, and at times the press and public opinion were used to pressure industrialists into reforms that would improve the safety and lives of their workers. Settlement sociologists sometimes took an active role in encouraging unionization as the best hope for workers to find a voice. Settlement workers used their standpoint epistemology to become spokespersons for their neighbors as they had first-hand knowledge of their problems and needs. Because so many problems of the Progressive Era were traceable to unbridled industrial growth and greed, settlement sociology was industrial sociology. The role of settlement residents and reformers in industrial sociology is nowhere more evident than in the official investigation into the Triangle Shirtwaist fire in New York. The official records of the Factory Investigating Commission provide abundant evidence that Henry Street researchers represented by Wald and her nurses and Kelley and her NCL staff repeatedly demonstrated the intersecting of quality-of-life with industrial work.

The National Consumers' League (NCL) was responsible for a number of studies that deserve recognition for laying the foundation of what was later to be labeled as industrial sociology. These works paved the way in collecting empirical data on the relationship between worker fatigue, working conditions in general, and productivity; some of the NCL research also contrasted different styles of management. They produced empirical evidence connecting the length of the work day with health and family life (Goldmark 1912, Frankfurter and Goldmark 1916). These are the very kinds of studies attributed to early male social scientists such as Elton Mayo and as being of later, post-World War I, origin. For example Madge's work on "pioneers in industrial sociology" traces its roots to England's Industrial Fatigue Research Board with the first study cited in the US being a 1917 study of women workers in a munitions plant during World War I where it was found that reducing work hours from twelve to ten cut accidents in half (1962:162–209). The only early settlement-related work mentioned in Madge's history is that of Josephine Goldmark who is credited with writing a 1920 report for the Public Health Service. He does not, however, mention the more relevant and much earlier, *Fatigue and Efficiency* (1912) by Goldmark, work carried out under the auspices of the National Consumers' League. By Madge's account, Industrial Sociology began in the US as Industrial Psychology with the establishment in 1926 of the Harvard Fatigue Laboratory and Harvard's Department of Industrial Research funded by Rockefeller funds in the Graduate School of Business Administration. Madge's recognition was no doubt based on Elton Mayo's now classic Hawthorne studies of the 1930s. Odum's brief history of industrial sociology in the US makes no mention of any of the Progressive Era work by women. Instead, he cited Arthur J. Todd as Director of Industrial Relations for B. Kuppenheimer and Company and his subsequent book, *Industry and Society* (1933) as establishing industrial sociology as a formal branch of the discipline (1951:306–308). Typical of the incomplete history of industrial sociology in the US is a recent text (Watson 2008) chronicling the sociology of work, workers, and industry as stemming from the European roots of Marx, Durkheim and Weber giving passing recognition to Chicago social interactionism but with no mention of settlement sociology thus continuing the politics of erasure.

Among the many works associated directly and indirectly with settlement sociology, two provide clear evidence of early contributions to industrial sociology. Both studies were sponsored by the National Consumers' League with Florence Kelley's leadership. The first, published in 1911 as *Making Both Ends Meet: The Income and Outlay of New York Working Girls*, was the work of Sue Ainslie Clark and Emily Wyatt and used interviews with large numbers of working women (some collected by the authors, some by other settlement workers) employed in two different venues and with different styles of management. Those women working under traditional management were employed in hospitals, hotels, garment shops, and laundries. Women working under a new, more "scientific" form of management were employed in a cotton mill, a bleachery, and a cloth-finishing factory. The researchers found that under the more "scientific" management wages were increased and fatigue decreased. The same study found that shorter working days and more rest periods increased worker productivity and worker satisfaction. The second study was done by Kelley's assistant, Josephine Goldmark, published in 1912 as *Fatigue and Efficiency: A Study in Industry* which one reviewer described as "the first systematic treatise on the dynamic relation of the worker to the work" (Hutchins 1913:30). This comprehensive work, introduced by Frederick Lee a physiologist at Columbia University, began by establishing the fact that fatigue is a physiological state with predictable impact on work performance. Goldmark assembled statistics from various work environments in Europe and the United States showing the dysfunctional effects of long working hours and other adverse working conditions on productivity. Some of the data are generic and some specific to particular kinds of industries. Most of the data are not gender-specific although wherever possible, Goldmark singled out women workers for their special effects and also examined some all-female industries. Prior to publication some of these data were used in several court cases to establish a scientific defense for protective labor legislation. The research drew heavily on interviews with workers in industries such as textiles, canneries, shoe making, and telephone service taking into account variables such as speed, monotony, and noise. Goldmark used secondary data from earlier European studies as well as primary data collected in the US, most of it by settlement workers. She provided scientific evidence that speed and long hours did not maximize worker output while at the same time documenting some of the adverse effects on women's health and secondarily on infant mortality and low birth rates (Goldmark 1912:91–96, Schachter 2002:563–578). Further, Goldmark looked at work-hour requirements, night work for women, and wages (Goldmark 1953:153–159). Her book quickly went to three printings and the final one included as appendices data collected to support adjudicatory appeals in cases involving worker hours and wages, and also the Supreme Court decision in *Mullen v. Oregon* (1908). These studies are selected from a much larger body of research conducted by the network of women associated with settlement sociology and whose contributions appear to be similar to and preceding those conducted by academic males who are generally recognized as the pioneers of industrial sociology.

Women's Networking and Public Sociology

Settlement workers developed a kind of subculture based largely on their networking through organizations, meetings, personal friendships, and visits. One of the strongest and most functional was that between New York and Chicago, particularly among the women of Hull House and Henry Street because of Kelley's experience with both and because of the personal friendship between Wald and Addams. The effectiveness of this network is perhaps most evident in the case of the Children's Bureau, a project of Wald and Kelley for years before it became reality. According to accounts of several biographers, it was a breakfast table interaction between the two women in 1905 that led eventually to the establishment of a national Children's Bureau. Apparently the vision began when Kelley voiced her outrage over a news story that the Secretary of Agriculture was being dispatched to the southern states because a boll weevil infestation was threatening the cotton crop. The two women commiserated that none of the atrocities reported daily as happening to children would call forth such a response from the federal government. Yet they questioned why, "If a quarter-inch insect that could destroy a cotton crop was worthy of federal investigation, should not the conditions that destroy children be worthy of an equal effort" (Duffus 1939:94–95, Siegel 1983:60)? Thus began a concerted effort for the establishment of a Children's Bureau, an agency with the capacity to investigate, collect, and analyze data where none existed, and an agency to educate the public and offer legislative proposals to make the world healthier and safer for children. The immediate need was seen for restrictions on child labor because of its impact on health and education. But equally important was a simple lack of data. At that time, it was not even known how many children were born in the United States each year. Similarly, no central data existed on infant mortality and morbidity.

Following the breakfast table conversation at Henry Street, events were set in motion that would eventually culminate in a federal Children's Bureau. Kelley took the first step in enlisting the support of Dr. Edward Devine, a Columbia University sociologist and head of the Charity Organization Society, and the National Child Labor Committee (NCLC) formed a year earlier at Kelley's initiative. In short order, Devine was able to secure a meeting for Wald with President Theodore Roosevelt who had many times been a visitor at Henry Street and knew of her work and reputation. He gave his support for a bill to establish a federal Children's Bureau, first introduced in Congress in 1906 where it languished for years despite wide-spread backing. It was not until 1912 that Congress passed the legislation and President Taft signed it into law creating the Children's Bureau. This goal, however, was accomplished because Wald and Kelley did not give up and did not allow their supporters to give up the fight in behalf of the nation's children. Their most valuable public voice, and the center of lobbying activity, was the male-dominated National Child Labor Committee that among its first actions hired Lewis Hine, a sociologist, photographer, and teacher at the New York Ethical Cultural School who was also an advocate of the use of photo journalism as a tool for social reform. His photographs remain today as a thorough and dramatic documentation of child labor and other social problems in the United States in the early twentieth century[6] (Jaycox 2005:256). Efforts of the NCLC to establish the Children's Bureau culminated with a symposium, and ample press coverage, as part of the Fifth Annual Conference on Child Labor held in Chicago in 1909 to which leading politicians, philanthropists, clergymen, and intellectuals were invited and featuring prominent speakers. Lillian Wald opened the symposium and was followed by Jane Addams and academic sociologists such as Charles Henderson of the University of Chicago and Samuel Lindsay of Columbia as well as businessmen and jurists (LDWP: Reel 24, B36, F1). Interestingly, Lillian Wald's papers preserved the program of this Chicago Symposium, dated January 21–22, 1909 as well as that of the White House Conference on the Care of Dependent Children, called by President Roosevelt and dated January 25–26 of the same year in

6 On September 2, 2012, Scott Paley, anchor of the CBS national news, included a segment on Hine's photography of child laborers in the first decade of the twentieth century.

Washington, D.C. Although the focus of the Symposium was on child labor and the Conference was broader in scope, both featured many of the same speakers and attendees (LDWP: Reel 24, B36, F1). It appears for supporters of the Children's Bureau that the Chicago Symposium was a warm-up for the latter.

Although Kelley was the driving force behind the idea of the Children's Bureau, she was impeded by her reputation as a socialist and because she sometimes "came on like gangbusters" (Muncy 1991:49). Thus, Wald took the public leadership role in the Children's Bureau project and solicited the help of the male-dominated NCLC of which both she and Kelley were members. Kelley, Wald, Addams, and Lindsay, who was also General Secretary of the NCLC at the time, drafted the first proposed legislation inclusive of all aspects of child welfare such as health, disease, labor, and education. It was the NCLC that first took the proposed bill creating the Children's Bureau to Congress in 1906 and for every year thereafter until it was finally passed in 1912. President Theodore Roosevelt convened the White House Conference on the Care of Dependent Children in Washington, D.C. with pressure from the NCLC and other groups. The Conference was apparently a means by which Roosevelt could put pressure on Congress as those invited were asked to make recommendations to the President on a number of issues relating to child welfare, including the need for the establishment of a children's bureau. Some 200 persons, a majority male, accepted invitations to attend the Conference. The only well-known settlement people in attendance were Jane Addams and Julia Lathrop of Hull House and Lillian Wald; Florence Kelley's name was not listed among those invited although some accounts put her at the conference and she was a speaker at the earlier Chicago Symposium (Muncy 1991: 46, Conference on the Care of Dependent Children (CCDC) 1909). All officers of the Conference were males, headed by Homer Folks of the New York State Charities and the National Child Labor Committee, Thomas Mulry, a New York banker, and Judge Julian Mack of Chicago. The male delegates were drawn largely from charitable and philanthropic organizations with a few judges, ministers, academics, and business moguls such as Julius Rosenwald and Andrew Carnegie. The academics included sociologists Edward Devine, Samuel Lindsay, and Charles Henderson. Booker T. Washington was the only recognizable name among black leaders present.

The Conference produced overwhelming support for a Children's Bureau, the only disagreement being over whether this government agency was to be confined to fact-gathering and non-editorial dissemination of facts. All were in agreement that the agency should be a clearing house on statistics pertinent to child welfare. The need was clear as it was repeatedly pointed out that the US had no systematic means of collecting vital statistics on births, infant mortality, industrial accidents, or contagious diseases. Most of the delegates, however, did not approve of the kind of agency favored by settlement people—that is, a bureau that would not only collect statistics but advocate for needed legislation and help governments to draft model statutes and push them through legislative bodies. Wald, introduced by Homer Folks as the "woman behind the bureau," was the most forceful speaker in spelling out what she saw as the appropriate role of a Children's Bureau. After stating the obvious, that the US was the only great nation that did not know how many children were born or died each year and from what causes, she went directly to the heart of the controversy about advocacy, "Only the Federal Government can cover the whole field and tell us of the children with as much care as it tells of the trees or the fishes or the cotton crops." She went on to point out that other countries have no problem in "using knowledge" under the leadership of trained specialists to achieve "efficient manhood through a well-guarded childhood" (CCDC 1909:204). Apparently, to mediate the two positions (clearing house restrictive versus expanded advocacy role), delegates were asked to debate and vote on the formation of a complementary "permanent organization," voluntary and privately funded, to be vested with the advocacy and reform agenda, modeled after groups such as the National Playground Association or the National Child Labor Committee. Among the recommendations that conferees submitted to the President, was formation of such an organization as well as a separate recommendation for passage of the bill pending before the Congress for establishment of a Children's Bureau within the Department of Interior and Commerce. The final legislation was signed into law on April 9, 1912 and mandated that the Children's Bureau "investigate and report...upon all matters pertaining to the welfare of children and child life among all classes of people." Indicative of the status of representatives of the NCLC, the President presented a signature pen to NCLC lobbyist Alexander McKelway (Lindenmeyer 1997: 26–27).[7] Although the men seemed to get credit for what the women had initiated and fought for, to Wald and Kelley, the end result was more important than public recognition.

The final bill was weaker than that initially drafted by Kelley, Wald, and Lindsey, seemingly making the Bureau into a census department for children, with no mandate to correct problems documented. In fact, Muncy, in her account of the Children's Bureau creation, conceptualized the difference between ideal

7 Indicative of the fear of Federal government control and preemptive authority over the family, the legislation passed in the Senate only after Texas Senator Charles Culbertson successfully attached an amendment stating that "no official or agent or representative of said bureau shall, over the objection of the head of the family, enter any private family residence under this act" (Lindenmeyer 1997:26).

and real as based on gender and "pure" versus "applied science," the latter at that time most often associated with women reformers, the former with male academics and the growing quest for "scientism" (1991:38–65). Taking this argument further, Muncy documents how the women were able to control and use the Children's Bureau as a "female dominion" in reform despite having come out of years of work with a relatively weak piece of legislation. Once the bill was signed into law, the women immediately began working the system, and did so quite successfully for their own agenda. Both Scott (2004:xviii-xxi) and Muncy (1991:38–65) give accounts of how the women's network essentially shaped the Children's Bureau to their vision of an agency of advocacy and reform, very unlike the neutral, data-collecting vision of some of their male colleagues and legislators. Their vision began to take shape with the appointment of Julia Lathrop as the first director of the Bureau and the first female director of such a government agency. Muncy traced the series of events that began almost immediately after the legislation was signed and culminated in Lathrop's appointment.

> [N]o one could have predicted that the new agency would establish the primacy of women in its area of public policy…many Congressmen expected that the Bureau's chief would be male, and the NCLC considered several men…. Jane Addams wired both Lillian Wald and President Taft to say that 'the Chicago group' supported Julia Lathrop's appointment to the new office…. Addams wrote more elaborately to Wald: 'It does seem to me a pity not to have a woman and a very able one in this position…. Let's try hard for a woman first'. Wald agreed and she persuaded the NCLC to support Lathrop's candidacy…. Taft sent Lathrop's appointment to the Senate where it received confirmation that same day (1991:47–48)

In the same vein, Scott wrote,

> When Congress finally adopted legislation to create the Children's Bureau and the president signed it in April 1912, members of the Hull-House network went into action. …Ironically, Lathrop, the firm advocate for the merit system, gained office through the political skills of her friends.
>
> SCOTT 2004:XVIII

Since there was little data to be collected from the various states and localities, the Bureau was right away launched into a research agenda, and Lathrop saw to it that it was the kind of research that would command action in such areas as infant mortality and child labor. With limited budget and staff, however, early research, data collection, and public education could not have been accomplished except for a vast army of volunteers, most of them females, that Lathrop with the help of the Hull House and New York connections could mobilize quickly in such groups as the General Federation of Women's Clubs, the National Federation of Settlements, the Consumers' League, the Association of Collegiate Alumnae, the Women's Christian Temperance League, and the National Child Labor Committee. Although funds were limited for research, Lathrop did send some contracts to the research team she had earlier assembled at the Chicago School of Civics and Philanthropy (MacLean and Williams 2012). The Bureau not only did basic sociological research, but also produced educational pamphlets—largely aimed at mothers—on such topics as birth registration, infant care, and the rights of children. The bureau also adopted new strategies for reaching the public: exhibits, posters, demonstrations, and later radio and film shorts (Muncy 1991:56). The power of the Bureau was demonstrated in Lathrop's sharp budget increase request for 1914–1915 fiscal year. Initially, the House Appropriations committee ignored her request and recommended the same level of funding as the year before. Again, Lathrop mobilized her community supporters through the New York-Chicago network and received her budget increase as requested. The other thing that Lathrop did to insure her agenda was to work the civil service system so as to hire largely from her women's network. She often made hires gender-specific to women by stipulating that workers would be interviewing mothers and women about sensitive topics such as child birth and breast feeding. Thus by 1919, of 169 Bureau employees, only 14 were males (Muncy 1919:51). However, remembering her days in Illinois when service institutions were victims of a political patronage system, Lathrop always advocated merit-based hiring. In fact her first two hires, an assistant bureau chief and the director of statistics were both males with experience in government departments known for their production of statistics, the census department and the Bureau of Labor (Lathrop 1912: 319). As evidence, however, that the Bureau was truly a female domain, when Lathrop retired in 1922, the second director was another Hull House woman, Edith Abbott who assumed the directorship with the support of her Chicago and New York colleagues.

Public Health, Medical Sociology, and Home Health Care

Lillian Wald is not typically thought of as a sociologist, nor do we attempt to establish her as such. However, she acted as a public sociologist in her day, not only from her post as head resident of Henry Street but also as one of a group of New York women who found a path to power in what Recchiuti (2007) labeled "social-science grounded, issue-oriented groups" that made a significant contribution to public sociology. Lillian Wald understood the many and complex linkages between health and economic and social conditions, and because of this understanding she brought to public awareness a "Millsian" conceptualization of public health. She did not leave health to be understood as an individual or personal matter. By her own observations, and no doubt by her exposure to other social settlements, Wald was early convinced that nursing was more than just medical. She contextualized problems associated with health and illness by consistently locating them in poverty, in the work place, in housing, in public education, and in the unnecessary spread of contagious diseases. In a 1911 speech before the International Conference of Settlements, she emphasized that "the nurse is required to make accurate account of social conditions which should be remedied" (LDWP: Reel 25, B38). In that same speech Wald catalogued a list of health-related milestones that she attributed to the tested practices and application of facts collected by "the American Settlement in New York." For example, the initiation of the public health nurse and her functions; school nurses employed by the city of New York; the training and regulation of midwives; and "industrial nursing" begun through a collaboration of Henry Street and the Metropolitan Life Insurance Company. By her own words, Wald intended to go beyond the scientific nursing founded by Florence Nightingale (for whom she had great respect) and take it to "the next interpretation in the relation of the nurse to the public rather than the individual or ward" (Daniels 1989:25). Wald explained that the work she and Brewster began they defined as "Public Health Nursing" and she went on to quote "the famous Dr. William H. Welch of Johns Hopkins University as declaring the public health nurse to be one of three original contributions that America has made to public health (Wald 1934:72–73).[8] By her social-economic-political location of health, by her role in public education about health, and by teaching prevention as well as treatment, Wald defined what was later to become the sociology of health and illness/wellness. One of her biographers wrote that "In the process of developing community health care, Miss Wald established the early concepts of preventive medicine and the treatment of the whole patient" (Siegel 1983:48).

Wald pioneered home health care by taking nursing to the people. By 1927, 250 trained nurses served 50,000 patients in Manhattan, Richmond and Bronx boroughs, making nearly half a million home visits a year (Kellogg 1927:778). Wald was adamant about treating the sick in their homes, a concept only

8 The other two "original contributions" identified by Welch were "the sanitation of the Canal Zone, [and] the State Tuberculosis Laboratories instituted by Dr. Hermann Biggs (Wald 1934:73).

recently making its way back into the practice of holistic medicine, and her statistical records showed a better recovery for in-home cases when compared with similar hospital cases (Siegel 1983:48). Wald also had a role in the establishment of medical sociology, with its emphasis on health professionals, because she was the first to offer nurse practitioners as home health care providers as well as in nurses' stations located in settlements and later in the public schools. Perhaps most important of all, she redefined the nurse-doctor relationship, always stressing that settlement nurses worked *with* not *for* physicians. In her first history of Henry Street, Wald discussed some of their early encounters with physicians and the diplomacy required to establish nurses' acceptance so that they could "work together as comrades" ([1915]1991:34). No doubt, much of Wald's success in public health was due to the fact that she relied on fact, persuasion, and personal charm. She knew that she could not alienate physicians; she did not directly challenge them but found ways to work around them, largely by taking her message about health directly to the public. Changing this subordinate-superordinate nurse-physician role also involved changes in nursing education and in the public perception of nurses. Wald's concept of public health nursing was spread throughout the United States and beyond, and Henry Street became one of the great centers of nursing education, routinely offering classes for visiting nurses (Daniels 1989:26). For many of these classes, Columbia University Teachers' College offered credit (LWP, B66). In fact, Wald wrote about the role of Henry Street in educational innovations at Columbia,

> offering opportunities for post-graduate training and experience in the newly opened field of public health nursing.... This department is in affiliation with the settlement. At least four important training-schools for nurses are now working under the direction of universities...to give education supplementary to the hospital training ([1915]1991:63–64).

Wald was elected the first president of the National Organization for Public Health Nursing and came to epitomize the public figure of nursing. She elevated the status of nurses as she worked to have them represented in all policy-making regarding public health issues, particularly with regard to families and children. She herself represented the voice of public health in many Progressive Era organizations whose mission it was to improve quality of life among the working classes. Wald proclaimed public health as "a part of the consciousness of the socially minded...and all problems, even economic ones, seem to be but a variant of health and knowledge of the requisites for the maintenance of health in the individual, the family, the community and the state" (LDWP 1911:

Reel 25, B38). Wald was also among those settlement leaders who worked internationally, at first in opening up training programs at Henry Street for nurses from Africa, Asia, Latin America, and Europe and later as a part of the women's international movement for peace. Siegel attributed Wald with helping to "seed public health nursing in every corner of the world" (1983:107).

Sociological Jurisprudence

Oliver Wendell Holmes Jr. and later Roscoe Pound became known as the theorists of sociological jurisprudence in the US by calling for judges to take into account non-legal matters as the "felt necessities of the time." Most legal scholars agree, however, that it was Louis Brandeis who became the "great practitioner" of sociological jurisprudence (Urofsky 2009:76). Some of these scholars also acknowledge that Brandeis gave legalistic form to the sociological substance supplied him by Florence Kelley and Josephine Goldmark (Piott 2006:109–126, Urofsky 2009). The underlying assumption of sociological jurisprudence is that the meaning or interpretation of the law should evolve in relation to the social needs of a people that are constantly changing. This assumes, of course, a human element—that is, that judges make decisions in social context, raising the question frequently posed by Florence Kelley: "Is the trouble really in the Constitution? Or is it in the judges"? (Goldmark 1953:179). Building on the assumption that the law can be used to protect the public, sociological jurisprudence establishes a reasonable connection between the law and public health, safety, and general welfare (Piott 2006:120, 136). Thus when Kelley, Goldmark and other colleagues at the NCL teamed up with Brandeis, they advanced sociological jurisprudence as they laid markers on a trail that eventually ended with judicial acknowledgment that the Constitution should protect social as well as individual rights (Goldmark 1953:143–159). The social rights in cases they argued had to do with the health, safety, and welfare of workers and by extension society at large. As a means of improving the quality of life for industrial workers in the United States, Kelley and her associates aimed to regulate hours, secure a minimum wage, and establish safety regulations in the work place. They made their case in the form of legal briefs filled with data drawn from industrial work situations in Europe and the United States, aggregate data interspersed with descriptive and memorable cases. They began with cases involving protective legislation passed at the state level that had moved up through the appeals process to the Supreme Court where arguments were couched in constitutional questions and legal precedents established.

In 1895, New York enacted the Bakeshop Act limiting the work hours of bakers to ten per day or 60 per week. The law was eventually tested before the US

Supreme Court as *Lochner v. New York* (1895) and the Court decided that the "due process" clause of the 14th Amendment guaranteed protection of personal rights as well as property rights and that "personal rights" included the right of an employee to enter into a work "contract" with his employer. In essence, the Court decided that bakers were capable of looking out for themselves in deciding whether to take a job requiring that they work more than allowed under the Backshop Act and that work hours could be restricted by statute "only in occupations proven injurious to the health" of the worker. In the Court's opinion, the State had not proven that excessive work hours for bakers were an endangerment. To decide in favor of the state in this case would unreasonably and unnecessarily interfere with an individual's right and liberty to contract with an employer. However, the decision seemed to leave the door open for a case that would prove long work hours were injurious to the health of workers. Thus, three years later in *Holden v. Hardy* (1898) the Supreme Court upheld a Utah law restricting the number of hours miners could be required to work without injury to their health. Encouraged by the Utah decision, Kelley decided to become involved in another case that would test the protective inclination of male decision-makers. She seized the opportunity to have the NCL manage the defense of *Mullen v. Oregon* (1908) involving a statute limiting the number of work hours of laundry women to 10 per day. The case had broad implications since 19 other states had similar statutes. She and Goldmark solicited Louis Brandeis of Boston (Goldmark's brother-in-law) as unpaid counsel for the NCL in defense of the Oregon law. He agreed but stipulated that he needed facts to establish that excessive work hours were injurious to the health of workers, in this case female workers. Kelley and Goldmark had only two weeks to assemble such data, their only help being NCL volunteers. The US had no such thing as records on "industrial medicine" or "industrial hygiene" and this was three years before Dr. Alice Hamilton of Hull House attended the Fourth International Congress on Occupational Poisons and described the position of the US as "not an occasion for national pride" (Goldmark 1953:155). Goldmark's later work on industrial fatigue grew out of her realization that there were no systematic data in the US. Thus she turned first to international sources and found the most substantial help in the reports of British factory inspectors and British medical commissions beginning as early as 1833. There she found records of experience with long and short hours of labor in France, Germany, Italy and Belgium and to this was added Kelley's knowledge of Engels' data on English factory workers. To the international data were added observations and statistics from the US, largely from settlement workers such as Kelley had collected in Illinois. Goldmark turned her initial findings over to Brandeis even as Kelley and others continued to collect data.

> What emerged from the whole were the contrasting pictures of misery and its alleviation. From the whole sordid, miserable record of exploited workers under unregulated hours, there stood out—clear and luminous—the regeneration that followed a more decent limitation of hours. But could this be shown in a legal document? It could, said Mr. Brandeis, because this part of the brief need not be legal at all. The legal argument he would present briefly in only a page or two. But in presenting the facts we could bring out the contrast buried in our compilation.... We would contrast evil and good; the dangers to health, safety, morals, and the general welfare from excessive hours; the corresponding benefits from shortened hours. Reiteration of the theme from country after country, state after state...was precisely what we needed to round out the picture.... And so the first 'Brandeis Brief' was completed.
>
> GOLDMARK 1953:157

The first Brandeis Brief was 104 pages with only two pages of legal argument and more than one hundred pages of factual evidence showing that long hours of work were dangerous to the health, safety, and well-being of women and that improvements could be made with changes in industrial work settings. While not explicit in the argument, the implication was clear: if the well-being of women were endangered, the nation was at risk since women, or rather their reproductive well-being, were the future of the nation. Most historians credit the Brandeis Brief with the decision of the Supreme Court upholding the Oregon statue. Brandeis put before powerful male decision-makers the same kind of information that Kelley and her colleagues had been compiling for years and the Court's unanimous decision established the acceptance of the use of sociological data as a means of legal augmentation and established that the law should evolve in relation to social needs (Piott 2006:120). This win, however, was not without controversy because the Oregon statute that the NCL fought to uphold was opposed by some feminists who saw it as protective legislation for women, thus a setback to their fight for equal rights. Nevertheless, over the next eight years forty-one states enacted laws in protection of working women (Piott 2006:136).

Once the value of the Brandeis Brief had been established in the Supreme Court and because the first one had been put together so hurriedly, Kelley and Goldmark set about building on the volume of work they had collected hastily for the first brief. With a grant from the Russell Sage Foundation, additional work was begun but was interrupted by the need to turn their attention to a case in Illinois challenging that state's ten-hour work week limitation on women. Thirteen years earlier when Kelley was Illinois State Factory Inspector, the State Supreme Court had overturned a similar statute in *Ritchie v. People* (1895), a decision that caused Kelley to resolve to "rescue the Fourteenth Amendment...from the perverted application upon which this decision rests" (Goldmark 1953:144). In preparing the Brandeis Brief for *Ritchie v. Wyman* (1910) this time was added the "abundance of new evidence" collected by Kelley and Goldmark and the document presented to the Illinois Supreme Court was over 600 pages (Goldmark 1953:162). In 1910 a favorable decision was handed down and Kelley took particular satisfaction in one sentence in the opinion, "What we know as men, we cannot profess to be ignorant of as judges" (Goldmark 153:162). Indeed, it appears that sociological jurisprudence was now established at both the state and national levels. Over the next several years the NCL participated in and gave support to cases in other state courts involving work hours in various occupations, for example retail stores, and in a New York case defending a statute regulating night work for women. An appellate court found in *Schweinler Press v. New York* (1915) that night work could be injurious to the health of women, and after much delay a similar decision was reached by the Supreme Court in *Radice v. New York* (1924). Results in all of these cases, both in state courts and in the Supreme Court were favorable. The cause of trying to insure a minimum wage for women, and ultimately for all workers, however met with less success. It was not until 1937, after Kelley's death, that the Supreme Court handed down a decision upholding minimum wage laws. In the meantime, however, some success was achieved by expanding protections from women to all workers.

In 1917, in the landmark *Bunting v. Oregon*, the Supreme Court upheld another Oregon law mandating a maximum 10 hour work day and requiring overtime pay beyond the 10 hour limit for all employees, thus expanding the protection given to women in *Muller v. Oregon*. By this time, Brandeis had been appointed to the Supreme Court and his friend and future Supreme Court justice, Felix Frankfurter, assumed the task of preparing briefs and working with the NCL. Thus the brief used in support of arguments for *Bunting v. Oregon* was authored by Frankfurter and Goldmark and with updates to the earlier briefs it was over a thousand pages, six pages of legal argument and 959 pages of facts and expert testimony about the evils of long hours of labor. The court ruled that the limitation on workers' hours and the requirement for overtime pay did not interfere with the individual's right to contract under the 14th amendment, thus reversing itself from *Lochner v. New York*. As the Brandeis Brief became widely acclaimed it was reprinted and distributed by the NCL and, as Goldmark reported, it "was in great demand from law schools and universities as well as from labor unions and libraries" (1953:159). Kelley raised special funds to cover the cost of the printing and it was actually critically reviewed in publications such as the *Political Science Quarterly* where it was evaluated as furnishing "an excellent model for future briefs on similar constitutional questions" (Powell 1916:471). Clearly Henry Street included some of our most important sociological antecedents who left behind prolific and profound artifacts.

CHAPTER 9

Greenwich House: The House that Mary Built

Like College Settlements, Greenwich House began with an organization, the Cooperative Social Settlement Society, founded in 1901 by Mary Kingsbury Simkhovitch. Unlike the all-female CSA, however, founding members, except for Simkhovitch, were all men: Bishop Henry C. Porter, Judge Eugene Philbin, Carl Schurz, Jacob Riis, Felix Adler, and Robert Fulton Cutting. Those who joined with Kingsbury to found Greenwich House were well known, well-connected, and assured a sound beginning for the settlement. The first donation, for example, came from Mrs. J. Pierpont Morgan (Kraus 1980:102). The aim of the founders was to establish and maintain "a Social Settlement or Social Settlements in the City of New Ywork, as centers for social, educational, and civic improvements, to be carried on in conjunction and association with the people residing in the neighborhoods where such Settlement or Social Settlements may be situated" (Simkhovitch 1938:88). Greenwich House was actually the only settlement founded by this Society and opened its doors on Thanksgiving Day, 1902 at 26 Jones Street in the most densely populated block on New York's lower west side in what is today known as Greenwich Village, with Mary Kingsbury Simkhovitch as head resident. The building had previously been a tenement and the Anarchist's Society once had its headquarters in what was to become the Greenwich House dining room (Briggs 2008:33). The primary ethnic populations in the area were Italian and Irish and African American migrants from the South although at the time the African Americans were moving out, replaced largely by Italian immigrants. Over the first two decades of the settlement the Irish became the dominant group but by the end of the First World War, they were outnumbered by the Italians in the eastern part of the Village. Greenwich House worked with blacks in its early years, although in deference to public sentiment, most activities were segregated. Later the settlement opened a facility on Cornelia Street so that blacks would have a place to meet without controversy (Briggs 2008: 42). Work among African Americans became more intense and more organized when Mary White Ovington arrived at Greenwich House in 1904.

In its first year, Greenwich House had nine residents to move in, 17 the following year, and a waiting list was developed. As in most settlements, residents were required to pay their own room and board and to participate in the social investigations and programs offered. For example, residents were expected to attend Tuesday evening meetings of the Social Reform Club founded by Edmund Kelly, a disciple of Tolstoy, who presided over discussions of issues and problems as well as proposed solutions (Simkhovitch 1938:71). Greenwich House initially occupied only one building at 26 Jones Street but in 1905 expanded to occupy additional buildings at 18, 20 and 28 Jones Street. In 1916, the Board authorized the construction of a new Greenwich House at 27 Barrow Street. Some of the old buildings were retained for special programs but two were sold to a group of residents who formed the first Cooperative Housing Society in New York (Simkhovitch 1938:179). Over the years the settlement was supported by many influential and wealthy individuals and families, names such as Vanderbilt, Whitney, Roosevelt, Carnegie, Phipps, Prentice, and Harriman. Despite loyal and influential supporters, however, there were times when national economic trends impacted Greenwich House and it faced the threat of mortgage foreclosure and the necessity of program reductions (Briggs 2008). Although always reliant on support from the upper classes, Greenwich House, nevertheless, maintained its grass roots involvement by means of a neighborhood council with direct input to the Board and to the Director (GHR: B23, F138).

Although Simkhovitch herself seems to have maintained a public profile somewhat more conservative than some other settlement workers, Greenwich House began with a socialist philosophy that led to attacking the structural causes of social problems and engaging in reform activities of a reconstructive nature. Above all else, Greenwich House stood for a better life for workers and toward that end marshaled efforts to achieve better health, wages, housing, recreation, and working conditions. Greenwich House saw many well-known personalities and public figures pass through its doors and some even took up residence. Classes and clubs heard lectures by the likes of Emily Balch and Elsie Hill on the subject of suffrage and women's rights. The future first lady Eleanor Roosevelt was a frequent visitor. Paul Kellogg, director of the Pittsburg survey and later editor of the *Survey*, was a resident for a time and after that a regular visitor as was early sociologist-anthropologist and feminist Elsie Clews Parsons. Frances Perkins who became Secretary of Labor under Franklin Roosevelt and the first female cabinet member lived at Greenwich House while a student at Columbia. The fact that such personalities lived in or visited Greenwich House may be reason for Crystal Eastman as a young resident to write her brother, Max,[1] "they are all cranks and reformers, and sooner or later

1 Crystal Eastman and brother, Max, were socialist-leaning and from a liberal and activist family where both parents were Congregational ministers. Crystal (1881–1928) was a lawyer, feminist, antimilitarist, and journalist who had worked for Paul Kellogg on the Pittsburg survey. She was one of the founders of the Women's International League for Peace and Freedom. Max (1883–1969) was a Greenwich Village activist while a student at Columbia where he earned a doctorate in philosophy with John Dewey. He was a writer, philosopher, and poet,

every really interesting up and doing radical...gets down to Greenwich House" (as quoted in Briggs 2008:92).

Greenwich House was networked with other settlements in the city with Simkhovitch serving on various committees and active in numerous organizations. Several of her writings mention cooperative endeavors with University and College Settlements and with Lillian Wald on nursing services. She worked with Florence Kelley in the National Consumers' League and the Committee on Congestion of Population commissioned by the mayor in 1905 and issuing a massive report in 1911. Simkhovitch was active in the Association of Neighborhood Workers in New York, in the National Conference of Charities and Correction, and in the National Federation of Settlements, at various times serving as president of these organizations. There was always a close if informal association between the settlement and Columbia University because of Simkhovitch's husband and other Columbia professors such as Henry Seager who lived for a time at Greenwich House, and Edwin Seligman, once president of Greenwich House Board, and John Dewey who headed their Education Committee. At least one Columbia faculty served on the Greenwich House Board almost every year. In 1929, the association with the University was formalized although the agreement specified that Columbia would provide no financial support (Simkhovitch 1938:223). Simkhovitch saw universities and settlements as having "a common field of interest in social structure and in social change both from an economic and from a sociological angle" (1938:223–224). She also saw the affiliation with Columbia as insuring that Greenwich House would endure over time even as community needs and settlement activities changed.

> Our theory is that a settlement is not an institution harboring activities but a stimulating center for rethinking and for new action in the light of new events. We might envision a time when all our present activities might be liquidated, but we are convinced the time will not come when a neighborhood center will cease to be needed, bringing to light as it does local desires and needs and presenting the views of all groups and interests with the intent of creating a common understanding and, as far as may be, a working agreement...(1938: 224–25).

During the second decade of the century those who became known as bohemians began moving into the Village: intellectuals, artists, nonconformists, and advocates of "free love" (Briggs 2008:11). Real estate agents began to exploit

---

and for a time editor of *The Masses*. He founded the Men's League for Women's Suffrage but in later life he moved away from liberal causes and became much more conservative.

this reputation leading to rising rents and eventually to a total change in the character of the area as immigrants found it unaffordable. Greenwich House, however, has endured to the present as a community center with two primary functions: social services and the arts. According to their website they specialize in support services for those suffering with HIV and AIDS, counseling services for substance dependency, and nursery and day care programs. Greenwich House's artistic programs in pottery, music, and drama are well known throughout the city and state (greenwichhouse.org, accessed July 12, 2014). The Simkhovitch philosophy that established and nourished Greenwich House for so many years is resilient and endures as reflected in the final sentence of her story of Greenwich House. "If I have...learned anything throughout these many years it is...that it is our common life that matters, and that to stay apart from it is the death of art, of politics and of religion" (1938:301).

Founder and Head Resident

Mary Kingsbury (1867–1951) was born to upper middle class parents in fashionable Chester Hill, Massachusetts near Boston, the oldest child and only daughter of Laura Holmes and Isaac Kingsbury, both from prominent New England families. Neighbors in Chester Hill had socially recognizable names such as Lowell and Lee, whose daughter later married Theodore Roosevelt. Mary grew up with grandparents and other extended family, heavily influenced by the local Congregational Church in which her family maintained a pew. Her father was wounded in the Civil War and returned home to spend the remainder of his life in some form of public service. Her mother was an educated woman who wrote poetry and was described by Mary as "an intellectual person" more worried by domestic duties than interested in them (1938:28). In her pursuit of higher education, Mary passed up the women's colleges, many of them located near Boston, in favor of attending the co-educational Boston University, only seven miles away from her home and to which for a time she commuted by train. Her autobiography notes a particular professor, Borden Bowne, who taught his students that Herbert Spencer, although "food" for most of her generation, was "unworthy of sustenance" (1949:9). After graduating Boston University, she taught high school Latin for two years (1938:41). She then entered Radcliffe College for graduate study because she wanted to learn more about social problems after her "glimpse of the West End's tenements" (1949:12). At Radcliffe, she was able to study with Harvard professors even though women could not enter that all-male institution. She took a course in sociology from Edward Cummings (1938:44) and was influenced by William Ashley in economic history where he stressed research and understanding social problems in light of their historical origins, and where, as she put it, "the drama of social change was unfolded" (1938:44–45). In one of her autobiographies, Simkhovitch wrote of the many influences that shaped her thinking and her life's work during her Boston years. She acknowledged, for example, the Rev. W.D.P. Bliss, editor of the *Encyclopedia of Social Reform*, Christian socialist, Fabianist, and pastor of the Anglican congregation known as the Brotherhood of the Carpenter in South Boston. She lived for a time at Denison House where she became acquainted with the Knights of Labor, at one time headquartered there, and was greatly impressed with their open forums on current topics and social-political theory. She praised head resident, Helena Dudley, as a leader capable of combining theory and practice. At Denison House she also met sociologist and activist Emily Balch, as well as socialist and later fellow member of the Companions of the Holy Cross, Vida Scudder (Simkhovitch 1938: 37–39). Briggs reported that on Sundays after church, these three would often attend Central Labor Union meetings "where they listened to various speakers on the latest crimes against workers" (2008:14). Kingsbury attended Philip Brooks' Trinity church where she worked with the African American population in St. Augustine's Chapel and led the Primrose Club, visiting in homes of blacks and discovering for the first time slum landlords.

After one year of study at Radcliffe, Kingsbury seized the opportunity to study at the University of Berlin with a scholarship offered by the Women's Education and Industrial Union (1938:46). Although women were not yet awarded degrees at the University of Berlin, they were allowed to attend all classes. Her study abroad followed the pattern of many male academics of that period for whom study in Europe was considered a requirement for the well-educated individual. Indeed, Kingsbury studied with some of the same professors as Albion Small, W.E.B. Du Bois, Richard Ely, and Robert Park; for example, Gustav Schmoller, Georg Simmel, and Adolf Wagner, who dismissed sociology as "the American science" (1938:51). Also studying in Berlin at the time were Beatrice and Robert Webb of the Fabian Society and the Independent Labor Party, Emily Green Balch, Charlotte Perkins Gilman; and Vladimir Simkhovitch who was to become Kingsbury's husband (1938:55). As was the custom in those days for middle and upper-class women, Kingsbury was accompanied to Europe by her mother who remained with her through her year of study after which they traveled to Paris and London where her mother left her in the company of Emily Balch to attend the International Socialist Trade Union Congress to which Balch had secured passes through a friend of Karl Marx's. After her time in Europe, Kingsbury returned to the States and settled in New York to attend Columbia University where she studied with Harvey Robinson and

Franklin Giddings and where sociology, economics, and history took on "reality and validity" along with a keenly felt need to widen her experience (1938:58). Thus, she welcomed the opportunity to move into the College Settlement on Rivington Street shortly after it opened and where she spent a year visiting tenements and "getting acquainted with the life of the East Side" (Simkhovitch 1949:30). She considered and discarded the idea of college teaching, deciding instead that her life's work would be focused on "the city's problems, and especially the life and fortunes of the great influx of Europeans to America" which she saw as far outweighing "in challenge and attraction the call to academic life" (1938:58). Kingsbury left College Settlement after one year to become head resident of the Friendly Aid House supported by All Souls Unitarian Church and their organization, the Friendly Aid Society. Within a few months, in early 1899, she married Vladimir Simkhovitch (and changed her name) who had followed her to the US, entered into an intensive study of English, and secured a faculty position at Columbia. They moved into an upper-floor apartment in the Friendly Aid House where they remained until 1902 and where their son, Stephen, was born. Their second child, Helena was born in 1903 at Greenwich House. In 1908, the couple purchased a farm in New Jersey which they owned until 1925 and where they spent many week-ends and summers and where their children lived for long periods of time with a governess or with Mary's parents who spent some of their retirement years there (1938:132–133). Simkhovitch explained that she left the Friendly Aid House because, "the Society's idea of the settlement as a charity was so uncongenial...that we began to think harder about the reason for our work, or, to put it rather grandiloquently, the philosophy of the settlement" (1938:88). No doubt, her consideration of the role of religion in settlement life was also a factor in her "philosophy" as she explained in her autobiography.

> I had given up the idea of a church settlement which I had vaguely thought of in Boston days, for I felt that there could hardly be such a thing. A church predicates dogma and a settlement was rather a tryout, an experience in which dogma might perhaps develop, but life would come first and dogma afterward.... I was drawn to the idea of plunging into life where it was densest and most provocative (1938:51).

With the establishment of Greenwich House, often referred to as "the House that Mary built," Simkhovitch attempted to put into practice her own philosophy of what a settlement should be. She also taught for a number of years at the New York School of Philanthropy where she passed her philosophy on to many students while providing them with hands-on experience at Greenwich House.

Along with Lillian Wald, Simkhovitch was one of the best known and respected women in New York. Her position on an issue was important. As with most of the settlement leaders, Simkhovitch left behind a trail of speeches and writings documenting the causes she cared about and worked for; some of these were in the form of scholarly presentations, others obviously intended for popular consumption.[2] She routinely spoke to civic groups, professional organizations, religious, and governmental bodies. She was appointed to serve on many committees and commissions at the local, state, and national levels. She was one of three women appointed by the mayor to the influential Committee of Fourteen, charged with investigating commercialized vice in the city. She, Frances Kellor, and Mrs. William Baldwin were three of a four-member Research Committee that investigated and wrote the final report, *Social Evil in New York City* (1910). One of her passions over the years was descent housing. She served for over 15 years on the New York City Housing Authority and considered her major accomplishment to be passage of the Wagner-Steagall Act (1937) that she co-authored with New York Senator Robert Wagner. Among other things, this legislation created the United States Housing Authority and provided subsidies to improve housing for low-income families. Simkhovitch also spoke and wrote frequently on the changing role of women. She gave a number of speeches on war and the role of settlements and universities in preparation (non-military) for war. Some of her best writings, popular and professional, were in defense of settlements and their unique role in American society. At one point (circa 1919), she described Greenwich House as "a neighborhood center…at the same time an institution for the development of democratic human relations. Thus the sociologist, the educator and the statesman all have a stake in its development" (GHR:B23, F138). Simkhovitch retired as head of Greenwich House, in 1946 at which time she was honored with a city-wide appreciation dinner at the Roosevelt Hotel. She continued to live at Greenwich House until her death in 1951. She was a member of Trinity Episcopal Church where her funeral was held. Her husband survived her and at her death received messages of condolence from across the city, the state, and the nation. One eulogist shared what he called Mary Simkhovitch's version of the second commandment that was also her version of the "neighborly relation."

> To voice their wrongs, to understand their problems, to stand by their side in their life struggles, to welcome their own leadership, to reveal to

2 Copies of many of Simkhovitch's speeches and writings are archived in the Greenwich House Papers at the Tamiment Library, Wagner Labor Collection, New York University and in the Mary Kingsbury Simkhovitch Papers at the Schlesinger Library of the Radcliffe Institute, Harvard Library.

> others who have not had this opportunity of direct contact, the inner character of situations that arise—is the primary task of the settlement.
>
> MKSP:B2, F26

The Simkhovitch Philosophy at Work

What apparently turned out to be a negative experience for Simkhovitch at the Friendly Aid House, no doubt, led her to gather support for beginning her own settlement. Her first step was to form the Cooperative that in 1902 founded Greenwich House. Franklin Giddings, then at Columbia, was the Society's first speaker and he endorsed what he saw as a natural link between sociology and the social settlement, emphasizing their research role: "for the sociologist had especially at heart the revelations the settlement might unearth not only of concrete fact but also of group understanding" (Simkhovitch 1938:86). With this new venture, Simkhovitch began to build on her vision of what a social settlement should be, a vision she pursued for more than four decades. The Simkhovitch collection at Radcliffe's Schlesinger Library includes a one-page, untitled and undated writing that appears to be her definition and philosophy of a social settlement. It reads as follows.

> The settlement is a group of people living and working in a definite area from a common center with a view to raising the standard of living, improving the cultural opportunities, and fostering the democratic way of life in that area. Its work is civic, social, and economic in character. Its method is the bringing together of all elements in the area for common purposes. Its task is, therefore, primarily that of community organization for the furthering of democracy. Our country is made up of neighborhoods. These neighborhoods are the training centers where people must learn to get along with one another, and where common purposes will unite people of widely different backgrounds. It is in these local areas that we see how legislation really works out in practice. These neighborhoods are testing grounds for wider forces, and at the same time the seedbeds for creative purposes. For what happens in these neighborhoods happens in the country as a whole. The settlement must understand local attitudes, always holding fast, however, to its own responsibility for the conduct of its work. Management should include representation from the local area. The activities of the settlement will change as public and private organizations develop. But while its form may change, the need for democratic community organization will continue as a basic factor in the life of America.
>
> MKSP:B3, F62

The fact that early settlements played a key role in the Americanization of European immigrants is no doubt reason for the emphasis on democracy and democratic values that appear to be prevalent in all of the settlements examined. Greenwich House remained true to this philosophy even as through the years various social forces and events impacted both the settlement and Greenwich Village. In her autobiography, for example, Simkhovitch discussed the controversies surrounding WWI and the fact that the National Federation of Settlements in 1917 went on record as supporting the war, although most viewed it as the lesser of two evils and some settlement leaders such as Addams were peace activists. Simkhovitch wrote of people of German origin suffering discrimination during WWI and of help offered them by Greenwich House. She lamented that the War left scars on the nation, Greenwich Village, and Greenwich House. As with most other settlements, Greenwich House was the center of neighborhood war efforts—preparedness, support, and recovery. Simkhovitch, however, drew the line in allowing the use of the settlement as a recruiting station for the enlistment of soldiers but believed that settlements should support all civil service work because that was what they did well (1938:181–196). For example, the Fuel Administration took up residence at Greenwich House and as a result they had a supply of coal for heating when it was in short supply during the War.

In 1917, Greenwich House settled into its new home at 27 Barrow Street where they celebrated their fifteenth anniversary with Thanksgiving dinner. The post-War and later depression era saw a mix of prosperity, growth, and hard times for the Village and for the settlement. The Village came to acquire its bohemian reputation that has stuck through the years and life in the settlement gave evidence of why the phenomenon of change permeated all of Simkhovitch's speeches and writings. While she typically embraced change as a part of the natural process of life, she lamented certain changes in the Village: "The old standards of the neighborhood were conventional, respectable, and traditional. The new group rejected standards and gave its loyal adherence to freedom and to experimentation" (1938: 201). Some blamed Greenwich House and their festivals, which became city-wide attractions, for calling attention to the Village and making it attractive to tourists and to nonconformists. After the War and with an improved economy, the arts began to flourish at Greenwich House and their music and art programs included a host of celebrities. On the down side, during the influenza outbreak of 1918, the tenement area of the Village experienced a thirty percent higher death rate than the city as a whole. The settlement sent out all available nurses and reported that "Practically every member of every family we visit needs physical care" (GHR January 1919, Monthly Reports: Reel 3, B3). The post-war era forced Greenwich House and other settlements to become more conservative and to defend themselves against charges that they were "hot beds" of Bolshevism and Communism. The settlement for the first time denied meeting space to groups that had earlier been welcome there. Such perceptions caused Simkhovitch to strike back in a *New York Times* (July 20, 1919) article in which she protested, "If the right to be neighborly is Bolshevism, let us know it. If the right of free assemblage and free speech is un-American, then history needs to be rewritten" (MKSP: B4, F72). Some organizations adopted "Americanization" programs as a means of countering charges of being un-American, but Simkhovitch refused to be drawn in.

> Foreigners do not enjoy going to night school.... People are too tired...it is ridiculous to prevent people speaking their own language...suppression of foreign newspapers is foolish and would mean...elimination of a great opportunity to bring foreigners in close touch with American life. [Instead]...establish forums in the language of the people themselves where public matters could be discussed.... Suppression never leads anywhere...there must be mutual understanding and building up of American life. There is no formal or mechanical method of Americanization.
>
> GHR NOVEMBER 1919, Minutes: Reel 2, B2

Although summoned to testify as part of the Lusk Committee's[3] anti-radicalism investigation, Simkhovitch provided only minimal cooperation. When questioned about Greenwich House forums where communism was discussed, she testified in defense of free speech (Simkhovitch 1938:211). When the Committee requested settlement records, she agreed to supply only census data on those in the neighborhood who were not English-speaking. Further, she wrote the Governor and appealed for his intervention in halting the work of the Committee. Nevertheless settlement women such as Wald, Kelley, and Simkhovitch were particularly vulnerable. Even Vice-President Calvin Coolidge called into question their patriotism and their susceptibility to foreign influences in an article entitled, "Are Reds Stalking Our College Women?" Around Washington, a "spider web chart" was circulated showing how many women's

3 The Committee, chaired by State Senator Clayton Lusk, was established in 1919 by the New York state legislature to investigate "seditious activities." For over a year the Committee gathered information on "radical groups" by conducting raids, confiscating documents, subpoenaing witnesses and organizational records. Their work ended with a report of more than 4,000 pages, in four volumes (Joint Legislative Committee 1920). The work of the committee largely involved scare tactics and led to only two criminal arrests of "anarchists" newspaper editors and several deportations.

organizations throughout the country "were involved in an interlocking directorate which formed a conspiracy to undermine the government." In some cities the Daughters of the American Revolution circulated a "blacklist" of women's organizations and in some cases individuals were singled out as targets (Wolfe 1975:391). In the post-war era, Greenwich House supported prohibition, perceiving alcohol and lack of alternative leisure-time pursuits as the source of many family problems. As a substitute for meeting spaces offered by neighborhood saloons, Greenwich House opened a restaurant, offering games and music exclusively for men. On another issue, Greenwich House was a strong supporter of the Constitutional Amendment giving women the right to vote. Overall, however, research and reform activities at Greenwich House were reduced some after World War I as the settlement moved more toward club activities and an emphasis on music, arts, and crafts. Writing about the period Briggs surmised,

> During this period, Greenwich House as a social settlement waned, while Greenwich House community center began to wax. Its main programs included recreational activities for the children and young adults, day-care services, and the better development of its pottery, music, and art departments.... Greenwich House provided less agency and more social service and recreation...[although] it continued to focus on the fundamental concerns to a decent standard of living, namely the right to adequate employment as well as housing (2008:316).

Despite what Briggs depicted as a role-change for Greenwich House, in 1926, Simkhovitch authored the widely read and used *Settlement Primer* published by the National Federation of Settlements. Under the heading of "Knowledge of the Neighborhood," she included a strong endorsement of research.

> The Neighborhood House must carry on a continuous survey of the neighborhood...always...delving deeper into the heart of its problems.... No year should be permitted to pass without some tangible and recorded addition, no matter how humble, in the field of social research.... While it is impossible for every worker to know the whole neighborhood, each individual worker should be thoroughly acquainted with some aspects of its life. Naturally the executive or head resident should bring together the knowledge of the whole group (1926:11).

The depression years brought many adjustments and changes for Greenwich House as was true for the country as a whole. During 1931 and 1932, the settlement exhausted its savings, cashed in insurance, failed to meet mortgage payments, and could provide callers with only emergency aid. As community needs grew, the resources with which the settlement had to work were exhausted. The Works Project Administration (WPA)[4] helped some, for example furnishing a teacher to continue the settlement's well-known music school. WPA employees were also used as leaders in recreation, adult and worker education, drama, arts and crafts.

Toward the end of her career, Simkhovitch evidenced some disillusionment with settlement activism and suggested the need to move away from neighborhood work to broad-based legislation and policy-making. She wrote in her autobiography,

> It was with dismay that I realized how little progress had been made and how slow it was likely to be. For the great mass of tenement dwellings in New York remained in their old congested squalor.... The slums were there as they had been for many decades.... Was there no answer? Surely the people as a whole, that is, government, must make this a major concern. It was then that I became convinced that the answer lay in this direction (1949:40).

Simkhovitch to some extent changed the focus of her efforts, attending more to city and statewide organizations with legislative and policy-making potential. In the 1930s, she ran for city council but was defeated. She became more active in the Public Housing Authority, serving for a time as vice-chair, and she joined the Public Affairs Committee in New York, "to learn and to act" (1949:40). Simkhovitch endorsed Franklin Roosevelt both for Governor of New York and for president, writing at one point that he was "bent on a course of action which will effect social change gradually and bring about a more equitable economic order without resorting to the disastrous conflict a more drastic change would entail" (GHR: B23, F17). Even with apparent changes in direction and decreased activism over time, Greenwich House contributed substantially to early sociological research on the problems of urban-industrial life, documenting needs in the areas of housing, health, education, and improved wages and working conditions. In addition, through the years, organizations, both popular and unpopular, found meeting space; diverse groups found a

4 The Works Project Administration was a depression era agency established in 1935 to put millions of unemployed persons to work, its goal at least one worker per family in cases of long-term unemployment. Its large projects employed mostly men in the building of roads, bridges, parks, and public buildings. Some of its smaller projects included funding for unemployed teachers, writers, artists, musicians, and actors.

gathering place, leisure time activities, and a forum for open discussions at Greenwich House.

Research and Sociological Work

Simkhovitch as Sociologist

As with most of the other settlement leaders, at times Simkhovitch identified herself as a sociologist and at other times as a social worker. Her work suggests that she saw the two as inseparable although toward the end of her career she seemed to be giving voice to social workers even though her training was that of sociologist. As with her peers, Simkhovitch saw the settlement itself as the sociological method for learning about social relationships and structural forces (1902:203). She was also fully aware of the importance of settlements in public education because of their use of what she called the inductive process of "understanding and interpreting and then acting" (1902:189–190). She defended the settlement as "a method" rather than a charitable institution and emphasized that settlement workers or any other workers finding themselves in the role of social reformers had to deal with facts which she warned if interpreted incorrectly would be "likely to give a setback to true progress" (1902:203). In a 1911 address before the National Conference of Charities and Correction (GHR: B22, F34), Simkhovitch expounded on the idea of the settlement as method that gives rise to theory. The speech reflects her sociological acumen and suggests that she had given considerable thought to how settlements function and endure over time. The result is a pragmatic theory and method of managerial efficiency incorporated in five "standards and tests." First, efficiency demands knowledge of the settlement district because "out of the substance of life itself the settlement creates such theory as it has." Quite simply, "if a settlement cannot answer any inquiry in regard to its neighborhood it is...inefficient." Second, the settlement method requires workers who love people and are capable of acquiring, without judgment, "wide knowledge of people of all sorts." Third, efficiency in settlements requires knowledge of social forces, "those political, legal, medical, educational, industrial and social problems which make up contemporaneous life." Fourth, a capacity for cooperation is essential in order to "connect the local with the central, the specific with the general." Finally, efficiency in settlement work requires some business acumen, some executive ability, because while humanitarian in objectives, a settlement's functional permanence is dependent on its efficiency as a business. Simkhovitch's skill as leader and tactician is evident in this speech as she began by connecting her message with themes, although very different from her own, of speakers that had preceded her, namely Jane Addams, Graham Taylor, Robert Woods, and Lillian Wald.

Although Simkhovitch's writings are wide-ranging, two consistent and overt themes connect all of her work—neighborhood and social change. These themes were always, whether consciously or unconsciously, filtered through the lens of personal experience and are very apparent in her speech on the occasion of her retirement as head of Greenwich House when she proclaimed, "Oh America, you are made up of myriad neighborhoods." And toward the end of her speech, she stated emphatically, "It is in these neighborhoods that the future is being fashioned day by day" (MKSP 1946: B2, F32). She had in common with Robert Woods her belief that the neighborhood was a microcosm of America and that positive growth and development must begin there. Her interest in change began in classes with William Ashley at Radcliffe where she summed up the importance of the concept and the process, "the knowledge that change is inevitable and is always taking place is the first step necessary for the practical sociologist" (1938:45–46). Unlike many people who as they age resist change, Simkhovitch embraced change and was acutely aware of the necessity for change as new challenges are presented. One of her writings reveals her reason for the consistent theme of change when she asked, "What is the nature of real reform?" Her answer, "the idea that change is possible" (1902:200–201). One should expect no less from this woman who—younger than friends such as Jane Addams and Florence Kelley and who lived longer than her peer, Lillian Wald—saw life as a process of change. Simkhovitch's father fought in the Civil War and she subsequently lived through the industrial-urban revolution, massive waves of immigration, two world wars, and the great depression. Change characterized her life.

Simkhovitch authored five books, three of them similar in form and content in that she worked from a groups or institutional paradigm. Simkhovitch's first and likely most important book, *The City Worker's World in America* (1917) was a working description of her Greenwich neighbors but with facts and application extending to the lives of the working poor in urban America. Beginning with the matter-of-fact observation that "our wage-earners are mainly foreigners and the life of the industrial family is the life of the immigrant or of his children," Simkhovitch set out to answer the question, "How does this important group of workers live"? (1917:5). The book is far more than a description of the interesting and peculiar characteristics of the foreign elements in the United States, although there is some of that. It is largely qualitative description with some statistics depicting the "industrial class" in terms of housing, education, work, leisure, health, politics, and religion. The work is less than objective because Simkhovitch obviously meant to present the strengths of urban workers and particularly of working families. She found industrial workers in her neighborhood to be a class in poverty with jobs and wages their only means of survival and with little or no recourse if these were interrupted. She described what we have come to know today as the working poor with 82 percent, by some estimates, living below subsistence level, (1917:166). She defined a minimum family income for that time as $1000 to $1200 per year, below which a family could be said to be living in poverty (1917:165). She explained that many families were crowded into small tenements because "overcrowding is to be preferred to insufficient food" (1917:166). Although Simkhovitch declared in the beginning of this book that "relatively speaking our country is still a classless land," she effectively located industrial families in their political-economic class in the broader context of US society (1917:1). Indeed, Simkhovitch's work shows a strain between her idealistic belief in a classless America and her first-hand awareness of class inequality. She wrote, "The hired man may still eat at the same table with his employer, the iron worker may still become a master of iron and of gold, the factory hand may yet become the boss" (1917:1). Yet in this same work, Simkhovitch described the large number of hard-working people living in poverty as measured by falling below an income that "insures a healthful life with a little margin" (1917:165). While decrying families dependent on wage-earning children, she estimated that "until the oldest child becomes an earner, the largest part of the working class in large cities is in poverty" (1917:166). She was disdainful of any notion that the working class "should labor for the benefit of the advantaged classes" and argued that an income standard was "a social necessity in just the sense and for precisely the same reason as in a cubic air space standard" (1917:169). At the same time, *City Workers* reflects Simkhovitch's philosophy of the organic whole—the well-being of workers is the well-being of America. No doubt the belief that we are all a part of a bigger whole was fundamental to her supporting the long battle for a national minimum wage which she argued for as an income standard and "a social necessity" (1917:169). Despite the presentation of grim facts in most of Simkhovitch's writings, there was optimism, often integrated with her thematic of change. For example, she did not deal with classes as static aspects of social structure but rather as dynamic elements of community life moving toward one entity, presumably as America absorbs their differences: "Classes are concentrated pools of action, which lose their identity as they become absorbed" (1940:72).

In *Group Life* (1940), Simkhovitch identified herself as a social worker and attempted "to present a picture of the primary forms in which humanity is enmeshed, with a view to seeing if they have any common direction" (1940:8). Although the label "social worker," had broader connotations at that time than now, the book contains little in the way of specifics that social workers would look for in working with groups to improve the quality or cooperative aspects of social life. The book is less applicable to social work as a form of case management than to providing an understanding of group organization and dynamics. She examined, through a sociological lens, primary groups such as family, school, play, clubs, church, and work, and then progressed to secondary groups such as race, class, labor, and lobbyists. One of the few suggestions directed specifically to social work practitioners is about class. She warned that because workers are usually drawn from the middle class they should be cautious about imposing their values "upon the people with whom they are dealing" (1940:72). Whether this truism had its beginning with Simkhovitch, it has become a staple of social work training today. Her last published book, *Here is God's Plenty* (1949) is similarly structured around community groups and institutions such as education, housing, recreation, the arts, welfare, politics, and religion but these are examined autobiographically as "the themes that have been the structure of my life" (1949:i). Two of her books stand out as different from the aforementioned three, *Neighborhood* (1938) and *Quicksand* (1942). *Neighborhood* is an autobiographical combination of personal and Greenwich House history and the two are, of course, inextricably interwoven in the march of time. *Quicksand* was co-authored with Elizabeth Ogg and, among Simkhovitch's writings, belongs in a class by itself. It is a case study effectively describing the chain of negative events associated with the illness of a family wage-earner and showing how, once income is disrupted, it is necessary to marshal public and private resources in order to set the family on a path to recovery, independence, and well-being.

Simkhovitch's work was characterized by optimism and positive future expectation even as she saw around her poverty and inequality. For example, she explained the title, *Here is God's Plenty,* as a reminder that the "vast abundance of America was truly 'God's Plenty'" (1949:i), this even though neither abundance nor plenty was available to most of the residents of her neighborhood. As a kind of closing philosophical statement in her last book, Simkhovitch proclaimed that "the essence of life is change, and it is only the adjustments that take place inside change that can give a working arrangement by which people can get on, recognizing and respecting one another's attitudes" (1940:84–85). Toward the end of her life, Simkhovitch wrote a final book that never made it into publication. A copy of the manuscript entitled, *Green Shoots*, is preserved in her personal papers and seems to be an updated version of *Here is God's Plenty*. Again, it focused on the themes of change and neighborhood analyzed and interpreted through the lens of personal experiences. In this final work, Simkhovitch offered what she calls "green shoots" as germinal seeds for the future. These were positive forces located in various aspects of

American life that she saw as potentials for building and developing in order to meet the challenges and needs of the last half of the twentieth century. She looked for and extracted positive themes even as the country was experiencing a building "cold war" and a burgeoning fear of Communism. As she explained her final work, "the intent is...to consider those small groups which are now experimenting in the fields of religion and community with a view to bringing about a more purposeful society." Her words are reflective of Simkhovitch's optimism and identity as pragmatist and sociologist. She viewed these "green shoots" as "the laboratory of the future" and as "worthwhile not only to the sociologist and philosopher but also to everyone who stubbornly refuses to give up faith in life." She identified these fertile seedbeds as on-going work relevant to families, education, race relations, labor, and government. At least one reviewer gave a rather harsh critique of *Green Shoots* and suggested substantial revisions. Simkhovitch died little more than a year later, leaving the manuscript unrevised and unpublished (MKSP: B5, F85–88).

Research by Residents

The 1906 Greenwich House Annual Report described research completed at Greenwich House as including "a careful and prolonged study of the Standard of Living in the neighborhood" and also a study of local housing conditions and their relation to school attendance. Four residents reportedly made a study of "home manufacturing," and another the "social treatment of drunkenness." These investigations, the Report explained, were efforts to understand the neighborhood, "but studies are subordinate to the flow of knowledge that emanates from the daily social relationship of the Settlement with the locality. In a hundred different ways, life pours in on the Settlement Household and creates a body of knowledge" (GHR: B1, F6). Again, this statement affirms the neighborly relations paradigm and the settlement-as-method means of collecting data with practical value. The Report also included an explanation as to how such information was used, citing the dissemination of published reports to interested organizations and individuals as well as official reports to various regulatory agencies such as the Board of Health, the Tenement House Department, the Child Labor Committee, the Superintendent of Schools, the Bureau of Factory Inspection, and the police. Finally, the Report stated the desire of Greenwich House to tell the story in daily conversations "of want, of accident, of economic difficulty, of cramped conditions that mark this quarter." In discussing settlement research in her history of Greenwich House, Simkhovitch said, "Public and private agencies kept us busy and intellectually alert by asking us for reports on various social phenomena, such as overtime for women in factories, which were incorporated in their own material used for practical measures of reform" (1938:151). Some of the earliest social investigations carried out at Greenwich House were published and disseminated by the settlement itself while others were published by some of the major presses of the day.

Emily Dinwiddie, Greenwich House resident and tenement inspector produced *The Tenant's Manual* (1903), a house publication representing a kind of survivor's guide for tenement living, focusing on health, sanitation, child care, child labor, and tenement laws. The manual also included resources and helpful information about legal assistance, opportunities for education and leisure time activities, and how to apply for citizenship. The *Manual*, clearly a public service, was reprinted many times, and was widely disseminated throughout the city. Another in-house publication, *A West Side Rookery*, by Elsa Herzfeld and Natalie Henderson, was a study of "the alley" where nine tenement buildings were located and described as housing immigrant families as well as "crooks, loafers, and bums" (1906:7). The study called attention to unacceptable living conditions in tenement dwellings, citing causes such as unemployment, insufficient income, old age, illness, and intemperance. A third in-house publication was *Public Art Education in New York* (1908) by Katharine Lord which, as the name suggests, was an effort to promote public appreciation of the arts, especially among the working classes. More scholarly works from Greenwich House were conducted by "fellows," mostly female, under the auspices of the Committee on Social Studies also known as the Greenwich House Committee on Social Investigation and later the Social Science Research Council. Under these changing names, this research oversight organization was privately funded and chaired for most of its existence by Columbia economist Edwin Seligman and, in addition to Simkhovitch, was comprised at various times of Columbia anthropologist Franz Boas, economist/sociologist Edward Devine, psychologist/anthropologist Livingston Farrand, sociologist Franklin Giddings, and political economist Henry Seager (Recchiuti 2007:91). In reflecting on the contributions of research carried out by settlements such as Greenwich House, Devine concluded that "innumerable studies were made in the causes of poverty and crime, the social aspects of...preventable diseases, the relation of mental defect and unsanitary housing and child labor and congestion of population to dependency and delinquency [and] the standard of living of workingmen's families" (Devine 1921:22–23).

In some cases because Committee/Council members were associated with other organizations, there was cooperative sponsorship of research. Such was the case with Lillian Brandt's study of *Five Hundred and Seventy-Four Deserters and Their Families* (1905). In this case, the sponsoring organization was the Committee on Social Research of the Charity Organization Society (COS) of New York rather than Greenwich House. At the time, however, Brandt was a

Greenwich House resident and a graduate student at the New York School of Philanthropy where she later taught. During a COS summer school program Brandt apparently impressed Edward Devine of the COS (also a member of the Greenwich House Research Committee) with her research on the social aspects of tuberculosis (1903). Brandt's competence in interpreting statistical and factual information led the COS to sponsor her next work on fathers who deserted their families. Data were supplied by 54 COSs in 25 cities in 15 states using standardized schedules supplied by Brandt. The result is a description of more than 500 families, grouped on a number of criteria, and followed from the time of the father's desertion until the time of data collection. Brandt provided many examples of the negative impact of desertion for wives and children and focused on the costs for public and private agencies attempting to meet their needs. While not leaving the deserter free of responsibility, Brandt nevertheless placed some blame on society and social agencies that refused help to families in need as long as the man was in the home, thereby motivating some, when out of work, to desert their families. She advocated laws in all states that would make men responsible for family support but also provide assistance for families in need, whether the father was in the home or not. She concluded,

> The main hope...for the solution of the problem, lies in the providing of decent living conditions, and fair opportunities for work, and in the education of this generation of children, and the next...in whatever makes for stability of character, for economic efficiency, for a realization of responsibility, and for a wholesome family life (1905:64).

Showing methodological sophistication, Brandt did not generalize her work to all families experiencing desertion. Rather, she stated simply, "The value of these records...is that they reveal the characteristics and circumstances of five hundred and seventy-four families who were compelled, by reason of the desertion of the husband and father, to ask for help of some sort" (1905:11).

Louise Bolard More, identified by Simkhovitch as having moved with her from the Friendly Aid House and as being a dietician and teacher of domestic science at Greenwich House, conducted the first study of wage earners' budgets, using detailed income-expenditure data collected by members of her Greenwich House Woman's Club (Simkhovitch 1938: 151). "They were so fond of her [More] that they gladly entered into the plan and kept painstaking records of their income and expenditures [and got others to do the same] over a period of several weeks" (Simkhovitch 1949:88). The pioneering work, based on the budgets of 200 wage-earning families, was described by Recchiuti 100 years later, as "a direct and purposeful attack on those in the conservative camp in the academy who held that the working poor were poor through some personal fault or from an inability to save." More collected "a mass of statistics demonstrating that low-paid working class men and women lived in poverty not because they were spendthrifts or lazy or of debased moral character, but because they earned so little that, even with the best efforts at frugality, they could seldom make ends meet" (Recchiuti 2007:91). More provided case studies of families to illustrate living conditions in several income categories, and for all she concluded, "Food is the most elementary necessity of life, but under city conditions it has been shown to be of secondary importance to rent, and often to insurance" (1907:265). This conclusion considered along with Simkhovitch's later pronouncement that "overcrowding is to be preferred to insufficient food" suggests that families had in common a lack of resources to provide for the essentials of daily life and were sometimes forced to give up one for the other. The completed work, *Wage-Earners' Budgets* (More 1907), was published by the Henry Holt Company. Still of value to sociologists today is the Preface to this volume, written by Franklin Giddings, known for his promotion of the use of statistics in early sociology. His writing is a lesson in elementary research methods and statistics and his praise of More's work indicates acceptance of settlement sociology as a legitimate part of the discipline. His comments are worthy of quoting at some length.

> Its results have been obtained by methods more thorough, painstaking, and critical than it has usually been possible hitherto to use. Statistical work, as we have known it, has had the great merit of dealing with large numbers in which small errors are to a great extent self-eliminated by mutual cancellation, but it has left much to be desired on the side of exact knowledge of the concrete facts numerically expressed. Of the figures set down in Mrs. More's tables it can be said that everyone stands for something not only certainly known but also critically scrutinized and weighted before being added to the general sum of information. This critical thoroughness has been rendered possible by the limitations of the inquiry, and by the character of the relations subsisting between the investigator and the families whose economic status has been recorded. The tables comprise statistical data pertaining to two hundred families only. The results therefore are at best only representative, possibly only indicative of the Social Economy of Wage-earners.
>
> GIDDINGS 1907:III–IV

In further comments, as the research statistician that he was, Giddings qualified More's findings, because she lacked a representative sample, while at the same time noting that they could be taken as an indictment of the existing social order.

> Thrift can be demonstrated or the 'existing social order' can be indicted for infamous cruelty to any extent desired, by the method of statistical selection. When, therefore, an inquiry, instead of covering all possible instances in a given population, is necessarily and confessedly based upon selected units, it is imperative from the standpoints alike of science and of common honesty that the selections shall be made by a strictly objective test, and that the nature of the test shall be explicitly made known....
>
> GIDDINGS 1907:IV

With this elementary lesson in statistics, Giddings went on to point out that while More may have had a biased "sample," those who completed the record keeping for her research were in all likelihood better off than those who did not participate as they were,

> ...somewhat above the average of the class in which their economic lot is cast.... Such families...'get on' somewhat better than others. Consequently, if Mrs. More's picture of the life of these families shows much hardship and a never-ceasing struggle to keep above that line below which poverty begins, we may be very sure that it is not an exaggerated portrayal of the social-economic life of the self-sustaining working people of New York City to-day.
>
> GIDDINGS 1907: IV

In other words, those who participated in More's research, however poor, were probably not the worst of the working class. More's research, along with her own, no doubt gave authority to Simkhovitch's testimony about poverty before the Factory Investigating Commission (NYFIC 1913. Vol 4:2269–2270) and also gave substance to the concept of a minimal standard of living, the origin of which came to be associated with Greeenwich House (Simkhovitch 1917:165).

Perhaps the best-known work of the Greenwich House Committee on Social Investigation is *Half A Man* (1911) authored by Greenwich Fellow, Mary Ovington (1865–1951). Ovington is remembered today for her activism in behalf of African Americans, but she was also a competent early social scientist. She came from a Unitarian family that supported abolition, women's suffrage, and other liberal causes. She was educated at Parker Institute and Radcliffe College. She helped to found the Greenpoint Settlement and served as its head resident until 1903 when she was appointed a Greenwich House Fellow and moved there to begin research on the status of blacks in New York City.[5] The work has many commonalities with that of More. Again, an academic member of the Committee, in this case Franz Boas, wrote the Foreword and just as the earlier work offers a repudiation of individual or family-caused poverty, this work offered a repudiation of the alleged equality of opportunity for blacks and whites. Boas also used the Foreword to declare that "no proof can be given of any material inferiority of the Negro race…the bulk of the individuals composing the race are equal in mental aptitude to the bulk of our own people" (1911:vii). Read now, more than 100 years later, Ovington's work is an impressive and thorough analysis of the black population of New York. It has been compared to Du Bois' work in Philadelphia but differs considerably in methodology and in conclusions, perhaps because Ovington, who was white, was less constrained than Du Bois who wished to avoid criticism of his own racial bias. Ovington's work utilized available secondary data backed by observations and examples drawn from interviews and personal interactions. She began her writing by locating blacks historically in the context of slavery, not so far removed that it had not been experienced directly or indirectly by most, and certainly it had impacted all blacks alive at that time. Wherever data were available, Ovington compared blacks with whites in New York, and sometimes she compared blacks in New York with those in the South, especially in cities such as Atlanta, where they lived in a legally segregated world. By comparison, black New Yorkers lived in de facto segregation. Ovington gave the reader a very complete description, quantitatively and qualitatively, of congested black tenements. She zeroed in on facts about infant mortality, with deaths outnumbering births, and with a summer infant mortality rate among Blacks as high as 400 per 1,000. Blacks in the New York labor force were found to be overwhelmingly servants and waiters with up to 90 percent of women working as domestics. Similar to Du Bois' conclusion in Philadelphia, Ovington declared that "The Negro in New York has one vital need, steady, decent work" (1911:206). For the most part blacks, regardless of their abilities, were denied the opportunity

---

5 While many of the settlement workers voiced support for racial justice and several such as Addams and Wald were active in the formation of the NAACP, some also accepted the status quo segregation of their day and directed their energies toward the betterment of immigrant populations and the whole of American society as they saw it, leaving the problems of the Negro race unattended. Ovington was different in that after hearing a speech by Booker T. Washington, racial justice became her life's work. Following residence at Greenwich House, she moved to the Tuskegee Apartments in the black San Juan Hill area of New York to begin settlement work and remained there until she left to help found the Lincoln Settlement in Brooklyn. She began a correspondence with W.E.B. Du Bois and became his life-time friend and an instrumental supporter in founding the NAACP (Barbuto 1999:162–163).

to fill good jobs. At various points in the book, Ovington acknowledged, and supported with comparative data, the fact that blacks were better off in New York than in the country as a whole and certainly in the South. However, she found them far from equal citizens as guaranteed by post-Civil War constitutional amendments and political rhetoric. The result: "[i]f we deny full expression to a race, if we restrict its education, stifle its intellectual and aesthetic impulses, we make it impossible fairly to gage its ability" (1911:220).

In her history of Greenwich House, Simkhovitch mentioned two other studies in this research chronology: *Industrial Survey* (1912) by Louise Hyman and an unnamed study of unemployment by Alice Carpenter. Based on Greenwich House Annual Reports, Briggs says about the former, "the major investigation of 1912 was…of factory conditions in the neighborhood conducted by Louise Hyman which was prompted by the Triangle Fire tragedy." The work, a survey of 80 factories, took a year to complete and documented over 600 persons working under unacceptable health and safety conditions (Briggs 2008:160). Resident Alice Carpenter studied and reported on unemployment in the Greenwich neighborhood in 1914, a time described by Simkhovitch as "the darkest winter that our settlement has known" (Briggs 2008:161). Among other published works of Greenwich fellows was *Old Age Poverty in Greenwich Village* (1915) by Mabel Nassau. Again, it followed the pattern of some earlier works with a Foreword by Henry Seager who praised Nassau for having supplied evidence of the need for a broad policy ensuring systemic assistance for the elderly. Nassau provided a brief description of 100 subjects, all over the age of 60, in the Greenwich Village neighborhood. She divided her subjects into six categories descriptive of their living conditions, health or disabilities, income and/or resources from family or charity, and whether they currently worked full or part time. To address the question often asked as to why people do not save for old age, she provided information on what these subjects did for a living and their earnings when they were employed, leaving little doubt as to why they did not save for old age. Nassau provided limited analysis of her data, and perhaps it was more effective to simply let the cases speak for themselves. In the end, Nassau raised the poignant question "When people have contributed all their lives to the industry of their state, should they be obliged at the end of their days to depend on charity" (1915:96)? Of course, even systematic and reliable forms of charity were lacking. A fear of institutions and a pauper's burial was found to haunt the elderly and churches and charitable agencies were unable to cope with their needs. Clearly this work was intended to address the growing debate about some form of public assistance for the elderly, especially the urban elderly who, lacking the extended family support system of many rural elderly, had emerged as a needy and often dependent class in America.

Some states had already passed "old age pension" programs as had many European countries. In the United States, the Socialist party had for many years supported a nation-wide "old age pension" as did the Progressive Party platform. Nassau reviewed the merits and demerits of proposals or plans for old-age assistance. It was not, however, until 1935 when this need was addressed for the nation as a whole with passage of the Social Security Act with its provisions for old age survivors and disability insurance and supplemental grants to states to provide for the needy elderly. However, the Greenwich House-Columbia researchers had made the case for such a policy much earlier. Henry Seager, wrote in his Introduction, that Nassau "supplies convincing proof of the need of some broad, constructive policy" (Seager 1915:6). Of course, Seager (1910) had earlier published the first book advocating a national social security system with a proposal containing many of the provisions included in the Social Security Act of 1935.[6]

Apart from the formal work of the settlement's research committee, residents, visitors and Simkhovitch conducted other research, much of it of practical use locally (Simkhovitch 1938: 151–152). For example, muckraking journalists used Greenwich House to launch investigations. Ida Tarbell known for her research and reporting on Standard Oil, perhaps leading to its breakup, lived and worked at Greenwich House in 1910 and 1911. Over the years a number of graduate students conducted research for theses and dissertations from Greenwich House. One example is "The Economic Condition in Relation to the Delinquency of Girls" by resident Josephine Roche (1911) a student in sociology and economics at Columbia. After leaving Greenwich House, Roche spent much of her career advocating for the rights of female workers, citing the Triangle Shirtwaist fire that took the lives of over 100 as having indelibly influenced her life and career (Briggs 2008:120). Many of the workers who perished in the fire were part of the Italian colony in the Greenwich community and the settlement mobilized to help the families. Close to home also, Gertrude Hummler studied the use of vacant lots for planting flower and vegetable gardens as well as compiling a report on needed tenement repairs. Arthur McFarlane investigated the working conditions of longshoremen and he and Gertrude Graydon made a study of the working conditions of office cleaners. Beginning in 1915, the settlement placed home visitors in some of the public schools attended by Greenwich children, and follow-up reports were provided to support the effectiveness of this work in reducing truancy.

6 Seager's work is included in its entirety today on the Social Security Administration's website (http://www.socialsecurity.gov/history/seager.html, accessed July 7, 2014).

By 1930, the Greenwich House Committee on Social Investigation had become the Social Science Research Council which funded Dr. Caroline Ware's ethnography of *Greenwich Village, 1920–1930* ([1935]1965), published with the acknowledgment that it was "Prepared under the auspices of Columbia University Council for Research in collaboration with Greenwich House." Simkhovitch reported that "about a hundred students, neighbors and associates from various racial and religious and political groups took part in the study" (1938:225). Ware, a member of the history faculty at Vassar College, recognized many of these people by name and credited them with specific materials in some chapters. By the time of Ware's research, the city of New York had grown around Greenwich Village leaving a complex urban neighborhood of somewhat separate sub-communities: ethnic (Irish, Italian, Jewish), a few "old American families," and a "bohemian community." Ware found the totality as well as its sub-communities as lacking in cohesiveness. Simkhovitch's optimistic appraisal of Ware's work was that it "brought to light valuable data to follow up" (1938:225). She reported other research continuing in the 1930s, such as a study of youth activities in the Greenwich neighborhood carried out by Frederic Thrasher of NY University. Simkhovitch welcomed research conducted from both within and outside the settlement, proclaiming in one of her books: "All these approaches to the problems which beset us in our neighborhood have been of use as we attempt to build up, step by step, a fuller local life" (1938: 233).

Feminist Pragmatism

There was a strong thread of feminism at Greenwich House, as Briggs reported with regard to the campaign for women's suffrage,

> ... Greenwich House acted as a leading institution not only locally in the Village but also city-wide, supporting several key efforts, speaking at the State Legislative meetings.... During the last few years of the decade, Greenwich House hosted some of the most recognized international suffragists and women's rights activists (2008:274–275).

Feminist activities at Greenwich House were not confined to the suffrage movement. For example, in 1915 a dinner was held in honor of feminist writer and sociologist Charlotte Perkins Gilman whom Simkhovitch had met in Germany. Other names associated with Greenwich House feminism were residents, guests, and frequently speakers such as Marie Jenney Howe, Crystal Eastman, Ida Tarbell, Elsie Clews Parsons as well as such international feminists as Eleanor Barton and Mary MacArthur of England. Another strain of feminism at Greenwich House was found in the Men's League for Women's

Suffrage headquartered at the settlement (Briggs 2008:138–140). Simkhovitch wrote of a group of men associated with Greenwich House whose names should be remembered because they endured "boos and cat-calls" when they marched for women's suffrage. She named, in addition to her husband, Charles Burlingham, James Harvey Robinson, James Lees Laidlaw, John Dewey, and Judge Hand (GHR: B23, F22). She wrote in some of her remembrances of going around and talking suffrage to men's social clubs and marching in parades (GHR: B22, F33). In fact, the writings and speeches of Simkhovitch show that she gave considerable attention to the changing role of women and to women's rights. One of her most scholarly papers is a lengthy address given in 1910 (to an unnamed audience) entitled, "Woman's Invasion of the Industrial Field" (GHR: B22, F33). It is packed with statistics on women's increased representation in the labor force and includes specific recommendations for changes needed to accommodate this "invasion." For example, she recommended legislation to improve working conditions and shorten work hours, further compulsory public education as well as education for efficiency and skill in the work force and for home and community life. She was also vocal in her support of women's trade organizations to strengthen demands for better wages and working conditions. Both pragmatism and feminism are evident in speeches incorporating her passion for descent housing. For example, in "A Woman's View of Housing," she argued from a traditional gender-role perspective that "housing is shelter for families, and women's interests, no matter how wide, stem from their primary responsibility for a sound home life" (MKSP: B4, F73). Years later, she argued for New York to have an all-female committee on housing,

> Surely housing is a natural major interest to women and yet, taken by and large, it is men who have been most active in this field. Architects, planners, real estate interests, financiers—in other words business in all its forms—have very naturally dominated in this field. We women are the ones who live in the houses, bring up our families there, and have a deep concern as to not only the structure but the neighborhoods in which we live.... Our guidance, both as homemakers and as citizens, is, therefore, of the greatest importance.
>
> MKSP: B4, F73

For Simkhovitch, women's right to vote was critical to their improved status in life as well as to a more progressive nation. Pragmatically, however, her argument was couched in gender-traditional reasoning.

> By giving women a vote you will be giving not something new but something larger, something that will connect her house-keeping with the house-keeping of the community...to make the home what it should be in education, health, recreation, and morality it is necessary for women to be able to choose their representatives.
>
> as quoted in BRIGGS 2008:125

Public Policy and the New York Scholar-Activist Network

While it is obvious that almost all settlement sociology had applied value, in the case of Greenwich House and the New York scholar-activist network, it is possible to draw direct lines from their work to the social reforms of President Franklin D. Roosevelt and the New Deal. For example, there was a significant representation of settlement people, and specifically those associated with Greenwich House, on the President's Committee on Economic Security whose work was important in passage of the Social Security Act. "Among the twenty-three who served were Helen Hall, president of the National Federation of Settlements [and Greenwich House resident]; Grace Abbott, vice-president of the Hull-House board [and recently retired from the Children's Bureau]; Gerard Swope, president of the Greenwich House board; and Paul Kellogg, Hall's husband, editor of the *Survey*, and resident at Henry Street" (Trolander 1975:87). Given the prominent role of settlements in progressive era reforms, it is understandable that Roosevelt tapped into this resource, particularly in New York. Many of FDR's trusted advisors, his "brains trust" were associated with Columbia University and with New York: Raymond Moley, Rexford Tugwell, Adolph Berle, Jr., and Harry Hopkins. All but Hopkins had ties to Columbia University and he had once been at Christodora House and worked as a "friendly visitor" in New York before becoming head of the Temporary Emergency Relief Administration (ERA) during the depression (Rosen 1972, Recchiuti 2007:109, Smith 2007:262–264). On a more personal level, FDR's mother, Sarah, was a Greenwich House supporter and financial contributor, and "well into her eighties...was a 'regular' at Greenwich House events" (Caroli 1998:226). After 1918, the Simkhovitchs owned a summer home in Maine, across the Bay of Fundy from the Roosevelts' Campobello and they attended some of the same social events (Caroli 1998:225). Eleanor Roosevelt and Simkhovitch worked together on a number of progressive causes, especially housing. Eleanor Roosevelt spoke at various housing conferences organized by Simkhovitch and used her newspaper column "My Day" to help convince the public that the government had a legitimate role in providing decent housing for all Americans. She was also instrumental in seeing that Simkhovitch had input in depression era recovery programs, in the Wagner-Steagall Housing Act, and in formation of the Housing Authority (Caroli 1998:226).

> Among Simkhovitch's most visible political accomplishments was prevailing upon Secretary of the Interior Harold Ickes to include in the 1933 National Industrial Recovery Act a provision that included support for federal public housing in public works projects as well as assisting in the writing of the Wagner-Steagall Housing Act of 1937.
>
> DENEEN 2001:61

Beyond the direct Roosevelt-Simkhovitch network, there were other linkages. Frances Perkins who was Roosevelt's Secretary of Labor was a previous resident of Greenwich House, worked on the Factory Investigating Commission, and was a colleague of Florence Kelley in the Consumer's League where she documented the conditions of women working in prestigious retail stores in New York (Recchiuti 2007:138–139). Much of the research conducted at Geenwich House provided a factual basis for legislation during the Roosevelt administration. Simkhovitch' study of city workers combined with the work of More, Nassau, and Brandt constituted a substantial body of empirical research on the working poor and gave substance to the concept of a minimum standard of living as a right for working Americans. Brandt's study of families without fathers was the beginning of documenting the need for mother's pensions eventually provided for in the Social Security Act of 1935.[7] Nassau's work on the old aged poor and an earlier work by her professor, Henry Seager (1910), paved the way for compulsory retirement insurance for workers in most industries and for assistance to states in providing for the needy (Douglas [1936]2000). More's work on family wages of the working poor (1907) demonstrated the tension between the essentials of rent and food. Simkhovitch's, work on *The City Worker's World* (1917) established the principle that workers are entitled to "a healthful life with a little margin," and she even ventured to specify a dollar amount as a minimum livable income (1917:165). Both works paved the way for New Deal legislation such as the Works Projects Administration that created federally subsidized jobs for the unemployed. As a more permanent solution, in 1938, Congress passed the first minimum wage law, a goal of the settlements for many years and clearly called for in More's research. In fact, Greenwich

---

7 This provision was at first known as Aid to Dependent Children, later as Aid to Families with Dependent Children, and as of 1996 as Temporary Assistance to Needy Families.

House was a part of the New York-Chicago network that by its research on workers, housing, health, and child labor provided the empirical foundation for redefining and reshaping the role of the government in ensuring a minimal standard of living for all, a right described by Simkhovitch as "a social necessity in just the sense and for precisely the same reason as in a cubic air space standard." Their research helped to differentiate between private (charitable) assistance and the "right" to a certain life-sustenance, a right that could only be met by government intervention as needs had grown too large to be met by private resources (Leff 1973:398). Leff illustrates this transition by tracing the development of mothers' pensions, a movement won not only by establishing a statistical need but also by presenting the solution as a business and moral proposition: moral in keeping the home and family intact, business in that financial security for families would reduce child neglect, prostitution, crime, school drop-outs, and child labor. The move for governments (local and national) to assume more responsibility for public relief was one that at certain junctures pitted settlements against organized charities because it seemed to imply they could not do the job or that they were remiss in meeting public needs (Leff 1973:402–403). The "assertion of a state responsibility involved a quantum jump in the line dividing the roles of public and private welfare agencies" and Greenwich House and other settlements led in making this leap (Leff 1973:411). Early empirical research such as was done from Greenwich House on wage-earners budgets, the African American population in New York, and on the needs of the elderly are just a few of the works that laid the foundation for a literature on poverty and inequality and established the need for government intervention at the national level.

CHAPTER 10

Recovering a Paradigm Lost: Public Sociology Then and Now

American sociology has a legacy of praxis in the social settlements of the Progressive Era, and from these voices of "sociologies past" a vision for social change has threaded its way into the present day call for a return to the publics from which we came. Settlement sociology is a legacy worthy of our reclaiming and examining for lessons to be learned for the future. This legacy emanates from the settlement paradigm of "neighborly relations" the essence of which was to settle in communities and bring a sociological perspective in advocating for reforms and for social justice. Settlement sociology was a method of sociological praxis combining theory, research and action to mitigate social problems and social inequality. There are continuities between our past and our present and roadmaps for the future, particularly in critical thought directed toward structural-level social inequality. Aspects of the settlement paradigm are present in contemporary feminist standpoint and reflexive epistemologies that compel researchers to gain understanding by becoming engaged participants with the communities or publics they seek to represent. By adopting the interests of community stake-holders as their own, researchers can better advocate for change. Such interest-driven work is unapologetically antithetical to the "value-neutral" stances promoted by early positivists. The settlement paradigm made no claim to value-neutrality; nonetheless, the scholar-activist never took up residence within a community with a specific agenda in mind. Rather through dialogue and in genuine neighborly relations settlement sociologists first discovered needs and issues and then let the interests of the communities they joined direct the work undertaken.

In this collective case study we examined the contributions of some of the most prominent settlements of the Progressive Era. Each made unique contributions to the development of American sociology and in keeping with the neighborly relations paradigm all shared a common vision for social democracy and social justice. Jane Addams was the strongest proponent of this paradigm and the major theorist associated with the school of settlement sociology. She saw those who voluntarily settled among the nation's poor as having a unique perspective and responsibility to give them voice. The settlement, she argued "has put itself into a position to see, as no one but a neighbor can see, the stress and need of those who bear the brunt of the social injury" (Addams [1895b]2004:184). Similarly Mary Simkhovitch wrote that "before any help can be given, the situation must be felt, realized and understood first hand.... Only that which is lived can be understood and translated to others" (1938:39). The aim of settlements was to educate and to advocate through permeation. Their projects for research and analysis were ultimately "a means for informing and mobilizing the American public to demand progressive change" (Lengermann and Niebrugge-Brantley 2002:18). Addams described the humanistic philosophy and settlement method of practice.

> It should demand from its residents a scientific patience in the accumulation of facts and the steady holding of their sympathies as one of the best instruments for that accumulation. It must be grounded in a philosophy whose foundation is on the solidarity of the human race, a philosophy which will not waver when the race happens to be represented by a drunken woman or an idiot boy. Its residents must be...ready to arouse and interpret the public opinion of their neighborhood. They must be content to live quietly side by side with their neighbors until they grow into a sense of relationship and mutual interests ([1892a] 2002:26).

The neighborly relations paradigm was informed by a critical pragmatism which continues to present a challenge for sociology today—that is, how to make knowledge meaningful, available, and useful to the public. A pragmatic science cannot be practiced quickly because mutual relationships of trust, respect and interest must evolve before scientific-based knowledge will be meaningful or useful to community members. This method of practicing science is generally incompatible with the "publish or perish" pressures of today's academic workplace. It should be obvious from this research that settlement sociologists did publish. They were prolific writers in diverse venues, but they wrote less for their peers than to engage various audiences or publics in their causes. Even the academic journals of the day were more geared to public consumption than is presently the case. For Addams the settlement sociologist had an uncompromising ethical obligation to seek knowledge to effect change. Her summary of settlement sociology in one of her autobiographies is simultaneously matter-of-fact, emotional, and non-apologetic in its ethical imperative. It also gave credit to settlements for their pioneering methods of practice.

> During its first two decades, Hull-House with other American settlements, issued various studies and fact-finding analyses of the city areas with which they were most familiar. The settlements had antedated by three years the first sociological departments in the universities and by ten years the establishment of the first Foundations so that in a sense we

> were the actual pioneers in field research. We based the value of our efforts not upon any special training, but upon the old belief that he who lives near the life of the poor, he who knows the devastating effects of disease and vice, has at least an unrivaled opportunity to make a genuine contribution to their understanding (1930:405–406).

In this passage Addams captures the essence of standpoint epistemologies that generate knowledge based on understanding the experiences and vantage points of those studied. Further Adams insisted that knowledge gained living among the poor should make a contribution to improving the lives of the poor.

Settlement Contributions to Sociology

Not only were settlements the first to recognize the importance of class inequality, a core proposition that permeates all of sociology, but they also contributed to substantive areas of the discipline. Regardless of theoretical inclination, most sociologists today will attest to the fundamental importance of understanding social stratification and the intersections of race-ethnicity, class, and gender. Yet, few are aware or acknowledge that it was settlement sociologists and not those in academe who laid this foundation of the discipline. In fact, of the attention given social stratification in the development of American sociology, House wrote, "the subject of social classes, class struggle, the sociological aspects or implications of socialism, and similar or related themes cannot be said to have had a prominent place" ([1936]1970:252). When sociologists did begin to pay some attention to social class it was because of two influences, "the general philanthropic and social-reform movement" and what some academics came to know as the "theory of conflict" ([1936]1970:252–253). Despite his acknowledgement of reform movements, House made no mention of settlement sociologists or of their works. He relied instead on the development of the theory of conflict as presented through its European roots to explain the evolution of class as an analytic concept. A perusal of three volumes dealing with the history of class in American sociology reveals no mention of social settlements even though their *raison d'etre* was to reduce the gap between the classes (Page [1940]1969, Gordon 1963, Grimes 1991). Nor do these histories recognize any of the prominent settlement sociologists, such as Jane Addams, Florence Kelley, or Robert Woods, for whom social class and economic inequality were central to their analysis of neighborhoods and of society. They were very clear in describing unequal life chances and the accompanying quality-of-life outcomes as the result of groups of people occupying unequal positions in relation to industry. Sociologists at the University of Chicago—for many the "real pioneers" of the discipline in the United States—described social class but did not use it as an analytic or causal variable.

Hull House sociologists, on the other hand, embraced the importance of social class and incorporated it into a theory of socializing democracy as they attempted to give voice and empowerment to the poor and working classes. The principles of democracy constituted social rights to which groups and entire classes of people as well as individuals were entitled. In their practice of feminist pragmatism and a standpoint methodology, settlement residents produced substantive works detailing a multiplicity of problems relating to urban-industrial growth. The Hull House residents used survey techniques and systematic observations to provide the earliest science of social problems and evidence of the intersections of race, class, and gender. From Hull House, Alice Hamilton pioneered a sophisticated and interdisciplinary industrial sociology documenting through on-site visits the impact of industrial hazards on workers. Her reports were used to advocate for policies and regulatory standards for worker protection. Chicago Commons' Graham Taylor theorized sociology as an early form of Christian pragmatism, propelling a social ethic to join religion and social action in solving the problems of the poor. His dissemination of sociological research through lectures, classes, and newspaper columns gave sociology a public face. In early studies of Chicago's stockyards, Mary McDowell defined environmental injustice and used local and international studies to advocate for a scientific method of garbage disposal. Research at the University of Chicago Settlement provides a prominent example of how public sociology can be censured by powerful and privileged stakeholders, in this case the meat packers. The South End House sociological laboratory laid out a daunting research agenda and accomplished it, taking sociological practice from the neighborhood to the nation and beyond, pioneering an urban ethnography that preceded and influenced the sociology developed some two to three decades later at the University of Chicago. The College Settlements Association (CSA) provided opportunities for educated women, giving them a voice, a purpose, and a career path by which they could help to close the gap between the classes. The CSA encumbered educated women with responsibility for making a difference in the world around them; they advocated for women; and they provided some of the earliest fellowships by which women could design and follow their own sociological projects. The CSA sponsored or was associated with such classic ethnographies as Emily Balch's *Our Slavic Fellow Citizens* ([1910] 1969) and W.E.B. Du Bois' *The Philadelphia Negro* (1899). Along with Du Bois and Eaton's work in Philadelphia, settlement sociologists provided the first empirical studies on black Americans: from Greenwich House in New

York, *Half A Man* (Ovington 1911); from Hull House and the Chicago School of Civics and Philanthropy, *The Colored People of Chicago* (Bowen 1913); and from South End House in Boston, *In Freedom's Birthplace* (Daniels 1914). The nurse's settlement on Henry Street in New York originated the concept and practice of public health and laid the ground work for today's medical sociology and for epidemiological studies that document the distribution of disease. For over 20 years, Henry Street was also home to the indomitable and prolific Florence Kelley who created a sociology of work and industry comprised of consumers, industrialists, and workers. Well networked with Chicago and New York reformers, and in her role as secretary of the National Consumers League, Kelley was one of the most active of the settlement sociologists. Her work always entailed gathering facts, lobbying for legislation in behalf of underrepresented groups, and extending sociological jurisprudence into new venues in her quest for justice. Finally, Greenwich House with its influential ties to New York's network of scholar-activists was successful in using sociological research to shape public policy in pursuit of the principle of a minimum quality of life as a social right.

The crux of settlement sociology was social justice, often referred to as "economic justice." The names of some of the biographies of settlement pioneers accurately describe their life pathways: *Jane Addams Pioneer for Social Justice* (Meigs 1970); Grace and Edith Abbott, *Two Sisters for Social Justice* (Costin 1983); *Graham Taylor: Pioneer for Social Justice* (Wade 1964); Florence Kelley, *Impatient Crusader* (Goldmark 1953); and *Robert A. Woods: Champion of Democracy* (Woods 1929). These pioneer sociologists were unafraid to stand on moral principles in their use of the sociological imagination to transform society. The secular morality of Florence Kelley existed alongside and was complementary to the Christian-based morality of social gospelers such as Robert Woods and Graham Taylor. Settlement sociology included two additional characteristics subsequently lost in disciplinary growth but with later attempts at reclamation. Interdisciplinarity and internationalism were both integral to the settlement method. The interdisciplinary working of settlement residents in research and reform projects was a natural outgrowth of communal living with its diversity of interests, education, and training. Although a majority of the young people attracted to settlements had studied religion or the social sciences, there were always those from other areas such as law, medicine, journalism and nursing. Addams at one point identified the diverse credentials of Hull House residents as including, among others, physicians, attorneys, newspaper men, business men, teachers, scientists, artists, musicians, and professors ([1910]2008:286–287). Robert Woods wanted to attract those of varied interests who would find their own niche in projects at South End House, but he regarded the whole as "a group of experts...living intimately together constantly stirring each other to fresh interest" ([1923]1970:43). Many of the sociological writings discussed in this work, in fact, resulted from interdisciplinary work and cooperation. Without question, volumes such as *Hull-House Maps and Papers* and *City Wilderness* were products of diverse settlement residents, each who wrote from his or her perspective, interest, background and training. However, the substance of these works was sociological as they described and analyzed groups—often defined by race/ethnicity, occupation, income, or gender—in their relations with the socio-political forces of industrialization and urbanization. The reader was able to grasp the whole of daily life in settlement neighborhoods because the descriptions and data were interdisciplinary—variously emphasizing working conditions, living conditions, health, families, politics, education, delinquency, social welfare, traditions and customs. Mary McDowell studied the scientific disposal of industrial waste in order to counter environmental injustice and to effect a healthier environment for her neighbors. The deplorable conditions in Chicago's stockyards finally came to the attention of public officials, even the President of the United States, because of the combined work of social scientists and journalists. At the Henry Street settlement a small regiment of visiting nurses worked with social scientists such as Florence Kelley and Josephine Goldmark in their crusades for better health, for justice in industry-worker relations, and in their injection of consumer responsibility into the alleviation of workplace exploitation. An impressive number of settlement women held not only degrees in one of the social sciences but also law, bringing a sociological jurisprudence into their work on behalf of immigrants, the poor, the old, and laborers—especially women and children. There is little doubt that the effectiveness and pragmatism of settlement sociology was due in large measure to the breadth and depth of its interdisciplinarity, a quality subsequently lost to sociology as it moved resolutely toward self-definition and scientific rigor (Mills 1959).

The majority of women and men who took up residence in the various settlement houses came from similar upper middle-class backgrounds, were college educated, had studied and/or traveled in Europe, and were fluent in more than one language. Their international or global interests were obvious in writings, speeches, and travels. They recognized the inter-relationships among nation states and promoted the importance and responsibilities of caring for the needy at home and in other nations. They recognized that much could be learned from socialistic economies and from the public welfare systems of nations providing safety net supports for citizens. Settlement workers thus shared an interest and propensity for the European immigrants who were to become their neighbors. Some of the head residents we have written about broadened their influence and interest beyond Western Europe. Lillian Wald for example traveled "around the world" and on several occasions spent time in Russia at the invitation of their public health service (1934:262). Following World War I, Robert and Eleanor Woods traveled world-wide on what he referred to as a "sabbatical." He wrote that their visit to Japan led to "a whole new sense of the meaning of the one human family" (SEHR 1921:B1, F83). Graham Taylor was said to have felt that his early education was inadequate because he had not traveled or studied in Europe and only after he hired a private tutor did he learn German (Wade 1964:40–47). In later life, as head resident of the Chicago Commons, Taylor and his wife made at least two trips to Europe financed by private benefactors. Although many settlement workers were European travelers that influence may have paled in comparison with the reality of their daily lives where they were surrounded by and interacted with immigrants from all of Europe. Settlement neighborhoods were global villages. As Lillian Wald said of her Henry Street community, "in thought and practice we live internationally" (1934:10).

Public Sociology Reclaimed

Many of the issues sociologists are grappling with today vis-à-vis relevance, insularity, identity, and exclusivity are not new but have their roots in the formative years of the Progressive Era. In his 2004 presidential address to the American Sociological Association, Michael Burawoy assessed the history and state of the discipline and promoted a renewed Public Sociology. He argued the need for sociology to regenerate its moral fiber by taking knowledge back "to those from whom it comes, making public issues out of private troubles" (2005a:5). Burawoy described the discipline of sociology in the US as an interdependent division of labor sharing a distinctive ethos rather than as an integrated whole. Located within "fields of power," sociology has historically experienced tensions and at times antagonisms among its various practitioners, particularly around the questions "for whom and for what do we pursue sociology?" (Burawoy 2005a:10–11). Burawoy's schemata includes four "ideal types" of sociological work or activity: public, policy, professional, and critical sociology. Although this typology has been criticized as rigid, hierarchical, elitist, and static (cf. Clawson et al. 2007), most contemporary sociologists can appreciate its utility and see themselves as involved in *one or more* of the activities described. Likewise, our assessment of the work of settlement sociologists suggests that while much of the work done was primarily what Burawoy has termed public sociology, settlements were engaged in each type of activity. In Burawoy's schemata *public sociology* seeks knowledge with the intention of providing solutions to social problems with direct input from those affected. It engages dialogue about fundamental values concerning pressing issues, reaching beyond the discipline and the university. It consists of two complementary types: *traditional* which is directed at an unspecified public at large and *organic* which has an identifiable public. Burawoy's exemplar of *traditional* public sociology is C. Wright Mills whose work had popular appeal, was relatively free of jargon as well as theoretical and methodological esotericism. Mills' message was meant to educate a thinking, critical public but his publics were general and diffuse with no particular audience defined. He spoke with moral authority, leaving little doubt as to what he perceived as the right or wrong course of action. He exhorted civic engagement from a public on the brink of becoming blasé and insensitive to pressing social issues. *Organic* public sociology, on the other hand, has an identifiable public, "visible, thick, active, local and often counterpublic" (2005a:7). Sociologists working in an anti-war movement or in a labor movement where there is an active dialogue between the sociologist and his/her publics provide examples of the organic. To Burawoy "publics" is plural because sociologists are about the business of defining human categories, any of which may become their publics. The broad debates in society can be informed by sociological work with small groups or categories of people. Historically, it might be argued that the American Social Science Association (ASSA) and Christian sociologists were doing traditional public sociology, the settlement workers organic. The ASSA and many of the social gospelers represented voices of authority from men who thought themselves in positions, to know what was in the best interest of society as a whole. Their advocacy of science was to legitimize their authority and their prescriptions for solving problems. Settlement sociologists, on the other hand, particularly the women, targeted specific categories: workers, immigrants, the poor, women, children, and the inadequately housed. With these publics they dialogued, observed, collected data, and advocated on their behalf. At some juncture, the organic and traditional public sociologies merge. Clearly, as the settlement workers began advocating for government programs and laws in behalf of publics such as women and child laborers they moved into the arena of traditional public sociology in behalf of all workers, and all families. The problems settlement workers observed and documented in reports and briefs were public problems not just the problems of individuals or small groups of people. The facts and their analyses of these facts took settlement sociologists before state legislative bodies, city councils, and into national and occasionally international arenas, and motivated them to lecture, write news articles as well as sociological reports directed to a mass and unspecified audience.

A second division of labor in Burawoy's typology is *policy sociology*, defined specifically as sociology in service of a goal defined by a client. Much of the early Christian sociology and some of the settlement house work were of this variety. For example, Holbrook's survey of the appropriate use of the label Christian Sociology was sponsored by an Institute of Christian Sociology. Several settlements made studies of the influence of saloons in their neighborhoods, and their findings became a part of the rationale of the national prohibition movement. In the Progressive period policy sociology was converted into public sociology, providing its "moral conscience." Settlement workers conducted research and compiled reports and briefs intended to impact judicial and legislative decisions for improving the lives of the disenfranchised and downtrodden. Values and reform were central to the practice of sociology in its policy-oriented form although the move toward value-neutral scientism propelled by academic elites was well underway. Moreover, the scientism movement impacted settlement workers, creating complexities in changing identities and definitions as they experienced competing allegiances to the emerging and diverging fields of sociology and social work and to professionalism (MacLean and Williams 2012).

Burawoy's third type of labor division, *professional sociology* is comparable to what we have referred to in this work as academic sociology. Burawoy notes that professional sociology "supplies true and tested methods, accumulated bodies of knowledge, orienting questions, and conceptual frameworks" (2005a:10). Professional sociology is the *sine qua non* of policy and public sociology because it provides legitimacy and expertise. Professional sociology is comprised of many subfields or specializations such as family, race/ethnic relations, criminology, and stratification, each with theories, conceptual frameworks, and research agendas. In other words, it is to professional sociology that we look for the foundations provided by methods, theory, and research, activities that are today typically carried out in the halls of academe. This conceptualization of sociology, of course, immediately comes under criticism as elitist, insulated, lofty, abstract and potentially irrelevant, tucked away as it often is in the "ivory tower" with professionals speaking or writing for each other but not for public consumption. It does, however, reflect the history of the discipline as recorded, taught and passed on with few modifications.

Finally, Burawoy addresses a fourth division of labor or activity, *critical sociology* which is to professional sociology what public sociology is to policy sociology. It is the conscience of professional sociology. It questions the foundations of accumulated knowledge and its "tried and true" methods, making visible embedded biases and limitations to orienting questions of inquiry and traditional methods. Critical sociology addresses the questions, *sociology for whom and sociology for what?* In answering the first question, it must be decided whether sociology is directed to other sociologists, to another audience, or to the public at large. For reform-minded and settlement sociologists of the

Progressive period knowledge and facts were to be practical and used to benefit people who needed help and who lacked voice. These sociologists addressed their knowledge to those with the power to effect change, including the public, corporate executives, and government officials.

Each of Burawoy's four types of sociology is firmly planted in the history of the discipline which began

> ...in the middle of the 19th century as a dialogue between ameliorative, philanthropic and reform groups on the one side, and the early sociologists on the other side. The latter often came from a religious background but they transferred their moral zeal to the fledgling secular science of sociology. After the Civil War the exploration of social problems developed through the collection and analysis of labor statistics as well as social surveys of the poor. Collecting data to demonstrate the plight of the lower classes became a movement unto itself that laid the foundations of professional sociology.... In its origins therefore, sociology was inherently public (2005a:19).

Burawoy's further nod to history takes sociology through a second stage of development beginning in the 1920s and continuing through World War II. Professional sociology in this period, particularly after WWI, was shaped in no small way by funding from foundations and other organizations including government agencies. Value-free knowledge-for-knowledge's sake came to be the mantra of this period. In order to produce the "objective," scientific facts that were demanded, sociologists developed more methodological rigor and trended toward statistical analyses of quantitative data. The third phase of Burawoy's chronology of sociological development is characterized by a dialogue, often rising to the level of conflict, between professional and critical sociologists. Theoretically, it was a conflict between structural functionalism and Marxist conflict theory, the former more firmly ensconced in the academic institutions of the day. While C. Wright Mills and his *Sociological Imagination* (1959) typically receive credit for initiating the era of critical sociology, in reality Robert Lynd opened the dialogue almost two decades earlier with his critique of the narrowing scope of sociology and its claims of value-neutrality. The disciplinary conflict mounted throughout the decade of the sixties and reached its crescendo in Alvin Gouldner's *The Coming Crisis of Western Sociology* (1970). Only after the social movements of the 60s and 70s was there a significant reconfiguration of the division of labor in sociology, one ushered in by critical theoretical conditions for change, and then in the 80s, by the political impetus created by the resurrection of market fundamentalism or neoliberalism (Burawoy

2007:242). According to Burawoy, these two conditions led to the current third-wave renaissance of public sociology. And as with the first-wave Progressive period, this reconfiguration made natural allies of critical and public sociologists. Burawoy thinks that the current state of American sociology brings the discipline full circle—back to public sociology from whence we came—and that we are ready for the challenge.

> Professional sociology has now reached a level of maturity and self-confidence that it can return to its civic roots, and promote public sociology from a position of strength—and engagement with the profound and disturbing global trends of our time. If the original public sociology of the 19th century was inevitably provincial, it nonetheless laid the foundation for the ambitious professional sociology of the 20th century, which, in turn, has created the basis for its own transcendence—a 21st century public sociology of global dimensions (2005a:20).

In a sense, settlement sociology was a holistic sociology in that it incorporated all four of Burawoy's categories. Drawing from a theory of social democracy that made intervention or reform as necessarily ethically (normatively) and politically driven, the settlement vision was to eradicate misery and pain associated with social inequality and poverty. This vision was grounded in the actual experiences and life worlds of the settlement sociologists who witnessed first-hand the brutal consequences of urban blight and poverty. They practiced public sociology of both a traditional and organic type, traditional in that it was intended to educate the public at large and to awaken a moral indignation when confronted with facts documenting the inequality and injustices endemic in a Christian-democratic nation. Settlement sociology was organic public sociology in that it was directed to specific audiences such as capitalists, legislators, labor organizers, or consumers—to those who could and should make a difference. Settlement sociology also took on some of the characteristics of Burawoy's policy sociology—that is sociology in service to a client-defined goal. In the case of settlements, their clients were often those without voice and whose goals were defined from a standpoint epistemology in terms of needs: women, children, workers, the elderly, lodgers, tenement dwellers, and immigrants. Settlement sociologists were also critical sociologists. In a massive number of publications, newspaper columns, and speeches they were the moral voice of sociology, seekers of social justice, and the conscience of the nation in the Progressive Era. Settlement sociologists worked for the people who had not yet acquired a voice or power in America or had been denied such because of poverty, illiteracy, gender, race or ethnicity. They worked for a more just society and for a descent standard of living for all. Finally, settlement sociology also included the seeds of Burawoy's professional sociology in that it supplied "true and tested methods, accumulated bodies of knowledge, orienting questions, and conceptual frameworks." Working within the neighborly relations paradigm settlement workers perfected and tested methodologies such as mapping, urban ethnography, epidemiology, and social surveys. They accumulated knowledge in foundational areas such as inequality and cultural pluralism; they clearly differentiated private troubles and public problems. In classic studies now erased or forgotten, they gave us knowledge specific to substantive areas such as labor relations, poverty, gender inequality, race relations, industrial relations, public health, environmental justice, social movements, and immigration. The conceptual framework that informed all of their work was a humanistic understanding of structural rather than individual causes of social problems. Their theoretical orientation was an overarching theory of social democracy, infused with feminist and Christian pragmatism grounded in an epistemology of neighborly relations.

Lessons Learned: Beyond the Ivory Tower

Settlement sociology provided a broad umbrella for research and reform as well as opportunities for teaching and contributing to the developing discipline of sociology. As Addams saw it, settlements had a unique responsibility to fill a void left by institutions of higher learning.

> It was the business of the universities...to carry on research.... It was the business of the colleges...to hand down knowledge that had thus been accumulated *and if they kindled an ardor for truth,* each succeeding generation would add to the building of civilization. It was the business of the settlements to do something unlike either of these things. *It was the function of the settlements to bring into the circle of knowledge and full life, men and women who might otherwise be left outside.* Some of these men and women were outside simply because of their ignorance, some of them because they led lives of hard work that narrowed their interests, and others because they were unaware of the possibilities of life and needed a friendly touch to awaken them. The colleges and universities had made a little inner circle of illuminated space beyond which there stretched a region of darkness, and it was the duty of the settlements to draw into the light those who were out of it. It seemed to us that *our mission* was just

> as important as that of either the university or the college (1930:404–405 emphases added).

Addams' perception of the role of settlements vis-à-vis institutions of higher education is astute and while environments have changed and lessons from history cannot be adopted wholesale, we believe there is still much salience in the settlement mission for sociological practice today. Settlements were about bringing "outsiders" into the full life of a social democracy. They expanded the "illuminated space," left narrow by colleges and universities, pulling in those left in the "region of darkness" created by poverty, urban blight, and exploitation. Settlements did this work through the careful gathering of information and empirical data about the communities or publics they viewed as left out, passed over, or exploited. The work done in the settlements contributed to the accumulation of knowledge, but the knowledge gained was to be useful in its application—it should "kindle an ardor of truth." Moreover the knowledge accumulated was *potentially* more representative than that generated by university research given the engagement of settlements with their publics. In this sense settlements provided an important corrective to the biased construction of knowledge produced by a small inner circle of "elite knowers" associated with academic social science. In seeking knowledge that could contribute to solving some of the problems of the underprivileged classes (knowledge for what and for whom) the settlement sociologists were able to develop innovative methodologies thereby broadening the knowledge base that would become academic sociology. Oberschall is one of the few historians to credit the settlements with their substantial contributions to empirical sociology.

> The first social research techniques as well as the bulk of empirical social research up to the war [WWI] were developed and conducted mostly outside of the universities by social workers, philanthropists, public health and charity workers, journalists and reformers and some academic social pathologists, all of them loosely allied in the social survey movement.... Many were socially committed, college-educated women.... The two most remarkable of these were Jane Addams and Florence Kelley (1972:216).

Of the early male academic sociologists, Oberschall said, they "were textbook writers, not researchers or writers of scholarly publications" (1972:214). Some histories of sociology erroneously give universities credit for establishing settlements as a part of their sociological work even though a majority had no formal affiliation with colleges or universities. For example, Nels Anderson makes such attribution in his account of the development of urban sociology: "as social science turned from the university to the slum.... They [settlements] bear witness to the fervent social idealism then pervading the university" (1929:268–269).

The "founding fathers" of sociology were seemingly of one accord that sociology should be useful although most were not willing to assume responsibility for predicting what action was needed or how it was to occur. Nor did these men go out and collect data to aid in their search for "natural laws." It was the women of Hull House and those residents associated with social gospelers such as Taylor and Woods who collected the first extensive data on urban problems, decades before such work was conducted by males at the University of Chicago. And in this pre-computer age research often involved hundreds and thousands of surveys painstakingly tabulated by hand. As Feagin and Vera point out,

> The fact that the women sociologists were pioneers in empirical sociology was occasionally noted in the 1910s and early 1920s by the men in the University of Chicago department of sociology, but later on these men criticized the early work as little more than social work or ignored it entirely. Subsequently, methods textbooks cited the technique of demographic mapping as the invention of male sociologists at the University of Chicago (2001:66–67).

As professional sociologists became committed to objectivity and value-free science those with settlement-like interests or reform agendas were excluded or marginalized. It was not until the 1950s that mainstream sociology in the United States was challenged from within by a revolt fed later by the social movements of the 1960s and 70s. Young sociologists, women and minorities, many of them students, demanded change, calling for abandoning the value-free science position and adopting a "relevant" sociology that attended to issues of social justice. Emphasis was placed on protecting academic freedom, exhorting sociologists to take a stance on social issues, applying research in the formulation of social policies, and encouraging interdisciplinary cooperation among the social sciences. One result of these debates within the *American Sociological Association* (ASA), was a break-away organization established in 1951, the *Society for the Study of Social Problems*, and in 1976, the founding of *The Association for Humanist Sociology*, professional organizations more openly political than the ASA (Bernard 1973:774, Morton et al. 2012). When value-free social science came under attack as part of the social movements of the mid-twentieth century, it was labeled "mechanomorphism" by critics such as Matson (1966) or as "methodological inhibition" by Mills (1959). There was some effort by a minority of social scientists to put people back into the research process and to recognize that value neutrality on the part of the investigator is only an ideal and not a realistic one (Gouldner 1962). By contrast, the essence of the standpoint epistemology of the settlements was a clear understanding that scientists can most effectively influence when they are influenced for only then can they speak from the perspective of those they seek to portray or represent. Jane Addams said it best when she wrote, "we came to define a settlement as an institution attempting to learn from life itself in which undertaking we did not hesitate to admit that we encountered many difficulties and failures" (1930:408). Echoing Addams sentiments years later, Madge wrote in his Introduction to *The Tools of Social Science*,

> If we assign a functional role to science, we may require social scientists not as detached referees basing their judgments on a set of universal theories, but as active engineers of social change in directions freely chosen by each community of interest; in this case, their ability to help will be partly determined by their own identification with their adopted community and with its aims (1965:xxi).

In a similar vein, Valentine wrote of the ethnographer, from an ethical position, as having "major obligations to the people he is studying" (1968:188). Sociologists such as Gouldner dismissed value-free sociology (1962) in favor of a critical and "reflexive sociology" (1970). Social scientists such as Madge (1965), Matson (1966), and Valentine (1968) were among the advocates of putting people (both those studied and those studying) back into the research process. While many young sociologists in the sixties and seventies embraced such ideas as new and as a refreshing change from functionalism and the value-free posture, these ideas were, in fact, put into play during the Progressive Era. Even though continuities of critical thinking and standpoint epistemologies have persisted throughout sociology's history, there is much to be gained from reexamining the settlement paradigm for the purpose of understanding the state of the discipline today while seeking a more relevant future. The third wave of sociology characterized by a renaissance in sensitivity to public practice is yet to be fully defined. Burawoy's four types of sociological labor are subject to reconfigurations and how these alliances will ultimately settle into a new hierarchy of knowledge is yet to be determined within the fields of power at play. Despite the pessimistic forecasts of some who view sociology as heading toward decline or even premature death, Burawoy argues that the accumulation of instrumental knowledge by professional sociologists is not threatened by the growth of reflexive and critical thinking. There are indeed many indications that the discipline is flourishing as the numbers of college majors and graduate degrees increase. And it does appear that the discipline is responding to Burawoy's call to reclaim public sociology, with as many as 150 colleges and universities offering certifications or specializations in public sociology (Morton et al. 2012). Sociology is alive and well, but will it impact our social worlds? For whom and for what are we producing sociologists?

Perhaps the lesson that resonates most clearly from settlement history is the importance of sociology's escaping insularity by finding a more expansive place for practice outside the academy. Most professional sociologists today make their living at colleges and universities although the majority of sociology graduates will not become college professors. Yet, we are still hard pressed to answer the perennial student question: *What can I do with a degree in sociology?* Perhaps it is time to be less timid in encouraging our students to make a difference, to go change the world, or at least some corner of it. There are today limited venues in which to practice sociology, and part of our professional work should be to create new spaces for such practice. Most organizations—corporate, social, religious, health, military or service—can benefit from the work of sociologists in gathering facts, analyzing those data, and recommending procedures, policies, and practices that are sensitive to human consequences and public perceptions. Indeed, the profession might accept responsibility for the infusion of the sociological imagination into all complex bureaucracies (Mills 1959). To broaden our definitions of sociological engagement and practice to include work that extends beyond writing textbooks and peer-reviewed articles will better support our students' idealistic desires to be change agents, perhaps beginning with local-level projects and community-based movements (cf. Morton et al. 2012). Sociologists and universities should consider putting their collective weight behind a program of national service—a natural venue of praxis for young sociology graduates. Baring national inscription, many students would eagerly "settle" in geographic or social communities as interns or residents if opportunities for service were made available. Upon graduation many of our students are not unlike the settlement leaders who went through a period of floundering even as they searched for meaningful work. Our professional societies and universities could actively build community partnerships as post-graduate training through service-learning appointments. Government incentives such as student loan pay-offs or forgiveness programs attached to community service would appeal to many humanistically-oriented liberal arts and social science students and have pragmatic appeal in today's economy.

The restrictive academic environment offers professional sociologists both hope and despair. There is hope because semester-after-semester students present us with fresh faces and renewed energies. Many in our introductory classes will know little to nothing of sociology, giving professors opportunity to draw from history lessons that will resonate for today and tomorrow. On the other hand, the academic-restrictive venue for professional sociologists is filled with many pitfalls. For example, we continue to teach the classical artifacts of European predecessors such as Durkheim, Weber, and Marx, but not the artifacts of our American, Progressive Era pioneers for social justice who left a trail of publications, speeches, and reforms as well as a model for civic engagement. For professional careers the academic environment creates demands and shifts priorities, making it difficult to nurture idealistic hopes for sociological praxis. While carrying heavy teaching loads, we must be concerned with publishing before the next evaluation cycle rather than with engaging in community projects and social movements or even researching our preferred topics. Too often our time is consumed in going to endless meetings where we often rehash the same tired subjects that have little to do with student learning or social progress. To avoid these pitfalls it is important that we carve out and prioritize spaces that allow us to nurture our visions for sociological practice. This will require new reward structures that enhance opportunities to practice our trade beyond the traditional academic criteria of classroom teaching, research, and publication. Innovative changes, for example, could include creation of "practice sabbaticals" to support partnerships for engaging in community projects and social movements. Morton et al. make a compelling case for revitalizing civic engagement and public sociology movements which they view as at cross-roads, one road leading to institutionalization and co-optation by conservative (elite university) forces, the other engaging community-based social movements toward greater radicalization.

> [L]acking strong social movements as shaping forces, the social justice potential for both civic engagement and public sociology must come from practitioners' links to community-based politics and social movement organizing. These connections are grounded in teaching and scholarship and in the real politics of everyday life—people, institutions, and communities. In promoting just such a direction for radical sociology, Bonilla-Silva (2006) echoes Marx's *German Ideology* suggesting one's position—where one lives his or her life and does his or her work—shapes one's consciousness. As Cornell West suggested over a decade ago, to avoid the dilemma of being a progressive intellectual whose professional work is restricted by academia and adds only to the resources and power of elite institutions, faculty must be "critical organic catalysts" functioning inside the academy but remaining grounded outside the

> academy in "progressive, political organizations and cultural institutions [that are] the most likely agents of social change in America."
>
> WEST 1993: 27, MORTON ET AL. 2012:6–7

While institutionalizing opportunities for greater civic engagement and applied practice carry hope for public sociology, history records that social reformers were often banished from the university rather than rewarded for their projects. Contemporary critics, while applauding university responses to social movements for greater civic engagement and public sociology, caution that institutionalization and professionalization often bring with them a conservative impulse. The end result may be that the language and politics of movements are co-opted in support of the status quo or professional elitism and do little to impact social justice (McAdam 2007, Morton et al. 2012). State, local, and federal politics that control educational funding and social programming are typically beyond the control of the profession; however, attempts to engage political stakeholders in the interest of progressive change and social justice must remain a professional agenda. In fact, if we fail to interject the sociological perspective into these broader debates we will lose opportunities to enhance professional relevance and students' opportunities to practice sociology. Even acknowledging that our work as progressive sociologists will be limited by professional agendas, organizational interests, and political environments we still have opportunity to use our individual and collective voices to raise the level of public consciousness among our various audiences. This is a central lesson we take from the settlement model of sociological praxis.

Sociological Predecessors and Progenies

In this research we have attempted to follow some semblance of the settlement model: investigating, disseminating what we have learned to our audiences, and finally making some recommendations for the road ahead. We have learned about our predecessors in sociology having studied many of their artifacts. We have been constantly amazed at the volume, quality and current relevance of the work left to posterity including quality-of-life reforms from the neighborhood to the national level. Although settlements did not solve all the problems of their day, they clearly made a difference and laid a path worthy of study and emulation. Over time, predecessors of settlement sociology have died while their collective works have yet to be fully explored and employed to keep them alive in our canon of knowledge. Successive generations of sociology students have yet to learn the value of early works such as those we have described because they have been erased, forgotten, or redefined as philanthropy or social work. This was not always the case. Looking through the archived papers of a first and second generation of academic sociologists such as Charles Henderson, Albion Small, and Ernest Burgess, for example, there were course syllabi with required readings that included settlement sociologists, particularly Addams and Woods. Their students wrote papers about the settlements, the "happening" places of their day. Settlement sociologists and social gospelers were invited to make presentations at ASA meetings and to publish in the AJS. Succeeding generations, however, discontinued recognition of settlement sociologists thus setting in motion the politics of erasure. What has survived is a politics of knowledge giving preference to European roots over American roots and to "scientific" roots over applied or reform roots and to male-produced over female-produced knowledge. Many introductory sociology textbooks today have bowed to a call for "diversity" by adding at least one female and one black—usually Jane Addams and W.E.B. Du Bois—to the history of our discipline. More often than not such names are an "add and stir" gesture or recognition for contributions to causes other than sociology per se—for example Addams to the peace movement and Du Bois for organizing the National Association for the Advancement of Colored People. Today typical teaching of sociology at both the graduate and undergraduate levels is without recognition of the depth and breadth of settlement sociology, if settlements are mentioned at all. The politics of erasure has effectively obscured and diminished this history. The reform roots of the discipline were erased as universities established legitimacy and purged faculty whose work was ideologically threatening, particularly as World War I and the Bolshevik revolution triggered a period of political fear and repression in the United States.

Neighborhood settlements reached their apex during the Progressive Era and began a gradual decline or change in function following World War I. Because of substantial real estate holdings and endowments, most of the large settlements, such as those we have profiled, survive but in different form and with different functions. The case studies examined in this volume reveal a transition from community settlement to community center, in most cases multiple-centers, and a change in target clientele from European immigrants to African Americans, Hispanics, and in recent years some Southeast Asians. Many of the original settlements have joined city-wide associations, each offering specialized services. Hull House, the most noble of all settlements, survives today only in museum artifacts. Shifts in the local demand for settlements can be attributed to changes in political ideology, community fund-raising, expanded work opportunities for women, and the professional separation and institutionalization of the disciplines of sociology and social work. Changing demographics were also relevant as settlements were largely geared to work with European immigrant populations that gradually achieved a degree of success and moved to better neighborhoods. Additionally, there were political forces involved in the demise of the residential settlement houses, places suspected of being "un-American" and their residents, anarchists. Just as value-neutral science offered political sanctuary for academics, case work provided protection for social workers as the onus of change was placed on individuals and families. With professionalization, sociology was claimed by academic departments in colleges and universities where it was taught as theory and practiced primarily as scientific and "value-neutral" research. As professionally trained social workers took over settlement work, it became a day job, not a way of life as it had been. Residents were replaced by social workers who came to community centers in the morning and left at the end of the work day, many not even living in the area. As careers opened up for women, they no longer had to create their own spaces and their own roles as they had in the early settlements. The social gospel gave way to more conventional denominational dominance with churches more inclined to financial support of social services than to actual provision of them. The ultimate aim of settlements was not only to inform but to fix in the public mind visions of what could be accomplished through restructured political and economic systems. Settlement sociology gave the public a comprehensive view of life in US cities and was always a work of conscience in pursuit of justice.

This collective case study demonstrates that it was not historical accident that women and social gospel men have been typified as "do gooders," recast in history as operating from a nonscientific reform orientation and largely erased from the history of sociology as told in its canonical textbooks. Such a reformulation of the past distorts the important contributions of settlements to sociology. Indeed their seamless union of theory, research, and action suggests that much of the bifurcated logic embedded in contemporary debates is artificial and misdirected. There is no inherent disconnect between prevailing scientific methods and efforts to find practical solutions to problems. There are important lessons to be learned from our predecessors. For we cannot practice a truly democratic sociology in the interest of our many publics without partnering with the groups we represent. Liberatory research methods require that power be shared and that the object of our studies and those who study them be situated socially, politically, and economically in the local communities and social worlds we seek to understand. This was the essence of the "neighborly relations" paradigm and community-based work that informed progressive settlement sociologists. They joined the communities of the disempowered in neighborhood associations, social clubs, labor unions, action leagues, or committees to learn the interests, needs, and world views of their neighbors.

According to Mills, the task and the promise of sociology is that it enables us to grasp simultaneously history and biography and the relations between the two within the social space we occupy. Settlement sociologists explored, understood, and explained the structure of society as they placed themselves and their life histories in the intersections of class—their own and that of their neighbors—in the intersections of power—capitalist and labor—and for some the intersections of gender as they spoke with authority in a male-dominated world. Settlements were about "social reconstruction" and about the actualization of feminist and Christian pragmatism via the neighborly relation in a stratified society. Settlement sociologists understood the social world and developed an enviable capacity to explain it theoretically, empirically, and juristically even as others did not see the world from their location. The Progressive Era was a unique time in history and it provided vastly different experiences for the upper-ten, for the poor laborer, and for the settlement worker. All had a part in shaping the social world in which we live today and those who practiced sociology played a major role in shaping our discipline.

Settlements cast a broad net during the Progressive Era. Residents were service providers, educators, researchers, and reformers. They were internationalist in a provincial society and were interdisciplinary as others were laying disciplinary boundaries. The case studies included in this volume present indisputable evidence of sociological work—foundational and substantively comparable to that which has made its way into the sociological canon. As academic peers were pursuing a "science of society," settlement sociologists were practicing that science. The scope of settlement sociology was inclusive of feminist pragmatist Jane Addams, jurisprudent Florence Kelley, Christian ethicist Graham Taylor, environmentalist Mary McDowell, Christian socialists Vida Scudder, ethnographer-scholar Robert Woods, public nurse Lillian Wald, and housing proponent Mary Simkhovitch. Each brought to the settlement his or her own unique life history yet collectively they understood structural inequality and the relations between their own lives and that of their neighbors. A major goal of the settlements, perhaps the major goal, was to reduce the distance between the classes. It was a time when the top ten percent of the population owned almost 70 percent of the nation's wealth. In today's global society one percent of the population controls over half of the world's wealth and in the US, the top one percent controls more than one third of the wealth. The poor and disadvantaged are still with us—just different populations in a different era, but no less worthy of fully sharing in a democratic society.

This work should be read as much more than a nostalgic journey through the past. We have reached back to examine some of the earliest pioneers of sociology who were also some of the strongest proponents of social justice. These settlement histories offer new and challenging lessons in community, social inequality, interdisciplinary cooperation, methodological reciprocity, and pursuit of justice. In revisiting these sociological predecessors, we become knowers of a little known history and beneficiaries of a sociological vision that impels each generation to find its own "settlement" for meeting the challenges and responsibilities of today and of the future.

APPENDIX A

Selected Works of the Chicago Women's School of Settlement Sociology

Collective Writings

1895 Residents of Hull House. *Hull-House Maps and Papers: A Presentation of Nationalities and Wages in a Congested District of Chicago, Together with Comments and Essays on Problems Growing Out of Social Conditions*. Boston: Thomas Y. Crowell

1906 Abbott, Edith, Mabel Gillespie,and Anne Withington. *History of Trade Unionism among Women in Boston*. Boston: Women's Trade Union League

1907 Hall, George, Arthur O. Lovejoy, Henry J. Harris, H. Wirt Steele, Edward W. Frost, Scott Nearing, I.A. Loos, C.B. Wilmer, Benjamin J. Baldwin, Charles L. Cone, A.J. McKelway, Millie R. Trumbull, Phebe T. Sutliff, Mrs. A.M. Beardsley, Florence L. Sanville, Mrs. Daniel Miller, Edith M. Howes, Florence G. Taylor, Catharine Avery, Geraldine Gordon, Florence Kelley, and Samuel McCune Lindsay. *Reports from State and Local Child Labor Committees and Consumers' Leagues. Annals of the American Academy of Political and Social Science*

1909 Wald, Lillian, Jane Addams, Leo Arnstein, Ben B. Lindsey, Henry B. Favill, Charles R. Henderson, Florence Kelley, and Samuel McCune Lindsay. *The Federal Children's Bureau: A Symposium*. Proceedings of the Fifth Annual Meeting of the National Child Labor Committee. *Annals of the American Academy of Political and Social Science*

1911 Addams, Jane, Henry Baird Favill, and Jean M. Gordon. *Child Labor on the Stage: A Symposium. Annals of the American Academy of Political and Social Science*

1914 Addams, Jane, Earl Barnes, Mary R. Beard, et al. *Women in Public Life*. Philadelphia: American Academy of Political and Social Science

1915 Addams, Jane, Emily Greene Balch, and Alice Hamilton. *The Women at The Hague*. New York: Macmillan

Publications by Jane Addams

Books

1902 *Democracy and Social Ethics*. New York: Macmillan

1907 *Newer Ideals of Peace*. New York: Macmillan

1909 *The Spirit of Youth and City Streets*. New York: Macmillan

1910 *Twenty Years at Hull-House*. New York: Macmillan

1912 *A New Conscience and an Ancient Evil*. New York: Macmillan

1916 *The Long Road of Women's Memory*. New York: Macmillan

1922 *Peace and Bread in Times of War*. New York: Macmillan
1925 *The Child, the Clinic, and the Court*. New York: New Republic Press
1930 *The Second Twenty Years at Hull-House*. New York: Macmillan
1932 *The Excellent Becomes the Permanent*. New York: Macmillan
1935 *My Friend, Julia Lathrop*. New York: Macmillan
1985 *On Education*. New York: Teachers' College Press

Articles and Published Speeches[1]

1880 (2002) "Bread Givers," in Jean B. Elshtain, ed., *The Jane Addams Reader*. New York: Basic Books

1881 (2002) "Casandra," in Jean B. Elshtain, ed., *The Jane Addams Reader*. New York: Basic Books

1986 "A Belated Industry," *American Journal of Sociology*

1893 "The Subjective Necessity of Social Settlements" and "The Objective Value of a Social Settlement," in Henry C. Adams, ed., *Philanthropy and Social Progress: Seven Essays by Miss Jane Addams, Robert A. Woods, Father J.O.S. Huntington, Professor Franklin H. Giddings, and Bernard Bosanquet*. New York: Thomas Y. Crowell

1894 (1912) "A Modern Lear," The *Survey*

1895 "Prefactory Note" and "The Settlement as a Factor in the Labor Movement," in Hull-*House Maps and Papers*. Boston: Thomas Y. Crowell.

1899 "Trade Unions and Public Duty," *American Journal of Sociology*

1899 "A Function of the Social Settlement," *Annals of the American Academy of Political and Social Science*

1902 "The Housing Problem in Chicago," (with De Forest) *Annals of the American Academy of Political and Social Science*

1904 "The Humanizing Tendency of Industrial Education," *The Chautauquan*

1905 "Problems of Municipal Administration," *American Journal of Sociology*

1905 "Recent Immigration: A Field Neglected by the Scholar," *University Record*

1905 "Child Labor Legislation—A Requisite for Industrial Efficiency," *Annals of the American Academy of Political and Social Science*

1906 "The Operation of the Illinois Child Labor Law," *Annals of the American Academy of Political and Social Science*

1907 "Public Recreation and Social Morality," *Charities and the Commons*

1907 "National Protection for Children," *Annals of the American Academy of Political and Social Science*

1 More of Addams unpublished speeches and writings are included in collected works (see e.g., Johnson 1960, Elshtain 2002b, and Bryan et al. 2003).

1908 Comment on "Class Conflict in America," *American Journal of Sociology*

1908 "Public Schools and the Immigrant Child," *Journal of Proceedings* National Education Association

1908 "The Chicago Settlements and Social Unrest," *Charities and the Commons*

1911 "The Social Situation," *Religious Education*

1911 "Ten Years' Experience in Illinois," *Annals of the American Academy of Political and Social Science*

1912 "Recreation as a Public Function in Urban Communities," *American Journal of Sociology*

1912 "The Progressives Dilemma? The New Party," *American Magazine*

1912 "My Experiences as a Progressive Delegate," *McClure's Magazine*

1913 "If Men Were Seeking the Franchise," *Ladies Home Journal.*

1914 "A Modern Devil Baby," *American Journal of Sociology*

1914 "Social Justice through National Action," speech published by the Progressive National Committee

1914 "The Larger Aspects of the Woman's Movement," *Annals of the American Academy of Political and Social Science*

1916 "War Times Challenging Woman's Traditions," *The Survey*

1917 "Patriotism and Pacifists in War Time," *City Club Bulletin*

1918 "The World's Food and World Politics," *Proceedings of the National Conference of Social Workers*

1919 "Americanization," *Publications of the American Sociological Society*

1921 "The Potential Advantages of the Mandate System," *Annals of the American Academy of Political and Social Science*

1926 "How Much Social Work Can a Community Afford?" *Proceedings of the National Conference of Social Workers.*

1928 "Pioneers in Sociology: Graham Taylor," *Neighborhood*

1928 "The Importance to America of the Josephine Butler Centenary," *Social Service Review*

1929 "The Settlement as a Way of Life," *Neighborhood*

1929 "A Toast to John Dewey," *The Survey*

1930 "John Dewey and Social Welfare," in H.H. Price, ed., *John Dewey: The Man and His Philosophy.* Boston: Harvard University Press

1930 "Aspects of the Woman's Movement," *The Survey*

1931 "Tolstoy and Gandhi," *Christian Century*

1932 "A Great Public Servant, Julia C. Lathrop," *Social Service Review*

1932 "How to Build A Peace Program," *The Survey*

1935 "Julia Lathrop and Outdoor Relief in Chicago, 1893–94," *Social Service Review*

1935 "Julia Lathrop's Services to the State of Illinois," *Social Service Review*

Publications by Julia Lathrop

Books and Reports

1884 *Our Toiling Children.* New York: Women's Temperance Publication

1903 *The Travesty of Christmas.* New York: National Consumers' League

1913 *Birth Registration: An Aid in Protecting the Lives and the Rights of Children.* Washington, DC: Children's Bureau Publication

1914 *Baby Saving Campaigns: A Preliminary Report on What American Cities are Doing to Prevent Infant Mortality.* Washington, DC: Children's Bureau Publication

1917 *Shall this Country Economize for or against its Children?* New York: National Education Association

1972 *The United States Children's Bureau.* New York: Ayer Publishing Co.

Articles

1894 "Hull House as a Sociological Laboratory," *Proceedings of the National Conference of Charities and Correction*

1895 "The Cook County Charities," in *Hull-House Maps and Papers.* Boston: Thomas Y. Crowell

1896 "What the Settlement Work Stands For," *Proceedings of the Conference of Charities and Correction*

1905 "Suggestions for Visitors to County Poor-houses and to Other Public Charitable Institutions," in *Public Charities.* Chicago: Committee of the Illinois Federation of Women's Clubs

1905 "The Development of the Probation System in a Large City," *Charities*

1910 "Pensions for Mothers," *Journal of Education*

1910 "Institutional Records and Industrial Causes of Dependence," *The Survey*

1912 "Introduction" to *The Delinquent Child and the Home* by S.P. Breckinridge and E. Abbott. New York: Russell Sage.

1912 "The Children's Bureau," *American Journal of Sociology*

1916 "The Highest Education for Women," *Journal of Home Economics*

1917 "The Public Protection of Maternity," *The American Labor Legislative Review*

1918 "Provisions for the Care of the Families and Dependents of Soldiers and Sailors," *Annals of the Academy of Political Science*

1919. "Income and Infant Mortality," *American Journal of Public Health*

1919 "Wage-Earning Women in War Time in the Textile Industry," *Journal of Industrial Hygiene*

1921 "Standards of Child Welfare," *Annals of the American Academy of Political and Social Science*

1925 "Federal Safeguards of Child Welfare: Child Welfare Has Become a World Concern—What is the Share of the United States?" *Annals of the American Academy of Political and Social Science*

1925 "The Background of the Juvenile Court in Illinois" and "The Defective *Child* and the Juvenile *Court*," in Jane Addams, ed., *The Child, the Clinic, and the Court*. New York: New Republic Press

Publications by Florence Kelley

Books and Pamphlets

1905 *Some Ethical Gains Through Legislation*. New York: Macmillan

1907 *Persuasion or Responsibility* (with Jane Addams). New York: National American Woman Suffrage Association

1910 *Twentieth Century Socialism: What It Is Not; How It May Come*. Florence Kelley, ed., New York: Longmans, Green

1913. *The Present Status of Minimum Wage Legislation*. New York: National Consumers' League

1914 *Modern Industry in Relation to the Family, Health, Education, and Morality*. New York: Longmans, Green

1925 *The Supreme Court and Minimum Wage Legislation*. New York: National Consumers League

1927 (1986) *Autobiography: Notes of Sixty Years*. Chicago: Charles H. Kerr

Articles

1882 "On Some Changes in the Legal Status of the Child since Blackstone," *International Review*

1882 "Need Our Working Women Despair?" *International Review*

1895 "The Sweating System," in *Hull-House Maps and Papers*. Boston: Thomas Y. Crowell

1895 "Wage-Earning Children" (with Alzina Stevens), in *Hull-House Maps and Papers*. Boston: Thomas Y. Crowell

1896 "The Working Boy," *American Journal of Sociology*

1898 "The Illinois Child-Labor Law," *American Journal of Sociology*

1898 "The United States Supreme Court and the Utah Eight-Hours' Law," *American Journal of Sociology*

1899 "Aims and Principles of the Consumer's League," *American Journal of Sociology*

1902 "Child Labor Legislation," *Annals of the American Academy of Political and Social Science*

1903 "An Effective Child-Labor Law: A Program for the Current Decade," *Annals of the American Academy of Political and Social Science*

1904 "Has Illinois the Best Laws in the Country for the Protection of Children?" *American Journal of Sociology*

1905 "Review of Poverty," *American Journal of Sociology*

1905 "Child Labor Legislation and Enforcement in New England and the Middle States," *Annals of the American Academy of Political and Social Science*

1906 "The Federal Government and the Working Children," *Annals of the American Academy of Political and Social Science*

1907 "Obstacles to the Enforcement of Child Labor Legislation," *Annals of the American Academy of Political and Social Science*

1908 "The Responsibility of the Consumer," *Annals of the American Academy of Political and Social Science*

1909 "Scholarships for Working Children," *Annals of the American Academy of Political and Social Science*

1909 "The Invasion of Family Life by Industry," *Annals of the American Academy of Political and Social Science*

1910 "New England's Lost Leadership," *Annals of the American Academy of Political and Social Science*

1911 "Minimum Wage Boards," *American Journal of Sociology*

1911 "Street Trades," *Annals of the American Academy of Political and Social Science*

1911 "Our Lack of Statistics," *Annals of the American Academy of Political and Social Science*

1911 "What Should We Sacrifice to Uniformity?" *Annals of the American Academy of Political and Social Science*

1911 "The Abolition of Child Labor," in *What Women Might do with the Ballot*. New York: National Women's Suffrage Association

1914 "Women and Social Legislation in the United States," *Annals of the American Academy of Political and Social Science*

1916 "Amending State Constitutions," *The Forerunner*

1922 "Industrial Conditions as a Community Problem with Particular Reference to Child Labor," *Annals of the American Academy of Political and Social Science*

1923 "Laborers in Heat and in Heavy Industries," *Annals of the American Academy of Political and Social Science*

1926 "My Philadelphia," *The Survey*

1927 "When Co-education was Young," *The Survey*

1927 "My Novitiate," *The Survey*

1928 "Leisure by Law for Women," *Social Service Review*

1929 "Labor Legislation for Women and Its Effects on Earnings and Conditions of Labor" (with Marguerite Marsh), *Annals of the American Academy of Political and Social Science*

1998 "Promoting A Dialogue: American Women Forge Ties with German Activism," in Kathryn K. Sklar, et al., eds., *Social Justice Feminists in the United States and Germany*. Ithaca, NY: Cornell University Press

Publications by Edith Abbott

Books and Reports

1909 *Women in Industry: A Study of American Economic History.* New York: D. Appleton

1911 *The Housing Problem in Chicago* (with Sophonisba Breckinridge). New York: Russell Sage

1912 *The Delinquent Child and the Home* (with Sophonisba Breckinridge). New York: Charities Publication Committee

1912 *Wage-Earning Women and the State: A Reply to Miss Minnie Bronson* (with Sophonisba Breckinridge). Boston: Equal Suffrage Association for Good Government

1915 *The Real Jail Problem.* Chicago: Juvenile Protective Association

1915 *Education for Social Work.* Washington, DC: US Government Printing Office

1916 *One Hundred and One County Jails of Illinois and Why They Ought to be Abolished.* Chicago: Juvenile Protective Association

1917 *Truancy and Non-Attendance in the Chicago Schools* (with Sophonisba Breckinridge). Chicago: University of Chicago Press.

1918 *Democracy and Social Progress in England.* Chicago: University of Chicago Press

1921 *The Administration of the Aid-to-Mothers Law in Illinois.* Washington, DC: Government Printing Office

1924 *Immigration: Select Documents and Case Records.* Chicago: University of Chicago Press

1926 *Historical Aspects of the Immigration Problem.* Chicago: University of Chicago Press

1930 *Social Welfare and Professional Education.* Chicago: University of Chicago Press

1931 *Report on Crime and the Foreign Born* (with Alida Bowler). National Commission on Law Observance and Enforcement. Washington, DC: US Government Printing Office

1931 *Social Welfare and Professional Education.* Chicago: University of Chicago Press

1936 *The Tenements of Chicago, 1908–1935* (with Sophonisba Breckinridge and other associates). Chicago: University of Chicago Press

1937 *Some American Pioneers in Social Welfare: Select Documents with Editorial Notes.* Chicago: University of Chicago Press

1940 *Public Assistance: American Principles and Policies.* Chicago: University of Chicago Press

1943 *Twenty-One Years of University Education for Social Service, 1920–1941* Chicago: University of Chicago Press

Articles

1904 "Wage Statistics in the Twelfth Census" *Journal of Political Economy*

1905 "Wages of Unskilled Labor in the United States, 1850–1990," *Journal of Political Economy*

1906 "Harriet Martineau and the Employment of Women in 1836," *Journal of Political Economy*

1906 "Woman Suffrage Militant: The New Movement in England," *The Independent*

1906 "History of Industrial Employment of Women in the United States: An Introductory Study," *Journal of Political Economy*

1906 "Employment of Women in Industries: Twelfth Census Statistics (with Sophonisba Breckinridge)," *Journal of Political Economy*

1907 "Municipal Employment of Unemployed Women in London," *Journal of Political Economy*

1907 "Employment of Women in Industries: Cigar-making: Its history and Present tendencies," *Journal of Political Economy*

1908 "History of the Employment of Women in the American Cotton Mills," *Journal of Political Economy*

1908 "A Study of Early History of Child Labor in America," *American Journal of Sociology*

1908 "The English Working-Woman and the Franchise," *The Atlantic*

1909 "Women in Industry: The Manufacture of Boots and Shoes," *American Journal of Sociology*

1910 "Chicago's Housing Problems II: Families in Furnished Rooms (with Sophonisba Breckinridge)," *American Journal of Sociology*

1911 "Housing Conditions in Chicago. III: Back of the Yards" (with Sophonisba Breckinridge), *American Journal of Sociology*

1911 "Chicago Housing Conditions. IV: The West Side Revisited" (with Sophonisba Breckinridge), *American Journal of Sociology*

1911 "Chicago Housing Conditions V: South of Chicago at the Gates of the Steel Mills (with Sophonisba Breckinridge)," *American Journal of Sociology*

1911 "Women in Industry: The Chicago Stockyards" (with Sophonisba Breckinridge), *Journal of Political Economy*

1911 "English Poor-Law Reform," *The Journal of Political Economy*

1913 "Public Pensions to Widows with Children," *American Economic Review*

1915 "Field Work and the Training of Social Workers," *Social Service Review*

1915 "Progress of the Minimum Wage in England," *Journal of Political Economy*

1917 "Charles Booth, 1840–1916," *Journal of Political Economy*

1917 "The War and Women's Work in England," *Journal of Political Economy*

1918 "Crime and the War," *Journal of the American Institute of Criminal Law and Criminology*

1918 "The Social Caseworker and the Enforcement of Industrial Legislation," *Proceedings of the National Conference on Social Work*

1926 "Training for the Policewoman's Job," *Woman Citizen*

1927 "The University of Chicago, Graduate School of Social Service Administration," *Social Service Review*

1927 "The Civil War and the Crime Wave of 1865–70," *Social Service Review*

1927 "Immigration Restriction: Economic Results and Prospects," *The American Economic Review*
1929 "The Webbs on the English Poor Law," *Social Service Review*
1934 "Abolish the Pauper Laws," *Social Service Review*
1935 "Jane Addams Memorial Service," *Proceedings of the National Conference of Social Work*
1936 "Public Welfare and Politics," *Social Service Review*
1938 "Poor Law Provision for Family Responsibility," *Social Service Review*
1938 "Is there a Legal Right to Relief?" *Social Service Review*
1939 "Grace Abbott: A Sister's Memories," *Social Service Review*
1941 "Work or Maintenance: A Federal Program for the Unemployed," *Social Service Review*
1943 "The Beveridge Plan and the American Way," *Social Service Review*
1947 "Three American Pioneers in International Social Welfare," *The Compass*
1948 "Sophonisba P. Breckinridge: Over the Years," *Social Service Review*
1950 "Grace Abbott and Hull House, 1908–21, Part 1," *Social Service Review*
1950 "Grace Abbott and Hull House, 1908–21, Part 2," *Social Service Review*
1952 "The Hull-House of Jane Addams," *Social Service Review*

Publications by Sophonisba Breckinridge

Books and Reports

1903 *Legal Tender: A Study in English and American Monetary History*. Chicago: University of Chicago Press
1911 *Finding Employment for Children Who Leave the Grade Schools to Go to Work* (with Edith Abbott and Anne S. Davis). Chicago: Hollister Press
1912 *The Delinquent Child and the Home* (with Edith Abbott). New York: Charities Publication Committee
1912 *The Child and the City*. Chicago: Chicago School of Civics and Philanthropy
1912 *The Modern Household* (with Marion Talbot). Boston: Whitcomb and Barrows
1913 *Handbook for Women Voters of Illinois* (with Alice Greenacre). Chicago: Chicago School of Civics and Philanthropy
1917 *Truancy and Non-Attendance in the Chicago Schools* (with Edith Abbott). Chicago: University of Chicago Press
1920 *A Summary of Juvenile Court Legislation in the United States* (with Helen Jeter). Washington, DC: Government Printing Office
1921 *New Homes for Old*. New York: Harper & Brothers
1924 *Family Welfare Work in a Metropolitan Community*. Chicago: University of Chicago Press

1927 *Public Welfare Administration of the United States.* Chicago: University of Chicago Press
1931 *Marriage and the Civic Rights of Women.* Chicago: University of Chicago Press
1933 *Women in the Twentieth Century.* New York: McGraw Hill
1934 *Social Work and the Courts.* Chicago: University of Chicago Press
1934 *The Family and the State.* Chicago: University of Chicago Press
1934 *Family Welfare Work in a Metropolitan Community.* Chicago: University of Chicago Press
1936 *The Tenements of Chicago, 1908–1935* (with Edith Abbott). Chicago: University of Chicago Press
1939 *The Illinois Poor Law and Its Administration.* Chicago: University of Chicago Press

Articles

1901 "Review of *Domestic Service,*" *American Journal of Sociology*
1905 "Two Decisions Relating to Organized Labor," *Journal of Political Economy*
1906 "Legislative Control of Women's Work," *Journal of Political Economy*
1907 "Review of *Women's Work and Wages,*" *American Journal of Sociology*
1910 "Neglected Widowhood in the Juvenile Court," *American Journal of Sociology*
1910 "Chicago Housing Problem: Families in Unfurnished Rooms" (with Edith Abbott), *American Journal of Sociology*
1911 "Housing Conditions in Chicago, III: Back of the Yards" (with Edith Abbott), *American Journal of Sociology*
1911 "Chicago Housing Conditions, IV: The West Side Revisited" (with Edith Abbott), *American Journal of Sociology*
1911 "Chicago Housing Conditions, V: South Chicago at the Gates of the Steel Mills" (with Edith Abbott), *American Journal of Sociology*
1911 "Women in Industry: The Chicago Stockyards" (with Edith Abbott), *Journal of Political Economy*
1911 "Beginnings of Child Labor Legislation," *The Survey*
1912 "Immigrant Lodger as a Factor in the Housing Problem," *Proceedings of the Conference of Charities and Correction*
1913 "The Color Line in the Housing Problem," *The Survey*
1914 "The Family in the Community, but Not Yet of the Community," *Proceedings of the Conference of Charities and Correction*
1914 "Political Equality for Women and Women's Wages," *Annals of the American Academy of Political and Social Science*
1915 "A Recent English Case on Women and the Legal Profession," *Journal of Political Economy*
1917 "Social Control of Child Welfare," *Proceedings American Sociological Society*
1923 "The Home Responsibilities of Women Workers and the 'Equal Wage'," *Journal of Political Economy*

1923 "Summary of the Present State Systems for the Organization and Administration of Public Welfare," *Annals of the American Academy of Political and Social Science*
1923 "Southern Pioneers in Social Interpretation: Madaline McDowell Breckinridge," *Journal of Social Forces*
1923 "The Home Responsibilities of Women Workers and the Wage," *Journal of Political Economy*
1925 "The Family and the Law," *Proceedings of the National Conference of Social Work*
1927 "Widows' and Orphans' Pensions in Great Britain," *Social Service Review*
1927 "Frontiers of Control in Public Welfare Administration," *Social Service Review*
1930 "Separate Domicile for Married Women," *Social Service Review*
1930 "Public Welfare Organization with Reference to Child Welfare Activities," *Social Service Review*
1932 "Children and the Depression," *Proceedings of the National Conference of Social Work*
1933 "University Women in the New Order," *Journal of the American Association of University Women*
1933 "The Activities of Women Outside the Home," in Wesley Mitchell, ed. *Recent Social Trends*, Vol. 1, New York: McGraw-Hill
1936 "The New Horizons of Professional Education for Social Work," *Social Service Review*
1936 "New Chapters in the History of the Courts and Social Legislation (with Grace Abbott)," *Social Service Review*
1938 "Social Workers in the Courts of Cook County," *Social Service Review*
1939 "Grace Abbott and Education for Social Work," *The Child*
1939 "Statutory Provision for the Commitment of Insane Persons," *Social Service Review*
1940 "The Government's Role in Child Welfare," *Annals of* the *American Academy of Political and Social Science*
1943 "The Law of Guardian and Ward with Special Reference to the Children of Veterans" (with Mary Stanton), *Social Service Review*

Publications by Grace Abbott

Books

1910 *Juvenile Court Laws in the United States: A Summary by States* (with H.H. Hart and T.J. Homer). Chicago: Charities Publication Committee
1917 *The Immigrant and the Community*. New York: The Century Company
1920 *The Immigrant and Coal Mining Communities of Illinois*. Danville, IL: Illinois Printing
1920 *The Educational Needs of Immigrants in Illinois*. Chicago: State of Illinois Immigrants' Commission

1924 *Immigration: Select Documents and Case Records*. New York: Ayer Publishing
1938 *The Child and the State*. New York: Greenwood Press
1941 *From Relief to Social Security*. Chicago: University of Chicago Press

Articles

1908 "The Chicago Employment Agency and the Immigrant Worker," *American Journal of Sociology*

1909 "The Immigrant and Municipal Politics," *Proceedings of the Cincinnati Conference on Good Government*

1909 "A Study of Greeks in Chicago," *American Journal of Sociology*

1909 "The Bulgarians of Chicago," *Charities and the Commons*

1911 "Recent Trends in Mothers' Aid," *Social Service Review*

1911 "Adjustment—Not Restriction," *The Survey*

1911 "Treatment of Aliens in the Criminal Courts," *Journal of the American Institute of Criminal Law and Criminology*

1915 "The Midwife in Chicago," *American Journal of Sociology*

1915 "Immigration and Crime," *Journal of the American Institute of Criminal Law and Criminology*

1916 "The Democracy of Internationalism," *The Survey*

1916, "Immigration and Crime," *Journal of the American Bar Association*

1918 "Mother's Aid," *Women's Bureau Monthly Newsletter*

1922 "Federal Aid for the Protection of Maternity and Infancy," *American Journal of Public Health*

1923 "Ten Years of Work for Children," *North American Review*

1924 "The Child Labor Amendment," *The North American Review*

1925 "History of the Juvenile Court Movement throughout the World," in Jane Addams, ed. *The Child, the Clinic, and the Court*. New York: New Republic

1926 "Trends in Juvenile-Delinquency Statistics," *American Institute of Criminal Law and Criminology*

1926 "Compulsory School Legislation and Vocational Guidance," *The Vocational Guidance Magazine*

1929 "Case Work Responsibility of Juvenile Courts," *Social Service Review*

1930 "Adoption," *Encyclopedia of the Social Sciences*

1930 "The Federal Government in Relation to Maternity and Infancy," *Annals of the American Academy of Political and Social Science*

1931 "The Children's Bureau: What it is and How it Works," *Medical Women's Journal*

1931 "Safeguarding the Child in America," *Current History*

1932 "Improvement in Rural Public Relief: The Lesson of the Coal-Mining Communities," *Social Service Review*

1932 "The Changing Position of Women," in C.A. Beard, ed. *A Century of Progress*. New York: Harper and Brothers

1932 "The Child," *American Journal of Sociology*

1933 "The Child," *American Journal of Sociology*

1933 "Human Cost of Unemployment," *American Labor Legislation Review*

1934 "What About Mother's Pensions Now?" *The Survey*

1936 "New Chapters in the History of the Courts and Social Legislation" (with S.P. Breckinridge), *Social Service Review*

1936 "The Juvenile Courts," *The Survey*

1936 "The Social Security Act and Relief," *University of Chicago Literary Review*

1936 "This Business of Relief," *Proceedings of the Delegate Conference American Association of Social Workers*

1936 "The Juvenile Court and a Community Program for Treating and Preventing Delinquency," *Social Service Review*

1939 "Federal Regulation of Child Labor 1906–38," *Social Service Review*

1939 "A Sister's Memories," *Social Service Review*

1939 "Federal Regulation of Child Labor, 1906–38," *Social Service Review*

Publications by Frances Kellor

Books and Pamphlets

1901 *Experimental Sociology*. New York: Macmillan

1904 *Out of Work*. New York: G.P. Putnam's Sons

1908 *Notaries Public and Immigrants*. New York: New York State Immigration Commission

1909 *Athletic Games in the Education of Women* (with Gertrude Dudley). New York: Henry Holt

1914 *Unemployment: A Program for Relief*. New York: North American Civic League for Immigrants

1915 *The Immigrants in America Review*, ed., Vols 1 and 2. New York: Committee for Immigrants in America

1916 *Straight America: A Call to National Service*. New York: MacMillan.

1917 *Industrial Americanization and National Defense*. New York: National Americanization Committee

1918 *The Americanization of Women*. New York: National Americanization Committee

1918 *Industrial Americanization*. New York: National Americanization Committee

1918 *Neighborhood Americanization*. New York: National Americanization Committee

1920 *Immigration and the Future*. New York: George H Doran

1921 The *Federal Administration and the Alien*. New York: George H Doran and Co.

1923 *The United States of America in Relation to the Permanent Court of International Justice of the League of Nations and in Relation to the Hague Tribunal.* New York: League of Nations

1924 *Security Against War* Vol. I: *International Controversies.* Vol. 2: *Arbitration, Disarmament, Outlawry of War* (with Antonia Hatvany). New York: MacMillan

1924 *Protocol for the Pacific Settlement of International Disputes* (with Antonia Hatvany). New York: League of Nations

1925 *The United States Senate and the International Court* (with Antonia Hatvany). NewYork: Thomas Seltzer

1934 *Arbitration in the New Industrial Society.* New York: McGraw-Hill

1941 *Arbitration in Action: A Code for Civil, Commercial and Industrial Arbitration.* New York: Harper and Brothers

1944 *Arbitration in International Controversy* (with Antonia Hatvany). New York: New York Commission to Study the Organization of Peace and the American Arbitration Association

1948 *American Arbitration: Its History, Functions and Achievements.* New York: Harper and Brothers

Articles

1898 "Sex and Crime," *International Journal of Ethics*

1899 "Criminal Anthropology in Its Relation to Criminal Jurisprudence," *American Journal of Sociology*

1900 "Criminal Sociology: The American vs. the Latin School," *The Arena*

1900 "Criminality among Women," *The Arena*

1900 "Psychological and Environmental Study of Women Criminals," *American Journal of Sociology*

1901 "The Criminal Negro," *Boy's Industrial School Journal*

1901 "The Criminal Negro: Some of his Characteristics," *The Arena*

1901 "The Criminal Negro: Advantages and Abuse of Southern Penal systems," *The Arena*

1901 "The Criminal Negro: Environmental Influences," *The Arena*

1901 "The Criminal Negro: Childhood Influences," *The Arena*

1901 "The Association of Ideas," *The Pedagogical Seminary*

1904 "Immigration and Household Labor," *Charities*

1905 "Southern Colored Girls in the North," *Charities*

1905 "Assisted Emigration from the South: The Women," *Charities*

1905 "Associations for Protection of Colored Women," *Colored American Magazine*

1906 "The Ethical Value of Sports for Women," *American Physical Education Review*

1907 "The Immigrant Woman," *The Atlantic Monthly*

1908 "Protection of Immigrant Women," *The Atlantic Monthly*

1911 "Needed: A Domestic Immigration Policy," *North American Review*
1914 "A New Spirit in Party Organization," *North American Review*
1914 "Justice for the Immigrant," *Annals of the American Academy of Political and Social Science*
1914 "Is Unemployment a Municipal Problem?" *National Municipal Review*
1915 "Who is Responsible for the Immigrant?" *The Outlook*
1915 "Immigrants in America: A Domestic Policy," *Immigrants in America Review*
1915 "National Americanization Day—July 4th," *Immigrants in America Review*
1915 "Survey of Adult Immigrant Education," *Immigrants in America Review*
1915 "Unemployment in our Cities," *National Municipal Review*
1915 "Unemployment and Immigration," *Annals of the American Academy of Political and Social Science*
1916 "Americanization by Industry," *Immigrants in America Review*
1916 "Americanization: A Conservation Policy for Industry," *Annals of the American Academy of Political and Social Science*
1916 "How to Americanize a City," *The American City*
1917 "Women in the Campaign," *Yale Review*
1917 "Industrial Americanization and National Defense," *North American Review*
1919 "What is Americanization?" *Yale Review*
1919 "Immigration in Reconstruction," *North American Review*
1921 "Immigration and the Future," *Annals of the American Academy of Political and Social Science*
1921 "Future Immigration," *North American Review*
1923 "Humanizing the Immigration Law," *North American Review*

Publications by Alice Hamilton

Books and Reports

1912 *Lead Poisoning in Potteries, Tile Works, and Porcelain Enameled Sanitary Ware Factories*. Washington, DC: Bureau of Labor Statistics
1913 *Hygiene of the Painters Trade* (with Charles P. Neil). Washington, DC: Bureau of Labor Statistics
1914 *Lead Poisoning in the Smelting and Refining of Lead. Washington, DC:* Bureau of Labor Statistics
1915 *Industrial Poisons Used in the Rubber Industry*. Washington, DC: US Department of Labor
1917 *Industrial Poisons Used or Produced in the Manufacture of Explosives*. Washington, DC: Bureau of Labor Statistics

1917 *Hygiene of the Printing Trades* (with Charles H. Verrill). Washington, DC: US Government Printing Office

1919 *Women in the Lead Industries*. Washington, DC: Bureau of Labor Statistics

1922 *Carbon Monoxide Poisoning*. Washington, DC: Bureau of Labor Statistics

1929 *Industrial Poisons in the United States*. New York: Macmillan

1934 *Industrial Toxicology*. New York: Harper

1940 *Occupational Poisoning in the Viscose Rayon Industry*. Washington, DC: Bureau of Labor Statistics

1943 *Exploring the Dangerous Trades*. Boston: Little Brown

Articles

1903 "The Fly as a Carrier of Typhoid: An Inquiry into the part Played by the House Fly in the Recent Epidemic of Typhoid Fever," *Journal of the American Medical Association*

1904 "The Toxic Action of Scarlatinal and Pneumonic Sera on Paramoecia," *The Journal of Infectious Diseases*

1904 "The Question of Virulence among the So-Called Pseudodiphtheria Bacilli," *The Journal of Infectious Diseases*

1905 "The Dissemination of Streptococci through Invisible Sputum," *Journal of the American Medical Association*

1906 "Further Studies on Virulent Pseudodiphtheria Bacilli" (with Jessie Horton), *The Journal of Infectious Diseases*

1907 "Pseudodiphtheria Bacilli as the Cause of Suppurative Otitis, Especially the Postscarlatinal," *The Journal of Infectious Diseases*

1907 "The Opsonic Index and Vaccine Therapy of Pseudodiphtheric Otitis," *The Journal of Infectious Diseases*

1907 "The Social Settlement and Public Health," *Charities and the Commons*

1908 "The Midwives of Chicago: A Report of a Joint Committee of the Chicago Medical Society and Hull House (with Rudolph Holmes et al.)". *Journal of the American Medical Association*

1908 "Inoculation Treatment of Gonorrheal Vulvo-Vaginitis in Children" (with Jean Cooke), *The Journal of Infectious Diseases*

1908 "Gonorrheal Vulvo-Vaginitis in Children: With Special Reference to an Epidemic Occurring in Scarlet-Fever Wards," *The Journal of Infectious Diseases*

1908 "On the Occurrence of Thermostable and Simple Bactericidal and Opsonic Substances," *The Journal of Infectious Diseases*

1908 "Industrial Diseases: With Special Reference to the Trades in Which Women are Employed," *Charities and the Commons*

1910 "The Value of Opsonin Determinations in the Discovery of Typhoid Carriers," *The Journal of Infectious Diseases*

1911 "Occupational Diseases," *Proceedings, National Conference of Charities and Correction*

1912 "What One Stockholder Did," *The Survey*

1915 "At the War Capitals," *The Survey*

1916 "Wartime Economy and Hours of Work," *The Survey*

1917 "Prostitutes and Tuberculosis," *The Survey*

1919 "Angels of Victory," *The New Republic*

1919 "Inorganic Poisons, Other than Lead, in American Industries," *The Journal of Industrial Hygiene*

1922 "The Growing Menace of Benzene (benzol) Poisoning in American Industry," *Journal of the American Medical Association.*

1924 "Protection for Women Workers," *The Forum*

1925 "What the American Woman Thinks: A Doctor's Word on War," *The Woman Citizen*

1927 "Witchcraft in West Polk Street," *The American Mercury*

1929 "Nineteen Years in the Poisonous Trades," *Harper's Magazine*

1931 "What about Lawyers?" *Harper's Magazine*

1932 "American and Foreign Labor Legislation: A Comparison," *Social Forces*

1933 "Below the Surface," *Survey Graphic*

1934 "The Plight of the German Intellectuals," *Harper's Magazine*

1940 "Shall We Feed Hitler's Victims?" *The Nation*

1944 "New Problems in the Field of the Industrial Toxicologist," *California and Western Medicine*

1948 "Forty Years in the Poisonous Trades," *Journal of Industrial Medicine*

APPENDIX B

A Comparison of Some Aspects of the Urban Sociology of South End House and University of Chicago Sociologists

Woods and Kennedy describing Boston's Growth Pattern, 1905–1914	Burgess Concentric Zone Theory Chicago, circa 1925
"A city is naturally round...its nucleus is the 'market', a downtown commercial and manufacturing quarter about which zone after zone is circlingly added as the population increases. The belt immediately about the business section...is given over to a circle of poor and crowded neighborhoods broken in one place by a downtown residential quarter illustrating wealth and social power. The outer edge of this inner belt...marks the confines of the 'old city'.... As the city grew the downtown business quarter requisitioned the residential streets of the old town, and was itself later hemmed in by a series of congested tenement districts...[an 'inner belt']" (Woods and Kennedy 1969:31). "As the growth of commerce and industry makes increasing demands on the innermost portion of the city, those factories which require a considerable amount of space...seek cheaper land on the outskirts of the city, and the older and more well-to-do inhabitants move away. The neighborhoods thus requisitioned naturally change character [freeing up] more liberal conditions for the workers" (Woods and Kennedy 1969:33). Thus a Zone of Emergence develops between the innermost tenement districts and the outlying suburbs. "[T]he neighborhoods of the Zone of Emergence impress one familiar with the downtown tenement communities as distinctly more habitable [than downtown tenements]" (Woods and Kennedy 1969:34)	"The typical processes of the expansion of the city can best be illustrated by a series of concentric circles which may be numbered to designate both the successive zones of urban extension and the types of areas differentiated in the process of expansion." (Burgess [1925] 1967:50). The tendency is for city growth to expand outward from its central business district (zone 1) in a series of expanding zones. "Encircling the downtown area there is normally an area in transition (zone 2)...." where housing is deteriorating and invaded by business and light manufacturing. A third area (zone 3) is an area of working men's homes, "inhabited by workers in industries who have escaped from the area of deterioration (zone 2) but who desire to live within easy access of their work. Beyond this zone is the 'residential area' (zone 4) of high-class apartment buildings or of exclusive 'restricted' districts of single-family dwellings. Still further, out beyond the city limits is the commuters' zone—suburban areas, or satellite cities—within a thirty-to-sixty-minute ride of the central business district" (Burgess [1925]1967:50).

Woods and Kennedy on Neighborhoods and Natural Areas as units of analysis, 1905–1914	Robert Park on Natural Areas and the city as a laboratory, 1929
"...[F]rom an economic, a political, and a cultural point of view, the districts...between the old city and the suburbs constitute a single sociological fact with a sharply defined significance and appeal" (1969:32). "One advantage of the much indented configuration of Boston is that most local sections of the city have at least in part a natural boundary. This is particularly true of the districts that make up the zone [of emergence]. Set off geographically like towns by themselves it is easy for them to retain something like town spirit" (1969:40). "Sociology as an art, no less than as a science, must find its primary essential data in the fully understood neighborhood—building, organically from the neighborhood, up to the nation" (Woods 1914:589–590).	"The city is, in fact, a constellation of natural areas, each with its own characteristic milieu, and each performing its specific function in the urban economy as a whole.... The metropolis is ...a great sifting and sorting mechanism [selecting] out of the population...the individuals best suited to live in a particular region and a particular milieu (Park [1929b]1967:9–10). "The city always has been a prolific source of clinical material for the study of human nature because it has always been the source and center of social change" (Park [1929b]1967:12).

References

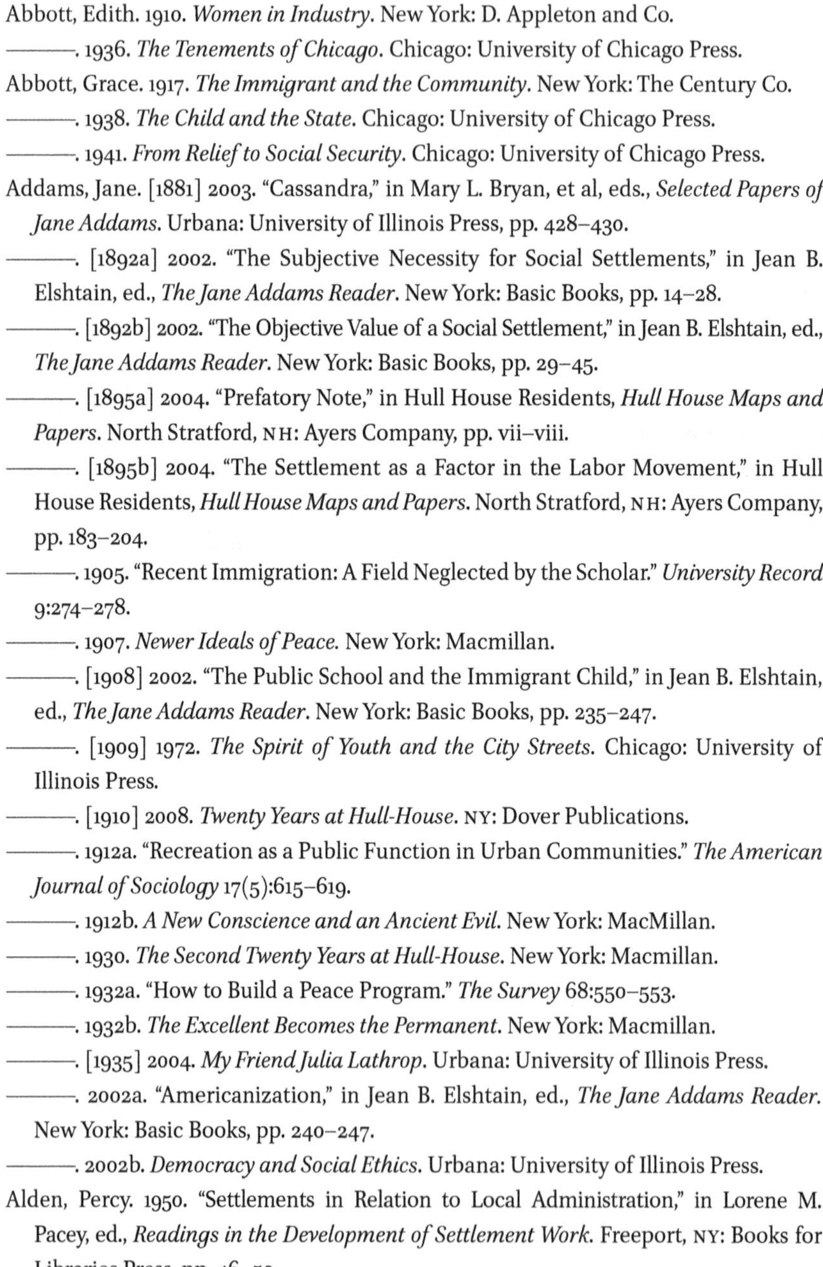

Abbott, Edith. 1910. *Women in Industry*. New York: D. Appleton and Co.

———. 1936. *The Tenements of Chicago*. Chicago: University of Chicago Press.

Abbott, Grace. 1917. *The Immigrant and the Community*. New York: The Century Co.

———. 1938. *The Child and the State*. Chicago: University of Chicago Press.

———. 1941. *From Relief to Social Security*. Chicago: University of Chicago Press.

Addams, Jane. [1881] 2003. "Cassandra," in Mary L. Bryan, et al, eds., *Selected Papers of Jane Addams*. Urbana: University of Illinois Press, pp. 428–430.

———. [1892a] 2002. "The Subjective Necessity for Social Settlements," in Jean B. Elshtain, ed., *The Jane Addams Reader*. New York: Basic Books, pp. 14–28.

———. [1892b] 2002. "The Objective Value of a Social Settlement," in Jean B. Elshtain, ed., *The Jane Addams Reader*. New York: Basic Books, pp. 29–45.

———. [1895a] 2004. "Prefatory Note," in Hull House Residents, *Hull House Maps and Papers*. North Stratford, NH: Ayers Company, pp. vii–viii.

———. [1895b] 2004. "The Settlement as a Factor in the Labor Movement," in Hull House Residents, *Hull House Maps and Papers*. North Stratford, NH: Ayers Company, pp. 183–204.

———. 1905. "Recent Immigration: A Field Neglected by the Scholar." *University Record* 9:274–278.

———. 1907. *Newer Ideals of Peace*. New York: Macmillan.

———. [1908] 2002. "The Public School and the Immigrant Child," in Jean B. Elshtain, ed., *The Jane Addams Reader*. New York: Basic Books, pp. 235–247.

———. [1909] 1972. *The Spirit of Youth and the City Streets*. Chicago: University of Illinois Press.

———. [1910] 2008. *Twenty Years at Hull-House*. NY: Dover Publications.

———. 1912a. "Recreation as a Public Function in Urban Communities." *The American Journal of Sociology* 17(5):615–619.

———. 1912b. *A New Conscience and an Ancient Evil*. New York: MacMillan.

———. 1930. *The Second Twenty Years at Hull-House*. New York: Macmillan.

———. 1932a. "How to Build a Peace Program." *The Survey* 68:550–553.

———. 1932b. *The Excellent Becomes the Permanent*. New York: Macmillan.

———. [1935] 2004. *My Friend Julia Lathrop*. Urbana: University of Illinois Press.

———. 2002a. "Americanization," in Jean B. Elshtain, ed., *The Jane Addams Reader*. New York: Basic Books, pp. 240–247.

———. 2002b. *Democracy and Social Ethics*. Urbana: University of Illinois Press.

Alden, Percy. 1950. "Settlements in Relation to Local Administration," in Lorene M. Pacey, ed., *Readings in the Development of Settlement Work*. Freeport, NY: Books for Libraries Press, pp. 46–59.

Alewitz, Sam. 1989. *"Filthy Dirty": A Social History of Unsanitary Philadelphia in the Late Nineteenth Century America.* New York: Garland Publishing.
Anderson, Elijah. 1996. "Introduction to the 1996 Edition of *The Philadelphia Negro*," in W.E.B. DuBois, *The Philadelphia Negro*. Philadelphia: University of Pennsylvania Press, pp. vix–xxxvi.
Anderson, Nels. [1923] 1961. *The Hobo*. Chicago: Phoenix Books University of Chicago Press.
———. 1929. "The Trend of Urban Sociology," in George A. Lundberg, et al, eds., *Trends in American Sociology*. New York: Harper Brothers, pp. 261–297.
Bachin, Robin F. 2004. *Building the South Side*. Chicago: University of Chicago Press.
Bailey, Thomas A. 1961. *The American Pageant*, 2nd. ed. Boston: D.C. Heath and Co.
Bain, Read and Joseph Cohen. 1929. "Trends in Applied Sociology," in George A. Lundberg, et al., eds., *Trends in American Sociology*. New York: Harper Brothers, pp. 344–388.
Balch, Emily Greene. [1910] 1969. *Our Slavic Fellow Citizens*. New York: Arno Press.
Bannister, Robert C. 1987. *Sociology and Scientism*. Chapel Hill, NC: University of North Carolina Press.
Barbuto, Domenica M. 1999. *American Settlement Houses and Progressive Social Reform*. Phoenix, AZ: Oryx Press.
Barker, John M. 1919. *The Social Gospel and the New Era*. New York: MacMillan Co.
Barnes, Harry E. 1925. *History and Prospects of the Social Sciences*. New York: A.A. Knopf.
———. 1948. *An Introduction to the History of Sociology*. Chicago: University of Chicago Press.
Barrett, James R. 1987. *Work and Community in the Jungle*. Urbana: University of Illinois Press.
Bascom, John. 1895. *Social Theory: A Grouping of Social Facts and Principles*. New York: Thomas Y. Crowell.
Berg, Bruce L. 2009. *Qualitative Research Methods for the Social Sciences*. Boston, MA: Allyn and Bacon.
Berger, Peter L. 1963. *Invitation to Sociology*. New York: Anchor Books.
Bernard, Jessie S. 1973. "My Four Revolutions: An Autobiographical History of the ASA." *American Journal of Sociology*, 78(4):773–791.
Bernard, Luther L. 1913. "Southern Sociological Congress." *American Journal of Sociology* 19(1):91–93.
Bernard, Luther L. and Jessie Bernard. 1943. *Origins of American Sociology*. New York: Thomas Y. Crowell.
Berson, Robin K. 2004. *Jane Addams: A Biography*. Westport, CT: Greenwood Press.
Blasi, Anthony J., ed. 2005a. *Diverse Histories of American Sociology*. Boston: Brill.
Blasi, A.J. 2005b. "The Sociology of William J. Kerby of Catholic University," in A.J. Blasi, ed., *Diverse Histories of American Sociology*. Boston: Brill, pp. 111–123.

Boas, Franz. 1911. "Introduction," in Mary Ovington, *Half a Man*. New York: Longmans, Green and Co., pp. vii–ix.

Bodo, John R. 1954. *The Protestant Clergy and Public Issues, 1812–1848*. Princeton, NJ: Princeton University Press.

Bonilla-Silva, Eduardo. 2006. "Towards a New Radical Agenda: A Critique of Mainstreamed Sociological Radicalism." *Contemporary Sociology* 35(2):111–114.

Booth, Charles. 1902–1903. *Life and Labor of the People of London*. New York: MacMillan.

Bowen, Louise De Koven. 1913. *The Colored People of Chicago*. Chicago: The Juvenile Protective Association.

———. 1917. *The Public Dance Halls of Chicago*. Chicago: Juvenile Protective Association.

Boydston, Jo Ann, ed. 1988. *John Dewey: The Later Works, 1925–1953. Essays, Reviews and Miscellany, 1939–1941*. Vol. 14. Carbondale: Southern Illinois University.

Boyer, Paul. 1992. *Urban Masses and Moral Order in America, 1820–1920*. Cambridge, MA: Harvard University Press.

Boyns, David and Jesse Fletcher. 2005. "Reflections on Public Sociology: Public Relations, Disciplinary Identity, and the Strong Program in Professional Sociology." *American Sociologist* 36(3–4):5–26.

Bramson, Leon. 1961. *The Political Context of Sociology*. Princeton, NJ: Princeton University Press.

Brandeis, Louis. 1918. *The Case against Night Work for Women*. New York: National Consumers' League.

Brandt, Lilian. 1903. "Social Aspects of Tuberculosis." *Annals of the American Academy of Political and Social Science* 21(1):65–76.

———. 1905. *Five Hundred and Seventy-Four Deserters and Their Families*. New York: Charities Organization Society.

Breckinridge, Sophonisba P. 1910 "Neglected Widowhood in the Juvenile Court." *American Journal of Sociology* 16(1):53–87.

Breckinridge, Sophonisba P. and Edith Abbott. 1911. "Housing Conditions in Chicago, III: Back of the Yards." *American Journal of Sociology* 16(4):433–468.

Breckinridge, Sophonisba and Edith Abbott. 1912. *The Delinquent Child and the Home*. New York: Russell Sage Foundation.

Breckinridge, Sophonisba. 1921. *New Homes for Old*. New York: Harper and Brothers.

———. 1923. "The Home Responsibilities of Women Workers and the 'Equal Wage'." *Journal of Political Economy* 31(4):521–543.

———. [1933] 1972. *Women in the Twentieth Century*. New York: Arno Press.

Briggs, Tracey. 2008. *Twenty Years at Greenwich House*. Ph.D. Dissertation, University of Toledo. ProQuest Information and Learning Co. http://search.proquest.com/docview/304458964, accessed June 16, 2014.

Brooks, John Graham. 1925. "Robert Archey Woods, 1865–1924." *The Survey* 53(March):732.

Brown, Mary E. 2012. "Jane Addams (1860–1935): Settling in the American City," in Patrick J Hayes, ed., *The Making of Modern Immigration*. Santa Barbara, CA: ABC-CLIO, LLC Books, pp. 1–10.

Bruere, Martha B. 1927. *Does Prohibition Work?* New York: Harper Brothers.

Bryan, Mary L.M., Barbara Bair, and Maree De Angury, eds. 2003. *The Selected Papers of Jane Addams*. Chicago: University of Illinois Press.

Bulmer, Martin. 1984. *The Chicago School of Sociology*. Chicago: University of Chicago Press.

Bulmer, Martin, Kevin Bales, and Kathryn K. Sklar. 1991. *The Social Survey in Historical Perspective 1880–1940*. New York: Cambridge University Press.

Burawoy, Michael. 2005a. "For Public Sociology." *American Sociological Review* 70(1):4–28.

———. 2005b. "Third-Wave Sociology and the End of Pure Science." *American Sociologist* 36(3–4):152–165.

———. 2007. "The Field of Sociology Its Power and Its Promise," in Dan Clawson, et al., *Public Sociology*. Berkeley, CA: University of California Press, pp. 241–258.

Burgess, Ernest W. [1925] 1967a. "Can Neighborhood Work Have a Scientific Basis?" in Robert E. Park and E.W. Burgess, eds., *The City*. Chicago: University of Chicago Press, pp. 142–155.

———. [1925] 1967b. "The Growth of the City," in Robert E. Park and E.W. Burgess, eds., *The City*. Chicago: University of Chicago Press, pp. 47–62.

Bushnell, Charles J. 1901–1902. "Some Social Aspects of the Chicago Stock Yards" Chs. I–IV. *American Journal of Sociology* 7(2–5):145–170, 289–330, 433–474, 689–702.

Bushnell, Horace [1843] 1916. *Christian Nature*. New Haven, CT: Yale University Press.

Calhoun, Craig, ed. 2007. *Sociology in America*. Chicago: University of Chicago Press.

Capitanio, Heather M. 2012. *Denison House: Women's Use of Space in the Boston Settlement*. Master's Thesis, Boston: University of Massachusetts. http://scholarworks.umb.edu/cgi/viewcontent.cgi?article=1000&context=masters_theses, accessed May 12, 2013.

Carnevale, Nancy C. 2009. *A New Language, A New World: Italian Immigrants in the United States 1890–1945*. Champaign, IL: University of Illinois Press.

Caroli, Betty B. 1998. *The Roosevelt Women*. New York: Basic Books.

Carrell, Elizabeth P.H. 1981. *Reflections in a Mirrow: The Progressive Woman and the Settlement Experience*. Ph.D. Dissertation, University of Texas at Austin. Ann Arbor: University Microfilms International.

Carson, Mina. 1990. *Settlement Folk*. Chicago: University of Chicago Press.

Chatfield, E. Charles. 1960 "The Southern Sociological Congress: Organization of Uplift." *Tennessee Historical Quarterly* 19(4):328–347.

Chicago Commission on Race Relations. 1922. *The Negro in Chicago*. Chicago: University of Chicago Press.

Clark, Sue A. and Edith Wyatt. 1911. *Making Both Ends Meet: The Income and Outlay of New York Working Girls*. New York: MacMillan and Co.

Clawson, Dan, Robert Zussman, Joya Misra, Naomi Gerstel, Randall Stokes, Douglas L. Anderton, and Michael Burawoy. 2007. *Public Sociology*. Berkeley: University of California Press.

Coghlan, Catherine L. 2005. "'Please Don't Think of Me as a Sociologist': Sophonisba Preston Breckinridge and the Early Chicago School." *The American Sociologist* 36(1):3–22.

Cohen, Rick. August 2, 2012. "Death of the Hull House: A Nonprofit Coroner's Inquest." *Nonprofit Quarterly*. http://charitableadvisors.blogspot.com/2012/08/death-of-hull-house-nonprofit-coroners.html, Accessed March 31, 2015.

Coit, Stanton A. 1892. *Neighbourhood Guilds: An Instrument of Social Reform.* London: Swan Sonnenschein and Co.

———. 1950. "The Neighborhood Guild Defined," in Lorene M. Pacey, ed., *Readings in the Development of Settlement Work*. Freeport, NY: Books for Libraries Press, pp. 21–28.

Collins, Patricia Hill. 1986. "Learning from the Outside Within: The Social Significance of Black Feminist Thought." *Social Problems* 33(6):14–32.

———. 1990. *Black Feminist Thought*. New York: Harper Collins.

———. 2000. "Black Feminist Epistemology," in Patricia Hill Collins, *Black Feminist Thought: Knowledge, Consciousness, and the Politics of Empowerment* (Revised Tenth Anniversary Edition). NY: Routledge, pp. 251–271.

Colwell, Stephen. 1851. *New Themes for the Protestant Clergy*. Philadelphia: Lippincott, Grambo and Co.

Commons, John. 1908. "Is Class Conflict in America Growing?" *American Journal of Sociology* 13(6):756–783.

Conference on the Care of Dependent Children (CCDC). 1909. *Proceedings*. Washington, D.C.: Government Printing Office. http://books.google.com/books?id=AAvTAAAAMAAJ&pg=PA224&dq=White+House+Conference+on+the+Care+of+Dependent+Children, accessed August 14, 2013.

Converse, Jean M. 1987. *Survey Research in the United States*. Berkeley: University of California Press.

Cook, Gary A. 1993. *George Herbert Mead: The Making of a Pragmatist*. Urbana: University of Illinois Press.

———. 2006. "George Herbert Mead," in John R. Shook and Joseph Margolis, eds., *A Companion to Pragmatism*. Blackwell Publishing: Malden, MA, pp. 67–78.

Cooley, Charles H. 1909. *Social Organization*. New York: Charles Scribner's Sons.

Costin, Lela B. 1983. *Two Sisters for Social Justice.* Urbana: University of Illinois Press.

Crane, Diana and Henry Small. 1992. "American Sociology since the Seventies," in Terence Halliday and M. Janowitz, eds., *Sociology and Its Publics.* Chicago: University of Chicago Press, pp. 197–234.

Cravens, Hamilton. 1971. "The Abandonment of Evolutionary Social Theory in America: The Impact of Academic Professionalization upon American Sociological Theory, 1890–1920." *American Studies* 12(2):5–20.

Cressey, Paul G. 1932. *The Taxi Dance Hall.* Chicago: University of Chicago Press.

Creswell, John W. 2013. *Qualitative Inquiry and Research Design*, 3rd ed. Thousand Oaks, CA: Sage Publications.

Cross, Robert D. 1958. *The Emergence of Liberal Catholicism in America.* Cambridge: Harvard University Press.

Crowell, F. Elisabeth. 1907. "The Midwives of New York." *Charities and the Commons* 17(January):667–677.

Daniels, Doris G. 1989. *Always a Sister: The Feminism of Lillian D. Wald.* New York: The Feminist Press.

Daniels, John. [1914] 1969. *In Freedom's Birthplace.* New York: Arno Press.

Darwin, Charles. [1859] 1964. *The Origin of the Species.* Boston: Harvard University Press.

Davis, Allen F. 1963. "The Campaign for the Industrial Relations Commission, 1911–1913." *Mid-America: An Historical Review* 45(4):211–228.

———. 1964. "Settlement Workers in Politics, 1890–1914." *The Review of Politics* 26(4):505–517.

———. 1972. "Introduction," in Jane Addams, *The Spirit of Youth and the City Streets.* Chicago: University of Illinois Press, pp. vii–xxx.

———. 2000. *American Heroine: The Life and Legend of Jane Addams.* Chicago: Ivan R. Dee.

———. 1984. *Spearheads for Reform.* New Brunswick, NJ: Rutgers University Press.

Deegan, Mary Jo. 1978. "Women and Sociology: 1890–1930." *Journal of the History of Sociology* 1:11–34.

———. 1987. "An American Dream: The Historical Connections between Women, Humanism, and Sociology, 1890–1920." *Humanity and Society* 11(3):353–365.

———. 1988. "W.E.B. DuBois and the Women of Hull-House, 1895–1899." *American Sociologist* 19(4):301–311.

———. 1990. *Jane Addams and the Men of the Chicago School.* New Brunswick, NJ: Transaction Publishers.

———. ed. 1991. *Women and Sociology.* Westport, CT: Greenwood.

———. 2002a. "The Feminist Pragmatism of Jane Addams," in Mary Ann Romano, ed., *Lost Sociologists Rediscovered.* Lewiston, NY: Edwin Mellen Press, pp. 1–19.

———. 2002b. *Race, Hull-House, and the University of Chicago*. Praeger: Westport, CN.

———. 2005. "A Private Trouble behind the Gendered Division of Labor in Sociology: The Curious Marriage of Robert E. and Clara Cahill Park," in Anthony J. Blasi, ed., *Diverse Histories of American Sociology*. Boston: Brill, pp. 18–39.

Delio, Ilia. 1995. "The First Catholic Social Gospelers: Women Religious in the Nineteenth Century," *U.S. Catholic Historian* 13(3):1–22.

Deneen, Patrick J. 2001. "Friendship and Politics: Ancient and American," in Peter D. Bathory and Nancy L. Schwartz, eds., *Friends and Citizens: Essays in Honor of Wilson Carey McWilliams*. Lanham, MA: Rowman and Littlefield, pp. 47–55.

Deutsch, Sarah. 2000. *Women and the City*. New York: Oxford University Press.

Devine, Edward T. 1921. *American Social Work in the Twentieth Century*. New York: Frontier Press.

Dewey, John. 1916. "Nationalizing Education." *Addresses and Proceeding of the National Education Association*.

Diliberto, Gioia. 1999. *A Useful Woman: The Early Life of Jane Addams*. New York: Scribner.

Diner, Steven J. 1970. "Chicago Social Workers and Blacks in the Progressive Era." *Social Service Review* 44(4):393–410.

———. 1975. "Department and Discipline: The Department of Sociology at the University of Chicago, 1892–1920." *Minerva* 13(Winter):514–553.

———. 1980. *A City and its Universities: Public Policy in Chicago, 1892–1919*. Chapel Hill, NC: University of North Carolina Press.

Dinwiddie, Emily. 1903. *The Tenant's Manual*. New York: Greenwich House Publications.

Dorrien, Gary. 2011. *Social Ethics in the Making*. Malden, MA: Wiley-Blackwell.

Douglas, Harlan P. 1909. *The Christian Reconstruction of the South*. Cambridge, MA: University Press.

Douglas, Paul H. [1936] 2000. *Social Security in the United States*. Washington, D.C.: Beard Books.

DuBois, W.E.B. [1899] 1996. *The Philadelphia Negro*. Philadelphia: University of Pennsylvania Press.

———. 1968. *W.E.B. DuBois: A Soliloquy on Viewing My Life*. New York: International Publishers.

Duffus, Robert L. (1939). *Lillian Wald: Neighbor and Crusader*. New York: Macmillan.

Eaton, Allen H. [1932] 1970. *Immigrant Gifts to American Life*. New York: Arno Press.

Eaton, Isabel. 1895. "Receipts and Expenditures of Certain Wage-Earners in the Garment Trades." *Journal of the American Statistical Association* 30(4):135–180.

———. [1899] 1996. "Special Report on Negro Domestic Service in the Seventh Ward Philadelphia," in W.E.B. DuBois, *The Philadelphia Negro*. Philadelphia: University of Pennsylvania Press, pp. 425–509.

Ehrenreich, John H. 1985. *The Altruistic Imagination.* Ithaca, NY: Cornell University Press.

Ellwood, Charles E. 1907. "How Should Sociology be Taught as a College or University Subject?" *American Journal of Sociology* 12(5):588–606.

Elshtain, Jean Bethke. 2002a. *Jane Addams and the Dream of American Democracy.* New York: Basic Books.

Elshtain, Jean Bethke, ed. 2002b. *The Jane Addams Reader.* New York: Basic Books.

Elson, Alex. 1954. "First Principles of Jane Addams." *Social Service Review* 28(1):3–11.

Ewing, James W. 1955. *Graham Taylor: Educator in "Life Rather than Literature."* BD Thesis, Chicago Theological Seminary. http://cts.kohalibrary.com/#/work/48338, accessed February 8, 2014.

Fabricant, Michael and Robert Fisher. 2002. *Settlement Houses under Siege: The Struggle to Sustain Community Organizations in New York City.* NY: Columbia University Press.

Fairbanks, Arthur. 1896. *Introduction to Sociology.* New York: Charles Scribner's Sons.

Faris, Robert E.L. 1945. "American Sociology," in Georges Gurvitch and Wilbert E. Moore, eds., *Twentieth Century Sociology.* New York: The Philosophical Library, pp. 538–561.

Feagin, Joe R. and Hernan Vera. 2001. *Liberation Sociology.* Boulder, CO: WestviewPress.

Feagin, Joe R. and Clairece C. Feagin. 2008. *Race and Ethnic Relations.* Upper Saddle River, NJ: Prentice Hall.

Fish, Virginia K. 1986. "The Hull House Circle: Women's Friendships and Achievements," in Janet Sharistanian, ed., *Gender, Ideology, and Action.* New York: Greenwood Press, pp. 185–227.

Fitzpatrick, Ellen. 1990. *Endless Crusade.* New York: Oxford University Press.

Frankfurter, Felix and Josephine Goldmark, 1916. *The Case for the Shorter Work Day,* Vols. 1 and 2. New York: The National Consumers' League.

Franklin, Donna L. 1986. "Mary Richmond and Jane Addams: From Moral Certainty to Rational Inquiry in Social Work Practice." *Social Service Review* 60(4):504–525.

Fremantle, William H. 1882. *The World as the Subject of Redemption.* London: Rivingtons.

Friedan, Betty. 1963. *The Feminine Mystique.* New York: W.W. Norton.

Furner, Mary O. 1975. *Advocacy and Objectivity.* Lexington, KY: University of Kentucky Press.

George, Henry. 1879. *Progress and Poverty.* New York: E.P. Dutton and Co.

———. 1891. *The Condition of Labor: Open Letter to Pope Leo XIII.* New York: United States Book Co. http://www.wealthandwant.com/HG/the_condition_of_labor.htm, accessed June 21, 2013.

Gibson, Campbell and Kay Jung. 2006. "Historical Census Statistics on the Foreign-Born Population of the United States: 1850–2000." US Census Bureau Population

Division. Working Paper No. 81. Washington, D.C.: US Census Bureau, accessed May 12, 2012.

Giddings, Franklin H. 1896. *Principles of Sociology*. New York: MacMillan Co.

———. 1899. "The Psychology of Society." *Science* 9:16–23.

———. 1907. "Preface," in Louise B. More, *A Study of Standards and Cost of Living in New York City*. New York: Henry Holt, pp. i–iv.

Gillin, John L. 1927. "The Development of Sociology in the United States." *Papers and Proceedings of the American Sociological Association*, 1926. Chicago: University of Chicago Press.

Gilman, Charlotte P. 1935. *The Living of Charlotte Perkins Gilman*. New York: D. Appleton-Century Company.

Gladden, Washington. 1886. *Applied Christianity*. Boston: Houghton, Mifflin and Co.

Goffman, Erving. 1961. *Asylums*. Garden City, NY: Anchor Books.

Goldin, Claudia and Lawrence F. Katz. 1999. "The Shaping of Higher Education: The Formative Years in the United States, 1890–1940." *Journal of Economic Perspectives* 13(1):37–62.

Goldmark, Josephine. 1912. *Fatigue and Efficiency*. New York: Russell Sage Foundation.

———. 1953. *Impatient Crusader*. Urbana: University of Illinois Press.

Goodspeed, Thomas W. 1916. *A History of the University of Chicago*. Chicago: University of Chicago Press.

Gordon, Milton. 1963. *Social Class in American Sociology*. New York: McGraw-Hill.

Gordon, Milton M. 1964. *Assimilation in American Life*. New York: Oxford University Press.

Gouldner, Alvin W. 1962. "Anti-Minotaur: The Myth of Value-Free Sociology." *Social Problems* 9(3):199–213.

———. 1970. *The Coming Crisis of Western Sociology*. New York: Basic Books.

Greek, Cecil E. 1992. *The Religious Roots of American Sociology*. New York: Garland Publishing.

Grimes, Michael D. 1991. *Class in Twentieth-Century American Sociology*. New York: Praeger.

Gwinn, Kristen E. 2010. *Emily Greene Balch: The Long Road to Internationalism*. Chicago: University of Illinois Press.

Hamilton, Alice. 1929. *Industrial Poisons in the United States*. New York: MacMillan.

———. 1943. *Exploring the Dangerous Trades*. Boston: Little, Brown Co.

Handy, Robert T., ed. 1966. *The Social Gospel in America, 1870–1920*. New York: Oxford University Press.

Haraway, Donna. 1988. "Situated Knowledges: The Science Question in Feminism and the Privilege of Partial Perspective." *Feminist Studies* 14(3):575–599.

Harding, Sandra. 1987. *Feminism and Methodology*. Bloomington: Indiana University Press.

———. 1991. *Whose Science, Whose Knowledge: Thinking from Women's Lives.* Ithaca, NY: Cornell University Press.

Harnish, Brandon. 2011. "Jane Addams's Social Gospel Synthesis and the Catholic Response." *The Independent Review* 16(1):93–100.

Hartsock, Nancy. 1983. "The Feminist Standpoint: Developing the Ground for a Specifically Feminist Historical Materialism," in Sandra Harding and Merrill B. Hintikka, eds., *Discovering Reality: Feminist Perspectives on Epistemology, Methodology, Metaphysics and Philosophy of Science.* Boston: D. Reidel Publishing Co., pp. 283–310.

Haskell, Thomas L. 2000. *The Emergence of Professional Social Science.* Baltimore: Johns Hopkins University Press.

Hayes, Samuel P. 1957. *The Response to Industrialism 1856–1914.* Chicago: University of Chicago Press.

Hedger, Caroline. 1906. "The Unhealthfulness of Packingtown." *The World's Work* 12(May–October):7507–7510

Henderson, Charles R. 1893. *An Introduction to the Study of the Dependent, Defective and Delinquent Classes.* Boston: D.C. Heath and Company.

Henking, Susan E. 1988. *American Protestantism and the Rise of American Sociology: A Contextual Study of Varieties of Secularization,* Vols. 1 and 2. A Dissertation Submitted to the Divinity School. University of Chicago.

Henking, Susan. 1992. "Protestant Religious Experience and the Rise of American Sociology." *Journal of the History of the Behavioral Sciences* 28:325–339.

———. 1993. "Sociological Christianity and Christian Sociology: The Paradox of Early American Sociology." *Religion and American Culture,* 3(1):49–67.

Herzfeld, Elsa and Natalie Henderson. 1906. *A West Side Rookery.* New York: Greenwich House Publications.

Higham, John. 1981. *Strangers in the Land.* Westport, CN: Greenwood Press.

Hill, Caroline Miles, ed. 1938. *Mary McDowell and Municipal Housekeeping: A Symposium.* Chicago: Millar Publishing Co.

Hofstadter, Richard. 1955. *The Age of Reform.* New York: Vintage Books.

Holbrook, Agnes Sinclair. [1895] 2004. "Map Notes and Comments," in Residents of Hull House, *Hull House Maps and Papers.* North Stratford, NH: Ayer Company Publishers, pp. 3–14.

Holbrook, Z. Swift. 1895. "What is Sociology?" *Bibliotheca* Sacra*: A Religious and Sociological Quarterly* 52:458–504.

Holden, Arthur C. [1922] 1970. *The Settlement Idea.* New York: Arno Press.

hooks, bell. 1984. *Feminist Theory: From Margin to Center.* Boston: South End Press.

Hopkins, Charles H. 1940. *The Rise of the Social Gospel in American Protestantism, 1865–1915.* New Haven: Yale University Press.

House, Floyd N. [1936] 1970. *The Development of Sociology.* Westport, CN: Greenwood Press.

Hull House Residents [1895] 2004. *Hull-House Maps and Papers*. North Stratford, NH: Ayer Company Publishers.

Hunter, Tera W. 1996. "Historical Note," in W.E.B. DuBois, *The Philadelphia Negro*. Philadelphia: University of Pennsylvania Press, pp. 425–426.

Hutchins, B.L. 1913. "Fatigue and Efficiency." *The Sociological Review* 6(1):30–42.

Jackson, Shannon. 2001. *Lines of Activity: Performance, Historiography, Hull-House Domesticity*. Ann Arbor, MI: University of Michigan Press.

Jaggar, Alison. 2008. *Just Methods: An Interdisciplinary Feminist Reader*. Bolder: Paradigm Publishers.

James, Edward T., et al. 1971. *Notable American Women 1607–1950*, Vol. 2. Boston: Harvard University Press.

James, William, 1910. "Review of *The Spirit of Youth and the City Streets*." *American Journal of Sociology* 15(4):550–553.

Jaques, William K. 1906. "A Picture of Meat Inspection." *The World's Work* 12(May–October):7491–7505.

Jaycox, Faith. 2005. *The Progressive Era*. New York: Facts on File.

Johnson, Emily Cooper, ed. 1960. *Jane Addams: A Centennial Reader*. New York: MacMillan.

Joint Legislative Committee (Lusk) Investigating Seditious Activities. 1920. *Revolutionary Radicalism: Its History, Purpose and Tactics*, Vols. 1–4. State of New York. Internet archive. http://archive.org/stream/revolutionaryrad02newyuoft/revolutionaryrad02newyuoft_djvu.txt, accessed June 17, 2014.

Joslin, Katherine. 2004. *Jane Addams: A Writer's Life*. Chicago: University of Illinois Press.

Kallen, Horace. 1915. "Democracy versus the Melting Pot." *The Nation* 100: 90–94, 217–220.

———. 1924. *Culture and Democracy* New York: Boni and Liveright.

Katz, Michael B. and Thomas J. Sugrue. 1998. *W.E.B. DuBois, Race, and the City*. Philadelphia: University of Pennsylvania Press.

Kelley, Florence. No date. "Notes on Sixty Years." Florence Kelley Papers, New York Public Library: B10, Fs 4–9.

———. [no date] 1998. "Kelley Reports of Women Factory Inspectors to a German Audience" in Kathryn K. Sklar, et al, eds., *Social Justice Feminists in the United States and Germany*. Ithaca, NY: Cornell University Press, pp. 96–104.

———. 1882a. "On Some Changes in the Legal Status of the Child since Blackstone." *The International Review* (Aug.):83–98.

———. 1882b. "Need Our Working Women Despair?" *The International Review* (Dec.):517–527.

———. [1887] 1986. "The Need of Theoretical Preparation for Philanthropic Work." in Kathryn K. Sklar, ed., *The Autobiography of Florence Kelley*. Chicago: Charles H. Kerr, pp. 91–104.

———. 1889. *Our Toiling Children*. Chicago: Woman's Temperance Publication.

———. [1895] 2004. "The Sweating-System," in Hull House Residents, *Hull House Maps and Papers*. North Stratford, NH: Ayer Company Publishers, pp. 27–45.

———. 1899. "Aims and Principles of the Consumers' League." *American Journal of Sociology* 5(3):289–304.

———. 1903. "An Effective Child Labor Law." *Annals of the American Academy of Political and Social Science* 21:438–444.

———. 1905. *Some Ethical Gains through Legislation.* New York: MacMillan.

———. 1986. *The Autobiography of Florence Kelley.* Chicago: Charles H. Kerr

———. 1998. "Women Factory Inspectors in the United States," in Kathryn K. Sklar, Anja Schuler, and Susan Strasser, eds., *Social Justice Feminists in the United States and Germany.* Ithaca, NY: Cornell University Press, pp. 95–104.

Kellogg, Paul U. 1927. "Settler and Trail-Blazer." *The Survey* 57 (March 15):777–780, LDWP, Biography, Reel 1, B1, NYPL.

Kellor, Frances. 1900a. "Criminal Sociology: The American vs. the Latin School." *The Arena* 23:301–307.

———. 1900b. "Criminality among Women." *The Arena* 24:516–524.

———. 1900c. "Psychological and Environmental Study of Women Criminals." *American Journal of Sociology* 5(4):527–543, 5(5):671–682.

———. 1901. *Experimental Sociology.* New York: MacMillan Co.

———. 1904. *Out of Work.* New York: G.P. Putnam's Sons.

Kemp, Virginia 1985. "Hull House: Pioneer Research during Its Creative Years." *Journal of the History of Sociology* 6(1):33–54.

Kennedy, Albert J. 1933. "The Saloon in Retrospect and Prospect." *Survey Graphic* 22:203–208.

Kennedy, John C. 1914. *A Study of Chicago's Stockyards Community III: Wages and Family Budgets in the Chicago Stockyards District.* Chicago: University of Chicago Press.

Kerby, W.J. 1900. "Priesthood and the Social Movement." *Catholic University Bulletin* VI:18–28.

Kim, Sukkoo. 2007. "Immigration, Industrial Revolution and Urban Growth in the United States, 1820–1920: Factor Endowments, Technology, and Geography" NBER Working Paper No. W12900. http://www.economics.uci.edu/docs/THD%20workshop/sp08/kim.pdf, accessed July 26, 2012.

Kingsbury (Simkhovitch), Mary. 1898. "Women in New York Settlements." *Municipal Affairs* 2:458–462.

Knight, Louise W. 2005. *Citizen: Jane Addams and the Struggle for Democracy.* Chicago: University of Chicago Press.

———. 2010. *Jane Addams: Spirit in Action.* New York: W.W. Norton.

Konvitz, Milton R. 1987. *The Legacy of Horace M. Kallen.* Cranbury, NJ: Associated University Presses.

Kraus, Harry P. [1970] 1980. *The Settlement House Movement in New York City, 1886–1914.* New York: Arno Press.

Lamarck, Jean-Baptiste. [1809] 1914. *Zoological Philosophy.* London: MacMillan and Co.

Lange, Brenda. 2008. *The Triangle Shirtwaist Factory Fire*. New York: Chelsea House.

Lannoy, Pierre. 2004. "When Robert E. Park was (Re)writing 'The City': Biography, the Social Survey, and the Science of Sociology." *The American Sociologist* 35(1):34–62.

Lasch-Quinn, Elisabeth. 1993. *Black Neighbors*. Chapel Hill: University of North Carolina Press.

Lathrop, Julia C. [1896] 1950. "What the Settlement Work Stands For," in Lorene M. Pacey, ed., *Readings in the Development of Settlement Work*. Freeport, NY: Books for Libraries Press, pp. 41–45.

Lathrop, Julia C. 1905. *Suggestions for Visitors to County Poorhouses and Other Public Charitable Institutions*. Chicago: Public Charities Committee of the Illinois Federation of Women's Clubs.

———. 1912. "The Children's Bureau." *American Journal of Sociology* 18(3):318–330.

———. 1919. "Income and Infant Mortality." *American Journal of Public Health* 9(4):270–274.

Latta, Maurice C. 1936. "The Background for the Social Gospel in American Protestantism." *Church History* 5(3):256–270.

Leach, William. 1989. *True Love and Perfect Union*. Middletown, CN: Wesleyan University Press.

Leff, Mark H. 1973. "The Mother's Pension Movement in the Progressive Era." *Social Service Review* 47(3):397–417.

Lengermann, Patricia M. and Jill Niebrugge-Brantley. 1998. *The Women Founders: Sociology and Social Theory, 1830–1930*. Boston: McGraw Hill.

———. 2002. "Back to the Future: Settlement Sociology, 1885–1930." *The American Sociologist* 33(3):5–20.

Lengermann, Patricia and Gillian Niebrugge. 2007. "Thrice Told: Narratives of Sociology's Relation to Social Work," in Craig Calhoun, ed., *Sociology in American*. Chicago: University of Chicago Press, pp. 63–114.

Leo, Pope XIII. 1891. *Rerum Novarum on Capital and Labor*. Encyclical of Pope Leo XIII, May 15, 1891. http://www.papalencyclicals.net/Leo13/l13rerum.htm, accessed June 17, 2014.

Levine, Donald N. 1995. *Visions of the Sociological Tradition*. Chicago: University of Chicago Press.

Levine, Harry G. 1983. "The Committee of Fifty and the Origins of Alcohol Control." *Journal of Drug Issues* 13(Winter):95–116.

Lewis, David L. 1993. *W.E.B. DuBois: Biography of a Race, 1868–1919*. New York: Henry Holt.

Lindenmeyer, Kriste. 1997. *A Right to Childhood: The U.S. Children's Bureau and Child Welfare, 1912–1946*. Urbana: University of Illinois Press.

Linn, James W. [1935] 2000. *Jane Addams: A Biography*. Urbana: University of Illinois Press.

Lissak, Rivka S. 1989. *Pluralism and Progressives: Hull House and the New Immigrants*. Chicago: University of Chicago Press.

Lopreato, Joseph and Timothy Crippen. 1996. *Crisis in Sociology*. New Brunswick: Transaction Publishers.

Luker, Ralph E. 1984. "Missions, Institutional Churches, and Settlement Houses: The Black Experience, 1886–1910." *The Journal of Negro History* 69(3/4):101–113.

———. 1991. *The Social Gospel in Black and White*. Chapel Hill, NC: University of North Carolina Press.

Lynd, Robert S. and Helen M. Lynd. 1929. *Middletown*. New York: Harcourt, Brace and World.

———. 1937. *Middletown in Transition*. New York: Harcourt, Brace and World.

MacLean, Annie M. 1925. *Modern Immigration*. Philadelphia: J.P. Lippincott.

MacLean, Vicky M. and Joyce E. Williams. 2005. "Sociology at Women's and Black Colleges," in Anthony J. Blasi, ed., *Diverse Histories of American Sociology*. Boston: Brill, pp. 260–317.

———. 2012. "Ghosts of Sociologies Past: Settlement Sociology in the Progressive Era." *The American Sociologist* 43(3):235–263.

Madge, John. 1962. *The Origins of Scientific Sociology*. New York: The Free Press.

———. 1965. *The Tools of Social Science*. Garden City, NY: Anchor Books.

Mallon, J.J. 1950. "Toynbee Hall: Past and Present," in Lorene M. Pacey, ed., *Readings in the Development of Settlement Work*. Freeport, NY: Books for Libraries Press, pp. 261–271.

Mann, Arthur. 1954. *Yankee Reformers in the Urban Age*. Cambridge: Harvard University Press.

Martindale, Don. 1958. "Prefatory Remarks: The Theory of the City," in Max Weber, *The City*. New York: The Free Press, pp. 9–62.

Mathews, Shailer. 1895. "Christian Sociology." *American Journal of Sociology* 1(1):69–78.

———. 1896. "The Process of Social Regeneration." *American Journal of Sociology* 2(3):416–432.

Matson, Floyd W. 1966. *The Broken Image*. Garden City, NY: Anchor Books.

Mattson, Greggor. 2007. "Urban Ethnography's 'Saloon Problem' and Its Challenge to Public Sociology." *City and Community* 6(2):75–94.

May, Henry F. 1949. *Protestant Churches and Industrial America*. New York: Harper and Brothers.

McAdam, Douglas. 2007. "From Relevance to Irrelevance: The Curious Impact of the Sixties on Public Sociology," in Craig Calhoun, ed., *Sociology in America*. Chicago: University of Chicago Press, pp. 411–426.

McClymer, John F. 1980. *War and Welfare: Social Engineering in America, 1890–1925*. Westport, CN: Greenwood Press.

McDonald, Lynn. 1993. *The Early Origins of the Social Sciences*. Montreal: McGill-Queen's University Press.

McDowell, Mary. 1914, 1927. *Autobiography*. MMSR, B1, F1.

———. 1923. "The Spirit of Social Service in Chicago." *University Record* 9:293–303, MMSR, B1, F3b.

———. 1938a. "City Waste," in Caroline M. Hill, ed., *Mary McDowell and Municipal Housekeeping*. Chicago: Millard Publishing Co., pp. 1–10.

McDowell, Mary M. 1938b. "Our Proxies in Industry," in Caroline M. Hill, ed., *Mary McDowell and Municipal Housekeeping*. Chicago: Millard Publishing Co., pp. 44–61.

McDowell, Mary. 1938c. "Prejudice," in Caroline M. Hill, ed., *Mary McDowell and Municipal Housekeeping*. Chicago: Millard Publishing Co. pp. 27–38.

McGerr, Michael. 2003. *A Fierce Discontent: The Rise and Fall of the Progressive Movement in America*. New York: Oxford University Press.

McKenzie, Roderick D. [1925] 1967. "The Ecological Approach to the Study of the Human Community," in Robert E. Park, Ernest W. Burgess, and R.D. McKenzie, eds., *The City*. Chicago: University of Chicago Press, pp. 63–77.

Meigs, Cornelia. 1970. *Jane Addams Pioneer for Social Justice*. Boston: Little Brown.

Melendy, Royal L. 1900. "The Saloon in Chicago." *American Journal of Sociology* 6(3):289–306.

———. 1901. "The Saloon in Chicago II." *American Journal of Sociology* 6(4):433–464.

Miller-Bernal, Leslie. 2000. *Separate by Degree*. New York: Peter Lang.

Mills, C. Wright. 1959. *The Sociological Imagination*. New York: Oxford University Press.

Montgomery, Caroline Williamson. 1905. *Bibliography of College, Social, University, and Church Settlements*. Boston: College Settlements Association, SC, MS 430, B1, F2.

Montgomery, Louise. 1913. *A Study of Chicago's Stockyards Community II: The American Girl in the Stockyards District*. Chicago: University of Chicago Press.

More, Louise Bolard. 1907. *Wage-Earners' Budgets: A Study of Standards and Cost of Living in New York City*. New York: Henry Holt.

Moore, Linda S. 1994. "Social Workers and the Development of the NAACP." *Journal of Sociology and Social Welfare* 21:125–137.

Morgan, J. Graham. 1969. "The Development of Sociology and the Social Gospel in America." *Sociological Analysis* 30(1):42–53.

———. 1980. "Women in American Sociology in the Nineteenth Century." *Journal of the History of Sociology* 2(2):1–34.

———. 1982. "Preparation for the Advent: The Establishment of Sociology as a Discipline in American Universities in the Late Nineteenth Century." *Minerva* 20(1–2):25–58.

Morton, Mavis, Corey Dolgon, Timothy Maher, and James Pennell. 2012. "Civic Engagement and Public Sociology: Two 'Movements' in Search of a Mission." *Journal of Applied Social Science* 6(1):5–30.

Moscowitz, Henry. 1911. "Music School Settlements." *The Survey* XXVI:458–465.

Muncy, Robyn. 1991. *Creating a Female Dominion in American Reform, 1890–1935*. NY: Oxford University Press.

Naples, Nancy. 2003. *Feminism and Method: Ethnography, Discourse Analysis, and Activist Research*. NY: Routledge University Press.

Nassau, Mabel. 1915. *Old Age Poverty in Greenwich Village*. New York: Fleming H. Revell.

National Child Labor Committee (NCLC). 1910. *Child Employing Industries: Proceedings of the Sixth Annual National Child Labor Committee*. New York: books.google.com, accessed February 11, 2013.

New York Factory Investigating Commission (NYFIC) Second Report, Vol. 4. 1913. Albany, NY: J.B. Lyon Co. books.google.com, accessed July 12, 2014.

New York Factory Investigating Commission (NYFIC) Fourth Report, Vol. 1. 1915. Albany, NY: J.B. Lyon Co. books.google.com, accessed July 12. 2014.

Nichols, Lawrence T., ed. 2005. "Special Issue on Public Sociology." *The American Sociologist* 36(1):3–4.

———. 2007. *Public Sociology: The Contemporary Debate*. New Brunswick, NJ: Transaction Publishers.

Nicholson, Philip. 2004. *Labor's Story in the United States*. Philadelphia: Temple University Press.

North, Cecil C. 1923. "The Settlement Horizon." *The American Journal of Sociology* 28(5):621–623.

Oberschall, Anthony. 1972. "The Institutionalization of American Sociology," in Anthony Oberschall, ed., *The Establishment of Empirical Sociology*. New York: Harper and Row, pp. 187–251.

Odum, Howard W. 1951. *American Sociology*. New York: Longmans, Green and Co.

Ovington, Mary W. 1911. *Half A Man*. New York: Longmans, Green and Co.

Pacey, Lorene M., ed. 1950. *Readings in the Development of Settlement Work*. Freeport, NY: Books for Libraries Press.

Page, Charles H. [1940] 1969. *Class and American Sociology: From Ward to Ross*. New York: Schocken Books.

Park, Robert E. 1914. "Review of in Freedom's Birthplace." *The Survey* 32:100.

———. 1915. "The City: Suggestions for the Investigation of Human Behavior in the City Environment." *The American Journal of Sociology* 20(5):577–612.

Park, Robert E. and Ernest W. Burgess. 1921. *Introduction to the Science of Sociology*. Chicago: University of Chicago Press.

Park, Robert E. [1925] 1967. "The City: Suggestions for the Investigation of Human Behavior in the Urban Environment." in Robert E. Park and Ernest W. Burgess *The City*. Chicago: University of Chicago Press, pp. 1–46.

Park, Robert E. and Ernest W. Burgess. [1925] 1967. *The City*. Chicago: University of Chicago Press.

Park, Robert E. [1929a] 1952. *Human Communities*. Glencoe, IL: The Free Press.

———. [1929b] 1967. "The City as a Social Laboratory," in Ralph H. Turner, ed., *Robert E. Park on Social Control and Collective Behavior*. Chicago: University of Chicago Press, pp. 3–18.

Phillips, Anna C. 1932. *Survey of the Communicable Disease Hospital Needs, Borough of the Bronx*. New York: City of New York.

Philpott, Thomas L. 1978. *The Slum and the Ghetto*. New York: Oxford University Press.

Piott, Steven L. 2006. *American Reformers, 1870–1920*. New York: Rowman and Littlefield.

Platt, Jennifer. 1994. "The Chicago School and Firsthand Data." *History of the Human Sciences* 7(1):57–80.

Pound, Roscoe. 1943. "Sociology of Law and Sociological Jurisprudence." *University of Toronto Law Journal* 5(1):1–20.

Powell, Thomas R. 1916. "The Case for the Shorter Work Day." *Political Science Quarterly* 31(3):469–471.

Randall, Mercedes M. 1964. *Improper Bostonian Emily Greene Balch*. New York: Twayne Publishers.

Rauschenbusch, Walter. 1917. *A Theology for the Social Gospel*. New York: Macmillan.

Rauschenbush, Winfred. 1979. *Robert E Park: Biography of a Sociologist*. Durham, NC: Duke University Press.

Recchiuti, John L. 2007. *Civic Engagement*. Philadelphia: University of Pennsylvania Press.

Reinharz, Shulamit. 1992. *Feminist Methods in Social Research*. NY: Oxford University Press.

Reisch, Michael and Janice Andrews. 2002. *The Road Not Taken*. New York: Brunner-Routledge.

Rhoades, Lawrence J. 1981. *A History of the American Sociological Association 1905–1980*. Washington, D.C.: American Sociological Association.

Riis, Jacob A. 1890. *How the Other Half Lives*. New York: Scribner's and Sons.

Rosen, Elliot A. 1972. "Roosevelt and the Brains Trust: An Historiographical Overview." *Political Science Quarterly* 87(4):531–557.

Rosenberg, Rosalind. 1982. *Beyond Separate Spheres: Intellectual Roots of Modern Feminism*. New Haven: Yale University Press.

Ross, Dorothy. 1992. *The Origins of American Social Science*. New York: Cambridge University Press.

———. 1998. "Gendered Social Knowledge: Domestic Discourse, Jane Addams, and the Possibilities of Social Science," in Helene Silverberg, ed., *Gender and American Social Science: The Formative Years*. NJ: Princeton University Press, pp. 235–265.

Rousmaniere, John P. 1970. "Cultural Hybrid in the Slums: The College Woman and the Settlement House, 1889–1894." *American Quarterly* 22(1):45–66.

Rowntree, Seebohm. 1901. *Poverty: A Study of Town Life*. London: Macmillan.

Russ, Charles T. 1960. *The Hartford Years of Graham Taylor 1880–1892 with Special Emphasis on His Association with the Fourth Church and the Hartford Theological Seminary*. STM Dissertation. Hartford, CN: Hartford Theological Seminary ProQuest Information and Learning Co. proquest.com, accessed July 20, 2013.

Ryan, Rosina McAvoy. 2006. *A Graduate School in Life: The College Settlement of Philadelphia*. Ph.D. Dissertation, Graduate School of Temple University. Ann Arbor, MI: ProQuest Information and Learning Co. proquest.com, accessed October 3, 2013.

Salmon, Lucy Maynard. 1897. *Domestic Service*. New York: Macmillan.

Sanborn, Alvan F. 1895. *Moody's Lodging House and Other Sketches*. Boston: Copeland and Day.

Sayles, Mary B. 1903. "Housing Conditions in Jersey City." *Annals of the American Academy of Political and Social Science* 21(supplement 16):1–72.

Schachter, Hindy L. 2002. "Women, Progressive-Era Reform, and Scientific Management." *Administration and Society* 34(5):563–578.

Schafer, Richard T. 2006. *Racial and Ethnic Groups*, 10th ed. Upper Saddle River, NJ: Prentice Hall.

Schultz, Rima L. 2007. "Introduction," in Residents of Hull House, *Hull-House Maps and Papers*. Urbana: University of Illinois Press, pp. 1–42.

Schutz, Alfred. 1967. *The Phenomenology of the Social World*. Evanston, IL: Northwestern University Press.

Schutz, Alfred and Thomas Luckmann. 1973. *The Structure of the Life World*. Evanston, IL: Northwestern University Press.

Schwendinger, Herman and Julia R. Schwendinger. 1974. *The Sociologists of the Chair*. New York: Basic Books.

Scott, Anne F. 1967. "Jane Addams and the City." *The Virginia Quarterly Review* 43(Winter):53–62.

———. 2004. "Introduction." *My Friend, Julia Lathrop*. Urbana: University of Illinois Press.

Scudder, Vida D. 1887a. "The Effect on Character of a College Education." *The Christian Union* 35(14):12–13, 15. VDSP, MS 140, Series III, B2, F2.

———. 1887b. "The Educated Woman as a Social Factor." *The Christian Union* 35(16):12–13. VDSP, MS 140, Series III, B2, F6.

———. 1890. "The Relation of College Women to Social Need." Paper presented to the Association of Collegiate Alumnae. VDSP, MS 140, Series III, B2, F3.

———. 1892. "The Place of College Settlements." *Andover Review* 18:339–350. VDSP, MS 140, Series III, B2, F1.

———. 1898. *Social Ideals in English Letters*. Boston: Houghton Mifflin.

———. 1900. "Colleges and Settlements." *Smith College Monthly* 6:140–143. VDSP, MS 140, Series III, B2, F1.

———. 1902. "Democracy and Education." *Atlantic Monthly* 89:816–822.

———. 1903. *A Listener in Babel*. Boston: Houghton Mifflin and Co.

———. 1911. "Class Consciousness." *Atlantic Monthly* 107:320–330, VDSP, MS 140, B2, F2.

———. 1937. *On Journey*. New York: E.P. Dutton.

Seager, Henry R. 1910. *Social Insurance: A Program of Social Reform*. New York: MacMillan.

———. 1915. "Introduction," in Mable Nassau, *Old Age Poverty in Greenwich Village*. New York: Fleming H. Revell, pp. 5–6.

Seigfried, Haddock C. 1991. "Where are All the Feminist Pragmatists?" *Hypatia* 6(Summer):1–19.

———. 1996. *Pragmatism and Feminism: Reweaving the Social Fabric*. Chicago: University of Chicago Press.

———. 2002. "Introduction to the Illinois Edition," in Jane Addams, *Democracy and Social Ethics*. Chicago: University of Illinois Press, pp. ix–xxxviii.

Shaw, G. Bernard. 1894. *Socialism: The Fabian Essays*. Boston: Charles E. Brown.

Shils, Edward. 1948. *The Present State of American Sociology*. New York: Free Press.

Shoemaker, Linda M. 1998. "Early Conflicts in Social Work Education." *Social Service Review* 72(2):182–191.

Sicherman, Barbara. 1984. *Alice Hamilton: A Life in Letters*. Cambridge: Harvard University Press.

Siegel, Beatrice. 1983. *Lillian Wald of Henry Street*. New York: MacMillan Publishing.

Silverberg, Helene, ed. 1998. *Gender and American Social Science*. Princeton, NJ: Princeton University Press.

Simkhovitch, Mary Kingsbury. 1902. "Friendship and Politics." *Political Science Quarterly* SVII(2):189–205.

———. 1917. *The City Worker's World in America*. New York: MacMillan.

Simkhovitch, Mary K. 1926. *The Settlement Primer*. New York: National Federation of Settlements.

———. 1938. *Neighborhood: My Story of Greenwich House*. New York: W.W. Norton and Co.

———. 1940. *Group Life*. New York: Association Press.

Simkhovitch, Mary and Elizabeth Ogg. 1942. *Quicksand*. Evanston, IL: Row, Peterson.

Simkhovitch, Mary K. 1949. *Here is God's Plenty*. New York: Harper and Brothers.

Sklar, Kathryn Kish. 1985. "Hull House in the 1890's: A Community of Women Reformers." *Signs* 10(4):658–677.

———. 1986. "Introduction" and "Florence Kelley," in *The Autobiography of Florence Kelley*. Chicago: Charles H. Kerr, pp. 1–15 and Back Cover.

———. 1995. *Florence Kelley and the Nation's Work*. New Haven, CN: Yale University Press.

———. 1998. "Hull-House Maps and Papers: Social Science as Women's Work in the 1890s," in Helene Silverberg, ed., *Gender and American Social Science*. Princeton, NJ: Princeton University Press, pp. 127–155.

Sklar, Kathryn Kish and Beverly W. Palmer, eds. 2009. *The Selected Letters of Florence Kelley, 1869–1931*. Chicago: University of Illinois Press.

Slayton, Robert A. 1986. *Back of the Yards*. Chicago: University of Chicago Press.

Small, Albion and George E. Vincent. 1894. *An Introduction to the Study of Society*. New York: American Book Co.,

Small, Albion. 1895. "The Era of Sociology." *American Journal of Sociology* 1(1):1–15.

Smith, T.V. and Leonard D. White, eds. [1929] 1968. *Chicago: An Experiment in Social Science Research*. New York: Greenwood Press.

Smith, Dorothy. 1974. "Women's Perspective as a Radical Critique of Sociology." *Sociological Inquiry* (44):7–14.

———. 1987. *The Everyday World as Problematic*. Boston: Northeastern University Press.

Smith, Jean E. 2007. *FDR*. New York: Random House.

Smyth, Newman. 1885. *Social Problems: Sermons to Workingmen*. Boston: Houghton Mifflin.

Snedeker, Ruth W. 1950. "An Experiment in Practical Christianity." SEHR, Series II, B1, F24.

Solomon, Barbara. 1972. *Ancestors and Immigrants*. Chicago: University of Chicago Press.

Spain, Daphne. 2001. *How Women Saved the City*. Minneapolis: University of Minnesota Press.

Sprague, Joey. 2005. *Feminist Methods in Social Research*. NY: Rowland and Littlefield.

Stackpole, Antoinette. 1961. *The American Social Settlement, 1890–1920*. Honors Thesis. Smith College, SC, Smith College Archives, B4, F3.

Starr, Ellen Gates. [1895] 2004. "Art and Labor," in Residents of Hull House, *Hull House Maps and Papers*. North Stratford, NH: Ayer Publishers, pp. 165–179.

Stbeightoff, Frank H. 1914. "Review of Wages and Family Budgets in the Chicago Stockyards Districts." *The American Economic Review* 4:951–952.

Stebner, Eleanor J. 1997. *The Women of Hull House*. New York: State University of NY Press.

Stein, Maurice R. 1960. *The Eclipse of Community*. New York: Harper Torchbooks.

Stivers, Camilla. 2000. *Bureau Men, Settlement Women*. Lawrence, KS: University Press of Kansas.

Streiff, Meg. 2005. *Boston's Settlement Housing: Social Reform in an Industrial City*. Ph.D. Dissertation, Graduate School of Louisiana State University. Baton Rouge, LA. http://etd.lsu.edu/docs/available/etd-06082005-101010/unrestricted/Streiff_dis.pdf, accessed June 17, 2014.

Strong, Josiah. 1893. *The New Era or the Coming Kingdom.* New York: Baker and Taylor.

———. 1902. *The Next Great Awakening.* New York: Baker and Taylor.

———. 1915. *The New World-Religion.* Garden City, NY: Doubleday, Page.

Sumner, William G. 1893. *What Social Classes Owe to Each Other.* New York: Harper and Brothers.

Sutherland, John F. 1973. *A City of Homes: Philadelphia Slums and Reformers, 1880–1918.* Ph.D. Dissertation, Graduate School of Temple University. Philadelphia, PA: University Microfilms Photocopy.

Swatos William H. Jr. 1984. *Faith of the Fathers: Science, Religion, and Reform in the Development of Early American Sociology.* Bristol, IN: Wyndham Hall Press.

Swift, Harold H. 1938. "As We Knew Her in the StockYards," in Caroline M. Hill, ed., *Mary McDowell and Municipal Housekeeping.* Chicago: Millar Publishing, pp. 115–119.

Talbert, Ernest L. 1912. *A Study of Chicago's Stockyards Community: Opportunities in School and Industry for Children of the Stockyards District.* Chicago: University of Chicago Press.

Talbot, Marion. 1910. *The Education of Women.* Chicago: University of Chicago Press.

Taylor, Graham. 1899. "The Social Function of the Church." *The American Journal of Sociology* 5(3):305–321.

Taylor, Graham. 1906a. "Social Tendencies of the Industrial Revolution," in Howard Rogers and Hugo Munsterberg, eds., *Congress of Arts and Science: Universal Exposition St. Louis, 1904.* Boston: Houghton, Mifflin, pp. 682–694.

———. 1906b. "The Industrial Viewpoint." *Charities and the Commons* 16(5):205–212.

———. 1908. "Is Class Conflict in America Growing?" *American Journal of Sociology* 13(6):766–770.

———. 1913. *Religion in Social Action.* New York: Dodd, Mead.

———. [1930] 1976. *Pioneering on Social Frontiers.* New York: Arno Press.

———. 1936. *Chicago Commons through Forty Years.* Chicago: Chicago Commons Association.

———. 1938. "Mary McDowell—Citizen," in Caroline M. Hill, ed., *Mary McDowell and Municipal Housekeeping.* Chicago: Millar Publishing, pp. x–xii.

Thomas, William I. 1923. *The Unadjusted Girl.* Boston: Little Brown.

Thomas, William I. and Florian Znaniecki. 1918–1919. *The Polish Peasant in Europe and America.* Boston: Badger.

Thrasher, Frederic M. 1927. *The Gang.* Chicago: University of Chicago Press.

Tibbitts, Clark. 1928. "A Study of Chicago Settlements and their Districts." *Social Forces* 6(3):430–437.

Tolman, Frank L. 1902. "The Study of Sociology in Institutions of Learning in the United States, I." *The American Journal of Sociology* 7(4):797–838.

Totenberg, Amy M. 1974. *Women Reformers from the Settlement Movement, 1889–1925.* Honors Thesis, Bachelor of Arts Degree, Radcliff College. Boston, MA: Archives and Manuscripts, Schlesinger Library.

Tower, Jay. 1961. "Crime and Punctuation." *Saturday Review* October 14, 1961:39.

Trachtenberg, Alan. 2007. *The Incorporation of America.* New York: Hill and Wang.

Traverso, Susan. 2003. *Welfare Politics in Boston, 1910–1940.* Boston: University of Massachusetts Press.

Trevino, A. Javier. 2011. "Program Theme: Service Sociology." *Service Sociology: Final Program.* Society for the Study of Social Problems.

Trolander, Judith A. 1975. *Settlement Houses and the Great Depression.* Detroit, MI: Wayne State University Press.

———. 1987. *Professionalism and Social Change.* New York: Columbia University Press.

———. 1990. "Introduction to the Transaction Edition," in Robert Woods and Albert Kennedy, eds., *The Settlement Horizon.* New Brunswick, NJ: Transaction Publishers, pp. vii–xxiii.

Turner, Stephen P. and Jonathan H. Turner. 1990. *The Impossible Science: An Institutional Analysis of American Sociology.* Newbury Park, CA: Sage Publications.

Tucker, William J. 1889. "Socialism under Democracy." *Andover Review* 12:205–214.

———. 1891. "The Authority of the Pulpit in a Time of Critical Research and Social Confusion." *Andover Review* 16:384–402.

———. 1915. "The Progress of the Social Conscience." *The Atlantic Monthly* 116(3):290–303.

———. 1917. "Twenty-Five Years 'In Residence'." *Atlantic Monthly* 119(5):640–649.

United States Commission on Industrial Relations (USCIR). 1916. *Final Report and Testimony Submitted to Congress* IV. Washington, D.C.: US Government Printing Office. https://archive.org/details/industrialrelatio4unitrich, accessed June 15, 2014.

United States Department of Labor. 1912. *Report on Condition of Woman and Child Wage Earners in the United States*, Vols. 1–19. Washington, D.C.: Government Printing Office. books.google.com, accessed April 12, 2014.

———. 1916. *Summary of the Report on Condition of Woman and Child Wage Earners in the United States.* Washington, D.C.: Government Printing Office. books.google.com, accessed January 28, 2013.

University of Chicago. 1910. *Annual Register.* http://books.google.com/books, accessed April 22, 2015.

Urofsky, Melvin I. 2009. *Louis Brandeis: A Life.* New York: Schocken Books.

Valentine, Charles A. 1968. *Culture and Poverty.* Chicago: University of Chicago Press.

Vicinus, Martha. 1985. *Independent Women: Work and Community for Single Women 1850–1920*. Chicago: University of Chicago Press.

Vidich, Arthur J. and Stanford M. Lyman. 1985. *American Sociology: Worldly Rejections of Religion and Their Directions*. New Haven: Yale University Press.

Vincent, George E. 1904. "Sociology." *Encyclopedia Americana* 14. New York: Americana Company.

Vittum, Harriet E. 1938. "Mary E. McDowell, Warrior against Prejudice," in Caroline M. Hill, ed., *Mary McDowell and Municipal Housekeeping: A Symposium*. Chicago: Millar Publishing, pp. 24–27.

Wade, Louise C. 1964. *Graham Taylor: Pioneer for Social Justice*. Chicago: University of Chicago Press.

Wald, Lillian D. 1901. "Nurses' Social Settlements." *American Journal of Nursing* 1(9):684–685.

———. 1902. "The Nurses' Settlement in New York." *American Journal of Nursing* 2(8):567–575.

———. 1905. "Medical Inspection of Public Schools." *Annals of the American Academy of Political and Social Science* 25(1):88–96.

———. 1906. "Organization amongst Working Women." *Annals of the American Academy of Political and Social Science*. 27:176–183.

———. [1915] 1991. *The House on Henry Street*. New Brunswick, NJ: Transaction Publishers.

———. 1934. *Windows on Henry Street*. Boston: Little Brown and Co.

———. 1941. Foreword: "We Called Our Enterprise Public Health Nursing" in Marguerite A. Wales, *The Public Health Nurse in Action*. New York: MacMillan:xi.

Wales, Marguerite A. 1941. *The Public Health Nurse in Action*. New York: MacMillan.

Ware, Caroline. [1935] 1965. *Greenwich Village*. Berkeley, CA: University of California Press.

Ware, Susan. 1993. *Still Missing: Amelia Earhart and the Search for Modern Feminism*. New York: W.W. Norton.

Warner Sam BassJr. [1962] 1969. "Preface to the First Edition," in Robert Woods and Albert Kennedy, eds., *The Zone of Emergence*. Cambridge, MA: MIT Press, pp. 1–30.

Watson, Tony J. 2008. *Sociology, Work and Industry*, 5th ed. New York: Routledge.

Webb, Beatrice. 1926. *My Apprenticeship*. London: Longmans, Green.

Webb, Sidney. 1887. *Facts for Socialists*. London: The Fabian Society.

Weber, Max. 1958. *The Protestant Ethic and the Spirit of Capitalism*. New York: Charles Scribner's Sons.

Weinberg, Julius. 1972. *Edward Alsworth Ross and the Sociology of Progressivism*. State Historical Society of Wisconsin: Madison, WI.

West, Cornell. 1993. *Keeping Faith: Philosophy and Race in America*. New York: Routledge.

White, George C. 1959. "Social Settlements and Immigrant Neighbors, 1886–1914." *Social Service Review* 33(1):55–66.

White, Ronald C. and C. Howard Hopkins. 1976. *The Social Gospel: Religion and Reform in Changing America.* Philadelphia: Temple University Press.

Williams, Daniel Day. 1970. *The Andover Liberals.* New York: Octagon Books.

Williams, Joyce E. and Vicky M. MacLean. 2005. "Studying Ourselves: Discipline-Building in Early American Sociology." *The American Sociologist* 36(1):111–133.

———. 2012. "In Search of the Kingdom: The Social Gospel, Settlement Sociology, and the Sociology of Reform in the Progressive Era." *Journal of the History of the Behavioral Sciences* 48(4):339–362.

Williamson, Caroline L. 1895. "Six Months at Denison House." *The Wellesley Magazine* 3(5):234–238.

Wilson, Howard E. 1928. *Mary McDowell Neighbor.* Chicago: University of Chicago Press.

Wirth, Louis. [1928] 1956. *The Ghetto.* Chicago: Phoenix Books University of Chicago Press.

———. 1947. "American Sociology, 1915–47." *American Journal of Sociology,* Index to Vols. 1–52:273–281.

Wolfe, Albert B. 1906. *The Lodging House Problem in Boston.* Boston: Houghton Mifflin.

———. 1907 "The Problem of the Roomer." *Charities and the Commons* 19(5):957–962.

Wolfe, Allis R. 1975. "Women, Consumerism, and the National Consumers' League in the Progressive Era, 1900–1923." *Labor History* 16(Summer):378–392.

Woodbridge, Alice L. 1893. "Our Working Women." *The Social Economist* 5:154–163.

Woods, Eleanor H. 1907. "Social Betterment in a Lodging District." *Charities and the Commons* 19(5):962–968.

———. 1916. *Report on Unemployment among Boston Women in 1915.* Boston: National Civic Federation Woman's Department.

———. 1929. *Robert A. Woods: Champion of Democracy.* Freeport, NY: Books for Libraries Press.

Woods, Katherine. 1891. "Queens of the Shop, the Workroom and the Tenement." *Cosmopolitan* 10:99–105.

———. 1895. "Accidents in Factories and Elsewhere." *Journal of the American Statistical Association* 32(4):303–321.

Woods, Robert A. 1891. *English Social Movements.* New York: Charles Scribner.

———. [1893] 1970. "University Settlements as Laboratories in Social Science," in Robert A. Woods, *The Neighborhood In Nation-Building.* New York: Arno Press, pp. 30–46.

———. 1893. "The University Settlement Idea," in School of Applied Ethics, ed., *Philanthropy and Social Progress.* Seven Essays Delivered during the Summer Session, 1892. New York: Thomas Crowell.

———., ed. 1895. *The Poor in Great Cities.* New York: Charles Scribner.

———. [1898] 1970. *The City Wilderness: A Settlement Study.* New York: Arno Press.

———. 1899. "University Settlements: Their Point and Drift." *The Quarterly Journal of Economics* 14(1):3–22.

———., ed. [1903] 1970. *Americans in Process: A Settlement Study*. New York: Arno Press.

———. 1906. "Democracy A New Unfolding of Human Power," in Students of Charles E. Garman, *Studies in Philosophy and Psychology*. Boston: Houghton, Mifflin, pp. 71–100.

Woods, Robert A. and Albert J. Kennedy, eds. [1911] 1970. *Handbook of Settlements*. New York: Arno Press.

———. eds. 1913. *Young Working Girls: A Summary of Evidence from Two Thousand Social Workers*. Boston: Houghton Mifflin.

Woods, Robert A. 1914. "The Neighborhood in Social Reconstruction." *The American Journal of Sociology* 19(5):577–591.

———. 1921. "The World Empire of the Disinterested." *Envelope Series* XXIV(1). SEHR, Series V. B1, F83.

Woods, Robert A. and Albert J. Kennedy. [1922] 1990. *The Settlement Horizon*. New Brunswick, NJ: Transaction Publishers.

Woods, Robert A. [1923] 1970. *The Neighborhood as Nation-Building*. New York: Arno Press.

———. 1950. "The Settlements' Foothold of Opportunity," in Lorene M. Pacey, ed., *Readings in the Development of Settlement Work*. Freeport, NY: Books for Libraries Press, pp. 154–175.

Woods, Robert A. and Albert J. Kennedy, eds. 1969. *The Zone of Emergence*. Cambridge, MA: MIT Press.

Wright, Carroll D., Victor Hugo, and Alfred S. Houghton. 1894. *The Slums of Baltimore, Chicago, New York, and Philadelphia*. Washington, D.C.: Government Printing Office

Zorbaugh, Harvey W. 1929. *The Gold Coast and the Slum*. Chicago: University of Chicago Press.

Archival Collections

AFDC – Anna F. Davies Collection
Lake Forest College Digital Collection
http://collections.lakeforest.edu/items/show/2904 Accessed June 13, 2014

AHP – Alice Hamilton Papers
Schlesinger Library, Radcliffe Institute
Harvard University

AWSP – Albion W. Small Papers
University of Chicago Special Collections Research Center

CCAR – Chicago Commons Association Records
Chicago History Museum

CSA – College Settlements Association
Internet Archive
Widener Library Collection, Harvard University

DHR – Denison House Records
Schlesinger Library, Radcliffe Institute

EGSP – Ellen Gates Starr Papers
Sophie Smith Collection, Smith College Archives.

EWBP – Ernest W. Burgess Papers
University of Chicago Special Collections Research Center

FCKP – Florence Cross Kitchelt Papers, 1900–1959
Sophie Smith Collection, Smith College Archives.

FKP – Florence Kelley Papers
New York Public Library

GHR – Greenwhich House Records
Tamiment Library. Robert F. Wagner Labor Archives. New York University

GTP – Graham Taylor Papers
Newberry Library Manuscript Collections, Chicago, IL

HHC – Hull House Collection
University of Illinois at Chicago

LDTP – Lea Demarest Taylor Papers, 1894–1969
University of Illinois at Chicago, Special Collections.

LDWP, CU – Lillian D Wald Papers
Columbia University Archives
Butler Library

LDWP, NYPL – Lillian Wald Papers
New York Public Library

Lillian Wald Papers on Microfilm, Reel 1, Biography
Lillian Wald Papers on Microfilm, Reel 24, Selected Writings and Speeches

MKSP – Mary K. Simkhovitch Papers
Schlesinger Library, Radcliffe Institute
Harvard University

MMSR – Mary McDowell Settlement Records, University of Chicago Settlement
Chicago History Museum Research Center

SC – Settlements Collection, 1883–1972
Sophie Smith Collection, Smith College Archives.

SEHR – South End House Records
Houghton Library, Harvard College Library

UCSLR – University of Chicago Service League Records
University of Chicago Special Collections Research

USEHR – United South End Settlement Records
Northeastern University, Boston, MA

VDSP – Vida Dutton Scudder Papers, 1883–1979
Sophie Smith Collection, Smith College Archives.

Other Internet Resources Used

Chicago Commons (chicagocommons.org)
Google Books (books.google.com)
Google Scholar (scholar.google.com)
Hamilton Madison House (hmhonline.org)
Henry Street Settlement (henrystreet.org)
Hudson Guild (hudsonguild.org)
Hull House Association (hullhouse.org)
Jewish Women: A Comprehensive Historical Encyclopedia (jwa.org/encyclopedia)
Social Welfare History Archives, University of Minnesota Libraries (lib.umn.edu/swha).
United South End Settlements (uses.org).
University Settlement (universitysettlement.org)
Wikipedia: The Free Encyclopedia (Wikipedia.org)

Subject Index

Name Index

www.ingramcontent.com/pod-product-compliance
Lightning Source LLC
Chambersburg PA
CBHW060019030426
42334CB00019B/2095

9781608466429